Death Notices from
Washington County, New York
Newspapers, 1799 - 1880

Mary S. Jackson
Edward F. Jackson

Heritage Books, Inc.

Published 1995 by

Heritage Books, Inc.
1540-E Pointer Ridge Pl.
Bowie, MD 20716
1-800-398-7709

ISBN 0-7884-0337-0

A Complete Catalog Listing Hundreds of Titles on
History, Genealogy and Americana
Available Upon Request.

Introduction

Newspapers are probably one of the most valuable and interesting sources for genealogy and are too often overlooked by researchers. Not only for the marriage and death notices that are published but many other articles are a valuable source of information. Some newspapers carry family histories of many of the local people. They also print sale of properties, notices of probate, advertising, personal items such as who is ill this week or who visited who, reunions, etc. They can be very entertaining as well as informative.

This volume contains death notices from Washington County New York newspapers from 1799 to 1880 abstracted from microfilm copies available at the New York State Library. Other copies may be available elsewhere. Although these newspapers were published in Washington County, they include notices for all the surrounding counties and the state of Vermont. They also include many notices for those people who moved to other towns in New York or to other states.

Vital records were being recorded by the Town Clerks in New York State beginning in 1880. However, recording was not mandatory until 1906. Before 1880 one of the best sources for these vital records are local newspapers for that time period. Verification of the information contained in these newspapers should be made by using a primary source whenever possible. Sometimes mistakes were made in printing and these newspapers are very old and sometimes very difficult to read. It is still one of the best sources available.

Notices may have been printed in more than one newspaper and occasionally there is a difference in either the age of the person or in the date given. When this happened it is indicated by giving both dates such as (May 1/7, 1850) rather than using duplicate notices. With this volume and its companion "Marriage Notices from Washington County Newspapers," it is possible to find information on three and four generations for some families.

List of Newspapers

County Post and North Star	1837
Granville Sentinel	1875 - 1877
Local Observer	August 1865
Northern Centinel	1799 - 1800
Northern Post	1804 - 1821
Salem Press	1850 - 1855
Salem Weekly Review	1877 - 1880
Sandy Hill Herald	1829 - 1876
Washington County Chronicle	1864 - 1870
Washington County Journal	1845 - 1850
Washington County News	1871
Washington County People's Journal	1854 - 1880
Washington County Post	1837 - 1879
Whitehall Chronicle	1851 - 1877
Whitehall Times	1864 - 1877

1

COUNTY POST AND NORTH STAR
January 4, 1837 - May 10, 1837

GOURLAY Jane in her 75th yr wife of Thomas in Hebron, NY December 23, 1836

GETTY Maria age 39y wife of Capt. John Getty in Hebron, NY December 22, 1836

IRVIN Susan infant dau of Richard and Mary in New York City January 20, 1837

BROWN Col. Caleb age 77y in Hartford, NY January 30, 1837

QUACKENBUSH Gerritt age 73y in Salem, NY February 7, 1837

CLEVELAND Palmer D. age 51y in Salem, NY February 21, 1837

MC CRACKEN Jackson age 22y in Salem, NY March 13, 1837

STILLWELL Margaret age 29/89y (Illegible) in White Creek, NY March 27, 1837

BLANCHARD (Mr. or Mrs. paper cut off) John age 39y in Salem, NY April 3, 1837

BROWN Mary dau of Joseph in Salem, NY April 11, 1837

SAVAGE Mrs. R. W. age 52y wife of John in Albany, NY April 16, 1837, formerly of Salem, NY and native of Lanesborough, Mass. where she was buried

CORNELL Allen age 60y formerly of Schaghticoke in Easton, NY April 23, 1837

HAWLEY Catherine Matilda in her 25th yr wife of David and dau of James HARVEY in Salem, NY May 5, 1837

GRAY Jane in her 28th yr dau of William F. in Salem, NY May 5, 1837

GRANVILLE SENTINEL
September 17, 1875 - September 6, 1877

HARRINGTON James Harvey age 38y in Cambridge, NY October 18, 1875

WILLIAMS Alice age 30y in N. Pawlet, Vt. October 26, 1875

MC BREEN Thomas J. age 20y in Wells, Vt. November 4, 1875

HURD Mrs. Betsey age 100y in Sandgate, Vt. November 6, 1875

MC LEAN Mrs. Ebenezer age 59y in Jackson, NY November 7, 1875

RANDALL Jonathan age 74y in Pawlet, Vt. November 18, 1875

JAMESON W. G. age 30y in Rutland, Vt. November 19, 1875

MILLIMAN Joseph age 82y in Cambridge, NY November 23, 1875

WHITE James A. age 76y 18d bro of George W. formerly of Girard, Pa. in Quindaro, Ks. September 26, 1875, born 1799 in Argyle, NY, went to Girard in 1873

AGAN Anna M. widow of Benjamin F. at son-in-laws John H. **WALLBRIDGE** in Saratoga Springs, NY December 20, 1875

WINCHESTER Gertie age 12y dau of Norman in Pawlet, Vt. December 25, 1875

SCOTT John Jr. age 28y in N. Pawlet, Vt. January 16, 1876

WATKINS Cornelia Bishop age 32y dau of H. N. **GRAVES** in Granville, NY January 18, 1876

CLEVELAND Charles Hubert son of D. A. in Pawlet, Vt. January 14, 1876

HOLLEY Mrs. George in Ft. Ann, NY January 22, 1876

KING Mrs. Sarah E. age 35y in Argyle, NY January 7, 1876

CRONK James in N. Hebron, NY January 22, 1876. Buried Granville, NY

GREEN Mrs. Ruth age 76y in Cambridge, NY January 21, 1876

NELSON Joel age 32y in W. Pawlet, Vt. February 1, 1876

MC MURRAY Francis age 65y in Cambridge, NY January 31, 1876

TEMPLE Roscoe Conklin age 2y 11m son of E. B. in Granville, NY February 20, 1876

HALL Abbie age 18y dau of Rev. George M. in Cambridge, NY February 25, 1876

GREEN Orvilla age 40y wife of William S. in Cambridge, NY March 1, 1876

POTTER James age 66y in Pawlet, Vt. February 26, 1876

WARNER Elisha abt 80y in Pawlet, Vt. February 27, 1876

COOPER Matilda age 40y wife of James M. in W. Hartford, NY February 28, 1876

WRIGHT Maria C. wife of Sidney W. in Cambridge, NY March 30, 1876

WARNER William H. age 25y 8m in Cambridge, NY March 25, 1876

HOPKINS Mrs. Cordelia age 71 of cancer in Dresden, NY March 17, 1876

BARRETT Anna age 82y relict of Jonathan F. in N. Granville, NY March 18, 1876. Leaves son J. B. of Sedalia, Mo. and dau Mrs. R. G. **DAYTON**

GOULD Mrs. Ebenezer in Hampton, NY March 28, 1876

BARNET Mrs. Amanda M. age 74y in Cambridge, NY April 5, 1876

WHITCOMB Reuben age 80y in Granville, NY April 14, 1876

PEMBER Orland in S. Granville, NY April 17, 1876

LEACH G. C. age 54y in Pawlet, Vt. April 16, 1876

ARCHER Miss Sarah age 78y in Cambridge, NY April 18, 1876

RICH Mrs. E. M. age 62y wife of Alonzo in Cambridge, NY April 20, 1876

STEWART Joseph age 30y in Eagle Bridge, NY May 1, 1876

GRIFFITH Freddie Elwin age 3m 2w son of E. V. and S. E. in Jamesville, NY May 3, 1876

BRIGGS Mrs. David age 88y in Ft. Ann, NY May 18, 1876

ROOT Miss Sally age 85y in Ft. Ann, NY May 19, 1876

MOODY William age 38y in E. Poultney, Vt. May 27, 1876. Wife and 7 children

MORRISON Samuel age 91y 8m 3d in Granville, NY June 7, 1876

RASEY Samuel age 17y in M. Granville, NY June 10, 1876

KRAUS Peter age 45y in Granville, NY June 14, 1876

BLANCHARD A. H. of Schodack, NY shot himself in Shushan, NY June 17, 1876

HUMPHREY John age 40y in M. Granville, NY June 19, 1876

WHEELER R. J. age 65y in M. Granville, NY June 26, 1876

HEATH Mrs. ____ age 86y in Granville, NY July 8, 1876

GUILDER Mrs. Stephen in Granville, NY July 5, 1876

LLOYD Elizabeth age 59y at son-in-laws John W. **THOMAS** in Granville, NY July 7, 1876

REYNOLDS Oliver age 59y of Granville, NY in Corry, Pa. August 10, 1876. Buried Granville

JONES infant child of Hugh R. Jones in M. Granville, NY August 21, 1876

MUNSON Miss Libbie in W. Hebron, NY August 27, 1876

HARLOW Weltha S. wife of Judson R. and dau of late Chauncey **GOODRICH** of Fairhaven, Vt. in Whitehall, NY September 11, 1876. Leaves 4 sons 2 of Michigan

HANNA Mattie J. age 18y in White Creek, NY October 23, 1876

HORTON Mr. ____ in White Creek, NY October 20, 1876

ROWE Mary age 78y in N. Granville, NY October 21, 1876

ELLIOT William age 50y in Whitehall, NY October 16, 1876

WILLIAMS E. age 44y in M. Granville, NY October 21, 1876

BELDEN ____ son of Levi in Putnam, NY October 20, 1876

LUDD Edward age 23y in Granville, NY October 24, 1876

KELLY Martin age 21y in Metheun, Mass. October 19, 1876. Buried Granville, NY

SKIFF Anna Mary age 17y dau of Samuel in Cambridge, NY November 2/12, 1876

WAIT Sanford age 66y in Granville, NY November 28, 1876

NICHOLSON Mrs. Charlotte age 73y in Cambridge, NY December 3, 1876

WHITCOMB Sebrina age 77y Mother of Mrs. Dr. **GOODSPEED** December 11, 1876

MAYER infant dau of John and Margaret in Granville, NY January 29, 1877

MORAN Frank age 17y in M. Granville, NY February 8, 1877

BEATTIE Thomas age 74y in Hebron, NY February 8, 1877

REYNOLDS Deacon Harrah in Granville, NY February 28, 1877. Born October 12, 1806 in Granville, NY. Wife died June 1876, leaves 2 sons H. J. of Rochester, NY and Rev. A. E. of Natick, Mass.

WARING Sybil age 86y widow of John in Hebron, NY February 25, 1877

ROBLER Truman age 81y in Granville, NY March 5, 1877

MC CLELLAN Lizzie age 31y wife of Donald in Hebron, NY February 27, 1877

MASON infant son of J. L. Mason in Granville, NY March 8, 1877

REYNOLDS Nathaniel in Hebron, NY March 9, 1877

WILLIAMSON Albert age 17y in Argyle, NY March 12, 1877

GRAHAM Mrs. Fanny age 66y in Putnam, NY April 25, 1877

EASTON Edith age 3y 9m 18d twin dau of A. and R. in Stockton, Cal. April 18, 1877

DAVIS Libbie age 8y dau of Richard in Granville, NY April 28, 1877

FAULKENBURY infant son of A. in Whitehall, NY April 23, 1877

WOODARD Mrs. Daniel age 82y in Granville, NY May 2, 1877

MC ARTHUR Margaret J. age 31y in Putnam, NY May 4, 1877

DELEHANTY Mrs. M. age 29y in M. Granville, NY May 28, 1877

GOODSPEED Winslow age 72y in Wells, Vt. May 29, 1877

HENDEE W. wife of E. B. formerly of Hebron, NY in Pittsford, Vt. May 24, 1877

SHERMAN Daniel age 59y in S. Granville, NY June 10, 1877

WHEATON Isaac C. age 68y in Pittsford, Vt. June 29, 1877

LOCAL OBSERVER (Ft. Edward)
August 10, 1865

BERRY David abt 24y at Ft. Edward, NY August 6, 1865

NORTHERN CENTINEL (SALEM, NY)
April 23, 1799 - December 23, 1800

STEVENSON James in his 60th yr in Salem, NY April 19, 1799

WARREN Mercy consort of Rev. Obed Warren in Salem, NY June 25, 1799

DICKENS Mrs. ____ age 105y in Salem, NY (newspaper date December 24, 1799) Married 66 yrs at age 28y. Husband died in his 96th yr

COWDEN James in Cambridge, NY July 30, 1800

NORTHERN POST (Salem, NY)
May 29, 1804 - April 5, 1821

BOYD Elizabeth wife of James of Argyle, NY suicide by hanging July 6, 1804

SMITH Amos age 13 son of Thadeus of Salem, NY at grist mill August 22, 1804

NICHOLSON Com. James at New York 69th September 2, 1804

LINN Rev. John Blair Pastor 1st Pres. Church in Phildelphia, Pa. August 30, 1804

WRAY George in Westfield, NY October 3, 1804

MC COY Jane consort of John and dau of Robert **MC MURRAY** in Salem, NY October 5, 1804

SMITH Ezra age 21y of Salem, NY in Lansingburgh, NY October 24, 1804

DUTCHER Elizabeth age 16y dau of Solomon (put an end to her life by drinking spirituous liquor) dated Greenwich, NY November 6, 1804

HOPKINS Sarah relict of David November 19, 1804

STREETER Daniel abt 12y son of John of Hampton, NY December 1, 1804

MC WHORTER Mathew in his 79th yr in Salem, NY December 12, 1804

HOBART John Sloss in his 67th yr in New York February 4, 1805

GLEASON Jacob of Benson, Vt. January 3, 1805

ANDREWS Loring formerly of Albany, NY in Charleston, SC October 19, 1805

FORT Lewis in his 23rd yr in Cambridge, NY November 2, 1805

DOUGLAS Capt. Nathan age 47y formerly of Danbury, Conn. in Hartford, NY March 17, 1806

WATSON James in his 56th yr in New York May 15, 1806

MC MURRAY Betsey consort of Robert of Salem, NY and dau of George **BARBER** of Cambridge, NY May 22, 1806

CARSWELL Margaret wife of Abner of Salem, NY June 14, 1806

WILLIAMS Gen. John age 53y 10m in Salem, NY July 22, 1806

PRINDLE Mary Ann wife of Sherman and dau of Maj. **BRADLEY** of Sunderland, Vt. in Sandgate, Vt. (newspaper date July 24, 1806)

EARL Nathaniel in Whitehall, NY March 3, 1807

CARSWELL Nathaniel in his 79th yr in Salem, NY March 25, 1807

GREEN Benjamin age 70y native of RI in Granville, NY March 13, 1807

MOFFIT Robert in his 34th yr Monday last (newspaper date May 7, 1807)

GAINE Hugh in his 81st yr in New York April 25, 1807

HICKOK Ezra age 71y in Lansingburgh, NY April 25, 1807

CLEAMANS Damaris in her 77th yr wife of Joseph in Whitehall, NY April 13, 1807. Husband in 80th yr died May 8, 1808

QUA Thomas to be executed August 12, 1807 for the murder of his wife. Born Ireland, leaves son age 9-10 yrs and dau age 7-8 yrs

MC FARLAND Daniel Jr. in Salem, NY June 21, 1807

AMES Fisher in Dedham, Mass. July 4, 1807

BARBER John Publisher of Albany Register rec. (newspaper date July 14, 1807)

CURTENIUS Mary age 37y dau of Peter I. in Cambridge, NY February 7, 1810

WINAN John R. in Albany, NY February 7, 1810

HAY Capt. James in Cambridge, NY March 7, 1810

WEBSTER Rebecca wife of James in Hebron, NY July 4, 1810

BROOME John (State Atty. General) age 72y in New York August 8, 1810

BEERS William P. Clerk of Albany Co. in Fairfield, Conn. (newspaper date August 16, 1810)

WEBSTER Alexander age 75y in Hebron, NY September 17, 1810

CLARK Mrs. Amos in Salem, NY (newspaper date September 20, 1810)

STILES Robert age 79y in Cambridge, NY November 7, 1810

SMITH Israel in his 52nd yr former Gov. of Vt. in Rutland, Vt. December 2, 1810

MC MULLEN Andrew age 46y in Salem, NY January 19, 1811

RIDER Zera in Salem, NY January 19, 1811

SAVAGE Esther consort of John of Salem, NY and dau of Timothy NEWELL of

Sturbridge, Mass. March 14, 1811

LAW John of Salem, NY June 9, 1811

RICH Polly consort of Jesse in Cambridge, NY June 11, 1811

GRAY Finley William age 8m son of William in Salem, NY July 18, 1811

COLE James in Salem, NY July 24, 1811

THOMAS Mrs. ____ in her 80th yr in Salem, NY August 10, 1811

HILL William in Cambridge, NY August 10, 1811

ENSIGN Mrs. Elizabeth in Easton, NY August 13, 1811

BURRITT William in Salem, NY September 22, 1811

SLOAN Jonas in his 36th yr in Salem, NY October 6, 1811

YOUNGLOVE Moses age 24y in Union village, NY November 28, 1811

PALMER Mr. ____ in Salem, NY December 2, 1811

MC CRACKEN Anna wife of Capt. George W. in Salem, NY December 9, 1811

MC WHORTER Mathew in Salem, NY February 7, 1812

RUSSELL Abel age 69y in Petersburgh, NY February 14, 1812

BECKER Maj. David P. in his 34th yr in Greenwich, NY March 16, 1812

LEE Polly formerly of Salem, NY in Westhaven, Vt. March 22, 1812

ALLEN infant child of Dr. Abram Allen in Salem, NY March 18, 1812

GILBERT Betsey age 26y dau of John in Sandgate, Vt. (newspaper date April 9, 1812)

VAN VALKENBURG Peter in his 19th yr son of Jacob in Salem, NY April 18, 1812

MARTIN A. April 21, 1812

BRANNAN Michael in Cambridge, NY April 21, 1812

HITCHCOCK James K. son of Zina of Sandy Hill, NY in Greenwich, NY (newspaper date May 14, 1812)

MASON Dr. Daniel in Hartford, NY May 2, 1812

STONE Asa son of Abner in Salem, NY May 18, 1812

RUTHERFORD John in his 41st yr in Lansingburgh, NY June 12, 1812

GANSEVORT Brig. Gen. Peter of US Army in Albany, NY July 2, 1812

LYTLE Eleanor in her 91st yr in Salem, NY July 16, 1812

MC MILLAN John in Salem, NY July 17, 1812

HILDRETH Mathias B. (State Atty Gen.) in Johnstown, NY July 11, 1812

WARFORD James P. age 31y son of late Rev. John of Salem, NY in Saratoga Springs, NY August 21, 1812

INGALLS Charles of Greenwich, NY in Colonie, NY September 2, 1812

PATTEN Nancy wife of Capt. Edward in Kingsbury, NY December 2, 1812

BRADLEY Ahaz son of Capt. Peter of Weston, Conn. in Hubbarton, Vt. December 16, 1812

PROUDFIT Ebenezer age 58y in Salem, NY January 2, 1813. Wife and 5 children

WRIGHT Alexander in his 45th yr in Salem, NY January 10, 1813

LOOKER John M. formerly of Salem, NY in Cincinnati, Ohio December 17, 1812

HOPKINS David in his 64th yr in Hebron January 27, 1813. Wife age 52y (no date)

WRIGHT Sarah in her 61st yr wife of Samuel in Salem, NY January 18, 1813

OLMSTEAD Aaron (Assembly of Columbia Co.) in Albany, NY January 26, 1813

DUNCAN John advanced age in Salem, NY February 4, 1813

LYTLE John abt 20y son of David February 7, 1813, and son of John PARISH abt 20 yrs same day

ROSS Mrs. ____ age 51y in Salem, NY February 14, 1813

LYTLE Mrs. Jane age 71y in Salem, NY February 15, 1813

ARMSTRONG Elizabeth wife of James in Salem, NY last week and James age 67y died February 25, 1813

BLOSSOM Benjamin in Salem, NY March 18, 1813

TACLES James advanced age in Salem, NY March 19, 1813

CROSSETT Mrs. ____ advanced age in Salem, NY March 19, 1813

MONCRIEF Hugh age 53y in Salem, NY March 28, 1813

THORN Stephen in Granville, NY March 20, 1813

HITCHCOCK Phineas Jr. in Hebron, NY March 24, 1813

MERRILL Chillson in Sandgate, Vt. March 22, 1813

KNAPP James in Sandgate, Vt. March 26, 1813

BROWN Salmon in Sandgate, Vt. March 27, 1813

ROOD Abijah age 33y in Salem, NY April 10, 1813

TOMB James age 57y in Salem, NY April 20, 1813

MONCRIEF Polly age 27y wife of William in Salem, NY April 21, 1813

COON ____ child of Rufus in Salem, NY April 22, 1813

HANNA John age 48y of Cambridge, NY in Granville, NY April 21, 1813

FAIRCHILD Jesse in Cambridge, NY April 24, 1813

BOTHEL Alexander age 70y in Salem, NY May 1, 1813

SAFFORD Samuel age 64y in Salem, NY May 4, 1813

HARSHA Miss Mary age 30y in Salem, NY May 5, 1813

VAN VALKENBURG Sarah in her 56th yr wife of Jacob in Salem, NY May 8, 1813

BARR Moses abt 16y in Salem NY May 12, 1813

MARTIN Sabra in her 23rd yr consort of Adam June 1, 1813

FAIRLEY John in his 70th yr in Salem, NY July 7, 1813

BILLINGS Margaret age 25y consort of Jesse L. in Salem, NY July 15, 1813

PROUDFIT Dr. James in Phildalphia, Pa. August 8, 1813

CLAPP Mrs. Stephen age 51y in Salem NY September 8, 1813

THOMPSON ____ age 3y son of William in Salem, NY September 8, 1813

PURDY Mills of Malone, NY in Plattsburgh, NY November 6, 1813

MC MURRAY James in Salem, NY January 19, 1814

MC MURRAY Robert in Salem NY January 23, 1814

WENDELL Cornelius of Cambridge, NY in Albany, NY February 27, 1814

SIMPSON Robert in his 81st yr in Cambridge, NY February 4, 1814

STEVENSON David in his 40th yr in Salem, NY February 22, 1814

PROUDFIT Dr. Daniel age 42y in New York February 27, 1814

CARPENTER Maj. Cyril age 47y in Granville, NY April 12, 1814

STEWART Alexander age 83y in Salem, NY (newspaper date June 9, 1814)

RUMSEY Timothy age 24y formerly of Hubbarton, Vt. at engagement at La Cole (newspaper date June 9, 1814)

TOMB Martha dau of Rev. Samuel Tomb in Salem, NY June 10, 1814

HARVEY Jonathan in his 25th yr in Salem, NY July 6, 1814

FOOT Ebenezer age 41y in Albany, NY July 21, 1814

ARMITAGE William in Hebron, NY July 22, 1814

DEXTER Rufus in Cambridge, NY July 22, 1814

PRATT Capt. Hiram in Cambridge, NY July 23, 1814

WOODWARD Daniel in Cambridge, NY July 24, 1814

LEE John in Greenwich, Ny July 29, 1814

SPENCER Capt. Ambrose Jr. late aide de camp to Maj. Gen. Brown at Manchester, Upper Can. of wounds from battle of Bridgewater August 5, 1814

SIMPSON Alexander age 85y in Salem, NY August 28, 1814

DUNNING Mrs. ____ wife of Z. Dunning in Salem, NY August 28, 1814

TERQUAND Jane wife of P. L. formerly of Salem, NY in New York September 22, 1814

SLARROW Mrs. ____ age 92y in Salem, NY October 9, 1814

LAW ____ age 16y son of Thomas in Salem, NY October 20, 1814

GRAHAM Mrs. ____ age 78y in Salem NY November 17, 1814

CONKEY Joshua age 80y formerly of Salem NY in Pawlet, Vt. November 30, 1814

GRAY infant son of David D. in Salem, NY December 17, 1814

BULKLEY Cynthia age 28y wife of Charles in Granville, NY December 10, 1814

BULKLEY Chester age 31y in Granville, NY December 15, 1814

ALLEN Dr. Ephraim age 49y in Salem, NY March 3, 1815

MC MURRAY Robert in his 38th yr in Salem, NY March 19, 1815

CARSWELL Esther in her 80th yr in Salem, NY May 22, 1815

WHITE Rebecca in her 48th yr in Salem NY June 10, 1815

GIBSON Dr. Samuel A. in his 33rd yr in Ticonderoga, NY July 9, 1815

TODD Phebe in her 25th yr consort of Jonathan in Granville, NY August 6, 1815

MC FARLAND James in his 57th yr in Salem, NY August 11, 1815

GRAHAM James age 29y in Salem, NY August 12, 1815

LADD James in Albany, NY August 14, 1815

MC ALLISTER John in his 84th yr in Salem, NY August 29, 1815

WALBRIDGE Thomas age 23y in Lansingburgh, NY August 29, 1815

CAMPBELL Miss Ann in Argyle, NY October 4, 1815

ROWAN Abraham in his 37th yr in Salem NY October 6, 1815

MAIRS Dr. John age 26y Surgeons mate US Navy (newspaper date October 12, 1815)

CRONK Solomon in Cambridge, NY (newspaper date November 23, 1815) Married 2 sisters, lived alternately with each wife 1 week, 13 children by each wife

MC CLEARY Dr. Daniel formerly of Salem, NY in Clarence, NY January 2, 1816

MURDOCK Huldah in her 32nd yr wife of Samuel in Salem NY January 22, 1816

RODMAN Daniel in his 32nd yr in Albany, NY January 26, 1816

GRAY Margaret in her 30th yr wife of William in Salem, NY February 14, 1816

MUNSON John abt 55y in Hebron, NY (newspaper date March 7, 1816)

MOORE Rev. Benjamin Bishop of Epis. Church in New York (newspaper date March

7, 1816

ADAMS Col. Pliny in Hampton, NY April 2, 1816

MARTIN Asa F. age 7m 4d son of Adam in Salem, NY April 13, 1816

FITCH Martin in his 23rd yr eldest son of Asa in Salem, NY June 1, 1816

ARMITAGE Thomas abt 55y in Hebron, NY last week (newspaper date May 4, 1820)

HARRIS Michael age 43y of Caldwell, NY in Warrensburgh, NY September 5, 1820

MORSE Benona age 50y in Whitehall, NY June 1, 1820

VAN VECHTEN Catherine age 55y wife of Abraham in Albany, NY September 10, 1820

STODDARD Charlotte age 35y wife of Dr. Israel Stoddard late of Whitehall, NY in Blakely, Ala. August 10, 1820

HEATH Mabel in her 65th yr wife of Joseph in Greenwich, NY October 29, 1820

HORTH Thomas age 99y 11m 10d in Hartford, NY October 27, 1820

PRATT Nathaniel C. in Plattsburgh, NY October 25, 1820

SALEM PRESS
May 21, 1850 - December 25, 1855

SCOTT Anna (**STEWART**) in her 32nd yr wife of James in Salem, NY May 9, 1850

SANFORD Henry formerly of Salem, NY in Durhamville, NY May 11, 1850

FRAZER Nancy age 29y wife of Dr. I. G. of Lansingburgh, NY at Fathers Thomas **GREEN** in Cambridge, NY July 1, 1850

STICKNEY Caroline in her 45th yr wife of William and dau of Theodore **STEVENS** formerly of Salem, NY in Fort Edward, NY June 11, 1850

GOODALE Josiah in his 28th yr in Jackson, NY July 16, 1850

BROWN James abt 64y in Arlington, Vt. July 14, 1850

GARDNER John J. abt 36 son of late Ishmeal N. of White Creek, NY at insane asylum in Utica, NY July 24, 1850

WELLS Austin abt 40 grandson of late Austin in White Creek, NY August 6, 1850

WELLS Laura age 53y dau of late Daniel in Cambridge, NY August 6, 1850

DWELLE Hamilton age 9y son of Alphonso in Greenwich, NY August 6, 1850

COURLEY Jane abt 40 wife of James in Hebron, NY August 10, 1850

LEWIS Mrs. Otto V. in Greenwich, NY last week (newspaper date August 27, 1850)

KENYON Mrs. John C. dau of Henry **SAFFORD** in Greenwich, NY last week (newspaper date August 27, 1850)

DUNBAR Phebe D. age 37y wife of William in Windsor, Vt. August 2, 1850

STEPHENS Ann Eliza Jane age 10y 9m 3d dau of John and Jane in N. White Creek, NY August 20, 1850

RICE Lemuel age 71y of N. White Creek, NY in Greenwich, NY August 15, 1850

WOLCOTT Charles N. age 5y 5m son of Dr. W. G. and Harriet A. in Whitehall, NY August 17, 1850

ROWLEY Col. Lee T. age 52y in Granville Corners, NY August 31, 1850

HARKNESS Mercy age 65y wife of Jacob in Salem, NY September 6, 1850

COREY Ann age 39y wife of Allen and dau of late David **WHIPPLE** of Union Village, NY at Schuylerville, NY September 6, 1850

TILTON Warren in his 78th yr of Union Village, NY at Albion, NY August 29, 1850

GRAHAM Fidelio F. age 1y 5m son of Fidelio F. and Letecia F. in Schuylerville, NY September 8, 1850

MC COLLISTER Charles age 51y formerly of Salem, NY in Chicago, Ill. August 12, 1850

NASH Isabella age 10y dau of Henry B. in Sandy Hill, NY September 6, 1850

HALE Mrs. ____ abt 90 in Jackson, NY September 8, 1850

OSGOOD Polly in her 67th yr at Ft. Edward, NY September 10, 1850

AUSTIN Mercy age 82y at son-in-laws Gen. E. **BULKLEY** in N. Granville, NY August 26, 1850

DOUGLAS Miss Fanny age 21y in Whitehall, NY August 31, 1850

SCOTT Anna Margaret age 10m 7d dau of James in Salem, NY September 9, 1850

GILCHRIST Mary E. in her 20th yr dau of Jarvis **MARTIN** in Salem, NY September 18, 1850

MARTIN William B. abt 50 in Orwell, Vt. September 13, 1850

COOK Anna Maria age 30y wife of Dr. John T. and dau of Samuel **GILMORE** of Cambridge, NY in Jewett City, Conn. September 15, 1850

BROWN Jane Maria age 18y dau of Dr. J. H. at Sandy Hill, NY September 11, 1850

SMITH Mrs. Eli age 45y in N. Hebron, NY September 28, 1850

KING George Henry age 13m son of Alexander B. of Kingsbury, NY in Troy, NY September 25, 1850

PRATT Caroline wife of Preston and dau of Lansing G. **TAYLOR** of Ft. Edward, NY in Troy, NY September 22, 1850

VAN VECHTEN Abram S. age 22y at Buskirks Bridge, NY October 8, 1850

KIMBALL Mrs. ____ age 57y relict of Col. E. formerly of Ft. Edward, NY at Comstocks Landing, NY October 7, 1850

AMIDON Mary Ann age 24y wife of Johnson at Sandy Hill, NY October 17, 1850

PATTERSON Robert Yule age 11y 4m son of William and Maria in Whitehall, NY October 6, 1850

MOWRY William H. in his 40th yr in Greenwich, NY October 22, 1850

FULLER Dwight Henry infant son of Sidney at Union Village, NY October 13, 1850

WHITESIDE Phineas age 50y formerly of Cambridge, NY in Weedsport, NY October 10, 1850

BEEBE Miss Charlotte in her 30th yr at Salem, NY October 7/9, 1850

CONGDON Caleb in his 38th yr at Eagleville, NY October 12, 1850

AUSTIN James P. infant son of Dr. James M. and Catherine of Lansingburgh, NY in Salem, NY October 26, 1850

YOUNG Hon. Samuel age 72y in Ballston Spa, NY November 3, 1850

BULL Dr. Mordecai L. in his 34th yr in S. Granville, NY November 4, 1850

BULL Mary age 72y wife of Mordecai in Greenwich, NY November 13, 1850

EDIE John abt 30y in Salem, NY November 15, 1850

HURD Mary age 22y 11m wife of Nathan and dau of Cyrus **PRINDLE** in Sandgate, Vt. (newspaper date November 26, 1850)

PRINDLE Amelia age 8m dau of Cyrus and Amy in Sandgate, Vt. November 6, 1850

GRAY Nathaniel near 80y in Camden Valley, NY November 12, 1850

DILLOWAY Samuel C. age 56y in N. Granville, NY November 4, 1850

BARBER Thomas age 64y formerly of White Creek, NY in Marshall, Mi. November 9, 1850

ROGERS Sarah age 70y relict of Samuel in Greenwich, NY November 29, 1850

HAY Eliza E. age 25y wife of Archibald B. in Schuylerville, NY November 26, 1850

JEWETT David B. age 40y in Middle Granville, NY November 30, 1850

ROBERTSON Col. John son of Thomas in Argyle, NY November 5, 1850

WOODWORTH Mrs. Aseneth age 81y in White Creek, NY December 25, 1850

BARKER George R. abt 50y formerly of Sandy Hill, NY in New York January 4, 1851

WATSON Augustus C. formerly of Whitehall, NY in California November 6, 1850

PARKER Charlotte in her 38th yr dau of Mathew **CORNELL** of White Creek, NY in Greenwich, NY January 8, 1851

FOSTER Mary Elizabeth in her 26th yr wife of Asil and dau of Francis **ROBERTSON** in Greenwich, NY January 8, 1851

MC NAUGHTON John in his 31st yr formerly of Union Village, NY in Delsfield, Wis. December 22, 1850

ALDRICH Lorenzo D. age 32y 10m in Lansingburgh, NY January 13, 1851

HATCH Hamilton in his 15th yr son of Dr. Ira formerly of Union Village, NY in Springfield, Mass. January 18, 1851

CROSBY Flavel age 81y at sons S. W. in N. White Creek, NY January 27, 1851

MC GEOCH James Edward age 10m son of George and Agnes in Jackson, NY February 2, 1851

MC LEAN Phebe abt 75y relict of James in Jackson, NY February 4, 1851

HILL David age 63y in Salem, NY February 11, 1851

PERKINS Margaret age 37y dau of Joseph in Rupert, Vt. February 11, 1851

MURDOCK Fidelia M. age 36y wife of Samuel in Salem, NY February 16/23, 1851

ROOT Dr. Leonard age 48y in Whitehall, NY February 19, 1851

ROGERS Beriah abt 70y in Whitehall, NY February 18, 1851

SLOCUM Mrs. Elizabeth age 81y in White Creek, NY January 15 1851

BAILEY Daniel W. age 28y of Greenwich, NY in Troy, NY February 16, 1851

COOK Benajah Jr. age 38y formerly of White Creek, NY in Jewett City, Conn. February 11, 1851

HOLMES Leroy age 34y son of Dr. Cornelius and Mary of Union Village, NY in California December 16, 1850

HOPKINS Grace age 93y relict of George in Salem, NY January 28, 1851

SAFFORD Nathan abt 70y in Salem, NY February 27, 1851

GANDEL Mortimer C. age 34y formerly of Ft. Edward, NY in Schenectady, NY February 26, 1851

COLLAMER Mrs. Sophiah age 66y formerly of Sandy Hill, NY in Michigan City, Ind. February 8, 1851

ROWE Rufus age 67y formerly of Granville, NY in Racine, Wis. February 19, 1851

MERRILL John abt 85y in Salem, NY March 16, 1851

SMITH John Fayette age 21y 7m at Fathers Dr. Horace in Granville, March 8, 1851

WARREN Janet age 13y dau of John R. in White Creek, NY March 18, 1851

CURTIS Alice L. age 51y wife of E. M. in N. White Creek, NY March 17, 1851

SMITH Benjamin in his 19th yr in White Creek, NY March 19, 1851

MILLIMAN Frank age 7m son of Elisha and Sarah J. in N. White Creek, NY March 20, 1851

WHITE William Wallace age 2y son of George H. in Union Village, NY March 20, 1851

KNAPP Sarah Maria age 11m adopted dau of A. H. and W. Maria in Union Village, NY April 1, 1851

MC DOUGAL John Blanchard age 1y 8m 9d son of A. L. and Mary J. in Salem, NY April 7, 1851

TILFORD Stephen abt 60y in Jackson, NY April 4, 1851

WOOD Edward age 38y in Cambridge, NY March 31, 1851

WARREN Caroline age 45y wife of John K. in White Creek, NY April 3, 1851

ROBERTSON Matilda age 48y wife of John B. in White Creek, NY April 5, 1851

AUSTIN Catherine abt 40y wife of Lewis in Salem, NY April 15, 1851

MC MANN Eliza age 24y wife of Michael in Salem, NY April 19, 1851

DAY Hosea age 71y in S. Granville, NY April 6, 1851

GETTY George in his 66th yr in Hebron, NY April 15, 1851

SPRAGUE Rebecca age 55y wife of Jourdan in Salem, NY April 25, 1851

DAROBY Miss Edetha abt 50y in Salem, NY April 24, 1851

BLAKE Robert in his 90th yr in E. Greenwich, NY May 1, 1851. Born "On the banks of the Water Liddle" in Scotland. Came here with parents at age 10.

SPRAGUE Simon age 31y in Salem, NY May 2, 1851

MC CLUSKEY Matilda age 36y in Salem, NY May 3, 1851

MACUMBER Daniel in his 77th yr in Cambridge, NY April 23, 1851

MACUMBER Mrs. Case in Cambridge, NY April 23, 1851

CORNELL Paul in his 93rd yr in White Creek, NY April 24, 1851

WHIPPLE Alvira age 14y dau of Robert in Cambridge, NY May 5, 1851

EVANS Mary Ann age 36y wife of William in Union Village, NY May 14, 1851

HARKNESS Southard age 44y in Salem, NY May 20, 1851

GRAY Isabella in her 64th yr relict of William F. formerly of Salem, NY at sons A. Gray in Philadelphia, Pa. May 18, 1851

CLEVELAND Moses age 65y formerly of Salem, NY in Prairieville, Wis. recently (newspaper date May 27, 1851)

SEELYE James age 25y in Schuylerville, NY May 21, 1851

ASHBY John J. age 1yr son of J. B. in Sandy Hill, NY May 24, 1851

MC FARLAND Mrs. Ellison age 79y relict of John in Jackson, NY June 8, 1851

ROWAN John age 17y son of A. M. & Mary in Argyle, NY May 11, 1851

CONKEY Joshua age 67y in Hebron, NY May 1, 1851

ALLEN Lieut. Amos of Continental Army at Ft. Ann, NY May 30, 1851

NELSON Joel age 68y at Ft. Ann, NY June 6, 1851

WOODWARD Rufus at Ft. Ann, NY June 9, 1851

LYONS Eliza (SHILAND) age 29y wife of Rev. David in Mineral Point, Wis. June 2, 1851

PERRY Ovando in 52nd yr in White Creek, NY June 13, 1851

KING Elizabeth age 25y wife of Thomas M. in Whitehall, NY June 23, 1851

KNIGHT John abt 25y in Whitehall, NY June 24, 1851

FOSTER Mrs. Ruth age 75y in Salem, NY July 1, 1851

LANGWORTHY Eliza wife of Sanford in Greenwich, NY June 28, 1851

CUNNINGHAM Mary Rebecca in her 26th yr in Cambridge, NY July 12, 1851

LAKIN Alexander in his 17th yr son of Lemuel in Salem, Ny August 8, 1851

PRATT Wait S. in his 40th yr in White Creek, NY July 19, 1851

WARNER Jane Ann age 2y 9m died July 25, 1851 and John Warner 8th yr died August 6, 1851, children of Abner K. and Martha in Jackson, NY

KERR Isabella age 60y wife of Robert in Jackson, NY July 30, 1851

DUBOIS Peter age 77y formerly of Jackson, NY in Milton, NY (newspaper date August 12, 1851)

WELLS Olive wife of Samuel in Cambridge, NY August 6, 1851

BOYD Thomas age 90y 1d in Salem, NY August 19, 1851

MURDOCK John in his 5th yr son of Samuel in Salem, NY August 28, 1851

BUTTON Polly in her 79th yr widow of Gideon of Hebron, NY at sons Charles N. in Jackson, NY August 26, 1851

ACKLEY Orrin in Cambridge, NY August 28, 1851

BULLOCK Else age 73y wife of Ephraim in Union Village, NY August 25, 1851

ROBINSON Melora age 1y 21d dau of George and Emily H. (FORBUSH) in Union Village, NY August 24, 1851

YOUNG Mrs. Eliza age 51y in Easton, NY August 25, 1851

MINER Phebe age 16y in Salem, NY September 11, 1851

FISHER Samuel J. age 61y in Rupert, Vt. September 9, 1851

MORRISON Mary abt 22y in Shushan, NY August 28, 1851

WARNER Henry Clay age 7y son of Jonathan in Jackson, NY September 2, 1851

NAYLOR Charles P. age 3m 4d son of Peter and Margaret in Salem, NY September 8, 1851

SKELLIE Margaret, head injuries from fall in E. Greenwich, NY September 8, 1851

BASSETT Russell age 67y in Salem, NY September 18, 1851

BRATT Mrs. Sarah age 27y in Union Village, NY September 13, 1851

ROGERS Samuel abt 40y in Granville, NY September 18, 1851

GRAY Miss Mary age 23y in M. Granville, NY September 19, 1851

LOWE Samuel J. Esq. in Chicago, Ill. September 16, 1851

WELLS Lewis abt 40y in Cambridge, NY September 29, 1851

FARRINGTON Daniel age 2y son of Rev. Thomas T and Mary M. in Hamptonburgh, NY September 21, 1851

BURROUGHS David age 47y in Greenwich, NY September 22, 1851

STEVENS Peter age 81y 3m in Hebron, NY September 4, 1851

LAMBERT James age 82y formerly of Cambridge, NY in Lansingburgh, NY October 18, 1851

LIDDLE Jemimah in her 27th yr wife of George in W. Rupert, Vt. October 24, 1851

COON Elizabeth M. age 27y dau of Rufus in Salem, NY October 27, 1851

INGALLS Susannah age 58y wife of Truman in Belcher, NY (newspaper date November 4, 1851)

WHITCOMB Harriet age 41y wife of Oliver in Salem, NY (newspaper date November 4, 1851)

LIDDLE George abt 30y in W. Rupert, Vt. November 1, 1851

BAKER Elisha D. age 80y in Queensbury, NY October 17/23, 1851

BARBER George M. son of John and Elizabeth in Jackson, NY October 16, 1851

COWAN Mrs. Elizabeth age 68y in Union Village, NY October 24, 1851

OTIS Richard age 69y at Ft. Ann, NY October 9, 1851

MC MILLAN Andrew abt 32y son of George of Argyle, NY November 2, 1851

COON Miss Elizabeth age 28y dau of Rufus & Mary in Salem, NY October 27, 1851

BILEL Julia age 4y dau of Charles and Emily in Belcher, NY October 4/5, 1851

WARFORD Margaret S. age 65y relict of Joseph of Salem, NY November 21, 1851

EASTON James P. age 29y of Rockville, Ill. at Fathers in Putnam, NY November 17, 1851

MARTIN Asa age 62y in Salem, NY December 1, 1851

BLISS Henry age 59y formerly of Greenwich, NY in Fountain Prairie, Wis. November 12, 1851

AIKEN Amos age 56y in Greenwich, NY November 29, 1851

MC COLLISTER Thomas age 28y son of Charles formerly of Salem, NY in Chicago, Ill. November 22, 1851

THOMPSON Periam Jr. in his 23rd yr bro of Benoni of Buffalo, NY in Ft. Ann, NY December 7, 1851

TILTON John age 64y formerly of Easton, NY in Mexico, NY December 6, 1851

WRIGHT Benjamin in Union Village, NY December 15, 1851

EPPS John H. B. age 7y 19d son of John and Eliza in Salem, NY December 25, 1851

GRAHAM John W. age 26y formerly of Jackson in Batavia, NY December 28, 1851

FOSS George age 19y of Sandgate, Vt. in Shushan, NY January 8, 1852

WILLETT Cornelius age 54y near Belcher, NY December 15, 1851

DAY Thomas P. age 2y son of Franklin and Ruth in Belcher, NY December 15, 1851

ROBERTSON Alexander age 63y in Salem, NY January 27, 1852

MC FARLAND James I. age 54y in Salem, NY January 21, 1852

MC FARLAND Joseph age 45y formerly of Salem, NY in New York January 23, 1852

LAW John Hamilton age 7m 17d son of Edward and Jennett in Salem, NY January 21, 1851

FORGEY Phillip age 89y in Salem, NY February 6/8, 1852

JACKSON Jane E. age 17y dau of James and Sophia in N. White Creek, NY January 17, 1852

SWEET Jeremiah age 89y a Revolutionary Soldier in Granville, NY February 1, 1852

DONALDSON Jane Ann in her 24th yr wife of James and dau of William **MC GEOCH** in Jackson, NY February 15, 1852

ALLEN Charles age 55y formerly of Salem, NY in Whitehall, NY February 13, 1852

MC NISH Ephraim abt 40y in Salem, NY February 15/22, 1852

THOMAS Hannah age 60y wife of David in Belcher, NY February 8, 1852

LAKIN Lemuel E. age 52y in Salem, NY February 27, 1852. Born Sandgate, Vt.

RUSSELL David age 12y son of William A. and Clarissa in Salem, NY February 28, 1852

CORNELL Patience age 26y wife of Thomas F. in White Creek, NY February 13, 1852

BISHOP Jedidah in her 8th yr dau of Elihu S. and Hannah in Jackson, NY February 11, 1852

STEARNS Mrs. Sarah in her 85th yr in Pawlet, Vt. February 28, 1852

WHITCOMB Thomas M. age 41y in Salem, NY March 10, 1852

HANNA Robert Alexander age 1y 11d son of Robert and Mary Ann in Salem, NY February 21, 1852

ROBERTSON Sylvia H. age 28y in White Creek, NY February 26, 1852

WOODWORTH Mary age 51y wife of Lott in N. White Creek, NY March 6, 1852

CHAMBERLAIN Lydia wife of John in Hebron, NY March 15, 1852

RUSSELL David age 12y son of William A. and Clarissa in Salem, NY February 28, 1852

MC CLELLAN Sarah Margaret age 5y 7m 16d dau of William and Margaret in Hebron, NY March 18, 1852

OSBORN Caroline age 25y wife of Henry of Glens Falls, NY at Fathers A. **MC**

ALLISTER in Salem, NY April 1, 1852

MARTIN Eunice age 70y relict of Moses in Salem, NY March 31, 1852

BULL Mrs. Martha Jane age 25y in Hebron, NY March 26, 1852

LIVINGSTON Thomas formerly of Cambridge, NY now Ft. Edward, drowned while trying to cross the Hudson River on ice April 11, 1852. Also, a companion not named

ROWAN Patrick brakeman on RR fell under train near Shushan, NY April 6, 1852

CAVANAUGH William, John **HURLEY** and John **CAFFREY** all killed by train near Granville, NY April 8, 1852

OSBORN Carrie age 25y wife of H. S. in Salem, NY March 31, 1852

CHAPMAN Ann L. age 17y wife of Perry and dau of late T. N. **WHITCOMB** in Salem, NY April 6, 1852

ELLSWORTH Roswell age 66y in S. Granville, NY March 28, 1852

VOLENTINE Daniel F. in his 2nd yr son of Clark and Asenette in Shushan, NY April 7, 1852

WILBUR Arathusa in her 42nd yr in Jackson, NY March 24, 1852

SMITH Platt of Ft. Ann, NY froze to death while intoxicated April 4, 1852

MARTIN Harriet age 7y 7m dau of Bradley of Shiawassee, Mi. in Salem, NY April 24, 1852

DRAPER Mary age 21y wife of George and dau of William **GRAY** in Sandgate Vt. April 21, 1852

CROSBY Lott Woodworth age 3y 9m son of S. W. and Betsey in N. White Creek, NY April 23, 1852

MARTIN Miss Eleanor age 68y in Salem, NY April 29, 1852

MONCRIEF Miss Sarah age about 28y in Sandy Hill, NY April 26, 1852

LYLE Lillian age 71y widow of Thomas of Antrim, Knockerboy, Ire. at son-in-laws Andrew **FOSTER** in W. Hebron, NY May 20, 1852

FLACK Wallace C. age 6y 11m son of John and Laurie in Argyle, NY May 6, 1852

WATKINS Martha A. age 22y in Jackson, NY May 6, 1852

WILKISON Gardiner age 84y in White Creek, NY May 24, 1852

CHASE Rebecca B. age 21y wife of Leroy in Cambridge, NY May 31, 1852

BARRETT Mrs. Charlotte in N. White Creek, NY June 2, 1852

NOTT Dr. Samuel in his 99th yr in Franklin, NY June 2, 1852

BRIGGS Mary in her 40th yr wife of Dennis in Shushan, NY May 16, 1852

BLAIR Phillip age 66y in N. White Creek, NY June 3, 1852

SKINNER Mary Ann in her 38th yr wife of Eli Jr. at Ft. Ann, NY June 3, 1852

GRAY Jenette abt 40y wife of Dr. Henry and dau of Alexander **BULLIONS** in N. White Creek, NY June 13, 1852

GRAHAM George B. abt 40y formerly of Washington Co. in Reynoldsburg, Ohio June 6, 1852

FLOOD Mr. beaten at house of ill fame in Sandy Hill, NY last week (newspaper date June 29, 1852)

MUSHET Margaret in her 88th yr in Argyle, NY June 5, 1852

STOTT John age 83y in Argyle, NY June 19, 1852

EGERY Sibbil age 73y at sons Joseph W. in Hampton, NY June 21, 1852

GOODRICH Alvin age 62y in Salem, NY June 26, 1852

BULL Mordecai age 77y in Hebron, NY June 24, 1852

PETTEYS Herbert C. son of H. C. and H. J. in Union Village, NY June 25, 1852

GRAY Kate Margaret age 15m dau of David S. and Margaret in Beltsville, Md. July 2, 1852

WESTON Ephraim age 83y in Salem, NY July 18, 1852

LANSING Jacob C. Esq. age 61y 6m in Lansingburgh, NY July 10, 1852, grandson of original patron of Lansingburgh.

QUICK Smith and J. **LA BONTA** in RR accident near Ft. Edward July 22, 1852

MONTGOMERY Jerome abt 30y son of John of Salem, NY hit by train July 29, 1852

WATSON William age 6m 1w 3d son of Nelson and Jane in Salem, NY July 30, 1852

LAW Elizabeth age 66y widow of Robert R. in Jackson, NY July 23, 1852

BURROUGHS Ephraim age 53y in Cambridge, NY July 16, 1852

CRONIN Eugene age 50y in Salem, NY August 6, 1852

DILLINGHAM Hannah age 24y dau of Joseph and Ruth of Granville, NY in Kingsbury, NY July 28, 1852

DYER Harriet age 35y wife of Martin D. in Union Village, NY August 10, 1852

BULL George C. age 1y 22d son of C. H. in Hebron, NY August 5, 1852

HALL William in his 79th yr in Cambridge, NY August 9, 1852

STEVENSON William abt 45y in N. Argyle, NY September 10, 1852

MC CANNER John age 42y in Salem, NY August 31, 1852

RUSSELL Thomas age 78y in White Creek, NY September 3, 1852

GANTZ George W. age 74y in Salem, NY September 23, 1852

BARBER Susannah age 72y relict of Gardner in Camden, NY September 27, 1852

BRAKENRIDGE Sarah widow of David late of Prescott at sons A. R. WARD in Smiths Falls, Canada W. September 14, 1852. Bro David RUSSELL of Salem, NY

CRONIN Ellen age 52y relict of Eugene in Salem, NY October 2, 1852

MILLER Mrs. Catherine in her 27th yr in Whitehall, NY September 26, 1852

NELSON Nehemiah age 62y in Granville, NY September 24, 1852

DENSMORE Mary A. in her 30th yr September 17, 1852 and Lydia E. in her 18th yr September 24, 1852, daughters of H. Densmore in Granville, NY

MINER Fanny Adams age 41y wife of A. L. and dau of late Abraham BEMAN of Hampton, NY in Manchester, Vt. September 15, 1852

BOYD Margaret in her 85th yr in Salem, NY October 9, 1852

SMART Elizabeth age 62y wife of James of Salem, NY in Pittstown, NY October 10, 1852

MARTIN Martha in her 66th yr wife of Andrew in Salem, NY September 15, 1852

FARLEND John engineer killed when train fell through bridge October 20, 1852

WAIT Zeba in his 82nd yr at Waites Corners, NY October 7, 1852. 8th son of William who settled Waites Corners in 1786

VOLENTINE George D. age 9m 20d son of Daniel and Sarah J. in Shushan October 19, 1852

EDGAR Jane Eliza age 3y 5m 8d dau of William and Mary H. in Salem, NY October 4, 1852

EDGAR James G. age 1y 14d in Salem, NY October 25, 1852

MC CLAUGHRY John Alexander in his 22nd yr formerly of Salem, NY on way to Oregon September 11, 1852

SHILAND John age 52y in Cambridge, NY November 7, 1852

CARNEY Arthur age 63y in Salem, NY November 11, 1852

LAMBERT Mary age 70y in Salem, NY November 22, 1852

WILSON Charles age 13m son of Nathan W. and Maria B. in Salem, NY November 4, 1852

FOWLER Sarah Elizabeth age 22y wife of Henry of Chicago, Ill. at Fathers John **WILLARD** in Saratoga Springs, NY November 13, 1852

BLISS Pelatiah age 31y only son of Luther in Lansingburgh, NY November 26, 1852

FREEMAN C. P. age 43y formerly of Salem, NY in New York December 3, 1852

GRAY Clarence age 5y 4m son of John W. and Caroline in Oak Grove, Wis. December 23, 1852

TUCKER Dr. James age 45y in Greenwich, NY December 29, 1852

DENNIS William in his 31st yr in Easton, NY December 30, 1852

MC LAUGHRY Rev. T. C. late of Cambridge, NY in Lisbon, NY January 6, 1853

BILLINGS Robert age 27y son of Chester in Salem, NY January 21, 1853

LORD Charles age 8m son of James and Harriet in Salem, NY January 21, 1853

ALGER Martha Elizabeth age 4m 4d dau of James T. and Mary in Salem, NY January 21, 1853

SHERMAN Marquis Lafayette age 5y 6m 16d son of William and Hannah in W. Rupert, Vt. January 23, 1853

LEAVENWORTH Josiah age 9y 5m son of John S. and Samantha in W. Rupert, Vt. January 23, 1853

KELLOGG Orrin age 4m 6d son of O. K. and M. A. in Union Village, NY February

3, 1853

ARCHIBALD Capt. Robert age 72y in Cambridge, NY February 18, 1853

HALLEY Phebe Vail age 14y dau of Ebenezer in Troy, NY February 11, 1853

WILSON ____ son of Eli G. kicked by horse in Hebron, NY February 8, 1853

BRUCE Asa abt 50y in Salem, NY February 21, 1853

STEVENSON William age 86y in Cambridge, NY February 20, 1853

ALLEN Charles age 70y in Belcher, NY January 25/29, 1853

MC CLEARY William abt 60y formerly of W. Rupert, Vt. between San Francisco and Utah. Formerly a mormon and brother-in-law of Joseph **SMITH**. Leaves a family in Fulton Co. Ill.

MC EACHRON Elizabeth age 5y 24d dau of James and Sarah in Hebron, NY February 7, 1853

CONEY James C. age 52y formerly of Jackson, NY in Etna, Ohio February 7, 1853

GOURLEY Thomas in his 21st yr son of James in Jersey City, NJ March 3, 1853

SAFFORD Margaret C. age 7y dau of William C. and Mary in Salem, NY March 26, 1853

PERKINS John abt 70y in Sandgate, Vt. March 27, 1853

HURD Lansing in his 47th yr in W. Sandgate, Vt. March 12, 1853

STEWART Joseph age 75y formerly of White Creek, NY in Washington DC February 27, 1853

GIBSON Margaret abt 65y formerly of Salem, NY in Chicago, Ill. February 17, 1853

HARRIS Ebenezer in Camden Valley, NY April 1, 1853. Born December 22, 1765 in Brooklyn, Conn. Married 1785 in Halifax, Vt. Lydia **SAWTELL** dau of Revolutionary Soldier. Lived E. Salem, NY 64 years

NAYLOR Mary Alice age 2m 8d dau of Peter and Margaret M. in Salem, NY April 8, 1853

GRAY Charlotte age 50y wife of David and dau of late James **HAWLEY** of Troy, NY in Camden Valley, NY April 9, 1853. Born 1803 in Salem, NY

CUMMINGS James age 80y in Hebron, NY April 8, 1853

DOBBIN Miss Sarah age 38y in Jackson, NY April 10, 1853

FELTON Mrs. M. S. G. age 45y formerly of Jeffrey, NH at bro O. T. **GILMAN** in Salem, NY April 2, 1853 and Mary age 72y Mother of O. T. died April 15, 1853

CRONIN Ellen age 8y 11m dau of Eugene and Ellen in Salem, NY April 14, 1853

HILL Mary age 1y 4m 23d dau of W. W. and Susan in Salem, NY April 14, 1853

MC DOUGAL Ellen age 1y 6m dau of A. L. and M. in Salem, NY April 10, 1853

AUSTIN Roxa age 15y dau of Lucius and Hannah in Camden Valley, NY May 6, 1853

CHASE Samuel age 56y in Salem, NY April 12, 1853

MARTIN Artemesia in her 60th yr wife of Aaron in Salem, NY May 12, 1853

OSBORN Henry Allen age 10m 18d son of Henry in Salem, NY May 11, 1853

MAHEW Sarah age 68y wife of Adonijah in Cambridge, May 13, 1853

SNYDER Elizabeth age 50y wife of George in Ft. Edward, NY May 20, 1853

HORTON Mrs. Jane Ann dau of James and Nancy **GETTY** of Hebron, NY in Hannibal, NY May 25, 1853

SCOTT Miss Christiana age 55y in Salem, NY June 2, 1853

GIBSON Jane age 2y 2m dau of A. C. and Eliza M. (**ROBERTSON**) in Salem, NY June 14, 1853

MC NISH Andrew age 49y in Salem, NY June 6, 1853

BLANCHARD Anthony I. age 84y in Salem, NY June 14, 1853. Born August 21, 1768 in New York of Huguenot family, married dau of late Gen. John **WILLIAMS**

YOUNG Robert E. age 30y 31d in Salem, NY July 5, 1853

STONE Horace P. age 32y in E. Greenwich, NY July 19, 1853

GIBSON Charles in his 4th yr son of James and Jane in Salem, NY July 22, 1853

STEVENSON James in his 24th yr in Argyle, NY July 18, 1853

ROUSE Lydia in her 72nd yr wife of Joseph in Argyle, NY July 21, 1853

ROGERS Henry Osborn in his 5th yr died July 14, 1853 and Sarah Elizabeth age 2yrs died July 16, 1853 children of Charles and Mary in Hebron, NY

REED Emily (**WILCOX**) age 34y and infant son, wife and son of Rev. V. D. Reed in Lansingburgh, NY July 26, 1853

WILLIAMSON William in his 19th yr in Argyle, NY August 7, 1853

SAFFORD Charlotte Ann age 1y 14d dau of Nathan F. and Betsy Ann in Salem, NY August 15, 1853

COOPER Mary age 61y wife of David in Salem, NY August 10, 1853 and dau Elizabeth 21y 4m 22d died August 24, 1853

MC CLELLAN Alexander age 28y 7m 13d in Hebron, NY August 11, 1853

WATKINS Henry age 40y in Cambridge, NY August 10, 1853

LAW John R. abt 85y in Jackson, NY August 16, 1853. Son George of New York

MILLINGTON Mrs. Eunice abt 22y in White Creek, NY August 16, 1853

ATWOOD Hannah G. age 78y widow of Z. Atwood in Salem, NY August 29, 1853

BEATTIE John W. abt 50y in Salem, NY September 10, 1853

SAVAGE Andrew M. age 23y late of Natchez, Miss. at Fathers in Argyle, NY September 12, 1853

LIDDLE Jane Eliza age 2y 4m 12d dau of John and Catherine in Salem, NY September 15, 1853

WALKER Emily E. age 24y wife of George in Danby, Vt. September 22, 1853

DOUGLAS Fanny M. age 37y wife of Dr. Horace Douglas formerly of Dorchester, Vt. in Salem, NY October 25, 1853

CLARK Martha age 51y widow of Horace in Middletown, Vt. October 29, 1853

FISHER Betsey age 61y widow of W. in Salem, NY November 1, 1853

RICE Ellis age 20y son of Shadrack and Eunice of Salem, NY in Virgil, NY November 7, 1853

GIBBS John son of Dr. Leonard Gibbs late of Granville, NY at Ft. Wagoner, Oregon from wounds received during encounter with Indians August 24, 1853

MC MILLAN William Engineer in RR accident December 9, 1853

STEVENSON Catherine E. age 37y wife of James and dau of late Col. **VAN BENTHUYSEN** of Warren Co. in Lansingburgh, NY December 7, 1853

WILLARD Margaret age 37y 7m wife of John N. of Troy, NY and dau of William **TOWNSEND** of Hebron, NY in St. Louis, Mo. November 24, 1853

CUNNINGHAM David H. age 23y 3m 8d in Cambridge, NY December 11, 1853

BEATY John in his 70th yr in Salem, NY December 22, 1853

CHAMBERS Cornelius in RR accident nr Schaghticoke, NY January 3, 1854

MC MILLAN James Andrew in his 11th yr son of Harvey and Julia Ann in Shushan, NY January 2, 1854

HARRIS Anna in her 59th yr wife of Amos in Jackson, NY December 29, 1853. Buried Camden Valley burying ground

WESTON Theodotia N. wife of L. W. in Peru, Ill. December 20, 1853

SAXE Edward A. age 2y 6m son of Rev. G. G. and H. K. M. in Salem, NY January 16, 1854

GRAHAM Fidelio D. age 31y formerly of Jackson, NY in Saratoga Springs, NY January 15, 1854

CORBETT Nancy M. in her 31st yr consort of J. H. in E. Greenwich, NY January 23, 1854

BARNES Charles E. age 1y 11m 8d son of William and Emmy J. in E. Greenwich, NY January 21, 1854

SAFFORD Agnes Cornelia age 7m dau of G. F. and Sarah in Salem, NY January 22, 1854

STEVENSON Thomas abt 75y in Salem, NY February 11, 1854

COOLEY Mary age 39y 2m wife of Seth and dau of James **INGALSBEE** of Hartford, NY in S. Hartford, NY January 23, 1854

FENTON Phila in her 46th yr wife of Andrew H. in Shushan, NY February 9, 1854

BENNETT Sarah age 90y at Sandgate, Vt. February 9, 1854

BARKER Walter F. age 43y in Leicester, Vt. February 8, 1854

ALDEN Francis age 23y son of William in Leicester, Vt. February 10, 1854

ARCHIBALD Eliza Margaret age 2y 7m dau of David T. and Margaret in Salem, NY February 27, 1854

EGERY Mary age 33y in Hampton, NY February 27, 1854

HEWITT Jennette age 22y 6m dau of James and Philanda in Hebron, NY February 26, 1854

MC CLELLAN Nancy age 49y 4m 3d wife of Gordon in Hebron, NY March 5, 1854

GRAHAM William G. in his 51st yr in Reynoldsburgh, Ohio January 18, 1854. Came to Salem, NY with father George in 1817

STEARNS Ann age 23y wife of William and dau of William **SCOTT** in Sandgate, Vt. March 9, 1854

BAILEY Mary age 45y wife of William in Rupert, Vt. March 24, 1854

PERRY Miss Sarah dau of Clark at female Seminary March 28, 1854

SCOTT Isabel K. age 24y wife of Charles of Salem, NY March 31, 1854

MC DOUGAL Daniel age 11m 23d son of Daniel and Mary in Salem, NY April 3, 1854

POTTER Nathaniel age 86y in Granville, NY April 14, 1854

MAIRS John age 46y formerly of Argyle, NY in Lansingburgh, NY April 26/28, 1854

MONTGOMERY Cordelia Frances age 8y 9m dau of James H. and Sarah in Lansingburgh, NY April 23, 1854 and James Augustus age 5y 3m died April 25, 1854

WATKINS Mrs. Susannah age 67y formerly of Salem, NY in Banksville, Ohio April 23, 1854

MC NAUGHTON Mrs. Nancy age 84y in Salem, NY May 23, 1854

BROWN Gratis age 75y wife of David in Rupert, Vt. May 10, 1854

CURTIS Amos age 86y in Pawlet, Vt. May 8, 1854

PERRY Martha age 7y dau of Hugh and Margaret in Salem, NY June 4, 1854

SMART Emily age 2y 4m dau of James and Jane in Salem, NY June 8, 1854

BECKWITH Henry age 76y in W. Granville, NY June 8, 1854

JONES Ann Eliza age 9m 25d dau of L. J. and Mary S. in Jasper Co. Miss. May 20, 1854

SHIPLEY Ella W. in her 21st yr wife of S. B. Shipley in Salem, NY July 10, 1854

MC MILLAN Julia Ann age 39y wife of Harvey in Shushan, NY July 15, 1854

CUMMINGS Chrisly in her 56th yr wife of Thomas in Putnam, NY July 16, 1854

BRITTON William in his 72nd yr in N. White Creek, NY July 21, 1854

STREETER Martha M. wife of Myron J. in W. Rupert, Vt. July 29, 1854

ALGER Elizabeth widow in her 80th yr June 9, 1854

CORBETT Jane E. age 31y wife of Elijah in Lansingburgh, NY August 10, 1854 and son Charles F. age 9m died August 17, 1854

FAIRLEY John in his 77th yr in Salem, NY August 20, 1854

VOLENTINE Aseneth wife of Clark K. and dau of Lott A. **WOODWORTH** of N. White Creek, NY in Shushan, NY August 15, 1854

MILLER Louisa age 9y 10m dau of Lewis and Marinda in Greenwich, NY August 28, 1854

SKELLIE Mary in her 21st yr in S. Argyle, NY August 28, 1854

KENYON Mary age 22y wife of Andrew at Fathers Clayton **YOUNG** in Easton, NY September 1, 1854

BARKLEY Joseph L. son of William H. of Salem, NY by accidental discharge of gun in Buffalo, Wis. August 23, 1854

CHAPMAN Mrs. Deborah age 67y in Salem, NY September 5, 1854

COGSHALL Thomas age 1y 10m son of Thomas and Harriet in Salem, NY September 8, 1854

BEATTIE Roxanna age 2y 2m dau of Robert and Elizabeth in Salem, NY September 16, 1854

WRIGHT Joseph age 83y one of the earliest settlers in Co. formerly of Salem, NY in Ft. Covington, NY August 20, 1854

COOPER David age 64y of Salem, NY in Oak Grove, Wis. while visiting his children (newspaper date September 19, 1854)

SHELDON Julius K. age 51y in Dorset, Vt. April 20, 1854 and wife Harriet H. age 50y died September 10, 1854

DOIG Margaret in her 4th yr adopted dau of James and Ann Eliza **CRUIKSHANK** in Salem, NY September 11, 1854

HARKNESS Jacob age 81y in Salem, NY September 22, 1854

CARSON William age 66y formerly of Salem, NY in Brutus, NY September 18, 1854

ROWLEY Laura widow of Col Lee T. suicide by drowning in Salem, NY September 23, 1854

CHERRY Catherine Ella age 3y 4m 5d dau of Alexander and Barbara in E. Greenwich, NY September 29, 1854

33

WATSON Catherine infant dau of Nelson and Jane in Salem, NY September 27, 1854

CRONIN Margaret D. age 17y 8m dau of late Eugene and Ellen in Salem, NY October 11, 1854

MC NAUGHTON Mary Jane age 3m 24d dau of Franklin and Elizabeth in Ontario, NY September 28, 1854

MC FADDEN James age 76y in Ft. Miller, NY September 5, 1854

MC MILLAN Robert age 19y in Argyle, NY October 8, 1854

NOYES Mary A. age 31y wife of E. P. in Salem, NY October 28, 1854

DICKINSON Eunice L. age 40y wife of Sylvanus in Salem, NY November 12, 1854

SCOVILL James M. age 1y 3m son of James P. and Nancy in Saratoga Springs, NY November 8, 1854

KANE Elizabeth age 17y wife of William and dau of Thomas BEATY in Salem, NY November 14, 1854

BLOUNT Susan S. in her 38th yr in Whitehall, NY November 19, 1854

FOWLER Jane age 70y wife of Francis L. in Salem, NY December 10, 1854

THOMPSON Margaret age 58y wife of David in Salem, NY December 16, 1854

ALLEN William Pitt age 47y in Whitehall, NY December 12, 1854

COOK Harriet age 30y wife of Isaac in Chicago, Ill. December 8, 1854

AGIN William age 30y accident at Bald Mountain, NY December 30, 1854

KING Huldah age 71y in Salem, NY December 27, 1854

FOSTER James age 94y in W. Hebron, NY December 12, 1854

AUSTIN Abner Jr. age 36y in Salem, NY February 3, 1855

MC ALLISTER Archibald age 69y in Salem, NY February 11, 1855

CRUIKSHANK Willaim Delaplaine age 5m 5d son of William in Cornwall, NY February 1, 1855

SKINNER C. G. age 22y in Whitehall, NY February 12, 1855

WHITE Dorcas Jane wife of John and dau of N. T. MUNSON of Hebron, NY in Somonauk, Ill. January 30, 1855

COWAN Moses age 64y formerly of Salem, NY in Leicester, Vt. February 21, 1855

MATHEWS Elizabeth in her 61st yr wife of Henry in Salem, NY March 5, 1855

DARROW Dennison age 78y 9m 8d in Hebron, NY March 7, 1855

BEATY Frances Elizabeth age 1y 8m dau of David and Nancy W. in Salem, NY March 7, 1855

DARROW Marriette (CHENEY) age 80y 2m 14d wife of James January 30, 1855

CRAWFORD David abt 40y in Hebron, NY March 24, 1855

CARSWELL Daniel age 81y in Argyle, NY April 1, 1855

HOPKINS Amos in his 66th yr in Rupert, Vt. April 20, 1855

REA Ann Eliza age 34y 4m 5d wife of John and dau of George and Elizabeth GETTY in Hebron, NY April 10, 1855

MC DOUGAL Eleanor age 78y in E. Greenwich, NY April 24, 1855

WATSON Nelson age 47y in Salem, NY May 18, 1855

WRIGHT Mrs. Nancy age 66y formerly of Salem, NY in Malone, NY May 7, 1855

MURDOCK Huldah L. age 26y 7m in Cambridge, NY April 1/8, 1855

BULLIONS Isabella (HARVEY) age 31y wife of Rev. David G. in Coila, NY May 19, 1855

BROWN Elizabeth age 78y relict of Dr. Seth Brown in Salem, NY June 27, 1855

HILL Mary Annette in her 16th yr dau of Abner in Salem, NY June 30, 1855

HOWE Abba Della age 12y dau of John and Caroline C. in Salem, NY July 20, 1855

SMITH Mrs. Ann age 60y of W. Troy, NY at bro Daniel HARKNESS in Salem, NY July 25, 1855

FOOT Erastus age 69y formerly of Granville, NY in Ontario, NY May 14, 1855

MC FARLAND Hannah Ellice in her 17th yr dau of William E. and Sarah in Jackson, NY August 14, 1855

DUNCAN Ruth age 67y relict of John in Salem, NY August 26, 1855

STEVENSON Martha age 48y wife of James B. in Salem, NY August 29, 1855

STEARNS Nancy age 54y wife of John in Pawlet, Vt. August 26, 1855

PROUDFIT Elizabeth age 74y widow of Ebenezer and sis of Col. John WILLIAMS in Salem, NY September 17, 1855

PROUDFIT William age 81y bro of Alexander in Salem, NY September 23, 1855

MC CRACKEN Sarah age 92y relict of John in Sandy Hill, NY September 11, 1855

LYTLE Andrew age 93y formerly of Salem, NY in Yorkville, Wis. September 7, 1855

BEATY James A. age 2y 3m son of James and Elizabeth in Salem, NY September 20, 1855

MC INTYRE Mary in her 82nd yr relict of John in Argyle, NY September 15, 1855

SAYLES Lydia A. formerly of White Creek, NY in Delevan, Wis. September 25, 1855

SWEENEY Patrick age 30y in Salem, NY October 5, 1855

RAYMOND Laura A. age 24y wife of Shepherd O. in Salem, NY October 16, 1855

SHELDON Jerusha age 77y wife of David in Rupert, Vt. November 16, 1855

LINCOLN Jane W. age 57y wife of John in Hebron, NY November 15, 1855

MC KIE James age 24y son of George in Cambridge, NY November 1, 1855

SKELLIE Robert abt 50y in Cambridge, NY October 26, 1855

BEEBE Ann age 62y wife of Roderick in Salem, NY November 27, 1855

SHEPPARD George W. age 47y in Chicago, Ill. November 21, 1855

BROWN Dr. George G. age 36y formerly of Hebron, NY in Canandaigua, NY November 19, 1855

HYATT James K. in his 57th yr in Battenville, NY December 12, 1855

ROBERTSON Anna Eliza age 64y wife of Rufus in Batavia, NY November 16, 1855. Born Salem, NY 1792 and removed to Leroy, NY in 1819. Buried Leroy

SALEM WEEKLY REVIEW
December 8, 1877 - December 30, 1877

COLE Maria S. age 52 wife of Daniel B. in Salem, NY November 19, 1877. Born January 1825, adopted by David BROWN of Rupert, Vt. Married November 1856.

FITCH Asa James age 25y 11d son of Dr. Asa in Salem, NY November 20, 1877

SAFFORD William C. age 71y in Salem, NY December 10, 1877

CARR Kate age 22y dau of Michael in Greenwich, NY December 16, 1877

MURDOCK Mrs. Jane age 69y 11m 14d in Salem, NY December 13, 1877

GRAHAM Ada age 26y wife of Frank H. in Salem, NY December 29, 1877

KING Thomas H. age 58y in W. Hebron, NY December 18, 1877

BEATY Ebenezer age 58y in Salem, NY January 1, 1878

HOFFERT Josephine age 2y 5m dau of Joseph and Josephine in Salem, NY January 7, 1878

TOZER Rev. Edward age 65y in Ft. Ann, NY December 31, 1878

BURKE Rebecca age 78y in Eaglesville, NY January 1, 1878

BROWN Thomas N. age 70y bro of Mrs. E. B. **HOYT** of Cambridge, NY in Dunellen, NJ December 29, 1877

O'NEIL Andrew abt 58y of Granvile, NY in the County Home December 26, 1877

JONES Hugh W. age 56y in Granville, NY January 6, 1878

RICE James age 67y in Pawlet, Vt. January 8, 1878

WOOD Mrs. Wealthy in Pawlet Vt. January 8, 1878

TOOLE Thomas age 80y in Sandy Hill, NY December 31, 1877

WILLIAMS Gertrude C. age 3m dau of T. E. and Sarah A. in Baxterville, NY January 5, 1878

FLYNN Mary E. age 26y wife of John and dau of Michael **CARR** of Greenwich, NY in Cambridge, NY January 15, 1878

GREEN Thomas age 19y son of James and Ruth in Cambridge, NY January 12, 1878

TIERNEY Thomas age 6y son of Patrick in White Creek, NY January 5, 1878

MC KIE Sophia (**WHITESIDE**) in her 84th yr widow of David of Cambridge, NY at son-in-laws Francis S. **THAYER** in Troy, NY January 21, 1878

SPERLE Matilda age 3y 6m dau of David in Baxterville, NY January 17, 1878

SMALLEY John age 71y in W. Rupert, Vt. January 24, 1878

GILMORE Eleanor age 75y 9m 11d wife of Martin in Cambridge, NY January 17,

HUTTON Martha age 30y dau of Thomas WEIR at Fitchs Pt., NY January 21, 1878

MONCRIEF Thomas age 68y in W. Rupert, Vt. February 1, 1878

HERRON James age 62y 7m 26d in Salem, NY January 25, 1878

ROBERTSON Ira age 74y in Camden Valley, NY January 26, 1878

TEFFT Willard age 72y in Greenwich, NY January 20, 1878

HATCH Willard age 74y of White Creek, NY at the County Home January 27, 1878

ROGERS William age 68y in Greenwich, NY January 22, 1878

FRENCH John age 38y at Lake, NY January 24, 1878

ROBERTSON Joseph age 61y at Argyle, NY January 23, 1878

LASHER infant dau of John A. and Sarah M. in Argyle, NY February 6, 1878

ELLIS Thomas age 59y formerly of Cambridge, NY in Ogden, NY February 4, 1878

PRATT Alonzo W. age 65y formerly of Kingsbury, NY in Westfield, NY January 25, 1878

KING Dennis age 80y in Hartford, NY January 30, 1878

STEWART Mary Jane age 49y in Argyle, NY February 10, 1878

AMES Reuben age 72y in Cambridge, NY February 7, 1878

MORGAN E. S. in his 70th yr in Hoosick Falls, NY February 21, 1878

TRUMBLE Mrs. Alexander age 73y in W. Rupert, Vt. February 17, 1878

LEARY Timothy age 2y son of Timothy and Honora in Cambridge, NY February 17, 1878

KENYON Mary age 26y wife of William in Easton, NY February 6, 1878

CHRISTOPHER John age 17y in Murray Hollow, NY February 15, 1878

HOGAN Patrick in Granville, NY February 11, 1878

HARRIS Relief age 91y widow of Samuel in Hartford, NY February 15, 1878

KING Eliza (QUINN) age 33y wife of George formerly of Salem, NY in Ft. Wayne, Ind. (newspaper date March 2, 1878)

MC GUIRE Mary Ann age 19y dau of Patrick and Hannah in Jackson, NY February 23, 1878

DORITY Daniel formerly of Jackson, NY in New York February 17, 1878

LIVINGSTON Alexander age 64y in Cambridge, NY February 26, 1878

MOREY Christopher age 80y in Salem, NY February 24, 1878

PALMER Mamie A. age 22y wife of Jesse in Greenwich, NY March 5, 1878

MC DERMOTT Rosa M. age 85y in Jackson, NY March 15, 1878. Sons Patrick and Michael

THOMPSON Miss Mary in her 52nd yr in Salem, NY March 20, 1878

MC FARLAND Nancy age 74y widow of Col. John Mc Farland and dau of late John **MC MURRAY** in Salem, NY March 21, 1878

AUSTIN David in his 48th yr in Utica, NY March 20, 1878

KINNE Lyman age 83y in Rupert, Vt. March 18, 1878

HARMON George S. age 53y in W. Rupert, Vt. March 18, 1878

SMITH Nancy age 83y at son-in-laws Enos P. **SHELDON** in Rupert, Vt. March 21, 1878

CALHOUN Mary L. in her 23rd yr at Lake, NY March 24, 1878

HOPSON Helen wife of Oliver R. in Wells, Vt. March 31, 1878

ROOT John R. age 68y in Rutland, Vt. April 9, 1878

ARNOTT Henry age 10y son of Morrison Arnott in Jackson, NY April 9, 1878

DONNELLY Richard age 50y in Salem, NY April 17, 1878

WOOD Louisa age 1m dau of Daniel and Eliza in Salem, NY April 17, 1878

CREIGHTON David age 71y in Salem, NY April 19, 1878

FIFIELD Eva M. age 2y 3m 11d dau of Frederick and Ella in Salem April 22, 1878

LEWIS Hettie age 24y 11m in W. Rupert, Vt. April 22, 1878

WILSON Miss Jane age 69y in W. Hebron, NY April 22, 1878

ARCHIBALD Hettie (**SKIFF**) in Hoosick Falls, NY April 23, 1878

MC CLELLAN James M. in his 74th yr at W. Hebron, NY April 24, 1878

ROBINSON Fanny age 25y dau of late B. F. of Salem, NY in Rutland Vt. April 26, 1878

BENTLEY Orr age 18y son of Abel H. in Sandgate Vt. April 23, 1878

PERRY Margaret age 67y wife of Robert in S. Argyle, NY May 6, 1878

MC KENZIE James age 79y at Green Island May 14, 1878. Buried Salem, NY

SPRAGUE Jane Ann age 65y wife of Lewis in Cambridge, NY May 16, 1878

MC NEIL Mrs. Moses age 43y of Argyle, NY at Utica Asylum May 8, 1878

NORTON George A. age 25y in Granville, NY May 4, 1878

RASEY Laura wife of Edwin S. in Granville, NY May 3, 1878

OWENS Kate age 28y in Granville, NY May 10, 1878

KEARNS Daniel age 5m son of Thomas and Bridget in Salem, NY May 12, 1878

MC CLINTOCK Patrick age 91y native of Antrim, Ire. in Salem, NY May 23, 1878

MOORE Calvin age 74y in Rupert, Vt. May 19, 1878. Born Rupert

COULTER Miss Elizabeth age 76y in N. Argyle, NY May 15, 1878

ELY Almira age 60y wife of William D. in Granville, NY May 22, 1878

HALL Mary E. age 50y wife of Sprague formerly of Salem, NY in Wamego, Ks. April 6, 1878

MC MORRIS Henry in his 35th yr in Salem, NY May 29, 1878

HAWLEY Betsey wife of Samuel in Granville, NY May 25, 1878

PIERSON Mrs. Melissa C. age 50y in Cambridge, NY May 27, 1878

QUINN Thomas age 33y in Pawlet, Vt. May 27, 1878

FERGUSON James age 70y in Salem, NY June 1, 1878. Born Jackson, NY

NORTON Ella A. age 40y wife of A. A. in Greenwich, NY May 31, 1878

BURTON Miss Sarah age 40y dau of J. G. in Rupert, Vt. June 4, 1878

MATTISON Lester F. age 5y died May 24, 1878 and Lulu S. age 3y died May 27, 1878 children of John and Sarah of White Creek, NY

DUNCAN David age 63y in Salem, NY June 11. 1878

PARISH Melvin son of late John Melvin in Jackson, NY June 7, 1878

WHEADON Anson in his 63rd yr in W. Pawlet, Vt. June 3, 1878

ANDREWS Edwin age 72y suicide in Salem, NY June 19, 1878

BENTLEY Esther age 5y dau of Abel in Sandgate, Vt. June 10, 1878

MC CLELLAN William G. age 77y in Cambridge, NY June 15, 1878

ROBERTSON James age 88y in Greenwich, NY June 21, 1878

BARTLETT Cornelia age 61y wife of Emri in Shushan, NY June 13, 1878

WOODARD Georgia A. age 30y wife of J. M. and dau of Mrs. J. W. **BOCKES** of Cambridge, NY in Dodge Center, Mn. June 8, 1878

NEWMAN John H. age 54y formerly of Cambridge, NY at sons in Sing Sing, NY June 19, 1878

WHALEN Edward age 38y at Fitchs Point, NY July 6, 1878

MITCHELL Carrie M. age 45y wife of Samuel in Salem NY July 9, 1878

SCOTT Miss Isabella age 73y in Salem, NY July 10, 1878

WING Hattie C. age 26y at Ft. Edward, NY June 28, 1878

BENNETT Eliza Ann age 47y wife of Daniel H. at Ft. Edward, NY June 28, 1878

NICHOLS Anna E. age 27y wife of Daniel B. in Argyle, NY July 6, 1878

GILCHRIST Nannie age 6y 1m 23d died June 7, 1878, Raymond age 4y 11m 11d died June 18, 1878, Cassie age 3y 2m 1d died June 19, 1878 and Manton age 2y 1m 5d died June 10, 1878, all children of John and Belle of Lake NY

HITCHCOCK Mary age 88y in Chicago, Ill. June 21, 1878. Born May 1, 1790 in Salem, NY dau of Alexander **TURNER** and grand daughter of James Turner one of the original settlers. Maternal Grandfather was James **MC CREA**.

LAMB Julia age 32y wife of William in Argyle, NY July 13, 1878

ROBINSON Mattie A. age 36y wife of Rev. James H. and dau of Walter G. **STEWART** of Lake, NY in Delhi, NY July 13, 1878

SMITH Mrs. Rebecca in her 88th yr in Hebron, NY July 13, 1878

NOXON Miss Celia M age 31y in Pawlet, Vt. July 13, 1878

HURD David age 81y 1m 27d native of Sandgate, Vt. and brother of late Truman in Springboro, Pa. June 6, 1878

GOULD Sophia age 33y 8m wife of Abram Gould and sister of Fred **KEGLER** of Salem, NY in Salt Lake City, Utah July 23, 1878. Native of Weinheim, Germany. Married 1875. Buried Salem, NY

MASTERS Anna (**TROWBRIDGE**) in her 82nd yr widow of Nicolas M. formerly of Schaghticoke, NY in Greenwich, NY July 23 1878

BLOSSOM Susannah age 63y wife of John in E. Greenwich, NY July 21, 1878

WEEKS Cyrus age 63y in Pawlet, Vt. July 18, 1878

HOYT Frederick D. in his 72nd yr in W. Arlington, Vt. July 17, 1878

FERGUSON Mary E. (**GIFFORD**) age 33y wife of James B. formerly of Cambridge, NY in Lowell Mi. July 4, 1878

BARNETT Thomas age 10y son of John S. in Jackson, NY July 31, 1878

MARTIN John Henry age 43y 6m 23d formerly of Salem, NY in Brooklyn, NY July 27, 1878

MC CLEARY Julia (**BEEBE**) in her 55th yr wife of James formerly of Salem, NY in Pittsfield, Mass. July 25, 1878

FARRER Charles age 69y in W. Rupert, Vt. July 20, 1878

DERBY Josiah age 67y in Dorset, Vt. July 18, 1878

BEVERIDGE John abt 80y in Jackson, NY July 30, 1878

BISHOP Dr. John in Salem, NY July 29, 1878. Born 1820 in Argyle, NY. Married 1849 Anna **SPRATT**

MARTIN Elizabeth age 74y widow of Chester in Salem, NY August 8, 1878

REYNOLDS James H. age 40y at Ft. Edward, NY August 3, 1878

MILLER Andrew age 5y son of James at Lake, NY July 31, 1878

DAVIS Mary Elizabeth age 41y widow of Henry W. and dau of late John H. **BOYD** of Whitehall, NY in N. Granville, NY August 1, 1878

EGERY Maggie age 25y dau of J. W. and Margaret in Salem, NY August 10, 1878

NUGENT John age 28y in Salem, NY August 12, 1878

GREGORY Clara age 8m dau of Thomas and Abbie in Salem, NY August 14, 1878

GREEN Janie M. (**WELLING**) age 23y 1m 16d wife of Ambrose in Cambridge, NY August 5, 1878

PRATT John L. age 64 yrs formerly of Salem, NY in Troy, NY August 20, 1878

NUGENT Patrick age 67y in Salem, NY August 17, 1878

HARWOOD Mrs. abt 70y widow of Joseph in Rupert, Vt. August 17, 1878

MC WHORTER W. M. formerly of Salem, NY in Kansas City, Mo. August 8, 1878

ENFIELD W. H. abt 55y in the County Home August 9, 1878

TURNER Cynthia age 31y 1m 27d wife of A. M. in Sandgate, Vt. August 14, 1878

BEEBE Albert S. age 9m 16d son of Edgar H. and Lucy W. in W. Rupert, Vt. August 21, 1878

DARROW Maggie age 21y suicide by drowning in N. Adams, NY August 18, 1878. Leaves two bro John and Robert and uncle Robert **MC DOWELL** of Hebron, NY

MILLER John age 59y in Salem, NY August 28, 1878

WARE Dr. Edward H. son of A. of Salem, NY in Acapulco, Mexico August 13, 1878. Born July 27, 1842 in Athens, Me. Married 1876 Eunice **TEWKSBURY** of San Francisco Cal.

LANSING William age 62y in Salem, NY September 6, 1878. Bro A. C. of Salem, sis Mrs. B. **BLAIR** and Mrs. James **VAN SCHOONHOVEN** of Lansingburgh, NY

STEELE Col. John J. age 82y in Salem, NY September 4, 1878

BASSETT Mrs. Eliza age 74y in W. Hebron, NY September 4, 1878

BAILEY John age 65y in W. Rupert, Vt. August 30. 1878

BASSETT Mrs. James age 80y in Chamberlains Mills, NY September 3, 1878

CARUTHERS Mrs. Jane age 67y in Salem, NY September 11, 1878

BROWN Alice age 7m dau of Henry V. and H. E. in Salem, NY August 30, 1878

MC FARLAND Harry age 6y son of John M. in Salem, NY September 3, 1878

BROMLEY Sabra age 58y in Schuyler Falls, NY September 6, 1878. Son Mack N. of Salem, NY

REID Peter age 85y in E. Greenwich, NY Septmber 6, 1878

GAILBRAITH Robbie age 7m son of Rev. G. T. in E. Greenwich, NY September

8, 1878

BEEBE ____ age 9m dau of John W. and Maria in Rupert, Vt. August 30, 1878

JOHNSON Louise age 30y wife of Allen E. and dau of Seneca W. **GIFFORD** in Greenwich, NY September 3, 1878

LARMAN William E. age 17y son of John and Laura F. in Salem, NY September 15, 1878

LYTLE Josie abt 2y son of Abram and Mary in Salem, NY September 19, 1878

POTTER Sally H. in her 85th yr wife of Joseph in Middle Falls, NY September 14, 1878. Sons Horace of Middle Falls and T. T. of Salem, NY, married 67 yrs

TAYLOR William age 29y at Eagle Bridge, NY September 14, 1878

POTTER Anna L. age 17y 6m in Cambridge, NY September 15, 1878

WALLACE Anna age 72y at Eagle Bridge, NY September 16, 1878

KELLEY Dennis age 4m son of Mark and Catherine in Cambridge, NY September 17, 1878

ROBERTS George Gaylord age 9y grandson of W. B. **BISHOP** in Cambridge, NY September 18, 1878

HAY John age 86y in Coila, NY August 29, 1878

MC AULEY Robert age 85y in Argyle, NY September 8, 1878

HUTCHINS Robert age 38y at Lake, NY August 31, 1878

PRATT Mrs. ____ age 78y in S. Argyle, NY September 18, 1878

ALLEN Cornelius L. age 78y in Salem, NY September 30, 1878

NELSON D. age 64y in Hebron, NY October 2, 1878

BLAIR Edwin age 72y in Williamstown, Mass. October 1, 1878, bro H. of Salem

BAIN Mrs. Hattie C. age 26y in Lakeville, NY September 28, 1878

LEARY Daniel age 25y in Salem, NY October 9, 1878

LYTLE Mary **(BEATY)** wife of Abram in Salem, NY October 11, 1878

ROGERS Helena in her 38th yr wife of A. B. in Granville, NY October 10, 1878

BEATTIE Mrs. Sarah age 80y 8m 7d October 14, 1878

KINNE Ella age 22y dau of Asa in Rupert, Vt. October 12, 1878

BROWN John age 73y formerly of Hebron, NY in Watertown, NY (newspaper date October 19, 1878)

BOYD Miss Susan C. formerly of Salem, NY at sis Mrs. W. H. **RYAN** at Ft. Covington, NY October 16, 1878

CRARY Kate (**HUESTIS**) age 34y in Troy, NY October 23, 1878

RANEY William T. age 40y in Shushan, NY October 20, 1878

CRONIN Eugene A. in Portland, Ore. October 14, 1878. Born August 9, 1841 in Greenwich, NY youngest of 6 children

MC CLEARY Minnie in her 16th yr dau of William in Salem, NY October 31, 1878

HOPKINS George age 59y in W. Rupert, Vt. October 28, 1878

BULKLEY Gen. Edward age 89y 9m 26d in N. Granville, NY November 3, 1878

BRIGGS George W. in his 69th yr in White Creek, NY November 3, 1878

FORT Susannah age 75y wife of Garrett in Cambridge, NY November 8, 1878

MOREHEAD Mary wife of W. D. and dau of Peter **WALSH** of Cambridge, NY in Mc Lean, Ill. October 29, 1878

LOURIE Laura E. in her 26th yr wife of William and dau of John **BURNETT** in Salem, NY November 14, 1878

ROWAN Archibald M. age 78y in Argyle, NY November 10, 1878

CONLEE Monroe age 53y in Greenwich, NY November 12, 1878

LUDLOW Elizabeth age 82y of Hebron, NY in the County Home November 10, 1878

ROBERTSON Theresa age 76y widow of Ira in Camden, NY November 1, 1878

WILLIAMSON William Henry age 37y formerly of Salem, NY in W. Rutland, Vt. November 18, 1878. Buried Salem, NY

DONLEE Henry age 25y in Granville, NY November 15, 1878

BOYD George L. age 19y in Argyle, NY November 13, 1878

LAW John T. age 85y in Shushan, NY November 28, 1878

WRIGHT Frank C. age 18y son of Clark in White Creek, NY November 6, 1878

LAMBERT Mary R. age 70y in Salem, NY December 5, 1878, son Dr. John Lambert

WILLIAMS Sarah R. age 30 wife of Erastus T. in Baxterville, NY December 6, 1878

MATTISON Julia age 7y dau of Bert and Fanny in White Creek, NY November 29, 1878

MATTISON Martha age 6y dau of Isaac and Eunice in White Creek, NY December 1, 1878

SHERIDAN Catherine age 59y in Hoosick Falls, NY December 9, 1878. Leaves dau Mrs. Patrick CONGDON of Salem, NY

DENNISON William abt 32y in Hebron, NY December 8, 1878

REID Harvey L. age 49y in N. Greenwich, NY December 9, 1878

LANT William A. abt 54y in Argyle, NY December 9, 1878

BARNES Mrs. Maria age 72y in Greenwich, NY December 8, 1878

DEAN Miss Margaret in her 65th yr in Cambridge, NY December 18, 1878

TUTTLE Mrs. C. M. age 44y in Cambridge, NY December 9, 1878

BRISTOL Polly age 82y wife of William at Ft. Edward, NY December 14, 1878

LIDDLE infant child of George and Mary J. in Salem NY December 23, 1878

GOODIN Susannah age 26y wife of Bradford and dau of George ROBINSON of Camden, NY in Hoosick, NY December 22, 1878

LARMAN Victoria age 37y wife of William C. in Salem, NY December 29, 1878

VOLENTINE George W. age 14y son of C. O. in Jackson, NY December 31, 1878

GETTY Chester L. age 56y in Hebron, NY January 7, 1879

HALL Elizabeth age 83y relict of Capt. John Hall in Argyle, NY January 5, 1879

VOLENTINE Jennie P. age 10y 8m in Cambridge, NY January 6, 1879

VOLENTINE Mattie age 17y in Cambridge, NY January 6, 1879

MAYNARD Rev. J. E. age 45y formerly of Hartford, NY in Busti, NY January 1, 1879

BAIN James W. age 59y in Argyle, NY January 2, 1879

THOMPSON Samuel age 45y formerly of Ireland in County Home January 6, 1879

RUSSELL David age 43y froze to death in Hebron, NY January 9, 1879

SPARKS Anna Maria in her 62nd yr wife of H. S. and dau of late David **COOPER** of Salem, NY in La Cresent, Mn. December 28, 1878

SHERMAN Zina age 75y in Cambridge, NY January 11, 1879

WELCH Mary E. age 3y 6m dau of Patrick in Coila, NY January 13, 1879

MC INERNEY John age 44y in Pittstown, NY January 14, 1879

LABOSIER Ida M. in Battenville, NY January 15, 1879

SHAW Miss Amy age 70y in Hebron, NY January 13, 1879

SCOTT John age 68y in W. Rupert, Vt. January 20, 1879

MC MURRAY John R. age 66y in Salem, NY January 26, 1879

KENNEDY Andrew abt 40y in Jackson, NY January 18, 1879

PRATT Mary A. age 69y at Buskirks Bridge, NY January 24, 1879

BRANT Mrs. William age 48y in W. Arlington, Vt. January 19, 1879

ROSS Maggie E. age 14y in Salem, NY February 4, 1879

SPERLE Julius W. age 5y 10m son of David in Baxterville, NY February 6, 1879

STEVENSON Miss Mary H. in her 79th yr dau of late Dr. James in Cambridge, NY February 6, 1879. Leaves brother Dr. Mathew Stevenson of Newburgh, NY

WILSON Samuel age 84y in W. Hebron, NY February 1, 1879

HAY James age 50y 8m in Hebron, NY February 4, 1879

RUSSELL John A. age 58y at Ft. Edward, NY January 29, 1879

NYE Dennis P. in his 62nd yr at Whitehall, NY January 30, 1879

BURKE Jennie age 11m dau of William and Frances in E. Greenwich, NY February 2, 1879

PRINDLE Jane widow of Edwin S. formerly of Salem, NY in Stillwater, NY February 7, 1879

SPERLE David in his 41st yr at Baxterville, NY February 14, 1879

LAWRENCE Peter age 84y in W. Rupert, Vt. February 14, 1879

BOSTON Samuel (colored) abt 73y in Salem, NY February 17, 1879

POTTER Rebecca age 76y in Salem, NY February 23, 1879, dau Mrs. B. F. BAKER

COY Mrs. Leslie at Lake, NY February 27, 1879

CLOUGH Willie age 11m 3d son of James and Mary in Salem, NY February 24, 1879

BARNES Mary (DOTY) age 72y wife of Dr. T. L. in Ukiah City, Cal. December 8, 1878, born Salem

BRAINARD infant son of S. Brainard in Shushan, NY February 13, 1879

FINCH Emma abt 20y dau of C. B. at Eagle Bridge, NY February 22, 1879

BURDICK Albert L. age 39y in White Creek, NY February 19, 1879

WRIGHT Mary age 67y widow of Alvah in Salem, NY March 4, 1879

PIERCE Dr. A. J. age 57y in Greenwich, NY March 3, 1879

STACKHOUSE Joseph age 67y in Cambridge, NY February 28, 1879

FOSTER Elizabeth age 38 wife of Joshua in Salem, NY March 2, 1879

BROWN Mary age 24y dau of John in W. Hebron, NY March 2, 1879

MACKLIN infant child of James and Sarah J. in Argyle, NY March 5, 1879

HATCH John Q. in his 30th yr in Hebron, NY March 3, 1879

LAKIN Mrs. W. H. age 50y in Salem, NY March 13, 1879

BARTHOLOMEW Thomas age 60y in N. Granville, NY March 2, 1879

HINDS Dr. J. R. age 47y in Harts Falls, NY March 8, 1879. Bro William in Greenwich, NY

FENTON Calvin age 63y in Greenwich, NY March 10, 1879

RIGGS Edward age 79y in Argyle, NY March 8, 1879

RICE Dr. James age 79y in Ft. Ann, NY March 5, 1879

ROGERS Sarah A. age 40y 7m 10d dau of James L. and Dianna in Salem, NY March 7, 1879

FOSTER Jemima age 69y in Shushan, NY March 15, 1879

BROWNELL Moses formerly of Troy, NY in Brooklyn, NY March 12, 1879

HILL Mrs. Harriet age 73y in Sandy Hill, March 15, 1879

ROGERS David age 79y in Hebron, NY March 21, 1879

MANUEL John Franklin age 2y 6m son of John W. and Libbie C. in Camden Valley, NY March 22, 1879

HILLS Asa age 87y in N. Hebron, NY March 10, 1879

WILSON Mrs. Martha age 85y in N. Argyle, NY March 11, 1879

GRAHAM Alexander age 89y in Argyle, NY March 13, 1879

DURLING Garrett abt 63y in Middle Falls, NY March 19, 1879

WILSON Andrew J. age 22y in Cambridge, NY March 18, 1879

SHEPHERD Laura age 80y 3w 3d widow of Capt. Russell Shepherd and Mother of Mrs. T. S. **CLEVELAND** of Jackson, NY in Westfield, Mass. March 18, 1879

MITCHELL George age 22m son of Nelson and Louisa in N. Hebron, NY March 6, 1879

HURD Henry age 79y in Belcher, NY March 17, 1879

MC MILLAN Andrew age 76y in W. Hebron, NY April 3, 1879

UPHAM Pauline B. wife of John formerly of Granville, NY and dau of late D. C. **BLOSSOM** of Pawlet, Vt. March 27, 1879

HOWE Luther J. age 34y formerly of Cambridge, NY in Pincoming, Mi. March 23, 1879

SISSON Mrs. Betsey H. age 73y at Eagle Bridge, NY March 27, 1879

JOHNSON George age 83y of Hartford, NY at sons in Hebron, NY April 6, 1879

POTTER Charles age 50y in Middle Falls, NY April 1, 1879. Bro Timothy J. of Salem, NY

ROSS John in his 88th yr in Argyle, NY April 6, 1879

BLOSSOM John age 66y in E. Greenwich, NY April 18, 1879

MURDOCK Mrs. Lavina in her 94th yr at Hebron, NY April 15, 1879

WHEELOCK Lysander age 63y of Greenwich, NY in Natick, Mass. April 10, 1879

BURCH Lyman age 4y in N. Hebron, NY March 21, 1879

LESTER Dr. George age 69y in N. Argyle, NY April 10, 1879

BAIN Mabel E. age 15m dau of James and Josephine in Argyle, NY April 11, 1879

HODGE Susan C. age 43y in Anaquasicoke, NY March 28, 1879

LUDDY Katie age 1y 10m 29d in Cambridge, NY April 15, 1879

KING Minerva age 72/79y in Cambridge, NY March 30, 1879

GRAY Herman C. age 3y 11m died March 17, 1879, Carrie age 9y 4m died March 18, 1879 and Jennie C. age 5y 8m died March 21, 1879, children of C. H. and M. A. Gray in Camden, NY

BENNETT James (colored) in his 67th yr in Salem, NY April 25, 1879

DORR Wallie age 4y son of Wallie formerly of Salem, NY in Brooklyn, NY April 24, 1879

HUTCHINS John F. age 66y 10m in White Creek, NY April 19, 1879

SMITH Samuel age 69y 11m 17d in Shushan, NY May 5, 1879

HOPKINS Thomas in his 61st yr at Argyle, NY May 3, 1879

LESTER John L. age 70y in N. Argyle, NY May 4, 1879

RYAN Anna age 11y in Cambridge, NY May 4, 1879

HORTON Terza age 76y in Cambridge, NY April 30, 1879

HARRIS Leonard age 72y in Hartford, NY April 27, 1879

FREEMAN Pliny age 81y formerly of Salem, NY in Ravenswood, NY May 12, 1879

COPELAND Alexander age 73y in Argyle, NY May 19, 1879

RANDLES Henrietta M. age 13y 6m dau of Samuel G. and Maggie B. formerly of Hebron, NY in Paxton, Ill. May 2, 1879

CRUIKSHANK Joe age 8m 23d son of Robert in Salem, NY May 27, 1879

WEBSTER Horace age 76y in Hebron, NY May 15, 1879

BUSHEE Jeremiah abt 71y in Pawlet, Vt. May 25, 1879

JOHNSON Mary Ann age 62y wife of John H. in Cambridge, NY May 18, 1879

STEWART Mary age 66y formerly of Argyle, NY in Cambridge, NY May 26, 1879

WHIPPLE Arrena M. age 24y in Cambridge, NY May 26, 1879

MURCH Maria age 61y wife of Richard in Greenwich, NY June 2, 1879

GRAY Elsie age 43y wife of Abel and dau of Daniel and Polly **BENTLEY** in Sandgate, Vt. May 29, 1879

NORTON John D. age 72y in Hartford, NY June 1, 1879

CHAPMAN Washington formerly of Lakeville, NY in Dorset, Vt. June 2, 1879

ELDRICH Ahira in 86th yr in Cambridge, NY June 5, 1879

FLETCHER Willie age 1y 9m son of David in Jackson, NY June 1, 1879

BISHOP Col. Linus D. age 51y in Ft. Edward, NY June 3, 1879

INGALLS Mary in her 78th yr relict of Charles in Greenwich, NY June 9, 1879

GOODRICH Mrs. G. A. age 76y in Battenville, NY June 10, 1879

POTTER Joseph age 87y in Middle Falls, NY June 17, 1879

SMITH Eli age 85y in S. Granville, NY June 14, 1879

SAFFORD Jennie age 38y wife of Charles in Cambridge, NY June 12, 1879

RUSSELL Roena age 87y wife of Ebenezer in White Creek, NY May 8, 1879

SHORTT John Forsythe age 27y son of Rev. J. B. in Cambridge, NY June 15, 1879

LE BARRON Sarah Jane age 43y wife of Michael in Cambridge, NY June 19, 1879

CAMPBELL Mrs. Jane age 32y in Hebron, NY June 15, 1879

BENSON Eva 21y 1m 2w dau of Hiram in Cambridge, NY June 19, 1879

FLOWERS Horace S. abt 63y in Salem, NY June 24, 1879

MADISON Beecher abt 20y son of late William of W. Rupert, Vt. in Jackson, NY June 22, 1879

LAMONT William age 20y in N. Argyle, NY June 23, 1879

HUIST Carrie E. age 33y wife of Dr. P. H. in Greenwich, NY June 26, 1879

MC CALL Hugh age 96y 8m in Rupert, Vt. June 23, 1879, born Scotland, served War of 1812

LUSK Rev. W. M. formerly of Cambridge, NY in Reedsborough, Wis. June 8, 1879

MC NEIL Mrs. Anna M. age 30y in E. Greenwich, NY July 4, 1879

DYER Joseph H. age 21y 7m 7d drowned in Nohawk River near W. Troy, NY (newspaper date July 12, 1879)

MC KIE Julia A. age 74y widow of William in Salem, NY July 16, 1879

TRAVERS James J. age 65y formerly of Anaquasicoke, NY in Oaks Grove, Wis. July 5, 1879

MC KNIGHT George age 80y in Arlington, Vt. July 14, 1879

FOSTER Mrs. Jane age 69y in Hebron, NY July 17, 1879

HUGHEY John age 56y in Argyle, NY July 23, 1879

SAFFORD Emma A. age 13m dau of Marvin F. and Mary J. formerly of Salem, NY in Oneonta, NY July 27, 1879. Buried Salem

SAVAGE Dr. James age 80y 10m in Argyle, NY July 25, 1879

QUACKENBUSH Alexander age 82y July 31, 1879

LIDDLE Ransom age 21y 10m in Salem, NY August 4, 1879

MERRILL Mrs. Lydia age 89y in Rupert, Vt. August 3, 1879

FLEMING Susie age 18y dau of Patrick in Salem, NY August 14, 1879

FOWLER Martha M. age 66y wife of Newman in Cambridge, NY August 2, 1879

HAWLEY Addison E. age 26y in Granville, NY August 13, 1879

BISHOP John C. age 66y in Granville, NY August 10, 1879

ABELL Caroline A. in her 62nd yr wife of Oliff in Ticonderoga, NY August 7, 1879

BINNINGER Maria age 63y widow of A. M. of Brooklyn, NY in Boonton, NJ August 8, 1879

SUYDAM Sarah age 65y wife of Riley V. in Saratoga Springs, NY August 16, 1879

FLEMING Ella age 21y dau of Patrick in Salem, NY August 16, 1879

WALSH Patrick age 72/77y at Fitchs Point, NY August 15, 1879

COMEGYS John Edward age 17y 10m formerly of Salem, NY in Chicago, Ill. August 12, 1879

SKINNER Talma age 10m 9d dau of L. S. and **Anna** F. in Burlington, Iowa August 12, 1879

PRATT Maria C. age 74y widow of Ira of Salem in Troy, NY September 2, 1879

GALE Warren age 6y 7m son of Curtis and Mary in Camden Valley, NY August 29, 1879

MORGAN William A. age 69y in Salem, NY September 8, 1879. Buried Troy, NY

HIGH Nathan formerly of Salem, NY in Seville, Ohio August 27, 1879. Born January 25, 1799 in Sandy Hill, NY. Married 1822 Maria **GRAY** dau of Nathaniel.

SWEET Agnes age 31y of Hebron, NY at brother-in-laws Elisha **HURD** in W. Rupert, Vt. September 8, 1879

CUNNINGHAM Cynthia T. (**FULLER**) age 56y at sis Mrs. William H. **SOUTHARD** in Salem, NY September 5, 1879

ROBERTSON Archibald in his 66th yr in Salem, NY September 19, 1879

BARKER John age 82y 4m in Cambridge, NY September 18, 1879

MAYNARD E. A. age 78y Father of Dr. W. B. of Salem, NY in Jamaica, Vt. August 6, 1879

HILL Frank I. 6w 1d son of W. W. and Mary B. in Salem, NY September 22, 1879

WILKINSON Truman age 63y in White Creek, NY September 16, 1879, buried Salem

SHERIDAN Mary age 6y dau of Patrick in Salem, NY September 19, 1879

ANDREWS Margaret abt 33y wife of Cleve in Danby, Vt. September 18, 1879

BEVERIDGE David age 74y in Hebron, NY September 12, 1879

BOWKER Martin formerly of Granville, NY in W. Pawlet, Vt. September 15, 1879

HAWLEY Etta age 19y dau of Elisha in W. Pawlet, Vt. September 25, 1879

CURTIS James A. age 30y formerly of Argyle in Wolcott, NY September 18, 1879

MASON Albert age 43 at brother-in-laws E. S. **SHERMAN** in Salem, NY September 24, 1879. Buried Brooklyn, NY

KENYON Harriet age 71y wife of Elisha in Jackson, NY September 18, 1879

MC GEOCH Robert age 58y in Argyle, NY September 12, 1879

GERMAIN George W. in his 81st yr of Albany, NY, formerly of Cambridge, NY in

Geneva, NY September 21, 1879

WELLS Martha H. **(MITCHELL)** wife of Austin H. in Albany, NY September 21, 1879

CLEVELAND Henry age 51y in Shushan, NY October 2, 1879

MC EACHRON Alexander in his 70th yr in Hebron, NY September 27, 1879

MC NAUGHTON Duncan R. age 81y formerly of White Creek, NY in Mumford, NY September 9, 1879

MANVILLE Taylor age 63y in Whitehall, NY October 2, 1879

DENSBURY Safety age 88y in Sandgate, Vt. October 2, 1879

WALKER Rhoda age 89y widow of Horatio in Manchester, Vt. October 11, 1879

HAYES Mary J. age 18y 9m in Sandgate, Vt. October 6, 1879

HOUGHTON John Alfred age 6m son of Alfred and Mattie in Cambridge, NY October 8, 1879

ACKLEY Irena age 74y wife of David W. in Salem, NY October 24, 1879

RIGGS Mrs. M. A. age 66y formerly of Argyle in Salem, NY November 3, 1879

MOORE Betsey **(SIMPSON)** age 81 widow of Andrew in Cambridge, NY November 3, 1879

HOUGHTON Andrew B. age 72y at Buskirks Bridge, NY November 9, 1879. Born Mass. Married Nancy **MONTGOMERY**

DICKINSON John son of Sylvanus of Salem, NY in Kansas City, Mo. November 14, 1879. Born April 2, 1841 in Salem, NY

RYAN Maria **(ROACH)** age 27y wife of John H. at Eagle Bridge, NY November 12, 1879

ROWLAND Garrads age 79y 9m in Jackson, NY November 20, 1879

WHEELER Hattie M. age 19y in M. Granville, NY November 11, 1879

GARVEY Eliza age 18y in N. Hebron, NY November 10, 1879

BARTLETT Sophia wife of Lyman age 79y in Shushan, NY November 7, 1879

SPRAGUE Caroline W. age 78y widow of Rev. D. G. in Salem, NY November 19, 1879. Buried Orange, NJ

BECKWITH Mary Banks age 32y in N. Granville, NY November 15, 1879

BAIN John Firman age 80y in Argyle, NY November 22, 1879

OVIATT David age 60y 9m in Jackson, NY November 27, 1879

CLARK John Albert age 40y in Coila, NY November 21, 1879

CHAMBERLAIN William C. age 23y in Salem, NY December 10, 1879

NOBLE Mary **(WHITNEY)** age 29y wife of Rev. C. F. in Argyle, NY December 7, 1879

SHIPLEY Sumner A. age 15m 3d son of Cornelius L. and Selina in Salem, NY December 12, 1879

ROTHDREM Albert age 16m 17d son of John and Mary in W. Rupert, Vt. December 21, 1879

BIGGART Mrs. Mary age 48y in Hampton, NY December 17, 1879

BLACK Archie age 13y 8m 16d son of Robert in W. Hebron, NY December 23, 1879

HAWLEY Elisha Jr. age 26y of W. Rupert, Vt. in Denver, Col. December 13, 1879

MOORE Charles H. age 62y in Greenwich, NY (newspaper date December 27, 1879)

TABER Emma M. age 23y wife of Hugh in White Creek, NY December 21, 1879

TRACY Theresa age 2y 9d dau of Dennis and Anna in Cambridge, NY December 22, 1879

MC MILLAN Margaret age 70y widow of Andrew in Cambridge, NY December 22, 1879

WATERS Earl age 75y in Jackson, NY December 27, 1879

FOWLER Blackman B. age 69y in Cambridge, NY December 12, 1879

SANDY HILL HERALD
May 12, 1829 - December 28, 1876
scatterd early issues

TARBELL Dudley M. age 24y in Sandy Hill, NY December 5, 1834

DUNSON Laura A. age 28 consort of John at Comstocks Landing, NY February 28, 1841

RODGERS Jane C. age 32y wife of George W. late of Vergennes, Vt. and dau of

Adonijah **EMMONS** late of Sandy Hill, NY in Detroit, Mi. February 18, 1841

BANCROFT Henry age 42y formerly of Albany in Sandy Hill, NY March 26, 1841

SHARP Holland found dead near Greenwich, NY April 1, 1841

STEWART Susan age 82y widow of Col. John at sons John C. in Ft. Edward, NY April 17, 1841

LAMSON Jonas in Sandy Hill, NY April 25, 1841

FINCH Darwin C. in his 21st yr at Shorum March 21, 1841

POTTER Amanda in her 31st yr wife of Joel F. in Pottersville, NY April 21, 1841

HOLBROOK Delia age 4y died April 25, 1841 and Jerome age 2y 7m died May 7, 1841 children of Lyman in Sandy Hill, NY

CLARK Sarah Frances age 4y 2m dau of Loreness and Belvia in Salem, NY April 22, 1841

PERRY Catherine age 9y dau of Rev. Joseph in Sandy Hill, NY May 22, 1841

COOK Warren abt 30y at Ft. Edward, NY May 13, 1841

PARMELEE J. C. of Talmadge, Ohio in Sandy Hill, NY June 29, 1841

ALLEN Sarah in her 86th yr in Kingsbury, NY July 1, 1841

PITCHER Montgomery P. age 28y in Sandy Hill, NY August 6, 1841

BENNETT Martha abt 38y wife of Hazen W. at Ft. Edward, NY August 17, 1841

CARPENTER Stephen age 63y in Sandy Hill, NY Agust 26, 1841

CRONKHITE Sarah S. wife of H. P. and dau of John **THOMAS** formerly of Sandy Hill, NY in Fonda, NY August 14, 1841

LEVENS Royal abt 50y formerly of Glens Falls, NY at Ft. Ann, NY October 5, 1841

FINN William abt 60y at Ft. Edward, NY October 8, 1841

NICHOLS Mrs. Mary age 22y in Sandy Hill, NY November 1, 1841. Deserted by her husband James G. Nichols

JACKSON Mrs. ____ age 46 in Sandy Hill, NY December 4, 1841

DUNHAM Giles E. age 28y formerly of Sandy Hill, NY in Hannibal, NY November 31?, 1841

BALL Charles age 19y in Sandy Hill, NY December 27, 1841

HENRY Robert C. age 32y drowned in Lake Champlain April 30, 1844

SHIPPARD Mrs. Elizabeth in her 60th yr in Argyle, NY May 30, 1844

WILSON Caroline age 22y wife of David and dau of late Carmi **DIBBLE** in Sandy Hill, NY July 4, 1844

BLANEY Mrs. Lydia age 42y in Sandy Hill, NY August 2, 1844

COOPER John H. age 40y in Sandy Hill, NY August 27, 1844

HOLBROOK Maj. Nahum in Sandy Hill, NY September 7, 1844

THOMAS John in his 76th yr late of Sandy Hill, NY at son-in-laws Mathew **HOPPER** in Plainfield, NJ September 11, 1844

PROUDFIT John W. age 45y in Salem, NY September 13, 1844

BUSH Juliette T. age 23y dau of late Amos T. at Ft. Ann, NY August 30, 1844

BARR Jonathan age 80y in Sandy Hill, NY November 12, 1844

BURCHARD A. C. suicide at Saratoga Springs, NY November 26, 1844

CHAPMAN Lucinda H. wife of John and dau of Thomas **ATKINS** formerly of Sandy Hill, NY in Center Taup, Ind. November 21, 1844

STEVENSON Rebecca in her 29th yr wife of James and dau of Mathew and Margaret **HALL** December 29, 1844

FERRIS William Henry age 11y in Sandy Hill, NY January 18, 1845

GOODRICH Asa in his 83rd yr in Whitehall, NY February 17, 1845

WOODWORTH Lydia Ann wife of S. P. and dau of Giles **BROWNELL** of Sandy Hill, NY in Wolcott, NY March 11, 1845

BROWN Jennett Moore age 17y dau of Daniel M. in Hartford, NY March 21, 1845

MATHEWS Henry in his 58th yr in Salem, NY March 29, 1845

ALLEN Dr. Abram age 81y in Salem, NY March 30, 1845

MOSS Charlotte in her 17th yr dau of Mrs. E. Moss March 21, 1845

FORBES Lydia L. age 7y dau of William and Esther G. of Ft. Edward, NY in Westhaven, Vt. May 29, 1845

HARVEY Sarah Elizabeth age 6y 6m 1d dau of George and Julia in Sandy Hill, NY May 27, 1845

CLARK John H. age 19y 4m son of Almon and Grace of Sandy Hill in Poultney, Vt. June 24, 1845

FAGAN Eveline age 21y 5m wife of M. L. in Sandy Hill, NY June 28, 1845

ROBERTSON Alvan age 40y in Salem, NY June/July 5, 1845

PARDEE Walter Clifton age 7y son of William H. and Susan B. drowned in canal at Ft. Edward, NY August 23, 1845

CLAPP Benjamin in his 65th yr at Argyle, NY September 19, 1845

BAKER Albert age 79y Revolutionary Soldier in Sandy Hill, NY September 22, 1845

DICKEY John H. age 19y 8m in Sandy Hill, NY December 3, 1845

PHILLIPS Ann Maria age 24y in Sandy Hill, NY December 21, 1845

PEFFERS John abt 70y in Sandy Hill, NY January 31, 1846

GRIFFITH Charles age 5y son of Ezra in Sandy Hill, NY February 1, 1846

HARRIS Samuel P. of Sandy Hill, NY in Schroon, NY December 6, 1846

PETERSON Jinnett age 65y wife of John at Ft. Edward, NY December 13, 1846

LOOMIS John abt 45y in Sandy Hill, NY December 14, 1846

FREEMAN Mary age 37y wife of Adolphus in Sandy Hill, NY January 24, 1847

THOMAS John age 34y in Sandy Hill, NY January 17, 1847

BIRD Thomas age 94y in Sandy Hill, NY February 9, 1847

NASH Adeline age 36y wife of H. B. in Sandy Hill, NY March 26, 1847

TAYLOR William age 22y son of David at Ft. Edward, NY June 4, 1847

PLATT Jane Eliza age 26y dau of late Isaac in Sandy Hill, NY June 6, 1847

WELLS William A. formerly of Washington Co. in Ontario County Poor House on Saturday (newspaper date Tuesday June 15, 1847 taken from Rochester Dailey Adv.)

CLARK Anson S. age 29y in Sandy Hill, NY June 16, 1847

BELDEN Hiram of Dresden, NY, Richard GILLETTE and John REYNOLDS of Ft. Edward, NY killed by lightning July 13, 1847

CLARK Martha age 21y dau of Benjamin in Sandy Hill, NY July 22, 1847

SKINNER Alexander age 24y in Sandy Hill, NY July 24, 1847

GRACE Jane Eliza age 24y wife of Moral and dau of Austin **ELMORE** at Ft. Edward, NY July 24, 1847

KNAPP son and daughter of Isaac Jr. drowned at State Dam west of village July 29, 1847 (taken from Glens Falls Republican)

KINGSLEY Freeland T. age 11m 23d son of Horace B. and Philena at Sandy Hill, NY August 21, 1847

MC NAUGHTON Duncan F. age 46y formerly of Washington Co. NY in Racine, Wis. August 25, 1847

BLACKMAN Glover age 39y in Keeseville, NY October 12, 1847

DIBBLE Susan age 16y dau of O. B. formerly of Sandy Hill, NY in Detroit, Mi. October 29, 1847

COLEMAN widow of Blackenridge Coleman in her 75th yr at sons Col. William Coleman in Sandy Hill, NY (newspaper date November 9, 1847)

BLACKMAN Sophia age 30y widow of Glover and dau of E. **RANSOM** in Sandy Hill, NY December 24, 1847

MOSS Simeon age 92y a Revolutonary Soldier in Sandy Hill, NY December 21, 1847

BLANEY John S. age 56y in Sandy Hill, NY January 13, 1848

MC CALL James age 53y in Ft. Edward, NY February 18, 1848

LAMSON Edwin C. age 19y son of late Jonas and Betsey in Sandy Hill, NY February 23, 1848

BEACH Titus age 72y in Sandy Hill, NY March 3, 1848

LOW Julia Louisa age 3y 8m dau of H. C. in Sandy Hill, NY March 3, 1848

GANDEL John in his 69th yr at Ft. Edward, NY April 1, 1848

EASTMAN William Alfred age 6y son of Rev. J. B. in Sandy Hill, NY April 8, 1848

WEEKS Mary age 34y wife of Randall C. in Sandy Hill, NY April 28, 1848

DOUBLEDAY Emma age 19m dau of Danvers in Sandy Hill, NY April 28, 1848

NORTHUP Alida age 16m dau of Lyman H. in Sandy Hill, NY April 30, 1848

PARKS Charles age 20m son of Brazilla in Sandy Hill, NY April 29, 1848

MOORE William age 8y son of Rev. W. W. Moore in Sandy Hill, NY May 6, 1848

MARTIN Harriet age 29y wife of Isaac in Ft. Ann, NY April 28, 1848

FORBES John abt 50y in Sandy Hill, NY May 21, 1848

CLARK Caroline age 2y dau of Loraness in Sandy Hill, NY July 4, 1848

BANCROFT Charlotte age 38y wife of George P. of Brooklyn, NY and dau of late Simeon **BARRY** in Sandy Hill, NY July 17, 1848

BAKER Margaret age 77y widow of Caleb in Sandy Hill, NY July 22, 1848

KEEFE Thomas native of Ireland drowned in Hudson River July 30, 1848

BROWNELL Giles in his 83rd yr in Sandy Hill, NY August 21, 1848

MATTISON Mary in her 76th yr widow of Job in Sandy Hill, NY August 27, 1848

ROOT Deborah age 25y wife of Warren at Ft. Ann, NY September 3, 1848

CORNING Lucy age 40y wife of Jason at Ft. Ann, NY September 4, 1848

STONE Warren age 36 printer in Utica, NY August 31, 1848

GEER Walter Jr. age 23y in Glens Falls, NY October 27, 1848

DIBBLE Catherine age 33y dau of late Hutton in Sandy Hill, NY October 30, 1848

BALDWIN Samuel H. age 39y of Cohoes, NY in Sandy Hill, NY January 11, 1849

ALDEN Felix age 68y in Sandy Hill, NY January 15, 1849

BENNETT Solomon abt 35y formerly of Sandy Hill, NY in Glens Falls, NY January 15, 1849

CASE George W. age 10y 7m son of Alfred and Almira in Saranac, NY January 8, 1849

COLE Lemuel P. age 36y formerly of Sandy Hill, NY in New York January 25, 1849

JOHNSON Samuel of Binghamton, NY formerly of Sandy Hill, NY in New Orleans, La. January 11, 1849

GREEN Thomas age 48y in Moreau, NY March 7, 1849

CARPENTER Miss Pamela age 33y in Sandy Hill, NY March 16, 1849

SMALLEY William abt 45y in Sandy Hill, NY March 20, 1849

JOHNSON Ann Maria wife of John L. formerly of Sandy Hill, NY in Granger, NY December 19, 1848

CARLTON Clark age 60y of Sandy Hill, NY in Hamilton Co. at dau April 14, 1849

CLARK Dr. Russell age 67y in Sandy Hill, May 30, 1849. Born Vt.

CLEVELAND James age 32y in Sandy Hill, NY July 8, 1849

HARRINGTON Harriet C. infant dau of Hosea and Caroline H. in Queensbury, NY August 20, 1849

WOODWORTH Warren L. age 33y formerly of Sandy Hill, NY in Cincinnati, Ohio August 10, 1849

TEFFT Mary age 23y wife of Henry and dau of Charles HARRIS in Sandy Hill, NY September 21, 1849

CROSS Theodore age 25y in Sandy Hill, NY September 22, 1849

PARRY Ellen age 23y dau of Rev. Joseph Parry in Sandy Hill, NY October 3, 1849

SWIFT Lucius A. age 36y in Fayetteville, NY September 21, 1849

HARRIS Refine age 25y in Sandy Hill, NY November 6, 1849

SHERRILL Darius age 66y in Sandy Hill, NY November 17, 1849

PARKER William H. age 62y 4m in Whitehall, NY November 27, 1849

KELLY Alonzo age 19y and bro Edwin age 17y drowned in Lake December 16, 1849

HARRIS Hannah age 94y formerly of Sandy Hill, NY at dau Mrs. BUTLER in Rutland, Vt. December 4, 1849

BENNETT Mary age 66y widow of Ezekiel in Reynolds Basin, NY November 14, 1849

CARPENTER Carmi age 23y in Sandy Hill, NY January 6, 1850

NASH Aurelis B. age 43y wife of Harvey S. in Sandy Hill, NY January 8, 1850

DICKEY Elizabeth W. age 48y in Saratoga Springs, NY February 5, 1850

HUGHES Jessie age 9m dau of C. Hughes in Sandy Hill, NY February 17, 1850

BEADLETONE Sally age 70y wife of Job in Queensbury, NY February 15, 1850

DIBBLE Miss Amelia A. E. in her 30th yr February 28, 1850

BAKER Elizabeth age 38y wife of Albert in Sandy Hill, NY April 13, 1850. Their son James Herbert age 10m 3d died April 5, 1850

CARPENTER Mrs. Stephen widow age 60y in Sandy Hill, NY April 13, 1850

CULVER Helen M. age 20y dau of Benjamin in Lansingburgh, NY April 21, 1850

CROSS Adeline in her 18th yr in Sandy Hill, NY April 25, 1850

LATIMER Jacob E. age 49y in Sandy Hill, NY April 27, 1850

CRAWFORD Elizabeth age 20y dau of John in Ft. Edward, NY May 21, 1850

VAUGHN Caleb in his 82nd yr at Ft. Ann, NY June 12, 1850

DUNSON Simeon M. age 36y at Granville Corners, NY June 11, 1850

MILLIMAN Hester age 55y wife of Thomas in Salem, NY August 1, 1850

HARRIS Orville age 15m son of Horace in Sandy Hill, NY September 26, 1850

KNAPP Desire age 39y wife of Marenus in Sandy Hill, NY October 17, 1850

WOODWORTH Mrs. Abel age 69y in Sandy Hill, NY October 18, 1850

TAYLOR Susan abt 50y wife of David in Ft. Edward, NY November 1/8, 1850

MC FADDEN John age 37y in Argyle, NY October 24, 1850

NORTHUP Anna age 76y relict of John H. in Hebron, NY December 4, 1850

CRANDALL Josephine M. age 8y dau of James H. in Ft. Edward, NY December 5, 1850

BURNHAM Charles A. age 2y 3m son of Rev. Jedediah in Sandy Hill, NY January 4, 1851

CHURCH Charles D. age 40y of Sandy Hill, NY in Maysville, NY January 1, 1851

TERRY Sarah Jane abt 23y dau of James **MC COY** in Ft. Edward, NY January 1, 1851

BREWSTER John of Illinois in Sandy Hill, NY January 22, 1851

VAUGHN Stephen in his 81st yr in Sandy Hill, NY February 22, 1851. Born Rhode Island, came to Washington Co. in 1793

HARRIS Lemuel of Sandy Hill, NY drowned nr Glens Falls, NY April 5, 1851

SHERRILL Sumner age 4y 2m son of James H. and Ellen A. in Schenectady, NY April 21, 1851

LOCKE Florence age 9m dau of S. E. and Helen in Sandy Hill, NY April 20, 1851

RIPLEY Seneca S. age 26y in W. Ft. Ann, NY April 23/26, 1851

WOODWORTH Hiram P. age 48y formerly of Sandy Hill, NY in Hennipen, Ill. May 23, 1851

WELLS Amos R. age 56y in Glens Falls, NY June 10, 1851

BANCROFT George P. abt 40y of New York in Ft. Edward, NY July 13, 1851

BURBANK Mrs. Polly age 54y in Schroon, NY (newspaper date July 22, 1851)

GRAY Mrs. Mary age 26 in Salem, NY. Also, Mrs. Ruth **FOSTER** age 74y in Salem, NY and Mrs. Josephine **GERART** age 20 in Glens Falls, NY (newspaper date July 22, 1851)

KINGSLEY Mrs. Abiah in W. Ft. Ann, NY July 15, 1851

DOIG Margaret age 36y wife of John in Salem, NY July 7, 1851

BREESE James bro of H. G. Breese of Sandy Hill, NY in Hoosick, NY May 7, 1851

KING Harriet Adelaide age 22y wife of Jeremiah B. and dau of late Simeon **BERRY** formerly of Sandy Hill, NY in Janesville, Wis. July 22, 1851

WILSON Lyman T. formerly of Glens Falls, NY in Albany, NY August 3, 1851

GRAVES Rufus age 59y in Granville, NY August 1, 1851

HITCHCOCK Samuel age 46y in Sandy Hill, NY August 14, 1851

TAYLOR Caroline wife of Lansing G. and dau of Daniel W. **WING** in Ft. Edward, NY August 20, 1851

BREESE Susan age 25y wife of John in Ft. Ann, NY August 20, 1851

CLARK Grace age 56y wife of Col. Almon in Sandy Hill, NY September 1, 1851

BREESE Sally age 64y wife of Maj. H. G. in Sandy Hill, NY August 31, 1851

JOHNSON Albert abt 35y in Whitehall, NY August 29, 1851

BALDWIN Laura B. age 56y wife of Judge in Glens Falls, NY September 4, 1851

MILLER Delinda wife of Moses in Ft. Ann, NY September 6, 1851

BUTTERFIELD Elijah age 89y in Hartford, NY September 17/24, 1851

PRINDLE James L. age 42y in Whitehall, NY September 10, 1851

SMALLEY Mary Ann in her 16th yr in Sandy Hill, NY October 1, 1851

MORGAN Erwin in his 40th yr in Battenville, NY September 30, 1851

MC CRACKEN Elizabeth age 74y formerly of Salem, NY in Mentz, NY September 27, 1851

MEEKER Miss Sarah D. age 28y in Salem, NY November 9, 1851

HARKNESS William age 2y son of William B. and Caroline in Salem, NY November 5, 1851

HARLOW Byron age 14y son of George C. in Whitehall, NY November 8, 1851

MC CLELLAN Isabella age 28y wife of Maj. William and dau of Rev. Alexander BULLIONS in Jackson, NY November 15, 1851

RACE Teresa in her 71st yr in Whitehall, NY November 11, 1851

COZZENS Mrs. W. L. age 26y in N. Granville, NY November 12, 1851

FORBES Harry abt 60y at Ft. Edward, NY November 30, 1851

PALMETEER Lucinda age 27y in Glens Falls, NY November 30, 1851

TEFFT Hannah wife of Caleb in Greenwich, NY (newspaper date December 12, 1851)

BURKE Hettie wife of Samuel in Greenwich, NY November 29, 1851

DEWEY Mrs. George abt 40y in Sandy Hill, NY December 9, 1851

WHITE James Henry age 23y son of Charles in Sandy Hill, NY December 12/19, 1851

BARREL Mary Jane age 18y dau of Cyrus in S. Hartford, NY December 2, 1851

STEVENSON Jane age 78y widow of Daniel in Argyle, NY November 19, 1851

MERRILL Sarah Elizabeth age 2y 2m dau of A. N. and Jane E. in Whitehall, NY December 17, 1851

ROBINSON Elizabeth C. age 5y dau of B. F. and Catherine in Salem, NY December 20, 1851

GIBSON Mrs. William age 60y near Belcher, NY November 13, 1851

CHURCH Daniel age 82y near Belcher, NY (newspaper date December 30, 1851)

NASH Oscar age 15y son of Harvey B. in Sandy Hill, NY December 30, 1851

GARDNER Mrs. ____ age 90y in Sandy Hill, NY December 30, 1851

ABRAMS Helen dau of Thomas of Lansingburgh in Argyle, NY December 20, 1851

KIRTLAND Miss Mary Jane age 28y in Whitehall, NY December 31, 1851

WHITNEY Jed S. age 30y of Whitehall, NY in Troy, NY January 1, 1852

WILLIAMSON James age 46y in Belcher, NY December 3, 1851

BEATTIE Jane H. age 21 near Belcher, NY (newspaper date January 13, 1852)

COOK Barnwell B. age 75y in Sandy Hill, NY January 13, 1852

BUCK Justice age 79y in Sandy Hill, NY January 5, 1852

CLEVELAND Mrs. Aaron age 76y in Salem, NY January 10, 1852

BILLINGS Horace in Arlington, Vt. January 3, 1852

WARNER Henry age 9y son of William in White Creek, NY December 24, 1851

WARNER John R. in Jackson, NY January 5, 1852

MEADER Margaret L. age 25y wife of Harvey M. of Union Village, NY at Ft. Miller, NY January 11, 1852

MC ARTHUR John age 79y in Jackson, NY December 31, 1851

BRAYTON John J. age 3m son of John and Maria in Belcher, NY January 19, 1852

PLATT Samuel R. age 38y in Sandy Hill, NY February 8, 1852

LUTHER Mary Jane age 19y wife of Curtis in Whitehall, NY January 30, 1852

BILLINGS William age 24y son of Chester in Salem NY January 29, 1852

WOODWARD Martha age 24y wife of Dr. A. T. in Whitehall, NY January 21, 1852

HALL Mary Jane age 25y wife of Joseph in Galesville, NY January 16, 1852

GRIFFITH Miss Sarah M. in her 40th yr in Lockport, NY January 22, 1852

HUGHES Lucy A. in her 28th yr wife of Charles and dau of Charles **STONE** formerly of Kingston, NY in Sandy Hill, NY February 11, 1852

NIMS Mrs. Warren abt 27y in Sandy Hill, NY February 8, 1852

GATES Mrs. Jacob abt 25y in Sandy Hill, NY February 11, 1852

EDDY Hiram age 51y in Whitehall, NY February 12, 1852

NAILER George age 6y son of Jacob in Greenwich, NY February 10, 1852

NELSON Dr. William G. in Cambridge, NY February 7, 1852

PARISH Mrs. Hiram age 54y in Jackson, NY February 11, 1852

ELLSWORTH Hannah age 67y wife of Roswell in S. Granville, NY February 2, 1852

ROBERTSON Betsey age 70y wife of Gilbert in Argyle, NY February 13, 1852

MILLER Susan abt 27y wife of David in Ft. Edward, NY February 12, 1852

MC EACHRON Mrs. Peter abt 65y in Argyle, NY February 12, 1852

BIGELOW Erastus age 27y son of Anson in Easton, NY February 20, 1852

CLARK Horace age 47y in W. Poultney, Vt. February 25, 1852

ORR Charles age 16y in Whitehall, NY February 21, 1852

SLADE Susan Amelia age 14y dau of M. H. in Hartford, NY March 14, 1852

MC NEIL Archibald in his 83rd yr in E. Greenwich, NY March 10/12, 1852

HUGHES Charles Walter age 10m son of Charles in Sandy Hill, NY March 28, 1852

WILSON Sarah in her 83rd yr relict of Nathan in Salem, NY March 19, 1852

CRARY John C. age 46y son of late John in Salem, NY March 21, 1852

PERRY Charles Md. in his 46th yr in Salem, NY March 22, 1852

SHAW Hiram age 57y in Hampton, NY March 28, 1852

PORTER Dr. Nelson age 59y in Whitehall, NY April 1, 1852

DOOLITTLE Cordelia age 8y dau of Silas and Cynthia in Ft. Edward, NY April 10, 1852

PALMETEER James age 68 in Glens Falls, NY April 14, 1852

ANDREWS Harriet age 54y in Union Village, NY April 6, 1852

HUBBARD Rev. E. B. age 52y of M. E. Church in Ft. Edward, NY April 22, 1852

BENTLEY Joseph abt 46y in Queensbury, NY April 21, 1852

VAUGHN Harriet age 30y in Union Village, NY April 17, 1852

DUTCHER Peter L. age 28y in Union Village, NY April 19, 1852

GREEN Samuel abt 35y in Whitehall, NY April 25, 1852

PECOR Basil age 52y in Whitehall, NY April 25, 1852

TEFFT Mrs. James age 64y in Galesville, NY May 10, 1852

BARNES C. W. age 18y in Ash Grove, NY January 20, 1852

BARNES Cornelius A. age 17y in Shushan, NY May 1, 1852

CAMERON James I. age 70y late sheriff Warren Co. in Caldwell, NY May 2, 1852

MASON Frank A. age 1y 10m son of Rev. J. T. in Galesville, NY June 12, 1852

FROST Matilda age 45y wife of Weston in Ft. Ann, NY June 10, 1852

SHEPHERD Eliza age 23y wife of Hugh in Ft. Ann, NY June 15, 1852

WARD Polly age 62y wife of Alfred in Belcher, NY June 16, 1852

TIMMERMAN Sarah Jane age 17y wife of Jesse and dau of Albert F. **HALL** formerly of Ft. Edward, NY in Lockport, NY July 8, 1852

BROUGHTON Martha D. age 3m dau of Joseph and Sarah near Belcher, NY (newspaper date July 27, 1852)

HOLEMAN Eolian Amelia age 3m dau of Dewitt in Sandy Hill, NY August 28, 1852

BUCK Elijah age 98y a Revolutionary Soldier in Sandy Hill, NY August 24, 1852

CRONIN Mrs. Elizabeth age 41 in Sandy Hill, NY September 9, 1852

CROSS J. Judson age 8m son of John G. and P. K. in Sandy Hill, NY December 7, 1852

GREEN Lucinda R. age 45y wife of Joseph and dau of Throop **BARNEY** of Sandy Hill, NY in New York November 9, 1852

DENTON Frances age 16y dau of Richard in Sandy Hill, NY December 23, 1852

WING Angeline B. age 42y wife of Abraham in Sandy Hill, NY January 5, 1853

JACKSON Frederick age 21y in Sandy Hill, NY January 12, 1853

ALLEN Mary A. age 32y wife of H. S. in Whitehall, NY January 19, 1853

RICE Silas H. age 40y in Salem, NY January 14, 1853

PARRY Lucy M. age 21y wife of John and dau of John MC INTYRE in Ft. Edward, NY January 25, 1853

CROSS Pamelia K. age 31y wife of John G. February 18, 1853

SHEPHERD Elizabeth age 2y 3d dau of H. in Argyle, NY February 1, 1853

RIPLEY Amy age 61y wife of James of Queensbury, NY in W. Troy, NY February 17, 1853

FINCH Jeremiah age 83y in Sandy Hill, NY April 2, 1853

CARLTON James Orville age 2y 4m son of Orville N. and Fanny E. in Sandy Hill, NY April 4, 1853

HALL William R. age 13y son of James in Argyle, NY February 18, 1853

WILLARD Elizabeth age 3y 9m dau of Henry and Maria in Ft. Edward, NY April 11, 1853

LUSEE Marcus Henry age 3y 9m son of James in Sandy Hill, NY May 8, 1853

FOILS _____ age 4y dau of John in Sandy Hill, NY May 7, 1853

KING Rev. David age 27y in Stillwater, NY May 15, 1853

BALDWIN Arabella wife of Hooker in Glens Falls, NY May 15, 1853

COLEMAN Capt. Alexander bro of Col. William of Sandy Hill, NY in San Antonio, Texas May 3, 1853

PHETTEPLACE John age 51y in Sandy Hill, NY June 11, 1853

BELL Warren age 73y in Ft. Edward, NY July 11, 1853

ROCKWELL Betsey age 73y widow of Judge Rockwell in Hadley, NY July 31, 1853

POTTER Freeman age 17y son of Erastus in Schroon, NY August 5, 1853

FISK Azariah age 80y in Sandy Hill, NY August 24, 1853

MATHEWS John age 13m son of William H. in Sandy Hill, NY September 26, 1853

POST Mrs. Alfred B. dau of William MC LAREN of Sandy Hill, NY in Florida, NY October 1, 1853

TAYLOR Lydia age 88y relict of Nathan in Hartford, NY October 7, 1853

STICKNEY Miss Mary age 28y in Sandy Hill, NY October 9, 1853

HALL Edgar age 14y 1m 6d son of Seneca and Mary in Sandy Hill, NY September 6, 1853

NICHOLS Nathan age 63y in Jackson, Mi. September 29, 1853

BAKER William T. age 52y in Sandy Hill, NY November 5, 1853

TAYLOR Margaret age 26y dau of David in Ft. Edward, NY November 10, 1853

ALDEN Joab age 63y in Sandy Hill, NY November 19, 1853

BELL Martha age 50y wife of Sidney in Sandy Hill, NY December 10, 1853

SHAW Winslow P. age 4y son of Samuel in Sandy Hill, NY December 27, 1853

CARRIER Jacob abt 70y in Sandy Hill, NY January 11, 1854

SKINNER Norman G. age 21y in Ft. Ann, NY January 1, 1854

ROBERTSON Isabella age 70y wife of Alexander in Ft. Miller, NY (newspaper date January 17, 1854)

MILLIMAN Julius B. age 10m in Argyle, NY January 8, 1854

HARRIS Zadoc age 85y in Hartford, NY February 2, 1854

MILLIMAN Henry Clay age 6y son of N. B.in Argyle, NY February 4, 1854

BACON Joseph age 56y in Ft. Ann, NY January 29, 1854

SLADE Lucina H. age 51y wife of Mason in Hartford, NY February 6, 1854

VAIL Isaac abt 78y in Sandy Hill, NY April 8, 1854

SAFFORD Rosa Ann age 6y dau of R. A. in Sandy Hill, NY April 8, 1854

BARDEN Jennett J. age 16y dau of Hiram W. in Argyle, NY April 3, 1854

BARNEY Sarah R. age 73y wife of Throop in Sandy Hill, NY May 4, 1854

SHERRILL Eliza R. age 5y 3d dau of George B. and Angeline in Sandy Hill, NY May 6, 1854

TAYLOR Lansing G. age 52 Pres. of Ft. Edward bank at Glens Falls, NY May 3, 1854

STROW William age 58y in Hartford, NY April 28, 1854

BURDICK Caroline L. age 54y wife of Albert S. in Granville, NY May 26, 1855

HARRIS Eugene age 12y son of Horace in Sandy Hill, NY June 25, 1855

KINGSLEY Duane age 6y son of Levi in W. Ft. Ann, NY July 14, 1855

GEER Walter abt 63y in Glens Falls, NY July 16, 1855

DAVIS Louisa age 28y wife of Abijah in Bolton, NY August, 6, 1855

TEFFT Charles Henry age 9m 4d son of Henry in Sandy Hill, NY August 19, 1855

WICKS Joseph age 84y in Sandy Hill, NY November 9, 1855

BARNEY Throop age 81y in Sandy Hill, NY November 20, 1855

BAKER Caroline R. age 41y dau of late E. D. in Queensbury, NY December 14, 1855

PHILLIPS Reid abt 80y in Sandy Hill, NY February 11, 1856

HOLMES Henry age 60y in Union Village, NY February 3, 1856

SHERWOOD Sally in her 71st yr consort of Col. Thomas A. in Ft. Edward, NY February 17, 1856

JUDSON Mrs. Lucretia age 80y in White Creek, NY February 18, 1856

BURTON George in Queensbury, NY February 19, 1856

SLEIGHT Sarah age 87y dau of John H. and Mary deceased of Fishkill, NY in Sandy Hill, NY February 23, 1856

DOUBLEDAY Olladine age 88y wife of Danvers in Sandy Hill, NY March 28, 1856

JOHNSON Lewis age 83y in Sandy Hill, NY March 24, 1856

COLE Darwin age 30y formerly of Sandy Hill, NY in New York April 16, 1856

NASH Augusta Imogene age 4y 6m dau of Harvey B. and Mary J. in Sandy Hill, NY May 2, 1856

MERRILL P. A. age 50y wife of Elam P. in Sandy Hill, NY May 19, 1856

CARSWELL Mary age 22y wife of William J. at Ft. Edward, NY May 27, 1856

CLARK Charles age 23m son of S. W. in Sandy Hill, NY July 1, 1856

WILTSIE Henry age 88y in Adamsville, NY July 10, 1856

CRONKHITE Dan age 70y in Queensbury, NY July 12, 1856

SHIPMAN Mrs. Harriet formerly of Sandy Hill, NY in Scriba, NY July 6, 1856

STEWART Rosanna age 14y dau of John C. in Ft. Edward, NY August 24, 1856

SMALLEY Porter age 81y in Sandy Hill, NY October 28, 1856

BOND Phebe Ann age 35y wife of Osro and dau of Samuel **DUNHAM** of Sandy Hill, NY in Oswego, NY October 24, 1856

MARSHALL Mrs. Mary age 97y 5m in Adamsville, NY October 31, 1856

SHERRILL Fanny age 48y wife of John F. in Caldwell, NY January 21, 1857

HOLMES Asa F. age 44y in Greenwich, NY February 4/5, 1857

VAN SANTVOORD Lucy age 15y dau of Rev. C. in Union Village, NY February 6, 1857

PALMER John age 74y in Cambridge, NY January 31, 1857

CLEVELAND Miss Margaret age 37y in Salem, NY January 30, 1857

CLARK Eleanor age 88y widow of Col. Thomas N. in Argyle, NY February 5, 1857

STRONG John age 67y in Sandy Hill, NY March 11, 1857

DOUBLEDAY Carmi Locke age 19m son of Harvey M. and Mary G. in Sandy Hill, NY March 12, 1857

ORCUTT Harvey A. abt 55y in Union Village, NY October 30, 1857

DIBBLE Melville C. age 50y of Sandy Hill, NY in Utica Asylum November 3, 1857

WILKIE Sylvester age 21y son of Israel of Queensbury, NY in Ticonderoga, NY November 11, 1857

MC MILLAN Mary age 42y wife of William in Jackson, NY December 26/29, 1857

JAMES Mary age 64y Mother of John B. **TEFFT** in Greenwich, NY December 17, 1857

SKELLIE Sarah Ann age 20y dau of John in Jackson, NY December 25, 1857

EVRETT Frances Mary age 28y wife of Rev. William Evrett and dau of Henry **GREEN** of Queensbury, NY at Williamsburgh January 3, 1858

BOOTH Mrs. age 54y wife of Deacon Booth at Ft. Edward, NY January 2, 1858

SHAW Harriet age 20y dau of Milton E. at Ft. Edward, NY January 6, 1858

MILLER John T. age 19y son of Jacob in Sandy Hill, NY January 12, 1858

STOUGHTON Mrs. Halsey W. age 68y in Ft. Edward, NY January 17, 1858

HARKNESS Daniel age 76y in Salem, NY January 19, 1858

SHERRILL Charles F. age 13y died January 31, 1858 and John F. age 3y 5m died February 11, 1858, sons of Mathew D. in Sandy Hill, NY

BARDEN Adin age 89y in Argyle, NY January 28, 1858

RICH Agnes age 38 wife of J. J. in Whitehall, NY January 25, 1858

EDDY Asa in his 65th yr of Whitehall, NY in Brattleboro Asylum January 18, 1858

THOMPSON Caroline Berry age 20y wife of Rev. Hugh M. in Portage, Wis. December 30, 1857

LEE Cornelia age 15y in Union Village, NY February 3, 1858

HEMINWAY infant son of Phineas age 6w in Salem, NY February 3, 1858

DAUGHRATY Augusta age 28y dau of George in Granville, NY January 31, 1858

WRIGHT Jane M. age 15y dau of Sidney W. in Granville, NY February 12, 1858

BARBER James age 71y in White Creek, NY February 10, 1858

BUTTERFIELD Harriet Sophia dau of Jeremiah formerly of Sandy Hill, NY in La Porte, Ind. February 12, 1858 by falling from chair

JONES Lucretia M. wife of W. F. in Glens Falls, NY February 14, 1858

AUSTIN Mrs. Martha age 93y at Ft. Ann, NY February 11, 1858

WALKER Juliette age 18y dau of Charles and Eunice in Granville, NY February 17, 1858

LITTLE Dr. Thomas in his 71st yr in Putnam, NY February 19, 1858

WATSON Alonzo abt 45y in Whitehall, NY February 24, 1858

WILBUR Henry age 19y son of Mrs. Polly Wilbur in Easton, NY February 14, 1858

WORTH Phebe age 64y in Easton, NY April 8, 1858

COGSHALL Clark in his 96th yr in Salem, NY April 7, 1858

FOSTER Andrew age 65y Hebron, NY April 11, 1858

WHITESIDE Mrs. Abigail age 76y in Cambridge, NY April 7, 1858

WATERS Worthy in 70th yr in Jackson, NY April 12, 1858

TEFFT Mary Louisa in her 9th yr dau of Henry in Sandy Hill, NY May 6, 1858

CLARK George age 4y 6m died May 3, 1858 and Fred age 1y 4m died May 8, 1858 sons of Noble W. and Maria G. in Sandy Hill, NY

PRESCOTT George age 13y son of G. A. in Sandy Hill, NY May 14, 1858

MATHEWS Susannah age 41y dau of Col. David in Sandy Hill, NY May 22, 1858

BUTTERFIELD Sherabiah age 16y son of Seamans in Libertyville, Ill. May 25, 1858

ROBERTSON Mary D. in her 36th yr dau of Alexander of Due West Abbeville, Dist. SC at bro in Albany, NY June 9, 1858

WALLS Mary Eliza in her 21st yr dau of James in Salem, NY July 17, 1858

BENDER Jane W. in her 51st yr widow of Henry in Sandy Hill, NY August 19, 1858

RING George age 28y in Glens Falls, NY September 10, 1858

CHOATE O. W. age 32y formerly of Ft. Edward, NY in Jericho, Vt. September 13, 1858

PITCHER Maj. M. S. in New York September 17, 1858, buried Sandy Hill,

WRIGHT Maj. James in his 56th yr at Mother-in-laws Mrs. **BAKER**, buried Sandy Hill, NY September 19, 1858

SWEET Ann Mahala age 25y dau of Daniel in Sandy Hill, NY September 22, 1858

CURTIS Mary Loeza nr 2yrs old died September 26, 1858 and Sarah Lissie died September 28, 1858, twin daughters of John W. and Hannah of Greenwich, NY

TALLMAN Lissie age 4m 19d in Sandy Hill, NY October 10, 1858

HAZARD John age 36y in Sandy Hill, NY October 13, 1858

PARIS Erskine Clark age 1y 14d son of Urias G. and Cordelia E. in Sandy Hill, NY October 22, 1858

BROWN Josiah age 24y son of Dr. J. H. in Sandy Hill, NY December 5, 1858

WEEKS Joseph age 77y in Sandy Hill, NY December 24, 1858

WESTON Frederick age 56y son of Roswell in Sandy Hill, NY December 27, 1858

HARRIS Estelle age 2m 21d dau of William D. and Frances in Kingsbury, NY January 21, 1859

COX Mrs. Arvilla age 51y 10m in Clintonville, NY February 15, 1859

HARRIS Thomas G. age 42y formerly of Sandy Hill, NY in Goshen, Ind. February 9, 1858

STOREY Mrs. Lydia age 69y in Sandy Hill, NY March 6, 1859

WELLS Sidney age 72y in Cambridge, NY March 1, 1859

BARNES Henry Jr. age 31y formerly of Washington Co. in Oxford, NY February 24, 1859

SHAY Michael age 40y in Easton, NY February 23, 1859

FISK infant son of Lewis A. and Frances age 4m in Sandy Hill, NY March 11, 1859

STOWELL Samantha age 56y wife of William in Sandy Hill, NY April 1, 1859

DONNELLY Charles L. age 25y in Smiths Basin, NY April 1, 1859

PLAISTED Eddie C. age 13y son of Widow Harriet in Sandy Hill, NY April 10, 1859

CROCKER Minerva wife of E. H. of Aberdeen, Miss. and dau of Col. William **COLEMAN** of Sandy Hill, NY in Sandy Hill April 14, 1859 and son William James died May 11, 1859

STILES Ransom age 68y in Argyle, NY April 20, 1859

PRATT Russell W. age 55y in Ft. Edward, NY May 19/20, 1859

COLBY Milo age 80y in Lincoln, Vt. March 21, 1859
GIBSON Roxanna age 68y wife of Nathan in Glens Falls, NY July 27, 1859

SHERRILL Polly age 73y widow of Darius in Sandy Hill, NY October 17, 1859

REYNOLDS Elizabeth W. age 49y wife of J. M. in Whitehall, NY November 16, 1859

COLLINS Merlyn age 56y in Whitehall, NY November 19, 1859

ROBERTSON Margaret age 34y dau of James in Greenwich, NY November 5, 1859

CORNELL Emeline M. age 29y 14d wife of Charles N. in Easton, NY November 12,

1859

BENSON Caroline age 35y wife of Simon in Easton, NY November 13, 1859

CAREY Samuel C. age 29y in Sandy Hill, NY December 23, 1859

CHALMERS J. M. age 30y in Whitehall, NY December 15, 1859

LYTLE James age 70y formerly of Ft. Edward, NY in New York January 31, 1869

HITCHCOCK Eunice age 91y wife of Collins in Kingsbury, NY January 4, 1860 and husband Collins in his 93rd yr died February 21, 1860

COON Russell B. in his 27th yr in Salem, NY February 11, 1860

WHITE Melissa in her 20th yr wife of Nathan at Comstocks Landing, NY February 21, 1860

MC KAY James of Glascow, Scotland in Union Village, NY January 27, 1860

DAVIS Philomelia age 22y wife of Isaac J. in Glens Falls, NY March 4, 1860

BEACH Mrs. Polly age 83y in Sandy Hill, NY June 13, 1861

KINGSLEY John Henry age 17y son of Levi of Wellsville, NY, formerly of Washington Co. at Campbell Hospital Washington DC June 14, 1864

BAKER Albert age 29y of the 3rd Iowa Cal. Co. G. at Little Rock, Ark. October 27, 1864

MC COY Capt. Robert E. at the 2nd Battle of Bull Run October 27, 1864. Buried Union cem. at Ft. Edward, NY

CARROLL Maggie age 25y dau of Owen in Queensbury, NY October 28, 1864

SHAW Milton Byron age 30y 2d son of Milton H. of Sandy Hill, NY at Ft. Edward, NY January 24, 1865. Mem. of 7th Reg. Heavy Artillery NYS Vol.

WHITE Sarah L. age 66y widow of Charles in Sandy Hill, NY March 8, 1865

FINCH Delia age 26y wife of D. J. and dau of Henry **LEWIS** in Sandy Hill, February 20, 1865

PARRY Mary age 44y dau of Elder J. of Sandy Hill, NY in Davenport, Iowa March 21, 1865

BERRY Simeon B. formerly of Sandy Hill, NY in Memphis, Tenn. Hospital January 19, 1865

DIBBLE Belva age 23y 2m dau of Horace and Louisa Sandy Hill, NY April 16, 1865

NELSON Helen M. age 25y in Hartford, NY May 17, 1865

CHURCH Lella Augusta 13m 9d dau of Harvey and Augusta in Sandy Hill, NY May 20, 1865

WARREN Mary R. age 45y wife of William of Moreau in Troy, NY June 18, 1865

KENYON William age 70y in Sandy Hill, NY June 23, 1865

BAKER Orrie E. age 28y 6m wife of Guilford D. formerly of Ft. Ann, NY and adopted dau of G. M. Baker of Sandy Hill, NY in Troy, Kansas June 20, 1865

WHITE Harvey age 21y of New York at bro Andrews in Argyle, NY June 25, 1865

BANE Harvey age 2y son of John and Sarah in Moreau, NY July 18, 1865

MORRISSEY Thomas abt 24y drowned near Sandy Hill, NY July 26, 1865

WOODWORTH Abel age 84y of Sandy Hill in Forrest Port, NY August 10, 1865

PHETTEPLACE Samuel age 81y in Sandy Hill, NY February 20, 1868

WESTCOTT Roxey (**KNOX**) in her 62nd yr wife of Henry in N. Argyle, NY March 6, 1868

TERRY Minnie Stevenson dau of Archibald and Frank E. in N. Argyle, NY April 1, 1868

JACKMAN Freddie H. 5y 8m 14d son of F. B. and Mary in Sandy Hill, NY August 1, 1868

METCALF Julia age 30y wife of Rev. J. E. in Ft. Ann, NY December 19, 1868

SCRIVER Ephraim age 79y in Argyle, NY December 29, 1870

SMITH Eliza age 40y wife of William in Granville, NY January 4, 1871

TODD Major John age 82y in Argyle, NY December 27, 1870

DE MOTT Mrs. ____ formerly of Sandy Hill, NY in Ft. Miller, NY January 2, 1871

STARKS Clarissa age 21y wife of Royal and dau of Nathan **FISH** who was killed at saw mill 19 yrs ago, in Comstocks Landing, NY January 4, 1871

MOORE Eliza age 67y widow of Judge Moore in Granville, NY January 8, 1871

PARKS Edwin H. age 23y son of M. B. and G. A. in Moreau, NY January 19, 1871

TAYLOR E. Orrie (**HAWKINS**) age 25y wife of Charles W. in Argyle, NY January 6, 1871

KINGSLEY Electa Ann age 53y sis of E. D. **CULVER** late of Greenwich, NY in Depere, Wis. December 8, 1870

MARTIN Levi age 1y 5m son of Pierce and Christian in Hartford, NY January 21, 1871

BLAKE Capt. Robert age 79y in E. Greenwich, NY January 6, 1871

PAYNE Charles age 73y in Moreau, NY January 12, 1871

SMITH Sarah Ann age 41y wife of John H. Jr. in Caldwell, Vt. January 3, 1871

WOOD Deborah E. age 78y formerly of Cambridge in New York January 2, 1871

JOSLIN Calvin age 88y in Queensbury, NY January 24, 1871

ALLEN Harriet (**BURDICK**) age 65y wife of King in Warrensburgh, NY January 23, 1871

PIERSON William A. age 63y in Sandy Hill, NY January 23, 1871

MC FARLAND Henry age 20y in Kingsbury, NY January 25, 1871

SWEET John age 77y in S. Granville, NY January 18, 1871

BEATY Nellie age 7y dau of David R. and Mary Jane in Salem, NY January 17, 1871

BULL Mrs. Nancy age 76y in M. Granville, NY January 25, 1871

BENNETT Mrs. Polly age 83y in Pattens Mills, NY January 27, 1871

MC OMBER Georgie age 1y 6m son of N. M. and Alvira in Ft. Edward, NY February 2, 1871

MICKLE Mrs. Cornelia age 27y grand daughter of Mrs. Silas **BAKER** of Ft. Ann, NY January 14/15, 1871

WILBUR Minerva age 84y Mother of Mrs. Willis **SWIFT** in Ft. Ann, NY January 21, 1871

MC FARLAND Henry in his 22nd yr in Ft. Ann, NY January 24, 1871

MURPHY Kate Elizabeth age 2m dau of Thomas and Margaret in Hebron, NY January 30, 1871

BUSTON Mrs. Mary Ann age 77y in Gansevort, NY February 6, 1871

TILFORD John in Argyle, NY February 11, 1871

DUNN Margaret wife of Ebenezer in Argyle, NY February 12, 1871

BRADY Christopher age 32y in Cambridge, NY February 3, 1871

THOMAS Catherine in her 59th yr in Johnsburgh, NY February 1, 1871

JENKINS Reynolds age 48y in Kingsbury, NY February 16, 1871

FISH Joseph age 70y in Kingsbury, NY February 16, 1871

ALLEN Larna in her 61st yr wife of Elihu in Kingsbury, NY February 22, 1871

TOWNE Jabez in his 73rd yr in Kingsbury, NY February 23, 1871

RANDALL Rev. Charles age 65y in Hartford, NY February 17, 1871

NELSON Flora age 10m dau of Horatio in Ft. Ann, NY February 2, 1871

BARTON Mial age 76y in White Creek, NY February 10, 1871

BAIN Archibald G. age 50y in Greenwich, NY February 14, 1871

ASHLEY Henry age 6y son of Jefferson and Demia Ann in Ft. Ann, NY February 4, 1871

QUA Martha age 47y wife of John in Hebron, NY February 11, 1871

FISK Willie age 18y son of Elijah in Sandy Hill, NY February 27, 1871

VAIL Mrs. Lucinda age 88y in Sandy Hill, NY February 26, 1871

BURT Paulina H. age 58y wife of Isaac T. in Queensbury, NY February 4, 1871

HALL John age 93y 6m Father of Seneca of Sandy Hill, NY in Bolton, NY February 22, 1871

HILL Levi age 17y in Salem, NY February 19, 1871

CUTTER John age 59y in Greenwich, NY February 17, 1871

HOLLEY Hannah C. age 45y wife of Jefferson in Cambridge, NY February 19, 1871

GALLOWAY John formerly of Cambridge, NY in Chautaugua, NY February 6, 1871

DEWEY Minnie age 19y in Kingsbury, NY March 7, 1871

PASCO Lydia age 76y in Ft. Ann, NY March 5, 1871

PORTER Mrs. Mary (ADAMS) age 35y formerly of Glens Falls, NY in Idaho City, Idaho February 15, 1871

DAHN Hannah M. age 51y wife of George in Whitehall, NY February 25, 1871

BAUMES Sarah age 36y in Easton, NY February 25, 1871

MATTISON Hannah age 96y formerly of Kingsbury in Scriba, NY February 14, 1871

SHEAR Mrs. Jasper in Putnam, NY March 2, 1871

VAUGHN Edwin A. age 42y of Brooklyn, NY formerly Sandy HIll, NY in Ft. Edward, NY March 22, 1871

LITTLE Lucy B. in her 33rd yr in Glens Falls, NY March 14, 1871

WELCH Thomas R. age 19y 3m son of Michael in Cambridge, NY March 12, 1871

HERRINGTON Kate W. age 22y in Greenwich, NY March 11, 1871

GUINNUP Alice M. age 8y dau of H. P. and Maria in Luzerne, NY March 12, 1871

HALL Ettie age 20y in Luzerne, NY March 5, 1871

SAYLES John age 70y of Albany, NY formerly of this Co. in White Creek, NY March 23, 1871

MC CLELLAN Dr. A. B. in Shanghai, China January 19, 1871

SKINNER John age 34y in Ft. Ann, NY March 21, 1871

GOW Dr. Archibald age 55y in Schuylerville, NY March 28, 1871

KNOX Willie age 1y 6m son of W. H. and E. A. in Glens Falls, NY March 19, 1871

FRASER Margaret age 62y in Whitehall, NY March 26, 1871

SOPER Mary age 15y dau of Burtis in Easton, NY March 25, 1871

GILSON Lucinda age 88y in Shushan, NY March 18, 1871

ELLIS Elizabeth age 22y dau of William in Argyle, NY April 1, 1871

LADD Lewis in his 74th yr in Glens Falls, NY March 24, 1871

WRAY Eliza age 42y dau of James and Susan in Whitehall, NY March 21, 1871

FISHER Frankie W. age 1y 3m 11d son of Frank and Ann in Whitehall, NY March 26, 1871

HOADLEY Elmar infant son of G. and C. in S. Bay, NY March 31, 1871

HYATT Nettie C. age 1y dau of Eugene and Maggie in Greenwich, NY April 1, 1871

CROCKER Sarah J. wife of R. K. in Cambridge, NY April 1, 1871

HANDY Seth P. age 51y in Easton, NY March 8, 1871

LEGGETT Joseph W. in his 77th yr in Chester, NY April 1, 1871

ROBERTS George Clark son of Harvey and Mary J. formerly of Sandy Hill, NY in Schenectady, NY February 10, 1871

MAXWELL Isaac in his 31st yr formerly of Putnam, NY in Chipmans Point, Vt. (newspaper date April 21, 1871)

LONG David age 58y formerly of Cambridge, NY in Glens Falls, NY April 11, 1871

SOMERVILLE Samuel in his 100th yr in Johnsburgh, NY April 4, 1871

ELLIS Mary age 80y widow of Enoch in Glens Falls, NY April 17, 1871

REYNOLDS Stephen age 77y in Granville, NY April 4, 1871

CORBETT John age 22y in M. Granville, NY April 15, 1871

JOHNSON John abt 80y in Greenwich, NY April 7, 1871

STEVENS Walter age 77y formerly of this Co. in Manchester, Mi. April 10, 1871

FLEMING Ellen age 33y in Cambridge, NY April 13, 1871

HALL Eunice in her 32nd yr wife of Ebenezer in Queensbury, NY April 19, 1871

MC DONALD Helen age 46y in Glens Falls, NY April 28, 1871

SNOW Lucinda age 87y in Cambridge, NY May 1, 1871

SHARPE Harry age 21m son of Harry and Mary J. (ROBERTS) of Brooklyn, NY formerly of Sandy Hill in Schenectady, NY May 8, 1871

BARTHOLOMEW Alva age 74y formerly of Whitehall in Benson, Vt. May 14, 1871

DIXSON William B. age 28y in Hebron, NY May 14, 1871

PORTEOUS Anna E. age 15y dau of Andrew in Luzerne, NY May 15, 1871

NORRIS Welcome in his 69th yr in Glens Falls, NY May 13, 1871

CARSWELL Elizabeth relict of David P. in Salem, NY May 8, 1871

WILLIAMS Griffith age 35y in M. Granville, NY May 7, 1871

STEVENS Russell age 73y in S. Bay, NY May 6, 1871

DENNISON James K. in Shushan, NY May 10, 1871

WASHBURN Della age 12y dau of Noah in Kingsbury, NY May 23, 1871

JENKINS Mrs. Jedediah age 81y in Pattens Mills, NY May 22, 1871

HEATH Miss Eliza age 55y in Argyle, NY May 16, 1871

POTVIN ____ age 8m son of Alfred in Sandy Hill, NY June 1, 1871

CARTER Louisa age 61y wife of John in Kingsbury, NY May 27, 1871

CARROLL Annie age 17y dau of Michael in S. Glens Falls, NY May 25, 1871

HALL Edward Hale age 42y formerly of Sandy Hill, NY in Schenectady, NY May 24, 1871

BROUGHTON Albert age 66y formerly of Hartford in Malone, NY April 11, 1871

HILL Peter age 68y 4m of Jackson, NY in Cambridge, NY June 1, 1871

ANDREWS Edwin M. son of Edwin in Greenwich, NY on 27th birthday May 25, 1871

HURLEY John age 83y in E. Salem, NY May 12, 1871

NOBLE Willie age 4m son of Dewitt and Josephine (**DUMOND**) in Whitehall, NY May 28, 1871

GOODWIN Mrs. Mary age 74y in Glens Falls, NY May 20, 1871

CUTTER Elizabeth age 97y in Ft. Ann, NY June 9, 1871. Came to Ft. Ann in 1780 age 5y. Married February 14, 1792 Capt. Benjamin Cutter a Revoltionary soldier, Mass. Reg. He died March 5, 1843 age 81

SIMPSON Miss Jennie in her 56th yr in Putnam, NY June 15, 1871

HALL Mary E. age 43y wife of Earl G. and dau of Rev. J. H. **BARBER** in Adamsville, NY June 12, 1871

LESTER James R. age 32y of N. Argyle, NY in Ft. Edward, NY June 10, 1871

BARKLEY Mrs. Henry in N. Argyle, NY June 11, 1871, husband died 6 months ago

BRANNOCK Mrs. Jane W. age 62y in Warrensburgh, NY June 5, 1871

TAYLOR Sarah age 61y wife of Samuel in Queensbury, NY June 4, 1871

FOSTER James age 75y in Argyle, NY June 19, 1871

WELLER Mrs. Gertrude in her 66th yr in Smiths Basin, NY June 16, 1871

PETTIS Sophia age 68y in Sandy Hill, NY June 24, 1871

MONAHAN John age 20y in Ft. Ann, NY July 3, 1871

MC CARTY Thomas age 26y in Glens Falls, NY July 6, 1871. Born Sandy Hill, NY

CRANE John age 35y in Ft. Edward, NY July 10, 1871

HARRIS Edith age 1y dau of George and Margaret in Ft. Edward, NY July 4, 1871

SHERMAN Lyman S. age 22y 3m 2d son of S. K. and D. A. in Sandy Hill, NY July 20, 1871

REYNOLDS John age 26y in Salem, NY July 9, 1871

AUSTIN Henry age 71 formerly of Hartford, NY in Mexico, NY June 19, 1871

DERBY Mrs. George F. in her 48th yr in Sandy Hill, NY July 28, 1871

WILTSIE Rosamond in Adamsville, NY July 18, 1871

BRISBIN Dr. Oliver in his 77th yr in Schuylerville, NY July 12, 1871

DURKEE Susie age 14y dau of Edmond and Charlotte in Ft. Edward, NY June 29, 1871

DAILEY Marvin P. age 2m 17d son of W. S. and Philindia C. in Sandy Hill, NY July 20, 1871

SMITH Lucy in her 83rd yr widow of Archibald formerly of Whitehall, NY in Anoka, Mn. April 20, 1871

SWIFT Birney age 53y in Ft. Ann, NY July 24, 1871

ALEXANDER Catherine age 60y wife of Jno. in E. Greenwich, NY July 25, 1871

LEDGERWOOD James M. age 29y in Putnam, NY May 11, 1871

THOMAS Jane age 42y wife of Amyles in Glens Falls, NY July 27, 1871

BOYD Mollie Elizabeth 10m 15d dau of S. G. and Kate M. in Glens Falls, NY August 3, 1871

MITCHELL Isabel age 76y widow of John in Cambridge, NY July 29, 1871

TURNER Matilda age 81 widow of James in Jackson, NY August 3, 1871

DOANE Franklin M. age 61 in White Creek, NY August 9, 1871

CARTER Miss Anne M. age 70y sis of Lewis in White Creek, NY August 3, 1871

FERRIS Cyrus L. age 71y in Sandy Hill, NY August 24, 1871. Lived here 40 yrs,

ATWOOD Henry C. Md. age 33y in Castleton, Vt. August 10, 1871

BEAMAN Rev. N. N. S. formerly of Hampton in Carbondale, Ill. August 8, 1871

WILLIAMS John formerly of Argyle, NY in Ft. Miller, NY August 12, 1871

DICK Morris age 90y in Hebron, NY August 27, 1871. Born Scotland 1781

HOOKER Samuel L. Md. age 43y formerly of Poultney, Vt. in Leroy, NY August 14, 1871

HAWKER Eda M. age 23y wife of William and dau of Col. John W. **SHEDD** of Leroy, NY in Clinton, Mo. August 17, 1871

LEDGERWOOD infant son of Alvira in Putnam, NY August 24, 1871

LANGDON Benjamin in Glens Falls, NY August __, 1871

VIELE Mrs. Phillip age 34y in Ft. Miller, NY (newspaper date September 8, 1871)

WILLIAMS John age 76y in Ft. Miller, NY August 13, 1871

POWELL Cornelia age 19y dau of Samuel in Granville, NY September 6, 1871

OVIATT Samie died September 3, 1871 and Frankie died September 5, 1871 twin sons of Thomas D. and Bell age 1y in Jackson, NY

LOVELOCK Margaret age 28y wife of Andrew in Cambridge, NY September 3, 1871

CUMMINGS Abbie wife of Thomas in Putnam, NY September 25, 1871

HAWLEY Asa age 66y in Whitehall, NY September 23, 1871

JONES William R. in his 67th yr in Granville, NY September 22, 1871

BRIGGS Nancy age 70y wife of James in Ft. Ann, NY September 18, 1871

GOODELL Joseph P. in Hartford, NY September 22, 1871

O'CONNOR Maurice age 76y in Sandy Hill, NY September 30, 1871

BARTHOLOMEW Betsey age 70y wife of Alva in Benson, Vt. October 1, 1871

CROCKER Elizabeth age 14m dau of E. H. and H. E. in Sandy Hill, NY October 8, 1871

CARLL Judge A. P. age 39y formerly of Argyle in Elko, Nev. September 21, 1871

DUDGEON Alexander age 72y in Salem, NY October 3, 1871

NELSON Horace N. age 18y 8m in Glens Falls, NY October 19, 1871

STEVENSON Rev. James age 31y 7m in Salem, NY October 18, 1871. Late pastor of the 2nd Pres. Church in Jersey City, NJ

CORBETT Willie S. age 16y son of W. C. in Chippewa Falls, Wis. October 6, 1871

QUACKENBUSH George W. in his 55th yr in Salem, NY October 30, 1871

HITCHCOCK Mary in her 69th yr in Ft. Ann, NY October 23, 1871

GRIFFIN Mrs. Charles in N. Granville, NY October 30, 1871

SMITH Daniel T. age 82y in Argyle, NY October 20, 1871

CUNNINGHAM Mrs. Mary age 67y in Sandy Hill, NY November 10, 1871

HAVILAND John Grant age 82y in Queensbury, NY November 4, 1871

TURNER Sally age 45y widow of Robert at brother-in-laws Capt. A. REED in Whitehall, NY November 7, 1871

PECK Martha in her 66th yr widow of Hermon in Glens Falls, NY November 1, 1871

BALL Sarah E. age 48y formerly of Sandy Hill in Brooklyn, NY November 12, 1871

MURPHY Margaret age 38y wife of Thomas in W. Hebron, NY November 17, 1871

STILES Henry age 21y in Sandy Hill, NY November 30, 1871

SWAIN Leona age 22y wife of Harvey in Hartford, NY November 20, 1871

MOWRY Nancy Ann in her 74th yr in Greenwich, NY November 29, 1871

TUCKER Miss Delia age 50y in Ft. Ann, NY November 16, 1871

BROWN Nora age 8y dau of Joseph in Ft. Ann, NY November 24, 1871

BLINN Mrs. Nancy age 73y in Whitehall, NY November 24, 1871

BENJAMIN William F. age 20y son of Duthan and Delinda in Whitehall, NY November 23, 1871

GILCHRIST Robert age 25y in Delphoe, Ohio December 6, 1871

WROTH Mrs. Louisa age 38y in Sandy Hill, NY December 6, 1871

PERRY Cyrus age 77y in Glens Falls, NY November 30, 1871

ROGERS H. Wallace age 16y son of S. T. in W. Hebron, NY December 6, 1871

SHAW David age 75y in Hebron, NY December 6, 1871

NORTON David S. age 34y in Sandy Hill, NY December 6, 1871

MC FARLAND Joseph age 58y 7m in Sandy Hill, NY December 11, 1871

SULLIVAN Mrs. Mary age 54y in Sandy Hill, NY December 20, 1871

ELDRIDGE Thomas in Sandy Hill, NY December 19, 1871

TALMADGE William age 57y in W. Ft. Ann, NY December 10, 1871

PARKS Henry L. age 33y in E. Whitehall, NY December 19, 1871

CORBETT Hattie D. age 13m 9d dau of Daniel and Jane H. in Putnam, NY December 9, 1871

MILLER John age 68y in Smiths Basin, NY December 30, 1871

GRIFFITH Samuel R. age 61y in Sandy Hill, NY December 28, 1871

REED Mary (**STEELE**) age 59y wife of Thomas in Argyle, NY January 3, 1872

SIMONDS Edgar age 34y in Sagetown, Ill. October 18, 1871

BARKLEY Samuel age 16y son of William J. in Hebron, NY December 26, 1871

CAMERON Daniel age 68y of Albany, NY at brother-in-laws John **GOURLIE** in Putnam, NY December 22, 1871

MC EACHRON James age 20y son of Peter H. in Argyle, NY December 30, 1871

SPRAGUE Mrs. Cornelia age 50y in Sandy Hill, NY January 14, 1872

KELLEY Mrs. Rose age 73y in Sandy Hill, NY January 13, 1872

WILTSIE Rodolphus age 64y in Adamsville, NY January 15, 1872

MC CLELLAN Col. William age 76y in Hebron, NY January 7, 1872

MARTIN Amy relict of Dr. Ansel Martin in Hartford, NY January 14, 1872

CLEARY Mrs. Ann age 48y in Sandy Hill, NY (newspaper date January 25, 1872)

LOVELAND Lottie age 13y 6m in Hebron, NY January 11, 1872

HALL Laura Augusta age 27y wife of Nathan in Whitehall, NY January 10, 1872

WAIT Mrs. Pamela age 80y Mother of Nelson W. in Sandy Hill, January 28, 1872

LARAWAY Edgar W. age 32y in Sandy Hill, NY January 30, 1872

NORTON Amarilla age 73y wife of William in M. Granville, NY January 24, 1872

STOCKWELL Nancy M. age 14y dau of David H. and Delia in Dresden, NY January 31, 1871

GRAHAM Thompson T. age 68y in Putnam, NY February 1, 1872

HAGUE George age 3y son of Richard in Hebron, NY January 28, 1872

WHITMAN Herbert age 28y in Salem, NY January 29, 1872

MC MURRAY Martha Jane age 33y in Argyle, NY January 14, 1872

BARKER Mary age 55y wife of Abram in M. Granville, NY February 5, 1872

FARNSWORTH William B. age 97y in Dresden, NY January 22, 1872

CROSS Hattie A. age 24y dau of S. J. and Ruby Ann in Sandy Hill, NY February 8, 1872

EASTON Lillie Mary age 7y dau of John and Janette in Putnam, NY January 31, 1872

MC MURRAY Robert age 69y in Argyle, NY February 1, 1872

MC MURRAY Marion age 19y in Argyle, NY February 2, 1872

GILCHRIST Duncan age 76y in Argyle, NY February 4, 1872

LUNDY John in his 23rd yr in Hebron, NY February 6, 1872

FOWLER Betsey age 84y 1m in Salem, NY February 3, 1872

HALL Mrs. Hannah in her 78th yr in Whitehall, NY February 14, 1872

WILSON Edward age 72y in Dresden, NY February 13, 1872

BELDEN Mrs. Calvin in her 73rd yr in Dresden, NY February 13, 1872

BUTTERFIELD Seamans age 1y formerly of Sandy Hill, NY in Libertyville, Ill. February 1, 1872

LOVE Moses P. age 55y in Ft. Edward, NY February 19, 1872

BETTS Royal C. Jr. in Granville, NY February 11, 1872

SMITH Charles F. in his 51st yr in Granville, NY February 22, 1872

WINEGAR Lucy age 44y in Ft. Ann, NY February 14, 1872

LAVY James age 69y in Hartford, NY February 19, 1872

HENRY Miss Mary age 80y in Argyle, NY February 25, 1872

MC COY Maria age 69y wife of William in Argyle, NY February 27, 1872

CREE John age 70y in N. Granville, NY March 1, 1872

MOSS J. M. age 54y in Sandy Hill, NY March 8, 1872

LILLIE Mrs. Mary age 77y in Putnam, NY February 26, 1872

GRAHAM John age 72 in Putnam, NY March 5, 1872

COPELAND Mrs. Alexander age 58y in Argyle, NY February 29, 1872

REID David abt 65y in S. Argyle, NY March 2, 1872

ROGERS Gardner age 78y in Hebron, NY March 9, 1872

JACKSON Betsey M. age 29y wife of G. P. in Sandy Hill, NY March 20, 1872

DICKINSON Ezra R. age 33y in Sandy Hill, NY March 8, 1872

MARSHALL Caroline P. age 50y wife of Ira in Glens Falls, NY March 1, 1872

COON Carrie May age 3m dau of James S. and May in Argyle, NY March 12, 1872

HILL Charity widow of Whiteside in N. Cambridge, NY March 8, 1872

BLASHFIELD Flavel age 73y in Salem, NY March 7, 1872

YARMER Napoleon Jr. age 21y in Sandy Hill, NY March 24, 1872

BURBY Thomas Edward age 5m son of Thomas in Dansville, NY March 23, 1872

BAIN Mrs. James age 86y in S. Argyle, NY March 16, 1872

BROWN Mrs. Eliza age 62y formerly of Queensbury, NY in Ft. Miller, NY March 12, 1872

GRANT Maranda age 67y widow of Rev. William in Whitehall, NY March 17, 1872

LUSHER Edward age 62y in Whitehall, NY March 18, 1872

STARKS Myron age 30y in Ft. Ann, NY March 12, 1872

PARKER E. W. age 66y in Whitehall, NY March 20, 1872

EASTON Ella Edith age 6y dau of Henry and Ann in Putnam, NY (newspaper date April 4, 1872)

ASHLEY George H. age 14y son of Warren and Sarah formerly of Ft. Ann, NY in Plato, Ill. (newspaper date April 4, 1872)

BENJAMIN Amy age 32y wife of Phineas in N. Whitehall, NY March 20, 1872

HURLEY Ellen in her 29th yr wife of James in Whitehall, NY March 27, 1872

SOUTHWORTH Alvira age 20y wife of Charles in Ft. Edward, NY March 12, 1872

RUGG Catherine age 83y in Glens Falls, NY March 21, 1872

CRANDALL Noel abt 65y in S. Hartford, NY March 31, 1872

HAWKINS William age 84y in Glens Falls, NY March 19, 1872

MC GINNIS Mrs. Catherine age 31y in Glens Falls, NY March 28, 1872

EDSON Dr. Alvin age 44y in Greenwich, NY March 25, 1872

WOODRUFF Harriet age 62y wife of Walter in Ft. Ann, March 20, 1872

CULVER Jennie age 19y dau of A. V. in Cambridge, NY March 29, 1872

SHERRILL Mary C. age 7y 9m dau of George B. and Angelina in Sandy Hill, NY April 8, 1872

SISSON Charles I. age 4m 13d son of B. F. and J. F. in Sandy Hill, NY March 24, 1872

HAWKS William age 84y 8m in Glens Falls, NY March 19, 1872

MALOY Thomas age 52y in Glens Fall, NY March 27, 1872

SALISBURY John age 74y formerly of Sandy Hill in Bethlehem, NY April 3, 1872

DONNIVAN Michael age 37y in Whitehall, NY April 1, 1872

KERSLAKE Albert E. age 3m son of Thomas in Salem, NY (newspaper date April 11, 1872)

HEMINGWAY Maynard age 57y in Ft. Ann, NY March 30, 1872

MC CLEARY Sarah age 82y in Salem, NY March 25, 1872

VAUGHN Mrs. Hannah age 83y Mother of H. B. in Sandy Hill, NY April 10, 1872

CHURCHILL F. A. age 33y in Sandy Hill, NY April 16, 1872

CULVER James age 75y in Sandy Hill, NY April 15, 1872

BABCOCK William age 72y in W. Ft. Ann, NY March 27, 1872

HEMINGWAY Minot W. age 52y in W. Ft. Ann, NY March 30, 1872

SWEET George age 26y in Whitehall, NY April 8, 1872

CARPENTER Jane E. age 52y wife of Nathan in Whitehall, NY April 4, 1872

PETTIBONE George age 67y in Whitehall, NY April 4, 1872

TREMBLEY Amelia wife of Vital of St. Louis, Mo. and dau of Antoine **RANOIS** of Whitehall, NY in Whitehall April 6, 1872

EDDY Mrs. Elizabeth age 82y in Queensbury, NY April 5, 1872

EDMONDS L. B. age 71y wife of James in S. Glens Falls, NY April 10, 1872

WELCH Edward age 50y in Salem, NY April 8, 1872

SMITH Emma Ann age 53y wife of Abram in Sandy Hill, NY April 20, 1872

MC GINNIS Michael age 14y in Sandy Hill, NY April 12, 1872

ALWELL Maggie age 4y dau of Phillip in Sandy Hill, NY April 12, 1872

POWERS A. T. age 25y late of Whitehall, NY in Adrian, Mi. April 12, 1872

CHURCHILL Patrick age 58y in Whitehall, NY April 18, 1872

CLEMENTS John D. age 58y in Dresden, NY April 18, 1872

PHELPS Orange age 65y in Ticonderoga, NY April 14, 1872

SEARLE John age 61y in Low Hampton, NY March 17, 1872

WEIR Garphelia R. age 23y dau of Capt. John Weir in Jackson, NY April 9, 1872

MC DOUGAL James age 74y in N. Argyle, NY April 7, 1872

WARNER Robert age 2y son of C. D. and A. E. in Cambridge, NY April 14, 1872

HOLMES Eugene age 23y in W. Ft. Ann, NY April 19, 1872

GOODALE Joseph age 82y in Whitehall, NY April 25, 1872

HUTTON Charles age 19y son of William and Mary in Putnam, NY April 19, 1872

REYNOLDS Benjamin abt 60y in Belcher, NY April 29, 1872

MOORE Alexander 18 son of Widow Moore in Putnam, NY April 17, 1872

HARRIS Simon D. age 57y formerly Queensbury, NY in Eckart, Ind. April 10, 1872

GUNN Daniel age 44y in Putnam, NY (newspaper date May 2, 1872)

NORTHUP Sarah age 72y relict of Gardiner in Hartford, NY April 20, 1872

DOWNS Isaac abt 80y in Hartford, NY April 20, 1872

MARTIN Levi age 78y in Granville, NY April 18, 1872

MURRAY Gertrude age 1y 12d dau of John L. and Ellen in Sandy Hill, NY April 1, 1872

EASTMAN Mrs. Betsey age 80y a pensioner of War of 1812 at residence of Calvin E. PEASE in Putnam, NY April 6, 1872

GREENOUGH Pluma wife of James in Whitehall, NY April 26, 1872

GALLIGAN Katie age 10y dau of Patrick in Glens Falls, NY April 28, 1872

AVERY Marsha J. age 20y dau of L. L. and Catherine formerly of Sandy Hill, NY in Troy, NY April 24, 1872

BURTICE Fannie age 12y in Ft. Ann, NY April 24, 1872

CLARK Frankie age 5y son of J. H. in Whitehall, NY April 20, 1872

BRENNAN John age 30y in Argyle, NY April 30, 1872

SHELDON Mrs. Joseph age 70y Mother of Mrs. E. H. GIBSON of Greenwich, NY in Fairhaven, Vt. April 25, 1872

SMITH Charles age 39y in Ft. Ann, NY April 21, 1872

MC CLELLAN Ophemia age 26y dau of John S. and Harriet in Hebron, NY April 25, 1872

VAUGHN William M. age 47y bro of H. B. of Sandy Hill, NY in Albany, NY May 14, 1872

PHILLIPS Emma F. age 26y 5m dau of Rev. J. and M. E. in Salem, NY May 14, 1872

SWEET Lottie age 10m 3d dau of John R. and Eliza in Sandy Hill, NY May 2, 1872

HYDE Frankie 1y 3m 21d son of Hiram and Josephine in Sandy Hill, NY May 14, 1872

STREETER Sarah W. age 25y wife of M. F. Md. in Pawlet, Vt. April 27, 1872

BACON Freddie F. age 20y in Whitehall, NY May 9, 1872

FLANDREAU Minnie G. 5m 10d dau of Daniel and Mary in Dresden, NY May 9, 1872

HURD Maria age 30y wife of Charles in Glens Falls, NY May 6, 1872

HAND Edward J. age 23y in Sandy Hill, NY May 20, 1872

TAYLOR Samuel age 80y in Sandy Hill, NY May 18, 1872

WILTSIE William Albert age 16y in Sandy Hill, NY May 5, 1872

DE FORRESTER Morris age 55y in Hampton, NY May 8, 1872

ROBERTS James age 24y drowned near Ft. Miller, NY May 15, 1872

HARVEY Catherine age 78y at son-in-laws D. GRIFFIN in Adamsville, NY May 10, 1872

KEEFE Danny age 3y 8m 9d son of John B. and Margaret L. in Glens Falls, NY May 15, 1872

ARMSTRONG James age 74y in Johnsburgh, NY May 19, 1872

BARBER Ralph age 84y in Dresden, NY May 22, 1872

BLANCHARD Stephen age 28y in Whitehall, NY May 17, 1872

MURRAY Mehittable age 76y wife of George F. in Whitehall, NY May 22, 1872

MONTGOMERY Lyman W. age 37y in Ft. Edward, NY May 18, 1872

LINDENDOLL Walter age 65y in Ft. Edward, NY May 17, 1872

HUTTON Ida Bell age 11y 4m dau of Robert R. and Mary L. in Putnam, NY June 8, 1872

HALL Elizabeth age 75y in Argyle, NY June 9, 1872

MC INTYRE John E. age 49y in Ft. Edward, NY June 9, 1872

WATERS Adelia age 12y 8m in Coila, NY June 12, 1872

OAKLEY Jennie B. age 6y 4m 5d dau of A. G. in Salem, NY June 12, 1872

FLETCHER Isaac age 83y in Jackson, NY June 1, 1872

VIRGIL Mrs. Hannah age 59y in Whitehall, NY June 4, 1872

BROWN Orcelia age 27y wife of Justus in Queensbury, NY June 11, 1872

PHELPS Chauncey age 3y son of N. G. in Schuylerville, NY June 5, 1872

CHASE Miss Jane age 54y in Johnsonville, NY May 15, 1872

TAYLOR Minerva age 17y in Kingsbury, NY June 20, 1872

BUCKLE William age 46y in Dresden, NY June 20, 1872

OSTRANDER Eugene age 5y in Dresden, NY June 21, 1872

KNIGHT Charlie age 6y 6m son of John and Calista in Whitehall, NY June 19, 1872

HOWE Mary age 33y wife of C. G. in Ft. Ann, NY June 11, 1872

BAKER Cinderilla age 64y wife of Henry in Cambridge, NY May 27, 1872

PARK Elora L. age 36y wife of Oscar in Hartford, NY June 23, 1872

MURRAY Lewis age 54y in Queensbury, NY June 25, 1872

TRUESDALE Seth age 61y in Bolton, NY June 16, 1872

SIMMONS Samuel E. age 52y in Ft. Edward, NY June 21, 1872

PIERCE Miss Emily age 63y in Whitehall, NY June 27, 1872

HALL Mary (**DEMAR**) age 48y wife of Enos in Jackson, NY June 9, 1872

COPELAND Sarah E. age 19y dau of Levi and Mary J. in Salem, NY May 30, 1872

HALL George M. Jr. age 21y in Cambridge, NY June 27, 1872

CAMPBELL W. O. age 71y in Anaquasicoke, NY June 14, 1872

SIBLEY Austin T. in his 6th yr son of Rev. A. W. in Sandy Hill, NY July 4, 1872. Born Woodstock, NH

CLARK Jane Maria wife of Dr. Erskine G. and dau of late William **MC DONALD** of Glens Falls, NY in Sandy Hill, NY July 10, 1872

GILMAN Capt. Zeb age 52 of Champlain, NY in Whitehall, NY July 5, 1872

MULHOLLAND Willie age 15m son of William and Catherine in Whitehall, NY July 5, 1872

MURPHY Helen Virginia age 1y 1m 11d dau of E. W. and Helen A. in Albany, NY

July 4, 1872

BARBER Amos age 51y in Whitehall, NY July 9, 1872, buried Dresden, NY

MOORE William age 75y in Hebron, NY July 7, 1872

KENYON William age 61y in Cambridge, NY July 4, 1872

RICHARDS Experience abt 70y in Greenwich, NY July 10, 1872

CARSWELL Nathaniel age 68y in Argyle, NY July 8, 1872

COTTRELL Anna W. abt 50y in Argyle, NY July 9, 1872

KEY David abt 25y in Argyle, NY July 10, 1872

CROCKER Lydia D. wife of Ezra and dau of late Daniel D. **SCOTT** of Queensbury, NY in Lake Mills, Wis. June 25, 1872

CARROLL Frank in Sandy Hill, NY July 23, 1872

COHEN Isaac age 23y at Lake George, NY July 19, 1872

BULLOCK Josephine L. (**SCOTT**) age 27y in Fairhaven, Vt. July 13, 1872

MC CARTY Nancy age 22y wife of Thomas at N. River June 14, 1872

BARRETT John and Richard age 2m twin sons of John and Ann in Whitehall, NY July __, and July 17, 1872

SAWYER Cornelia H. age 22y wife of Allen C. in Whitehall, NY July 16, 1872

BRENNAN William age 36y in Whitehall, NY July 18, 1872

MC GOUGH Katie age 12y in Sandy Hill, NY August 4, 1872

SIMONS Henry W. age 1y son of Stephen and Matilda in Ft. Edward, NY July 28, 1872

DONALDSON Samuel in his 89th yr in Argyle, NY July 29, 1872

WOOD Charles age 60y in Argyle, NY July 30, 1872

ROBINSON Mary Jane age 43y wife of Zenas of Argyle, NY in Ballston Spa, NY July 18, 1872

CARROLL Francis age 29y son of late Owen in Sandy Hill, NY July 23, 1872

PERRY Francis S. age 16y son of Francis and May in Sandy Hill, NY August 11, 1872

BLAKE Carrie age 16m dau of George and Mary in Sandy Hill, NY August 11, 1872

MONAHAN Mathew age 32y in Hartford, NY August 14, 1872

BENNETT Hollis K. age 10m 11d son of Dr. H. K. in Whitehall, NY August 6, 1872

HOYT Guy age 4m 3d son of T. G. and A. M. in Warrensburgh, NY August 10, 1872

BARKER Helen age 33y wife of Charles in Adamsville, NY August 14, 1872

KINSLEY Susan M. age 21y wife of Duane in Whitehall, NY August 8, 1872

MULLIGAN Margaret age 45y in Easton, NY August 13, 1872

MC GOWAN Miss M. E. age 24y in Easton, NY August 13, 1872

MC GEOCH Janet age 83y widow of Alexander in Argyle, NY August 6, 1872

BATES Myra Luella age 6m in Whitehall, NY August 12, 1872

GEORGE Mrs. Sylvania age 89y relict of Daniel in Whitehall, NY August 15, 1872

WRIGHT Alvah age 6y 1m died August 15, 1872 and Jennie age 5y died August 15, 1872 children of John and Melissa in Salem, NY

CONKLIN Abram age 86y of Sandy Hill, NY in Hartford, NY August 25, 1872

WILLIS Berty age 6m son of Edwin and Lucy in Sandy Hill, NY August 27, 1872

BILLOTDOUX Chester age 35y in Sandy Hill, NY August 25, 1872

PECK Miss Sarah age 20y in Sandy Hill, NY August 21, 1872

DAVIS Charlotte E. in Sandy Hill, NY August 30, 1872

BROOKS Lewis age 34y in Sandy Hill, NY September 10, 1872

ALLEN Alpha age 63y wife of Joseph in Whitehall, NY August 26, 1872

OSGOOD Henry H. age 34y in Whitehall, NY August 29, 1872

WHITE Olive age 25y wife of Chester in Ft. Ann, NY August 26, 1872. Infant dau age 6d died August 21, 1872

TAYLOR Miss Mary L. age 32 in Argyle, NY September 10, 1872

SARGENT Lucinda M. age 25y wife of Harrison in Whitehall, NY September 3, 1872

DURKEE Angeline in her 55th yr in Salem, NY September 12, 1872

BURNETT Lillie A. age 4m dau of H. and M. in Putnam, NY September 16, 1872

WRIGHT Robert in his 88th yr in Putnam, NY September 20, 1872

COOK Harvey age 84y in Kingsbury, NY September 19, 1872

MOREHOUSE D. Ray in his 29th yr in Greenwich, NY September 12, 1872

COLVIN Ann E. age 38y wife of Dearstill in Glens Falls, NY September 20, 1872

GALUSHA Mrs. Russell in Ft. Edward, NY September 17, 1872

COLLINS ___ age 1m dau of John H. and Sarah J. in Whitehall, NY September 16, 1872

SWIFT Hiram age 18y son of Willis in Ft. Ann, NY September 5, 1872

ELLIOTT Dency age 80y widow of Laban in Kingsbury, NY September 19, 1872

CORNELL James S. age 75y 5m 14d in N. Argyle, NY September 27, 1872

WRIGHT Johnie age 1y 8m son of John A. and Lucy in Pacific City, Iowa September 13, 1872

SWEET Sarah age 50y wife of Charles in N. Granville, NY September 30, 1872

MC FERRON Mr. L. age 40y in Whitehall, NY September 23, 1872

GIBBS Mr. Ozell age 47y in Whitehall, NY September 25, 1872

REID Anna age 28y wife of Joseph and dau of George **ASHLEY** in W. Hebron, September 20, 1872

WHITE Henrietta age 32y dau of John **EARL** in Ft. Ann, NY September 23, 1872

CHAMPLIN David in his 86th yr in Queensbury, NY September 28, 1872

BASSETT Pope T. age 21y son of John W. in Ft. Miller, NY September 27, 1872

DAYTON Robert age 21y son of R. G. in N. Granville, NY October 6, 1872

MC DONNELL Mary Ellen age 4y 7m dau of John in Dresden, NY September 3, 1872

WING Asamel age 49y in Ft. Edward, NY October __, 1872

BACON Ezra age 56y in Whitehall, NY October 8, 1872

TAYLOR Cyrus age 83y in S. Granville, NY October 13, 1872

TILFORD James age 84y in Argyle, NY October 4, 1872

DURKEE Sidney age 62y in Ft. Edward, NY October 5, 1872

SANDERS Laura age 52y at bro William **ALLEN** in Whitehall, NY September 28, 1872

ALLEN D. B. age 60y in Whitehall, NY October 30, 1872

DURKAN Mary age 60y in Sandy Hill, NY October 20, 1872

WHITE J. T. age 27y in Verona, Iowa October 7, 1872

MILLETT J. L. age 26y in Whitehall, NY October 16, 1872

INGALLS Mary age 33y wife of J. J. formerly of Granville, NY in Poultney, Vt. October 16, 1872

MC MOORE Alexander age 87y in S. Bay, NY October 20, 1872

BARBER Mrs. ____ age 80y relict of Ralph in Dresden, NY October 18, 1872

GILMAN Almira B. age 61y relict of Dr. O. P. in Salem, NY October 16, 1872

CRAWFORD Franklin A. age 21y in Ft. Edward, NY October 25, 1872

REYNOLDS Miss Maggie age 19y in Hebron, NY October 29, 1872

STEVENS W. H. age 65y in Whitehall, NY October 29, 1872

BURROUGHS Mary L. age 29y dau of O. C. and Louisa in Elkhart, Ind. (newspaper date November 7, 1872)

BECKWITH Oliver P. age 27y formerly of Whitehall, NY in Hydesville, Vt. October 18, 1872

LIDDLE Fannie B. age 27y in M. Granville, NY November 1, 1872

BASSETT F. M. age 67y formerly of Ft. Miller, NY in Culpepper, Va. October 27, 1872

MARTIN William age 54y in Hartford, NY October 31, 1872

DE GARMO Willie age 19y son of William R. and Rhoda in Ft. Miller, NY October 30, 1872

DUNCAN Mrs. Janette age 65y in Whitehall, NY October 27, 1872

EAGER Mary Ella age 15y in Whitehall, NY October 30, 1872

MC FARLAND Martha age 29y in Salem, NY November 1, 1872

LEET Susan J. age 34y in Ft. Edward, NY November 15, 1872

JOHNSON Frank age 26 in Whitehall, NY November 18, 1872

PECK Ansel age 78y in Whitehall, NY November 19, 1872

FARNHAM Polly (**FRISBIE**) age 79y wife of William L. in Poultney, Vt. November 15, 1872

KING Catherine in her 64th yr wife of Hugh in Ft. Edward, NY November 18, 1872

MC DOUGAL John S. age 76y in Argyle, NY November 12, 1872

KELLY Mrs. Ellen age 56y in Sandy Hill, NY November 30, 1872

ELLIOTT Polly age 78y relict of Daniel in Kingsbury, NY November 25, 1872

HOWARD Abial W. age 77y in Ft. Ann, NY November 20, 1872

STAY Mrs. Sylvester in S. Argyle, NY November 21, 1872

NORTON Eliza J. age 71y wife of Alvah in Hartford, NY November 21, 1872

RIVERS ____ only dau of George age 10y in Sandy Hill, NY December 5, 1872

ALLEN Peleg age 75y in Sandy Hill, NY December 11, 1872

BRADT Harriet A. age 43y wife of V. Z. formerly of Ft. Ann, NY in Albany, NY December 2, 1872

FISH Amanda age 60y in S. Bay, NY December 1, 1872

HITCHCOCK Alfred F. age 95y in Moreau, NY December 5, 1872

SPENCER Ambrose age 66y 3m in Albany, NY December 11, 1872

WEST George P. age 26y in Glens Falls, NY December 17, 1872

WEST James age 47y in Glens Falls, NY December 2, 1872

FULLER John age 81y at Ft. Miller Bridge, NY December 6, 1872

STEVENS William 2nd age 65y in Ft. Ann, NY December 11, 1872

BILLETT Hattie Annabelle 2w 4d dau of J. F. and Nellie in Whitehall, NY December 1, 1872

MURRAY Dr. John W. B. age 83y native of Scotland in Granville, NY November 29,

1872

COLVIN James L. age 68y formerly of Sandgate, Vt. in W. Day, NY December 18, 1872

HILLS Polly age 78y wife of Asa in N. Hebron, NY December 18, 1872

BEATTIE Louise age 27y wife of William J. of Hartford, NY in Cambridge, NY December 13, 1872

MC COLLUM Viola age 16y formerly of Ft. Ann, NY in Lansingburgh, NY December 10, 1872

DENTON Sidney E. age 30y in Troy, NY December 23, 1872

NORTHUP Miss Ada M. age 30y in Sandy Hill, NY December 23, 1872

SHERRILL Henry C. age 42y native of Sandy Hill, NY in Washington, DC December 31, 1872

BLAWIS Dr. J. P. age 37y in Ft. Miller, NY December 16, 1872

MORGAN Joseph W. age 54y in Moreau, NY December 24, 1872

ST JOHN William age 53y in Whitehall, NY December 18, 1872

STEWART Isaac age 54y in Whitehall, NY December 17, 1872

STARKS James age 27y in Comstocks Landing, NY December 29, 1872

ALLEN Florence age 1y 9m 10d dau of Charles N. and Jennie A. (**BAXTER**) in Comstocks Landing, NY December 14, 1872

MEEKER Rev. B. J. age 57y in W. Sandlake, NY January 3, 1873

HARRIS William Franklin age 1y son of Horace W. in Sandy Hill, NY January 8, 1873

TAYLOR Pamela J. age 21y dau of William S. of Green Bay, Wis. at uncles N. W. **WAIT** in Sandy Hill, NY January 11, 1873

GOSS Emma age 91y 8d widow in Kingsbury, NY January 8, 1873

STEVENSON Frances W. formerly of Cambridge in Geneva, NY January 14, 1873

BENTLEY Elisha abt 70y in Kingsbury, NY January 15, 1873

LAVEY Thomas in Glens Falls, NY January 15, 1873

YOUNG Masie age 1y 5m son of Ira H. and Lucy M. in Ft. Edward, NY January 3,

1873

MC KEACHIE Robena age 84y wife of George in Argyle, NY December 31, 1872

LAPHAM Mary Ann age 73y in Glens Falls, NY January 10, 1873

COLLAMER L. B. age 62y of Sandy Hill, NY in Davenport, Io. December 28, 1872

AUSMENT William age 87y in Kingsbury, NY January 4, 1873

ROGERS Thomas only son of John in Black Brook, NY January 21, 1873

JILLSON Betsey age 86y relict of Stephen in Whitehall, NY January 15, 1873

BAILEY Mary (HICKS) age 32y formerly of Ft. Ann, NY in Akron, Ohio January 12, 1873

BURTON Lydia age 96y in Caldwell, Vt. January 4, 1873

WILLETT Joseph age 51y in Glens Falls, NY January 10, 1873

COTTON Lois age 85y in Ft. Ann, NY January 10, 1873

KEY Robert in Argyle, NY January 12, 1873

CLEMMONS Kate age 64y in Dresden, NY January 29, 1873

NICHOLS Mrs. ____ age 90y in Ft. Miller, NY January 14, 1873

EMMONS Mrs. Benjamin age 70y in Sandy Hill, NY January 27, 1873

MC MILLAN Mary Ann age 35y wife of James in Argyle, NY January 20, 1873

ROSS Henry Erwin age 1y son of Erwin and Jennie in Ft. Edward, NY January 27, 1873

LYONS Mr. M. age 25y in Putnam, NY January 6, 1873

DIBBLE Dr. Henry E. formerly of Sandy Hill, NY in New York February 2, 1873

CROSIER Hannah age 22y dau of James in Hebron, NY January 31, 1873

HANNA David age 13/16 son of Andrew in N. Argyle, NY January 31, 1873

BUTLER Edward age 47y in Cambridge, NY January 26, 1873

WELLS William in his 80th yr in E. Whitehall, NY January 26, 1873

LANDON Cassius D. age 33y in Brooklyn, NY January 27, 1873

BOYINGTON Lucy C. age 61y of Whitehall, NY in Utica, NY January 29, 1873

FERGUSON Alexander F. age 77y in S. Argyle, NY January 25, 1873

BARBER Mary Ann dau of James MC LAUGHLIN of Sandy Hill, NY in Red Oak, Iowa February 1, 1873

WHITNEY Maria age 22y wife of Benjamin in Sandy Hill, NY February 11, 1873

HOLBROOK Tryphena age 94y 27d widow of Levi in Boston, NY January 24, 1873. Born Norfolk Co. Mass. married there about 1800, lived Hartford, NY 15 yrs

COOK Walton M. age 44y at brother-in-laws Robert CRONK in Sandy Hill, NY February 8, 1873

GILBERT Alvira age 40y wife of Josiah in Comstocks Landing, NY January 27, 1873. Dau Nancy age 18y died January 30, 1873 and son Herbert age 10m died January 31, 1873

NORTON Russell age 90y 3m formerly of Cambridge, NY in New Haven, NY January 16, 1873

BUEL Mary V. age 29y wife of Ad A. formerly of Whitehall, NY in New York January 31, 1873

BASCOM Franklin age 55y 6m in Whitehall, NY February 2, 1873

CLAPP Catherine age 88y at dau Mrs. D. G. NORRIS in Glens Falls, NY February 9, 1873

BINGHAM John age 66y in Sandy Hill, NY February 11, 1873

SLOCUM Mrs. Sarah age 87y in Hartford, NY February 6, 1873

NORTHUP Fred H. age 33y in W. Albany, NY February 15, 1873

BECKWITH Hon. H. W. age 61y in W. Granville, NY February 3, 1873

BENTON Lucinda age 63y wife of Alvah in Ft. Ann, NY February 4, 1873

BOTTOM ____ child of Mr. and Mrs. Bottom in Whitehall, NY February 2, 1873

SHIPPY Stephen in his 70th yr in Glens Falls, NY February 7, 1873

HURLEY James in his 8th yr in Glens Falls, NY February 3, 1873

BERRIGAN Mrs. Julia age 70y in Sandy Hill, NY February 26, 1873

THOMPSON Ebenezer age 33/83y in Adamsville, NY February 27, 1873

SARGENT Amos L. in his 82nd yr in Ft. Edward, NY February 19, 1873

CROSS Pamela age 77y relict of Theodore in Kingsbury, NY (newspaper date February 27, 1873)

NORRIS Frank dau of Rev. Edward **TOGER** in Ft. Ann, NY February 17, 1873

ADAMS Freeland G. age 19y son of Joseph in S. Bay, NY February 17, 1873

ANDERSON ____ age 17y dau of Thomas in Putnam, NY February 18, 1873

SMALLEY Jerome H. age 38y in Kingsbury, NY February 21, 1873

BROWN Clark age 55y formerly of Kingsbury in Glens Falls, NY February 26, 1873

HOLBROOK Altha wife of Joel in Glens Falls, NY February 17, 1873. Born July 19, 1786 in Wellington, Conn., married 1813 came to Hartford, NY 1817. 2 children

DAILEY Mrs. Betsey age 80y in N. Granville, NY March 1, 1873

ELDRIDGE Edward age 83y formerly of Hoosick, NY in Ft. Edward, NY February 20, 1873

LAVOY Miss Emma age 25y in Whitehall, NY February 24, 1873

NORTHUP Lieut. Edward S. in Sioux City, Iowa March 4, 1873. Born December 25, 1844 in Sandy Hill, NY. Enlisted in 44th NY Vol. in 1861

BURTON Samuel C. age 44y in Sandy Hill, NY March 6, 1873

HUNTLEY Helena B. age 12y only child of William and Frances formerly of Sandy Hill in Lock Haven, NY February 12, 1873

WATKINS Mary J. age 42y in Granville, NY February 27, 1873

JILLSON Joseph age 84y in Whitehall, NY March 7, 1873

TEFFT Amos age 69y in Greenwich, NY March 3, 1873

BAKER John Henry age 43y 4m in Plattsburgh, NY March 10, 1873. Born Washington Co. NY, married 1858 dau of Benjamin **FERRIS** of Sandy Hill, NY. Wife Helen in her 41st yr died March 14, 1873. Both buried Sandy Hill, NY

DOUGHERTY Dennis age 63y in Sandy Hill, NY March 18, 1873

WELCH Mary Amanda (**SMITH**) age 29y wife of Theodore in Minneapolis, Mn. March 6, 1873

CRAWFORD Theodore age 32y in Ft. Edward, NY March 11, 1873

GARRETT Jennie H. age 28y wife of Dr. J. S. in Glens Falls, NY March 14, 1873

KELLY Thomas F. age 30y in Glens Falls, NY March 19, 1873, born New London, Conn. oldest of 5 children

HOLBROOK Lyman age 76y in Bellingham, Mass. (newspaper date March 20, 1873)

PROUTY Lydia in her 80th yr in Glens Falls, NY March 13, 1873

HOLCOMB George Emerson age 5m 13d son of Dr. B. R. in Whitehall, NY March 13, 1873

RICHARDSON Eddie R. age 3y 3m in Granville, NY March 14, 1873

JOSLIN Sarah age 3y in Cambridge, NY March 14, 1873

HAY Isaac age 89y 10m 7d at son-in-laws William P. LINCOLN in Hebron, NY March 6, 1873

SMITH S. Ann (NEFF) age 28y wife of Frederick in Hebron, NY March 1, 1873

O'CONNOR Jane in her 78th yr in Salem, NY March 15, 1873

SHEA James killed on tracks near Hydesville, NY March 17, 1873

JILLSON Mrs. Hannah age 82y in Glens Falls, NY March 22, 1873

BROWN Joseph R. age 15y son of Samuel and Sophia in Whitehall, NY March 21, 1873

MASTERS Nicolas M. age 82y in Greenwich, NY March 28, 1873

ROBERTS Mr. ____ age 57y in Whitehall, NY March 25, 1873

KING Phebe age 52y in Salem, NY March 13, 1873

REYNOLDS Amos age 78y in Luzerne, NY March 20, 1873

JALET Edward age 4y in Whitehall, NY April 3, 1873

RICH Lucy age 10m dau of Joseph in Whitehall, NY April 1, 1873

MC ENERY Joanna age 36y wife of Michael in Cambridge, NY March 28, 1873

DOWNS Fred age 24y and Patrick MOYNIHAN age 27y killed on RR near Cambridge, NY March 20, 1873

NORCROSS Abby age 85y in Glens Falls, NY April 7, 1873

RIORDAN Abby age 41y wife of Cornelius in Hartford, NY April 15, 1873

JENKINS Lyman age 57y in Queensbury, NY April 15, 1873

FERGUSON Eliza age 60 in S. Argyle, NY March 24, 1873

HOYT Mary E. age 34y 3m 5d wife of William H. in Poultney, Vt. April 6, 1873

MATHEWS Abraham age 84y in Argyle, NY April 7, 1873

NORTON Jacob age 76y in Bolton, NY April 2, 1873

BECKWITH Oliver age 2y son of Anson M. and Lora in Whitehall, NY April 10, 1873

LARKIN Bertie age 9y 5m son of John E. and Frances drowned in Argyle, NY April 11, 1873

FULLER Mrs. Harmon age 42y in Stony Creek, NY April 14, 1873

LOVELAND George age 89y in Johnsburgh, NY March 25, 1873

ALLISON Mrs. Harriet age 67y in Glens Falls, NY April 2, 1873

EDGAR Walter age 77y in N. Argyle, NY April 10, 1873

RANDALL Rev. Moses age 81 formerly of Warren Co. in S. Wales, NY April 17, 1873

SKINNER Charles age 26y son of Sylvester and Sarah in Ft. Ann, NY April 13, 1873

STANTON Miranda age 62y widow in Bolton, NY April 11, 1873

BENNETT Charlotte C. age 60y wife of H. and dau of late Benjamin **CLARK** of Sandy Hill, NY in Sandy Hill April 27, 1873

BROWN Charley age 8y son of John in Sandy Hill, NY April 26, 1873

LUSCOMB Jesse Y. age 16y 10m in Ft. Edward, NY April 20, 1873

JOHNSON Walton age 4y son of William and Nettie in Sandy Hill, NY April 27, 1873

HARVEY William age 84y in Ft. Ann, NY April 29, 1873

LAMB Nathan age 77y of Greenwich, NY in the County Home April 17, 1873

MC NEIL James age 90y in Argyle, NY April 21, 1873

MILLER Sarah M. age 36y wife of Stephen in Glens Falls, NY April 14, 1873

JOHNSON David age 53y formerly of Glens Falls, NY in Lodi, Ill. (newspaper date

May 1, 1873)

THOMAS Susan age 77y at son-in-laws D. F. NYE in Whitehall, NY April 25, 1873

SMITH Georgie age 3m 15d son of George W. L. and Selina in Smiths Basin, NY (newspaper date May 1, 1873)

KILBOURN Edward age 22y son of Norman in Whitehall, NY April 28,1873

GEORGE Cornelius in his 85th yr in E. Whitehall, NY April 20, 1873

BURBY Margaret age 45y wife of Thomas in Dansville, NY (newspaper date May 8, 1873)

DONEGAN Daniel age 65y in Glens Falls, NY May 1, 1873

LEARY Patrick age 60y in Glens Falls, NY May 1, 1873

DILLON John in his 54th yr in Salem, NY April 28, 1873

BECKWITH Carrie L. age 19y dau of Louisa M. and late Henry of W. Granville, NY in Lebanon, NH April 29, 1873

CORNELL Catherine age 57y wife of Sidney in N. Argyle, NY May 1, 1873

ROOT William age 17y son of Henry S. and Jane in Ft. Ann, NY April 25, 1873

DOUGLAS Wilbur F. age 18y in Whitehall, NY May 6, 1873

SHORTT John age 56y bro of Rev. W. B. of Cambridge in New York May 1, 1873

CARSWELL Jemmie age 4y son of Gideon and Esther in Argyle, NY April 25, 1873

ROBERTSON Maria age 84 widow of James P. in Cambridge, NY May 4, 1873

MC FARLAND Caroline A. age 50 wife of Samuel in Cambridge, NY May 3, 1873

SULLIVAN Georgie J. age 4m 13d son of John and Eliza in Cambridge, NY May 5, 1873

BARBER John age 75y in Jackson, NY May 6, 1873

PALMER Charlotte age 52y in Cambridge, NY May 7, 1873

BAKER Mary age 22y wife of Samuel in S. Argyle, NY May 1, 1873

BAKER Sarah D. age 27y dau of Royal W. and Eliza in Ft. Ann, NY May 8, 1873

RUSSELL Eddie in his 4th yr son of Mark and Mary in S. Bay, NY May 8, 1873

WARD Martha J. dau of William H. of S. Hartford, NY May 6, 1873

BAKER Sarph age 40y wife of E. W. in Sandy Hill, NY May 20, 1873

MONTY George H. age 3y 4m son of Benjamin K. of Gr. Haven, Mi. in Sandy Hill, NY May 14, 1873

VAVIER Emily age 58y in Sandy Hill, NY May 21, 1873

MANSFIELD E. L. age 63y in Kingsbury, NY May 17, 1873

BELDEN Rev. Henry in Westhaven, Vt. May __, 1873

HARRIS Lent F. age 75y in Pattens Mills, NY May 11, 1873

MC KEE Edward age 49y in Ft. Edward, NY May 9, 1873

BARKER Perry C. age 85y in S. Glens Falls, NY April 29, 1873

MURPHY Coolidge B. age 70y in Sandy Hill, NY May 27, 1873

MILLER Dr. William H. age 52y in Sandy Hill, NY May 23, 1873

BUGBY Lorrina age 73y in Sandy Hill, NY May 24, 1873

MAGEE Calvin in his 73rd yr in Salem, NY May 12, 1873

TANNER Mrs. Harvey age 53y in Bolton, NY May 17, 1873

FLOYD Samuel E. age 37y in Whitehall, NY May 22, 1873

JUCKET Reuben age 75y in Whitehall, NY May 22, 1873

AKIN Samuel in Whitehall, NY May 16, 1873

STODDARD Sarah Maria age 22y wife of Goodsell in N. Granville, NY May 9, 1873

BRANNAN Thomas age 34y in Sandy Hill, NY May 29, 1873, in US Art. Civil War

WYMAN Joseph would be 99 on July 17, 1873 in W. Ft. Ann, NY June 1, 1873

MILLER Julia E. age 26y at Kings St. May 30, 1873

GRAHAM Eleanor in her 37th yr wife of William in Putnam, NY May 26, 1873

TILFORD Sarah A. in her 26th yr wife of John in Whitehall, NY May 30, 1873

KILBOURN Mary age 46y wife of Norman in Whitehall, NY May 30, 1873

CHRISTIE Jane abt 65y in the County Home May 26, 1873

SHERMAN James M. age 56y in Ft. Ann, NY May 21, 1873

MADDEN Mrs. Margaret age 73y in Glens Falls, NY June 5, 1873

WHITE Sarah in her 43rd yr wife of John in E. Whitehall, NY June 6, 1873

SHEEHAN Jennie age 13y in W. Granville, NY June 1, 1873

WOODCOCK Israel abt 44y in Schuylerville, NY May 27, 1873

CAVANAUGH Barney age 75y in Cambridge, NY May 30, 1873

WELLS Jane age 53y wife of Joseph of Easton, NY in New York May 31, 1873

DEIDRICK Alonzo age 68y in Putnam, NY May 23, 1873

GARDNER Matie age 36y wife of Rufus in Sandy Hill, NY June 13, 1873

KING Olive age 1y 4m 7d dau of Benjamin and Mary A. in Sandy Hill, NY June 16, 1873

BURDICK Minnie L. age 6y dau of J. H. and Thea in Glens Falls, NY June 11, 1873

WHITE Sarah (PARISH) age 42y wife of John in Whitehall, NY June 6, 1873

REYNOLDS Moses in his 67th yr in Dresden, NY June 12, 1873

RIGNEY William in Salem, NY June 8, 1873. Parents resided Ft. Edward, NY

ROBERTSON Ellery S. age 26y in Cambridge, NY June 12, 1873

QUINLAN John age 14m died May 11, 1873, David age 4y 10m died June 7, 1873, Mary age 9y died June 9, 1873 chidren of Michael and Mary in Pawlet, Vt.

BELDEN Fred S. age 30y in Whitehall, NY June 11, 1873

GOODRICH Miss Mary A. age 22y in S. Hartford, NY June 13, 1873

FORT Abbie R. age 70y in Moreau, NY June 21, 1873

BEADLE Mrs. Fanny age 76y in Whitehall, NY June 15, 1873

LIVINGSTON Mrs. Arathusa in her 76th yr in Whitehall, NY June 16, 1873

FAXON Charles H. age 33y in Glens Falls, NY June 18, 1873

BERRY John S. age 56y formerly of Sandy Hill, NY in Toledo, Ohio June 9, 1873

INGALLS Thomas in his 41st yr in Greenwich, NY June 18, 1873

MC EACHRON Alexander age 12y in Argyle, NY June 11, 1873

DAVIS Syrle age 69y in Granville, NY June 11, 1873

SPENCER William H. age 30y late of 123rd Reg. in Greenwich, NY June 15, 1873

MARTIN George C. age 70y in Hampton, NY June 9, 1873

DEPOT Mrs. J. B. age 44y in Sandy Hill, NY June 26, 1873

CRONKHITE Mrs. Ann age 78y in Sandy Hill, NY June 28, 1873

BROWN Helen M. age 21y wife of Levi in Sandy Hill, NY July 3, 1873

DEAUGA Mrs. Harriet age 25y in Sandy Hill, NY June 20, 1873

VAUGHN Howard B. age 19m son of Freeland and Elizabeth formerly of Sandy Hill, NY in Saratoga, NY June 27, 1873

BARBER Jacob age 55y in Whitehall, NY June 24, 1873

COUMEY William age 45y in Whitehall, NY June 24, 1873

BEEBE Mrs. Ann M. age 73y widow of Seymour in E. Hartford, NY July 1, 1873

THOMPSON Fred H. age 22y in Glens Falls, NY June 23, 1873

DICKINSON Ephraim age 83y in Caldwell, NY June 19, 1873

MC EACHRON Frank age 20y dau of Charles in Argyle, NY June 25, 1873

TREMBLEY Mitchell age 82y in Sandy Hill, NY July 18, 1873

KNAPP Ira age 68y formerly of Granville, NY in Watertown, NY June 26, 1873

JONES Morris son of Ebenezer of Granville, NY in Nashville, Tn. (newspaper date July 10, 1873)

SMITH Mrs. Joseph age 25y in Putnam, NY July 3, 1873

MACE Julia A. age 42y in Glens Falls, NY June 26, 1873

COTTRELL Nathaniel in his 81st yr in White Creek, NY June 25, 1873

SHELDON Dr. N. Edson age 68y in Glens Falls, NY July 3, 1873

WRIGHT Harriet F. age 24y wife of Edward in Glens Falls, NY July 1, 1873

SPRAGUE James in his 22nd yr in Salem, NY June 26, 1873

FASSETT Mrs. Mary age 65y 8m in Cambridge, NY June 29, 1873

HALL Desire D. age 49y in Cambridge, NY June 25, 1873

DONAVAN Catherine age 19y wife of Michael in Glens Falls, NY July 10, 1873

WATERS Mrs. ____ age 55y in E. Salem, NY July 7, 1873

MC CARTHY Timothy abt 60y in Cambridge, NY July 5, 1873

LADD Perry G. in Bensons Landing, Vt. July 8, 1873

TEFFT ____ age 6w dau of Andrew J. in Whitehall, NY July 8, 1873

GASTON Fremont age 16y son of O. and Elizabeth A. in Salem, NY July 3, 1873

CARTER George Henry age 16m son of Francis and Mary Caroline formerly of Whitehall, NY in Utica, NY July 11, 1873

ARMSTRONG Robert C. Md. age 71y formerly of Cambridge, NY in Sandwich, Ill. July 12, 1873

CLAPP Benjamin age 54y in Salem, NY July 11, 1873

LANSING Arcabinda age 26y wife of U. J. in Greenwich, NY July 13, 1873

WILDER Abel G. age 64y in Greenwich, NY July 13, 1873

MC LAUGHLIN Mrs. James age 89y in Putnam, NY July 16, 1873

BRAYTON Sarah age 77y Mother of Mrs. Simon **FLAGLER** of Sandy Hill, NY in Oneonta, NY July 21, 1873

GRAVES Rev. Oliver age 80y in Olmsteadville, NY July 10, 1873

BUCKLEY Mary age 78y wife of Gen. Edward in N. Granville, NY July 18, 1873

CULVER David C. age 86y in Lockport, NY July 17, 1873. Born 1787 in Hebron, Conn., lived Sandy Hill, NY. Served War of 1812

HALL Mrs. Rachel age 76y in W. Ft. Ann, NY July 29, 1873

DAVIS Thomas age 31y son of Edward in Whitehall, NY July 28, 1873

LEET Rollin C. age 4m son of Charles and Prudence in Whitehall, NY July 21, 1873

COLBY Margaret age 30y wife of Abner in Shushan, NY July 16, 1873

SMITH Angeline age 60y wife of Sanford in Saratoga, NY July 22, 1873

BULLOCK Miss Susan age 73y in Greenwich, NY July 18, 1873

GREEN Allen age 73y in Cambridge, NY July 17, 1873

BULL Kittie F. age 26y 10m 16d wife of R. C. in Cambridge, NY July 20, 1873

WILBUR Allen age 79y in Easton, NY July 7, 1873

EDDY David H. age 49y in Moreau, NY July 22, 1873

VAN KIRK Ann age 14y dau of William in Greenwich, NY July 13, 1873

MC CARTY Timothy age 60y in Jackson, NY July 7, 1873

DARDIS William age 20y in Ft. Edward, NY July 31, 1873

MC MOORE Mrs. Sally in her 81st yr in Ft. Ann, NY July 27, 1873

MORGAN James age 59 in Glens Falls, NY August 1, 1873

MC CUNE Mary age 33y in Glens Falls, NY July 31, 1873

MURRAY John age 41y in Glens Falls, NY August 2, 1873

TRAVERS Nicolas Bennington in his 84th yr in Ft. Miller, NY July 21, 1873. Two sons Dr. W. H. and Dr. L. of Providence and Enos of Glens Falls, NY

MC INERNEY Timothy age 3y son of Patrick in Cambridge, NY July 30, 1873

CORNELL Willie F. age 7m son of E. M. and Mary in Sandy Hill, NY August 11, 1873

COPELAND Hannahette age 87y wife of Benjamin in Ft. Ann, NY August 9, 1873

STEWART Margaret age 63y wife of Wiley formerly of Ft. Ann, NY in Gansevort, NY August 3, 1873

FITZGERALD Kate Elizabeth age 16y in Glens Falls, NY August 1, 1873

DOTY Annie M. in her 30th yr in Glens Falls, NY July 29, 1873

PARKS Hiram in his 71st yr in Moreau, NY August 8, 1873

WESTCOTT Daniel L. age 9y in Caldwell, NY July 22, 1873

WILLIAMS Lucretia in her 76th yr widow of Frederick S. of Schuylerville, NY at son-in-laws Judge **DAVIS** in Glens Falls, NY August 11, 1873

WAIT Albert age 21y in Cambridge, NY August 4, 1873

WILLIAMSON Robert age 50y in Putnam, NY August 17, 1873

DWIGHT Mary age 52y wife of S. L. in Whitehall, NY August 17, 1873

SAUNDERS Harry age 70y formerly of Whitehall in Trenton, Mi. August 2, 1873

HOWLAND Cornelia age 10m dau of Lansing M. and Hattie C. in Ft. Edward, NY August 22, 1873

FISHER Elizabeth Ann age 31y wife of Nathaniel W. in Glens Falls, NY August 18, 1873

GRAY John age 86 in the County Home August 2, 1873

ALLEN Georgie age 9w son of J. A. in Whitehall, NY August 31, 1873

QUA John age 50y in Hartford, NY September 3, 1873

ADAMS Lucy age 71y relict of Robert in Whitehall, NY August 8, 1873

COLIGAN Mrs. M. age 63y in Whitehall, NY August 5, 1873

GRIFFIN Bartholomew age 78y in Kingsbury, NY August 5, 1873

MANSFIELD Ellen age 22y in W. Ft. Ann, NY September 3, 1873

TOUSLEY Charles B. age 39y of Amsterdam, NY in Ft. Edward, NY September 13, 1873

PARMETER Emeline A. age 47y 10m in Ft. Edward, NY September 6, 1873

SHARROCK Clara age 4w dau of George and Sarah in Cambridge, NY September 12, 1873

STEVENSON Mary E. age 6m dau of Daniel W. and Maggie in Argyle, NY September 10, 1873

TOWSLEY Charles of Keesville, NY in Ft. Edward, NY September 13, 1873

MC NEIL Anna M. age 10y dau of David and Catherine in Argyle, NY September 15, 1873

FOSTER Priscilla age 41y wife of Henry in Sandy Hill, NY September 25, 1873

BLANCHARD Mrs. Deby age 74y in Putnam, NY September 20, 1873

DEAN Lorenzo age 56y in S. Glens Falls, NY September 22, 1873

CONANT George P. age 54y in Ft. Edward, NY September 24, 1873

COFFIN Folger age 51 in Caldwell, NY July 5, 1873

CHAPMAN Mary age 73 widow of William of Troy, NY in Salem, NY September 25, 1873. Names one dau Mrs. Daniel B. **COLE** of Salem, NY

LUTHER Henry Augustus age 9m son of F. L. in Granville, NY September 12, 1873

ROSS Eunice age 76y widow of John in Argyle, NY September 18, 1873

CULVER Sarah M. age 36y wife of Thomas in Cambridge, NY September 18, 1873

MON GARVIN Maggie age 17y of W. Hebron in Greenwich, NY September 21, 1873

BARRY Edward age 15y in Sandy Hill, NY October 4, 1873

WOODARD Mary L. age 6y 8m in Smiths Basin, NY September 26, 1873

MEAD Gildeon T. in his 54th yr in Chester, NY September 20, 1873

BLAIR John age 44y in Ft. Edward, NY October 3, 1873

NOLAN Ellen age 33y wife of John in Whitehall, NY September 28, 1873. Infant son died October 3, 1873

BROWN Hattie L. age 5y dau of Horatio and Hattie F. in Ft. Ann, NY September 20, 1873

WOOD H. K. age 59y in White Creek, NY October 2, 1873

DIMMICK Eliza M. age 44y wife of William in Cambridge, NY September 28, 1873

MOREY Elia A. age 20y wife of Carlos E. in Ft. Edward, NY October 3, 1873

CONKLIN Elizabeth age 35y wife of James H. in Ft. Edward, NY October 3, 1873

MURPHY Lydia age 20y dau of Michael in Whitehall, NY October 10, 1873

OFFENSEND Helena age 7y dau of David in Westhaven, Vt. October 11, 1873

WHITNEY Silas P. age 60y in Whitehall, NY October 11, 1873

ALDEN Mrs. Sally age 82y in Smiths Basin, NY October 1, 1873

ARCHIBALD Fannie M. age 28y wife of Andrew Jr. and dau of H. W. **BENNETT** of Glens Falls, NY in Ft. Edward, NY October 15, 1873

GILLIS John age 75y in Argyle, NY October 8, 1873

CRUIKSHANK James M. age 64y in Salem, NY October 14, 1873

HUGHES Catherine age 21y in Jackson, NY October 3, 1873

MERRIAM Martha age 56y in Granville, NY October 4, 1873

FLACK James H. age 83y in Argyle, NY October 23, 1873

MARTIN Joseph H. age 33y in Whitehall, NY October 21, 1873

BARRY Thomas age 28y in Whitehall, NY October 23, 1873

HALLARD Elizabeth age 72y in Cambridge, NY (newspaper date October 30, 1873)

STEVENS Polly age 68y relict of William in S. Bay, NY October 18, 1873

HUTCHINSON Rev. William age 79y in Sandy Hill, NY November 6, 1873

WRIGHT John N. age 66y in Sandy Hill, NY November 4, 1873

PIKE Willie D. age 4y 21d son of William H. in Glens Falls, NY October 31, 1873

FRASER Pollyette age 64y wife of Ora in Greenwich, NY October 30, 1873

SELLECK Mary age 71y widow of Aaron in Greenwich, NY October 26, 1873

ALLEN William R. late of 2nd NY Vet. Cav. in Glens Falls, NY October 15, 1873

BOGART William age 10y in Whitehall, NY November 3, 1873

LEE Almar age 35y in Whitehall, NY November 8, 1873

FERRIS Diana age 68y in Sandy Hill, NY November 19, 1873

DENNIS Mrs. Phebe Ann age 40y in Sandy Hill, NY November 9, 1873

BENTON Alvah age 67y in Ft. Ann, NY November 17, 1873

BORDEN Lewis age 76y in Whitehall, NY October 14, 1873

SMITH John L. age 74y in Whitehall, NY November 27, 1873

BARTHOLOMEW Phebe J. wife of Jerome in Dresden, NY November 21, 1873

BEATY Fannie J. age 57y wife of Samuel in Salem, NY November 18, 1873

CARLTON Alida S. age 19y dau of Orville N. in Sandy Hill, NY November 29, 1873

STILLSON Eli age 66y in M. Granville, NY November 24, 1873

FAXON Sidney B. age 68y 4m in Hartford, NY November 29, 1873

WASHBURN Elizabeth age 77y 8m in Hartford, NY November 22, 1873

BROWN Sally Ann in her 57th yr wife of Isaac S. formerly of Glens Falls, NY and dau of late Barber **WILLIAMS** formerly of Queensbury, NY in Sacramento, Cal. November 24, 1873

BEEBE Julius age 59y in Shushan, NY November 22, 1873

KENYON Martha age 75y 19d wife of Joseph C. in Elgin, Ill. November 2, 1873

CAIN Lucinda A. age 49y wife of William in Whitehall, NY December 9, 1873

CROSS Oscar A. age 19y son of S. O. and Ruby Ann in Kingsbury, NY December 12, 1873

LESTER William age 28y in the County Home December 13, 1873

PETTEYS Joseph age 60y in the County Home December 15, 1873

CHURCHILL Otis age 67y in Ft. Edward, NY December 12, 1873

HODGEMAN F. D. age 61y in Ft. Edward, NY December 14, 1873

HULL Erastus age 63y in Ft. Edward, NY December 8, 1873

MASON Isaac age 72y in Sandy Hill, NY December 22, 1873

AUSTIN John D. age 87y at the Onieda December 16, 1873

SMITH Anna age 63y wife of Major F. Smith in Queensbury, NY December 7, 1873

WILSON Nathan W. age 82y in Salem, NY December 6, 1873

NELSON Samuel age 82y formerly of Hebron, NY in Cooperstown, NY December 13, 1873

KNOWLSON Henry age 3y 6m son of Dr. J. in Granville, NY December 8, 1873

CARTER John age 71 in Sandy Hill, NY December 24, 1873

STEARNS Helen Estella age 13y dau of Samuel in Sandy Hill, NY December 23, 1873

BROUGH Sarah age 29y wife of Rev. D. in Argyle, NY December 28, 1873

FLACK Mary age 73y widow of John W. in N. Argyle, NY December 31, 1873

HARSHA Susan age 45y wife of David of Young America, Ill. in Argyle, NY January 4, 1874

DERBY George F. age 56y in Akron, Ohio December 31, 1873

HALL Hannah age 77y relict of John November 19, 1873

JENKINS Dr. Samuel age 58y in Queensbury, NY December 29, 1873

MORAN Mrs. Nella E. age 65y in Cambridge, NY December 24, 1873

MC NISH James in his 26th yr in Salem, NY December 23, 1873

WOOD Samuel age 78y in Greenwich, NY December 20, 1873

ROGERS Charles age 73y in Sandy Hill, NY January 13, 1874

POWERS Walter age 31y in Sandy Hill, NY January 9, 1873

MILLER George W. age 57y formerly of Hampton, NY in Monticello, Mn. January 5, 1873

FULLER Orasmus age 22y son of Alexander in Moreau, NY December 21, 1873

O'CONNOR Daniel age 80y in Whitehall, NY January 10, 1874

WATERS Cornelia age 32y in Whitehall, NY January 8, 1874

CARPENTER C. W. age 63y widow of D. N. of Mass. in Sandy Hill, NY January 18, 1874

HUGGINS Nancy in her 68th yr wife of John in N. Argyle, NY January 21, 1874

CARSWELL Amanda M. age 26y wife of Benjamin in Argyle, NY January 13, 1874

NICHOLS C. D. age 61y in Whitehall, NY January 7, 1874

WATERS Peter age 88y in Whitehall, NY January 15, 1874

POOR Margaret A. age 43y wife of Clark in White Creek, NY January 9, 1874

BENSON Delia W. age 13y dau of Sidney W. and Mary in Greenwich, NY January 10, 1874

WADHAMS Clara D. age 18y 7m in Greenwich, NY December 30, 1873

FISHER Flora age 2y 2m dau of Stephen R. in Cambridge, NY January 9, 1874

VAUGHN Allen age 68y at Kings St. NY January 19, 1874

UNDERWOOD Charles Clements age 3m son of Charles M. and Kate W. (CLEMENTS) in Ft. Edward, NY January 26, 1874

EMMONS Harriet S. age 84y 5m 20d relict of A. formerly of Sandy Hill, NY in Detroit, Mi. January 20, 1874

NORTON Frank age 32y in Ft. Edward, NY January 26, 1874

WYMAN Joseph Jr. age 52y in Ft. Edward, NY January 26, 1874

MC LEARY Patrick age 27y in Salem, NY January 22, 1874

DOREN William E. age 26y in Whitehall, NY January 31, 1874

HENNESSY Patrick age 48y in Whitehall, NY January 31, 1874

PLUE Stillman R. age 29y in Whitehall, NY January 28, 1874

LESTER David age 90y in N. Argyle, NY February 8, 1874

BARRETT Jonathan age 84y in N. Granville, NY January 30, 1874

BARNES Julia age 14y dau of late Capt. D. E. in Glens Falls, NY February 1, 1874

RODGERS Harriet age 69y in Glens Falls, NY February 7, 1874

WEED Joseph age 10y 10m son of George C. in Ticonderoga, NY January 31, 1874

STREETER Dennie Adelbert age 15m son of R. A. and H. E. in Ft. Edward, NY February 7, 1874

MILLER Squires age 80y in Whitehall, NY February 10, 1874

TOWNER John age 84y in Luzerne, NY February 12, 1874

DE KALB Ruth E. in N. Granville, NY January 31, 1874

ROGERS Harriet Leavens age 69y in Glens Falls, NY February 7, 1874

HAWLEY David age 65y in Salem, NY February 5, 1874

BURT Jerome B. age 59y in Whitehall, NY February 6, 1874

SIMPSON John age 69y in Putnam, NY February 10, 1874

SHATTUCK Joseph age 35y in Ticonderoga, NY January 31, 1874

BAKER Miss Keziah age 74y in Sandy Hill, NY February 25, 1874

HINES Susannah age 89y in Glens Falls, NY February 13, 1874

OWEN Edward age 70y in Argyle, NY February 1, 1874

BAIN John age 20y son of Andrew in Kanes Falls, NY February 16, 1874

WILLIS Nancy age 87y widow of Allen of Pawlet, Vt. in Granville, NY February 11, 1874

HUYCK ____ age 8m child of William and Jane in Ft. Ann, NY February 13, 1874

LEONARD Thomas Jr. bro of Rev. J. F. of Sandy Hill, NY in Albany, NY March 1, 1874

LYONS John age 68y in S. Bay, NY February 27, 1874

GETTY Mrs. Elizabeth age 93y in Salem, NY February 24, 1874

QUACKENBUSH Cornelia age 93y in Salem, NY February 25, 1874

WILLIAMS Eliza age 86y in Easton, NY February 23, 1874

STILES Mrs. Matilda age 27y in Sandy Hill, NY March 7, 1874

LA DEGRUSH Mrs. Isabel age 30y in Welch Hollow, NY March 10, 1874

WINEGAR Chester age 80y in Welch Hollow, NY March 2, 1874

HOGLE Sally age 81y widow of Barney in Luzerne, NY February 26, 1874

MC NEAL Lucy age 33y wife of George in Ft. Edward, NY February 28, 1874

KNOX Libbie age 30y wife of Charles in Glens Falls, NY February 7, 1874

TURNER Lucinda age 68y wife of John formerly of Ft. Ann, NY in Cleveland, Ohio March 5, 1874

LAMBERT Jennie Martin age 17y dau of Josiah PARISH in Hebron, NY February 24, 1874

FLANDREAU Mary age 38y wife of Rev. Daniel in Dresden, NY March 6, 1874

MC EACHRON Maggie age 36y wife of Frank in Argyle, NY February 27, 1874

MC DOUGAL Ann C. age 76y relict of John S. in Argyle, NY February 27, 1874

DENNISON William age 1y 10m son of William in Argyle, NY March 1, 1874

DUERS infant son of Zenas at Moss St. March 18, 1874

SHARP John H. in Putnam, NY February 27, 1874

DURKEE Harriet W. age 14y in Ft. Edward, NY March 7, 1874

COLLINS infant dau of Patrick in E. Hartford, NY March 13, 1874

SMITH Elisha P. age 76y in Easton, NY March 1, 1874

GRAHAM Miss Jane age 49y in Argyle, NY March 12, 1874

BUCKBEE Orville age 14y in Glens Falls, NY March 11, 1874

CROCKER Anna age 78y in Cambridge, NY March 9, 1874

HILL Miss Eliza age 64y in Greenwich, NY March 11, 1874

LEWIS Henry age 72y in Sandy Hill, NY March 25, 1874

VAUGHN Lucy age 84y in Kingsbury, NY March 22, 1874

ROGERS Miss Martha age 60y in S. Glens Falls, NY March 13, 1874

COPELAND Eleanor age 93y relict of John in Argyle, NY March 19, 1874

CARR Ann age 77y of Hudson, NY at son-in-laws James KNICKERBOCKER in Argyle, NY March 19, 1874

WALDRON William G. age 90y in N. Creek, NY March 7, 1874

CROW Michael age 50y in Victory Mills, NY March 12, 1874

HASTINGS Elijah age 75y in Salem, NY March 16, 1874

HAWKS Mary Jane age 28y 5m in Sandy Hill, NY March 30, 1874

HANNA Robert age 62y in Sandy Hill, NY April 1/2, 1874

SHAW Nathaniel age 55y formerly of Warren Co. in Lock Haven, Pa. March 11, 1874

BARDEN Alvira P. age 30y wife of Asa and dau of S. O. CROSS at Kings St. April 3/8, 1874

KINNEY Joseph age 74y in Argyle, NY April 2, 1874

HUGHEY Sally age 89y relict of Joseph in Argyle, NY April 1, 1874

TRAPHAGEN Sarah age 72y in Glens Falls, NY March 14, 1874

FINCH Mary in her 23rd yr wife of Lewis in Greenwich, NY March 20, 1874

VAN NESS M. A. in her 76th yr in Greenwich, NY March 30, 1874

GRAY Rachel age 90y formerly of Cambridge, NY in Troy, NY March 31, 1874

DONAHUE Eliza age 35y in Ft. Edward, NY March 24, 1874

SELFRIDGE Oliver age 52y in Battenville, NY April 1, 1874

SOREL George age 1y in Whitehall, NY April 5, 1874

HART Mrs. Amelia age 59y in White Creek, NY March 31, 1874

HILMAN Miss Susan age 24y in Ft. Ann, NY April 9, 1874

BRIGGS David age 85y in Ft. Ann, NY April 2, 1874

MC GHEE Mrs. Marion age 85y in Willsborough Falls, NY April 8, 1874

OWENS Mrs. Phebe age 29y wife of John in M. Granville, NY April 10, 1874

CRANDALL John age 83y in Greenwich, NY April 7, 1874

BECKWITH Ida age 19y 6m wife of Carl in Whitehall, NY April 14, 1874

PRATT Cynthia age 77y widow of David in Cambridge, NY April 3, 1874

HARRIS Marvin C. age 62y in Kingsbury, NY April 23, 1874

DOUBLEDAY Mrs. H. L. age 48y in Macedon, NY April 23, 1874

PARTRIDGE Frederick age 16y in Sandy Hill, NY April 21, 1874

COLLINS George age 73y in Whitehall, NY April 15, 1874

COLBY Catherine abt 35y of Jackson, NY in the County Home April 13, 1874

LEE William age 35y in Glens Falls, NY April 16, 1874

WOODWORTH Charles age 58y in Jackson, NY April 13, 1874

BEVERIDGE Elizabeth D. age 64y wife of David in W. Hebron, NY April 12, 1874

CHAPMAN Samuel age 85y in Northumberland, NY April 15, 1874

EDMONDS James abt 76y in Glens Falls, NY April 11, 1874

BUSWELL James age 75y in Glens Falls, NY April 21, 1874

WANDELL Mrs. Polly age 95y in Argyle, NY April 23, 1874

NORTON Hiram abt 40y in M. Granville, NY April 26, 1874

COWAN H. R. in his 65th yr in Salem, NY April 21, 1874

MOREHOUSE Mrs. William age 72y in Salem, NY April 16, 1874

QUACKENBUSH Mrs. Mary age 92y in Granville, NY April 23, 1874

CASE Lottie M. age 20y wife of Darwin G. in Ft. Edward, NY April 9, 1874

JOHNSTON Josephine age 27y wife of James L. in Ft. Edward, NY April 14, 1874

JOHNSTON Landon A. age 1y 8m in Ft. Edward, NY April 16, 1874

JOHNSTON Herbert E. age 4y 4m in Ft. Edward, NY April 23, 1874

JACKSON Freddie age 11m 10d in Sandy Hill, NY April 27, 1874

VANDENBURGH Carrie age 8y dau of George and Cornelia in Sandy Hill, NY May 3, 1874

RAMSEY infant son of James age 6m in Argyle, NY April 22, 1874

MOORE Lemuel H. age 39y in Salem, NY April 28, 1874

MC EACHRON Jane Ann age 36y 8m in Salem, NY April 26, 1874

MORGAN Mary Helen age 25y 3m 28d dau of Mathew **BURDICK** in Battenville, NY April 15, 1874

MARTIN Eddie age 15m son of Harvey and Mary in Greenwich, NY April 16, 1874

BARR Mrs. Elizabeth in her 86th yr in Greenwich, NY April 11, 1874

PARKER Allen age 68y in Shushan, NY April 22, 1874

DYER I. Gardner age 32y son of John K. of White Creek, NY April 20, 1874

MC EACHRON Ann C. age 60y wife of Alexander in Davenport, NY April 9, 1874

ROACH Patrick age 25y in White Creek, NY April 22, 1874

ROBERTSON John in his 81st yr brother of George of Cambridge, NY in Newark, Ohio (newspaper date May 7, 1874)

FAXON Zelia May (**GILBERT**) in her 43rd yr formerly Mrs. Thomas **VALENTINE** of Washington Co. in Little Rock, Ill. April 18, 1874

DENNIS Mrs. Mary age 63y in Schuylerville, NY April 28, 1874

ALDRICH John age 64y 1m 17d in Bloomington, Wis. April 14, 1874

DEIDRICK Henry age 72y in Putnam, NY May 2, 1874

CANE Mrs. Margaret in Hampton, NY May 4, 1874

BOYCE Ira age 74y in Sandy Hill, NY May 12, 1874

LITTLE Alden age 50y in Ft. Edward, NY May 2, 1874

ROZELL Katie B. age 21m dau of Myron and Martha in Ft. Edward, NY April 28, 1874

AMES Newton H. age 53y in Whitehall, NY May 8, 1874

CRANDALL James age 69y in Caldwell, NY May 6, 1874

GRIFFIN Seneca J. abt 55y in Easton, NY May 6, 1874

NOONAN Willie age 4y in M. Granville, NY May 7, 1874

MILLIMAN Mrs. Tempa age 80y in White Creek, NY May 7, 1874

WILLIAMS Hugh age 74y in M. Granville, NY May 10, 1874

JONES Deborah age 3y and Eliza Ann age 18y died May 1, 1874, children of Richard and Rebecca in M. Granville, NY

TAYLOR Benjamin H. age 61y in Greenwich, NY May 15, 1874

SNYDER John B. age 68y in Argyle, NY May 13, 1874

ROGERS Anna age 6y dau of Thomas and grand dau of Hon. John Rogers all of Black Brook, NY May 11, 1874

WHITE Nancy age 51y in Argyle, NY May 15, 1874

CAPERS Mrs. Amanda B. age 65y in Cambridge, NY May 10, 1874

WELLS Mary A. age 54y formerly of Gloversville, NY at son-in-laws George BRIGGS in Sandy Hill, NY (newspaper date May 28, 1874)

WROTH Fred Leroy age 7m son of John and Margaret in Sandy Hill, NY May 12, 1874

ROBINSON Lyman age 81y in E. Lake George, NY April 20, 1874

IRISH Duane age 19y in E. Lake George, NY May 1, 1874

SHIELDS Adeline age 28y wife of William in Luzerne, NY May 19, 1874

MATHEWS Ella Ida age 7y 4m 25d dau of Robert and Jane in Whitehall, NY May 20, 1874

HOPKINS George age 71y in Salem, NY May 17, 1874

COFFIN Robert A. age 37y in Cambridge, NY May 16, 1874

SPENCER Warren age 54y in Ticonderoga, NY May 14, 1874

COPELAND John Younglove age 73y son of Weeks in Old Soldiers Home near Washington DC April 17, 1874. Reared Saratoga Co. NY. Enlisted near 50 yrs ago

DUNSMORE David age 61y in Kingsbury, NY May 31, 1874

LOUDEN William age 67y in Argyle, NY May 19, 1874

HOWISON Mrs. Margaret in her 85th yr formerly of Greenwich, NY in Somonauk, Ill. April 29, 1874

DICKINSON Silas in Bolton, NY May 26, 1874

HURD Olive age 76y wife of Merritt in Cambridge, NY May 23, 1874

NICHOLSON Eddie age 16y in White Creek, NY May 23, 1874

STOWELL William age 74y in Sandy Hill, NY June 10, 1874

PERKINS Mary Augusta age 50y dau of Dr. N. P. COLVIN formerly of Sandy Hill, NY in Clyde, NY May 20, 1874

RAMSEY George B. age 65y in Glens Falls, NY June 5, 1874

GROARK Michael age 74y at Lake George, NY June 5, 1874

HULETT Welcome age 93y in Dresden, NY May 27, 1874

DEYO Lydia age 39y wife of David in Whitehall, NY June 5, 1874

KENNEDY Edward age 7y in Whitehall, NY June 7, 1874

BLOSSOM Artemus age 74y of Argyle, NY in the County Home (newspaper date June 11, 1874)

BEVERIDGE Alexander age 81y in W. Hebron, NY June 2, 1874

JENKINS Lulu age 4y in Shushan, NY May 24, 1874

VAN VECHTEN Mrs. age 80y widow of Garrett in Easton, NY June 1, 1874

IVES Lavinia wife of Hiram in S. Cambridge, NY May 29, 1874

SLOCUM Mary age 57y wife of Lewis of Easton, NY in Lockport, Mass. May 31, 1874

DAVIS Hannah age 7y in M. Granville, NY May 30, 1874

BLASHFIELD Mrs. M. M. age 48y wife of James in Salem, NY June 4, 1874

COLLINS Maggie age 8y in Salem, NY May 27, 1874

HOLMAN William age 20y native of Ft. Ann, NY in Canada June 7, 1874

KETCHUM John age 78y in Argyle, NY June 15, 1874

BAIN Maria age 60y widow in S. Argyle, NY June 12, 1874

BAKER Mrs. ____ age 22y in M Granville, NY (newspaper date June 18, 1874)

CONANT Mary age 13y dau of Elisha in Hebron, NY June 4, 1874

MAGEE Mrs. Mary I. in W. Hebron, NY May 27, 1874

SEARLE Hannah age 94y in Greenwich, NY (newspaper date June 18, 1874)

HAWLEY Ephraim age 87y in Warrensburgh, NY June 11, 1874

CULVER Mrs. Amanda age 60y widow of Erastus in Pawlet, Vt. June 4, 1874

SKINNER William age 58y in Argyle, NY June 17, 1874

RASEY Eva Louisa age 17y in M. Granville, NY June 18, 1874

THOMPSON A. A. formerly of Hartford, NY in Troy, NY June 4, 1874

PECK Fanny Viola wife of Henry T. formerly of Troy, NY and dau of Leander TREADWAY of Phildelphia, Pa. in Newark, NJ June 12, 1874

GALLOT David age 76y of Easton, NY in the County Home June 11, 1874

BLOSSOM Henry age 51y in Pawlet, Vt. June 20, 1874

RISING Hannah age 63y wife of Moses in Cambridge, NY June 5, 1874

GRAY Alonzo age 76y in Salem, NY June 16, 1874

ARMSTRONG Caroline age 35y 3m wife of J. A. formerly of Argyle, NY and dau of James and Abigail CARL in Winnebago City, Mn. June 13, 1874

WILSON Agnes (PARK) age 21y wife of Samuel in Hebron, NY June 11, 1874

BAILEY Harden age 87y lacking one day in Smiths Basin, NY June 28, 1874

WHITCOMB Mrs. Esther age 38y in S. Granville, NY June 25, 1874

PECOR Willie O. R. age 11y in Whitehall, NY June 27, 1874

SCOTT Mrs. Margaret A. age 50y in Argyle, NY June 23, 1874

ROBERSON Mrs. Elberta H. age 46y in Queensbury, NY June 16, 1874

LENORD Henry age 88y in M. Granville, NY June 25, 1874

NELSON Levi age 93y formerly of Warrensburgh, NY in Manchester, Iowa June 5, 1874

BARNES Jane in her 22nd yr in Greenwich, NY June 22, 1874

BACHELDER Hattie age 18y dau of Ira in Sandy Hill, Ny July 4, 1874

FONDA Mary (HALL) age 28y formerly of Sandy Hill, NY in St. Albans, Vt. July 2, 1874

RANGER Fanny Mary age 47y in Glens Falls, NY July 7, 1874

LEIGH Joseph age 88y in Argyle, NY July 12, 1874

MURRAY Mary Ann age 41y in Whitehall, NY July 5, 1874

BAKER Amos in Warrensburgh, NY June 21, 1874

HUMPHREY Mrs. ____ age 55y of Whitehall, NY in the County Home July 5, 1874

WILLIAMSON dau of James age 4y died July 2, 1874 and a son of James age 4y died July 3, 1874 in Argyle, NY

TEFFT Mary age 16y dau of Augustus and Mary in Sandy Hill, NY July 20, 1874

SARGENT Jessie age 10m 21d dau of Edmond T. and Fidelia in Sandy Hill, NY July 9, 1874

KELLY Susan age 1y 4m dau of Peter and Katie in Sandy Hill, NY July 18, 1874

SULLIVAN Mary age 26 of Kingsbury, NY in the County Home July 19, 1874

BRAYMAN Seth age 70y in Argyle, NY July 19, 1874

PROUDFIT Abigail (HAZARD) age 73y widow of Rev. John W. in New Brunswick, NJ July 10, 1874

WEAVER Kendrick age 54y formerly of Sandy Hill in St. Albans, Vt. July 26, 1874

BARNES Emily T. age 71y in Hartford, Conn. July 21, 1874

PERKINS Lillie age 12y in Whitehall, NY July 27, 1874

FERGUSON R. age 82y in Whitehall, NY July 25, 1874

TABOR Mrs. William in Schuylerville, NY July 21, 1874

GARRITY William age 65y in Sandy Hill, NY August 1, 1874

GOWRAN Freddie age 1y in Sandy Hill, NY August 3, 1874

FLACK Lillie E. age 39y of Stockbridge, Mass. formerly of Argyle, NY in Unadilla, NY (newspaper date August 6, 1874)

CAMPBELL Sue P. age 33y in Ft. Edward, NY July 27, 1874, buried Poultney, Vt.

BROWN Rosa age 14y in Glens Falls, NY July 28, 1874

RIFENBURG Daniel W. age 36y in Sandy Hill, NY August 13, 1874

MC MURRAY S. Ellen age 16y in Argyle, NY August 8, 1874

DARROW Frank age 17y dau of Josiah in Cambridge, NY August 5, 1874

STEELE Estella age 25y in Salem, NY August 2, 1874

SHUMWAY Dr. Samuel age 81y in Whitehall, NY August 8, 1874

MC KIE George M. age 29y 3m 17d in Cambridge, NY August 13, 1874

CUTHBERT Robert age 70y in N. Argyle, NY August 11, 1874

BEEKER George age 26y in the County Home August 17, 1874

CLARK Mary age 85y widow of Joseph in Salem, NY July 26, 1874

ASHLEY infant son and dau of William in Whitehall, NY August 13, 1874

GORDON Mrs. B. age 35y in Whitehall, NY August 15, 1874

SWAIN Cynthia age 79y in Glens Falls, NY August 21, 1874

STEBBINS Theodoric age 60y in Caldwell, NY August 21, 1874

RASEY Etta age 3m in M. Granville, NY August 21, 1874

SMITH William age 58y in Salem, NY August 20, 1874

HISTED John Franklin age 10m 15d formerly of Salem, NY in Schenectady, NY August 1, 1874

BELGARD ____ son of Joseph age 4y in Whitehall, NY August 24, 1874

CARTER Carrie age 21y wife of Robert in Sandy Hill, NY August 22, 1874

STYLES Mrs. Louisa age 79y relict of Samuel in Ft. Miller, NY August 28, 1874

ROBINSON William age 67y bro of late James in Ft. Edward, NY August 27, 1874

ROOD Daniel age 66y in Greenwich, NY August 26, 1874

SANFORD Catherine age 75y in Glens Falls, NY August 27, 1874

BENTLEY Mary J. age 46y in Queensbury, NY August 21, 1874

CARPENTER ____ dau of Samuel age 6y in Whitehall, NY August 24, 1874

SMITH Libbie age 21y wife of Eugene in Salem, NY August 25, 1874

CHAMBERLAIN Dora E. age 14m 6d in Putnam, NY September 6, 1874

SEBRING John age 81y in N. Argyle, NY September 2, 1874

HITCHCOCK Caroline age 73y formerly of Glens Falls, NY in Cleveland, Oh. August 12, 1874

MURRAY infant son of Michael in N. Granville, NY August 29, 1874

CURRAN Thomas age 35y in New York September 11, 1874

PATTEE Emma L. age 19y 7m in Sandy Hill, NY September 10, 1874

HOLBROOK Asa in Oxford, Mass. September 9, 1874

RUTHERFORD John age 72y formerly of Washington Co. NY in Caledonia, Oh. August 12, 1874

HANEY Betsey age 61y wife of David in Sandy Hill, NY September 13, 1874

UNDERHILL Bloomer age 59y in Sandy Hill, NY September 15, 1874

WILLIAMS John S. age 33y in W. Hebron, NY September 16, 1874

GILCHRIST John age 62y in Hebron, NY August/September 27, 1874

HENRY George age 80y in S. Argyle, NY September 12, 1874

ADAMS Carrie age 26y 6m in S. Glens Falls, NY September 9, 1874

REED Johnie age 8y in Whitehall, NY September 18, 1874

BARBER ____ son of Melancton age 18y in Dresden, NY September 17, 1874

LAMB Lydia Jane age 21y in Whitehall, NY September 14, 1874

GREEN Almira age 78y in Cambridge, NY September 11, 1874

WHITCOMB Nancy age 45y wife of Silas in Sandy Hill, NY September 28, 1874

CARSWELL Daniel S. in his 64th yr in Ft. Edward, NY September 23, 1874

MIDDLETON Richard age 84y in N. Granville, NY September 22, 1874

POWELL John age 40y in Granville, NY September 16, 1874

IRICK Matilda age 78y in Greenwich, NY September 11, 1874

SISSON Sylvia R. M. age 67y in White Creek, NY September 21, 1874

ALLEN Sarah E. age 4m 21d in Salem, NY September 18, 1874

HUNTER Col. Robert E. age 87y in Hamilton Twp. NJ September 27, 1874

LESTER Mary E. age 42y in Adamsville, NY October 2, 1874

MEECH Lydia Clark age 88y formerly of Glens Falls, NY in Burlington, Vt. September 29, 1874

GRIFFIN Oliver age 99y formerly of Washington Co. in Mason, Mi. August 30, 1874

ROBERTS Albert H. age 25y 5m in Glens Falls, NY September 28, 1874

RANDALL Rhoda age 86y in Shushan, NY September 28, 1874

NORTON Addie E. age 12y in Whitehall, NY October 5, 1874

REID Libbie age 4y in S. Argyle, NY September 29, 1874

PROUTY Hannah age 95y in Low Hampton, NY October 3, 1874

BELL Mary age 9y in Ft. Ann, NY September 22, 1874

BARKER Carrie age 14y dau of David in Easton, NY September 23, 1874

DERBY Emma age 35y in Easton, NY September 27, 1874

MC CUNE Mertie age 3m dau of Frank in Whitehall, NY September 28, 1874

BISHOP John age 86 Veteran of War of 1812 in Argyle, NY October 19, 1874

KISSEL Ella age 1y 9m dau of William and Mary F. in Ft. Edward, NY October 13, 1874

CRANNAL Jerusha A. age 44y wife of Robert in Glens Falls, NY October 8, 1874

BAZINET Elizabeth age 26y wife of Joseph in Glens Falls, NY October 18, 1874

REID Mrs. R. L. age 34y in Whitehall, NY October 16, 1874

COLEMAN Noah age 75y in Ft. Ann, NY October 7, 1874

ROSS James age 67y in Salem, NY October 4, 1874

MAZNER Mrs. Lewis age 42y in N. Granville, NY October 5, 1874

WILLARD Mrs. Lucy J. age 53y in Fairhaven, Vt. October 6, 1874

WILTSIE Warren D. age 33y in Adamsville, NY October 24, 1874

BROUILETTE Rachel wife of Moses and dau age 1y 6m formerly of Sandy Hill, NY both drowned near Montreal, Canada October 24, 1874

WILLARD Henry age 50y in Ft. Edward, NY October 18, 1874

CLEMMONS infant dau of A. B. and A. in Dresden, NY October 5, 1874

HALE Oliver would be 80y on October 22 in Putnam, NY October 19, 1874

LAPE Mrs. Polly E. age 76y in N. Argyle, NY October 21, 1874

BUTLER Thankful age 74y in Queensbury, NY October 4, 1874

BRAYTON Lesolina Julia age 8m at E. Lake George, NY September 28, 1874

COWLES Zina H. age 79y in Glens Falls, NY October 19, 1874

WHITNEY Rufus in N. Granville, NY October 13, 1874

BOMBARD Delia age 19y 4m wife of Alfred in Sandy Hill, NY October 30, 1874

DOUBLEDAY Betsey in her 80th yr widow of Daniel of Kingsbruy, NY at sons H. M. in Farmington, NY (newspaper date November 5, 1874)

MICKLE Jacob A. age 38y in W. Ft. Ann, NY October 18, 1874

FITZGERALD John T. son of P. J. and Mary Jane in Troy, NY November 4, 1874

HOSFORD Harlow age 78y in Poultney, Vt. October 28, 1874

WILSON Mrs. Sarah age 79y in Poultney, Vt. October 29, 1874

WHITLOCK Jeremiah age 77y in Galway, NY October 15, 1874

CRONKHITE Miss L. age 76y in Sandy Hill, NY September 26, 1874

HEARLIHY Patrick age 25y in Glens Falls, NY November 4, 1874

LEWIS Stephen age 40y in Ft. Edward, NY November 2, 1874

CRANNELL Levi age 45y in Ft. Edward, NY October 31, 1874

MC GREGOR Charlotte B. age 77y wife of John in Ft. Edward, NY November 1, 1874

MUNN William age 47y in N. Greenwich, NY November 5, 1874

BAIN Mrs. Margaret age 75y in Argyle, NY November 7, 1874

HAGGART Mrs. Duncan age 64y in Saratoga Springs, NY November 5, 1874

WILCOX Freddie age 2y 3m 18d in Queensbury, NY October 24, 1874

WAIT Jane V. age 29y wife of H. R. in Whitehall, NY November 6, 1874

WILCOX Oliver age 86y in Greenwich, NY November 3, 1874

VAUGHN Dewitt C. age 58y in Kingsbury, NY November 11, 1874. Wife age 58y died November 10, 1874

CRAMER Mrs. Elizabeth age 51y in M. Granville, NY October 31, 1874

LAW Lena age 79y in Granville, NY November 12, 1874

ALSTON Ester (LAUDER) age 22y wife of E. J. at French Mountain, NY November 5, 1874

HOLMES Henry age 21y formerly of Kingsbury in Barry, Mi. November 19, 1874

LINENDOLL Mrs. Walter age 64y in Ft. Edward, NY November 9, 1874

WAIT Thomas E. age 24y in Coila, NY November 18, 1874

CHASE William J. abt 40y in Easton, NY November 10, 1874

JOHNSON Elnor age 75y in Waits Corners, NY November 3, 1874

PRINDLE Abigail age 75y in Poultney, Vt. November 7, 1874

BROWN Jerusha age 60y wife of George W. in Poultney, Vt. November 18, 1874

BANNEN Thomas age 13y son of Eugene at French Mountain, NY November 27, 1874

ALSTON Elizabeth age 73y wife of John at French Mountain, NY November 23, 1874

ROCKWELL Jeremy age 65y in Luzerne, NY November 23, 1874

ORTON Esther age 82y in Glens Falls, NY November 11, 1874

BROWN Virginia age 9y dau of George at French Mountain, NY November 12, 1874

GOODICH Sylvester age 67y in Dresden, NY November 22, 1874

MC ARTHUR William age 57y in Putnam, NY November 21, 1874

MONELLE ____ age 6y dau of Peter in Whitehall, NY November 27, 1874

AUSTIN Julia E. age 19y in Cambridge, NY November 22, 1874

PADDEN Mrs. Robert abt 40y in Ft. Ann, NY November 11, 1874

ROBERSON Benjamin age 51y in Cambridge, NY November 21, 1874

NELSON Neolia age 30y in Sandy Hill, NY December 6, 1874

BARNEY Leonard age 10m son of George and Mary in Sandy Hill, NY December 5, 1874

LANT Duncan R. age 48y in Argyle, NY December 5, 1874

CAIN John W. in N. Argyle, NY December 1, 1874

HARVEY Eliza age 9y in Glens Falls, NY November 28, 1874

KNOX Mrs. Palina age 62y in Glens Falls, NY November 28, 1874

OGDEN Mary age 32y and her sister Catherine **LOCKHART** age 17y both in Glens Falls, NY November 26, 1874

MABBIT Willie T. age 5y son of T. G. in Whitehall, NY December 5, 1874

LA POINTE ____ age 13y son of Joseph in Whitehall, NY December 5, 1874

FORTIN Cora age 3y dau of Charles in Whitehall, NY December 11, 1874 and dau Lillie age 7y and Julia age 8y died November 24, 1874

MC CREEDY Evaline age 71y in Schuylerville, NY December 2, 1874

HUBBARD Mary C. age 47y in Shushan, NY December 1, 1874

LAUGHLIN Peter age 47y in White Creek, NY November 30, 1874

HOPKINS Levi age 67y formerly of Hebron in Philadelphia, Pa. December 2, 1874

129

VAN SHAICK Annice age 17y dau of George W. and Martha in Sandy Hill, NY December 1, 1874

HERRICK Rufus age 85y Vet. of War of 1812 in Moreau, NY December 14, 1874

ANTHONY Mrs. C. age 52y formerly of Sandy Hill, NY in Bennington, Vt. December 14, 1874

BUTCHER Mr. ____ Pastor Methodist Church in Ft. Ann, NY December 14, 1874

HOPE Clarissa age 39y wife of Joseph in Whitehall, NY December 11, 1874

MARTIN Alwyne age 63y in Whitehall, NY December 14, 1874

SWEET ____ son of Mr. ____ Sweet age 12y in Whitehall, NY December 15, 1874

WILSON Mary Ann age 11y dau of David in Whitehall, NY December 12, 1874

PARISH Seth age 57y in Ft. Edward, NY December 6, 1874

CLARK Eliza abt 50y formerly of Easton in Saratoga Springs, NY December 6, 1874

REYNOLDS Helena age 7y dau of Daniel in Easton, NY November 22, 1874

DRESSER Rose M. age 26y wife of Benjamin in Kingsbury, NY December 17, 1874

MANNIS Hiram age 36y of Underhill, Vt. in Ft. Edward, NY December 20, 1874

CHEESMAN Sarah F. age 24y wife of Charles E. in Ft. Edward, NY December 21, 1874

PAIR Edward age 36y at res. of John Pair in Ft. Edward, NY December 22, 1874

CHESTNUT Johnie age 7y son of William and Lydia at Lake George, NY December 12, 1874

FITZGERALD Catherine age 62y in Glens Falls, NY December 15, 1874

GAVIN Mannis age 22y in S. Glens Falls, NY December 20, 1874

REID James age 1y 5m son of William J. in S. Argyle, NY December 17, 1874

LARKIN Mrs. Nancy age 77y in Argyle, NY December 17, 1874

STOLIKER Mrs. Mary A. age 45y in Greenwich, NY December 10, 1874

LAMPMAN S. wife of John in Greenwich, NY December 7, 1874

BURDICK Clark age 74y in the County Home December 11, 1874

PERRY Alphia age 70y wife of Delevan in White Creek, NY December 16, 1874

AUSTIN Mary Jane age 32y 9m wife of John and dau of Horace **PRATT** in Cambridge, NY December 17, 1874

HIEDDLISTON Josephine age 26y wife of William in Ft. Ann, NY December 24, 1874

WILLIAMS Henry age 24y in Durkeetown, NY December 28, 1874

TILLOTSON Augusta age 33y wife of D. C. in Glens Falls, NY December 23, 1874

THURBER William age 65y in Whitehall, NY December 19, 1874

MARTIN F. B. age 5y son of Horace in Whitehall, NY December 19, 1874

ARNOTT George B. age 30y in Salem, NY December 23, 1874

MC CORMICK Mary age 37y in Boston December 20, 1874

BROWNELL Esther age 86y in Cambridge, NY December 18, 1874

GILL Theodore M. age 26y in Whitehall, NY December 30, 1874

WOOD Alonzo age 72y in Hartford, NY January 11, 1875

LIVINGSTON Iva Dell age 3y 7m dau of Joseph in Whitehall, NY January 19, 1875

HOYT Nathan Bennett age 58y in Whitehall, NY January 11, 1875

BOYLE infant son of James age 5m in Whitehall, NY January 9, 1875

CHILSON Willie age 2y son of James in Whitehall, NY January 6, 1875

KENHART George age 79y of Argyle, NY in County Home December 11, 1874

HOUTTIN Myer abt 70y of White Creek, NY in the County Home December 9, 1874

STEVENS Freeland J. age 21y son of Gardner and Maria in Ft. Ann, NY December 28, 1874

MORAN John age 51y in Cambridge, NY January 13, 1875

DOWNS A. P. age 51y in Sandy Hill, NY January 22, 1875

CARLTON Smith abt 70y of Granville, NY in the County Home January 18, 1875

LAVEY Mrs. Betsey age 68y in E. Whitehall, NY January 21, 1875

BOGART Sarah L. age 7y and Mary F. age 1y 7m children of Joseph in Whitehall,

NY January 25, 1875

WILCOX Laura age 22y 2m 18d in Queensbury, NY January 7, 1875

FIELDING Gershom W. age 76y in Caldwell, NY January 4, 1875

WHITE Nancy age 17y dau of Edward and Jane in W. Ft. Ann, NY January 26, 1875

DELORINE ____ age 5y dau of Simeon in Whitehall, NY January 30, 1875

BUGBY William age 21y formerly of Ticonderoga, NY in Trenepolean, Wis. January 5, 1875

HOLMES Ann C. Mother of William M. in Greenwich, NY February 2, 1875

SMITH Phillip V. N. native of Cambridge, NY in Clyde, NY December 14, 1874

SEELEY Nathan age 78y 5m 23d in White Creek, NY January 24, 1875

MEAD Deborah D. in Glens Falls, NY January 30, 1875

BUTCHER Mary age 6y dau of late Rev. Butcher in Ft. Ann, NY February 4, 1875

BARRELL Cyrus age 71y in S. Hartford, NY February 5, 1875

HAYNES Sophia age 79y in Whitehall, NY February 3, 1875

HOLCOMB Charlotte age 54y wife of John in Whitehall, NY February 3, 1875

BRADSHAW Freddie age 10y in Whitehall, NY February 7, 1875

HUNT Hiram K. age 74y in Westhaven, Vt. February 5, 1875

TRULL Williard age 74y formerly of White Creek, NY in Brooklyn, NY December 30, 1874

GREEN William age 72y in Hampton, NY February 4, 1875 and wife Maria age 73y died February 5, 1875

HARVEY Spencer age 80y in Hampton, NY February 7, 1875

GRAHAM Jane age 80y in Coila, NY February 2, 1875

BOMBARD ____ age 1y child of Eli in Sandy Hill, NY February 15, 1875

BROWNELL Oliver abt 71y of Kingsbury, NY in County Home February 10, 1875

CARPENTER Henry C. age 32y in Glens Falls, NY February 11, 1875

CRANDALL Walter C. age 18y in Queensbury, NY October 27, 1874

CRANDALL Eva G. age 45y in Queensbury, NY February 10, 1875

CRANDALL Martha A. age 21y in Queensbury, NY February 15, 1875

GILL Ella age 13y in Ft. Ann, NY February 8, 1875

DUNN Thomas age 3y died January 25, 1875 and Maggie age 2y died February 3, 1875 children of Thomas in Ft. Ann, NY

HARRIS Moses age 69y in Ft. Ann, NY February 10, 1875

DANIELS son age 1y died February 6, 1875, son age 6y died February 13, 1875 and dau age 3y died February 15, 1875, children of A. Daniels in Whitehall, NY

GOODALE Bradshaw age 66y in Whitehall, NY February 16, 1875

WILLIS Amasa age 96y in Belcher, NY February 5, 1875

AKIN Eliakim age 80y in Cambridge, NY February 8, 1875

JOY Richard age 84y in Ft. Ann, NY February 13, 1875

EGGLESTON Andrew age 87y in Hebron, NY February 21, 1875

WOOD Rev. J. Wesley age 62y in E. Poultney, Vt. February 20, 1875

BARBER ____ age 4y dau of J. in Whitehall, NY February 20, 1875

DELON George E. age 10y 7m in Whitehall, NY February 20, 1875

DUGAN ____ age 2y dau of P. Dugan in Whitehall, NY February 21, 1875

MORRIS Martha Jane age 4y in Whitehall, NY February 22, 1875

TEFFT Pliny C. age 21y in Cambridge, NY February 17, 1875

MURPHY Timothy age 67y in Salem, NY February 16, 1875

RATHBONE Elta age 18y in Easton, NY February 12, 1875

BUCKLEY Sylvia age 87y in Easton, NY February 8, 1875

SALTER Isabella age 68y in Saratoga Springs, NY February 23, 1875

KETCHUM Amanda age 75y in Argyle, NY February 18, 1875

DE KALB infant son of George age 4m in N. Granville, NY February 26, 1875

SHAW Mrs. Betsey age 78y in Luzerne, NY February 20, 1875

BURNETT Phebe R. age 19y 9m in Salem, NY February 14, 1875

RIPLEY William age 15y in Cambridge, NY February 13, 1875

LAWLESS Mrs. Ann age 69y in Glens Falls, NY March 7, 1875

JOHNSON Melvin age 25y in W. Ft. Ann, NY March 8, 1875

HASKIN Genie age 7y in W. Ft. Ann, NY February 25, 1875

SPICER Felia age 7y in W. Ft. Ann, NY March 1, 1875

ASHLEY Mrs. Nancy age 72y in Ft. Ann, NY February 28, 1875

MC FARLAND John A. age 73y 5d in Royalton, Ohio February 15, 1875

BARKER Edward age 75y in Easton, NY February 25, 1875

ALLEN Charles H. age 43y in Salem, NY March 1, 1875

ROBINSON Belle M. age 25y in Glens Falls, NY March 11, 1875

BROWN Esther age 60y wife of G. C. in Ft. Ann, NY March 16, 1875

MURRAY Hiram age 65y in Reynolds Corners, NY March 14, 1875

WELCH Horace age 64y in Whitehall, NY February 28, 1875

FRENCH Calvin age 68y in Bolton, NY March 8, 1875

RIFENBURG John age 82y in Sandy Hill, NY March 22, 1875

BARKLEY Infant child of John in Argyle, NY March 15, 1875

BOYNTON Edmond age 55y formerly of Whitehall in New York March 15, 1875

BROUGHTON Katie age 8y 5m 6d dau of P. A. in Whitehall, NY March 18, 1875

SNOW Frankie age 1y 5m son of Samuel in Whitehall, NY March 22, 1875

WILSON Josiah age 88y in Salem, NY March 15, 1875

STEELE Jennie T. age 19y in Salem, NY March 18, 1875

MORGAN William age 30y in Easton, NY March 10, 1875

FOLGER Daniel age 8y in W. Pawlet, Vt. March 14, 1875

POLLOCK Joseph age 4y in Cedar Rapids, Iowa March 17, 1875

BAIN Andrew age 45y in W. Ft. Ann, NY March 16, 1875

JENKINS Julia age 30y in Welch Hollow, NY March 14, 1857

MC LAUGHLIN Martha age 80y in Ft. Ann, NY March 22, 1875

HARVEY Willie age 2y son of Joel in Ft. Ann, NY March 18, 1875

HOLMES J. J. age 64y formerly of Sandy Hill, NY in Joliet, Ill. March 8, 1875

BUTTS Mrs. Phebe age 89y in Greenfield, NY March 22, 1875

ADAMS Angelia R. age 37y 5m in Whitehall, NY March 27, 1875

BARNES Eliza Ann age 50y in Ticonderoga, NY March 19, 1875

LEWIS Bettie M. age 17y in Ticonderoga, NY March 12, 1875

BARBER Lyman age 69y in Poultney, Vt. (newspaper date April 1, 1875)

PATZ Rhoda L. formerly of Washington DC at Moss St. April 3, 1875

CARTER Dr. Erwin formerly of Kingsbury, NY in Geneva, Mi. March 31, 1875

ORCUTT Eber age 72y in W. Ft. Ann, NY March 23, 1875

GRAHAM John age 83y in Argyle, NY March 24, 1875

SHARP William age 76y of Greenwich, NY in the County Home March 27, 1875

LAMB Mr. ____ age 74y of Granville, NY in the County Home March 28, 1875

WASHBURN Ella age 21y wife of Isaac in Whitehall, NY April 2, 1875

VANNIER Ellen age 34y wife of Norman in Whitehall, NY April 6, 1875

BEDELL Delight age 63y in in S. Granville, April 3, 1875

LEWIS Josiah age 75y in Poultney, Vt. March 27, 1875

RIPLEY Franklin age 21y in Queensbury, NY March 26, 1875

SLADE Mrs. Lucy H. age 66y in Hartford, NY April 7. 1875

O'BRIEN Mary age 76y in the County Home April 1, 1875

HAZARD Levi age 73y in the County Home April 7, 1875

MC FARREN Abiser age 73y in Whitehall, NY April 10, 1875

BRISTOL Albert G. in Whitehall, NY April 11, 1875

LEAK Mrs. B. age 78y in Whitehall, NY April 6, 1875

EARL Fred age 2y in Whitehall, NY April 12, 1875

WOLCOTT Manda age 57y in Ticonderoga, NY April 4, 1875

DUGAN Mrs. Mary age 39y in Cambridge, NY April 5, 1875

ALDEN Cornelia age 52y in Sandy Hill, NY April 5, 1875

WESTCOTT Mrs. William age 65y at Kings St. April 18, 1875

VIELE Emma age 21m dau of D. M. and Mary in Ft. Edward, NY April 5, 1875

FERRIS Sarah V. age 65y in Glens Falls, NY April 14, 1875

GURNEY Bessie age 17m at French Mountain, NY March 30, 1875

LEAVENS Jeremy R. age 40y in Glens Falls, NY April 13, 1875

STEBBINS Barbara age 38y in Glens Falls, NY April 12, 1875

MC QUARN Hugh age 73y in Argyle, NY April 14, 1875

COOK Nettie age 25y wife of H. G. in Argyle, NY April 15, 1875

RENOIS Antoine C. age 21y in Whitehall, NY April 15, 1875

FERRY D. Frank age 45y in Whitehall, NY April 12, 1875

PATTERSON Mrs. M. age 67y in Westport, NY April 14, 1875

O'NEIL Mary E. age 9y in Whitehall, NY April 20, 1875

GOURLAY Mrs. Grace age 80y in W. Hebron, NY April 9, 1875

CORNISH Fonrose age 29y in Poultney, Vt. April 16, 1875

BOYLE Mrs. Kate age 43y in Schuylerville, NY April 11, 1875

MC FARLAND Mrs. Martha age 70y in Cambridge, NY April 8. 1875

GARDNER Edgar age 47y in Troy, NY April 25, 1875

GILBERT Eva J. age 4y in Kingsbury, NY April 21, 1875

TUBBS Phebe age 80y formerly of Luzerne, NY in Greenfield, NY April 22, 1875

SMITH Mrs. ____ age 62y sis of Father James **WHYTE** in Ft. Edward, NY April 26, 1875

HALL Estelle age 2y adopted dau of George in Argyle, NY April 18, 1875

MONARQUE infant son of Frank in Whitehall, NY April 21, 1875

MONTY Mary E. age 2y in Whitehall, NY April 23, 1875

CAMPBELL ____ age 4y dau of James in Whitehall, NY April 24, 1875

ROGERS Lemuel age 75y in M. Granville, NY April 17, 1875

LLOYD Ellis age 67y in M. Granville, NY April 24, 1875

WHITLOCK Bertha age 2m son of Arthur and Eliza in Salem, NY April 2, 1875

LOFTER John age 32y in Salem, NY April 17, 1875

SHATTUCK Calvin of Amsterdam, NY in Ft. Edward, NY April 26, 1875

JONES Dennis age 78y of Whitehall, NY in Poughkeepsie, NY April 28, 1875

LOOMIS Amos age 61y in Whitehall, NY April 29, 1875

BELLEVILLE Josephine age 19y in Whitehall, NY May 2, 1875

STRONG George E. age 8y son of Marshall in Whitehall, NY May 2, 1875

DUGAN Mary age 25y wife of Henry in Whitehall, NY May 2, 1875

CARPENTER Myron age 21y in Saratoga, NY May 10, 1875

CARLTON Luther J. age 47y in Sandy Hill, NY May 11, 1875

FRENCH Miss Annie age 14y dau of James formerly of Washington Co. in Sandwich, Ill. May 2, 1875

WASHBURN Zina age 66y in Ft. Ann, NY April 23, 1875

AXTELL Solomon F. age 3y in Ft. Ann, NY April 24, 1875

BARTHOLOMEW Mary S. age 62y in Whitehall, NY May 7, 1875

COLLINS Miss Mary age 38y in Whitehall, NY May 9, 1875

DONALDSON Samuel age 87y in Whitehall, NY May 10, 1875

WOOD Mrs. Julia age 68y in Whitehall, NY May 10, 1875

GREEN Mrs. Harriet L. age 49y in Jackson, NY April 24, 1875

MC KIE Mrs. Lucy A. age 63y in Cambridge, NY April 25, 1875

THOMAS Ellen J. age 18y in Salem, NY May 1, 1875

MONTY Sarah Louisa age 31y wife of Daniel and dau of Joseph **PARRY** in Sandy Hill, NY May 19, 1875

TUCKER Mrs. Mary J. age 27y in Sandy Hill, NY May 15, 1875

PERRY Louis Sr. age 56y in Sandy Hill, NY May 19, 1875

YOUNG Edwin C. age 43y in Ft. Edward, NY May 11, 1875

MC INTYRE Daniel age 75y of Ft. Edward, NY in the County Home May 17, 1875

MURPHY Mary age 24y of Whitehall, NY in the County Home May 7, 1875

MC COLLEY Harris age 75y of Ft. Ann, NY in the County Home May 7, 1875

HASTINGS William age 71y in Ft. Ann, NY May 4, 1875

GLEASON Theodosia age 56y relict of Thomas in Luzerne, NY May 9, 1875

GIBSON Henry age 56y in Whitehall, NY May 15, 1875

COLEMAN Nelson B. age 25y in Whitehall, NY May 12, 1875

KINDONAH Anthony age 85y in Westhaven, Vt. May 15, 1875

MANVILLE Mrs. Julia age 79y in Whitehall, NY May 18, 1875

LEDGERWOOD Aggie age 28y in Putnam, NY May 15, 1875

BALANTINE George W. age 34y late of US Army in Martin Tx. January 29, 1875

HARRIS Rufus age 82y in Kingsbury, NY May 21, 1875

SWIFT George age 30y in Ft. Ann, NY May 23, 1875

MC FADDEN Thomas age 47y in Ft. Miller, NY May 24, 1875

GRIFFIN Ann Eliza age 30y drowned in Ft. Miller, NY May 25, 1875

KING Joseph age 68y in Argyle, NY May 15, 1875

FARRELL ____ age 8m child of John in Whitehall, NY May 25, 1875

LANGDON Laura age 6m dau of Edward and Marion in Poultney, Vt. May 13, 1875

BROWNELL Mrs. Anna age 84y in Easton, NY May 19, 1875

FONDA John age 85y in Schuylerville, NY May 14, 1875

BURNETT James A. age 26y in Salem, NY May 6, 1875

CAMPBELL Eliza age 28y wife of Hugh in Salem, NY May 16, 1875

DONAHUE Jane age 74y in Cambridge, NY May 15, 1875

WHITNEY Mrs. Anna M. age 34y in Sandy Hill, NY May 28, 1875

CROSS Walter E. in Kingsbury, June 3, 1875

INGALSBEE Aaron age 78y in Dunhams Basin, NY June 1, 1875

CRANNELL Hettie age 7y in Ft. Edward, NY May 31, 1875

HARRIS Betsey R. age 74 widow of Oliver of Hartford, NY In Ft. Edward, NY May 20, 1875

BAKER Mary A. in Glens Falls, NY May 12, 1875

KINNEY David A. age 4y in Whitehall, NY May 28, 1875

KELLOGG Edith age 8y dau of M. Kellogg in Whitehall, NY June 1, 1875

HAWLEY infant son of F. S. in Cambridge, NY May 30, 1875

WARNER Mrs. Sarah age 69y in Cambridge, NY May 28, 1875

BURNETT Joseph age 59y in Cambridge, NY May 28, 1875

HAWLEY Fannie age 39y in Cambridge, NY May 23, 1875

BRAINARD Nettie M. age 5y of Sandy Hill, NY in Poultney, Vt. May 30, 1875

INGALSBEE Carrie age 36y wife of L. L. of Adamsville, NY June 5, 1875

ALLEN Mrs. Robert age 54y in Ft. Edward, NY June 4, 1875

HARMON S. J. age 49y formerly of Ft. Edward, NY in New York May 31, 1875

TROMBLEAU ____ age 9y son of Eli in Whitehall, NY June 6, 1875

DIMES William Jr. age 18y in Whitehall, NY June 6, 1875

PARKER Henry W. age 54y formerly of Whitehall, NY in Erie, Pa. May 30, 1875

BALDWIN Sophie age 26y wife of C. H. in Ticonderoga, NY June 3, 1875

WOODWORTH Alfred age 37y in Cambridge, NY June 6, 1875

WAIT Eliza age 65y in White Creek, NY May 31, 1875

COWAN Elizabeth age 2y in Jackson, NY June 10, 1875

MC LIN Mary L. age 22y in Argyle, NY June 9, 1875

WASHBURN Lillie age 10y in Welch Hollow, NY June 5, 1875

FRENCH Mrs. Susan age 74y in N. Granville, NY June 6, 1875

SIMMONS Alonzo age 73y in Redding Ctr. NY June 5, 1875

VAYETTE Eddie age 6y in Whitehall, NY June 10, 1875

LEIGH Joseph H. age 68y in Salem, NY May 23, 1875

FITCH Charles Horace age 19y in Salem NY June 3, 1875

GRIFFIN Michael age 65y in Cambridge, NY June 8, 1875

JACKSON Thomas age 63y in Jackson, NY June 4, 1875

CAMPBELL Sarah age 1y in Jackson, NY June 8, 1875

MACKLIN Mrs. John in S. Argyle, NY June 10, 1875

BURCH Benjamin K. age 65y in Slateville, NY June 6, 1875

BURKE Daniel age 34y in White Creek, NY June 12, 1875

CHRISTOPHER James age 57y in White Creek, NY June 13, 1875

MC CABE Michael age 61y in Cambridge, NY June 21, 1875

GAMBLE Willie A. age 4m in Cambridge, NY June 10, 1875

AUSTIN Miss Sarah P. in Cambridge, NY June 12, 1875

RANGER Betsey age 77y in Glens Falls, NY June 14, 1875

FARRELL Jerry L. age 17y in Glens Falls, NY June 21, 1875

NUMAN Phebe age 99y in Glens Falls, NY June 19, 1875

PARO John age 40y in Argyle, NY June 24, 1875

MERRIAM Edward S. age 50y in Argyle, NY June 23, 1875

CONWAY John age 56y in Argyle, NY June 21, 1875

SINOTT Thomas age 58y in Whitehall, NY June 27, 1875

BARBER Betsey age 78y in Jackson, NY June 23, 1875

HANNAN James age 76y in Ft. Edward, NY June 29, 1875

NEWCOMB Abram age 61y in Luzerne, NY June 28, 1875

STEWART Lydia age 7y dau of J. Stewart in Whitehall, NY July 5, 1875

LARAVAN ____ age 5m child of Stephen in Whitehall, NY July 4, 1875

STOVER Martin age 60y in S. Argyle, NY June 27, 1875

CLARK Robert S. age 57y in Salem, NY June 12, 1875

WHITE Mary E. M. age 36y dau of Charles in Spencertown, NY June 3, 1875

GOURLEY Alex age 57y in Putnam, NY June 28, 1875

BEAURDEN ____ age 2y dau of Joseph in Whitehall, NY July 10, 1875

MURRAY Nellie age 1y 9m in Ft. Edward, NY June 29, 1875

HILLS James age 45y at French Mountain, NY July 9, 1875

ANGEVINE Henry age 55y in Hampton, NY July 9, 1875

WILCOX Orlando age 67y at Schroon Lake, NY July 4, 1875

POTTER Ann Lizzie age 14y dau of Erastus and Jane in Plattsburgh, NY June 26, 1875

ASHTON Mrs. Mary age 73y in Jackson, NY June 29, 1875

THOMAS Maranda **(PHELPS)** age 45y wife of Inman in Cambridge, NY June 24, 1875

DURKEE R. age 55y in Sandy Hill, NY (newspaper date July 22, 1875)

SHIELDS Eliza age 50y in Argyle, NY July 8, 1875

ALLEN Joseph age 77y in Whitehall, NY July 20, 1875

TOBEY Mrs. Lovet age 71y in Granville, NY July 13, 1875

MC CLELLAN Minerva age 63y wife of William G. in Cambridge, NY July 8, 1875

BURHANS Benjamin P. age 77y in Warrensburgh, NY July 16, 1875

CLEMENTS Sarah M. wife of D. H. formerly of Ft. Edward, NY in Brooklyn, NY July 1, 1875

HAND Mary S. infant dau of William H. and Sarah S. formerly of Ft. Edward, NY in Portland, Me. July 16, 1875

DAY Martha age 76y formerly of Glens Falls, NY in Newago, Mi. May 10, 1875

HUBBELL Mary Finn age 31y in Ft. Edward, NY July 18, 1875

CROSBY Miss Polly age 86y in Tarrytown, NY July 16, 1875

PARKS Harmon age 12y in Hartford, NY July 25, 1875

HARVEY Emily age 6y dau of Joel of Ft. Ann, NY in Whitehall, NY July 24, 1875

STEARNS Stephanus age 76y in N. Granville, NY July 8, 1875

WOODARD Sarah age 57y in W. Hebron, NY July 17, 1875

HOAG Elizabeth age 75y in Easton, NY July 10, 1875

DENNISON Isabella (THOMPSON) age 67y in Salem, NY July 4, 1875

LA FARR ____ son of Louie drowned in Ft. Edward, NY July 31, 1875

BURNS Dr. George C. age 58y in Shushan, NY July 31, 1875

SANDS Miss Nancy Jane age 28y in Glens Falls, NY July 28, 1875

BRADLEY Francis age 19m in Caldwell, NY July 12, 1875

HILLS Nathan in Hebron, NY July 12, 1875

COSHBURN ____ age 4m son of Henry in Whitehall, NY August 2, 1875

WALTERS Benjamin age 23y in Ft. Edward, NY August 10, 1875

POWERS Mrs. Mary age 30y in Ft. Edward, NY August 2, 1875

BAILEY Lyman age 61y in Ft. Ann, NY August 8, 1875

WILSON Thomas age 87y in Hampton, Ny August 6, 1875

BARER infant son of George in Whitehall, NY August 3, 1875

PLATT Estella M. age 5y in Whitehall, NY August 4, 1875

MURRAY infant son of John in Whitehall, NY August 8, 1875

DUNSTON infant son of G. H. in Whitehall, NY August 8, 1875

YARTER Alfred age 7m died August 13, 1875 and Albert M. age 7m died in Sandy Hill, NY August 17, 1875

MOSS Charles age 6y in Sandy Hill, NY August 16, 1875

LOCKE Mrs. Harriet M. age 69y in Glens Falls, NY August 16, 1875

KNOX Fred P. age 24y in Glens Falls, NY August 6, 1875

PRICE Charles age 95y at Lake George, NY August 16, 1875

HERBERT D. age 66y in Whitehall, NY August 13, 1875

HALL Nathan age 38y in Whitehall, NY August 12, 1875

BARBER George age 30y in Whitehall, NY August 14, 1875

ARCHAMBAULT Antoine age 72y in Whitehall, NY August 16, 1875

SHAW Mrs. John age 61y in Greenwich, NY August 7, 1875

AUSTIN Cynthia C. age 55y wife of J. P. in Moreau, NY August 18, 1875

GOKEY Augustus age 28y in Whitehall, NY August 22, 1875

CARR Carrie E. age 6y in Ticonderoga, NY August 16, 1875

CLARK Mrs. Elsie age 27y in Poultney, Vt. (newspaper date August 26, 1875)

LYNCH ____ age 4m son of John in Poultney, Vt. August 10, 1875

ALLEN ____ age 6m son of T. P. in Poultney, Vt. August 9, 1875

BUTLER ____ age 5m son of Edward in Poultney, Vt. August 20, 1875

THOMPSON John age 71y in Poultney, Vt. August 21, 1875

STEVENSON Miss Anna age 22y in Troy, NY August 19, 1875

NEWBURY Robert age 7m 3d in Glens Falls, NY August 21, 1875

GILCHRIST Rollin age 4m son of O. F. and E. J. in Ft. Edward, NY August 21, 1875

DENNIS Emma age 2m dau of Benjamin and Helen in Smiths Basin, NY August 21, 1875

MC ARTHUR Ida age 19y in Putnam, NY August 22, 1875

HILL Susan S. age 61y in Schuylerville, NY August 27, 1875

BUCK Mrs. Hannah M. age 39y dau of Mrs. D. DUERS of Sandy Hill, NY in Farmington, Mn. August 10, 1875

GARDON James in Ft. Edward, NY September 1, 1875

HOLBROOK Nahum age 35y son of Joseph E. and Mary in Homewood, Ill. (newspaper date September 9, 1875)

MORRELL William A. age 14y in Sandy Hill, NY September 12, 1875

MORRELL Amos B. age 3y in Sandy Hill, NY September 15, 1875

MORRELL Carrie B. age 12y in Sandy Hill, NY September 18, 1875

BURNHAM Mrs. Harriet age 71y in Moreau, NY September 11, 1875

POTTER Martha age 65y wife of Benjamin formerly of Ft. Ann, NY in N. Geneva, Wis. August 27, 1875

WELLS ____ age 3y son of Frederick in Whitehall, NY September 10, 1875

HURLEY Ora Gertrude age 7m in Jackson, NY September 8, 1875

HOWELL Phebe M. age 12y in Ticonderoga, NY September 8, 1875

SHEPARDSON Aruna age 80y Vet of War of 1812 in Benson, NY October 12, 1875

BARTON Minnie age 3y of Ft. Edward, NY in Amsterdam, NY October 14, 1875

VAN GREER Mrs. Henrietta age 83y in Glens Falls, NY October 17, 1875

HAMMOND Courtney age 22y in Caldwell, NY October 21, 1875

BYERS Mrs. Hannah age 90y in N. Argyle, NY October 11, 1875

SKELLIE Mary age 5w dau of John and Bridget in Ft. Miller, NY October 20, 1875

HAY Jane age 64y in Lakeville, NY October 17, 1875

CLAPP Dr. John age 80y in Salem, NY October 18, 1875

HAGGART Mrs. ____ age 29y in Salem, NY October 15, 1875

FITTS Mary C. B. age 28y wife of Friend B. formerly of Glens Falls, NY in New York October 27, 1875

FANCHER Arthur age 28y formerly of Glens Falls, NY in Abilene, Ks. October 17, 1875

WRIGHT Chattie T. age 7m dau of Silas and Nellie B. formerly of Sandy Hill, NY in Brooklyn, NY November 9, 1875

BROWN Charles age 6y son of Charlotte in Sandy Hill, NY November 10, 1875

RIFENBURG Dan age 16m son of W. W. and Minnie in Sandy Hill, NY November 9, 1875

MAXFIELD __ age 1y dau of William and Mary in Whitehall, NY November 3, 1875

LA BARGE ____ age 18m child of Samuel in Whitehall, NY November 4, 1875

HARLOW ____ age 2y child of M. Harlow in Whitehall, NY November 4, 1875

SOLES Gay D. age 11y son of Ira in Whitehall, NY November 7, 1875

WATERS ____ age 3y dau of Henry in Whitehall, NY November 6, 1875

MILLER Nellie wife of W. H. and dau of Fordyce **FOSTER** of Sandy Hill, NY in Newburgh, Md. November 10, 1875

WALKER Mrs. Lucy D. age 29y in Warrensburgh, NY November 6, 1875

DEWEY Hima age 2m son of Heaman A. and Maria in Sandy Hill, NY November 23, 1875

ELDRIDGE Ellis age 88y of Adamsville, NY in Bolton, NY November 16, 1875

DUBOIS Cornelius age 76y in Luzerne, NY November 16, 1875

WATERS ____ age 2y son of E. in Whitehall, NY November 13, 1875

HARLOW Willie age 3y 7m in Dresden, NY November 4, 1875

HEATH Lois W. age 71y in Shushan, NY November 16, 1875

ARMS Cynthia G. age 83y in Glens Falls, NY December 2, 1875

DEAN Mrs. Mary A. age 32y in Luzerne, NY November 27, 1875

WATERS Ida age 6y in Dresden, NY November 26, 1875

MAYNARD Horace G. age 56y formerly of Hartford, NY in Ross, Ohio (newspaper date December 9, 1875)

CROMWELL Dr. James age 64y in Caldwell, NY December 7, 1875

LABRUM Mary age 29y wife of William in Ft. Miller, NY December 10, 1875

WATERS ____ age 3y son of John in Whitehall, NY December 10, 1875

SLIGHT Alexander age 81y in Dresden, NY December 12, 1875

GIBBS Silas L. age 68y in Ticonderoga, NY December 4, 1875

NILES Mrs. Nathaniel M. in White Creek, NY December 11, 1875

FOOT Eliza C. age 74y formerly of Sheffield, Mass. at son-in-laws D. K. SAVAGE in Osborns Basin, NY (newspaper date December 16, 1875)

CAREY William age 60y bro of Robert C. of Sandy Hill, NY in Bolton, NY December 21, 1875

BACHELDER Charles age 12y in W. Ft. Ann, NY December 17, 1875

MILLER Solomon age 90y in W. Ft. Ann, NY December 18, 1875

CARVER Caroline M. age 54y in Whitehall, NY December 16, 1875

CHAPMAN Frankie age 11y in Dresden, NY December 9, 1875

HILL Eliza age 17y in Ft. Ann, NY December 23, 1875

SANBORN Ellen R. age 43y dau of Joseph P. BALDWIN in Sandy Hill, NY December 27, 1875

BURT Farren age 25y in Ticonderoga, NY December 21, 1875

DENNIS John P. age 53y in Argyle, NY December 24, 1875

TAYLOR Mrs. John C. age 80y in Argyle, NY December 24, 1875

BATEMAN George age 72y in Thurman, NY December 15, 1875

FULLER Frank infant son of Louis in Cambridge, NY December 26, 1875

DURKEE Mrs. Halsey abt 53y in Ft. Edward, NY December 29, 1875

CANFIELD Mrs. Sally age 94y in Luzerne, NY December 26, 1875

INGRAHAM Edward P. age 19y in Glens Falls, NY December 22, 1875

SIMPSON Elizabeth age 33y in Glens Falls, NY December 30, 1875

PETERS Mrs. Ruth age 82y in Glens Falls, NY December 29, 1875

HUMPHREY Abbie L. age 21y in Whitehall, NY December 30, 1875

LEWIS John age 54y in Ticonderoga, NY December 30, 1875

SCHERMERHORN Mrs. Agnes age 88y in Cambridge, NY December 26, 1875

ADAMS Mercy age 85y in White Creek, NY December 28, 1875

KING Mrs. Sarah E. age 35y in Argyle, NY January 7, 1876

MC DOUGAL Mrs. John B. age 70y in S. Argyle, NY January 10, 1876

BAIN Margaret age 68y wife of Hugh in S. Argyle, NY January 6, 1876

CLARO Catherine abt 55y of Whitehall, NY in the County Home January 11, 1876

FREEBORN Lewis age 2y in White Creek, NY January 3, 1876

PARTRIDGE Frederick age 4y in Sandy Hill, NY January 19, 1876

LANGEVIN Philomene (**COULTER**) age 24y wife of Ezra in Ft. Edward, NY January 11, 1876

CROAK James age 67y in N. Hebron, NY January 15, 1876

HALE Emma age 16y in Hartford, NY January 12, 1876

RODD Ella Dee age 6y in Whitehall, NY January 12, 1876

WELLS Julian A. age 5y in Whitehall, NY January 17, 1876

LA PORTE Mrs. A. age 30y in Whitehall, NY January 2, 1876

BATES Smith C. age 19y in Whitehall, NY January 16, 1876

WHEELER Gertie age 5y in Whitehall, NY January 17, 1876

VAN WORMER Mrs. Calvin in W. Ft. Ann, NY January 14, 1876

MAHAR Hannah wife of Bennett in Salem, NY January 10, 1876

DUNDON Margaret age 35y in Salem, NY January 7, 1876

TURNER Ella M. age 26y in White Creek, NY January 10, 1876

RAINEY Mrs. Anna age 61y in Cambridge, NY January 3, 1876

STOCKTON Mrs. Ellen age 72y in Chester, NY December 30, 1875

WELLS Cordelia age 32y wife of J. H. and dau of Benjamin **LESTER** of Hartford, NY in Sandy Hill, NY January 23, 1876

CARROLL Mrs. Rosa age 74y in Sandy Hill, NY January 23, 1876

FERGUSON Jefferson age 35y of Whitehall, NY in County Home January 22, 1876

DRAPER Isaac age 64y of Hartford, NY in the County Home January 25, 1876

BECKER Peter age 65y of Easton, NY in the County Home January 25, 1876

HAWLEY Curtis age 84y in Hartford, NY January 22, 1876

WILLIAMSON ___ age 5y son of Joseph in Whitehall, NY January 18, 1876

THOMPSON D. B. age 72y in Salem, NY January 16, 1876

BISHOP Mrs. Cornelia age 32y in Granville, NY January 18, 1876

SWEET Freeborn age 4y in White Creek, NY January 19, 1876

TURNER Hattie E. age 9y in White Creek, NY January 15, 1876

THORNTON Walter age 14y in Oak Hill, NY January 15, 1876

CAMERON Major Duncan age 50y in Hadley, NY January 18, 1876

RAMSEY Mrs. Sarah age 27y in Luzerne, NY January 16, 1876

ANDERSON Rufus age 84y in Harrisena, NY December 15, 1875

BRADLEY Silas Jr. in Adamsville, NY January 31, 1876

ROGERS George E. age 56y of Hebron, NY in the County Home January 30, 1876

CLARK Sophia age 78y in Lake, NY January 31, 1876

DURREN Libbie age 18y in Caldwell, NY January 24, 1876

PHILBROOK Mrs. Joseph age 55y in Ft. Ann, NY January 27, 1876

STEVENS Sybil age 87y wife of William in Ft. Ann, NY January 25, 1876

SMITH Pearl V. age 2y 18d son of Martin W. and Cornelia V. in Granville, NY January 18, 1876

JILLSON Minnie F. age 22y in Whitehall, NY January 27, 1876

HAWLEY Phoebe age 95y in Whitehall, NY January 22, 1876

JOHNSON Frances age 36y wife of Milo in Whitehall, NY January 21, 1876

COOK Bertrand A. age 22m in Whitehall, NY January 23, 1876

THOMAS Carrie age 13y in Salem, NY January 25, 1876

BEATTIE John F. age 62y in Salem, NY January 25, 1876

WARD John age 65y in Easton, NY January 21, 1876

GORHAM Mary age 67y in Easton, NY January 19, 1876

COTTRELL Mary age 75y in Greenwich, NY January 25, 1876

CROSS Miss Ida M. age 23y in Kingsbury, NY January 6, 1876

WADE William age 35y formerly of Sandy Hill in Baldwin, Iowa January 5, 1876

WHEELER Rollin age 7y son of John in Whitehall, NY January 29, 1876

BARTHOLOMEW Bertha age 13y in Whitehall, NY February 2, 1876

ROLAND Henry Haman age 10m son of V. E. and L. C. in Cambridge, NY February 3, 1876

HENNELY Mary age 31y wife of Thomas in Jackson, NY February 6, 1876

ALEXANDER John age 10y died February 5, 1876, Carrie age 4y February 6, 1876 and Charles age 8y died February 7, 1876 children of Robert in Lake, NY

CLOUGH Jessie age 4y dau of Elijah in Lake, NY February 4, 1876

WAGNER Estella age 2y formerly of Easton, NY in Cohoes, NY February 4, 1876

BRIGGS James age 90y formerly of Ft. Ann, NY in Brooklyn, NY (newspaper date February 17, 1876)

STEWART Isabella age 79y wife of John M. in Argyle, NY February 13, 1876

PALMER Lydia W. age 54y in the County Home February 10, 1876

BARKLEY Miss Jennie age 65y in N. Argyle, NY February 8, 1876

WIGGINS Hugh age 64y in N. Argyle, NY February 7, 1876

CLIFFORD ____ age 15m son of N. Clifford in Whitehall, NY February 7, 1876

HAY Alexander age 83y in Greenwich, NY February 6, 1876

HOUGHTALING John age 72y in Easton, NY February 6, 1876

DENNIS Mrs. Marilla age 75y in Easton, NY February 2, 1876

THORNTON Margaret A. age 5y in Burskirks Bridge, NY February 6, 1876

MC DONALD ____ age 7m 24d dau of James and Gertrude in Glens Falls, NY February 17, 1876

HAMILTON Mrs. Andrew age 85y in Argyle, NY February 12, 1876

RANDLES Sarah A. age 40y in Argyle, NY February 13, 1876

MC FARLAND Marjory age 82y in Salem, NY February 13, 1876

FLAHERTY Mary age 72y in Greenwich, NY February 12, 1876

TOOHEY Mary age 18y in N. Greenwich, NY February 15, 1876

MC LEAN Mrs. Jane H. age 52y in Jackson, NY February 11, 1876

STARBUCK James E. age 23y in Chester, NY February 8, 1876

ARCHER John age 70y in N. Argyle, NY February 19, 1876

MC KEACHIE George age 88y in N. Argyle, NY February 19, 1876

REYNOLDS Mrs. Alexander in S. Argyle, NY February 13, 1876

MORSE Grace age 5y in Greenwich, NY February 18, 1876

BIGGART James age 60y in Kingsbury, NY February 29, 1876

MC NULTY Mary E. age 17y in Ft. Edward, NY February 17, 1876

MC MILLAN James age 46y in Argyle, NY February 23, 1876

RANDLES James age 3y in Argyle, NY February 23, 1876

CARVER Stephen age 86y in Whitehall, NY February 19, 1876

GRISWOLD Nellie A. age 17y in Whitehall, NY February 21, 1876

LATTIMORE Samuel age 44y in Glens Falls, NY February 19, 1876

HAGGERTY Edward age 26y in S. Glens Falls, NY February 16, 1876

CHAMPIN W. N. age 22y in Greenwich, NY February 19, 1876

CHERRY Frank age 29y in E. Greenwich, NY February 21, 1876

GATES infant son of George D. in Cambridge, NY February 17, 1876

SCRIBNER Mr. ____ age 67y in the County Home March 5, 1876

TURK Jacob age 65y of Hartford, NY in the County Home March 3, 1876

MC CORMICK Catherine E. age 38y in Whitehall, NY February 28, 1876

WEST Anna age 9y in Salem, NY February 18, 1876

WRIGHT William age 21y in Greenwich, NY March 1, 1876

TEFFT Mrs. Laura F. age 68y in Greenwich, NY February 28, 1876

WELCH Mrs. Bridget age 80y in Bald Mountain, NY February 28, 1876

HALL Miss Abbie age 18y in Cambridge, NY February 25, 1876

STOWELL C. C. age 61y in Sandy Hill, NY March 14, 1876

RICE James Jr. age 44y in Ft. Ann, NY March 13, 1876

THOMPSON Caleb age 80y in Ft. Ann, NY March 8, 1876

YOLT M. age 63y in Whitehall, NY March 12, 1876

GREGORY Aaron age 28y in Whitehall, NY March 12, 1876

CORBETT James J. age 2y in Whitehall, NY March 12, 1876

MOORE Mrs. Andrew formerly of Ft. Ann, NY in Saratoga, NY (newspaper date March 16, 1876)

MC NAUGHTON Susannah age 76y in Argyle, NY March 3, 1876

COOPER Matilda age 40y in W. Hartford, NY February 28, 1876

O'DELL Benjamin age 78y in Glens Falls, NY March 4, 1876

BAILEY Mrs. Franklin age 43y in Ft. Ann, NY March 11, 1876

GRIFFIN Edward age 24y in Ft. Ann, NY March 12, 1876

FILLMORE Cullen A. age 3y in Whitehall, NY March 10, 1876

DAVIS Frederick age 21y in Easton, NY March 3, 1876

BARR William D. age 27y in Cambridge, NY March 7, 1876

ENSIGN Mrs. Nancy G. age 48y in Greenwich, NY March 4, 1876

CLARK Felix age 71y in Greenwich, NY March 3, 1876

MC DOUGAL Elsie age 89y in Jackson, NY March 4, 1876

SHEEHEY Thomas age 27y in White Creek, NY March 2, 1876

DERMODY Julia in Salem, NY March 16, 1876

WOOD George S. age 34y in Whitehall, NY March 16, 1876

HOLMES Carroll M. age 15y son of William E. in Greenwich, NY March 10, 1876

BARRY Kate age 60y in Greenwich, NY March 10, 1876

BRAYTON Susan age 73y in Easton, NY March 13, 1876

DAILEY Andrew age 56y in Easton, NY March 13, 1876

ABEAL Sybil in Easton, NY March 14, 1876

SMITH Martha E. age 33y in Cambridge, NY March 14, 1876

MAYNARD Anna age 80y relict of Horace in S. Hartford, NY March 21, 1876

ADAMS Sally age 69y in Whitehall, NY March 17, 1876

HOPKINS Cordelia age 71y in Pike Brook, NY March 17, 1876

MILLER Louis age 70y in Kingsbury, NY March 21, 1876

DURKEE Charles age 75y in Argyle, NY March 27, 1876

FORD James age 62y in Argyle, NY March 20, 1876

BARRETT Mrs. Anna age 82y in N. Granville, NY March 18, 1876

BOIES Miss Ella age 17y in N. Granville, NY March 16, 1876

NICHOLSON Mary Ann age 55y wife of Samuel in Greenwich, NY March 18, 1876

BENNETT ____ child of Exody Jr. in Greenwich, NY March 20, 1876

HAY James age 87y in Lakeville, NY March 21, 1876

WARREN William age 25y in Cambridge, NY March 25, 1876

MORRISSEY Mary Ann age 22y of Salem, NY in the County Home March 27, 1876

JONES David age 6w in the County Home March 20, 1876 (born County Home)

HICKEY Cora age 2w in the County Home March 24, 1876 (born County Home)

DINGS Sarah F. age 52y widow of John of Hartford, NY in Middletown, Vt. March 18, 1874

STILES William age 35y of Sandy Hill, NY in Hudson River Hospital, Poughkeepsie,

NY March 29, 1876

LYONS Sarah Louise age 34y wife of William H. at Kings St. March 29, 1876

CONGDON Mrs. Eunice age 63y in Ft. Ann, NY April 2, 1876

WILSON Mrs. Jane age 70y in N. Granville, NY March 26, 1876

BEATTIE Miss Sarah age 72y in Salem, NY March 28, 1876

WRIGHT Maria age 60y in Cambridge, NY March 24, 1876

BECKER Belden N. age 28y in Easton, NY March 29, 1876

BARREN Samuel age 85y formerly of Hartford, NY in Arlington, Vt. (newspaper date April 6, 1876)

ROBINSON Fannie age 9m in White Creek, NY March 31, 1876

GRAHAM Jane age 76y of Argyle, NY in the County Home April 3, 1876

DAVIDSON Sarah Ann age 20y in Dunhams Basin, NY April 7, 1876

PEARSONS Helen in Ft. Edward, NY April 8, 1876

WEATHERHEAD Mrs. Almira age 58y in Glens Falls, NY April 9, 1876

MURDOCK Allen age 71y in Glens Falls, NY April 8, 1876

BAILEY Adlie age 4y son of A. S. in Whitehall, NY March 31, 1876

BARNETT Mrs. Amanda age 74y in Cambridge, NY April 5, 1876

ENGLISH Jane Ann age 56y in Cambridge, NY April 1, 1876

ELLIS B. V. age 61y formerly of Cambridge, NY in Lyons, NY April 4, 1876

WETHERBEE Pauline age 70y in Dresden, NY April 2, 1876

DENNIS Erastus age 85y in Easton, NY March 31, 1876

BUEL Orrin age 74y in Easton, NY April 3, 1876

ACKLEY Eunice age 46y in Stony Creek, NY March 31, 1876

HILL Clarissa age 60y widow of Peter of Coila, NY in Albany, NY April 10, 1876

LOOMIS Mrs. J. W. age 27y in Whitehall, NY April 10, 1876

BARRETT William Richard age 2y in Whitehall, NY April 4, 1876

BALDWIN Stella age 18m in Whitehall, NY April 14, 1876

BROWN Sarah F. age 27y wife of George S. in Glens Falls, NY April 9, 1876

COMSTOCK Eliza (BREWSTER) age 65y widow of Peter in Port Kent, NY April 13, 1876

STEWART Mrs. Betsey age 84y in Westhaven, Vt. April 14, 1876

COLE Charles H. age 9y in Granville, NY April 7, 1876

VAN BUREN William age 38y in Greenwich, NY April 5, 1876

CLEVELAND James age 79y in Greenwich, NY April 12, 1876

MACK Mary M. formerly of Granville, NY in New York April 4, 1876

PARK Jane abt 70y formerly of Hartford, NY in W. Liberty, Iowa March 9, 1876

SHIPARD Mrs. Henry in Ft. Edward, NY April 25, 1876

SMITH Walter age 29y in Ft. Edward, NY April 25, 1876

WRIGHT Mrs. Julia age 37y in Smiths Basin, NY April 20, 1876

GRIFFIN Mrs. Viola age 27y in Smiths Basin, NY April 14, 1876

COBB Janett age 71y in Whitehall, NY April 22, 1876

PEMBER Orland in S. Granville, NY April 17, 1876

HAMLIN Mrs. Nancy M. age 73y in Glens Falls, NY April 17, 1876

DOBBIN Samuel age 87y in Greenwich, NY April 18, 1876

RICH Mrs. E. M. in Cambridge, NY April 20, 1876

MC CARD Mrs. Maria age 76y in Moreau, NY May 3, 1876. Funeral at bro Melville PARKS

VALENTINE Mrs. Margaret A. age 67y in Ft. Edward, NY April 22, 1876

HUTCHINSON Rebecca age 57y in Argyle, NY April 26, 1876

ALEXANDER Mrs. Maggie A. age 25y in Lake, NY April 27, 1876

ROBINSON Mrs. Mary age 22y in Glens Falls, NY April 27, 1876

GATES Kellum age 63y in Warrensburgh, NY April 12, 1876

BENNETT/BURNETT Jabez age 80y in Greenwich, NY April 24, 1876

WILLIAMS Miss Mary A. age 39y in Argyle, NY April 17, 1876

ARCHER Miss Sarah age 78y in Cambridge, NY April 18, 1876

WHITCOMB Reuben age 80y in Granville, NY April 14, 1876

ROBERTSON Jeremiah age 70y in Greenwich, NY April 15, 1876

LANGWORTHY Dr. James age 86y in Greenwich, NY April 16, 1876

BAILEY Daniel H. age 57y in Cambridge, NY April 18, 1876

HARWOOD Seymour D. age 22y in Rupert, Vt. April 18, 1876

DILLON Jason age 45y in Salem, NY April 26, 1876

CONNORS Kate age 46y in Salem, NY April 25, 1876

HOADLEY William age 37y in Middletown, Vt. April 13, 1876

PRICE Mrs. Sarah age 85y at Lake George, NY May 4, 1876

FITCH Mrs. Hannah age 71y at Saratoga Lake, NY April 27, 1876

RATHBONE ____ age 2y dau of William in N. Granville, NY April 25, 1876

SHEY Charles age 45y in Cambridge, NY April 29, 1876

GORDON Mrs. Elizabeth age 83y in Easton, NY April 30, 1876

CLARK Martha Jane age 38y in Ticonderoga, NY April 30, 1876

BARNARD Frederick J. age 81y in Albany, NY May 6, 1876

RAYMOND James age 94y in Slateville, NY April 25, 1876

WALLACE Mrs. Lydia age 88y in Lake, NY May 8, 1876

BURDETT Israel age 85y in Whitehall, NY May 4, 1876

INGRAHAM Herman age 57y in Whitehall, NY May 5, 1876

PATTERSON Dr. J. Frank age 35y of Glens Falls, NY in Troy, NY (newspaper date May 11, 1876)

CHURCHILL Charles P. in Ft. Edward, NY May 13, 1876

CUSHMAN Susan age 94y widow of Comfort A. in Ft. Edward, NY May 15, 1876

MC KEE Mrs. Mary age 91y in Ft. Edward, NY April 29, 1876

SWEENEY Patrick age 51y of Ft. Edward, NY in the County Home May 14, 1876

ANTHONY Elijah S. age 69y in Easton, NY May 5, 1876

HIGGINS Stephen age 64y in Warrensburgh, NY May 2, 1876

MC ARTHUR Peter age 79y in Jackson, NY May 8, 1876

COLLINS Mrs. Mary age 52y in Salem, NY May 6, 1876

HODGSON Adam C. age 50y in Johnsburgh, NY May 1, 1876

PAGE Elizabeth S. age 30y formerly of Greenwich in Brooklyn, NY May 15, 1876

CLARK Miranda B. age 84y widow of Benjamin of Sandy Hill, NY in Ballston, NY May 15, 1876

LIVERMORE Mrs. Louisa age 74y in Ft. Miller, NY May 10, 1876

PERRY Mr. ____ age 78y in Ft. Miller, NY May 14, 1876

GILL Mrs. Mary B. age 37y in Greenwich, NY May 14, 1876

SNELL John D. age 51y in Easton, NY May 15, 1876

GLASBY Hugh age 76y of Easton, NY in the County Home May 16, 1876

WELLING Maria age 73y in Easton, NY May 15, 1876

WRIGHT Rebecca age 73y in Salem, NY May 13, 1876

CENTER Mrs. Sheldon age 60y in Cambridge, NY May 14, 1876

LAMBERT Ruth (infant) in Cambridge, NY May 21, 1876

LANE Miss M. A. age 19y in Sandgate, Vt. May 30, 1876

SMITH Jennie E. age 17y dau of Harvey in Kingsbury, NY May 27, 1876

POLLOCK Sarah E. age 29y in Argyle, NY May 25, 1876

STEVENS Catherine age 76y wife of Lewis in Ft. Edward, NY May 29, 1876

SLOCUM Warren abt 50y in S. Hartford, NY May 22, 1876

MC MILLAN Mrs. George age 39y in Salem, NY May 25, 1876

ROOT Sally age 83y in Ft. Ann, NY May 19, 1876

MC INTOSH Mrs. S. age 84y in Camden, NY May 24, 1876

NAYLOR Jacob age 59y in Greenwich, NY May 21, 1876

NASH Mrs. Henry age 77y in N. Granville, NY May 27, 1876

MC NUTT Dr. Hiram of Warrensburgh, NY in Holton, Ks. May 3, 1876

LAUDER Mrs. Margaret age 61y at French Mountain May 16, 1876

BURDICK Mrs. Molly age 68y in Thurman, NY May 11, 1876

HOLLENBECK Mrs. Mary L. age 69y in Sandy Hill, NY June 6, 1876

WELLS Delia S. age 1y dau of E. S. and E. in Sandy Hill, NY June 2, 1876

WILLIS Charles H. age 5m 15d son of Henry H. in N. Granville, NY May 31, 1876

HEWITT Mrs. Mary A. age 29y in Eagle Bridge, NY June 3, 1876

RICE Mrs. Betsey Ann age 59y in Cambridge, NY June 2, 1876

DOHERTY Mary Ann age 15y in Ft. Edward, NY June 2, 1876

MONROE Charles age 2y son of Ira and Sarah in Salem, NY May 15, 1876

BRIGGS Mrs. David age 88y in Ft. Ann, NY May 18, 1876

DECKER Heman age 52y in Battenville, NY May 25, 1876

MC KENZIE Sarah age 89y in N. Greenwich, NY (newspaper date June 8, 1876)

MORSE Joseph age 83y in E. Poultney, Vt. May 12, 1876

GREEN Rufus H. age 77y in E. Poultney, Vt. May 14, 1876

SCUDDER Joel R. and 83y in E. Poultney, Vt. May 17, 1876

LEE Patrick age 56y of Kingsbury, NY in the County Home May 22, 1876

PRATT Daniel S. age 55y in Cambridge, NY May 31, 1876

FULLERTON Janette age 39y wife of W. H. in Factory Point, Vt. May 26, 1876

KELLENY Maria age 20y sis of Louis of Sandy Hill, NY in Montreal, Canada June 11, 1876

HALL John age 6y son of William D. in Argyle, NY June 11, 1876

TABOR George age 65y of Ft. Edward, NY in the County Home June 9, 1876

LAVY John age 13y son of John in Whitehall, NY June 8, 1876

PRICE Col. Walter W. age 56y at Lake George, NY June 5, 1876

NASH Marion E. age 54y in Glens Falls, NY June 5, 1876

VANDENBURGH Clarence age 25y in Glens Falls, NY June 1, 1876

MC CABE Mrs. Eliza age 77y in Glens Falls, NY June 5, 1876

MEAD Stephen H. age 68y in Pattens Mills, NY June 7, 1876

FRENCH infant son of Frederick age 5m in W. Hoosick, NY June 7, 1876

KEATING John T. age 6y in White Creek, NY June 6, 1876

LOSSEE J. D. age 83y in Quaker Springs, NY June 6, 1876

VAN TASSEL Mrs. Emma age 24y in Dunhams Basin, NY June 21, 1876

FLAGLER Mrs. E. age 84y in Queensbury, NY June 8, 1876

GRAY Gracie F. age 2y in Hartford, NY June 14, 1876

PARKER Nellie age 21y in Whitehall, NY June 14, 1876

HOWE John age 64y in Granville, NY June 13, 1876

CLARK Ransom age 60y in Hartford, NY June 11, 1876

BARKLEY Mrs. Sarah age 74y in Salem, NY June 11, 1876

PARISH Daniel age 71y in Salem, NY June 9, 1876

PENDERGRASS Robert age 35y formerly of Argyle, NY in Troy, NY June 11, 1876

REYNOLDS Hannah wife of Harry in Whitehall, NY June 19, 1876

BLANEY Henry S. age 43y in Dunhams Basin, NY June 13, 1876

BRAYTON Rebecca age 81y at Kings St. June 25, 1876

LANT infant dau of M. H. and Amanda in Argyle, NY June 22, 1876

MURRAY Francis age 14y in Sandy Hill, NY July 4, 1876

RICE Mrs. Rowena age 78y in Glens Falls, NY June 29, 1876

MC OMBER Hattie E. age 23y formerly of Hartford in Albany, NY June 28, 1876

REYNOLDS Mrs. Calvin age 21y in Hague, NY June 15, 1876

MC GINN Michael age 28y in Johnsburgh, NY June 30, 1876

VAN BUREN Hannah age 11y in Greenwich, NY June 17, 1876

REYNOLDS Delia in Easton, NY June 17, 1876

GANNON James age 78y in Cambridge, NY June 22, 1876

VAN KIRK Mrs. Catherine age 83y in Greenwich, NY June 25, 1876

SHARP Harvey age 1y in Salem, NY June 13, 1876

BOTTOM Mrs. Edward age 31y in Whitehall, NY July 9, 1876

BARTLETT Lucinda age 60y in Chestertown, NY June 18, 1876

GRAY David D. age 31y in Detroit, Mi. June 21, 1876

ROBBINS James formerly of Granville, NY in Dover, Del. June 27, 1876

INMAN Abigail W. age 76y widow of Isaiah in Hampton, NY July 5, 1876, born 1800 in Fairhaven, Vt.

GUILDER Mrs. Stephen in Granville, NY July 5, 1876

LLOYD Mrs. Elizabeth E. age 59y in Granville, NY July 7, 1876

LINDSAY Mrs. Annie F. age 24y in Argyle, NY July 7, 1876

MC KINNEY Elsie age 15y in Salem, NY July 11, 1876

ROBINSON Freelove Ann age 72y in Galesville, NY July 5, 1876

SHERWOOD Georgia M. age 21y in Easton, NY July 6, 1876

DUGAN Kate age 19y in Ft. Edward, NY July 18, 1876

NORTON Louisa J. age 23y in Queensbury, NY July 13, 1876

KENYON Charles R. age 32y in Glens Falls, NY July 21, 1876

LIVERMORE ____ age 9m dau of Josiah and Sarah in Ft. Miller, NY July 19, 1876

HALL Earl age 45y in Adamsville, NY July 23, 1876

LEWIS Melia (**HUBBELL**) age 28y at Lake George, NY July 14, 1876

HARRINGTON Deborah age 16y in Cambridge, NY July 12, 1876

LAPAN Mrs. Edward age 45y in Sandy Hill, NY July 29, 1876

WARD Miss Frankie age 16y in S. Hartford, NY July 27, 1876

ROCHESTER Walter age 63y of Rouses Point in Northumberland, NY July 29, 1876

CURLEY Mrs. Sarah age 43y in Smiths Basin, NY July 29, 1876

FISH Fastino age 26y 10m dau of Merrill W. and Caroline in Chester, NY July 22, 1876

CHASE William age 72y in Easton, NY July 22, 1876

SHAW Cora age 3y 1m 18d died July 14, 1876 and Sarah Mary age 8y died July 17, 1876 children of John and Katie in Jackson, NY

PECK Emeline age 64y in Glens Falls, NY July 26, 1876

BURTON Richard age 26y in Sandy Hill, NY August 6, 1876

HASKELL Daniel age 2y in Argyle, NY July 30, 1876

NORTHUP Mrs. Solomon age 78y in Gansevort, NY August 8, 1876

GIBSON William age 78y in N. Argyle, NY August 3, 1876

BENNETT Delia C. dau of James late of Warrensburgh, NY in Chemung, NY July 28, 1876

COOK J. R. age 9m 6d in Whitehall, NY July 30, 1876

WHITBECK Henry age 66y formerly of Easton in Milwaukee, Wis. July 12, 1876

HODGE Amasa age 74y in Cambridge, NY July 28, 1876

PRATT Eliza age 6m in White Creek, NY August 3, 1876

ROGERS Kittie age 7m dau of Frank and Cornelia in Rutland, Vt. August 5, 1876

STARBUCK Hiram age 59y in White Creek, NY August 5, 1876

HALL John age 76y in Adamsville, NY August 5, 1876

MC COY James age 36 of Ft. Edward, NY in Brasher Falls, NY August 14, 1876

CORBETT Mrs. Ellen age 22y in Whitehall, NY August 7, 1876

PECK Benjamin age 61y in Glens Falls, NY August 8, 1876

COON Thomas P. age 60y in Salem, NY August 8, 1876

CULVER Nathan age 61y formerly of Cambridge in Syracuse, NY August 4, 1876

GREEN Ellen L. age 17y dau of John E. and Julia in Cambridge, NY August 10, 1876

JOB Herbert F. age 13m in Schuylerville, NY July 31, 1876

BULLARD J. Augustus age 54y in Riverside, NY August 4, 1876

HARRINGTON Louie age 17m in Cambridge, NY August 9, 1876

THOMAS Sidney age 34y in Sandy Hill, NY August 23, 1876

WIGGINS James age 19y in Smiths Basin, NY August 23, 1876

KEAYS Mrs. Mary age 40y in Ft. Edward, NY August 14, 1876

ROZELL Miss Lotta age 34y in Ft. Edward, NY August 12, 1876

TAYLOR Alexander age 74y of Argyle, NY in the County Home August 20, 1876

STICKNEY Mrs. Martha J. age 24y in Durkeetown, NY August 14, 1876

CONANT Duane age 32y formerly of Granville in Jersey City, NJ August 10, 1876

MARTIN Jane age 44y wife of Robert in Hebron, NY August 14, 1876

BATES William A. age 60y of Greenwich, NY in Binghamton, NY August 12, 1876

OBER Gracie A. age 13m in Ft. Edward, NY August 18, 1876

FONDA W. A. formerly of Glens Falls, NY in St. Albans, Vt. August 23, 1876

PEER Willie age 4y in Bolton, NY August 23, 1876

GLEASON Mrs. Mary age 54y in Ft. Edward, NY August 22, 1876

ROUSE George in Northumberland, NY August 17, 1876

SWEET George age 21y in Northumberland, NY August 19, 1876

PECKHAM Garrison age 18y in Easton, NY August 17, 1876

AUSTIN N. P. age 67y in Granville, NY August 24, 1876

IRVING Anna V. age 14m in Smiths Basin, NY September 3, 1876

MC ARTHUR Thomas L. age 24y in Putnam, NY September 5, 1876

HAMLIN Mrs. Louisa M. age 26y in Glens Falls, NY August 29, 1876

CAMERON Grace age 6m in Stony Creek, NY August 20, 1876

WEBB Edward in Glens Falls, NY August 28, 1876

MARSHALL Willie S. age 2y in Pattens Mills, NY August 29, 1876

MUNSON Miss Libbie age 25y in E. Hebron, NY August 27, 1876

GRANT Andrew age 77y in Whitehall, NY August 29, 1876

BARTHOLOMEW Justus age 63y in Whitehall, NY August 30, 1876

MC QUEEN James age 64y formerly of Luzerne, NY in Glendale, Wis. August 12, 1876

KILLIAN Lawrence in Ft. Edward, NY September 8, 1876

SMITH _____ age 16y son of Rufus in Ft. Edward, NY September 11, 1876

PALMER Mary Jane age 50y in W. Ft. Ann, NY August 26, 1876

BARBOUR Martha in W. Granville, NY September 3, 1876

HOGAN _____ child of Michael in M. Granville, NY September 4, 1876

THOMAS Mrs. Owen in M. Granville, NY September 5, 1876

ROGERS Hiram age 72y in Hebron, NY August 31, 1876

WESTCOTT Nicolas age 78y in W. Rupert, Vt. September 7, 1876

FOWLER William age 76y in White Creek, NY August 29, 1876

COWAN Jane age 75y in Argyle, NY August 28, 1876

NEWTON Orpha (JENKINS) age 23y in Kingsbury, NY September 12, 1876

RICHARDS E. B. age 93y in Glens Falls, NY September 15, 1876

RICH William C. age 53y in Ft. Edward, NY September 10, 1876

MONROE Almira age 30y in White Creek, NY September 12, 1876

MARSHALL Mrs. Robert age 81y in Jackson, NY September 13, 1876

TERRY Moses age 92y in Whitehall, NY September 19, 1876

AMIDON Mary S. wife of Dr. A. O. in Ticonderoga, NY September 12, 1876

ELDRIDGE John age 56y formerly of Hartford in Danforth, Iowa August 26, 1876

162 **WASHINGTON COUNTY NEWSPAPERS**

GILCHRIST William L. age 64y in Hebron, NY September 16, 1876

YULE Edward D. age 2y son of George P. in W. Ft. Ann, NY September 11, 1876

CONKEY Daniel age 67y in Salem, NY September 17, 1876

GOULD Mary A. age 88y wife of Abram in Shushan, NY September 19, 1876

QUACKENBUSH Catherine age 49y in Buskirks Bridge, NY September 20, 1876

DUGAN Mrs. A. age 27y in Glens Falls, NY October 2, 1876

NORRIS Mrs. Nancy A. age 47y in Glens Falls, NY September 28, 1876

BOCKES James A. age 69y in W. Hebron, NY November 8, 1876

DE FOREST Edith age 20y 7m wife of Alfred in Ft. Edward, NY November 6, 1876

STARBUCK Edward of Chester, NY in Ft. Ann, NY November 1, 1876

MILLS Ceylon I. age 11m in S. Schroon, NY October 21, 1876

WING George W. age 50y in Sandy Hill, NY November 20, 1876

COOPER Mrs. Elizabeth age 64y in Sandy Hill, NY November 21, 1876

BETTS Mrs. Juliza age 36y in Easton, NY October 21, 1876

OWENS Morris age 42y in Poultney, Vt. November 15, 1876

MEINBURG Moses age 86y in Poultney, Vt. November 15, 1876

MILLIMAN Charles L. age 19y in Ft. Edward, NY November 19, 1876

WATSON Varney age 85y in Ft. Ann, NY November 17, 1876

COTTRELL Daniel age 64y in Oconomowoc, NY October 30, 1876

MC NITT Mrs. B. F. age 45y in Cambridge, NY November 27, 1876

KELLY Mark age 9y in Cambridge, NY December 9, 1876

SAFFORD Gideon age 67y in Argyle, NY December 1, 1876

WOOD Rev. N. B. age 63y in Hartford, NY December 8, 1876

LA POINTE Mrs. Steve Jr. age 24y in Ft. Miller, NY December 12, 1876

WOODWORTH Benjamin F. age 56y formerly of Sandy Hill, NY in Wende, NY December 9, 1876

CHENEY Mrs. Elizabeth age 25y in Glens Falls, NY December 16, 1876

TRAPHAGEN Jonathan age 77y in Glens Falls, NY December 19, 1876

CARRIGAN Nellie age 5y and Dot age 16m died December 12, 1876 chidren of J. B. and S. J. in Hartford, NY

WASHINGTON COUNTY CHRONICLE
December 23, 1864 - October 28, 1870

MOON Betsey Elizabeth age 5m 1d dau of Francis and Catherine in Whitehall, NY December 18, 1864

LESTER Samuel in N. Argyle, NY October 2, 1868

RATHBUN Marietta age 21y wife of William in Whitehall, NY December 20, 1868

TISDALE Susan age 21y dau of H. G. Tisdale in Whitehall, NY December 29, 1868

BARTHOLOMEW Harvey age 57y February 10, 1870

CLARK J. F. in his 74th yr at son-in-laws Lemuel WILSON in Whitehall, NY February 24, 1870

THAYER Warren A. age 3y 11m 4d son of T. W. in Whitehall, NY March 21, 1870

WILLETT Mrs. Addison in N. Granville, NY March 28, 1870

SHUMWAY Col. Doty in his 87th yr in N. Granville, NY April 2, 1870

COZZENS Lewis in Ft. Ann, NY April 3, 1870

KING Hannah in her 78th yr relict of Thomas in Whitehall, NY April 12, 1870

CONNORS William W. age 39y in Whitehall, NY April 13, 1870

LEGGIN Francis abt 40y April 6, 1870. Mem. of 169th Reg. NY Vol.

WENTWORTH Harry age 67y in M. Granville, NY April 30, 1870

SUTHERLAND Robert age 58y in Dresden, NY May 3, 1870

BAILEY Susan A. age 18y in Ft. Ann, NY April 30, 1870

WASHBURN James age 17y in Ft. Ann, NY May 2, 1870

LYONS Rebecca R. in her 39th yr wife of A. T. Lyon May 8, 1870

WOOD Edward Henry infant son of James M. and Empia May 23, 1870

MOSHER Austin age 62y in Ft. Ann, NY May 29, 1870

MC INTYRE Mary wife of John in Hebron, NY February 17, 1870

CARSON Jessie age 1y 12d dau of Newton in Hebron, NY May 9, 1870

GILCHRIST Sarah age 36y 4m wife of Duncan in Hebron, NY May 30, 1870

WASHBURN Frank J. age 10m 19d son of William B. and F. J. in Whitehall, NY May 28, 1870

JORDAN Edward age 72y in Ft. Ann, NY June 5, 1870

FARR Col. James in his 76th yr at Ft. Ann, NY June 2, 1870

BILLINGS George W. age 24y son of William J. and Betsey M. in Westhaven, Vt. June 5, 1870

THOMAS Samuel age 81y in Ft. Ann, NY June 27, 1870

BAILEY Lusie M. in Ft. Ann, NY April 30, 1870

SMITH Mary E. **(DOIG)** age 23y wife of Henry in Whitehall, NY July 15, 1870

BECKWITH Charles Platt age 1y 10m 19d son of A. G. in Whitehall, NY July 19, 1870

GREEN William Morris age 4y 6m son of Patrick and Bridget in Whitehall, NY July 20, 1870

BENJAMIN Charlie age 3y 10m son of Harry and Mary in Whitehall, NY August 1, 1870

VAUGHN Thomas D. age 56y in Whitehall, NY August 7, 1870

HIXSON Lucy age 72y 6m in Queensbury, NY August 15, 1870

DAY Mary A. widow of Orson formerly of Whitehall nr Stanton, Ks. July 18, 1870

LOWELL Jesse Esq. in his 74th yr in N. Granville, NY August 10, 1870

BRIGHAM Clara C. age 3y 6m dau of J. M. and M. E. in Whitehall, NY August 12, 1870

COWAN Claude age 6m son of William H. and Phoebe S. in Bensons Landing, Vt. August 6, 1870

HALL Ira age 74y in Ft. Ann, NY August 8, 1870

LEACH Clara Antoinette age 2m dau of V. W. and M. E. in Whitehall, NY August

18, 1870

KEITH Lyman B. age 66y in Otsego, Iowa August 21, 1870. Born Jackson, NY, lived at Ft. Ann and buried in Ft. Ann, NY

BACKUS Rufus abt 75y in N. Granville, NY August 30, 1870

WING Laura age 65y wife of R. D. in M. Granville, NY August 30, 1870

UTTER J. Melville age 38y in Amsterdam, NY August 29, 1870

BORTLE Josephine B. age 36y 11m in Whitehall, NY August 20, 1870

HART Nettie age 3y 9m 6d of Putnam, NY in Argyle, NY August 16, 1870

MURPHY Timothy in his 20th yr in Whitehall, NY September 12, 1870

WRAY Electa B. age 78y wife of Garrett in W. Granville, NY September 11, 1870

MONARQUE John age 14m 12d son of Joseph in Whitehall, NY September 15, 1870

NICHOLS Julia age 26y wife of A. E. in Whitehall, NY September 20, 1870

STRONG Isaac Newton abt 40y September 23, 1870

TERRY Eli abt 50y in Whitehall, NY September 24, 1870

MASON Mrs. Charles L. in N. Granville, NY September 23, 1870

STAFFORD Seymour age 39y 5m 27d October 7, 1870

RATHBUN Cyrus Eugene age 18m son of George and Josephine October 4, 1870

CONANT Mrs. Alonzo age 52y in Granville, NY October 10, 1870

MURRAY Millie age 6y 9m dau of John and Catherine in Whitehall, NY October 19, 1870

BULL ____ age 5m dau of J. D. in Ft. Ann, NY October 18, 1870

WASHINGTON COUNTY JOURNAL (Union Village)
January 2, 1845 - December 30, 1849

LARABEE John age 90y Revolutionary Soldier at Centre Falls, NY January 28, 1845

BIGELOW Anson in his 44th yr at Easton, NY January 25, 1845

HATCH Mary L. age 2y 6m 10d dau of Dr. in Union Village, NY January 25, 1845

YOUNG Elizabeth Ann dau of Alanson F. and Clarissa in Union Village, NY

February 7, 1845

PRENTISS Miss Harriet age 42y dau of Luke of Union Village, NY in Brattleboro, Vt. February 7, 1845

DEUEL Mrs. _____ age 70y in Union Village, NY February 17, 1845

REYNOLDS Zachariah age 90y a Revolutionary Soldier at Ft. Miller, NY February 15, 1845

MOWRY William age 65y native of Woodstock Conn. in Union Village, NY March 23, 1845

SHELDON Mary in her 53rd yr wife of Caleb in Easton, NY March 17, 1845

LANGWORTHY Rue age 33y wife of Seth in Union Village, NY March 13, 1845

KETCHUM A. Biron age 3y 7m 8d son of Henry in Galesville, NY March 30, 1845

BURROUGHS David age 78y in Union Village, NY April 3, 1845

COLEMAN Obed M. in his 28th yr in Saratoga Springs, NY April 5, 1845

WRIGHT Martin Lee age 8m 9d son of Dr. William and Eliza Ann Wright in Cambridge, NY March 27, 1845

CARPENTER Miss Deanthy age 30 in Union Village, NY April 10, 1845

BROWNELL Elijah age 64y in Easton, NY April 18, 1845

GRAY Lyman age 33y in Salem, NY May 2, 1845

STONE Harriet age 28y wife of Henry R. and dau of Smith and Fanny **HURD** in Union Village, NY May 19, 1845

TILTON Anson age 43y in Union Village, NY May 21, 1845

WHELDON Mariann age 3m dau of Darius and Abigail in Easton, NY May 5, 1845

HASTINGS David S. abt 36y in Salem, NY May 13/15, 1845

PIERCE Eleanor age 35y wife of Juline late of Madison Co. NY and dau of Comfort and Sally Ann **BARBER** of Union Village, NY in N. Greenwich, NY July 22, 1845

DUNHAM Anna in her 20th yr dau of Nathum in Jackson, NY July 30, 1845

SAFFORD Caroline age 11y dau of John in Union Village, NY August 22, 1845

LAWTON Daniel age 26y in Union Village, NY August 26, 1845

CHUBB Henry Clay age 1y 2m son of Simon N. and Lydia in Union Village, NY September 13, 1845

MC DOUGAL Margaret Jane age 13 dau of Joseph and Jane in S. Argyle, NY September 23, 1845

DURHAM Stephen age 73y formerly of Washington Co. in Wilson, NY November 6, 1845

CLARK Mercy age 36y wife of James E. in Schuylerville, NY December 1, 1845

MATHEWS Charles Sidney age 1y 4m son of Abraham Jr. in Ft. Miller, NY December 13, 1845

AUSTIN Ann A. in her 23rd yr wife of A. Austin Jr. in Salem, NY January 2, 1846

NEWCOMB Solomon age 65y in Waterbury, Vt. December 23, 1845

KITTLE Simon age 72y in Union Village, NY January 9, 1846

PATTERSON John age 54y 11m in Union Village, NY January 21, 1846

LOOMIS Content E. age 28y dau of late Eben **CRANDALL** in Greenwich, NY February 2, 1846

MATHEWS Samuel age 77y formerly of Union Village, NY at Ft. Henry January 16, 1846

SAFFORD Harriet age 74y widow of Joseph in Union Village, NY January 20, 1846

WHITCOMB Eleanor Frances age 6m dau of Thomas and Jane at Lake, NY January 29, 1846

HOOD Harriet age 1y 9m 5d dau of James and Eliza at Lake, NY January/February 24, 1846

ROBERTSON Francis in his 83rd yr in Union Village, NY March 15, 1846

CRARY Sarah Jane age 7y 6m dau of John C. and Sarah in Salem, NY April 1, 1846 and dau Eleanor age 9y 3m 13d died April 11, 1846

GRAY James P. age 26y son of late D. D. Gray in Salem, NY April 7, 1846

CRUIKSHANK Catherine in her 15th yr dau of Rev. William in Canterbury, NY April 11, 1846

FULLER John C. in his 9th yr son of Sidney and Eliza Jane in Union Village, NY May 7, 1846

NEWBURY James B. in his 41st yr in Union Village, NY May 3, 1846

DUNBAR Elizabeth age 72y 15d wife of Robert H. formerly of Albany, NY in Argyle, NY May 27, 1846

POTTER Ward B. in his 28th yr in Galesville, NY June 14, 1846

WILLIAMS John Jr. age 37y of Salem, NY in Philadelphia, Pa. June 14, 1846

ALLEN Jonathan age 89y in Cambridge, NY June 23, 1846

BLISS Sarah E. in her 13th yr in Union Village, NY July 2, 1846

PRENTISS Susan age 72y wife of Luke in Union Village, NY July 11, 1846

MC FARLAND Abner A. age 20y son of Daniel and Martha formerly of Salem, NY in Peekskill, NY June 28, 1846

DILLINGHAM William H. in his 46th yr in Granville, NY July 5, 1846

HARKNESS Henry C. age 1y 6m son of William B. and Caroline in Whitehall, NY July 16, 1846

GILSON Mary Marie age 27y 11m at Uncles A. **CHASE** in Cambridge, NY July 7, 1846

MC FARLAND Margaret Mother of William in Salem, NY July 29, 1846

GRANGER Judge of Saratoga Co. on Champlain Canal boat August 1, 1846

RUSSELL Emeline M. age 32y 20d wife of Solomon W. in Union Village, NY July 25, 1846

BAILEY Samuel age 18y son of Titus in Schuylerville, NY August 16, 1846

VAN SCHAICK Gerrett I. in his 74th yr in Easton, NY August 2, 1846

MARTIN Elizabeth age 23y dau of Andrew in Salem, NY August 3, 1846

STOWELL Francis L. age 76y in Salem, NY August 25, 1846

FISHER Margaret A. age 25y dau of George in Union Village, NY August 27, 1846

SANDERSON John H. age 56y in Sunderland, Vt. August 21, 1846

GIDLEY Benjamin age 21y 11m 12d at fathers in Saratoga Co. NY August 24, 1846

MORRIS Mary Lucy age 2y 4m dau of Rev. H. in Union Village, NY September 13, 1846

GALE John age 77y in Galesville, NY September 29, 1846

169

WOODARD Mrs. E. in Union Village, NY September 29, 1846

BRIGGS Daniel age 27y in Easton, NY September 19, 1846

WOODWORTH Wealthy Ann age 48y wife of Ira in White Creek, NY October 2, 1846

RUSSELL Caroline M. age 10m 2d dau of Jehiel and Harriet in Union Village, NY October 9, 1846

ASHTON Rebecca age 11y 18d dau of James in N. Argyle, NY October 13, 1846

NORTON Mabel age 46y wife of Alexander in Union Village, NY November 7, 1846

WHITE Henry Clay age 17m son of George W. in Hebron, NY October 27, 1846

CORLISS Sarah S. age 15y dau of Hiram in Union Village, NY December 2, 1846

RUSSELL Frances Maria age 6m dau of Seymour and Maranda in Greenwich, NY December 13, 1846

SKINNER Nathan age 78y in Cambridge, NY December 21, 1846

REMINGTON Benjamin in Greenwich, NY December 15, 1846

WHIPPLE Mary age 29y wife of Charles in Greenwich, NY December 26, 1846

CLEGG John age 21y in Schaghticoke, NY December 23, 1846

LAWTON Mr. ____ age 69y in Greenwich, NY January 1, 1847

WEIR Mrs. John A. age 29y in Centre Falls, NY December 30, 1846

SHILAND Mary age 47y wife of John in Cambridge, NY January 7, 1847

WINNEY Peter age 86y in Greenwich, NY January 15, 1847

ROGERS Louisa in her 28th yr dau of Thomas in Ft. Edward, NY January 12, 1846

TICE William age 75y in Greenwich, NY January 21, 1847

DOYLE John age 34y formerly of Greenwich, NY in Buffalo, NY January 20, 1846

AUSTIN Sarah dau of Abner in Salem, NY January 23, 1847

BAILEY Titus in Schuylerville, NY January 21, 1847

TEFFT Mrs. John H. age 34y in Greenwich, NY February 1, 1847

GRIFFIN John H. age 59y in Greenwich, NY February 12, 1847

BARBER Joseph abt 23y son of Comfort in Greenwich, NY February 19, 1847

KNAPP Charles Russell age 5y 4m son of Alanson H. and W. Maria in Greenwich, NY March 9, 1847

HYDE Edward age 3y 5m son of Benjamin in Greenwich, NY March 7, 1847

SHEARER Catherine Elizabeth age 2y 1d dau of Volney in Ft. Edward, NY January 30, 1847

STALKER Mrs. Rev. Douglas in N. Argyle, NY March 5, 1847

REED Archibald age 34y of Cambridge, NY in Argyle, NY February 27, 1847

STEWART Robert in his 31st yr in Salem, NY March 1, 1847

ENOS Sibbil age 72y widow of Capt. Andrew of Leicester, Vt. in Salem, NY March 9, 1847

MORRELL Rachel age 24y wife of Robert in Greenwich, NY March 20, 1847

BURDICK Ephraim age 72 in Easton, NY March 20, 1847

WHELDON Peter B. age 27y in Easton, NY April 17, 1847

FISHER Garrett W. in his 37th yr in Cambridge, NY April 16, 1847

BILLINGS Jesse I. in his 67th yr in Whitehall, NY April 3, 1847

CLARK Elizabeth in her 83rd yr in Jackson, NY May 10, 1847

TEFFT Capt. Benjamin age 73y in Greenwich, NY May 21, 1847

VAN NESS Catherine age 29y wife of James in Greenwich, NY May 24, 1847

CROSSY Charles Henry age 1y 5m son of Dr. Joseph B. and Almira in Greenwich, NY June 1, 1847

STEVENS Mercy A. age 36y dau of James S. **TEFFT** in Galesville, NY May 31, 1847

FAIRCHILD Zerua age 84y widow of Jesse at son-in-laws Samuel **RUSTE** in White Creek, NY June 11, 1847

MOWRY Sarah G. age 15y dau of Leroy and Catherine in Greenwich, NY May 29, 1847

NEWBURY Jeremiah age 83y in Greenwich, NY June 25, 1847. Settled here 1773

WARNER William in his 10th yr son of Asaph in Jackson, NY June 21, 1847

CARL James Hamlin age 6y son of James in Argyle, NY July 3, 1847

CULVER Mrs. Catherine abt 30y in Jackson, NY July 2, 1847

BARKER Jane A. age 33y wife of Robinson W. in Troy, NY July 12, 1847

BLISS Dwight S. age 20y formerly of Greenwich, NY in Poultney, Vt. June 5, 1847

CORNELL Mary in her 20th yr dau of Mathew in White Creek, NY July 20, 1847

MC LEARY John age 70y in Jackson, NY July 22, 1847

AKIN Oscar in his 25th yr in White Creek, NY July 21, 1847

GRISWOLD Sarah dau of Leroy MOWRY in Greenwich, NY June 29, 1847

BARKER Caroline Amelia age 2y dau of P. L. and Mary A. in Greenwich, NY August 3, 1847

DUTCHER Solomon age 87y Revolutionary Soldier in Greenwich, NY August 12, 1847

ROBINSON Lyman abt 40y formerly of Greenwich in Stillwater, NY August 13, 1847

STARKEY Joseph Edwin age 1y 6m son of Joseph E. and Jane in Greenwich, NY August 14, 1847

SPRAGUE Henry W. Md. age 30y in Whitehall, NY August 9, 1847

BEATY Isabella age 35y in Cambridge, NY August 12, 1847

CORNELL Abraham abt 55y formerly of Greenwich in Troy, NY August 21, 1847

VIELE Simon in his 78th yr at Ft. Miller, NY August 30, 1847

MOORE George P. age 51y in Greenwich, NY September 13, 1847

FAIRLEY John 2nd age 54y in Salem, NY September 1, 1847

LATIMER Nicolas in Salem, NY September 11, 1847

BARBER Amelia age 31y dau of Perry C. and Lydia in Troy, NY September 24, 1847

SHEPHERD Emily in her 35th yr wife of Franklin and dau of Comfort and Sally BARBER in Greenwich, NY September 29, 1847

CARPENTER Maria age 22y dau of John in Greenwich, NY September 30, 1847

CARPENTER Mehitable age 47y wife of John T. in N. Greenwich, NY September

29, 1847

SIMPSON Ebenezer abt 34y in Jackson, NY September 28, 1847

MASON Mary age 2y dau of I. I. Mason and Sarah E. HOLMES in Troy, NY October 11, 1847

WARFORD Joseph in his 69th yr in Salem, NY October 11, 1847

YOUNG Charles abt 20y in Salem, NY October 9, 1847

LARKIN Nathan in his 33rd yr in Salem, NY October 4, 1847

BARKER Lydia age 57y wife of Perry C. in Troy, NY October 17, 1847

MILLER Perry age 77y in Greenwich, NY October 30, 1847

WRIGHT D. W. Prin. Argyle Academy last wk (newspaper date November 4, 1847)

POTTER Sarah Ann age 14y dau of Stephen and Sally in Galesville, NY November 1, 1847

MC FARLAND John age 83y 10m in Jackson, NY November 17, 1847, came from Scotland 1784

LARKIN Caroline C. age 33y in Salem, NY November 19, 1847

REYNOLDS George E. abt 10y son of Hart in Galesville, NY December 12, 1847

MARSH Alzina A. age 14y dau of Hiram in Schuylerville, NY December 11, 1847

BAILEY Ruby age 23y dau of Titus in Schuylerville, NY December 11, 1847

PRATT Ruth age 63y wife of Daniel H. in White Creek, NY December 1, 1847

MOSHER Charles R. age 51y in Easton, NY December 19, 1847

SKINNER Reuben in his 76th yr in Granville, NY January 4, 1848

SMITH Sarah age 64y wife of Daniel and sister of H. EMMONS of Greenwich, NY in Clarenceville, Vt. (newspaper date January 20, 1848)

AUSTIN Susannah in her 23rd yr dau of Abner in Salem, NY January 14, 1848

TEFFT Nathan age 71y in Greenwich, NY January 24, 1848

EDDY Electa age 36y wife of Walden in Greenwich, NY January 29, 1848

DENNIS Electa age 19y wife of Edward and dau of Rev. STEAD in Galesville, NY January 30, 1848

NOBLE Polly age 55y formerly of Greenwich, NY in Rupert, Vt. January 27, 1848

CLAPP Miss Amelia in her 31st yr dau of Constant January 13, 1848

WATSON Lydia Maria age 13m dau of James and Emeline in Galesville, NY January 31, 1848

HEATH Consider age 32y formerly of Greenwich in Racine, Wis. January 31, 1848

FENTON Mrs. Martha age 63y in Greenwich, NY February 10, 1848

RICHARDS Erastus age 34y in Galesville, NY February 14, 1848

MC GILL Patrick in his 34th yr in Cambridge, NY February 6, 1848

MOORE Keziah age 35y wife of Charles H. in Greenwich, NY February 13, 1848

INGALLS Mary age 25y wife of Charles R. in Greenwich, NY February 23, 1848

SKINNER Phoebe age 69y relict of Nathan in White Creek, NY February 16, 1848

HORTON Jonathan K. age 72y of Greenwich, NY at sons in Cincinnati, Ohio February 22, 1848

GARVIN Emerett age 9m dau of Ephraim T. and Elizabeth in Greenwich, NY February 23, 1848

YOUNG Mrs. John age 33y in Easton, NY March 2, 1848

LAMBERT Thomas Scott age 2y 6m son of Rev. A. B. in Salem, NY March 4, 1848

SAFFORD Charlotte age 42y wife of Henry in Greenwich, NY March 18, 1848

BARNARD Mrs. Betsey age 34 wife of John H. in Greenwich, NY March 26, 1848

SHELDON Asa age 87y formerly of Greenwich, NY in Utica, NY March 19, 1848

TEFFT William age 34y in Greenwich, NY March 30, 1848

WILLIAMS Phillip H. age 51y in Greenwich, NY April 7, 1848

WELLS Joseph age 67y resident of Salem, NY in Constantine, Mi. rec. (newspaper date April 13, 1848)

FROST Abigail age 72y wife of Ezra in Greenwich, NY April 15, 1848

FENTON Joseph age 63y in Galesville, NY April 18, 1848

DUNBAR Miss Sarah age 25 dau of late John in Union Village, NY April 27, 1848

WARNER Phillip in his 83rd yr in Jackson, NY April 15, 1848

MEAD Mrs. _____ age 62y in Greenwich, NY April 30, 1848

CORBETT Elijah abt 57 yrs in Jackson, NY April 26, 1848

BROWNELL Mehettabel age 25y wife of H. K. in White Creek, NY April 30, 1848

WILMARTH Leander formerly of Greenwich, NY in Glens Falls, NY May 9, 1848

LANGWORTHY Jason age 55y in Greenwich, NY May 28, 1848

CROCKER Eliza (HOWE) in her 29th yr wife of Rev. A. B. Crocker in Schaghticoke, NY May 1, 1848

BRYANT William age 54y in Greenwich, NY June 3, 1848

DOBBIN Thomas in his 23rd yr in Jackson, NY June 1, 1848

SHAW Cornelius in his 66th yr in Easton, NY June 24, 1848

MC NAUGHTON Esther Ann age 43y wife of Gen. John Shaw and dau of John **CRARY** in Salem, NY June 24, 1848

HOLMES Joseph postmaster in Greenwich, NY July 1, 1848

HEWLET Nehemiah age 84y Revolutionary Soldier in Granville, NY August 4, 1848

PRENTISS Luke age 11m son of Horace in Greenwich, NY August 21, 1848

COFFIN Louise age 3y 4m died August 21, 1848 and Nelson age 14m died August 23, 1848, children of Thomas in Easton, NY

BLAWIS Peter age 60y in Easton, NY July 29, 1848

WOODRUFF Miss Selina age 29y in Easton, NY August 29, 1848

TILFORD Isabella age 3y dau of Robert and Mary Ann in Jackson, NY September 1, 1848

REMINGTON Hannah age 68y wife of David in Greenwich, NY September 18, 1848

YOUNG Miss Polly T. age 26y at parents in Warren Co. NY September 16, 1848

FERGUSON Alexander B. in his 14th yr in Jackson, NY September 16, 1848

TAYLOR Miss Jane age 20y in Greenwich, NY September 24, 1848

COLLINS Dr. William A. in Battenville, NY September 23, 1848

WHELDON infant son of Francis B. age 10m in Easton, NY September 19, 1848

CARPENTER Lyman age 39y in Greenwich, NY October 11, 1848

SPRAGUE Mrs. Martha age 28y in N. Greenwich, NY October 15, 1848

WILMARTH Clara age 8m dau of Edwin and Almira in Greenwich, NY October 16, 1848

ADAMS Mary E. age 3y 6m in Greenwich, NY October 30, 1848

LITTLEJOHN Susan T. age 26y wife of Harrison G. in Greenwich, NY November 14, 1848

BROWNELL Ann Eliza age 28y wife of James and dau of Henry **BLISS** in Greenwich, NY November 25, 1848

PERRINE John age 60y in Jackson, NY October 31, 1848

MILLS William R. in Argyle, NY November 7, 1848

WILSON James H. age 18y in Easton, NY December 24, 1848

WHELDON Jabez age 84y in Easton, NY December 31, 1848

ROBERSON Nancy age 23y wife of Barber in Greenwich, NY January 5, 1849

YOUNGLOVE Lucas age 82y formerly of Cambridge, NY in Trenton, NY January 17, 1849

BUEL Julia E. in her 17th yr formerly of Washington Co. NY at uncles Orson Buel near Cumberland January 5, 1849

WHYTE Rev. Archibald age 93y in Argyle, NY January 6, 1849

BENTON Charlotte E. age 43y wife of Henry in Troy, NY February 23, 1849

HALL Mary age 71y wife of William in Cambridge, NY March 20, 1849

PRENTISS Edwin J. age 10m son of John M. and Ann in Greenwich, NY April 18, 1849

BARBER Comfort in Greenwich, NY April 11, 1849

MC INTYRE Isabel in her 20th yr in Greenwich, NY April 16, 1849

PRENTISS William age 15y son of Horace in Greenwich, NY April 13, 1849

MC ALLISTER Frances age 9m 20d dau of John M. and Seraph H. (**STEVENSON**) in Cambridge, NY April 13, 1849

CURTIS Janet age 2y 10m 15d dau of William D. and Mary A. in Warren, Wis. April 15, 1849

BARNHAM Roxy age 50y wife of Noadiah in Greenwich, NY May 11, 1849

BROWNING John F. age 42y in Easton, NY May 10, 1849

DAMON Levi age 47y in Greenwich, NY May 15, 1849

PARKER Calvin L. age 55y in Hartford, NY April 28, 1849. Wife and 4 children

CLARK Alfred age 25y at Lake, NY May 29, 1849

WHITESIDE Mrs. Margaret in her 96th yr in Cambridge, NY June 9, 1849

OSBORN Mrs. Mary age 25y in Greenwich, NY June 25, 1849

MARVIN Mary in her 44th yr wife of Jarvis in Salem, NY June 13, 1849

STUART Mrs. Mary in her 62nd yr at sons C. D. in New York June 29, 1849

SCOTT Elizabeth in her 60th yr wife of William in Sandgate, Vt. July 31, 1849

VANDERWERCKER Charlotte in her 19th yr wife of James and dau of Elisha **WALLER** of Greenwich, NY in Ft. Miller, NY August 20, 1849

GRIDLEY Caroline age 24y wife of H. C. and dau of Daniel T. **REED** of Saratoga Springs, NY in Saratoga Springs, NY August 12, 1849

MIENER Melissa age 64y wife of David in Greenwich, NY (newspaper date September 6, 1849)

GEER Mrs. Frances age 59y in Troy, NY September 6, 1849

NORTON Mrs. Rebecca in her 84th yr in Greenwich, NY September 16, 1849

MC CALL Henry C. age 1y 6m son of William A. and Adelia E. in Greenwich, NY September 20, 1849

DYER Mrs. Phebe age 57y of Greenwich, NY in Springfield, Mass. October 3, 1849

TABER Parmelia in her 43rd yr wife of Sidney and dau of Simeon and Merriam **TAYLOR** in Greenwich, NY October 24, 1849

MC KALLOR Archibald in his 65th yr in Argyle, NY December 13, 1849

POTTER John age 33y in Greenwich, NY December 20, 1849

WILSON Susan E. age 20y dau of Osborn in Greenwich, NY January 18, 1850

CLARK Miss Elizabeth in her 25th yr in Greenwich, NY February 17, 1850

ROWELL Lemuel abt 68y in Greenwich, NY February 19, 1850

HENRY Caroline B. age 60y wife of Col. William of Chicago, Ill. dau of late Consider WHITE of Troy, NY in New York January 11, 1850. Buried Greenwich,

BRADLEY Clarinda age 27y wife of Charles in Greenwich, NY March 6, 1850

WRIGHT John age 84y in Jackson, NY February 25, 1850

EVANS Rebecca in her 45th yr wife of Benjamin in Greenwich, NY March 8, 1850

ROOD Nathaniel age 45y in Greenwich, NY March 15, 1850

KENYON John Henry age 15m son of John in Greenwich, NY March 18, 1850

MC MILLAN Mary in her 33rd yr in Argyle, NY March 19, 1850

LEONARD Lucy wife of Rev. J. Leonard former pastor of M. E. Church in Greenwich, NY and dau of Nicolas and Lucy COOK of Wallingford, Vt. in Cohoes, NY April 7, 1850. Born April 27, 1807 and married October 3, 1826

MILLER Miss Martha J. age 24y in Greenwich, NY April 25, 1850

LUCAS Elizabeth in her 86th yr relict of David in Easton, NY May 13, 1850

SHERMAN Mrs. ____ age 78y in Easton, NY June 26, 1850

MC FARLAND Margaret age 24y 10m dau of Daniel and Jane in Jackson, NY June 24, 1850

COWAN David M. formerly of Washington Co. in Cleveland, Ohio June 13, 1850

HALL William Jr. age 45y of Cambridge, NY in San Francisco, Cal. July 11, 1850

GILCHRIST Mrs. Mary E. in her 20th yr dau of Jarvis MARTIN in Salem, NY September 13, 1850

FULLER Dwight Henry infant son of Sidney died October 13, 1850 and dau Frances L. in her 9th yr died October 24, 1850 in Greenwich, NY

KITTLE Sarah age 72y in Greenwich, NY November 23, 1850

SKIFF Benjamin in Easton, NY November 23, 1850

MC CALL William A. in his 29th yr in Hebron, NY November 12, 1850

BAILEY Asa age 86y in Greenwich, NY December 15, 1850

WASHINGTON COUNTY NEWS
March 25, 1871 - September 16, 1871

RUSSELL Alida age 88y relict of David March 15, 1871

HOVER Cornelia A. age 28y wife of John in Cambridge, NY March 16, 1871

JEWETT Eloise (CAMERON) age 31y wife of L. Paul in Glens Falls, NY March 17, 1871

PARKS Steven age 92y in Whitehall, NY March 16, 1871. Born November 4, 1779 in Conn. Three wives, 11 children, 4 living. Names Isaac and A.

CODY Catherine Elizabeth 7m 17d dau of James and Mary in Whitehall, NY March 11, 1871

DODELIN Josette would be 100y in 4 weeks, wife of Joseph who is about 20 years younger, at son-in-laws John **JALET** in Whitehall, NY April 7, 1871

FACTO Johnie age 6y 3m 5d son of George and Jane in Whitehall, NY April 12, 1871

BEMIS Elias H. age 52y in N. Granville, NY April 18, 1871

COLE _____ age 4y dau of John and Thursday April 25, 1871

THOMPSON Anna (GILBERT) age 87y wife of Jacob in Whitehall, NY April 16, 1871. Born June 1782 in Cavendish, Vt.

MOREHOUSE William age 80y in Whitehall, NY May 3, 1871. Born 1791 in Ausable, NY. Served War of 1812. Names son Henry C. of Whitehall

LUTHER Curtis C. age 80y 3m 10d in Whitehall, NY May 9, 1871

CARRINGTON John age 71y in Whitehall, NY June 13, 1871

SIMPSON Agnes age 94y in Putnam, NY July 16, 1871. Born Scotland

WASHINGTON COUNTY PEOPLE'S JOURNAL
January 5, 1854 - December 30, 1879

EVANS Harriet age 22y in Greenwich, NY December 29, 1853

PROUDFIT Susan relict of Alexander at son-in-laws Richard **IRVIN** in New York December 25, 1853

WYATT Jane Elizabeth in her 26th yr wife of George in Schuylerville, NY January 2, 1854

BOWEN Allison age 19m 13d son of Uriah and Margaret I. in Greenwich, NY January 17, 1854

NEWTON Clarissa age 66y in Greenwich, NY January 16, 1854

ROOD Frances age 17y in Greenwich, NY January 13, 1854

MOSHER Miss Ann in Greenwich, NY January 17, 1854

LAGER Chloe in her 90th yr at sons Charles S. WRIGHT in Greenwich, NY January 13, 1854

WESTON Theodotta age 30y wife of L. W. in Peru, Ill. December 20, 1853

POTTER Amos age 74y in Greenwich, NY January 20, 1854

GRAHAM F. B. in Saratoga Springs, NY January 15, 1854

EMMONS Horatio Jr. age 37y of Greenwich, NY in California October 9, 1853

WHYTE William Albert age 2y 4m son of Thomas and Mary in Greenwich, NY January 23, 1854

MC MORRIS Mary in her 20th yr dau of Thomas in Jackson, NY January 22, 1854

MILLER Fanny M. age 41y wife of David in Greenwich, NY February 7, 1854

RICHARDS Maria age 45y in Greenwich, NY February 5, 1854

LOURIE Mary Sophia age 26y wife of Alexander and dau of Anson BIGELOW of Easton, NY in Jackson, NY February 4, 1854

VOLENTINE Thomas in Jackson, NY January 30, 1854

VOLENTINE Leonard in Jackson, NY February 3, 1854

MILLIMAN Henry Clay age 6y son of N. B. in Argyle, NY February 4, 1854

BOYD James abt 33y in Salem, NY February 12, 1854

CALHOUN Mary Jane age 14y 24d in Greenwich, NY February 15, 1854

BIGOT Jane age 17y in Bennington, Vt. February 25, 1854

HERRINGTON Edgar abt 4y son of Bentley in Easton, NY February 28, 1854

CRUIKSHANK Rev. William age 56y formerly of Salem, NY in Cornwall, NY February 20, 1854

DAWLEY Simon age 38y in Geenwich, NY March 13, 1854

WILCOX Mrs. Oliver age 59y in Easton, NY March 8, 1854

LOOMIS Sarah age 84y in Centre Falls, NY March 19, 1854

WALKLEY Sarah Mary age 4y 10m 10d dau of B. W. in N. White Creek, NY March 11, 1854

SMITH Caroline wife of James in Easton, NY February 20, 1854

MC DOUAL Jane in Jackson, NY April 3, 1854

BAIL Henry age 24y in Greenwich, NY March 31, 1854

MORSE Ella P. age 21m 15d dau of Sidney and Sarah A. in Greenwich, NY April 12, 1854

TOMPKINS Jerome age 10m son of L. P. and Eliza A. in Greenwich, NY April 12, 1854

YOUNG Henry C. age 24y in Easton, NY April 13, 1854

CORLISS Julia age 16y dau of Nathan Corliss in Easton, April 11, 1854

JOHNSON Olive infant dau of Juda Maria in N. Easton, NY April 16, 1854

STEWART Joseph K. age 22y in Greenwich, NY April 22, 1854

CHAMBERLAIN Martha age 25y wife of William in Salem, NY April 19, 1854 and dau Margaret age 3m died April 2, 1854

HEGEMAN Jacob Andrew age 18y 3m son of William and Louisa C. in Easton, NY April 20, 1854

CRANDALL Bridget age 67y in Greenwich, NY April 24, 1854

BARNETT William age 27y in Greenwich, NY May 9, 1854

WATERS Albert F. age 1y 5m son of Edwin S. and Ellen M. in Greenwich, NY May 12, 1854

TIMMERMAN Mary E. age 21y formerly of Argyle, NY at Aunts Mrs. H. B. SCOTT in Waterford, NY May 20, 1854

MASTERS Mary Elizabeth age 8y 10m dau of John T. and Mary E. in Greenwich, NY May 28, 1854

FULLER Sarah age 2y dau of Sidney and Eliza A. formerly of Washington Co. in Arlington, Mi. May 24, 1854

HYATT Sarah in her 83rd yr relict of John in Battenville, NY June 14, 1854

ROBINSON Emma Alvincy age 1y 3m dau of Benjamin and Elizabeth in Easton, NY June 4, 1854

TEFFT Allen E. age 22y in Greenwich, NY June 18, 1854

NEWCOMB Irenaeus P. age 40y in Easton, NY May 27, 1854

BOGGS Mrs. Sarah age 70y in Greenwich, NY June 11, 1854

CRANDALL Harriet wife of Dr. F. S. in Greenwich, NY June 28, 1854

FISHER George age 58y in Easton, NY July 3, 1854

TABER Mrs. George age 44y in Greenwich, NY July 4, 1854

MC DOUAL Sarah age 86y of Cambridge, NY in Schuylerville, NY June 28, 1854

NEWCOMB Mary Elizabeth age 41y wife of Dr. John E. and dau of late John GALE in Whitehall, NY July 1_, 1854

MC NEIL John A. in his 49th yr of Argyle, NY in Ft. Edward, NY July 16, 1854

SOUTHWORTH George age 12y in Greenwich, NY July 8, 1854

SHELDON Caleb in his 70th yr in Easton, NY July 15, 1854

WILMARTH Mary B. age 49y wife of Enoch in Greenwich, NY August 6, 1854

TEFFT Ellen N. in her 16th yr dau of Simeon and Abigal formerly of Greenwich, NY in Fairview, Iowa July 31, 1854

HUNT Mrs. Nancy age 68y wife of William formerly of Argyle, NY at son-in-laws Peter BAIN in Fairview, Iowa August 5, 1854

DWELLE Abner age 43y formerly of Greenwich, NY in Onondaga Co. NY August 19, 1854

WHIPPLE Herman C. age 1y 1m son of Job T. and Maria in Greenwich, NY September 8, 1854

THOMPSON Margaret age 8y 2m 13d dau of Andrew and Eliza in Jackson, NY September 8, 1854

BAILEY Mrs. Nancy in Greenwich, NY September 12, 1854

KENYON Mrs. Eliza abt 36y wife of Solomon in Greenwich, NY September 10, 1854

HYATT widow of Jacob formerly of Greenwich in Hoosick, NY September 11, 1854

WADE Thomas age 25y in Greenwich, NY September 14, 1854

MANYARD Elizabeth (colored) age 10y 4m dau of John and Sarah in Greenwich, NY October 2, 1854

HOLMES Charles Henry age 21y son of Henry in Greenwich, NY October 9, 1854

CRANDALL Edward in his 3rd yr formerly of Greenwich, NY in Greenfield, NY October 9, 1854

TEFFT Jennie age 1y 9m dau of Simeon B. formerly of Greenwich, NY in Fairfield, Iowa September 1, 1854

MC FARLAND Robert age 25y son of Daniel in Jackson, NY September 27, 1854

DEAN Joel age 80y in Cambridge, NY October 11, 1854

STEEL Rev. Henry age 80y in Galesville, NY October 18, 1854

DENNIS Charles age 78y in Galesville, NY October 19, 1854

HARWOOD Fanny wife of Rev. J. Harwood formerly of the Troy Conference in Meigs Co. Ohio October 3, 1854 and dau Fanny A. age 18y died July 31, 1854

WADE Sarah Jane age 16y in N. Greenwich, NY October 29, 1854

HOLLISTER Caroline M. in her 25th yr in Easton, NY October 23, 1854

WILLIAMS Mrs. ____ age 90y in Battenville, NY November 19, 1854

EPPS Walter Kelly age 9m 4d son of John and Eliza in Greenwich, NY November 25, 1854

WATERS Ziba W. in her 62nd yr formerly of Greenwich, NY at son-in-laws James V. **PARKER** in W. Bloomfield, Clinton Co. NY October 16, 1854

WOODS Capt. William age 32y formerly of Cambridge, NY in Earlville, Ill. November __, 1854

TEFFT Ruhama age 85y widow of David at son-in-laws Capt. Lyman **WOODARD** in Battenville, NY December 13, 1854

ARCHIBALD John Robert age 18y formerly of Greenwich, NY in Chelsea, Mass. September 30, 1854

BURDICK Rozella age 45y wife of Willard in Greenwich, NY December 23, 1854

GILSON Otis in his 55th yr in Battenville, NY January 7, 1854

BAKER Jonathan in his 49th yr in Greenwich, NY December 3, 1854

HILL Nancy age 84y in Cambridge, NY January 14, 1855. Names son Peter

CRANDALL Dr. Simeon F. age 56y in Greenwich, NY January 30, 1855

TEFFT James age 79y formerly of Easton, NY in Eden, NY January 17, 1855

SALTER Charles age 4y son of John and Priscilla in Jackson, NY February 13, 1855

TOBEY Elizabeth in her 32nd yr wife of Henry M. and dau of Abram **BURREL** in Greenwich, NY February 11, 1855

THOMPSON Jennett age 31y wife of James in Jackson, NY February 18, 1855

LOCKWOOD Mrs. ____ abt 65y in Greenwich, NY March 5, 1855

ROGERS Bronson age 41y in Greenwich, NY March 26, 1855

BROWNELL Pernel age 33y dau of George of Easton, NY in Cambridge, NY March 20, 1854

ROBINSON Amos age 71y formerly of Greenwich, NY in Niagara Co. NY recently (newspaper date March 29, 1855)

TEFFT Elizabeth age 87y relict of William in Greenwich, NY April 8, 1855

FREEMAN Croesa (colored) age 76y in Greenwich, NY April 9, 1855. Born September 14, 1778 in Lyme, Conn.

LANGWORTHY Harriet age 33y wife of Sanford in Jackson, NY April 1, 1855

SHILAND David age 43y in Cambridge, NY March 15, 1855

GREEN John abt 72y in Cambridge, NY March 22, 1855

STILES Susannah R. in her 18th yr dau of Ransom in Argyle, NY April 14, 1855

HANNA Mary Ann age 42y wife of Robert in Salem, NY March 17, 1855

CRANDALL Uberto age 5m son of Thomas and Elizabeth in Greenwich, NY April 30, 1855

WHIPPLE Welcome age 51y in Greenwich, NY May 9, 1855

BULLIONS Mary wife of Rev. Alexander in Coila, NY April 30, 1855

LEWIS Green R. age 49y in Galesville, NY May 2, 1855

YOUNG Mary R. age 2y 3m 13d dau of Zadoc and Nancy in Easton, NY May 2, 1855

ARCHER Margaret in her 76th yr in Cambridge, NY April 12, 1855

ARNOTT Sarah B. age 33y wife of William in Jackson, NY May 9/10, 1855

FISHER Mrs. Delight in her 85th yr at Ash Grove, NY May 13, 1855

COOK Mary in her 30th yr wife of Cortland C. and dau of Hiram **CORLISS** in Greenwich, NY May 29, 1855

WHIPPLE Miss Ruth age 62y in Greenwich, NY June 2, 1855

WARREN Hiram abt 53y in Hustisford, Wis. May 15, 1855

MC KINNEY Elizabeth in her 71st yr at dau in Saratoga Co. NY May 16, 1855

MILLER Margaret Cornelia age 17y dau of Robert I. and Eliza in Cambridge, NY May 24, 1855

BURDICK Caroline L. age 34y in Granville, NY May 26, 1855

SEARLE Josephine in her 5th yr dau of Samuel T. and Cornelia F. of Schuylerville, NY in Key Port, NJ (newspaper date June 21, 1855)

CLARK Rusha age 37y wife of Aaron formerly Washington Co. in Racine, Wis. May 28, 1855

FROST Roxanna W. age 58y wife of Daniel formerly of Green Co. in N. Orange, Mass. June 30, 1855

BIGELOW Erastus age 91y in Greenwich, NY July 15, 1855

HILL Alexander age 49y in Cambridge, NY July 15, 1855

GARDEPHE Modest age 31y in Greenwich, NY July 31, 1855

POTTER Thomas age 24y in Galesville, NY July 27, 1855

REMINGTON Hannah age 28y wife of Morgan in Galesville, NY August 2, 1855

WALMARTH Betsey age 46y wife of Bela in Greenwich, NY August 27, 1855

MC KALLOR Virginia M. widow of Archibald of Argyle, NY in Galloway, Ill. August/September 3, 1855

CHICHESTER Rev. Elijah in his 78th yr in Lansingburgh, NY August 28, 1855

COFFIN Benjamin age 79y in Easton, NY September 7, 1855

ROBINSON Sally Taylor age 63y formerly of Thompson, Conn. at son-in-laws George **FORBUSH** in Greenwich, NY September 21, 1855

SPENCER Elenora age 26y in Greenwich, NY September 22, 1855

WELCH Charles age 21y son of David in Battenville, NY September 22, 1855

DAYTON Roxanna age 59y relict of Mulford in Granville, NY October 2, 1855

WRIGHT David in his 23rd yr son of John F. in Greenwich, NY October 19, 1855

FROST Ezra age 80y formerly of Washington Co. in Hoosick Falls, NY October 19, 1855

WHELDON Harriet age 20y wife of Francis J. in Easton, NY October 25, 1855

DINGS Abram in his 81st yr in Argyle, NY October 19, 1855

WILMARTH Louisa wife of Thomas formerly of Greenwich, NY in Hartland, Vt. recently (newspaper date November 1, 1855)

BURROUGHS John age 56y formerly of Cambridge, NY in Belvedere, Ill. October 25, 1855

ARNOLD Sophia M. age 18y in Greenwich, NY October 26, 1855

EGGLESTON Elizabeth wife of Horace in Schenectady, NY November 26, 1855

FULLER Henry age 56y in Greenwich, NY December 26, 1855

SHEARER Ruth age 63y at sons James L. **DAVIDSON** in Greenwich, NY December 19, 1855

ROSS Thomas age 73y in Greenwich, NY January 5, 1856

ROOD Mrs. Mercy in her 56th yr in Greenwich, NY January 6, 1856

MC CLELLAN Chester age 45y in Jackson, NY January 24, 1856

ANTHONY William (colored) age 36 in Greenwich, NY February 9, 1856

COON Rufus age 78y in Salem, NY January 21, 1856

GETTY Isaac age 86y in Salem, NY February 9, 1856

BEEBE William age 26y in Salem, NY January 30, 1856

MANNING James E. age 28y in Greenwich, NY February 18, 1856

BURNETT Robert in his 55th yr in Blissfield, Miss. February 6, 1856 and Jane Burnett age 18y in Blissfield August 19, 1855

AUSTIN Edmund age 48y in Whitehall, NY February 23, 1856

FONDA Jacob D. age 62y formerly of Greenwich, NY in Schaghticoke, NY March

3, 1856

BUGBEE William age 70y in Granville, NY March 8, 1856 and wife Sophia formerly of Ft. Miller, NY in Granville March 10, 1856

CORNELL Gideon age 67y in Greenwich, NY March 25, 1856

RICHARDS Ingraham age 43y in Easton, NY March 25, 1856

BENNETT Nancy age 52y wife of Benjamin in Greenwich, NY April 1, 1856

HEMSTREET Orly A. son of Alonzo and Elizabeth M. in Cambridge, NY March 28, 1856

RATHBONE Patience age 88y at dau Mrs. Ann **BROWNELL** in Easton, NY March 23, 1856

STEVENSON Mary age 76y widow of Thomas in Salem, NY March 24, 1856

BEATTIE Thomas age 76y in Salem, NY March 29, 1856

TIMMERMAN Mrs. E. age 80y at sons Stephen in S. Argyle, NY April 8, 1856

MARSHALL Deborah age 22y wife of Alexander and dau of Nathan **CRANDALL** in Greenwich, NY April 13, 1856

HAWLEY Sally in her 70th yr wife of Joseph in Salem, NY April 14, 1856

STEWART Caroline age 13y dau of James and Elmira in N. Argyle, NY April 7, 1856 and dau Mary Helen age 17y died April 3, 1856

MC NAB Katherine abt 23y dau of Andrew and Janet in Greenwich, NY February 1, 1856

HUTTON Margaret age 78y in Greenwich, NY April 17, 1856

OWEN Jacob formerly of Greenwich, NY in Rutland, Vt. April 27, 1856

MARTIN Jane age 8y 5m dau of A. B. and S. B. **LAMBERT** in Salem, NY April 18, 1856

ROUSE William H. age 51y in Argyle, NY April 4, 1856

CLARK Thomas N. age 79y son of Ebenezer in Argyle, NY April 19, 1856

GRAY Mrs. Catherine age 35y dau of late William F. formerly of Salem, NY in Philadelphia, Pa. April 8, 1856

HEGEMAN William in Easton, NY May 7, 1856

CHURCH Lydia age 102 yrs in the County Poor House May 6, 1856

MOTT John R. in his 71st yr in Schuylerville, NY May 14, 1856

WHELDON Mrs. Lucy in her 70th yr at Victory, NY May 12, 1856

TURNER James formerly of Salem, NY in Sandgate, Vt. May 15, 1856

BENTLEY Nathaniel age 61y in the County Poor House May 14, 1856

RICE Ann Eliza age 17y dau of Harvey and Sarah in Jackson, NY May 11, 1856

FITCH Lucinda in her 68th yr relict of William in Salem, NY May 21, 1856

BEATY David in his 68th yr in Salem, NY May 26, 1856

STEWART Alexander in his 26th yr formerly of Lake, NY in Hasting, Minn. May 23, 1856

NOYES Hannah T. in her 67th yr wife of William in Greenwich, NY June 16, 1856

JONES Carlos D. in New York City June 17, 1856

FLETCHER Simeon age 64y in Greenwich, NY June 30, 1856

HASTINGS Lydia Louisa in her 13th yr in Salem, NY June 21, 1856

CARTER Charles age 4y 4m son of Col. Andrew and Eliza **(THOMPSON)** in Easton, NY June 30, 1856

BRYANT James age 35y formerly of Greenwich, NY in Arlington, Vt. July 20, 1856

ROOT George 1y 10m 11d son of Henry and Mary Jane in Easton, NY July 22, 1856

WASHBURN Charles age 9y 10m son of Lewis in Galesville, NY August 1, 1856

PEABODY Almira S. age 52y wife of Charles in N. Pownel, Vt. July 10, 1856

ALLEN Caroline S. in her 49th yr wife of Dr. George in Salem, NY August 4, 1856

FENTON Herbert Duane age 4y 6m son of Calvin and Harriet in Greenwich, NY August 19, 1856

HERRINGTON Almira age 11y dau of Bently in Easton, NY August 17, 1856

STEELE Margaret abt 60y wife of William in Salem, NY August 14, 1856

THOMPSON Seth A. age 48y formerly of Washington Co. in Samanouk, Ill. July 10, 1856

DENNIS Mrs. Edward in Galesville, NY September 8, 1856

HYATT Deborah in her 50th yr widow of James K. of Battenville, NY in Battle Creek, Mi. August 21, 1856

CHEESEBRO Emeline age 39y in Greenwich, NY September 27, 1856

KNAPP Polly E. age 70y Mother of A. H. Knapp of Greenwich, NY in Brooklyn, NY September 27, 1856

WILLIAMS Matilda M. in 20th yr wife of C. H. C. and dau of John and Eliza A. LEE of Greenwich, NY in New York October 16, 1856

ROGERS Julia age 44y wife of Harvey J. in Galesville, NY October 20, 1856

SEYMOUR James H. age 64y formerly of Salem, NY in Napaneck, Ulster Co. NY October 15, 1856. Leaves dau Mrs. Elsie **ARCHIBALD** of Greenwich, NY

CRANDALL Simeon age 44y in Easton, NY November 9, 1856

BOSWORTH Elizabeth age 40y wife of Robert in Hartford, NY November 2, 1856

ROTCH Hannah age 30y wife of William in Easton, NY October 23, 1856

MC WHORTER Alexander age 66y in W. Hebron, NY October 29, 1856

WILSON James B. age 32y in W. Hebron, NY October 26, 1856

ROTCH William Henry in his 40th yr in Salem, NY October 29, 1856

SAFFORD Jacob age 42y in Greenwich, NY December 1, 1856

CULVER Eunice age 75y 8m widow of Rev. Phineas in Burlington, Vt. November 20, 1856

WILCOX Ella Tryphena age 6m dau of Hiram K. and Sarah F. in Easton, NY December 2, 1856

GRANDY Roswell age 25y formerly of Greenwich, NY in Keesville, NY November 16, 1856

ALLEN Gilbert age 72y in M. Granville, NY December 12, 1856

ALLEN Mrs. Sarah age 63y in M. Granville December 15, 1856

HAMMOND Fred F. age 23y in Greenwich, NY November 30, 1856

SMART Mary Ann in her 38th yr wife of Peter in Hebron, NY December 30, 1856

BEATTIE Mary age 42y wife of Thomas in Hebron, NY December 19, 1856

SMALLEY Esther age 70y wife of John F. formerly of Salem, NY in Hebron, NY January 2, 1857

HILL Albert age 5y son of Gurnham and Eunice in Jackson, NY December 25, 1856

LEE Eliza in her 51st yr wife of John in Greenwich, NY January 8, 1857

LARKIN Clarissa in her 70th yr wife of John in Salem, NY January 7, 1857

EARLEY Clementine in her 34th yr wife of George W. and dau of Col. William **HENRY** of Greenwich, NY in Algonquin, Ill. December 4, 1856

DELAVARGE Dorus age 69y in Easton, NY January 13, 1857

SHAW Daniel age 74y in Galesville, NY January 16, 1857

YOULEN Thomas age 20y son of Benjamin and Rachel in Salem, NY January 13, 1857

HURD Polly in her 53rd yr wife of Humphrey in Rupert, Vt. January 5, 1857

ROGERS Dr. Heman age 70y formerly of Washington Co. in Dunn, Wis. December 25, 1856

MC GEOCH John near Lakeville, NY January 14, 1857

BEATTIE Thomas in his 65th yr in Salem, NY January 24, 1857

MC NEIL Robert in Cambridge, NY January 20, 1857, born February 26, 1789 in Argyle, NY

CLEVELAND Margaret age 37y dau of Aaron in Salem, NY January 30, 1857

GRAY Anson age 44y formerly of Salem, NY in Philadelphia, Pa. January 22, 1857

MARSTON Anna wife of William and dau of Jesse K. **MANNING** in Troy, NY last week (newspaper date February 12, 1857)

PALMER John age 74y in Cambridge, NY January 31, 1857

HURD Carrie A. age 6y 8m dau of Hopson and Martha in Cleveland, Ohio February 2, 1857

STONE Ethan age 68y in Manchester, Vt. February 2, 1857

SHERWOOD Eulalie age 2y 10m 11d dau of Darius and Sarah in Greenwich, NY February 6, 1857

THOMPSON Hannah age 78y in Jackson, NY February 19, 1857. Leaves two sons Col. Andrew and James

NILES Catherine in her 73rd yr widow of Elisha in Easton, NY January 28, 1857

MILLER Charles age 2y 8m son of William and Elizabeth and grand son of William **MC ADOO** in Greenwich, NY February 23, 1857

WEEKS Thomas age 25y in Greenwich, NY March 10, 1857

GREELEY Raphael Cilland age 64y 12d only remaining son of Horace and Mary Y. C. Greeley in New York February 28, 1857

MAXWELL Jennett age 88y in Jackson, NY March 17, 1857, from Scotland 1784

HARRIS Amos age 65y in Salem, NY (newspaper date March 19, 1857)

SHEFFIELD Joseph age 74y in Greenwich, NY March 14, 1857

SHEPHERD Rebecca age 77y wife of Prentiss in Greenwich, NY March 30, 1857

WOODARD Nancy age 50y wife of Lyman in Battenville, NY April 14, 1857

THOMPSON David T. age 59y formerly of Salem, NY in Blue Earth Co. Minn. March 22, 1857

SAFFORD William age 59y in Greenwich, NY April 17, 1857

LUNDY William in his 73rd yr in Argyle, NY April 10, 1857

LYNCH Miss Ellen age 29y in White Creek, NY April 6/8, 1857

RICE Joseph M. in his 26th yr only son of Harvey in Jackson, NY March 21, 1857

MINER Mary C. in her 26th yr wife of C. S. Miner Jr. and dau of Col. E. W. **CLAPP** in Jackson, NY April 3, 1857

ADAMS Elizabeth age 75y wife of Hosea in Greenwich, NY April 29, 1857

PEALING John age 43 in Greenwich, NY May 3, 1857

SHELDON Mary in her 72nd yr wife of Thomas in W. Rupert, Vt. May 10, 1857

WILCOX Cortes age 45y in Greenwich, NY May 13, 1857

BROWN Mrs. Amy abt 80y in Greenwich, NY May 21, 1857

LEE Mary Jane age 27y in Greenwich, NY May 23, 1857

SHERMAN John T. age 1y 10m son of Caleb and Caroline in Greenwich, NY May 20, 1857

BENNETT _____ age 3m son of Benjamin and Laura in Greenwich, NY May 22, 1857

MOREY Jonathan in his 67th yr in Cambridge, NY May 20, 1857

REYNOLDS Livona N. age 27y dau of Nahum and Lydia in Galesville, NY May 25, 1857

POLLARD Miss Susan in her 65th yr in Galesville, NY June 1, 1857

MILLIMAN N. B. Jr. age 2y in Argyle, NY May 9, 1857

ROGERS Mary age 48y in Hebron, NY May 31, 1857

GUILD Martha D. C. in her 83rd yr Mother of C. C. **COOK** in Greenwich, NY June 16, 1857

STONE Col. Reuben age 87y in Greenwich, NY June 13, 1857

TEFFT Mrs. Nancy age 74y in Galesville, NY June 14, 1857

DENNIS John age 73y in Cambridge, NY June 12, 1857

MIX Phebe age 71y wife of Joseph in Greenwich, NY June 19, 1857

ALLEN Joseph in his 60th yr in Greenwich, NY June 27, 1857

FLETCHER Miss Frances B. in Greenwich, NY June 19, 1857

CLAPP Jane in her 71st yr wife of Stephen in Salem, NY July 13, 1857

HARSHA John in his 73rd yr in S. Argyle, NY June 28, 1857

HOWE Luther J. in White Creek, NY August 9, 1857

RICHARDS Thomas in his 66th yr in Greenwich, NY August 15, 1857

PATTERSON Robert in his 87th yr in Putnam, NY August 18, 1857

FRENCH Benjamin in his 79th yr in Putnam, NY August 20, 1857

KING John age 12y 8m 25d son of William H. and C. J. in Argyle, NY August 9, 1857

FIELDING John age 59y in Galesville, NY September 3, 1857

FISK Olin age 5y 4m 6d son of Rev. J. Fisk and E. **PHILLIPS** in N. White Creek, NY August 30, 1857

AUSTIN Elizabeth in her 31st yr dau of Abner and Susan in Salem, NY September 7, 1857

BREWER John Henry age 16m died September 11, 1857 and Julia age 5m 11d died

September 21, 1857, children of Leroy and Manima of Greenwich, NY

SCHERMERHORN Willie F. age 6m 10d son of Charles and Jenny in Luzerne, NY September 2, 1857

CONLEE James age 89y in Greenwich, NY October 7, 1857

WHIPPLE Maria wife of Job T. in Deerpark, NY October 1, 1857

MOWRY ____ son of William P. and Elizabeth in Greenwich, NY September 4, 1857

HOGABOOM Jacob age 77y in Greenwich, NY September 11, 1857

GARDEPHE Mrs. Caroline age 28y in Greenwich, NY October 17, 1857

ARCHIBALD Harvey S. age 24y in Greenwich, NY October 23, 1857

RUSSELL Clarissa age 42y wife of William A. in Salem, NY October 21, 1857

HENRY Miss Ann in her 23/33rd yr formerly of Greenwich, NY in Saratoga Springs, NY October 28, 1857 (one issue gives age as 23rd yr and one gives 33rd yr)

BARBER Daniel age 33y in Centre Falls, NY November 6, 1857

REED Charles in his 16th yr son of Owen in Centre Falls, NY November 8, 1857

WOODS Andrew age 37y in Cambridge, NY November 8, 1857

ROBINSON Robert C. age 42y formerly of Greenwich, NY in Pittsfield, Mass. November 5, 1857

YOUNG Clayton age 57y in Easton, NY November 25, 1857

JAMES Judith in her 83rd yr widow of Joseph in Cambridge, NY November 13, 1857

CORNELL Deborah age 35y wife of Charles and dau of Roderick **BEEBE** of Salem, NY in Easton, NY November 15, 1857

LEE Thomas age 27y in Greenwich, NY November 29, 1857

DUNLAP Barberry J. age 53y wife of Peter in Easton, NY November 26, 1857

MARTIN Lansing age 49y formerly of Salem, NY in Rockford, Ill. November 8, 1857

HARTSHORN Jedidiah age 73y in Greenwich, NY November 27, 1857

ROBINSON Martha widow of Gen. Henry of Bennington, Vt. in Troy, NY November 29, 1857

WHITE Mary A. age 28y 6m wife of Thomas formerly of Greenwich, NY in New

York December 1, 1857

ARCHIBALD David T. age 49y in Salem, NY Decemer 5, 1857

BARBER Alpheus age 83y in Greenwich, NY January 10, 1858

SMALL Eleanor L. age 48y wife of James E. in Cambridge, NY December 31, 1857

DEUEL Mary H. wife of Derastus formerly of Cambridge, NY at Ft. Covington, NY December 31, 1857

SCOTT Peter abt 55y in White Creek, NY January 2, 1858

RUGGLES Mrs. ___ age 91y 3m Mother of Ruel at Ft. Edward, NY January 3, 1858

GRAY Rebecca P. wife of David and sis of Rev. Dr. **LAMBERT** of Salem, NY in Salem February 3, 1858

MC DOUGAL Miss Maria in her 77th yr in Greenwich, NY February 7, 1858

GRAHAM Ann age 19y 3m dau of John and Susan in Putnam, NY February 12, 1858

LARABEE Benjamin in Easton, NY February 6, 1858

ANTHONY Jesse in his 66th yr late of Easton, NY in Troy, NY February 16, 1858

PREO Mary Melissa age 1y 4m 18d dau of John and Mary in Easton, NY February 27, 1858 and dau Ida May age 1y 5m died March 21, 1858

FARNHAM Louisa C. in her 55th yr dau of Justin formerly of Salem, NY in Chatham, NY February 11, 1858

CHAMBERS Florence age 1y 2m dau of Thomas and Hannah in Greenwich, NY March 4, 1858

GILBERT Jeduthan in his 94th yr in Centre Falls, NY March 5, 1858

WHITNEY Jane in her 40th yr wife of Isaac in Mequoketa, Iowa March 8, 1858

COWAN Ann Eliza age 26y wife of Charles H. and dau of late Dr. Archibald **MC ALLISTER** of Salem, NY in Buffalo, NY March 14, 1858. Buried in Salem

MARTIN George C. in his 50th yr in Jackson, NY February 26, 1858

SAFFORD Agnes Cornelia age 3m 10d dau of Gideon F. and Sarah in Salem, NY March 1, 1858

HENRY Mrs. ____ age 92y in Argyle, NY March 28, 1858

KING Charles Joseph age 2y 3m son of Joseph and Mary in Ft. Edward, NY March

25, 1858

REYNOLDS John P. age 76y formerly of Washington Co. in Hamilton, Ohio March 27, 1858

QUACKENBUSH Lucy Jane wife of John W. and dau of Joseph **WALKER** of Saratoga, NY in Easton, NY April 10, 1858

WHIPPLE Hiram age 40y son of Daniel formerly of Greenwich, NY in Quincy, Ill. March 22, 1858

RUSSELL Derrick C. age 30y of Salem, NY in Houston, Texas April 1, 1858

MOSHER Phillip age 33y in Easton, NY April 20, 1858

TILTON Ephraim in his 89th yr in Greenwich, NY May 10, 1858

POTTER Mrs. Sarah abt 80y in Cambridge, NY May 10, 1858

WHEELOCK Solomon B. age 40y formerly of Washington Co. in Springfield, Ill. May 3, 1858

PROUDFIT Mary in her 91st yr widow of Dr. Andrew in Argyle, NY May 22, 1858.

HILLMAN Mary Jane age 17y dau of George and Chloe in Greenwich, NY May 29, 1858

KNAPP Edwin Rush age 1y 1m 8d son of Henry I. and Julia Ann in Greenwich, NY May 21, 1858

CORLISS Almy H. age 54y wife of Dr. Hiram in Greenwich, NY June 5, 1858. Native of New Medford, Mass.

ALLEN Clementine age 59y at sons William C. in Greenwich, NY June 9, 1858

DENNIS Edward age 34y in Schuylerville, NY June 1, 1858

DURHAM Polly age 78y at sons Anson in Salem, NY June 6, 1858

HANNA Nancy in her 87th yr in Salem, NY June 2, 1858

MC LEAN Henry R. age 56y in Jackson, NY July 5, 1858

RATHBONE Kinyon in Easton, NY July 19, 1858

PETTEYS Permelia Ann age 5m dau of Ephraim and Elizabeth in Cambridge, NY July 7, 1858

COON Charles age 1y 2m son of James S. and Jane C. in Argyle, NY July 12, 1858

MADDEN Mary C. age 1y 2m 2d dau of Boyd and Margaret in Argyle, NY July 18, 1858

MILLER David in his 55th yr in Greenwich, NY July 24, 1858

BENNETT Welthy in her 89th yr in Greenwich, NY July 26, 1858

CURTIS Philo age 75y 2m 10d formerly of Salem in Greenwich, NY August 1, 1858

BARBER Nellie age 80y relict of Edward in Brooklyn, NY July 31, 1858. Buried Greenwich

DEWEY Caroline age 36y dau of Benjamin BARBER in E. Poultney, Vt. July 26, 1858

DICKINSON Matilda age 55y 5m at son-in-laws Alexander GIFFORD in Argyle, NY August 9, 1858

ATWOOD Silas in his 61st yr in Salem, NY August 5, 1858

SANTEE Fanny A. in her 9th yr in Greenwich, NY August 13, 1858

WILCOX Daniel age 65y in Greenwich, NY August 16, 1858

BARBER Ann age 25y wife of Thomas late of Greenwich, NY in Rutland, Vt. August 15, 1858. Buried in Greenwich

HORTON Elizabeth (TICE) age 77y relict of Jonathan in Greenwich, NY August 22, 1858. Born Tarrytown, NY. Leaves son H. V. of Cincinnati, Ohio

MILLER Mararet M. in her 22nd yr in Jackson, NY August 16, 1858

FLETCHER Horace B. in his 31st yr in Schuylerville, NY August 22, 1858

KNAPP Emma Estella age 4m 10d dau of Henry and Jerusha in Greenwich, NY August 28, 1858

WILLIAMS Betsey age 78y wife of Stephen B. in Easton, NY September 10, 1858

HAWLEY Joseph in his 84th yr in Salem, NY September 13, 1858

REID William in his 24th yr in Argyle, NY September 5, 1858 and Anna Margaret in her 17th yr, children of Alexander and Ann

BROWN Ann W. age 39y in Jackson, NY September 11, 1858

CHAPIN John age 41y in N. Easton, NY September 26, 1858

STONE Reuben Franklin age 47y formerly of Greenwich and Jackson, NY in Racine, Wis. October 7, 1858

RITTER Mrs. Charlotte C. age 29y 11m 9d dau of James S. **HAWLEY** in Troy, NY October 13, 1858

ROGERS Charles Henry age 3y 9m died September 24, 1858 and Mary Frances age 9y 8m died October 12, 1858 in Alexandria, Va. children of James S. and Amanda M.

WYLIE Margaret age 27 wife of James in Greenwich, NY November 29, 1858 and dau Margaret age 1w 6d died November 2, 1858

BASSETT Mary age 24y wife of William in Greenwich, NY November 6, 1858

MILLER Martha abt 60y in Jackson, NY November 20, 1858

SEYMOUR Alvira age 61y wife of Isaac N. in New York November 25, 1858

GLOVER Mereb E. age 26y wife of Charles B. in Orangeburg, SC December 1, 1858

RANDALL Chandler age 36y formerly of Greenwich, NY in San Jose, Cal. October 8, 1858

TABER Mary abt 25y in Greenwich, NY December 27, 1858

WHALEY James age 73y in Greenwich, NY January 4, 1859

PECK Seth in his 80th yr in Hampton, NY December 5, 1858

WOODWORTH Martha L. in her 29th yr wife of George W. formerly of Salem, NY in Cleveland, Ohio January 10, 1859

BLANCHARD Mrs. Susannah in her 19th yr in Salem, NY January 19, 1859

SEAVER Martha J. in her 33rd yr wife of Julius and dau of James **HERRON** formerly of Hebron, NY in Darien, Wis. January 17, 1859

HARVEY Mary in her 90th yr widow of Maj. James in Salem, NY January 20, 1859

SPRAGUE Lucy in her 37th yr in Salem, NY January 26, 1859

BREWER Lucy age 23y wife of William in Greenwich, NY February 6, 1859

DAVIS James W. in his 29th yr in Lansingburgh, NY January 28, 1859

GUILD Jane M. in her 29th yr wife of J. Henry and dau of Nathan **BURTON** in Rupert, Vt. February 1, 1859

STEWART Caroline age 14y dau of Walter G. and Eunice in Greenwich, NY February 16, 1859

NEWTON Adelia abt 40y wife of Lorenzo D. in Ft. Edward, NY February 3, 1859

THORPE Susan age 74y in Greenwich, NY February 24, 1859

HOYSRADT Matilda D. age 23y wife of H. W. in Ft. Edward, NY February 15, 1859

BLAKELEY Warren age 29y in Greenwich, NY February 27, 1859

HARKNESS Jane age 76y widow of Daniel in Salem, NY December 12, 1858

STEWART Annie Mary age 4y dau of John and Ann in Greenwich, NY March 16, 1859

INGALLS Augusta age 23y wife of D. L. in Salem, NY March 13, 1859

MC MILLAN Elizabeth in her 67th yr wife of John in Salem, NY March 27, 1859

MORSE Elvira age 60y at son-in-laws Norman T. **ANDREWS** in Greenwich, NY April 6, 1859

PLACE Susannah age 75y 10m wife of Godfrey in Greenwich, NY March 25, 1859

SHELDON Miss Mary in her 90th yr in Troy, NY March 28, 1859

WILLIS Caleb age 92y formerly of Greenwich, NY in Palermo, NY March 31, 1859

ROGERS Mrs. Deloss age 39y in Victory, Saratoga Co. NY April 5, 1859

TAYLOR Sarah M. age 32y wife of James M. and dau of Prentiss **SHEPHERD** formerly of Greenwich, NY in San Francisco, Cal. March 12, 1859

GILLIS Cornelia M. age 10y dau of George in Argyle, NY April 10, 1859

GILMAN Osceola B. son of Dr. O. P. Gillman in Salem, NY April 14, 1859

FITCH Ida Myra dau of Charles L. and Cynthia in Cambridge, NY March 28, 1859

ALMY Mrs. _____ age 91y in Greenwich, NY April 18, 1859

ROBINSON Mary Elizabeth age 14m 4d dau of B. F. and Catherine in Salem, NY April 5, 1859

ROBERTSON James abt 80y formerly of Jackson in Spafford, NY February 26, 1859

MC MILLAN Mrs. Elizabeth age 66y in Hebron, NY March 28, 1859

MC ARTHUR Rev. James son of Peter in Jackson, NY April 15, 1859

POTTER James in Galesville, NY May 9, 1859

MEAD James age 9m son of James and Irene in Easton, NY May 30, 1859

THORN John age 15y son of S. B. and C. A. at Bald Mountain, NY May 27, 1859

VAN VECHTEN Hermon in his 88th yr in Schuylerville, NY May 26, 1859

WATERS Edwin S. age 33y formerly of Greenwich, NY in Mequoketa, Iowa May 28, 1859

REYNOLDS Kittie P. age 3y 2m dau of Hiram and Margaret Ann in Easton, NY June 2, 1859

SHERWOOD Darius J. in his 31st yr in Greenwich, NY June 17, 1859

WILBUR Esther wife of Job in Easton, NY June 23, 1859

JOHNSON Sarah age 53y wife of Chauncey P. in Greenwich, NY June 29, 1859

CAPEN Eleanor **RANDALL** age 33y wife of John L. formerly of Greenwich, NY in Philadelphia, Pa. July 9, 1859

WHITE Amasa S. age 74y in Freeport, Ill. June 24, 1859

HOWARD Archibald in Battenville, NY July 8, 1859

MOWRY Kate Noyes age 8y 7m dau of Leroy and Catherine in Greenwich, NY July 28, 1859

FORSYTHE Joseph Md. age 27y 4m in Salem, NY July 23, 1859

BENNETT Samuel age 80y in Greenwich, NY August 20, 1859

MC FARLAND Martha age 35y wife of Abner in Greenwich, NY August 22, 1859

COLE Sarah age 62y widow of Benjamin in Salem, NY August 23, 1859

STEWART Cora M. age 7m 3d dau of John and Clementine in Greenwich, NY September 10, 1859

MC NEIL William in his 61st yr in E. Greenwich, NY September 12, 1859

CLARK Cordelia abt 40y wife of John W. in Argyle, NY September 10, 1859

STEWART George in his 74th yr in Greenwich, NY September 15, 1859

NEWBURY Jane E. age 39y yr wife of James R. in Galesville, NY September 17, 1859

LONG Mrs. Meribah T. age 50y in Greenwich, NY September 25, 1859

TAYLOR Delia age 25y wife of D. W. and dau of James A. **WHIPPLE** of Greenwich, NY in Ft. Edward, NY September 25, 1859

CROSBY Watson age 83y in Brattleboro, Vt. September 24, 1859

ARMSTRONG Thomas R. age 1y 10m son of Archibald and Mary in Argyle, NY September 16, 1859

STOVER Melissa age 8y 11m died October 22, 1859 and Minerva age 7y 1m 8d died October 23, 1859, children of Rev. Ensign Stover of Albany, NY

COLE Sarah in her 17th yr dau of late David T. ARCHIBALD in Salem, NY October 18, 1859

WALES Henry N. age 50y in Schaghticoke, NY October 16, 1859

EASTON Eliza Ott wife of Alton H. formerly of Albany, NY in St. Louis, Mo. October 13, 1859

SCOTT Dr. John B. in his 40th yr formerly of Greenwich, NY in Rupert, Vt. October 27, 1859

GRAVES Mary age 19y dau of H. N. and E. L. in Granville, NY October 24, 1859

HYDE Benjamin in his 81st yr formerly of Washington Co. in Dunkirk, NY November 9, 1859

CROSBY Almira age 41y wife of Dr. J. B. in Greenwich, NY November 22, 1859

WILLARD Eliza C. age 65y wife of John in Saratoga, NY November 25, 1859

HEATH Sidney age 69y formerly of Greenwich in Henry Co. Ill. October 19, 1859

BATES Merritt age 22y son of Rev. M. in N. White Creek, NY January 6, 1860

EVANS William age 61y in Greenwich, NY December 21, 1859

LA POINTE Rozilla age 26y wife of Octavus in Greenwich, NY January 29, 1860

WENDELL Clarence L. age 25y of Bald Mountain, NY at Fathers in Charlton, NY January 25, 1860

HYDE Lois age 77y widow of Benjamin in S. Hartford, NY January 27, 1860

FRANKLIN Laura Ann age 13y dau of William B. and Ann in Galesville, NY January 16, 1860

MC INTOSH Alexander abt 80y in Salem, NY January 21, 1860

BROUGHTON Elizabeth in her 33rd yr in Granville, NY January 23, 1860

CARSWELL George P. age 3y son of William J. drowned in Hudson River near Ft. Edward, NY January 28, 1860

MC CAY James age 32y formerly of Glascow, Scot. in Greenwich, NY February 27, 1860

TUBBS Simeon age 84y 11m 4d formerly of Easton in Wilton, NY February 17, 1860

ANDREWS Jane age 36y wife of N. T. in Greenwich, NY March 5, 1860

FISK Mary Emmons age 40y wife of Warren and dau of William E. BURNHAM of Greenwich, NY in Hoosick Falls, NY February 29, 1860

STEVENSON William age 54y son of late William in Cambridge, NY February 18, 1860. Names brother James M.

CHURCH Mary age 21y died January 25, 1860 and Delia age 18y died February 25, 1860 daughters of Mrs. Mary Church in Ft. Ann, NY

WHIPPLE Munroe age 18m 28d son of Henry and Mary W. in Greenwich, NY March 18, 1860

TAYLOR Ann Eliza age 27y wife of H. R. of Apalachicola, Florida and dau of Rev. T. SEYMOUR of Waterford, NY in Troy, NY February 26, 1860

JACKSON Cobus age 113 yrs in Waterford, NY February 22, 1860

VANDERWARKER Lucy age 77y in Northumberland, NY March 13, 1860

DUNHAM Daniel in his 99th yr a Revolutionary Soldier formerly of Kingsbury, NY in Mexico, NY February 13, 1860

PARK Nathan F. age 65y formerly of Salem, NY in Jackson, NY March 18, 1860

BARDEN Hiram Austin age 19y 4m in Argyle, NY March 11, 1860

MURDOCK Russell age 16y son of Samuel in Salem, NY March 25, 1860

BARKER Amy T. age 59y wife of John in N. Granville, NY March 24, 1860

BURDICK Abbie A. age 28y wife of Rev. C. F. in Albany, NY March 23, 1860

BULLOCK Ephraim in his 89th yr in Greenwich, NY April 6, 1860

VAN VECHTEN Walter in his 81st yr in Schuylerville, NY April 1, 1860

MOBBS Adelaide (BLISS) age 27y wife of James F. and step dau of H. V. MIDDLEWORTH in Sandy Hill, NY March 28, 1860

DOUBLEDAY Catherine age 45y wife of Horace in Kingsbury, NY March 29, 1860

WILLIAMS Jerusha age 76y in Ft. Edward, NY March 28, 1860

EAGER Hattie age 1y 4m dau of Abram and Mary formerly of Washington Co. in Galesburg, Ill. March 24, 1860

DIBBLE Aseneth in her 82nd yr relict of Carmi in Sandy Hill, NY April 3, 1860

TENANT Huldah age 94y in Sandy Hill, NY April 3, 1860

MONAHAN John age 7m 13d son of Timothy and Lucy in Greenwich, NY April 15, 1860

OATLEY Ida L. age 5y dau of Albert and Jane in Greenwich, NY April 20, 1860

CAMPBELL Maria age 28y in Greenwich, NY May 2, 1860

BRITT Henry Warren age 4y son of Jerry and Mary Ann in Greenwich, NY May 7, 1860

KIMBALL William Herbert in his 8th yr son of E. W. and Julia A. in Ottawa, Ill. May 2, 1860

SPRAGUE Ann age 11y dau of Joseph in Salem, NY May 12, 1860

WALKER Polly age 74y wife of Warren formerly of Greenwich, NY in Victory, NY May 21, 1860

WILDER Arthur Tappan age 23y late of Greenwich, NY in N. Dixmont, Me. May 21, 1860

LOOKER Helen Augusta age 11y dau of Eleazor and Clarissa in Easton, NY May 24, 1860

TOMPKINS Eugene 1y 6m 3w 3d son of Liscom and Eliza Ann in Greenwich, NY June 8, 1860

TRUMAN John age 75y in Salem, NY June 3, 1860

SPRAGUE Horace formerly of Greenwich, NY in Amsterdam, NY rec. (newspaper date June 21, 1860)

CRANDALL David age 78y in Greenwich, NY June 16, 1860

COGSHALL David in his 76th yr in Malta, Saratoga Co. NY June 12, 1860

TEFFT Susan age 39y wife of Henry in Sandy Hill, NY June 12, 1860

JOHNSON Asa age 98y 11m 26d in White Creek, NY July 5, 1860

CARPENTER Elizabeth age 50y wife of Whipple in Greenwich, NY July 4, 1860

POTTER Joseph Boies age 6y 6m son of Joseph and Catherine in Greenwich, NY July

4, 1860

DE RIDDER Catherine A. age 52y widow of Henry in Easton, NY June 24, 1860

STONE Sarah (**BUCKINGHAM**) age 73y relict of Ethan of Arlington, Vt. in Greenwich, NY July 26, 1860

GRAY Harry age 55y in Arlington, Vt. July 20, 1860

LEIGH Louisa age 8y 2m 5d died July 20, 1860 and Annie age 2y 2m 22d died July 24, 1860, children of Joseph H. and Betsey in Salem, NY

BETHUNE Joanna in her 92nd yr widow of Divie in New York July 28, 1860

STEVENSON James W. of St. Paul, Minn. son of late William of Coila, NY August 1, 1860. Born February 13, 1833 in Coila, NY

JOHNSON Emeline age 25y 11m 3w 4d wife of Alonzo in Greenwich, NY August 10, 1860

HOPKINS David age 34y in Argyle, NY August 5, 1860

MERRITT John B. in Whitehall, NY August 12, 1860

WILLIAMS Lyman age 6y son of Martin and Mary M. in Salem, NY July 27, 1860

MC CREEDY Charles age 21y in Schuylerville, NY July 18, 1860

KENYON Stephen age 53y formerly of Greenwich in Davisburg, Mi. August 13, 1860

KNAPP Ervin age 2m son of Francis Z. and Prudence in Greenwich, NY August 15, 1860

THOMPSON Hugh in his 67th yr in Salem, NY August 10, 1860

WHEADON Miss Sarah in her 93rd yr in Hebron, NY August 14, 1860

REID Anna in her 64th yr wife of William in N. Greenwich, NY August 16, 1860

ARMSTRONG Archibald in his 61st yr in Argyle, NY August 22, 1860

DANIELS Anna M. age 1y 2m dau of George W. and Elizabeth in Greenwich, NY August 25, 1860

DIBBLE Oscar J. H. age 48y formerly of Greenwich, NY in Columbus, Ga. July 20, 1860

LATIMER Edmond C. age 31y formerly of Salem, NY late of Brooklyn, NY in Hebron, NY August 29, 1860

BEADLE Hannah age 97y in Greenwich, NY September 5, 1860

MORGAN William M. age 48y in Greenwich, NY September 12, 1860

CULVER Oscar F. age 39y in Cambridge, NY September 11, 1860

FISHER David age 55y in White Creek, NY September 12, 1860

ROBERSON Eunice age 62y wife of Jeremiah in Greenwich, NY September 18, 1860

KENYON Sam C. in his 23rd yr in Greenwich, NY September 23, 1860

SMITH George M. age 67y formerly of Green Co. in New Albany, Ind. September 13, 1860

VAN BUREN Cornelius in his 83rd yr in Easton, NY September 17, 1860

BISHOP Isaac J. age 40y in Granville, NY September 8, 1860

CHAPMAN Eliza C. age 58y wife of Henry formerly of Greenwich, NY in Rockford, Ill. September 22, 1860

MORSE Catherine age 48y wife of Daniel in Galesville, NY September 27, 1860

HITCHCOCK Noble C. in his 86th yr in Kingsbury, NY October 4, 1860

DUFF James A. age 30y in S. Argyle, NY October 6, 1860

RICH Myra in her 66th yr wife of Ebenezer in Salem, NY October 7, 1860

FINCH Cynthia age 26y wife of Charles B. in Wallingford, Vt. October 13, 1860

SPARHAWK Rufus S. in his 29th yr in Greenwich, NY November 8, 1860

NEWCOMB Dr. J. E. age 51y in Whitehall, NY October 29, 1860

CONLEE Polly age 77y relict of James in Greenwich, NY November 20, 1860

BARBER Harper in Centre Falls, NY November 18, 1860

HARWOOD Ruby age 83y widow of Oliver in Rupert, Vt. October 26, 1860

SPRAGUE Samuel in his 57th yr in Glens Falls, NY November 4, 1860

ATWOOD Maggie S. age 24y of Lansingburgh in Salem, NY November 10, 1860

FREEMAN Phineas age 56y formerly of Salem, NY in New York November 13, 1860

MC CLAUGHRY Rosamond age 37y wife of Thomas and dau of late Col. A. MC WHORTER in E. Greenwich, NY October 20, 1860

MILLER Loeza age 12y dau of Frank and Jennette in Greenwich, NY November 28, 1860

BRUCE Abel Wilder age 65y in Cambridge, Mass. November 28, 1860

MC GINNIS Thomas age 71y in Schuylerville, NY November 1, 1860

OSBORN Richard age 82y in Greenwich, NY November 30, 1860

CHURCH Charles age 4y 8m 17d son of Henry and Malvina in Greenwich, NY October 30, 1860

CROWL James H. age 45y formerly of Salem in Cleveland, Ohio October 17, 1860

MC ALLISTER Archibald age 48y formerly of Salem, NY in Buffalo, NY October 19, 1860

BREWER Ann in her 38th yr wife of Horace in Greenwich, Ny December 15, 1860

REMINGTON David age 88y in Greenwich, NY December 15, 1860

ROGERS Eben in his 74th yr in Greenwich, NY December 20, 1860

COOK Abigal age 65y in Greenwich, NY December 30, 1860

JACKSON Charles age 30y formerly of Greenwich in Castleton, Vt. January 4, 1861

GIDDINGS Rev. Charles age 42y in Victory Mills, NY December 30, 1860

ROGERS Dolly in her 92nd yr widow of Nathan in Greenwich, NY January 8, 1861

CONLEE Miss Amanda H. age 30y in Greenwich, NY January 3, 1861

CALDWELL Mary E. age 21y dau of Joseph and Susan in Troy, NY January 6, 1861

MC KIE George age 70y in Cambridge, NY January 15, 1861

ALLEN Margaret Ann age 37y wife of Charles A. and dau of Billings **BLAKELEY** of Xenia, Ohio in Greenwich, NY January 20, 1861

ROBERTSON Charles Nelson age 9y son of George L. and Charlotte in Greenwich, NY January 26, 1861

BAIN Jane Ann wife of Peter formerly of Argyle in Monroe, Iowa December 19, 1860

PARRY Fanny age 20y dau of Rev. Joseph in Sandy Hill, NY January 17/24, 1861

COX Job in his 82nd yr in Cambridge, NY February 9, 1861

MC WHORTER Sally age 66y widow of Col. Alexander in W. Hebron, NY January

21, 1861

MILLER David in Jackson, NY January 21, 1861

MOSHER Margaret J. age 34y in Easton, NY February 13, 1861

FREEMAN Alfred age 68y formerly of E. Greenwich in New York February 8, 1861

CHAPMAN Lucy in her 19th yr dau of Henry and Eliza C. formerly of Greenwich, NY in Rockford, Ill. February 9, 1861

FENTON Emma age 25y in Cambridge, NY February 15, 1861

BINNINGER Joseph age 45y formerly of Salem, NY in New York January 2, 1861

FULLER Clarissa age 54y relict of Henry in Greenwich, NY March 4, 1861

BIGELOW Mary age 78y in Greenwich, NY March 12, 1861

STEWART David Rhodes age 12y son of Solomon and Maria L. in Greenwich, NY March 1, 1861

WEST Julius A. age 4y 9m died January 6, 1861, William J. age 6y 6m died January 31, 1861 and Charles E. age 2y 9m died February 20, 1861, children of Moses and Mary J. in Salem, NY

ACKLEY Solomon in his 88th yr in Jackson, NY February 25, 1861

HODGEMAN Angeline age 51y wife of Frederick in Ft. Edward, NY March 16, 1861

SMALLEY Chauncey B. age 56y in Sandy Hill, NY March 16, 1861

DUNCAN Lucy Jane age 2y 8m dau of William S. and Sarah Ann in Greenwich, NY March 31, 1861

BULL Keziah in her 91st yr at son-in-laws James MOTT March 21, 1861

MERRILL Franklin M. age 43y in Schuylerville, NY April 1, 1861

BAKER Charles age 8y son of Reuben and Laura in Salem, NY March 28, 1861

WATERS Barber age 45y in Jackson, NY March 25, 1861

TAYLOR Simeon age 81y in Greenwich, NY April 19, 1861

TAYLOR Mrs. Betsey Lee age 52y dau of Simson Taylor in Greenwich, NY April 22, 1861

GAVETTE Marianne age 43y wife of Asel in Greenwich, NY April 11, 1861

MERRILL Fanny age 6y in Schuylerville, NY April 24, 1861

MOWRY Mary C. age 26y wife of William L. in Greenwich, NY May 3, 1861

VAN VRANKEN Sally abt 68y wife of Samuel in Salem, NY April 22, 1861

PRATT Maria W. age 25y in Cambridge, NY (newspaper date May 9, 1861)

BLANCHARD Anthony age 59y son of A. I. in Salem, NY May 1, 1861

PORTER James H. age 45y in N. White Creek, NY April 4, 1861

MOTT Walter Md. age 40y 3d in Moreau, NY April 17, 1861

PRENTISS Adeline A. age 23y dau of Gilman and Almira in Greenwich, NY May 18, 1861

BAIN George A. in his 13th yr son of John B. in S. Argyle, NY May 16, 1861

LEWIS Samuel age 64y in Jackson, NY May 23, 1861

WRIGHT Charles S. abt 70y at Bald Mountain, NY May 21, 1861

SILL James Henry age 25y son of Zachariah in Hartford, NY May 11, 1861

MEADER Mrs. Nancy in Greenwich, NY June 3, 1861

FINCH Mrs. Mary age 55y in Salem, NY May 25, 1861

BULL Henry age 65y in Granville, NY May 28, 1861

CLARK Betsey age 53y dau of late Benjamin in Sandy Hill, NY June 6, 1861

SPAULDING Curtis C. age 51y formerly of Rockingham, Vt. in Salem, NY June 9, 1861

MADDEN Rachel age 23y of Battenville, NY in the County Home May 26, 1861

BURKE John abt 80y at Bacon Hill, NY June 14, 1861. Father of Capt. Martin J. Burke who was killed in Mexican War.

CRANDALL Samuel in his 86th yr veteran of War of 1812 in Greenfield, NY (newspaper date July 4, 1861)

HUNT Sarah wife of Lekas in Cambridge, NY June 27, 1861

HILL Jane in her 15th yr in Greenwich, NY July 7, 1861

CHAMBERS William John age 27y formerly of Greenwich, NY on board U. S. gunboat Mystic March 28, 1861

WRIGHT Mary Jane age 27y 6m 6d wife of Daniel V. in Northumberland, NY July 21, 1861

WHITTAKER Harriet age 50y in Greenwich, NY July 29, 1861

WILCOX Nelson H. age 5y 3m son of Harvey and Ann Sophia in Greenwich, NY August 12, 1861

LAMPSON Caroline Melissa age 7y dau of Henry and Caroline in Greenwich, NY August 11, 1861

ALLEN Anna Mary age 8y dau of John and Jane in Greenwich, NY August 16, 1861

WILCOX Charles age 8m son of Hiram K. and Sarah Frances in Easton, NY August 16, 1861

WESTON Roswell in his 88th yr in Sandy Hill, NY August 18, 1861

VORCE Freeman age 83y in Sandy Hill, NY August 19, 1861

STEWART David age 58y in Centre Falls, NY August 16, 1861

BASSETT William J. in his 29th yr son of Pardon in Greenwich, NY August 31, 1861

GRANGER Porter age 9m and Herbert age 2y 2m both died August 30, 1861, children of Henry and Maria in Greenwich, NY

STOVER Georgia H. age 6y 8m 17d son of George and Mary A. in N. Greenwich, NY August 15, 1861

MANYARD Sarah Frances (colored) age 5y 11m 3d dau of John R. and Cornelia Ann in Greenwich, NY August 21, 1861

JILLSON Emma 18m 14d dau of H. J. of Battenville, NY August 29, 1861

MANYARD Mary Emily age 8y 4m 6d dau of Samuel and Betsey in Greenwich, NY September 7, 1861

JONES George W. age 9m 24d son of Alfred and Anna E. in Greenwich, NY September 9, 1861

WILCOX Sarah Jane age 32y wife of Edmond D. in Greenwich, NY September 21, 1861

MANYARD Sarah age 57 wife of John in Greenwich, NY September 27, 1861

DOBBIN Margaret age 90y widow of William in Greenwich, NY September 27, 1861

STEAD Charles Henry age 1y 3m son of Henry and Sarah formerly of Galesville, NY in Grand Rapids, Ill. October 5, 1861

DENNIS Sarah in her 29th yr wife of Deranzel in Greenwich, NY October 16, 1851

DENNIS Adelaide age 23y wife of Marvin in Greenwich, NY October 19, 1861

BUROUGHS Antoinette age 22y wife of Allen in Easton, NY October 24, 1861

NORTON Edgar age 28 in N. White Creek, NY October 26, 1861

CONLEE Allen age 22y 9m in Easton, NY November 13, 1861

KITTLE David S. age 53y formerly of Greenwich in Troy, NY November 17, 1861

MC MURRAY William age 24y son of Ebenezer in Salem, NY November 5, 1861

BAKER Charles G. age 56y in N. Granville, NY November 21, 1861

BASSETT Pardon age 55y in Greenwich, NY November 27, 1861

MORSE Etta Louisa age 7y 9m 3d adopted dau of Sidney and Mary A. at Bald Mountain, NY died November 26, 1861 and dau Sarah Alamanda age 3y 3m 9d died November 28, 1861

WILSON Nathan A. age 18y 9m 6d son of Nathan W. of Salem, NY in Washington DC November 22, 1861

RUSSELL David in his 81st yr in Salem, NY November 22, 1861

FENTON James Edwin age 23y at Seminary Hospital in Georgetown, DC November 29, 1861

ROBINSON Sarah age 92y relict of Francis in Galesville, NY December 4, 1861

MILLER Frederick age 2y 1m son of Joseph and Susan in Greenwich, NY December 17, 1861

SHELDON Isaac in his 74th yr in Rupert, Vt. December 8, 1861

PARISH Mrs. _____ age 81y in Greenwich, NY December 21, 1861

MORSE Cora Augusta age 10m 12d dau of Sidney and Sarah at Bald Mountain, NY December 12, 1861

CRANDALL Elizabeth **(LATHAM)** age 33y wife of Thomas in Greenwich, NY December 28, 1861

BRADLEY Francis A. age 33y formerly of Green Co. in St. Louis, Mo. (newspaper date January 2, 1862)

BARTLETT Emery D. age 39y in Cambridge, NY December 21, 1861

JOHNSTON John W. age 33y of Hebron, NY in Ft. Edward, NY December 21, 1861

PARKER John M. age 1y 8m 27d son of Robert and Olive in Salem, NY December 24, 1861

GRAVES Fidelia in her 80th yr wife of Asael in Salem, NY December 4, 1861

DOOLITTLE George H. age 7y 8m son of Charles and Mary A. in Easton, NY December 24, 1861

BAKER Charles Edwin age 1y 2m 12d son of Rev. John E. Baker and Carrie **STEVENS** in Arkport, NY January 4, 1862

TIMMERMAN Stephen in his 50th yr in Argyle, NY January 23, 1862

MARTIN James I. in his 45th yr in Salem, NY January 18, 1862

WHITE Spencer R. age 48y in Greenwich, NY January 30, 1862

DYER Miss Ruth age 74y at bro John K. in White Creek, NY January 10/16, 1862

KNAPP Henry Sr. age 55y in Greenwich, NY February 8, 1862

WRIGHT Polly age 76y in Greenwich, NY January 25, 1862

DUBOIS Koert in Easton, NY February 6, 1862

WILCOX Betsey in her 70th yr relict of Daniel in Greenwich, NY February 10, 1862

BENEDICT Aurelia age 55y wife of Samuel of Arlington, Vt. in Greenwich, NY February 19, 1862

CARPENTER John age 85y in Greenwich, NY February 24, 1862

WELLS Lucinda age 55y formerly of Greenwich in Racine, Wis. January 27, 1862

RODGERS James age 1y 5m 18d son of John F. and Elizabeth **GROVE** in Albany, NY February 22, 1862

HARTSHORN Susannah W. abt 35y in Greenwich, NY March 2, 1862

CRANDALL Sylvia Ann age 50y wife of Nathan R. in Greenwich, NY February 19, 1862

NORTON Carrie age 4m dau of Franklin and Caroline in Greenwich, NY March 14, 1862

HILL Whiteside in his 81st yr in Cambridge, NY March 7, 1862

STEWART Jane I. age 25y dau of James in Greenwich, NY April 4, 1862

SOMES Elizabeth abt 25y dau of late Jonas in Greenwich, NY April 2/3, 1862

WHIPPLE Alice age 80y wife of Otis in Easton, NY April 3, 1862

DELAVARGE Lewis age 47y in Easton, NY April 3, 1862

ATWOOD Jane in her 63rd yr wife of E. G. Atwood of Salem, NY in Birmingham, Conn. March 15, 1862

MURDOCK Peter age 66y in Salem, NY March 22, 1862

SHEPHERD Samuel T. in his 76th yr at Ft. Miller, NY March 29, 1862

O'DELL Barbara in her 77th yr relict of Simeon at Ft. Miller, NY March 29, 1862

FARMER Mc Guire abt 45y at Ft. Miller, NY April 10, 1862

DUNLAP Georgie T. age 3y 8m 16d child of Henry H. and Laura M. in Easton, NY April 10, 1862

KNAPP Alanson age 1y 8m son of T. H. and Sarah Y. in Brooklyn, NY April 17, 1862

KITTLE William S. in his 65th yr in Greenwich, NY April 25, 1862

BURCH Clarissa age 76y wife of Henry in Easton, NY May 7, 1862

VAN VALKENBURG Charles in his 23rd yr of Co. C. 44th Reg. NY Vol. at Annapolis, Md. April 28, 1862

CAMPBELL Archibald age 72y in Centre Falls, NY June 8, 1862

WOOD Elizabeth age 8y died May 11, 1862 and John age 7y died June 9, 1862, children of Joseph and Mary in Greenwich, NY

BOWEN John abt 50y in White Creek, NY May 26, 1862

HILL Nancy age 47y wife of James and dau of Andrew **MARTIN** in Argyle, NY May 30, 1862

LEWIS Margaret (**HARVEY**) age 66y wife of G. A. Lewis in Gorham, NY June 15, 1862. Buried with 1st husband in Salem, NY

LANGWORTHY Sanford abt 60y in Greenwich, NY June 28, 1862

DAWLEY Parmelia age 54y wife of George in Greenwich, NY July 5, 1862

WRIGHT John age 53y of Co. I 77th Reg. NY Vol. of Greenwich, NY July 21, 1862

SMART Rev. John G. abt 60y formerly of Coila, NY in Brandon, Vt. July 18, 1862

REMINGTON Gardner age 93y in Easton, NY July 19, 1862

SPRAGUE Gibson age 23y son of William and Susan in Greenwich, NY July 8, 1862

HATCH Albert S. in St. Louis, Mo. July 17, 1862. Born September 1, 1839 in Ft. Ann, NY

LUTHER Mary Libbie in her 7th yr dau of Almond and Jennett in Easton, NY July 22, 1862

BAIN William J. in his 22nd yr son of Peter of Argyle, NY in the 93rd Reg. NY Vol. on the steamer 'State of Maine' July 7, 1862

TAYLOR Thomas W. age 15y 10m son of William of Cambridge, NY at the battle of Saratoga Station, Va. July 29, 1862

CURTIS Hannah C. age 43y wife of John W. and dau of Moses M. and Susannah **WHITE** in Greenwich, NY August 8, 1862

ELDRICH Mrs. Job in Easton, NY rec. (newspaper date August 14, 1862)

MOBBS James F. of Sandy Hill, NY at son-in-laws John H. **BEACH** (newspaper date August 14, 1862)

GALE R. M. widow of John formerly of Galesville, NY in Sheboygan, Wis. August 26, 1862. Buried Union Village, NY

TULL Jesse abt 65y in Greenwich, NY August 29, 1862

MILLER Sarah in her 87th yr widow of Perry in Greenwich, NY September 9, 1862

RICE John age 14y son of Mrs. J. A. Rice of Salem, NY in Jackson, NY September 1, 1862

REMINGTON George age 66y in Easton, NY September 13, 1862

RICHEY Alexander N. age 31y son of William of W. Rupert, Vt. in San Francisco, Cal. August 1, 1862

MORRISON Samuel age 87y 3m 24d in Battenville, NY October 12, 1862

HARRIS Joshua Jr. age 76y 6m in Kingsbury, NY September 27, 1862

HARRINGTON John age 35y son of Peleg in Greenwich, NY October 16, 1862

BAIN John P. abt 45y in S. Argyle, NY October 20, 1862

RICHARDSON Harriet A. age 48y relict of A. B. in Argyle, NY October 13, 1862

FAIRLEY Hugh age 73y in Salem, NY October 9, 1862

DEAN Abby H. age 7y dau of Seymour and Alice in Easton, NY November 1, 1862

WALSH Carrie Mary age 11y 5m dau of John and Fannie in Argyle, NY October 26, 1862

SHERMAN Peleg age 62y in Greenwich, NY November 18, 1862

NORTON Alexander age 64y of Easton, NY (newspaper date November 27, 1862)

HARTNETT Bartlett age 56y formerly of Greenwich, NY in Ellenboro, Wis. November 19, 1862

WHITE Robert age 17y son of John and Eunice in Greenwich, NY December 26, 1862

MILLIMAN Thomas age 70y 8m in Ft. Edward, NY January 1, 1863

DEAN Jennie age 3y dau of Lorenzo in Ft. Edward, NY December 31, 1862

OSBORN Charles M. age 26y of Schuylerville in Albany, NY December 30, 1862

ARCHIBALD John abt 53y in Argyle, NY January 6, 1863

EAGER Eugene M. in his 6th yr son of Abram and Mary in Galesburgh, Ill. November 9, 1862

WROATH Isadorah age 11y dau of William and Margaret in Schuylerville, NY January 17, 1863

MILLER Peter age 34y of Easton, NY at Camp Union Mills, Va. January 10, 1863

GREEN Sarah age 15/45y dau of Mrs. Margaret Green of Cambridge, NY at E. Hampton, Mass. January 26, 1863

BARBER Banjamin in his 66th yr at Centre Falls, NY February 10, 1863

STEVENSON Dr. James age 92y in Cambridge, NY February 14, 1863

MORSE Mary L. age 23y 5m in Galesville, NY February 3, 1863

DONALDSON Jane age 53y wife of Nicholas N. and dau of James **STEWART** late of N. Argyle, NY in Owattonna, Wis. (newspaper date February 26, 1863)

WILCOX Martha age 9y died February 25, 1863, Lucy age 21y died March 7, 1863, Daniel age 15y died March 8, 1863, Sarah Jane age 4y died March 15, 1863, Orrin T. age 23 died March 18, 1863, Thurston M. age 10y died March 20, 1863 all of diptheria, children of Thurston and Sarah Wilcox of Greenwich, NY

BISHOP William age 84y in Easton, NY March 1, 1863

THOMPSON Isaac age 48y in Annaquasicoke, NY February 28, 1863

SCOTT William J. age 25y of Cambridge, NY near Stafford Court House, Va. February 23, 1863

ROGERS Nelson abt 25y of Canada East in Salem, NY March 15, 1863

GRAY Sarah A. age 76y widow of David P. in Salem, NY March 6, 1863

MATHEWS Hannah age 90y at Saratoga Springs, NY March 24, 1863. Names sons John A. and Allen Corey

SWIFT Wyatt R. age 66y at Schaghticoke Point, NY March 30, 1863

TEFFT Eliza wife of Asel formerly of Greenwich, NY in Troy, NY April 7, 1863

ADAMS Clark age 66y in Greenwich, NY April 17, 1863

WALLER Mrs. Ella J. age 22y 2m 13d dau of Jehiel RUSSELL in Greenwich, NY May 1, 1863

WHIPPLE Hattie Louise age 1y 2m 18d dau of Henry and Mary J. in Greenwich, NY May 2, 1863

SHERMAN Abraham age 86y 9m of White Creek, NY in Hoosick, NY May 3, 1863

DEAN Jane age 73y wife of Dr. Solomon Dean in White Creek, NY April 28, 1863

DUNLOP James abt 45y in N. White Creek, NY April 30, 1863

MC LEAN Rachel in her 87th yr widow of Thomas in Cambridge, NY April 28, 1863

CLAPP Mrs. Lois age 72y in N. White Creek, NY April 24, 1863

RUSSELL Elizabeth (TAYLOR) age 30y wife of Marlin W. in Stillwater, NY December 10, 1862

NOBLE Charles Holmes age 2y 8m 24d son of Henry and Sarah B. in N. White Creek, NY April 28, 1863

FAXON Zelia Amanda age 7y 1d dau of Rodney D. and Permelia in Greenwich, NY May 4, 1863

BREWER Lottie age 3y died May 7, 1863 and Leroy age 5y died May 14, 1863, children of Leroy and Manima Brewer in Greenwich, NY

BREWER Simon age 19y son of Horace in Greenwich, NY May 15, 1863

LYONS Holmes in his 81st yr formerly of Greenwich, NY at son-in-laws B. F. ROSS in Ela, Ill. April 26, 1863

DUNTON Roxanna age 84y wife of Josiah in N. White Creek, NY May 10, 1863

NORTON Franklin age 29y Lieut. Col. in 123rd Reg. NY Vol. son of William Henry Norton at Chancelorville (newspaper date May 28, 1863)

EDIE Jane age 35y wife of Peter in Easton, NY April 15, 1863

LONG Charity (**RUSSELL**) age 64 wife of Edward at sis Mrs. J. M. **HALL** in Argyle, NY June 1, 1863

FENTON Sarah E. age 17y dau of Calvin and Harriet in Greenwich, NY June 9, 1863

EDDY Willie W. age 3y 10m son of Jeremiah and Ruth in Greenwich, NY June 14, 1863

ROOD Seth in his 85th yr in Greenwich, NY June 25, 1863

SHELDON Jane age 63y wife of John in Easton, NY June 20, 1863

DIMMICK Libbie in her 22nd yr at Saratoga Springs, NY June 11, 1863

SOUTHWORTH Joseph in his 73rd yr in Greenwich, NY June 30, 1863

WHITE Catherine age 54y wife of Dr. Charles J. in Hebron, NY June 22, 1863

BRYANT Nahum in Galesville, NY (newspaper date July 9, 1863)

ADAMS Hosea age 82y in Greenwich, NY July 14, 1863

JOHNSON Hiram age 24y in Greenwich, NY July 10, 1863

COLFAX Evelyn E. age 40y formerly of Argyle, NY wife of Schuyler in Newport, RI July 10, 1863

FROST Daniel age 77y formerly of Greenwich in Canterbury, Conn. July 18, 1863

YOUNG Catherine A. age 41y 5m wife of Hilon in Easton, NY July 23, 1863

HEATH Edward H. age 19y of Wis. Reg. son of late Consider Heath of Greenwich, NY near Gettysburg July 4, 1863

CLARK Edward Russell age 7m son of C. H. and Amelia in Greenwich, NY August 24, 1863

DE RIDDER Cornelius age 57y in Schuylerville, NY August 27, 1863

MOSHER Mary L. age 79y in Easton, NY August 1, 1863

GIBBS Leonard age 63y in Greenwich, NY September 12, 1863

DEAN Melissa age 45y wife of Corbin C. in Greenwich, NY September 11, 1863

CLARKE Rhoda Louzeta age 1y 10m 21d died July 13, 1863 and Gaylord H. age 12w 2d died September 9, 1863, children of Gaylord J. and Helen F. and Grand children of Allen and Ann **(WHIPPLE) COREY** formerly of Greenwich, NY

AMES Amelia in her 23rd yr wife of Chauncey in Greenwich, NY October 2, 1863

RUSSELL Ada C. age 29y wife of William A. in Salem, NY September 19, 1863

BASSETT James in his 81st yr at Ft. Miller, NY October 7, 1863

BROCK Mrs Elizabeth age 77y formerly of Greenwich, NY in Sandy Hill, NY October 9, 1863

PRENTISS Gilman age 63y in Greenwich, NY October 13, 1863

SCHOFIELD Anna age 56y wife of Lewis N. in Greenwich, NY October 24, 1863

WHIPPLE Otis age 86y in Easton, NY October 29, 1863

MEADORS Ira B. in his 22nd yr grandson of late Ira **BRAGG** formerly of Ft. Miller, NY in Newark, NJ January 1, 1864

ARNOTT Mrs. James age 55y in Jackson,NY January 19, 1864

LUTHER Jennett age 34y wife of Almond in Easton, NY January 19, 1864

HERRINGTON John age 4y 1m 11d son of Ezekiel and Catherine in Easton, NY January 16, 1864

RUSSELL Thaddeus age 84y in N. White Creek, NY January 18, 1864

WOLF Caroline in her 31st yr wife of Michael in Greenwich, NY January 21, 1864

REYNOLDS Mary age 68y wife of John in Greenwich, NY January 26, 1864

GILES Maria age 43y wife of Thomas in Greenwich, NY January 30, 1864

CRARY Sarah in her 56th yr widow of John C. in Salem, NY January 22, 1864

DOBBIN Nealie age 1y dau of John W. and Annie **(WELLS)** in E. Greenwich, NY January 16, 1864

ROBERTSON Alexander in his 87th yr at Ft. Miller, NY January 29, 1864

SCRIPTURE Mr. ____ in his 101st yr in Moreau, NY February 12, 1864

BETTS ____ age 8m child of James in Moreau, NY February 15, 1864

NORTON Willie age 2y 9m son of William S. and Mary F. in Ft. Edward, NY February 16, 1864

YOUNG Addie M. age 2y 7m dau of Ira H. and Lucy M. in Ft. Edward, NY February 16, 1864

HARRINGTON John in his 89th yr at sons Ezekiel in Easton, NY February 28, 1864

TEFFT Seneca M. age 19y 18d son of Simeon B. and Abigal formerly of Greenwich, NY in Army at Ft. Harney, Neb. February 26, 1864

HUTTON Willie W. age 7m 12d son of Alex and Martha in Greenwich, NY March 9, 1864

NEWBURY James R. in his 59th yr in Galesville, NY March 14, 1864

POTTER Sara Matilda age 19y at uncles Gardner **TEFFT** in Greenwich, NY March 17, 1864

TEFFT Kinyon age 43y formerly of Greenwich, NY in Victory, NY March 18, 1864

CRANDALL Eudora age 5y dau of Thomas in Easton, NY March 18, 1864

TIBBITS John age 100y 20d at sons William in Troy, NY March 20, 1864

CUBIT Thomas age 78y in Greenwich, NY March 25, 1864

WRIGHT Emma age 17y dau of John F. in Greenwich, NY March 25, 1864

MC GATHEN William age 76y in Greenwich, NY March 23, 1864

RICHARDS Tommy age 3y 6m son of Andrew in Greenwich, NY March 25, 1864

BLAKELEY Billings age 66y in Greenwich, NY March 29, 1864

SUTFIN Susan M. in her 18th yr in Schuylerville, NY March 29, 1864

BROWN Seth C. age 61y in Salem, NY March 28, 1864

COON Jane C. age 37y wife of James F. in Argyle, NY April 6, 1864

HOAG Betsey abt 35y wife of Jonathan and dau of Jeremiah **ROBERSON** in Easton, NY April 9, 1864

CLARK Mrs. Stephen A. age 52y in Greenwich, NY April 10, 1864

HARRISON a son of Mrs. John Harrison age 4/5y in Greenwich, NY April 7, 1864

COTTRELL Thomas in his 76th yr in Greenwich, NY April 16, 1864

MASON Emma in her 17th yr dau of Rev. J. O. in Greenwich, NY April 24, 1864

WHIPPLE Catherine age 47y wife of William in Easton, NY May 1, 1864

PETTEYS Ephraim age 77y in Cambridge, NY April 28, 1864

PRENTISS Gilman in his 64th yr in Greenwich, NY May 5, 1864

HILL Mrs. Sarah in her 78th yr in Greenwich, NY May 8, 1864

EMMONS Horatio in his 86th yr in Greenwich, NY May 30, 1864

COON William age 55y in Salem, NY May 29, 1864

FREEMAN Pernal in his 92nd yr in Cambridge, NY May 31, 1864

WESTON Theodore R. age 46y in Salem, NY June 9, 1864

HENRY Pamelia age 76y in Greenwich, NY June 6, 1864

CLAPP Aseneth in her 80th yr widow of Benjamin in Argyle, NY May 28, 1864

ROBINSON Helen Libbie age 1y 6m dau of Sanders and Maria in Cambridge, NY June 24, 1864

GALE Lydia F. age 58 wife of F. A. in Greenwich, NY July 11, 1864

REYNOLDS John age 72y in Greenwich, NY July 14, 1864

WOLF Mrs. Lany age 53y in Lansingburgh, NY July 15, 1864

INGALLS Thomas K. age 55y in Greenwich, NY July 26, 1864

BREWER Alzina age 13y dau of Anson and Elizabeth in Greenwich, NY July 30, 1864

MULLIGAN William J. in his 33rd yr in Greenwich, NY July 20, 1864

MORSE Alice age 1y 6m 25d dau of Sidney and Sarah A. in Galesville, NY July 25, 1864

BRADLEY Jesse age 78y in Greenwich, NY August 20, 1864

LEIGH Julia Mairs age 18y dau of late Jesse S. in Argyle, NY August 15, 1864

THOMPSON Hiram A. age 50y 1m 16d formerly of Greenwich, NY in Newark, NJ August 21, 1864

REYNOLDS Maria C. wife of Almon F. September 11, 1864

CURTIS Mary Ann age 42y wife of William D. in Garden Valley, Wis. September 14, 1864

SHERWOOD William B. age 65y in Greenwich, NY October 4, 1864

HENRY John B. age 27y grandson of John **BARNARD** of Greenwich, NY in Lanesborough, Mass. September 29, 1864

COON Sarah age 1y 2m 15d dau of James E. in Argyle, NY September 18, 1864

HOAG Abbie G. age 27y dau of Robert in Easton, NY October 11, 1864

SELLECK Perry M. age 40y in Greenwich, NY October 24, 1864

CLOSSON Stephen age 95y 9d in Easton, NY October 9/14, 1864

MILLS Stephen age 72y in Easton, NY October 18, 1864

OSBORN Diantha L. age 38y wife of Rev. Richard Osborn formerly of Greenwich, NY in Champion, NY November 1, 1864

NEWTON Ephraim H. age 77y in Cambridge, NY October 26, 1864

REYNOLDS Amanda P. age 34y in Greenwich, NY November 22, 1864

BARBER Mrs. widow of Benjamin of Greenwich, NY at son-in-laws Horton **TEFFT** in Jackson, NY November 18, 1864

FENTON Edna age 21y dau of Calvin in Greenwich, NY December 16, 1864

DECKER Nancy age 15y dau of Jacob and Mary Ann in N. White Creek, NY December 6, 1864

CAULKINS James M. age 35y formerly of Greenwich, NY in New York December 26, 1864

TEFFT Nathan S. age 91y at son-in-laws Miles **ADAMS** in Salem, NY December 25, 1864

DAICY John H. in his 28th yr of Hartford, NY at Military Hospital near Atlanta, Ga. July 22, 1864. 1st Lieut. in Co. E. 123rd Reg. NY Vol.

BLACKMAN Cornelia age 22y 2m wife of Horace and dau of Mrs. Delia M. **STONE** formerly of Greenwich, NY in Paris, Wis. December 31, 1864

TINGUE Lottie age 1y 6m dau of George and Emma in Greenwich, NY January 11, 1865

SHELDON Libbie G. age 24y dau of John in Easton, NY January 19, 1865

HOLMES Cornelius in his 91st yr in Greenwich, NY January 29, 1865

TILLOTSON Joshua S. age 69y at son-in-laws John **BARNARD** in Lanesborough, Mass. January 23, 1865

CORNELL Mary age 34 wife of Hiram K. in Greenwich, NY February 7, 1865

MASON Dr. F. P. age 46y in Greenwich, NY February 27, 1865

REYNOLDS Mrs. ____ age 81y in Hartford, NY February 23, 1865, sons Hiram and Abram

WOLF John M. age 33y in Hospital in Jefferson, Ind. February 7, 1865

SHILAND Ann age 46y in Cambridge, NY February 26, 1865

KENYON Ada age 3y 3m 2d dau of Andrew H. and Jane A. in Greenwich, NY February 20, 1864

ROBERTSON Gilbert age 86y at sons William D. in Argyle, NY February 11, 1864

SKINNER Alice age 39y 3m wife of William in Argyle, NY January 23, 1865

VAN KIRK Albert age 15m son of Norman and Kate in Greenwich, NY March 8, 1865

WRIGHT Dr. Austin H. Missionary in Oroomiah, Persia January 4, 1865

COOK Frederick A. in his 24th yr son of C. C. of Greenwich, NY in Providence, RI March 20, 1865

CRANDALL Alexander age 73y in Easton, NY March 15, 1865

WHELDON Tabitha in her 89th yr widow of Peter in Easton, NY March 24, 1865

TEFFT Phebe Jennie age 7y 5m dau of Lewis and Margaret in Galesville, NY March 2, 1864

WHITE John W. age 42y in Greenwich, NY April 3, 1865

WILDER Mrs. Elisabeth age 54y 10d in Greenwich, NY April 5, 1865

MEAD Mrs. ____ age 63y at bro Henry R. **OWEN** in Greenwich, NY April 8, 1865

CORNELL Jonathan in his 69th yr of Galway, Saratoga Co. NY at son-in-laws Daniel **EDDY** in Greenwich, NY April 22, 1865

GUNN Abigal H. in her 64th yr wife of C. J. in Greenwich, NY April 24, 1865

STEWART Betsey age 85y in Cambridge, NY April 23, 1865

WRIGHT David S. in his 63rd yr in Greenwich, NY April 27, 1865

ALLEN Mrs. _____ age 85y widow of George in Easton, NY April 28, 1865

COLLINS John age 37y late of Greenwich, NY in Troy, NY May 5, 1865

OSBORN Byron C. in his 23rd yr formerly of Wabash, Ind. son of John C. formerly of Greenwich, NY in Stockton, Cal. March 30, 1865

REYNOLDS Hart age 82y in Greenwich, NY May 12, 1865

PHELPS William H. of Cambridge, NY with Co. I. 123rd Reg. NY Vol. in Hospital at Savannah, Ga. April 1, 1865.

BENTLEY John C. formerly of Greenwich, NY in Co. K. 16th Reg. at Petersburgh September 16, 1864

EVANS Joseph age 36y formerly of Greenwich in Schaghticoke, NY May 18, 1865

ADAMS Willie Herbert age 7y 2m in Galesville, NY May 22, 1865

WEIR Emeline age 21y in Salem, NY May 19, 1865

BENDON James age 20y of Greenwich, NY in Co. D. 146th Reg. in Hospital at City Point, Va. April 6, 1865

STEELE Emma age 8y 10m dau of Rev. J. in Greenwich, NY June 22, 1865

STEWART Robert age 66y in Salem, NY June 20, 1865

ATWOOD Samuel age 25 in Salem, NY June 15, 1865

QUACKENBUSH Miss Helen in her 73rd yr in Salem, NY June 15, 1865

COZZENS Betsey E. age 72y widow of William F. in Greenwich, NY July 24, 1865

HARRINGTON Charles age 90y 3m 10d in Easton, NY July 23, 1865

BENNETT Horace age 55y in Galesville, NY July 29, 1865

INMAN Ezekiel age 83y in S. Argyle, NY July 28, 1865

EMMONS Sarah age 81y widow of Horatio in Greenwich, NY August 4, 1865

SPARHAWK Arthur in his 14th yr son of Dexter and Calphurna C. in Greenwich, NY August 10, 1865

BABCOCK Leroy H. age 27y in E. Greenwich, NY August 15, 1865

CARTER Sarah J. age 22y in Salem, NY August 27, 1865

SMALL Jennett age 82y widow of James in Jackson, NY August 25, 1865

DUNLAP James age 79y in Arlington, Vt. August 24, 1865

KENT John age 70y in White Creek, NY August 28, 1865

BURNHAM William Emmons in his 71st yr in Greenwich, NY September 8, 1865

HATCH Gideon G. age 33y in Greenwich, NY September 8, 1865

WHITE Emeline age 30y wife of D. W. in Greenwich, NY September 19, 1865

WILCOX Seymour son-in-law of John BARNARD of Greenwich, NY in Lanesborough, Mass. September 6, 1865

PETTEYS Harvey E. abt 55y in Greenwich, NY September 21, 1865

LANSING Lucinda A. age 28 wife of Uriah J. in Greenwich, NY September 24, 1865

KENYON Anna abt 30y wife of Clark H. in Greenwich, NY September 21, 1865 and dau Carrie in her 8th yr died October 1, 1865

CROSBY Joseph B. in his 53rd yr in Greenwich, NY October 1, 1865

LATHAM Barber K. age 66y formerly of Greenwich, NY in Port Byron, NY September 14, 1865

BELL Ebenezer age 55y in Greenwich, NY October 16, 1865

SHEPHERD Franklin age 63y in Greenwich, NY October 9, 1865

RICE Emily age 29y wife of C. H. and dau of Taber TEFFT formerly of Greenwich, NY in Charleston, Ill. October 11, 1865, son Eddie age 1y 10m died October 13, 1865

PIERCE Dolly T. age 32y wife of Dr. A. G. in Greenwich, NY October 28, 1865

OSBORN John C. age 50y formerly of Greenwich, NY in Peru, Ind. October 24, 1865

CROSBY Flavel age 61y formerly of White Creek in Palatine, Ill. October 24, 1865

CLARK Sophia T. age 58y wife of Isaac D. formerly of Greenwich, NY in Wattsburg, Pa. October 31, 1865

BREWSTER Sophronia M. age 25y dau of E. H. of Worthington, Mass. in Greenwich, NY November 22, 1865

BREWER Horace age 46y in Greenwich, NY December 3, 1865

WILSON Mary Jane age 5y dau of Robert and Martha E. in Greenwich, NY

November 12, 1865

WILSON Margaret Ann age 7y 7m dau of Andrew and Margaret in Greenwich, NY November 28, 1865

YOUNG Rhoda age 62y widow of Clayton in Easton, NY December 9, 1865

SIMPSON Frances H. age 28y 4m wife of John and dau of James **CONLEE** formerly of Greenwich, NY in Springfield, Mi. (newspaper date December 14, 1865)

DUDLEY Victorine age 19y dau of Joseph and Martine in Greenwich, NY December 4, 1865

MASON Orlie age 4y 5m son of Andrew and Margaret in Greenwich, NY December 15, 1865

KENYON Lewis age 37y in Greenwich, NY December 28, 1865

SHELDON John age 77y 6m in Easton, NY December 22, 1865

WALKER Martha age 71y widow of James in Greenwich, NY December 31, 1865

WRIGHT Morgan age 44y in Greenwich, NY December 28, 1865

CRANDALL Samuel age 53y in Greenwich, NY January 8, 1866

HATCH Mary V. wife of Dr. Ira formerly of Greenwich, NY in Chicago, Ill. January 4, 1866

MC FARLAND Ebenezer C. age 25y son of late Daniel A. in Salem, NY January 14, 1866

PARKS Barzilla in his 74th yr in Sandy Hill, NY January 4, 1866

DOBBIN Fanny (**LEIGH**) wife of James formerly of Argyle, NY in Fairbault, Minn. December 29, 1865

ROBERSON Ancil age 56y in Greenwich, NY January 22, 1866

BODGE Charles C. age 17y son of David C. at Bald Mountain, NY January 24, 1866

HATCH George age 52y at Ft. Miller, NY January 29, 1866

YOULEN Benjamin age 86y in Salem, NY February 1, 1866

BOIES Joseph age 83y in Greenwich, NY February 11, 1866

LAMBERT Hannah age 56 in Greenwich, NY February 11, 1866

CRANDALL Prudence in her 77th yr in Easton, NY February 16, 1866

WALLER Elisha age 83y February 24, 1866

PETTEYS David in his 70th yr in Cambridge, NY March 9, 1866

KENYON John C. age 45y in Greenwich, NY March 14, 1866

BINNINGER Henry L. age 23y 11m 3d son of Isaac in Salem, NY March 6, 1866

MOREHOUSE Elizabeth **(KNIGHT)** in her 21st yr wife of Henry C. in Granville, NY March 18, 1866

SNELL Desire age 68y wife of Peter in Easton, NY April 2, 1866

STEWART Hattie V. age 2m dau of John and Clementine in Greenwich, NY March 27, 1866

HERRINGTON Infant son of Bentley in Easton, NY March 30, 1866

DE RIDDER widow of Prince abt 100y former slave of this state in E. Greenwich, NY April 3, 1866

ROBERTSON Isabel in her 59th yr wife of Alvin in Salem, NY March 23, 1866

LEWIS Amos P. age 41y in E. Greenwich, NY March 10, 1866

SHERMAN Seeley in his 83rd yr in Salem, NY March 25, 1866

KENYON Esek age 21y in White Creek, NY March 21, 1866

GRIFFIN Margaret age 23y wife of E. J. in White Creek, NY March 16, 1866

DAWLEY Ann Loezia age 4y 1m 9d dau of William and Ellen in Greenwich, NY April 9, 1866

SIMPSON Eunicy age 40y wife of John H. in Greenwich, NY April 14, 1866

SIPPERLY Abraham L. infant son of Dr. John Sipperly in Easton, NY April 14, 1866

BUTLER Robertson in his 83rd yr in Easton, NY April 4, 1866

FULLER Jennie S. age 25y wife of Lewis in Salem, NY April 8, 1866

TRULL David age 60y in White Creek, NY April 9, 1866

ROBINSON Hiram age 59y formerly of Greenwich, NY in Hoosick, NY May 1, 1866

CLAPP Ambrose age 54y formerly of Salem, NY in Easton, NY April 29, 1866

WEBSTER R. wife of Charles abt 65y in Hebron, NY April 22, 1866

WRIGHT Alexander age 66y died April 11, 1866 and brother Tobias age 79y in Edgerton, Ohio died April 17, 1866, both formerly of Salem, NY

AUSTIN Ruth age 56y wife of James in Cambridge, NY May 10, 1866

WELCH John age 83y formerly of White Creek, NY in Darlington, Canada West (newspaper date May 31, 1866)

COLE Alida C. age 27y wife of Norman in Glens Falls, NY May 20, 1866

SMART James age 7y son of Hugh and Frances in Salem, NY May 27, 1866

HEATH Lodica in her 68th yr wife of Stephen G. in Salem, NY April 8, 1866

SAFFORD William M. abt 60y formerly of Salem in W. Pawlet, Vt. May 31, 1866

PRATT Asa age 50y in White Creek, NY June 12, 1866

ENGLISH William L. age 72y in Easton, NY June 19, 1866

HERRINGTON Michael abt 60y in Easton, NY June 20, 1866

WILSON John in his 89th yr in Hebron, NY May 30, 1866

WILCOX Sarah age 77y widow of Thurston in Greenwich, NY June 23, 1866

STOVER Ensign age 18y in Greenwich, NY June 23, 1866

COOK Leonard in Easton, NY June 25, 1866

COTTRELL Mary age 77y widow of Thomas in Greenwich, NY July 7, 1866

JACKSON Bradford B. age 40y in Stillwater, NY July 10, 1866

FOSTER John in Greenwich, NY July 15, 1866

CROCKER Elizabeth in her 72nd yr in Cambridge, NY July 19, 1866

JONES Mary E. age 2y 1d dau of Alfred J. and Ann in Greenwich, NY July 26, 1866

BASSETT Alexander abt 50y in Cambridge, NY July 30, 1866

VOLENTINE Joel age 74y formerly of Jackson, NY in Bennington, Vt. July 17, 1866

ROBINSON Mrs. Charles abt 30y in S. Argyle, NY July 7, 1866

MARSHALL David abt 40y in Cambridge, NY July 26, 1866

COLLINS Mrs. Jane in her 78th yr in Greenwich, NY August 27, 1866

PHILLIPS Jennie in her 28th yr wife of Thomas and dau of Robert and Hester **SHANNON** of Argyle, NY in Saratoga Springs, NY August 15, 1866

KERR Jennett age 73y in Salem, NY August 19, 1866

VAN DYNE Miss Mary age 55y in Greenwich, NY September 4, 1866

STANLEY Arthur H. infant son of Theodore S. and Eunice in N. Argyle, NY August 22, 1866

FOLLETT Emily F. wife of Joseph L. and dau of J. H. **BARNARD** in Greenwich, NY September 8, 1866

WALKER Warren in his 87th yr formerly of Washington Co. at son-in-laws George **HALLAND** in Victory Mills, NY September 5, 1866

CAMERON Huldah age 48y formerly of Greenwich, NY in Glens Falls, NY August 27, 1866

HENRY Mary Eliza age 5y dau of James L. and Fannie S. in Sturgeon, Ill. August 30, 1866

BUDD Jacob S. bro of Mrs. Walden **EDDY** of Greenwich, NY in Madison Parish, La. August 25, 1866

WILCOX Rebecca age 42y relict of Cortes near Memphis, Tenn. August 23, 1866

JOHNSON Hester (colored) age 83y in Greenwich, NY September 11, 1866

HITCHCOCK Sarah G. age 52y in Salem NY September 5, 1866

JENKINS Augusta M. age 20y dau of Charles and Margaret in Battenville, NY August 20, 1866

LAW Hannah M. age 22y dau of David in Salem, NY September 10, 1866

STANLEY Benajah Burnett age 6y son of Darius and Sarah in Shushan, NY September 8, 1866

HORTON Sumner age 15y son of Abraham and Margaret (**BAUMES**) in Greenwich, NY September 28, 1866

HALL Elizabeth age 74y in Cambridge, NY September 29, 1866

WEIR Rosilla age 23y dau of Alonzo in Jackson, NY September 29, 1866

FENTON Seneca age 38y formerly of Greenwich, NY in Leavenworth, Ks. October 24, 1866

GRANT Hattie A. age 17y in Sandy Hill, NY October 22, 1866

STEWART John age 40y in Lakeville, NY October 27, 1866

BROWN Isachar Holmes age 55y in Greenwich, NY November 9, 1866

ROSEBUSH Adolphus abt 28y Pvt. in Co. A. 123rd Reb. NY Vol. in Greenwich, NY November 11, 1866

WILLIAMS Sarah Jane age 32y in Greenwich, NY November 10, 1866

MC NAMARA John age 21 at res. of Daniel **BARBER** in Easton, NY November 4, 1866

PERRY Hugh in his 86th yr in Salem, NY November 1, 1866

WEEKS Helen in her 5th yr dau of Charles and Susan in Greenwich, NY November 20, 1866

MAIN Joseph age 65y in Easton, NY November 18, 1866

RUSSELL Solomon W. age 66y in Salem NY October 28, 1866

COLLINS Emma E. age 1y 4m dau of Thomas formerly of Greenwich, NY in Troy, NY November 26, 1866

BLANCHARD Anthony age 36y son of late Anthony and Elizabeth of Albany, NY in Salem, NY November 24, 1866

HURD Reuben age 30y in Sandgate, Vt. November 17, 1866

DAWLEY Ellen age 24y wife of Morgan in Greenwich, NY December 4, 1866

DUNTON Josiah in his 90th yr in Cambridge, NY November 25, 1866

SWEET Mrs. Betsey L. age 56y dau of Rev. Daniel **TINKHAM** in Cambridge, NY December 2, 1866

SELFRIDGE Mary Jane age 39y wife of Oliver in Coila, NY December 7, 1866

WOODARD George age 68y in Easton, NY November 28, 1866

TOMPKINS Eliza age 38y wife of Lascom P. in Greenwich, NY December 21, 1866

DWELLE Betsey age 64y wife of Alphonso in Greenwich, NY December 24, 1866

REYNOLDS Jimmie age 1y 6m 10d son of William and Mary Augusta in Greenwich, NY December 22, 1866

BORDEN Smith age 88y in Easton, NY December 1, 1866

FILE Eliza J. age 46y in Easton, NY December 6, 1866

ROGERS James age 87y in Greenwich, NY December 8, 1866

BARBER Lyman age 61y in Jackson, NY December 21, 1866

VAN BUREN Gilbert age 26y in Greenwich, NY January 1, 1867

BAKER Mary age 87y widow of E. D. Baker and Mother of E. D. of Sandy Hill, NY at French Mountain, NY December 9, 1866

SKINNER Eli in his 69th yr at Ft. Ann, NY December 16, 1866

BAKER Reuben age 73y in Easton, NY November/December 29, 1866

LANSING Almira M. age 43y wife of W. at fathers John **MACE** in Ausable, NY December 30, 1866

CARTER Mrs. Hannah age 53y in Centre Falls, NY January 4, 1867

BASSETT Mary in her 86th yr widow of James at Ft. Miller, NY rec. (newspaper date January 31, 1867)

KENNEDY Anna Mary age 32y wife of Dr. L. W. and dau of late William **STEVENSON** in Coila, NY January 10, 1867

SHURTLIFF Laura in her 63rd yr wife of Rev. Asaph Shurtliff formerly of Greenwich, NY in Troy, NY January 31, 1867

ROWAN William R. age 76y in Brooklyn, NY January 21, 1867. Buried Salem, NY

CHERRY Oliver in his 29th yr son of James of E. Greenwich, NY in Sacramento, Cal. December 22, 1866

WRIGHT Alva in his 62nd yr in Salem, NY February 4, 1867

WRIGHT Dr. Daniel S. in his 65th yr in Whitehall, NY December 31, 1866

ALLEN Sarah dau of C. L. Allen of Salem, NY in Albany, NY January 29, 1867

PATTISON John age 88y 3m 23d formerly of Ft. Miller, NY in New York February 6, 1867. Buried Ft. Miller

PRENTISS Elizabeth age 23y dau of Gilman and Almira in Schaghticoke, NY October 16, 1866

CLAPP Phebe in her 77th yr wife of Dr. John Clapp in Belcher, NY January 23, 1867

LAMBERT Boardman age 23y son of A. B. in Hoosick Falls, NY December 11, 1866

SHERWOOD Thomas A. age 80y in Ft. Edward, NY February 20, 1867

PARDO James age 32y in Whitehall, NY February 27, 1867

CALHOUN Susan in her 51st yr wife of James in Greenwich, NY March 9, 1867

DENNIS Martha in her 60th yr wife of Seneca in Galesville, NY March 23, 1867

WING Charles age 76y in Shushan, NY March 19, 1867

CORLISS Roxena age 67y wife of Nathan in Easton, NY April 5, 1867

BALL Sylvanius age 29y at father-in-laws Harvey **BREWER** in Greenwich, NY April 6, 1867

HUTTON John age 57y in Greenwich, NY April 8, 1867

HANSOM Rev. H. W. age 54y in E. Dorset, Vt. March 24, 1867

WILSON Elizabeth age 47y widow of Capt. H. S. in Sandy Hill, NY March 30, 1867

RICHEY Elishaby P. age 59y wife of William and dau of late Justin **FARNHAM** of Salem, NY in W. Rupert, Vt. March 19, 1867

SCHERMERHORN James S. age 37y in S. Argyle, NY March 26, 1867

SKINNER Ann age 70y at son-in-laws Dr. Morgan **COLE** in Greenwich, NY February 19, 1867

BABCOCK Henry D. in his 66th yr formerly of Marcy, NY in Galesville, NY April 15, 1867

MC COLLUM Margrette wife of William and dau of John and Isabel **STEWART** in Argyle, NY April 4, 1867

HASKELL D. D. in his 44th yr April 23, 1867

WRIGHT Mary age 28y dau of John F. in Greenwich, NY April 29, 1867

MOORE Archa age 9m son of William H. and Anna E. in Galesville, NY April 20, 1867

STEWART Emma age 21y dau of James in Greenwich, NY May 4, 1867

BOSWORTH Jabez age 92y formerly of Greenwich, NY in Troy, NY May 5, 1867

RITTER William age 45y in Troy, NY May 5, 1867

OATLEY wife of G. Oatley and dau of Robert **LANGWORTHY** of Greenwich, NY in Salem, NY May 10, 1867

BAYLE Luke age 35y in Greenwich, NY May 19, 1867

HENRY Julia age 19y adopted dau of Alexander and Isabella in S. Argyle, NY May 7, 1867

HAWLEY Ella B. age 4y 5m dau of Fletcher and Ann in Danby, Vt. May 13, 1867

CONWAY Mary age 70y in Cambridge, NY May 25, 1867

BREWER Mary age 23y widow of Horace in Greenwich, NY June 7, 1867

ROBINSON Francis age 74y in Greenwich, NY June 7, 1867

FOSTER Marian age 16y dau of Allen in Greenwich, NY July 7, 1867

LANSING Anna age 4y 8m dau of Austin F. and Sarah E. in Schuylerville, NY June 25, 1867

BEATY Nancy age 73y widow of John in Salem NY July 12, 1867

BINNINGER W. S. age 28y 6m 9d of Milwaukee, Wis. at fathers Isaac W. in E. Salem, NY August 1, 1867

SCHUYLER Pharoah abt 70y in Easton, NY August 1, 1867

HAZARD Carrie E. age 4y dau of Leonard G. and Caroline in Greenwich, NY August 5, 1867

COTTRELL Horace age 46y in Easton, NY August 14, 1867

MC FARLAND William E. in his 64th yr in Jackson, NY August 11, 1867

LAPMAN Mary age 15y in Jackson, NY August 11, 1867

BAKER Solomon in his 71st yr in N. Easton, NY August 25, 1867

COZZENS Nancy M. in her 52nd yr at Ft. Ann, NY August 19, 1867

SMITH Solomon in his 78th yr in N. Hartford, NY August 19, 1867

TABER Joseph age 72y in Easton, NY August 27, 1867

TEFFT Sarah P. age 53y wife of Gardner in Greenwich, NY August 31, 1867

KETCHUM John age 94y in Cambridge, NY August 10, 1867

MOORE Harriet G. age 41y wife of James in Salem, NY September 2, 1867

ROBERTSON Rebecca age 33y dau of late Alvin in Cambridge, NY August 28, 1867

HOPKINS Sally age 75y wife of Amos in W. Rupert, Vt. August 19, 1867

HOPKINS Walter H. age 3m 2d son of F. W. and Frances in W. Rupert, Vt. August 18, 1867

MUHALL James age 80y at Ft. Edward, NY September 14, 1867

SHEFFIELD Polly age 86y of Greenwich, NY in County Home September 12, 1867

BARTHOLOMEW Lemuel in his 77th yr in Dresden, NY August 24, 1867

SPENCER Mrs. Fayette L. age 42y in N. Granville, NY September 7, 1867

CULVER Jane age 70y wife of Isaac in Jackson, NY September 18, 1867

LEWIS Benjamin age 53y of Rupert, Vt. in Poultney, Vt. September 1, 1867

HULSKAMP Sophia age 32y wife of Theodore in New York September 9, 1867

MURCH Electa in her 66th yr wife of Bectus in Greenwich, NY October 1, 1867

WRIGHT George age 78y in Jackson, NY October 3, 1867

WEIR Clementine age 21y dau of John A. in Salem, NY October 14, 1867

NORTHUP Mary F. in her 31st yr wife of Henry in Easton, NY September 30, 1867

GIFFORD Allen age 9m 24d son of Gideon G. and Catherine M. in Easton, NY September 16, 1867

SHERMAN Mrs. Mary age 72y in Greenwich, NY October 12, 1867

ANDREWS Sarah L. age 19y 5m 23d dau of E. in Greenwich, NY October 17, 1867

PARKER Morgan W. age 43y in Greenwich, NY October 20, 1867

ALLEN Annie in her 74th yr widow of Elisha in W. Rupert, Vt. September 23, 1867

CARMAN Ellen A. wife of C. W. and dau of H. B. NORTHUP of Sandy Hill, NY at sea on way to San Francisco, Cal. September 22, 1867

HOLMES Mary in her 80th yr widow of Dr. Cornelius in Greenwich, NY October 27, 1867 (next issue gives date of October 24, 1867)

BOSWORTH George H. age 29y in Greenwich, NY October 27, 1867

CROSBY Sarah Maria age 53y wife of Samuel W. in Cambridge, NY October 23, 1867

FLAHERTY Hannah age 19y in Jackson, NY October 27, 1867

WHIPPLE Mrs. Wealthy in her 104th yr in Greenwich, NY November 1, 1867

BROWN Dr. Warren age 69y in Granville, NY October 23, 1867

POTTER John age 74y in Greenwich, NY November 10, 1867

WATSON Josephine A. in her 25th yr wife of William D. and dau of D. and S. M. **KENYON** in Greenwich, NY November 13, 1867

HAWLEY Esther Ann age 43y wife of Hiram in Arlington, Vt. November 14, 1867

DAVIS Mrs. Charity age 60y in Greenwich, NY November 15, 1867

NILES Josie S. age 26y wife of Walter C. in White Creek, NY November 12, 1867

LARMAN Hannah L. age 31y wife of William in Cambridge, NY November 14, 1867

SPARHAWK Delia E. in her 17th yr in Greenwich, NY December 1, 1867

BISHOP Hayden age 16y son of late Elihu and Hannah B. in Jackson, NY November 17, 1867

MOORE Mary abt 70y wife of Archibald in Greenwich, NY December 6, 1867

SOULE Mrs. Nancy age 80y Mother of Rev. F. A. Soule of Greenwich, NY in La Grange Mo. January 2, 1868

GLEASON Erastus age 64y formerly of Greenwich, NY in Waucans, Ill. (newspaper date January 16, 1868)

FISHER Joseph in his 77th yr native of England in Greenwich, NY January 21, 1868

FISH Sarah Jane age 24y 5m dau of Ephraim **BRADEY** of Greenwich, NY in New Castle, Upper Canada West January 18, 1868

ABEL David over 80y near Saranac Lake, NY January 7, 1868

CARPENTER Maria age 63y wife of Daniel in Corinth, NY December 1, 1867

BURROUGHS Elizabeth age 65y relict of Ephraim in Cambridge, NY January 27, 1868

PHILLIPS Thomas of New York at res. of Robert **SHANNON** in Argyle, NY February 7, 1868

MC EACHRON John age 70y in N. Argyle, NY February 7, 1868

PIERSON William age 63 of Glens Falls, NY in Staffordshire, Eng. January 13, 1868

WEED Charles B. age 17y in Glens Falls, NY February 24, 1868

HUGHES Minnie R. age 10y dau of Charles in Sandy Hill, NY February 26, 1868

BOYCE Lydia age 73y 3m of Danby, Vt. at Battenville, NY February 26, 1868

HALL Mrs. Robert G. abt 66y in Argyle, NY March 10, 1868

SALTER John Henry abt 15y son of John in Jackson, NY March 9, 1868

CULVER Carrie age 1y 9m dau of Stephen and Lucy E. **(SMITH)** in New York March 7, 1868. Buried Greenwich, NY

BRINDLE Maria M. age 31y in Argyle, NY March 20, 1868

HILLMAN Mathew in his 82nd yr in Jackson, NY March 20, 1868

ROGERS Charlotte M. age 53y wife of Archibald in Easton, NY March 26, 1868

NORTON Charles Henry age 9y son of Leroy in Greenwich, NY March 22, 1868

WILSON Ann **(COLLINS)** in her 45th yr wife of David formerly of Greenwich, NY in Troy, NY March 20, 1868

ALLEN Jeannette B. age 40y relict of William C. and dau of late Billings **BLAKELEY** in Greenwich, NY April 9, 1868

MC GEOCH Mrs. Robert in S. Argyle, NY April 15, 1868

BUEL Mrs. Sally formerly of Greenwich, NY in Saratoga Springs, NY April 15, 1868

BEATTIE Mrs. Peter age 70y in Argyle, NY April 26, 1868

MASTERS Leroy Mowry age 16y son of John T. and Mary E. in Greenwich, NY May 5, 1868

HALL Eliza age 12y adopted dau of Marshall **MURCH** formerly of Greenwich, NY in N. Bennington, Vt. May 8, 1868

LAMONT George age 23y in N. Argyle, NY May 7, 1868

MADDEN Mary dau of Boyd in N. Argyle, NY May 10, 1868

STEWART John G. son of William of Jackson, NY in Enterprise, Fl. April 29, 1868

DWELLE Horton age 35y in Greenwich, NY June 7, 1868

ANGWINE Elizabeth in her 92nd yr wife of Isaac in Mt. Pleasant, NY April 22, 1868

SCHOOLHOUSE Jacob age 10y son of Charles and Fanny in Greenwich, NY June 9, 1868

HARRINGTON Hannah age 82y relict of Peleg of Easton, NY at dau Mrs. Jape **CROWNER** in Greenwich, NY June 17, 1868

CLARK Adeline Amelia age 31y 5m 27d wife of C. H. and dau of Jehiel and Harriet **RUSSELL** in Greenwich, NY June 21, 1868

BARRETT Josiah age 74y in Greenwich, NY June 21, 1868

SELFRIDGE William age 83y in S. Argyle, NY June 17, 1868

DURKEE Walter in Argyle, NY June 26, 1868

HOLLINGSWORTH Eliza Ann (**ALLEN**) formerly of Greenwich, NY in Lewisburgh, Ohio July 6, 1868

MILLER Mattie age 27y in N. Greenwich, NY July 15, 1868. Buried Argyle, NY

MC MULLEN Mrs. John abt 75y in S. Argyle, NY July 15, 1868

MOSHER Arnold age 12y son of Dennis in N. Argyle, NY July 14, 1868

STEVENS Phillip Edwin age 6m 13d son of E. R. and Ruth in Greenwich, NY August 2, 1868

ADAMS Charles H. age 25y in Greenwich, NY August 4, 1868

TEFFT Rennie N. age 2y 11m son of Caleb and Helen in Ft. Miller, NY August 24, 1868

STEWART John in his 17th yr in Bald Mountain, NY August 31, 1868

WILCOX Willie age 10m son of Hiram and Sarah in Greenwich, NY August 7, 1868

FAXON Leroy K. in his 23rd yr drowned in Cowans Lake, NY August 8, 1868

DOWD John age 50y in Greenwich, NY August 20, 1868

PRENTISS Ann age 55y wife of J. M. in Springfield, Vt. August 21, 1868

COZZENS George H. in his 54th yr formerly of Greenwich, NY in Saratoga Springs, NY August 24, 1868

MARTINDALE Desire age 63y in Saratoga Springs, NY September 19, 1868

BAUMES Margaret age 62y 5m 10d wife of Abram in Greenwich, NY September 28, 1868

WILCOX Orrin R. age 41y formerly of Greenwich, NY in Dover, Del. September 25, 1868

BARBER Ella age 17y dau of Daniel in Greenwich, NY November 4, 1868

DURHAM Ezra age 53y in Bald Mountain, NY November 3, 1868

WHITE Alice Albertice age 15y dau of Benjamin and Caroline November 10, 1868 and Julia A. age 18y eldest dau died November 13, 1868

SOUTHWORTH Emma (or Anna) Mary age 40y dau of late Joseph in Greenwich, NY November 14, 1868

WHITE Benjamin T. age 50y in Greenwich, NY November 20, 1868

LONG Isabelle age 22y wife of Thomas/Thadeus in Greenwich, NY November 24, 1868

MC NEIL Catherine Eliza age 3y died November 13, 1868 and Daniel M. age 5y died November 15, 1868 children of Neil M. in Argyle, NY

CUTHBERT John W. abt 38y in Argyle, NY November 24, 1868

SHIPHERD James H. abt 24y in Argyle, NY November 28, 1868

GILCHRIST Andrew in his 99th yr in Hebron, NY November 28, 1868

CAREY Isaac J. age 40y in Belcher, NY December 3, 1868

MC EACHRON Eliza/ Ella age 80y wife of James in Argyle, NY December 11, 1868

issues missing 1869 - 1873

ROOT Mrs. Matilda in her 94th yr in Hebron, NY December 24, 1874

STEWART Margaret age 77y widow of George in Salem, NY December 29, 1874

LANT Henry G. age 68y in Argyle, NY December 27, 1874

COCHRANE Edward A. age 55y in Winhall, Vt. November 25, 1874

SEAMAN Stephen age 93y in Schuylerville, NY December 29, 1874

WELLS Elijah age 76y bro of late Leonard of Cambridge, NY in Buffalo, NY December 23, 1874

CRANDALL Asher A. age 47y in Cambridge, NY December 25, 1874

HALL George M. age 67y in Cambridge, NY December 28, 1874

PERO Mary A. age 67y wife of A. in Whitehall, NY December 29, 1874

HEWITT Frankie A. age 25y wife of Adelbert in Ft. Edward, NY December 26, 1874

COY Nellie age 3y dau of C. P. in Easton, NY January 1, 1875

MEADER Helen age 20y wife of W. L. in Easton, NY January 9, 1875

BATES Deborah N. age 78y in Greenwich, NY January 14, 1875, buried Weymouth, Mass.

WHIPPLE W. W. age 77y at son-in-laws Job G. **SHERMAN** in Greenwich, NY January 11, 1875

ADAMS John age 86y in Easton, NY January 12, 1875

MC NISH William in his 77th yr in Salem, NY December 31, 1874

NAUGHTON Mary age 36y formerly of Salem, NY in New York December 31, 1874

LARMON William age 90y in Cambridge, NY December 30, 1874

BURNS Catherine age 78y in Cambridge, NY (newspaper date January 21, 1875)

DAVIS Lydia Lee age 50y wife of Henry M. in Salem, NY January 14, 1875

HAY Alexander/Andrew age 59y in Lake, NY January 2, 1875

MURRAY John F. age 7y 7m died December 28, 1874, George F. age 11y 7m died December 29, 1874, Katie age 5y 6m died December 31, 1874, Hattie E. age 13y died January 1, 1875, Eva J. age 9y 3m died January 2, 1875, William H. age 6y 4m died January 3, 1875, Ida age 17y died January 6, 1875, and Emma age 15y died January 8, 1875, children of E. B. Murray in Whitehall, NY

FLATTEY Michael age 50/80y (illegible) in Easton, NY January 5, 1875

BAIN John A. age 18y son of James Jr. in Argyle, NY January 6, 1875

BESHART George age 70y of Argyle, NY in the County Home December 16, 1874

LACKEY Mrs. Peggy age 70y in Hartford, NY January 4, 1875

MARSHALL Mrs. Jane age 54y in Victory Mills, NY January 3, 1875

FAXON Mrs. Mary age 91y in Greenwich, NY January 27, 1875

BAGGOT Katie age 16y in Victory Mills, NY January __, 1875

WOOD Mrs. Alonzo age 73y in Hartford, NY January 11, 1875

WHALEY Samuel age 78y in Ft. Miller, NY January 7, 1875

STEVENS Freeland G. age 21y son of Gardner and Maria in Ft. Ann, NY December 28, 1874

WILCOX Mrs. Sanford age 22y in Glens Falls, NY January 7, 1875

DIXON E. B. age 67y in Hartford, NY January 14, 1875

CARTER Josephine age 74y wife of L. D. in Dresden, NY January 8, 1875

HOLT Nathan Bennett age 58y in Whitehall, NY January 11, 1875

HALL George W. age 64y formerly of Cambridge, NY in Chenango Forks, NY January 14, 1875

ODBERT Mattie E. age 37y wife of George E. in Salem, NY January 15, 1875

LONG Kate wife of Lucius in Greenwich, NY January 30, 1875

HOLMES Ann Caroline widow of Henry and dau of William and Lydia **MOWRY** in Greenwich, NY February 3, 1875. Born October 13, 1809 in Easton, NY

SELEE Nathan age 78y in White Creek, NY January 24, 1875

INGALLS Ebenezer age 73y in Whitehall, NY January 25, 1875

KENNEDY Mrs. M. age 65y in Whitehall, NY January 24, 1875

HILL Gilson age 68y in Kingsbury, NY January 24, 1875

WEIR Lena S. age 27y dau of Abram in Greenwich, NY February 6, 1875

LARKIN Ann M. age 35y wife of William in E. Greenwich, NY February 7, 1875

PLATT Frances D. age 28y wife of Orson F. in Galesville, NY February 6, 1875

DAY Nancy wife of William in Belcher, NY February 5, 1875

BURDICK Daniel age 14m son of Orley L. and Matilda in Rodman, NY January 13, 1875

ANDREWS Arnie age 88y in Pittstown, NY February 6, 1875

VIELE Peter age 70y in Ft. Miller, NY (newspaper date February 11, 1875)

HARFOR Robert age 60y in S. Argyle, NY January 30, 1875

RICE John age 64y in Argyle, NY January 30, 1875

HALL Mrs. Atherton age 72y in Whitehall, NY February 1, 1875

ANTHONY Andrew age 54y in Cambridge, NY February 3, 1875

BEATTIE ____ age 5m son of James H. in N. Argyle, NY January 18, 1875

REID John abt 70y in Argyle, NY January 31, 1875

HARPER Robert in S. Argyle, NY January 30, 1875

MC MAHON Mary age 94y in Jackson, NY January 29, 1875

WILLIAMSON Nancy age 18y in Greenwich, NY February 12, 1875

HARRINGTON Richard age 78y in Easton, NY February 11, 1875

SMITH William age 75y in N. Granville, NY February 8, 1875

REBELA Mrs. Thomas abt 50y in N. Granville, NY February 1, 1875

BLAIR infant dau of Lewis in N. Granville, NY February 6, 1875

MC INTYRE Agassis age 1y 5m son of Lewis C. and Rosa M. (HITCHCOCK) in Buskirks Bridge, NY February 10, 1875

TALLMAN Mrs. B. F. age 53y formerly of Sandy Hill, NY in Glens Falls, NY January 24, 1875

ESMAN Ludiwig age 73y in Cambridge, NY February 13, 1875

CHAMBERS Dennis age 66y in Cambridge, NY February 14, 1875

OVIATT Nancy age 74y in Jackson, NY February 15, 1875

WOODWORTH Louisa A. age 48y in Jackson, NY February 13, 1875

FERRIS Benjamin F. age 82y in Sandy Hill, NY February 15, 1875

COOPER Miss Mary E. age 41y in Sandy Hill, NY February 14, 1875

MOORE Carrie infant dau of George and Alice in Sandy Hill, NY February 16, 1875

CRAMER Miss Mary age 74y in Grangerville, NY February 9, 1875. Sis Mrs. Calvin REID

WHITE Susannah age 84y widow of Moses H. in Greenwich, NY March 1, 1875

HARRIS Charles Jr. age 62y in Sandy Hill, NY February 19, 1875

BANCROFT George age 38y son of late Laysel in Ft. Edward, NY February 18, 1875

KETCHUM Amanda age 75y widow of John in Argyle, NY February 18, 1875

GILMAN Charles O. T. age 34y in Salem, NY February 22, 1875

BURNETT Phebe R. age 19y 9m dau of John and Sarah M. in Salem, NY February 14, 1875

BROWN Valentine age 30y son of George at French Mountain, NY February 18, 1875

PERCY Ransom age 80y in Hartford, NY February 17, 1875

RICE Mrs. Catherine age 81y in Sandy Hill, NY March 2, 1875

PALMER Mary Ann age 58y wife of William in Sandy Hill, NY March 4, 1875

GANTZ Mrs. Sarah age 81y in Salem NY March 1, 1875

MC KALLOR Anthony age 83y in Argyle, NY March 2, 1875

REID Mrs. Donald age 32y in Argyle, NY February 28, 1875

WILLIAMS Mrs. Betsey age 62/82 in Easton, NY March 17,1875

ROGERS Nettie wife of Deliverance and dau of John **BISHOP** in Granville, NY March 13, 1875

BOOL Margaret C. age 58y widow of William B. in Salem, NY March 11, 1875

SHERMAN Mrs. Lucy age 75y in Cambridge, NY March 3, 1875

HANRIHAN Mrs. Mary age 33y in Jackson, NY March 10, 1875

HARVEY George age 23y son of Heber and Jane in Kingsbury, NY March 8, 1875

WARK Mary age 42y in Whitehall, NY March 1, 1875

SHATTUCK Mrs. Roswell age 42y in Dresden, NY March 2, 1875

CROCKER Sarah wife of J. D. formerly of Cambridge, NY in Langley, Va. March 2, 1875

BROUGHTON Mrs. Hannah age 79y in Ft. Ann, NY March 14, 1875

BARKLEY Florence age 2m 2w dau of John A. and Fanny in Argyle, NY March 15, 1875

MYGATT Mrs. Dina age 74y in Whitehall, NY March 11, 1875

PERCIVAL Mrs. Sally O. age 79y 4m in Whitehall, NY March 11, 1875

COZZENS Earl M. age 66y in Greenwich, NY April 1, 1875

ROBERTSON John A. age 23m son of Duncan and Alice in S. Argyle, NY March 29, 1875

THOMAS Miss Lucy age 88y in Easton, NY March 24, 1875

SNOW Frankie age 1y 3m son of Samuel in Whitehall, NY March 22, 1875

AMLOW _____ age 4y son of A. in Whitehall, NY March 22, 1875

BAKER Betsey age 56y in Pumpkin Hook, NY March 23, 1875

WALSH Hannah age 18y in N. Argyle, March 22, 1875

CHAMBERS Cynthia age 28y in Jackson, NY March 17, 1875

CULVER Harvey age 71y formerly of Whitehall, NY in Vassar, Mi. March 19, 1875

KNICKERBOCKER Sarah M. age 31y wife of H. H. in Argyle, NY March 12, 1875

ALMY Miss _____ age 86y in Greenwich, NY April 7, 1875

THOMAS Everett E. age 17y 6m in Greenwich, NY April 7, 1875

DOOLITTLE Orlando F. age 36y in Schuylerville, NY March 24, 1875

HOLMES J. J. age 64y formerly of Sandy Hill, NY in Joliet, Ill. March 8, 1875

KENYON Joel age 40y in N. Argyle, NY March 27, 1875

WILLIAMS Mrs. Clarissa age 66y in Salem, NY March 27, 1875

HALL James age 78y n Argyle, NY March 28, 1875

HASTINGS Mrs. Martha in her 88th yr in Greenwich, NY April 4, 1875

SHERMAN Adly in N. Greenwich, NY April 2, 1875

TERRY Seth H. age 76y in Greenwich, NY April 6, 1875

HAMLIN Sarah age 95y Mother of Mrs. A. M. **ROWAN** in Argyle, NY April 4, 1875

CALHOUN John A. age 75y in Greenwich, NY April 9, 1875

VAN NESS Matilda in Center Falls, NY April 3, 1875

TEFFT Cathern Ann age 49y wife of Amos M. and only dau of Joseph and Maria **BENSON** in Galesville, NY April 9, 1875

WICKS Albert M. age 64y in Easton, NY April 13, 1875

BENNETT Alice A. age 21y in Greenwich, NY April 21, 1875

STEWART James age 75y in Greenwich, NY April 21, 1875, born Ireland came here 5 yrs ago. Wife Eliza/Almira age 66y died April 18, 1875

MALBY Alexander age 73y in Greenwich, NY April 14, 1875

MILLER Susan age 48y wife of Joseph in Greenwich, NY April 16, 1875

KENYON Sarah Jane age 36y wife of Harper in Greenwich, NY April 10, 1875

SHAW John S. age 71y in Middle Falls, NY April 16, 1875

MC CLELLAN Elizabeth P. age 64y in Greenwich, NY April 25, 1875

GILBERT Benjamin R. abt 80y in Middle Falls, NY April 29, 1875

WILBUR Job age 78y in Easton, NY April 26, 1875

BULSON Olive A. age 49y wife of Lodowick in Greenwich, NY May 2, 1875

HALE ____ age 2y adopted dau of George in Argyle, NY April 26, 1875

CUBIT Martha age 46y wife of Richard in Greenwich, NY May 8, 1875

CHUBB Simon M. age 56y in Greenwich, NY May 11, 1875

MALONEY John age 68y in Easton, NY May 6, 1875

OWEN Miss Eleanor age 62y in Easton, NY May 14, 1875

COLONNEY Lizzie age 18y in S. Cambridge, NY May 14, 1875

FOSTER Sidney age 69y in Greenwich, NY May 24, 1875

BARNES Alzina in Greenwich, NY May 20, 1875

EDDY Daniel age 58y in Easton, NY May 30, 1875

SEDDON Jessie Culver age 3y 16d in Greenwich, NY May 31, 1875

SISSON Constant age 84y in Easton, NY June 2, 1875

SAFFORD Eva age 8y in Ft. Edward, NY May 28, 1875

FLYNN ____ age 17m dau of John in Cambridge, NY May 18, 1875

HARRIS Ira age 88y in Kingsbury, NY June 3, 1875

ROZELL Capt. John age 63y in Ft. Edward, NY June 1, 1875

POTTER Ann Lizzie age 13y dau of Erastus and Jane of Greenwich, NY in Plattsburgh, NY June 26, 1875

HEMINGWAY Mrs. ____ in Sandy Hill, NY June 20, 1875

TOWNSEND Mrs. Phebe in S. Hartford, NY June 17, 1875

MEADER Eliza age 65y wife of Robert in Easton, NY July 11, 1875

HILLMAN Ephraim age 73y in Broadalbin, NY June 26, 1875

PATTERSON Eliza A. age 49y wife of Benjamin in S. Greenwich, NY July 23, 1875

FURSMAN Jesse B. age 65y in Easton, NY July 5, 1875

GRANGER Asa age 19y son of Henry in Greenwich, NY July 26, 1875

SHAW Mrs. John age 61y in Greenwich, NY July 7, 1875

LAWRENCE twins abt 10m of L. L. in Granville, NY August 8, and August 9, 1875

ADAMS Mrs. Catherine age 82y 5m 7d in Westhaven, Vt. August 19, 1875

BULKLEY Alfred age 68y in Granville, NY August 13, 1875

COOPER Eunice A. age 49y in Hartford, NY August 20, 1875

PARKS Timothy age 74y in Hartford, NY August 22, 1875

VOSBURGH Mrs. Margaret age 68y in Whitehall, NY August 20, 1875

HILL Mrs. Susan S. age 61y in Schuylerville, NY August 6, 1875

GILCHRIST Archibald age 69y in N. Argyle, NY August 21, 1875

ROBERTSON Miss Mary in N. Argyle, NY August 21, 1875

HAY Ellen wife of J. W. in Hebron, NY August 16, 1875

MC CALL Mrs. Elizabeth age 37y in Salem, NY (newspaper date September 2, 1875)

DEWEY R. King age 56y in Cambridge, NY August 23, 1875

GREEN Hannah age 72y in Coila, NY August 23, 1875

HOLMES John S. age 62y in W. Ft. Ann, NY August 18, 1875

LIVINGSTON Louise age 64y 2m wife of Alexander and Mother of James H. formerly of Cambridge, NY in Hoosick Falls, NY August 23, 1875

CLARK Thomas in Easton, NY August 20, 1875

MC KEE Cynthia Ann age 48y in Arlington, Vt. August 27, 1875

DYER John K. age 70y in White Creek, NY August 28, 1875

HAGGERTY Mary Agnes age 1m in Cambridge, NY August 28, 1875

MC SHANE Peter age 78y in Sandy Hill, NY August 29, 1875

HAMMOND Mary age 64y in Ft. Edward, NY September 1, 1875

WILSON Mathew age 60y in Ft. Edward, NY August 30, 1875

VIELE Eddie D. age 16y 3m 2d son of D. M. in Ft. Edward, NY September 1, 1875

COOLEY James Clark age 15y 4m son of Dr. Leroy C. drowned in Argyle, NY September 1, 1875

MASTERS Nicolas Merritt Mowry 1st and only remaining son of John T. and Mary E. in Greenwich, NY September 10, 1875. Born August 22, 1842, married June 6, 1866 Mary **HARVEY** of Cincinnati

LANGLUS George abt 3y in Greenwich, NY September 13, 1875

TORENTO Willie age 1y 4m son of Lewis and Eliza Jane in Battenville, NY September 9, 1875

CAMERON Cynthia abt 53y in Stony Creek, NY August 29, 1875

HACKETT Mrs. Mary J. age 45y in Glens Falls, NY August 15, 1875

FARR Hannah age 80y relict of James in Ft. Ann, NY September 3, 1875

FOWLER David age 63y in White Creek, NY September 6, 1875

RAY Alanson age 75y in Cambridge, NY September 3, 1875

HALL James M. age 65y in Argyle, NY September 4, 1875

BARRETT Mrs. Annis age 75y in Dresden, NY August 19, 1875

MC LACHLAN Eliza age 23y in Whitehall, NY September 4, 1875

JACKSON Mrs. Mary age 77y in Whitehall, NY September 6, 1875

MALTHANER Edward M. age 9m 6d in Salem, NY September 9, 1875

AUSTIN Lena age 5m 10d dau of George and Carrie in Salem, NY September 3, 1875

THOMPSON Sherman age 24y son of late David in Rupert, Vt. September 4, 1875

MARTIN Mrs. Almira formerly of Salem, NY in Marcy, NY August 27, 1875

ALLEN Henry age 6m 15d son of John D. and Charlotte in W. Rutland Vt. September 2, 1875

KEESE Peter in his 78th yr in Saratoga Springs, NY (paper gives date as October 12,

1875, date of issue September 23, 1875)

COCHRANE Sally C. age 57y wife of Isaac N. in Fairmount, Ks. August 11, 1875

CLARK James R. age 72y in Victory Mills, NY September 3, 1875 formerly of Greenwich, NY

MORELL William A. age 14y in Sandy Hill, NY September 12, 1875

MORELL Amos B. age 3y in Sandy Hill, NY September 15, 1875

WHITCOMB Bessie age 6m dau of Charles and Elizabeth in Salem, NY September 14, 1875

SKELLIE Mrs. Maria age 72y in Coila, NY September 11, 1875

BLANCHARD Adda age 19y in Shushan, NY September 14, 1875

CENTER Sheldon age 68y in White Creek, NY September 12, 1875

PRATT Mary Leah age 4m 8d in White Creek, NY September 13, 1875

STARBUCK William A. age 31y in White Creek, NY September 14, 1875

WILSON Levinus age 43y in Cambridge, NY September 8, 1875

ROGERS Joseph age 80y in N. Ferrisburgh, Vt. August 26, 1875

ROOD Ann age 67y widow of Daniel in Greenwich, NY September 26, 1875

BURT Margaret age 75y in Northumberland, NY September 26, 1875

CROWL Rev. J. F. age 51y in Schaghticoke, NY September 14, 1875

WARNER George in N. Granville, NY September 13, 1875

WILSON infant child of Edward in N. Granville, NY September 13, 1875

NASH infant child in Rev. Charles Nash in N. Granville, NY September 17, 1875

SILL E. E. age 52y bro of Mrs. Mary **JOHNSON** of Sandy Hill, NY in Rochester, NY August 19, 1875. Sis Miss Lydia G. Sill age 63y died Moreau, NY September 7, 1875

HALE Harriet age 40y in Argyle, NY September 16, 1875

HILL George W. age 61y in S. Granville, NY September 3, 1875

WARREN George age 69y in N. Granville, NY September 13, 1875

CONNEY Thomas age 34y in Whitehall, NY September 18, 1875

TRUMBULL Miss Mary age 17y in Sandy Hill, NY September 27, 1875

HALL Alexander age 75y in Hartford, NY September 29, 1875

HALL James E. in Hartford, NY September 28, 1875

TINKEY infant dau of David in Argyle, NY September 28, 1875

RILEY Oliver age 6y in Whitehall, NY September 25, 1875

SHOVE Peter age 65y in Whitehall, NY September 26, 1875

VEAZIE J. age 75y in Whitehall, NY September 27, 1875

DWINNELL George age 24y in White Creek, NY September 25, 1875

SHERMAN Fidelia age 70y widow of Peleg in Jackson, NY October 7, 1875

TRIMBLE Mary J. age 16y 9m dau of Alexander and Margaret in Salem, NY September 27, 1875

FORREST Bertha I. age 14m 26d dau of Darwin and Maria in Salem, NY September 31?, 1875

WATERS ____ age 7y son of John in Whitehall, NY October 3, 1875

QUACKENBUSH David age 77y in Buskirks Bridge, NY October 5, 1875

SWEET Charles H. age 34y in Walloomsac, NY October 5, 1875

MC GOURLIE Grace age 30y in S. Hartford, NY October 2, 1875

MC AULEY Robert age 9y 10m son of John in Argyle, NY September 28, 1875

HALE Hattie age 18y dau of Robert and Mary in Argyle, NY September 30, 1875

WELCH Albert age 1y in Jackson, NY September 29, 1875

GATES George H. age 4y in White Creek, NY October 3, 1875

LYONS John age 5y son of Edward, NY in Whitehall, NY September 28, 1875

SHIELDS George age 5y son of Edward in Whitehall, NY September 15, 1875

TAYLOR Blanch V. dau of Zeliff and Nellie in Sandy Hill, NY September 26, 1875

REED Thomas S. son of William of New York and Grandson of Alexander **CATLIN** late of Kingsbury, NY in New York September 28, 1875

MILLER Mrs. David age 45y in Ft. Edward, NY October 6, 1875

HAY Jane in her 64th yr in Lakeville, NY October 17, 1875

VAN SCHAICK Gerritt in his 73rd yr in E. Greenwich, NY October 14, 1875

YOUNG May A. age 16y in Sandy Hill, NY October 7, 1875

EMPY F. N. age 73y in Ft. Ann, NY October 6, 1875

BEEKMAN Mrs. E. J. age 31y of Glens Falls in Schaghticoke, NY October 3, 1875

KNIGHT Harry J. age 19y in Glens Falls, NY October 6, 1875

BLANCHARD Ida Bell in Dresden, NY October 10, 1875

WAIT Horace Richard age 3y in Whitehall, NY October 8, 1875

PATTEN Florence age 11y in Ft. Edward, NY October 8, 1875

WHITESIDE Margaret E. age 66y wife of Thomas C. in Cambridge, NY October 6, 1875

BYRNE Mrs. Hannah age 90y in N. Argyle, NY October 11, 1875

OSBORN Mrs. Richard in her 88th yr in Greenwich, NY October 20, 1875

CLAPP Dr. John age 89y in Salem, NY October 15, 1875

EAGER Mary A. (NORTON) age 46y wife of Abram formerly of Greenwich, NY in Galesville, Ill. October 5, 1875

DERBY George Hamilton age 3m son of J. H. and M. S. in Sandy Hill, NY October 18, 1875

BLANCHARD infant dau of Charles in Dresden, NY October 19, 1875

SAWYER ___ age 10y dau of William in Whitehall, NY October 18, 1875

WARN Mary abt 45y wife of Orville of White Creek, NY in the County Home October 6, 1875

BEVIS Mrs. Elizabeth age 52y 6m in Salem, NY September 23, 1875

BARTON Minnie age 3y 11m dau of Ferris E. and Mattie A. of Ft. Edward, NY in Amsterdam, NY October 19, 1875

HERRINGTON James Harvey age 38y in Cambridge, NY October 18, 1875

PHELPS Jennie L. age 21y wife of Jesse B. in Fairhaven, Vt. October 18, 1875

ROBERTS Gertrude age 21y wife of John in M. Granville, NY October 20, 1875

REED Mrs. Sally in Whitehall, NY October 22, 1875

WATERS ____ age 6y son of William in Whitehall, NY October 23, 1875

ELLAGAPIN George in Cedar Rapids, Mi. October 2, 1875

CLAPP Col. Ephraim William age 85y in E. Salem, NY October 24, 1875

JOSLIN Emma E. age 23y 7m wife of Henry P. in Hoosick, NY October 26, 1875

CROZIER Margaret age 90y in N. Argyle, NY October 13, 1875

DENNIS Seneca age 76y in Middle Falls, NY November 7, 1875

ROGERS James abe 85y at Bald Mountain, NY November 6, 1875

BROWN Willie W. age 7y in Sandy Hill, NY October 22, 1875

BROWN Austin S. age 3y in Sandy Hill, NY October 30, 1875

LAPHAM Elisha age 83y in M. Granville, NY October 29, 1875

WILLIAMS Alice age 30y in N. Pawlet, Vt. October 26, 1875

BROWN Mrs. Sarah W. age 79y in Cambridge, NY October 25/26, 1875

ASHTON William age 86y in Salem, NY October 29, 1875

YARTER Agnes in Sandy Hill, NY October 15, 1875

YARTER Mary age 7y in Sandy Hill, NY October 20, 1875

YARTER Marcella age 5y in Sandy Hill, NY October 28, 1875

SNYDER Mrs. Martha age 33y in Sandy Hill, NY October 26, 1875

NELSON Orestus age 34y in Sandy Hill, NY October 27, 1875

HUDSON Mrs. Charles in her 26th yr in Hebron, NY October 27, 1875

BROWN Merrit in his 62nd yr in Hebron, NY November 6, 1875

LANSING Barent Bleecher age 74y in Greenwich, NY November 19, 1875

PRINDLE Lazarus G. age 83y in Argyle, NY November 9, 1875

HALL Mrs. William D. age 35y in Argyle, NY November 10, 1875

HOPKINS Miss Susie age 19y in Argyle, NY November 15, 1875

MC DOUGAL Mrs. Amos age 60y in S. Argyle, NY November 15, 1875

INMAN Louise age 19y in S. Argyle, NY November 16, 1875

MC LEAN Martha age 59y 6m wife of Ebenezer in Jackson, NY November 7, 1875

WAIT Sarah A. age 48y wife of Edward C. in Coila, NY November 9, 1875

ALLEN Moses age 76y of Ft. Edward, NY in the County Home November 6, 1875

QUINN Hannah age 32y wife of Michael in White Creek, NY November 7, 1875

SHEPPARD Cleveland age 22y in Depere, Wis. NY November 11, 1875

CHANDLER Mrs. Augustus age 81y in Granville, NY November 14, 1875

NOBLE Wilbur age 14y in Whitehall, NY November 20, 1875

WHEELER _____ age 3y son of Napoleon in Whitehall, NY November 22, 1875

SHERMAN Evva E. age 3y 10m dau of Nathaniel and Phebe in Pittstown, NY November 24, 1875

DALTON Patrick age 56y in Easton, NY December 6, 1875

STEWART Mercy Maria **(DUNLAP)** age 51y wife of William in Easton, NY December 5, 1875

MC NISH John age 85y in Cambridge, NY December 2, 1875

SHEDD Isaac age 71y in Buskirks Bridge, NY November 25, 1875

HILLMAN Mrs. Jane age 42y in Cambridge, NY November 26, 1875

HAVILAND Joseph age 82y in Queensbury, NY November 26, 1875

ELDRIDGE Albert age 61y formerly of Hartford, NY in Stephentown, NY (newspaper date December 9, 1875)

KENYON Ambrose H. age 70y in Greenwich, NY December 8, 1875

RYAN Mrs. Martha age 75y in Buskirks Bridge, NY December 12, 1875

THOMAS David age 44y of Johnsonville, NY in Easton, NY December 11, 1875

MC GEOCH Mrs. Eleanor age 67y in N. Greenwich, NY December 2, 1875

SHAW Warren age 23y in Ft. Edward, NY November 26, 1875

INMAN Jenks age 89y in S. Argyle, NY December 5, 1875

MAYNARD Horace G. age 53y formerly of Hartford, NY in Ross, Ohio (newspaper date December 16, 1875)

CRANDALL Edna A. (**BUCKLEY**) age 24y in Greenwich, NY December 23, 1875

CROWL Emma L. age 13y 5m dau of late Rev. J. F. in Schaghticoke, NY December 22, 1875

LABRUM Mrs. Maggie age 20y in Ft. Miller, NY December 10, 1875

RYDER Lizzie age 8y died November 27, 1875 and Laura age 15y died November 30, 1875 children of Mrs. E. Ryder in N. Granville, NY

SPENCER Fayette G. age 60y in Granville, NY December 9, 1875

SLIGHT Alexander age 81y in Dresden, NY (newspaper date December 23, 1875)

ADAMS Miss Kate L. age 30y in Greenwich, NY December 30, 1875

MOYNIHAN Bridget age 29y 6m wife of Patrick in Salem, NY December 16, 1875

BAKER William R. age 82y in Thurman, NY December 15, 1875

GREEN John in his 82nd yr in Glens Falls, NY December 17, 1875. Wife age 71y

LANSING Lydia age 23y of Greenwich, NY in the County Home December 13, 1875

PENDERGRASS James age 76y in Argyle, NY December 20, 1875

MORRIS Henry age 5y son of John and Ellen in Whitehall, NY December 17, 1875

BASCOM Hermonie age 6y dau of R. E. in Whitehall, NY December 18, 1875

SULLIVAN Ellen age 75y in Smiths Basin, NY December 20, 1875

BLINN _____ age 3y dau of Eben in Whitehall, NY December 21, 1875

DALTON Clara age 8y 9m dau of Lewis in Whitehall, NY December 17, 1875

SMALLEY Nancy age 90y in N. Argyle, NY December 20, 1875

STEWART Miss E. in Salem, NY December 24, 1875

(missing issues January through July 1876)

WILCOX Jesse age 48y in Ft. Miller, Ny July 22, 1876

VAUGHN Mrs. Washington age 50y in Ft. Ann, NY July 22, 1876

CASTLE Mrs. Maria age 62y in Whitehall, NY July 15, 1876

BRIGGS infant child of Royal in Whitehall, NY July 22, 1876

BLANCHARD infant child of Henry in Whitehall, NY July 22, 1876

HAYNER Otis age 71y in Easton, NY July 30,1876

EDDY Nathan age 67y in Easton, NY July 27, 1876

HILLMAN Ira Martin age 58y in Bald Mountain, NY August 6, 1876

BATES William A. abt 60y of Greenwich, NY in Binghamton, NY August 12, 1876

CARRINGTON Luke H. age 8m son of Luke H. in Whitehall, NY August 6, 1876

MC NEIL Alexander age 42y in E. Greenwich, NY August 12, 1876

WILLIAMS Eli P. age 83y in E. Greenwich, NY August 14, 1876

MC GHEE _____ age 9m child of Richard in Whitehall, NY August 11, 1876

FEELEY infant child of Martin in Whitehall, NY August 11, 1876

LAMPRA infant child of George in Whitehall, NY August 11, 1876

HOLCOMB _____ age 7y child of John in Whitehall, NY August 13, 1876

MELLON _____ age 1y 1m 11d child of John in Whitehall, NY August 15, 1876

RODD Solomon age 77y in Whitehall, NY August 15, 1876

BALDWIN Mary A. wife of Benjamin in Whitehall, NY August 18, 1876

MASON George B. age 21y 5d son of Charles L. in Granville, NY August 13, 1876

WAIT Mary Ellen age 1y dau of Rev. A. A. in Sandy Hill, NY August 17, 1876

LANGWORTHY Eva C. wife of H. C. at Mothers Mrs. Mary E. BIGGART in Kingsbury, NY August 14, 1876

BROWN Willie age 5m in Ft. Edward, NY August 13, 1876

PACKETT George age 24y of Whitehall, NY in the County Home August 14, 1876

SHANKS Ethel Harriet age 5m 15d dau of Robert in Greenwich, NY August 26, 1876

HUNT James in Brooklyn, NY August 27, 1876

GRANT Andrew age 77y in Whitehall, NY August 29, 1876

LAMPHIER Mrs. Abigail age 71y at India Lake, NY August 18, 1876

COGSHALL Mrs. Sarah age 93y in Easton, NY September 4, 1876

RUSSELL William A. son of David and Alida (**LANSING**) in Salem, NY September 1, 1876. Born Salem, NY December 5, 1812, married January 25, 1834 Clarissa **MC KILLIP**. She died October 21, 1857 age 42y. Married (2) February 27, 1860 Ada **CALDWELL** who died September 19, 1863 age 29y. Married (3) November 15, 1865 Mattie **FOX**, surviving

SHILAND Miss Mary J. age 39y in Greenwich, NY September 11, 1876

DE LONG Mrs. David age 27y in Easton, NY September 11, 1876

BRADLEY Rachel age 44y wife of David formerly of Greenwich, NY in Manuatea, Ks. September 1, 1876

BRESNAHAM Mrs. Margaret age 43y in Sandy Hill, NY September 5, 1876

MC TAGUE Mrs. Patrick in Sandy Hill, NY September 5, 1876

TASEY George age 64y in N. Greenwich, NY September 18, 1876

HILLS Frank M. age 21y in Hartford, NY September 25, 1876

DALTON Mrs. L. age 73y in Whitehall, NY September 22, 1876

COGSHALL Arnold B. age 73y in Cambridge, NY October 1, 1876

DUNN Murty age 62y in Greenwich, NY September 19, 1876

HITCHCOCK Miss Hattie age 24y dau of late Rev. P. M. in Pottersville, NY October 2, 1876

NICHOLS Daniel age 80y 10m 28d at dau Mrs. Charles **ROGERS** in Rockport, Mass. September 16, 1876

LANGDON Samuel in Greenwich, NY October 20, 1876. Born February 1, 1811 in Kingsbury, NY to Orthodox Quakers 8th of 9 children, 1 sis, 3 bro living

OATLEY Albert G. in his 46th yr in Salem, NY November 2, 1876

SMYTHE Mary Mc Cree (**CONGER**) wife of Rev. Henry E. in Greenwich, NY November 12, 1876

HAVILAND Charles abt 60y formerly of Easton in Saratoga, NY October 27, 1876

BAKER Patience age 74y widow of Simeon in Easton, NY November 5, 1876

BUTLER Moses age 78y in Easton, NY November 7, 1876

MARTIN Lydia (**CLARK**) age 84y 2m 19d widow of Kenyon of Argyle, NY in Hartford, NY November 7, 1876

MONROE Joseph age 101y 1m in Whitehall, NY November 7, 1876

WATERS infant son of Merritt in Whitehall, NY November 8, 1876

BUSTARD infant son of William age 15m in Whitehall, NY November 9, 1876

BURROUGHS Henry abt 50y in Greenwich, NY November 22, 1876

HAZARD Amelia age 17y dau of Leonard in Greenwich, NY November 7, 1876

WILSON Fayette in his 61st yr in Salem, NY November 17, 1876

FORT Garrett age 76y in S. Cambridge, NY November 28, 1876

CHANDLER Enos Sr. age 71y in Greenwich, NY November 15, 1876

SHERMAN Caroline age 57y wife of Caleb in Greenwich, NY December 8, 1876

BROWN William age 78y formerly of Saratoga Co. father-in-law of A. A. **MOORE** of Greenwich, NY in Watervliet, Mi. December 10, 1876

LINDLOFF Stewart F. age 5m Grandson of G. W. **FAIRBANKS** of Greenwich, NY in Bennington, Vt. December 15, 1876

POWERS John age 87y in Easton, NY December 24, 1876

BAILEY Louden age 75y in Kingsbury, NY December 16, 1876

COPELAND Elizabeth (**BROWN**) age 35y in Argyle, NY December 17, 1876

HILL Libbie age 3y dau of Samuel and Sarah in Schuylerville, NY December 13, 1876

POTTER George age 6y son of George and Harriet in Schuylerville, NY November 29, 1876

LOOMIS Benjamin M. age 70y in Cambridge, NY December 19, 1876

WHITE Harriet A. (**FENTON**) age 42y wife of John W. in Cambridge, NY December 16, 1876

BEATTIE William J. age 32y in Cambridge, NY December 19, 1876

BROWN Joseph M. age 82y in Cambridge, NY December 18, 1876

MC MULLEN Mrs. Christian F. age 71y in Shushan, NY December 20, 1876

WILLIAMS Mrs. Mary age 74y in S. Argyle, NY December 18, 1876

PRATT Ira in Salem, NY December 24, 1876

PAIR Sophia Willett age 39y wife of John in Ft. Edward, NY December 26, 1876

STEELE Thomas son of Daniel T. in Salem, NY December 27, 1876

SIMPSON Chloe **(HARMON)** age 80y in W. Rupert, Vt. December 21, 1876

CURTIS Gracie age 1y 8m dau of Mc Endrick and Mary in Schuylerville, NY December 25, 1876

WELCH Eunice age 5y dau of John R. and Abbie R. in Schuylerville, NY December 22, 1876

MC LENATHAN Ruth E. age 23m dau of W. H. and M. Amelia, Grand dau of late Rev. N. H. **WOOD** in Hartford, NY December 16, 1876

CARRIGAN Willie age 5m died December 12, 1876 and Dot age 16m died December 13, 1876, only children J. H. and N. J. in Hartford, NY

COPELAND Clara age 31y wife of Theodore in Hebron, NY December 29, 1876

RICE Robert A. age 48y in Cambridge, NY January 3, 1877

CULVER Miss Surena age 45y in Cambridge, NY December 23, 1876

PRATT Ira J. age 7y 8m son of Andrew K. and Hannah J. in Cambridge, NY December 30, 1876

HAGGERTY Mrs. Bridget age 75y in S. Cambridge, NY December 14, 1876

SMITH Etta dau of John W. and Harriet in Cambridge, NY January 2, 1877

MC NAB Andrew age 83y 1m 14d in E. Greenwich, NY December 30, 1876

CULVER Jonathan formerly of Greenwich in Iowa City, Iowa December 29, 1876

PADDEN Morica age 74y wife of William in E. Greenwich, NY January 1, 1877

SLOAN Israel age 75y in Easton, NY January 9, 1877

KENYON Lester age 10m son of William and Mary in Cambridge, NY January 9, 1877

WHEELER Edward brother-in-law of A. J. **FENTON** in Poughkeepsie, NY January 9, 1877

NORTON Elizabeth **(PERINE)** age 72y 1m 10d wife of Reuben M. in Chicago, Ill.

January 3, 1877

BROUGHTON Mrs. Harriet age 76y 6m in E. Poultney, Vt. January 4, 1877

COMSTOCK Thomas in his 78th yr in Cambridge, NY January 18, 1877

LEWIS William A. age 24y in Easton, NY January 23, 1877

WELLING Herman D. age 25y in S. Cambridge, NY January 23, 1877

PETTEYS John D. abt 62y in Easton, NY January 23, 1877

BROWNELL Smith H. in Shushan, NY January 21, 1877

GILBERT Samuel age 76y in Shushan, NY January 18, 1877

REYNOLDS Mrs. Jane age 69y in Greenwich, NY January 28, 1877

CORNELL Caleb A. age 55y in Easton, NY January 29, 1877

BARRETT Mary age 18y 10m wife of Harmides in Whitehall, NY January 26, 1877

CHASE Rev. Hiram age 75y 11m of Troy Conference in Los Angeles, Ca. January 9, 1877

LONG Rev. Chester age 83y in Salem, NY January 23, 1877

CARTER Miss Polly age 72y in Salem, NY January 24, 1877

HARRIS Chester age 75y of Warren Co. NY in Ft. Edward, NY January 19, 1877

STICKLES Henry M. age 75y 6m in Clavarack, NY January 20, 1877

RENOIS L. N. age 21y in Whitehall, NY January 29, 1877

HAY Marrgaret age 77y in Greenwich, NY February 1/5 1877

LAMBERT John at Greenwich Hotel February 6, 1877

COMSTOCK Miss Eunice age 71y in Cambridge, NY January 27, 1877

BADGER Mary E. in her 25th yr in Ft. Edward, NY January 28, 1877

GAY Joel in his 78th yr in White Creek, NY January 29, 1877

FULLER Freeman A. age 72y in Cambridge, NY January 29, 1877

COTY Clement in Sandy Hill, NY January 29, 1877

COON Mrs. Mary age 54y at Kings St. January 29, 1877

FLAGLER Lydia widow of Titus in Adamsville, NY January 27, 1877

GLEASON Eddie age 6m son of John and Mary in Greenwich, NY February 14, 1877 and son Jimmie age 6m died February 22, 1877

GLADSTONE Rev. J. F. age 37y in E. Greenwich, NY February 12, 1877

GRAY Henry C. age 68y in Cambridge, NY February 10, 1877

MC CREEDY Katie May 8y 1m 15d dau of Samuel and Mary in Schuylerville, NY February 5, 1877

BARKER Mrs. George R. age 87y in Granville, NY February 5, 1877

PALMER Mrs. Robert age 28y in Salem, NY February 3, 1877

WINN James W. age 21y in Ft. Edward, NY January 30, 1877

SHAW infant dau of John in Greenwich, NY February 19, 1877

DENNIS Lonnie in son of of S. H. in E. Greenwich, NY February 16, 1877

BOGART Coty age 66y in Salem, NY February 21, 1877

MORRIS Frank age 17y in M. Granville, NY February 8, 1877

FOSTER Allen age 63y in Greenwich, NY February 18, 1877

CAMERON Mrs. ____ age 90y in Greenwich, NY February 18, 1877

VIALL Matilda in her 74th yr wife of Ira in Harts Falls, NY February 19, 1877

LYONS M. age 25y in Whitehall, NY February 16, 1877

GOODMAN Mrs. R. age 69y in Whitehall, NY February 15, 1877

REYNOLDS Harry age 70y in Whitehall, NY February 20, 1877

TABER Mira A. age 28y wife of Charles in Easton, NY March 1, 1877

CENTER Mrs. ____ in Hebron, NY February 9, 1877

TILFORD Maggie L. age 27y 11m 27d wife of J. S. and dau of late Rev. James **BALLANTINE** of W. Hebron, NY in Saginaw, Mi. January 30,1877

MC INTYRE Lavina age 5m dau of Robert H. and Cynthia in Argyle, NY February 19, 1877

MURPHY Edward age 24y in Arlington, Vt. February 18, 1877

ROBERTSON Zenas age 73y in Cambridge, NY February 20, 1877

SMALL James E. age 62y in Coila, NY March 6, 1877

MAYNARD Betsey in Greenwich, NY March 7, 1877

REARDON Kate age 84y in Greenwich, NY (newspaper date March 8, 1877)

WAGER Sarah widow of Hector formerly of Greenwich, NY in Schoolcraft, Mi. February 21, 1877

ANDREWS Darwin formerly of Greenwich, NY in Racine, Wis. March 3, 1877. Born Arlington, Vt. March 4, 1810, married Catherina PURDY dau of Levi who died April 3, 1841. Went west with dau 22 yrs ago

KENYON Sarah age 84y in Easton, NY March 18, 1877

FINNIGAN Mary age 16y in Victory Mills, NY March 18, 1877

NORMAN Mrs. Mary age 45y in Greenwich, NY March 26, 1877

MC NITT Miss ____ in E. Greenwich, NY March 28, 1877

WILCOX N. O. age 45y formerly of Greenwich in Minneapolis, Mn. March 20, 1877

PALMER Mrs. Olive in Whitehall, NY March 27, 1877

KINGSLEY Frederick age 56y in Whitehall, NY March 20, 1877

PREVILLE infant child of John in Whitehall, NY March 21, 1877

ST CLAIR ____ age 17m dau of E. in Whitehall, NY March 23, 1877

LA BARGE Samuel age 39y in Whitehall, NY March 24, 1877

MORRIS Anna A. age 29y wife of H. D. in Salem, NY March 29, 1877

WRIGHT Eliza (SAFFORD) age 88y 6m widow of Z. F. formerly of Pawlet, Vt. in Berrien Springs, Mi. (newspaper date April 5, 1877)

ACKLEY Catherine age 78y in Cambridge, NY March 23, 1877

THOMAS Emery age 2y of Whitehall, NY in the County Home March 21, 1877

SHAW Nellie age 6y of Hebron, NY in the County Home March 26, 1877

STEVENSON Mrs. Jane age 86y in Argyle, NY March 24, 1877

SELFRIDGE George E. age 24y of Argyle, NY killed by cars in Joliet, Ill. March 6, 1877

WRIGHT Rispy F. age 37y wife of Jerome in Cambridge, NY March 20, 1877

NORMAN Samuel A. age 69y 11m 2d in Valatie, NY March 19, 1877

HOES Henry age 16y son of Christopher and Jane R. in Valatie, NY March 23, 1877

ST CLAIR Alice age 2y in Whitehall, NY March 24, 1877

DAVIS Edward age 79y in Whitehall, NY April 2, 1877

DEWEY Charles age 33y in Comstocks, NY March 30, 1877

MONAHAN John age 18y in Ft. Ann, NY March 30, 1877

POLLEY Clarissa age 77y wife of Jonathan in Whitehall, NY March 30, 1877

CARRINGTON Polly age 72y in Whitehall, NY March 31, 1877

MOORE Martha age 57y wife of C. B. in Greenwich, NY April 12, 1877

SMITH Deborah age 70y wife of Harvey in Easton, NY April 8, 1877

MC LAUGHLIN ____ child of Mr. ____ in Greenwich, NY April 10, 1877

CRANDALL Mary Jane wife of Philander in Greenwich, NY April 10, 1877

DAVISON James T. in Greenwich, NY April 16, 1877

HUTTON ____ child of Mrs. Abbey Hutton in E. Greenwich, NY April 17, 1877

SALISBURY Orson in Greenwich, NY April 17, 1877

SHARPE H. E. in Cambridge, NY April 15, 1877

BAKER Sherman abt 32y of Victory Falls, NY nr Hoosick Falls, NY (newspaper date April 19, 1877)

LEE Noah L. formerly of Greenwich, NY in Glens Falls, NY April 13, 1877

WILEY Rev. Thomas age 30y formerly of Hebron, NY in Martin, Mi. April 3, 1877

BARNES Charles age 78y of Jackson, NY in the County Home March 5, 1877

MOSHER Thomas age 70y of Easton, NY in the County Home April 6, 1877

LEE Rachael age 75y of Argyle, NY in the County Home April 9, 1877

WALLER Hiram age 77y in Hartford, NY March 29, 1877

GRISWOLD Paul C. age 31y in Whitehall, NY April 10, 1877

GAUVREN Miss Rosa age 21y in Whitehall, NY April 7, 1877

DE KALB Mrs. George A. age 21y in N. Granville, NY March 28, 1877

PRATT Edwin age 33y of Easton in Denver, Col. (newspaper date April 19, 1877)

TERRY infant son of Edwin in Cambridge, NY April 4, 1877

CLARK Lenora age 17y wife of Peter in Hartford, NY March 28, 1877

WYATT William age 51y in Easton, NY April 13, 1877

DARROW Jerusha age 31y in Easton, NY April 12, 1877

HOAG Miss Mary S. age 20y in Easton NY April 20, 1877

DOBBIN Mrs. Miller age 82y in Lakeville, NY April 19, 1877

WRIGHT Betsey age 72y in Ft. Miller, Ny April 23, 1877

MEADER Libbie age 64y in Easton, NY April 22, 1877

THOMPSON Mary age 53y wife of D. F. in Granville, NY April 24, 1877

THOMAS Sarah wife of William H. and sis of Alfred **BULKLEY** of Granville, NY in Rochester, NY April 19, 1877

BEACH Abbie age 76y wife of John H. in Sandy Hill, NY April 25, 1877

SISSON Walter W. age 4m son of B. F. in Cambridge, NY April 13, 1877

DENNIS Mrs. Hannah age 73y in Whitehall, NY April 23, 1877

ROSEKRANS Enoch Huntington in his 69th yr in Glens Falls, NY May 1, 1877

GUNN Charles J. in his 75th yr in Greenwich, NY May 1, 1877

DENNIS George C. age 66y in Argyle, NY May 1, 1877

GRAHAM Jane age 80y wife of John in N. Argyle, NY May 1, 1877

FULLER Sidney age 70y formerly of Greenwich, NY in Mattawan, Mi. May 6, 1877

ADAMS James H. in Greenwich, NY May 16, 1877. Born December 17, 1848

MC COY Robert age 77y in Ft. Edward, NY May 12, 1877

CLOSSON Alexander age 56y formerly of Ft. Edward in Cohoes, NY May 1, 1877

SLOAN Michael in his 21st yr in Greenwich, NY May 12, 1877

EDDY Richard L. in his 44th yr in Easton, NY May 11, 1877

LAMPMAN Hopy age 62y in Battenville, NY May 11, 1877

MC MILLAN Katherine age 81y relict of Frank in Argyle, NY May 15, 1877

REYNOLDS Merritt age 32y in Whitehall, NY May 12, 1877

HALL Alma T. age 34y in Cambridge, NY May 6, 1877

SMART Daniel S. Md. in Fredericksburg, Tx. May 15, 1877. Brother Rev. J. G. of Greenwich, NY. Buried in Cambridge, NY

SWEET Burdick G. age 59y in S. Hartford, NY May 18, 1877

MOSHER Hannah L. in her 56th yr wife of Eugene of Rochester, NY and dau of late Daniel **ANTHONY** formerly of Greenwich, NY in Leavenworth, Ks. May 12, 1877

BELCHER Catherine S. (**QUACKENBUSH**) wife of E. in Newark Valley, NY May 10, 1877

LEWIS Willie age 11y in Jackson, NY May 2, 1877

BABCOCK Mrs. Laura age 68y in Greenwich, NY May 25, 1877

WRIGHT Mrs. Sarah age 58y in Greenwich, NY May 26, 1877

HOLBROOK Peter age 71y in Sandy Hill, NY May 27, 1877

SHAW Mary R. age 25y in Sandy Hill, NY May 23, 1877

YULE Miss Eva age 22y 1m 11d in Whitehall, NY May 31, 1877

WELLS Lucinda age 88y wife of William of Whitehall, NY in Clarendon, Vt. May 30, 1877

BALLOU Eliza age 45y widow of Joseph in Whitehall, NY May 29, 1877

RIGNEY Mrs. ____ age 54y widow of Thomas in Ft. Edward, NY May 24, 1877

SOWEL William in his 63rd yr in Wilton, Wis. April 29, 1877, son Alfred L. in his 19th yr only son of William and Margaret died May 5, 1877

KEECH Rosalia M. age 6y 5m adopted dau of I. B. in Ft. Ann, NY June 5, 1877

STILES Augustus age 68y in Whitehall, NY June 11, 1877

WILSON Everet A. age 28y 7m 17d in Whitehall, NY June 12, 1877

NORTON Mr. A. A. abt 40y in E. Greenwich, NY June 19, 1877

WEBB Alvira in her 62nd yr wife of Abel S. in Fitchs Point, NY June 8, 1877

MC INTYRE William age 74y in W. Hebron, NY June 7, 1877

WHITTAKER Fred abt 25y in Easton, NY June 1, 1877

BULSON Ludwig age 56y in Greenwich, NY June 22, 1877

BRADLEY ____ dau of Eugene in Greenwich, NY June 25, 1877

CRANDALL ____ child of Philander in Greenwich, NY June 26, 1877

HILLMAN ____ age 13y son of Lafayette in Jackson, NY June 22, 1877

YOUNG Henry J. age 24y in Greenwich, NY June 17, 1877

DOTY Edward age 49y in Whitehall, NY June 20, 1877

BARRETT Mrs. David Jr. age 49y in Dresden, NY June 21, 1877

MOREHOUSE Mrs. Lucinda F. age 54y in Fairhaven, Vt. June 17, 1877

ANTHONY Daniel age 77y in Greenwich, NY July 12, 1877

REYNOLDS Susan age 68y in Greenwich, NY July 7, 1877

GOLDEN ____ child of Mr. ____ in Easton, NY July 7, 1877

WING N. H. age 70y in Greenwich, NY July 13, 1877

TERHUNE Nancy age 75y in Northumberland, NY July 13, 1877

CHASE Eunicy age 75y in Easton, NY July 15, 1877

BOGART Joseph age 72y in Whitehall, NY July 9, 1877

ATWELL Lillie E. age 24y wife of Frank S. and dau of A. C. **HOPSON** of Whitehall, NY in Port Henry, NY July 19, 1877

COLLINS Orange age 56y in Whitehall, NY July 22, 1877

FOWLER Catherine E. age 50y wife of Charles A. in Greenwich, NY July 29, 1877

BARRELL Abram age 78y formerly of Greenwich, NY in Bellville, NY July 26, 1877

HARDEN Catherine M. age 30y wife of James In Troy, NY August 3, 1877

HUMPHREY Thomas age 13y son of Alexander in Battenville, NY August 13, 1877

JOICE William age 33y in Sandy Hill, NY August 7, 1877

CARPENTER Adolphus age 9y in Sandy Hill, NY August 3, 1877

SPAULDING Squire in his 79th yr in N. Granville, NY August 6, 1877

HINDS Thomas age 54y in Salem, NY August 8, 1877

WESTINGHOUSE J. H. age 56y in Johnsonville, NY August 14, 1877

STYLES Henry in Easton, NY (newspaper date August 23, 1877)

BURGESS ____ child of N. in Greenwich, NY August 23, 1877

MOORE Mrs. ____ age 77y in Ft. Ann, NY August 20, 1877

OVIATT Miss Olive age 63y in Shushan, NY August 17, 1877

WARNER Orson V. age 65y in N. Colebrook, Conn. August 1, 1877

LAUGHLIN William Joseph age 20m in Ft. Edward, NY August 11, 1877

KETCHUM H. W. age 72y in Ft. Edward, NY August 14, 1877

LANGWORTHY P. H. age 64y in Sandy Hill, NY August 11, 1877

SARGENT Alonso J. age 56y formerly of Sandy Hill, NY in Drummerston, Vt. July 28, 1877

MC GOLDRICK James age 22y in Hartford, NY August 11, 1877

PAYNE Charles age 37y (colored) of Cambridge in the County Home August 14, 1877

LA HUE Mrs. Belle age 27y in Whitehall, NY August 12, 1877

CAMPBELL Miss Maria age 59y in Argyle, NY August 10, 1877

WHEELER Evaline relict of Charles formerly of Whitehall, NY in Indianapolis, Ind. August 8, 1877

SCOTT Mrs. Permelia age 77y in Whitehall, NY August 20, 1877

NOBLE A. E. age 66y 4m widow of Adonijah S.in Cambridge, NY August 21, 1877

LEE Lillie age 11m dau of B. G. and Hattie A. in Cambridge, NY August 16, 1877

ELLIS Margaret age 79y in Cambridge, NY August 18, 1877

HODGEMAN Hobart E. age 9m son of A. C. in Ft. Edward, NY August 20, 1877

KELLY Mrs. Joseph in Salem, NY August 24, 1877

DRAKE John age 60y in Easton, NY August 24, 1877

CARTER Minnie E. age 9m 20d dau of L. D. in Dresden, NY August 27, 1877

EARL James age 65y in Whitehall, NY August 27, 1877

LOCKE ____ child of Benjamin in Easton, NY August 24, 1877

LARABEE ____ child of Seth in N. Greenwich, NY September 2, 1877

WHEELOCK ____ age 1y child of S. B. in Greenwich, NY September 4, 1877

RAY ____ age 1y child of Thomas in Jackson, NY September 5, 1877

MORROW Elizabeth wife of Robert in Lakeville, NY August 24, 1877

BARDEN John abt 26y in Rupert, Vt. August 24, 1877

OATMAN Frederick age 20y son of Isaac J. in Belcher, NY August 19, 1877

BURDICK Allen age 71y in White Creek, NY August 25, 1877

MULLEN James J. age 21y in White Creek, NY August 25, 1877

LANE David H. abt 49y in Ft. Edward, NY August 25, 1877

CAREY Mrs. Maria age 77y of Ft. Edward, NY in Belcher, NY August 24, 1877

MOORE Louisa age 38y wife of A. W. in Ft. Edward, NY August 29, 1877

HAY Jessie in Greenwich, NY September 9, 1877

BELDEN ____ dau of widow Belden in N. Greenwich, NY September 11, 1877

CORLISS Dr. Hiram in his 84th yr in Greenwich, NY September 7, 1877

DAWLEY Carrie E. in her 17th yr in Greenwich, NY September 7, 1877

CURTIS Mrs. Benjamin in E. Greenwich, NY September 8, 1877

ALMY Thomas J. age 63y in N. Easton, NY September 11, 1877

STRONG Augustus age 52y in Sandy Hill, NY September 4, 1877

NORTON Catherine age 78y in Hartford, NY September 8, 1877

WILCOX Harvey age 50y in Easton, NY September 19, 1877

GAILBRAITH ____ child of Rev. in E. Greenwich, NY September 18, 1877

HODGE Josephine age 28y wife of J. S. in N. Granville, NY August 29, 1877

SMITH Edward abt 28y in W. Sandgate, Vt. September 1, 1877

ROGERS Evaline (**HAY**) age 46y wife of Wilson in W. Rupert, Vt. September 5, 1877

VAUGHN Miss Belle age 22y adopted dau of Henry **THOMAS** in Sandy Hill, NY September 6, 1877

OATMAN Lyman formerly of Hartford, NY in Angola, NY September 9, 1877

HENRY James in his 71st yr in Argyle, NY September 9, 1877

OVERACKER George Walter age 11m son of G. W. in Cambridge, NY September 9, 1877

VAN VECHTEN Walter in his 54th yr in Buskirks Bridge, NY August 16, 1877

MACKOIT Charles Linus age 5m in Salem, NY September 3, 1877

DUNLAP Peter C. age 81y in Watersville, Ontario, Can. August 28, 1877

BELL Stephen age 16y son of James and Hannah in Durkeetown, NY September 10, 1877

CURTIS James age 58y in Cambridge, NY September 12, 1877

PARKER Joseph age 11y son of Robert and Olive in Lakeville, NY September 20, 1877

O'NEIL William age 16y son fo Patrick in Quaker Springs, NY September 22, 1877

WILBUR Hattie M. in her 28th yr wife of W. J. in Ausable, NY September 15, 1877

AUSTIN Mary A. age 65y wife of Augustine in Westhaven, Vt. September 18, 1877

COLEMAN Robert age 64 in Whitehall, NY (newspaper date September 27, 1877)

SARGENT Henry G. age 54y in Ft. Ann, NY September 20, 1877

KING Eliza (**PALMER**) age 41y wife of B. W. formerly of Hartford in Ft. Edward, NY September 15, 1877

RUSSELL Fred C. age 25y in White Creek, NY September 2, 1877

LEAVENS Celina Elizabeth age 65y 6m wife of Thurlow in Glens Falls, NY August 13, 1877

BAKER Laura D. age 58y wife of Isaac V. in Comstocks Landing, NY September 24,

FREEMAN Charlotte B. age 80y widow of Marvin in Salem, NY September 26, 1877

HORTON H. J. age 38y in Cambridge, NY September 25, 1877

FLETCHER Rebecca age 40y wife of David in Jackson, NY September 19, 1877

BURKE Michael age 25y in Cambridge, NY September 20, 1877

DOUGAN Timothy age 6y 6m son of Henry in Cambridge, NY September 20, 1877

PRATT Fanny L. age 50y in S. Cambridge, NY September 22, 1877

WHITESIDE Henry age 80y in S. Cambridge, NY September 20, 1877

JACKWAY Lucinda age 40y wife of William in Westhaven, Vt. September 22, 1877

WILCOX Jesse age 17y in N. Granville, NY September 23, 1877

MC NALL Johnie son of Charles in Whitehall, NY September 24, 1877

CURTIS Clark E. age 35y in Washington DC September 28, 1877

PARKER Lida Mary age 8y in Lakeville, NY (newspaper date October 4, 1877)

FERGUSON Edmond age 78y in Easton, NY October 3, 1877

WHYTE Archibald age 55y in Argyle, NY October 1, 1877

HOLLISTER Phebe age 76y in Easton, NY September 27, 1877

LA BARGE Mrs. Alexander age 23y in Whitehall, NY September 29, 1877

WILCOX Phebe (**KENYON**) age 43y wife of Edson D. in Greenwich, NY October 6, 1877

BELL Nelson age 21y 6m son of Sidney and Martha drowned at Ft. Edward, NY (newspaper date October 11, 1877)

ROGERS Ella age 24y wife of E. H. Jr. of New York at bro William **COLEMAN** in Sandy Hill, NY October 1, 1877

REILLY John age 73y in Sandy Hill, NY September 27, 1877

BRADLEY Mrs. Elias P. age 83y of Adamsville, NY at son-in-laws Dewitt **WASHBURN** September 22, 1877

STEWART Miss Jane age 63y in Argyle, NY September 29, 1877

LILLIE Mrs. William age 30y in Putnam, NY September 30, 1877

HILL Miss Betsey age 80y in W. Hebron, NY September 26, 1877

JACQUITH Stephen M. age 53y in Schuylerville, NY September 25, 1877

CAULKINS Emma L. age 14y at Bacon Hill, NY October 4, 1877

MC CABE Mrs. Catherine at Bald Mountain, NY October 9, 1877

WOODWORTH William age 28y 10m son of Calvin V. K. formerly of White Creek, NY in N. Cohocton, NY September 2, 1877

POWELL Mrs. William age 65y in Ft. Edward, NY October 2, 1877

QUA George abt 75y in Hebron, NY October 5, 1877

HOYT Emma wife of Frank B. in Cambridge, NY October 11, 1877

HEFFRON Jane age 80y in Salem, NY October 6, 1877

STRONG Mrs. ____ age 86y relict of John in Sandy Hill, NY October 7, 1877

PRINDLE Norman age 77y in Sandy Hill, NY October 9, 1877

TABER Albert age 33y of Ft. Edward, NY in the County Home October 3, 1877

HAGGART Andrew age 72y in Argyle, NY October 7, 1877

BARBER ____ age 17y son of Ralph in Dresden, NY October 11, 1877

LOOMIS Harriet age 19y in Whitehall, NY October 21, 1877

MILLINGTON Anna Louise infant dau of Dr. and Mrs. J. in E. Greenwich, NY October 19, 1877

BOYCE Willie age 6y 3m son of Charles and Lillie in Sandy Hill, NY October 12, 1877

FITZGERALD Delia age 5y dau of Daniel in Ft. Edward, NY October 21, 1877

BOWER Mrs. William age 55y in Hartford, NY October 22, 1877

MULHOLLAND Angeline age 25y in Whitehall, NY October 12, 1877

SWEET Mrs. C. age 28y in Whitehall, NY October 14, 1877

SAWYER Miss Viola age 16y in Ticonderoga, NY October 14, 1877

DALTON Catherine age 45y in M. Granville, NY October 10, 1877

CUMMINGS George age 2y son of William M. and Louisa in Putnam, NY October 21, 1877

BAKER Miss Mary age 19y in Hartford, NY October 22, 1877

THOMAS ___ age 2m child of Henry and Katie in Whitehall, NY October 27, 1877

SNELL Thomas age 80y 1m 8d in Cambridge, NY October 18, 1877

MC LEAN John age 5y 5m in Cambridge, NY October 31, 1877

BECKWITH Louise age 21y dau of late Henry W. and Louisa M. in W. Granville, NY November 3, 1877

WOODWORTH Mattie Evans age 4y 11m dau of George and Mary in Easton, NY November 18, 1877

EGGLESTON Alice wife of James A. in Aurora, Ill. November 10, 1877

MILLER Garet age 69y in Easton, NY November 26, 1877

COTTRELL Adam age 79y 6m of Easton, NY in Albany, NY November 26, 1877

REMINGTON Jenks age 77y in Easton, NY November 26, 1877

STORY Frank age 22y in Whitehall, NY November 9, 1877

RICHARDSON Emma age 19y in Whitehall, NY November 17/19, 1877

IRISH Mary L. age 28y in Eagle Bridge, NY November 19, 1877

MATTISON Stella J. age 4y in White Creek, NY November 18, 1877

REYNOLDS Annie age 20y 9m in Granville, NY November 13, 1877

MC INTYRE Patrick age 79y in Sandy Hill, NY November 12, 1877

RAND Mrs. Amanda age 53y in Ft. Edward, NY October 31, 1877

DINGS Peter age 74y in Lakeville, NY October 24, 1877

MIDDLETON Lewis age 68y in S. Hartford, NY November 20, 1877

ROCKWELL Jane age 55y in Whitehall, NY November 18, 1877

BECKWITH Mrs. David age 54y in Whitehall, NY November 14, 1877

SCHLEYER Frederick in Hebron, NY November 16, 1877

EDIE Jennett age 58y in E. Salem, NY November 12, 1877

LIVINGSTON Rebecca age 57y in Cambridge, NY November 14, 1877

CARPENTER Martha age 18y in Eagle Bridge, NY November 14, 1877

DUTCHER Sarah age 57y wife of Salem in Camden Valley, NY November 1, 1877

ALEXANDER Maxwell age 68y in Jackson, NY November 10, 1877

JOHNSON Lewis E. age 21y 9m 27d in Whitehall, NY November 27, 1877

CULVER Eugene age 5y in Whitehall, NY November 23, 1877

WILLIAMSON Andrew age 70y in Putnam, NY November 12, 1877

REID John Henry age 27y 10m in Belcher, NY November 23, 1877

BLOWERS James age 55y 6m 10d in White Creek, NY December 5, 1877

ALMA John age 25y in W. Ft. Ann, NY November 28, 1877

HAVILAND James age 36y formerly of Pittstown in Easton, NY December 11, 1877

ROGERS Thomas in his 94th yr at Bald Mountain, NY December 19, 1877

VANDENBURGH Willie age 3w 2d son of Edwin and M. Libbie in Cambridge, NY December 14, 1877

WARN William E. age 38y 11m in Cambridge, NY December 17, 1877

LEGGETT Daniel age 79y formerly of Easton, NY in Saratoga Springs, NY December 9, 1877

REYNOLDS Sarah Mary age 16y dau of John B. and Martha in Hebron, NY December 18, 1877

RICHARDSON Henry H. age 48y formerly of Ft. Ann, NY in Troy, NY December 2, 1877

WALLER Truman age 69y in Hartford, NY December 13, 1877

TOOMB Abigail age 74y in the County Home December 7, 1877

O'BRINE Eddie C. age 4w son of Daniel and Annie in Ft. Ann, NY December 17, 1877

POLLOCK Rahamah wife of William of Agyle in Hebron, NY December 23, 1877

CURTIS Jane E. age 57y wife of Erastus in Schaghticoke, NY December 24, 1877

COLIN William M. age 35y in Sandy Hill, NY January 1, 1878

ALLEN John S. bro of James Mathew of Sandy Hill, NY in Norwich, NY December 12, 1877

BAILEY Ebenezer age 58y in Salem, NY January 1, 1878

WOODARD ____ abt 8y dau of Chancey and Ellen in Rupert, Vt. (newspaper date January 10, 1878)

EDDY Adeline age 80y relict of Samuel in Comstocks Corners, NY January 9, 1878

MC MILLAN Martha age 83y relict of George in Argyle, NY January 6, 1878

SMITH Henry age 85y 10m in Dunhams Basin, NY January 2, 1878

TOOHEY Thomas in N. Greenwich, NY January 1, 1878

ASHLEY Helen M. age 35y wife of W. A. in Ft. Edward, NY January 3, 1878

CUSENBARK William formerly of Sandy Hill, NY in Flint, Mi. January 13, 1878

WATERS Mrs. Mary age 79y 9m 17d formerly of Greenwich, NY in Mequoketa, Iowa December 29, 1877

DEVINE Margaret B. age 53y wife of Seth of Kingsbury, NY January 24, 1878

ALLEN Jonathan W. age 77y in Griswolds Mills, NY January 7, 1878

PRENTISS Horace age 78y formerly of Greenwich, NY in Hoosick Falls, NY February 5, 1878

BURDICK Mathew in his 84th yr in Battenville, NY February 11, 1878

IVES Deborah N. age 82y widow of Hiram in S. Granville, NY February 2, 1878

WHITNEY Fanny F. age 47y wife of Willard W. formerly of Greenwich, NY in Mequoketa, Iowa February 9, 1878

STILLMAN Ruth M. age 36y wife of Dr. S. L. in Greenwich, NY February 20, 1878

HARDEN John age 24y in Hartford, NY January 30, 1878

STOUGHTON Timothy age 94y in Ft. Edward, NY February 21, 1878

EDWARDS Amy age 65y wife of Daniel in Greenwich, NY February 18, 1878

CASE Albert age 14y in Johnsonville, NY February 26, 1878

NORTON Mrs. Charles age 80y in M. Granville, NY February 26, 1878

MORA Christopher age 81y in Lake, NY February 20, 1878

POTTER Anson age 50y in M. Granville, NY February 22, 1878

NEWELL Richard age 92y in M. Granville, NY February 21, 1878

GOWAN Julia age 68y in Sandy Hill, NY February 19, 1878

ELLIS Thomas Jr. age 83y in Durkeetown, NY February 13, 1878

HARRIS Mrs. ____ age 91y Mother of S. M. **MC DONALD** in Hartford, NY February 15, 1878

DONALDSON Mrs. Elizabeth age 68y in Whitehall, NY February 22, 1878

BARRETT Dennis age 31y in Dresden, NY February 23, 1878

WELLS Truman age 65y in N. Pawlet, Vt. February 26, 1878

HURTUBIS Joseph age 63y in Whitehall, NY February 25, 1878

DE RIDDER Mary age 59y 9m 7d wife of A. G. L. in Easton, NY February 17, 1878

DIXON Mary in her 12th yr in Easton, NY March 10, 1878

SHERMAN Warren age 62y in Easton, NY March 8, 1878

THORNE L. C. age 44y in Granville, NY March 4, 1878

STOCKWELL Nancy M. age 4y 1m dau of William in Dresden, NY March 9, 1878

MAXFIELD Charles age 20m son of William and Mary in Whitehall, NY February 22, 1878

WOOD Isaac E. in his 51st yr in Whitehall, NY March 7, 1878

ADAMS Mrs. Martha age 80y in N. Ft. Ann, NY March 5, 1878. Son Martin H.

HAYWARD Mary Jane age 50y 10m wife of L. A. formerly of Grenwich, NY in Warsaw, NY March 9, 1878

ROBINSON Mrs. Elizabeth age 35y in Belcher, NY February 26, 1878

TEFFT John age 66y in Sandy Hill, NY March 8, 1878

SMITH Abram age 67y in Sandy Hill, NY March 8, 1878

MASON Fanny age 62y at Kings St. March 6, 1878

LA ROSE Joseph age 67y in Smiths Basin, NY March 11, 1878

ROBERTS Mrs. John in Granville, NY March 7, 1878

GILBERT Henry Coleman in his 22nd yr in Ft. Edward, NY March 12, 1878

VIELE Amanda W. age 34y in Ft. Miller, NY March 16, 1878

PERRY Dr. A. formerly of S. Easton, NY March 16, 1878

WARREN George age 40y in N. Granville, NY March 19, 1878

HILL William M. abt 40y in S. Granville, NY March 20, 1878

MAXWELL Eliza age 40y wife of James March 15, 1878

HAYWARD T. W. age 52y of Whitehall, NY in the County Home March 16, 1878

OATMAN ____ age 2y dau of Henry in Sandy Hill, NY March 15, 1878

AUSTIN Jenny A. age 7m 14d dau of T. E. in Whitehall, NY March 17, 1878

MILLETT Lizzie age 3y 1d dau of George in Whitehall, NY March 15, 1878

HANKS infant child of Dr. and Mrs. Hanks in Whitehall, NY March 24, 1878

VANDENBURGH Mrs. Garrett age 70y in Easton, NY March 23, 1878

JOHNSON William H. in his 68th yr in Whitehall, NY March 22, 1878

STEVES Melinda age 28y in S. Bay, NY March 11, 1878

GILCHRIST Clara age 17y in Hebron, NY March 12, 1878

HODGE Cora died March 5, 1878 and Hattie died March 22, 1878 children of Hiram and Nancy A. in Eagle Bridge, NY

HALL Peter abt 25y in Easton, NY March 1, 1878

HERRINGTON Emma age 10m dau of Edward D. and Jane A. in Hoosick, NY March 28, 1878

BROUGHAM Mrs. Ann G. age 75y in Ft. Edward, NY March 23, 1878

JEFFERS James in his 48th yr in N. Greenwich, Ny March 29, 1878

VAN LONE Sarah age 70y in Whitehall, NY March 27, 1878

SUTHERLAND Charles age 10y in Dresden, NY March 27, 1878

GIBSON Jonas age 73y of Greenwich, NY in Poultney Vt. April 5, 1878

HUNT Wealthy age 75y in Buskirks Bridge, NY (newspaper date April 11, 1878)

PHALEN Ellen age 23y in Durkeetown, NY April 3, 1878

WING Benjamin in his 86th yr at sons Harvey S. in Granville, NY March 27, 1878

HURTUBIS ____ age 7m child of Albert in Whitehall, NY April 5, 1878

TUCKER Mary age 42y wife of George in Ft. Ann, NY April 2, 1878

KNAPP Prudence age 40y wife of Frank formerly of Greenwich, NY in Troy, NY April 10, 1878

ROBINSON Ruth age 8m dau of H. and Emma J. in Greenwich, NY April 17, 1878

OSBORN Eliza widow of John C. formerly of Greenwich, NY, sis of Charles **RAINEY** in Somerset, Ind. rec. (newspaper date April 18, 1878)

FISHER Emma age 16y of Ft. Ann, NY in the County Home April 8, 1878

BECKWITH Reed age 83y in Whitehall, NY April 8, 1878

VANCE ____ age 20m child of Isaac in Whitehall, NY April 11, 1878

THOMAS Mary S. age 57y in Whitehall, NY April 12, 1878

CARTER Mrs. Thankful M. age 73y in Whitehall, NY April 13, 1878

HILL Jennie B. age 27y 10m wife of H. D. W. C. in Whitehall, NY April 15, 1878

CUNNINGHAM Mrs. J. age 70y in Ft. Ann, NY April 14, 1878

GETTY Ebenezer age 71y in Hebron, NY April 9, 1878

MC CREARY Freddie E. age 10y 8m 25d son of Joseph J. and Margaret A. in Cambridge, NY April 3, 1878

BLINN ____ age 6m dau of Eben in Whitehall, NY April 21, 1878

VAUGHN Albert age 47y in Ft. Ann, NY April 21, 1878

DWYER Patrick age 60y in Victory Mills, NY April 22, 1878

CONNORS Kate abt 8y dau of J. in Victory Mills, NY April 17, 1878

MOORE Thomas age 77y in Whitehall, NY April 26, 1878

MONTA C. M. age 5y in Whitehall, NY April 29, 1878

WATERS ____ age 6m son of Lewis in Whitehall, NY April 25, 1878

WHITESIDE Emily dau of Henry in S. Cambridge, NY April 27, 1878

KING Edward Joseph age 9y in White Creek, NY April 20, 1878

BLOSSOM Benoni age 66y in N. Granville, NY April 23, 1878

TRIPP William abt 75y of Argyle, NY in the County Home April 18, 1878

ORR Frank age 9y son of W. H. in Whitehall, NY May 4, 1878

AUSTIN Augustin age 70y in Whitehall, NY May 5, 1878

KING James age 73y at Kings St. April 27, 1878

LAVEY Parick age 27y in Ft. Edward, NY April 20, 1878

JONES Keziah age 74y widow of William R. in Granville, NY April 30, 1878

EARL Frances J. age 25y wife of J. D. of Ft. Ann, NY in Teas, Mi. April 9, 1878

BURNETT Alvira age 65y in Cambridge, NY April 25, 1878

BROWN Elisha age 83y in Ft. Ann, NY May 6, 1878

LA BARGE ____ age 3y son of A. in Whitehall, NY May 10, 1878

PERRY Margaret age 67y wife of Robert in Argyle, NY May 6, 1878

SLOCUM Katie age 8y dau of Lewis and Cornelia in Eagle Bridge, NY May 11, 1878

WILLARD Mrs. George age 76y in Ft. Miller, NY (newspaper date May 23, 1878)

CRONIN Mrs. Timothy in Pattens Mills, NY May 12, 1878

MAHAR Edward age 6y in Schuylerville, NY May 14, 1878

CLAYTON infant child of Mrs. Jerry Clayton in Rupert, Vt. May 19, 1878

PERRY Laura age 29y wife of Abner J. in Wells, Vt. April 17, 1878

SCALLY Ella age 19y in Wells Vt. May 19, 1878

DRAVEY Nancy age 27y wife of Michael in Ft. Edward, NY May 21, 1878

JUCKETT Lawrence age 52y in Whitehall, NY May 18, 1878

MC CALLUM ____ age 4m son of William in Argyle, NY May 21, 1878

JONES George T. age 68y in Greenwich, NY May 4, 1878

NORTON Sarah M. age 40y 11m wife of Albert A. in Greenwich, NY May 31, 1878

ELDRIDGE Eugene age 35y formerly of Cambridge, NY in Manitowoe, Wis. May 25, 1878

SMITH Ebenezer age 47y at Mothers Mrs. R. **HAYNES** in Albany, NY May 21, 1878

PERRY Henry age 15y of Granville, NY in the County Home May 22, 1878

LIENDOLL Dewitt age 9y drowned at Ft. Edward, NY May 21, 1878

HUBBARD E. W. age 40y in Wells, Vt. May 26, 1878

CROHAN Bridget age 50y in Granville, NY May 27, 1878

LENT Howard in Easton, NY May 26, 1878

HALL William age 84y in Hartford, NY May 31, 1878

PRATT Samuel Deming age 62y in White Creek, NY May 31, 1878

HAWKINS Edwin age 35y 7m 19d in Shaftsbury, Vt. May 29, 1878, dau Susan H. age 8y 10m 14d died May 19, 1878 and son Eddie F. age 4y 6m 9d died June 6, 1878

STREEVER Uldrick age 82y in Argyle, NY June 9, 1878

MASON Russell age 79y in Kingsbury, NY June 8, 1878

BURR Charlie age 2y in Smiths Basin, NY June 7, 1878

HARDEN E. P. age 62y in Hartford, NY June 11, 1878

HALL Jane **(DAYTON)** age 54y wife of David formerly of Granville, NY in Duanesburg, May 29, 1878

COLE Emery abt 60y in Ft. Edward, NY June 15, 1878

PARISH Melvin in his 34th yr son of John in Jackson, NY June 7/11, 1878

PATCH Anna J. **(HAXTON)** in Sutherland Falls, Vt. June 11, 1878

BAKER Ransom age 70y in Hartford, NY June 12, 1878

MOTT Abbie H. age 83y widow of John K. at dau Mrs. **LEWIS** in Schuylerville, NY June 18, 1878

DENNIS Jesse age 9y son of D. D. in Greenwich, NY (newspaper date July 4, 1878)

COOK Mrs. Myra age 70y in Granville, NY June 26, 1878

PERKINS Mrs. Emma age 52y in Putnam, NY June 12, 1878

SMITH Levi age 62y in Putnam, NY June 18, 1878

TEFFT Hiram age 86y in Whitehall, NY June 16, 1878

MILLETT Anna Jane age 5y dau of George in Whitehall, NY June 17, 1878

WRIGHT Caroline B. dau of Dennis HARRIGAN in Whitehall, NY June 20, 1878

JONES Susie E age 9y 7m 28d died June 8, 1878, Maud age 8y 3m 9d died June 9, 1878 and Mary H. age 6y 11m 25d died June 25, 1878 children of John Jr. in Whitehall, NY

KEEFE Michael son of Michael in Greenwich, NY July 11, 1878

THOMPSON Rev. John in his 78th yr in Saratoga Springs, NY July 9, 1878

SEARLE William G. age 24y son of J. B. and A. M. in Wilton, NY June 30, 1878

MC COTTER Hannah age 77y 14d wife of Hugh formerly of Whitehall, NY in Madison, Conn. July 5, 1878

RHODES Mrs. Anna age 102y in Dresden, NY July 8, 1878

WALLACE Josephine S. age 33y wife of Marcus and dau of John H. JOHNSON in Cambridge, NY June 14, 1878

STEWART William age 95y in Kingsbury, NY July 1, 1878

HAMLIN Lent age 80y in Monroe, NY June 20, 1878

NICHOLS Mrs. Rosa age 60y in Ft. Miller, NY June 30, 1878

MC FERRON Mrs. Seth age 55y in Whitehall, NY July 9, 1878

HARRINGTON Joseph T. age 50y in Kingsbury, July 3, 1878

DE RUSSIA Charles age 9y drowned at Queensbury, NY July 5, 1878

WARREN Pamelia age 60y wife of Samuel B. in S. Granville, NY June 29, 1878

HUMPHREY Mrs. R. age 42y in Poultney, Vt. June 30, 1878

ROBINSON Bessie age 7m 8d dau of George and Elizabeth in Schuylerville, NY July 13, 1878

TOOHEY Harriet age 8m 20d dau of Thomas and Mary in Schuylerville, NY July 15, 1878

FLOOD Eugene in Sandy Hill, NY July 16, 1878

CONNELLY Lorenzo age 20y in S. Cambridge, NY July 8, 1878

HUNTINGTON Daniel F. abt 55y in Dresden, NY July 16, 1878

MILLER Electa M. age 45y in Hampton, NY July 16, 1878

JILLSON Bessie Louisa age 3y 2m 1d dau of H. C. in Whitehall, NY July 21, 1878

COATS Margaret age 73y in Whitehall, NY July 18, 1878

CARPENTER Peter A. age 7m son of Peter and Martha in Ft. Edward, NY July 21, 1878

MC INTYRE Mary age 75y in Sandy Hill, NY July 26, 1878

MASON Julia age 75y in Sandy Hill, NY July 22, 1878

TAYLOR Polly age 90y in Kingsbury, NY July 20, 1878

MC NAMARA Johanna age 18y 8m in Whitehall, NY July 27, 1878

MILLER James age 9y son of James in Lakeville, NY August 7, 1878

DURKEE John K. age 53y son of John in Durkeetown, NY July 28, 1878

DURKEE Lucy Ann age 1y 3m dau of Harrison and Roselia in Durkeetown, NY July 25, 1878

TELFAIR Mrs. Nancy age 82y in Schuylerville, NY July 29, 1878

PURDY Willie age 19y 1m 17d son of Jerome in Schuylerville, NY July 28, 1878

BUEL Sarah A. age 64y wife of Julio in Whitehall, NY August 2, 1878

GRANT infant child of Andrew in Ft. Ann, NY August 3, 1878

TEFFT Hiram Jr. age 45y drowned in Whitehall, NY July 31, 1878

BURBANK Roxana age 79y in N. Granville, NY July 24, 1878

GRANGER Luther age 55y at S. Bay, NY July 31, 1878

MILLER _____ age 3y child of J. in Lake, NY August 12, 1878

TORENTO _____ age 8y child of Mr. Torento in Battenville, NY August 9, 1878

COVE Henry C. age 7y in Ft. Ann, NY August 7, 1878

DOHERTY J. age 26y in Ft. Ann, NY August 5, 1878

DAVEY C. F. age 58y in New York August 12, 1878

COON James S. age 60y in Saratoga Springs, NY August 11, 1878

OTT Friend James age 40y in Greenwich, NY August 17, 1878

ARNOLD Christopher son-in-law of late John **BARNARD** of Greenwich, NY in Fox Lake, Wis. August 13, 1878

CONE Henry Clay age 3y son of Harlan P. in W. Granville, NY August 7, 1878

BURTON Elijah age 64y in W. Rupert, Vt. August 3, 1878

TEFFT Mary C. age 45y in Sandy Hill, NY August 11, 1878

PECK Samuel R. in Sandy Hill, NY August 14, 1878

HILL Laura A. age 52y wife of C. P. and Mother of A. S. of Whitehall, NY at Isle Le Motte August 12, 1878

MC FARLAND Elizabeth age 75y in Ft. Edward, NY August 18, 1878

GRANGER Willie age 2y 6m son of Elias in Ft. Ann, NY August 18, 1878

RYAN Thomas age 40y in Whitehall, NY August 26, 1878

LANGWORTHY Lydia age 5y 2m dau of P. B. and B. T. in Greenwich, NY August 18, 1878

HUTCHINS Emma age 38y wife of Robert in Lake, NY August 31, 1878

METCALF Mrs. M. age 89y in Schuylerville, NY August 28, 1878

MC KEE Mrs. Eliza abt 50y in Ft. Edward, NY August 24, 1878

RICE Caroline age 64y in Ft. Ann, NY August 25, 1878

FULLER Anna D. age 23y in Ft. Miller, NY August 24, 1878

MC GRATH Julia age 64y in Hampton, NY August 14, 1878

BALDWIN Celia age 7y died August 7, 1878 and Georgia age 5y died August 15, 1878 children of Amos and Ann in White Creek, NY

DAVIS Stella age 15y in Bolton, NY August 14, 1878

BENTLEY Jane Ann age 60y in White Creek, NY August 23, 1878

RANDLES Maggie M. age 7y dau of Robert and Frank in Argyle, NY August 24, 1878

NORTON Anna age 74y widow of David in M. Granville, NY August 31, 1878

LEE Eliza age 53y widow of Chester in Granville, NY August 31, 1878

CROWN Nellie age 11y dau of E. M. in Greenwich, NY September 11, 1878

TEFFT ____ age 6y child of Martin in Greenwich, NY September 8, 1878

CORAS ____ age 7y child of John in Vly Summit, NY (newspaper date September 12, 1878)

GEOLIN infant dau of Mr. and Mrs. Geolin in Sandy Hill, NY August 31, 1878

DE GRUSH infant dau of J. E. in Sandy Hill, NY August 31, 1878

SMITH Mabel age 3m 2w dau of Eugene R. and Annie E. in Salem, NY September 12, 1878

BROWN ____ age 7m dau of Henry F. and H. E. in Salem, NY August 30, 1878

GIFFORD Dr. J. J. age 28y at fathers in Caledonia, Wis. September 8, 1878. Son-in-law of Azor **CULVER** of Cambridge, NY

BENSON Lydia age 83y Mother of Hiram in White Creek, NY September 9, 1878

HAM Mrs. Electa age 84y in Cambridge, NY September 15, 1878

GLINN Mary age 66y wife of E. in Whitehall, NY September 24, 1878

HASKELL Frank age 6y in Argyle, NY September 16, 1878

NEWTON Mary age 80y widow of Asahel in Hartford, NY September 14, 1878

WARREN Louise in her 54th yr widow of J. B. in Granville, NY September 28, 1878

FILLMORE Alevia age 14y 1m dau of L. H. in Whitehall, NY September 28, 1878

MATHEWS Mrs. Jane age 82y in Whitehall, NY September 18, 1878

CONNORS Kate age 24y in Schuylerville, NY September 26, 1878

CHITTY Charles W. age 58y in Ft. Edward, NY September 25, 1878

ROBERTSON Robert age 73y formerly of Cambridge, NY in Summitville, Iowa September 29, 1878

LOWBER Ellen A. widow of John formerly of Bald Mountain, NY at bro William

M. FERGUSON in Washington, DC September 22, 1878

CARRINGTON Levi age 46y 4m in Whitehall, NY October 9, 1878

DIBBLE Clella (REED) in her 60th yr widow of B. L. of Whitehall, NY at son-in-laws Levi BULLIS in Decorah, Iowa (newspaper date October 17, 1878)

AUSTIN Mary A. age 23/33y wife of George A. in Salem, NY October 6, 1878

BECKWITH William Gould son of late Henry W. in Granville, NY October 18, 1878

MC GINNIS Mark age 50y in Sandy Hill, NY October 14, 1878

WATERS Mrs. E. A. age 35y in Sandy Hill, NY October 11, 1878

CORCORAN Frank age 7y son of Michael in Sandy Hill, NY October 17, 1878

BELL John age 81y in French Mountain, NY October 10, 1878

BURGESS Estelle age 7w dau of Loan and Eliza in N. Hoosick, NY September 25, 1878

SUTFIN Derrick age 59y in Northumberland, NY October 8, 1878

COX Elizabeth age 84y in Schuylerville, NY October 15, 1878

FREIDENBURGH Mrs. Tobias in Middle Falls, NY October 28, 1878

MATTISON Martha age 37y wife of Hiram C. in Dunhams Basin, NY October 26, 1878

WINN Roxanna age 72y in Dresden, NY Ocotber 8, 1878

WILSON Lucy age 82y in Hampton, NY October 24, 1878

CAVANAUGH Mary age 68y in Cambridge, NY October 22, 1878

BEAUCHAMP Willie age 8y in Ft. Edward, NY October 25, 1878

GLENHOLMES Frank age 78y in Argyle, NY November 10, 1878

SWEET Charles A. age 59y in N. Granville, NY November 10, 1878

BRADLEY Mary age 19y in Ft. Edward, NY November 9, 1878

ROGERS Anna P. age 60y wife of James in Whitehall, NY November 18, 1878

SHAW Ira age 27y in Whitehall, NY November 23, 1878

TERRY Albro age 22y in Whitehall, NY November 24, 1878

JOHNSON Mrs. Jane age 61y in Whitehall, NY November 24, 1878

KNIGHT Henry H. age 46y in Whitehall, NY November 24, 1878

GETTY Agnes age 74y relict of John at bro F. **CRAIG** in Putnam, NY November 14, 1878

DEYO Jonathan age 43y in Northumberland, NY November 21, 1878

LEE Lewis age 26y in Ft. Miller, NY November 23, 1878

SNODY Mrs. William age 71y in Dresden, NY November 30, 1878

FOX Joseph age 62y in Sandy Hill, NY November 29, 1878

BENWAY Mrs. Moses age 40y in Sandy Hill, NY November 30, 1878

FOX Margaret age 23y in Sandy Hill, NY December 5, 1878

PARKER Asa age 88y in S. Granville, NY November 24, 1878

DONNELLY Walter J. age 44y in Troy, NY December 3, 1878

JERRAM Frank age 9y son of John and Mary in Cambridge, NY November 22, 1878

RUSSELL Ebenezer age 86y 5m in White Creek, NY November 30, 1878

BRIGGS Garrie L. age 3y son of Charlie and Libbie in White Creek, NY December 1, 1878

HOLMES Fannie P. wife of Richard S. and dau of John **OLMSTEAD** in Auburn, NY December 9, 1878

SKINNER Fannie age 4y died November 22, 1878 and Earle age 8m died December 22, 1878 children of Fortunatus and Frank in Greenwich, NY

WILBUR Jonathan in N. Easton, NY December 23, 1878

BROWN Clarence M. age 22y in Eagle Bridge, NY November 29, 1878

HOWE Spencer age 76y in Ft. Edward, NY December 4, 1878

MILLER Mrs. A. A. age 51y in Sandy Hill, NY December 15, 1878

GATES Jacob age 62y in Dunhams Basin, NY December 18, 1878

MC SHANE James in Smiths Basin, NY December 11, 1878

SULLIVAN Frank age 7y in Victory Mills, NY December 12, 1878

DUGAN Hugh age 81y in Cambridge, NY December 2, 1878

DOLLARD Alice age 1y in Cambridge, NY December 19, 1878

MC GRATH David age 5y in Cambridge, NY December 21, 1878

RUNDELL Ira age 38y in Buskirks Bridge, NY December 25, 1878

DAVIS Owen age 21y in Granville, NY December 25, 1878

GILBERT Margaret (**INGERSOLL**) age 81y in Pittsford, Vt. (newspaper date January 2, 1879)

STARKS Freddie L. age 12y in Ft. Edward, NY December 17, 1878

WILLIAMS Mrs. Julia A. age 74y in Beloit, Ks. December 17, 1878

FREEMAN Allie age 8y dau of George L. and Annie in Ft. Edward, NY December 18, 1878

CURTIS Thomas age 79y in the County Home December 31, 1878 (inmate for 23 yrs)

CAYZOR George age 5y in Ft. Ann, NY December 27, 1878

SNELL Mrs. Esther Ann age 45y in Easton, NY December 20, 1878

VAN SHAICK Mrs. Tina age 80y in Easton, NY December 21, 1878

AYOTT Jessie age 19y in Wells, Vt. January 5, 1879

WILLIAMS Chauncey E. age 46y in Rutland, Vt. January 6, 1879

LOUPRETTE Joseph age 3y in Glens Falls, NY December 26, 1878

MC DONALD Mrs. R. E. age 54y in Stroudsburg, Pa. December 20, 1878

GREEN Henry age 83y in Glens Falls, NY December 27, 1878

VAN DEUSEN David age 82y in Glens Falls, NY January 1, 1879

RIPLEY Myron age 62y in Fenton, Mi. (newspaper date January 16, 1879)

CALDWELL Mrs. Eliza in her 81st yr in Whitehall, NY January 10, 1879

BAUMES Edward age 14y son of Adam and Lucine in Schuylerville, NY January 14, 1879

WATSON Rev. Elisha age 57y at sons in Schenectady, NY January 4, 1879

BEADLE Ida E. age 9y 6m 25d dau of Zina W. and Mary D. in Easton, NY January

11, 1879

ALLEN John R. age 31y formerly of Greenwich, NY in Saratoga Springs, NY January 1, 1879

HOAG Mrs. Sylvia age 74y in Easton, NY January 8, 1879

BUTTERFIELD Sylvester age 48y in Ash Grove, NY January 6, 1879

KETCHUM Harry Gray age 13y in Cambridge, NY January 4, 1879

NILES Mary age 74y in White Creek, NY December 28, 1878

GUY Mrs. George age 87y in Sandy Hill, NY January 10, 1879

SCOTT Dr. William E. age 70y formerly of Sandy Hill, NY in Buffalo, NY January 5, 1879

LAPHAM Hattie age 17y in Glens Falls, NY January 6, 1879

ALLEN David in his 80th yr in Granville, NY January 11, 1879

RODGERS Rev. R. K. age 82y (Pastor of Pres. Church in Sandy Hill, NY 10 yrs) at Athens, Ga. January 12, 1879

MOON Etta M. age 1y at E. Lake George, NY January 10, 1879

OSSMAN Miss Lucinda in Hampton, NY January 18, 1879

DWYER Thomas age 28y in Greenwich, NY January 20, 1879

SAFFORD Carrie E. age 32y in Easton, NY February 4, 1879

WELLING ____ age 2y child of Edgar in Easton, NY January 30, 1879

BARRY John in Center Falls, NY January 28, 1879

GILMAN Abijah age 76y in Easton, NY January 25, 1879

HANDY Lydia age 87y Mother of Thomas in Easton, NY January 15, 1879

FORT Lewis age 75y in Easton, NY January 30, 1879

SMITH Anna age 79y in Shaftsbury, Vt. January 25, 1879

GRIFFIN Jay age 20y in Sandy Hill, NY January 26, 1879

DUERS Mrs. Jane age 79y in Sandy Hill, NY January 27, 1879

DILLON Thomas age 65y in Sandy Hill, NY January 26, 1879

BURNHAM Mary Ann age 73y in Sandy Hill, NY January 8, 1879

BEST Walter H. in his 17th yr son of Walter formerly of Salem, NY at the Elm Grove Hotel on Albany Rd. January 21, 1879

BLACK Miss Jane age 63y in Whitehall, NY February 4, 1879

HAWLEY Mrs. Anna age 77y at son-in-laws J. W. **ESTY** in Whitehall, NY (newspaper date February 6, 1879)

WILSON Stephen D. age 5y of Charles H. and Maggie in Whitehall, NY February 2, 1879

GRIFFIN William age 17y of Ft. Edward, NY in the County Home February 5, 1879

GIFFORD Susannah age 86y widow of Ira in Schaghticoke, NY February 1, 1879

BENNETT Nancy (**HOLLENBECK**) age 69y 23d wife of James in Ft. Edward, NY January 23, 1879

GANNON Peter age 64y in Cambridge, NY February 1, 1879

DUGAN George Edward age 1y 6m son of Henry and Margaret in Cambridge, NY February 1, 1879

MC CARTY Mrs. Mary age 22y in Schuylerville, NY February 8, 1879

WROATH William age 54y in Schuylerville, NY February 5, 1879

MIDON John age 85y nr Slyborough, NY February 1, 1879, born Ireland, buried Granville, NY

ORCUTT Chester abt 47y in Hartford, NY January 30, 1879. Served 123rd Reg. NY Vol. wounded in leg at battle of Peachtree Creek

MERRILL Frederick V. in his 76th yr in Easton, NY February 10, 1879

WILCOX Elijah age 4y son of Stephen in Easton, NY February 17, 1879

WHEELER F. A. age 47y in Fairhaven, Vt. February 6, 1879

COLTON David B. age 52y 4m 6d in Fairhaven, Vt. February 10, 1879

HAVENS Mary J. age 55y in Westhaven, Vt. February 9, 1879

DEUEL H. D. age 47y in Sandy Hill, NY February 6, 1879

PECK Melinda age 71y in Northumberland, NY February 8, 1879

RELIHAN Johanna age 78y in White Creek, NY February 12, 1879

CARPENTER Daniel age 56y in Tomhannock, NY February 15, 1879

MC GAHEN Mrs. ____ age 91y in N. Greenwich, NY February 18, 1879

WALKER William age 88y in Whitehall, NY February 16, 1879

SHELDON Fred age 2y son of Don and Amelia in Hebron, NY February 6, 1879

MUNSON Lettie in her 8th yr dau of James in Hebron, NY February 6, 1879

HOWE ____ age 5m 13d dau of James in Ft. Edward, NY January 30, 1879

BELL Mrs. Zina age 61y in Ft. Edward, NY February 4, 1879

SILL Zachary age 86y in Hartford, NY February 15, 1879

HALE Hannah wife of George in Argyle, NY February 15, 1879

KEEFE Richard age 35y in Buskirks Bridge, NY February 14, 1879

HERRINGTON Deborah age 65y in W. Hoosick, NY February 15, 1879

SHELDON Sarah P. age 57y wife of John P. in Fairhaven, Vt. February 17, 1879

VAN TASSEL Hiram age 38y formerly of Sandy Hill, NY in Conklingville, NY February 17, 1879

GILBERT Hiram B. age 78y in Kingsbury, NY February 5, 1879

VANDENBURGH Mary dau of Rev. J. E. **KING** in Ft. Edward, NY February 11, 1879

ELLSWORTH Emma age 16y in Victory Mills, NY February 16, 1879

ROSE Maggie E. age 14y in Salem, NY February 4, 1879

ROWLEY Michael in M. Granville, NY February 12, 1879

HATCH Munson abt 2y son of Milo and Olive in Hebron, NY February 16, 1879

TEFFT Mary A. age 52y widow of Allen F. formerly of Greenwich, NY and dau of Isaac **WESTCOTT** in Stillwater, NY February 20, 1879

OWEN Jane (**HILL**) age 55y wife of Henry R. formerly of Greenwich, NY in Minturn, Iowa February 17, 1879

GLEASON ____ child of John in Easton, NY February 23, 1879

DONALDSON Judge N. M. in Owatonna, Mn. February 7, 1879. Born November 12, 1809 in N. Argyle, NY. Married (1) Jane **STEWART** in N. Argyle, married (2)

Emily S. **STRONG** in 1864. 2 children Mary and Bessie

NEWBURY Jennie E. age 26y in New York February 25, 1879 buried Middle Falls

CAMPBELL Hattie age 15y in Whitehall, NY March 2, 1879

PENNIMAN A. G. age 80y in Battenville, NY February 28, 1879

THORPE Louisa age 57y in Greenwich, NY February 5, 1879

WALLACE Thomas age 24y in Lake, NY March 5, 1879

BRAYTON Bettie age 32y in Kingsbury, NY February 23, 1879

GATES Joseph age 70y in Kingsbury, NY February 24, 1879

COOK Olive A. age 50y wife of Chester and dau of J. H. **NORTHUP** of Sandy Hill, NY in Ft. Edward, NY February 16, 1879

WOOD Helen age 57y wife of John D. in Fairhaven, Vt. February 26, 1879

KENNEDY Katie age 20y in Greenwich, NY March 8, 1879

HALLUM Mary age 89y at son-in-laws Hiram C. **RATHBONE** in Easton, NY March 11, 1879

SKINNER Franklin B. age 45y formerly of Greenwich, NY in Northeast, Pa. March 8, 1879. Bro Courtland

MARTIN Janette age 32y in N. Granville, NY March 1, 1879

BARTHOLOMEW W. of Dresden, NY in N. Granville, NY March 2, 1879

COATS Mary wife of John in N. Granville, NY (newspaper date March 13, 1879)

OGDEN Nelson P. age 18y in Buskirks Bridge, NY February 27, 1879

HUMPHREY Ebenezer age 32y in S. Granville, NY March 1, 1879

MC EACHRON Margaret age 72y wife of John J. in Argyle, NY February 26, 1879

BORDEN Daniel in Argyle, NY March 3, 1879

FOSTER Elizabeth age 38y in Salem, NY March 2, 1879

BECKER Harmon age 76 in Easton, NY March 14, 1879

HEWITT ____ child of David in Greenwich, NY March 12, 1879

BAKER Mrs. Silas age 84y in Ft. Ann, NY March 5, 1879

FLANNERY James age 35y in Whitehall, NY March 8, 1879

LACCA Mrs. Charlotte M. age 76y in Whitehall, NY March 10, 1879

DOUGLAS Nelson age 65y in Whitehall, NY March 10, 1879

PIERCE Mrs. Julius ae 72y in Whitehall, NY March 10, 1879

FLACK Edmond R. age 39y in the County Home March 7, 1879

CREIGHTON ____ age 3w son of George in Argyle, NY March 6, 1879

BRISTOL Mrs. Silas nr Ft. Miller, NY March 6, 1879

FOSTER Mrs. George and child in Shushan, NY March 3, 1879

NORMAN Caroline M. age 68y in Elyria, Ohio February 27, 1879. 2 children Mrs. George C. **WASHBURN** of Elyria and Mrs. M. J. **OATMAN** of Cambridge, NY

PRUYN Ann age 83y in Buskirks Bridge, NY March 9, 1879

SHELDON Pearl S. age 14m in W. Rupert, Vt. March 6, 1879

RASTALL Mrs. E. age 72y in Schuylerville, NY March 8, 1879

PENNOCK Mrs. Sarah in Schuylerville, NY March 7, 1879

ROGERS Mrs. Walter age 78y in Ft. Edward, NY March 14, 1879

FOURNEY Susie L. age 19y in Whitehall, NY March 14, 1879

GRANT Charles age 49y in Whitehall, NY March 17, 1879

BRETT Jonnie age 10y son of George in Whitehall, NY March 17, 1879

ABEL Louisa (**LOVERIN**) age 67y 6m wife of Asa in Whitehall, NY March 16, 1879

ALLORE Mrs. ____ age 64y in Whitehall, NY March 16, 1879

RENCAUD Mrs. Napoleon age 25y in Whitehall, NY March 16, 1879

QUINN Mrs. James age 85y in N. Granville, NY March 16, 1879

WOODRUFF Walter age 60 in Ft. Ann, NY March 19, 1879

GRAHAM James age 85y in Ft. Edward, NY March 13, 1879

BISHOP Caroline H. age 56y wife of William D. in Cambridge, NY February 28, 1879

TUCKER Mrs. Lyman abt 90y in Spraguetown, NY March 21, 1879

MC NEIL Edwin age 80y in Whitehall, NY March 21, 1879

AMES Caroline A. age 52y 1m 4d wife of Almon in Canton, Ill. March 15, 1879

WILBUR ____ child of Stephen in Easton, NY March 24, 1879

FLYNN Bridget in Easton, NY March 31, 1879

ROOT Rollin age 22y in Hebron, NY March 19, 1879

STEWART Leonard age 3m 16d son of John W. and Mary C. in Sandy Hill, NY March 20, 1879

MOORE Abel W. age 66y in Ft. Edward, NY March 20, 1879

LAWRENCE Eliza age 65y of Gansevort, NY in Sandy Hill, NY March 21, 1879

GRACE Frank age 26y in Glens Falls, NY March 20, 1879

PINE Elizabeth age 63y in Glens Falls, NY March 25, 1879

BRAYMAN Nellie age 2y in Glens Falls, NY March 17, 1879

BEEBE Laura Ann in Glens Falls, NY March 25, 1879

DAVEY Mrs. Albert age 73y in Fairhaven, Vt. March 23, 1879

BURNS Bridget age 62y in Fairhaven, Vt. March 25, 1879

KING Laura age 26y dau of John D. in Benson, Vt. March 19, 1879

BARTHOLOMEW George S. age 31y in Whitehall, NY March 29, 1879

FITCH Prof. Asa Md. in his 70th yr in Fitchs Point, NY April 8, 1879

TODD James I. age 11y son of Thomas D. in Waterloo, Neb. March 26, 1879

HARRIS May age 9m dau of Ira and Carrie in Kingsbury, NY March 26, 1879

SPENCER Mrs. Warren age 55y in Ticonderoga, NY March 20, 1879

MARTIN Mrs. Fannie age 45y in Glens Falls, NY March 18, 1879

BALDWIN James age 87y in Glens Falls, NY March 25, 1879

HALL John R. age 32y in Warrensburgh, NY March 21, 1879

WRIGHT ____ age 1y 3m dau of H. A. and D. C. in E. Hartford, NY April 2, 1879

WILSON Warren age 65y in Hampton, NY April 1, 1879

SHEPPARD Harvey age 62y in Fairhaven, Vt. April 3, 1879

LOURIE Mrs. Jennett in her 87th yr relict of George and dau of Thomas **BEVERIDGE** in Jackson, NY April 11, 1879. Sons T. B. and J. L.

BURNHAM Noadiah age 63y of Greenwich, NY in Natick, Mass. April 10, 1879

DAVIS Gardner age 62y in Quaker Springs, NY April 9, 1879

CARRIER Katie age 23y in Sandy Hill, NY April 5, 1879

HAUNSBERRY Michael age 47y in Hoosick Falls, NY April 6, 1879

GILMORE Laura (**MEEK**) age 28y 5m 22d wife of W. J. formerly of Cambridge, NY in Lawrence, Ks. March 27, 1879

WILSON Delia age 34y wife of Andrew in Ft. Edward, NY April 2, 1879

JOHNSON George age 83y of Hartford, NY at sons in Hebron, NY April 6, 1879

CARROLAN Rosa age 27y wife of John formerly of Salem, NY in Brooklyn, NY April 6, 1879

ARNOLD Gertrude age 13y dau of late O. A. in Harts Falls, NY April 13, 1879

ALLEN Stephen age 98y in Crandalls Corners, NY April 14, 1879

FRENCH Mrs. Laura age 60y in S. Argyle, NY April 21, 1879

NULTY ____ age 6y dau of George in Easton, NY April 17, 1879

TUCKER Samuel age 81y in N. Greenwich, NY April 18, 1879

MEADER Burt abt 80y in Easton, NY April 13, 1879

COLE Mary age 79y in Whitehall, NY April 2, 1879

PIERCE Mary age 16m dau of D. T. and Marietta in Argyle, NY April 15, 1879

BAKER Sarah age 84y in Valley Falls, NY April 4, 1879

BARNES Frederick age 2y in Eagle Bridge, NY March 17, 1879

DURFEE Lura V. age 2m 15d dau of M. and V. in Easton, NY March 20, 1879

MC FADDEN Blanche Louisa age 2y 10m dau of T. F. and A. L. in Cambridge, NY April 10, 1879

ALEXANDER James age 84y in Sandy Hill, NY April 13, 1879

BRISLEN Daniel age 87y in Ft. Edward, NY April 15, 1879

WARNER John in S. Hartford, NY April 13, 1879

HOOKER Phillip age 83y in Whitehall, NY April 12, 1879

RANSOM Royce age 2y in Whitehall, NY April 12, 1879

MC COTTER Mrs. Susan in Whitehall, NY April 15, 1879

DUNN Lillian A. in her 17th yr in Harts Falls, NY April 17, 1879

LINSENBARTH Charles age 22y son of Fred of Salem, NY in Brooklyn, NY April 24, 1879

MURCH Lettie age 5y in Greenwich, NY April 28, 1879

AUSMENT Alonzo age 63y in Sandy Hill, NY April 17, 1879

TANNER Mary age 28y dau of Luther PIKE in Ft. Edward, NY April 20, 1879

HERRINGTON Solomon age 67y in Kingsbury, NY April 10, 1879

SKINNER Mrs. Amanda/Aurelia oldest sis of Mrs. L. J. HAWLEY and Mrs. C. MORGAN of Salem, NY in Cincinnati, Ohio April 13, 1879

JACKSON James in his 50th yr formerly of Greenwich, NY in Deerfield, Mi. April 24, 1879

STOUGHTON Elizabeth (HALL) widow of Fisher in Ft. Edward, NY April 25, 1879

HEWITT Mrs. Dr. in Ft. Edward, NY April 26, 1879

DAILEY Mrs. Prudy E. age 74y in Sandy Hill, NY March 23, 1879

RENAUD Mrs. Delia age 57y in Whitehall, NY April 24, 1879

TIERNEY William age 73y in Whitehall, NY April 25, 1879

BLANCHARD Kittie age 2y 4m dau of Alfred and Libbie in Whitehall, NY April 29, 1879

BENJAMIN Freddie H. age 2y son of P. S. in Whitehall, NY April 26, 1879

MC GORTY Miss Rose age 19y in Whitehall, NY April 29, 1879

ROOT Phelia W. age 70y in Greenwich, NY May 6, 1879, funeral at son-in-laws John RICHARDS

WILSON Arthur E. age 5y 3m 22d died May 2, 1879 and Charlie age 8y died May 5, 1879, children of John and Fannie in Easton, NY

HILL Prince in his 74th yr bro of Jemima and Jesse Hill March 29, 1879

HURD Minnie age 8y dau of L. F. formerly of Greenwich, NY in Lee, Mass. April 25, 1879

KENNEDY Michael at Bald Mountain, NY May 13, 1879

BOULDER Mrs. Martha age 40y in N. Easton, NY May 10, 1879

HAMILTON Freeland/Russell age 7y 6m son of Frank and Margaret in Cambridge, NY April 25, 1879

HALL infant child of Barnes in Argyle, NY May 8, 1879

PARTRIDGE Cyrus age 66y in Ft. Edward, NY May 3, 1879

DURKEE Archibald age 72y in Durkeetown, NY May 3, 1879

SWEET Charles age 8y in Whitehall, NY May 3, 1879

HASTINGS Alpheus age 73y in Greenwich, NY May 5, 1879

GOODELL Frederick age 76y in Fairhaven, Vt. May 6, 1879

WHITE Nancy age 88y relict of Charles in N. Whitehall, NY May 9, 1879

WRIGHT Charles age 28y in Whitehall, NY May 8, 1879

NICHOLS Carrie F. age 2y 6m 6d dau of Milo and Jane C. in Whitehall, NY May 5, 1879

WOOD Stephen age 76y in Whitehall, NY May 7, 1879

GRAULICH Lizzie age 4y dau of J. Phillip in Whitehall, NY May 12, 1879

MC ALLEY Joseph in Sandy Hill, NY May 9, 1879

ROGERS John age 66y in Moreau, NY May 11, 1879

KINNE Mahala age 97y wife of John G. in Ft. Edward, NY May 10, 1879

MC GHIE Mary abt 55y wife of William F. in Whitehall, NY May 16, 1879

WARNER Betsey in Leicester, NY April 22, 1879. Born March 9, 1804 in Buckland, Mass. dau of Nathaniel **WILDER**, married February 12, 1826. Leaves husband Daniel, 3 children Thomas of Cohocton, NY, Henry H. of Washington Co. and Mrs. E. S. **PERRY** of Knowlesville, NY

NORTON Warren age 65y formerly of Cambridge, NY in Chicago, Ill. May 12, 1879

ALLEN Mrs. Loren age 44y in Sandy Hill, NY May 18, 1879

DOOLITTLE Mrs. Silas age 55y in Sandy Hill, NY May 21, 1879

HUMPHREY Mrs. John age 70y in M. Granville, NY (newspaper date May 29, 1879)

PRICE Elias W. in M. Granville, NY (newspaper date May 29, 1879)

DAWLEY Nellie F. age 5y 7m died May 18, 1879 and Jesse M. age 3y 3m died May 29, 1879, children of Morgan and Martha in Easton, NY

JOYCE Johnie age 1y 6m son of John and Bridget in Greenwich, NY May 30, 1879

KELLY Joseph age 77y in Salem, NY May 27, 1879

CONGDON E. Morgan age 40y in Schaghticoke, NY May 24, 1879

SMITH Charles age 6y in Greenwich, NY June 7, 1879

MESICK Mrs. E. D. age 45y in Valley Falls, NY June 8, 1879

BUSH John age 19y in Victory Mills, NY June 1, 1879

LEE Rene Bell age 14m dau of G. B. and Hattie A. in Cambridge, NY June 2, 1879

BARTLETT Joseph age 64y in Greenwich, NY June 13, 1879

PERRY Joseph age 85y in Sandy Hill, NY June 7, 1879

SMITH Fannie age 71y wife of Elijah in Whitehall, NY June 13, 1879

SMITH Nathan age 59y in Whitehall, NY June 9, 1879

FACTO George adopted son of Obed NORTON in Whitehall, NY June 6, 1879

RATHBONE Perlina age 77y in Easton, NY June 16, 1879

BAKER Sophia age 61y wife of Daniel in Ft. Miller, Ny June 27, 1879

HUIST Anna abt 9y dau of Dr. P. H. in Greenwich, NY June 27, 1879, infant child died July 9, 1879

BLAIR Alexander age 60y in Greenwich, NY July 8 1879

PATTERSON George S. age 28y son of B. S. of Greenwich, NY in Troy, NY July 4, 1879

CORNELL Lucy A. age 58y wife of Madison in Sandy Hill, NY June 24, 1879

TISDALE Capt. H. G. age 75y in Whitehall, NY July 6, 1879

FISHER Jenny age 16y in Cambridge, NY July 7, 1879

KING Jonathan age 67y in Coila, NY July 1, 1879

HOAG Stephen age 95y in White Creek, NY July 8, 1879

CORLISS Tistram age 81y in Easton, NY July 19, 1879

CRANDALL Mrs. Asa age 52y in Easton, NY July 18, 1879

HARDY Willie age 3y 3m son of Abraham in Whitehall, NY July 12, 1879

OSBORN Joseph age 76y in Schuylerville, NY July 15, 1879

AKIN Jennie age 30y wife of Charles C. and dau of Alexander **ROSS** in Johnsonville, NY July 15, 1879

RELIHAN Daniel age 35y in Buskirks Bridge, NY July 4, 1879

SPENCER Edwin age 10y son of S. S. of Troy, NY in Greenwich, NY July 21, 1879

WILSON Allie age 12y son of John in Greenwich, NY July 27, 1879

GRAHAM Mary E. age 30y wife of William in Bald Mountain, NY July 27, 1879

MOORE Clarinda age 78y wife of Alex C. in Cambridge, NY July 23, 1879

DURLING Willie in his 11th yr in Greenwich, NY August 3, 1879

KENYON _____ age 6y dau of Otis in N. Greenwich, NY August 1, 1879, wife died August 6, 1879

ROURKE Mary age 50y in Easton, NY August 4, 1879

WRIGHT John in his 48th yr in Greenwich, NY August 13, 1879

BARTLETT Elizabeth age 52y wife of Mathias in Belcher, NY July 23, 1879

BRODIE Mary A. age 2m 6d dau of Patrick and Mary Ann in Cambridge, NY August 1, 1879

WILSON Johnie age 6y 6m 17d son of John and Lucindy in Granville, NY August 5, 1879

DONALDSON Margaret Ellen wife of Benjamin in Argyle, NY August 3, 1879

WESTFALL Ernest Howe age 1y 10m 18d son of D. M. and Susan in Cambridge, NY August 10, 1879

LOOMIS Mary M. age 56y wife of Henry in Whitehall, NY August 15, 1879

REYNOLDS Schuyler age 72y 3m 11d at sons in Maquoketa, Iowa August 8, 1879. Born Washington Co. bro of Porter (dec) of Middle Falls, NY, 3 children living

LEE ____ abt 5y dau of Elisha in Greenwich, NY August 25, 1879

ROBINSON William B. age 69y in Pawlet, Vt. August 24, 1879

EGAN ____ child of Michael and Mary of Brooklyn in Salem, NY August 19, 1879

PERRY Evaline age 58y widow of Dr. A. of Easton, NY in Granville, NY August 17, 1879

HARDEN Mrs. S. H. age 64y in S. Hartford, NY August 15, 1879

BIGGER Mrs. Rev. Samuel in Putnam, NY August 13, 1879

DWINNELL Mrs. Betsey in her 76th yr in White Creek, NY August 10, 1879

LEARY Charles in Ft. Edward, NY August 17, 1879

PRENTISS Amelia in her 43rd yr dau of Horace and Mary in Hoosick Falls, NY August 22, 1879

DAVIS Freddie age 2y 8m son of Edward, NY in Greenwich, NY September 9, 1879

RUSSELL Albert age 22y in White Creek, NY August 23, 1879

CUMMINGS Darwin L. age 12y son of William A. and Calista in Putnam, NY August 30, 1879

COLEMAN Norah age 76y widow in Ft. Ann, NY August 23, 1879

MAXFIELD George age 28y in Ft. Ann, NY August 23, 1879

BAXTER Mrs. John age 78y in Ft. Ann, NY August 31, 1879

LANSING Jennie infant dau of G. V. P. and Carrie M. in Ft. Ann, NY September 9, 1879

SPARHAWK Dexter age 70y in Greenwich, NY September 24, 1879

GALLUP Fred age 11y son of Wyatt and Harriet of Stillwater, NY in Easton, NY September 9, 1879

NICHOLS Ann M. age 56y wife of Louis in Lansingburgh, NY September 21, 1879

POWERS Mrs. Joseph abt 40y in Sandy Hill, NY September 7, 1879

NELSON Ada age 18y in Whitehall, NY September 14, 1879

THOMAS Anna age 24y in Glens Falls, NY September 2, 1879

FRENCH Betsey **(RANDALL)** age 72y wife of Warren in Greenwich, NY September 28, 1879

BENNETT George age 4y son of Benjamin in Greenwich, NY September 27, 1879

BECKER Corona age 33y dau of Henry in Easton, NY September 26, 1879

MERRIAM Polly B. abt 60y wife of S. B. in Whitehall, NY September 30, 1879

BAKER Mrs. Lucretia age 77y in Granville, NY October 5, 1879

MURPHY Mary age 3y dau of Thomas and Abbie in Granville, NY October 2, 1879

PEISTER Robert age 76y in Argyle, NY September 24, 1879

BROUGHTON Amos age 76y in Ft. Ann, NY October 6, 1879

DOLAN Thomas abt 80y in S. Granville, NY September 21, 1879

MONTGOMERY William age 57y in Ft. Edward, NY September 27, 1879 and wife Jane A. age 56y died September 28, 1879

GOURLEY Ellen A. age 55y of Putnam, NY in the County Home October 2, 1879

THOMAS Oliver abt 70y of Whitehall, NY in the County Home October 6, 1879

BRIDGEFORD Lottie age 10y 2d dau of William and Catherine in Cambridge, NY October 5, 1879 and son Thomas age 12y died October 12, 1879

RANDALL David age 74y in Greenwich, NY October 22, 1879

JEMINSON John age 69y in Hoosick Falls, NY October 13, 1879

HOWLAND Jennie age 20y 11m 5d in Schuylerville, NY October 11, 1879

SCHERMERHORN Carrie age 10y grand dau of Hiram **CLARK** in Clarks Mills, NY September 14, 1879

FORD Mary Agnes age 42 relict of James in Argyle, NY October 9, 1879

AKIN Hannah age 82y 10d Mother of James in Cambridge, NY October 14, 1879

O'BRIEN Patrick Joseph age 6y son of Thomas in Cambridge, NY October 13, 1879

NORTHUP Willie age 7m son of James M. in Hartford, NY October 9, 1879

BROWNELL Matie age 10y dau of Hiram and Hettie in Easton, NY October 15, 1879

MARTIN Horace age 74y in Warsaw, NY October 22/29, 1879

COLLINS Iona (INGALLS) wife of Russel J. in N. Granville, NY November 7/8, 1879

BAIN G. B. age 56y in New York November 6, 1879

BAIN John Mc Intyre in S. Argyle, NY November 10, 1879

WELLS Samuel P. age 35y in Whitehall, NY November 9, 1879

SCOTT Henry in Granville, NY November 5, 1879

LEWIS Mrs. Henry of Sandy Hill, NY in New York November 6, 1879

COLEMAN Warren B. age 45y in Sandy Hill, NY November 4, 1879

ROGERS infant son of J. C. in Sandy Hill, NY November 4, 1879

STARLETT Sophia age 80y in Shushan, NY November 8, 1879

MOONEY Francis T. age 11y in Hartford, NY October 30, 1879

DECKER John D. Md. age 22y in Cambridge, NY November 2, 1879

MC CLELLAN Paul Lamotte age 10m 7d son of Mory L. and Sarah in Eagle Bridge, NY November 11, 1879

MC ENERY Anna age 19y dau of Michael in Cambridge, NY November 13, 1879

MC NISH Maria Urlaville age 9y 2m 23d dau of James and Lorinda in Greenwich, NY November 21, 1879

TEFFT Betsey F. in her 60th yr in Center Falls, NY November 20, 1879

HOYT Clara Hollis age 2y 4m dau of Harvey and Maria and grand dau of Zalmon FENTON of Cambridge, NY in Eagle Bridge, NY November 3, 1879

PALMER Effie May (STEVENS) age 24y 6m 8d wife of J. E. in Cambridge, NY October 16, 1879

FERGUSON Polly Mother of James E. in Jackson, NY November 7, 1879

MIDDLETON George A. age 21y in Hartford, NY November 15, 1879

HILLS Mrs. Hannah of Hartford, NY in the County Home November 8, 1879

GATES Jackson age 42y in Eagle Bridge, NY November 14, 1879

HALL David age 60y in Sandy Hill, NY November 17, 1879

SHARP Jennie age 11y dau of Hugh in S. Argyle, NY November 13, 1879

BLOOD Mrs. ____ age 87y Mother of Martin in Ft. Ann, NY November 17, 1879

BAIN Casper age 82y formerly of Argyle, NY in Oneonta, NY November 16, 1879

DAWLEY Gertie age 2y 2m in Greenwich, NY November 22, 1879

MULLEN Michael in his 70th yr in Whitehall, NY November 20, 1879

TERRY John age 13y drowned in Whitehall, NY November 19, 1879

BECKER Howard age 9y 5m 10d son of Edward and Mary Ann in Cambridge, NY November 25, 1879 and Freddie age 16y 1m 4d died December 7, 1879

BROWN Benjamin age 81y in Ft. Ann, NY November 17, 1879

BURCH Mrs. Catherine age 44y in Greenwich, NY December 3, 1879

VANDERWARKER Mrs. Leonard abt 65y in Ft. Miller, NY November 25, 1879

YATES Mrs. C. E. of Albany, NY in Ft. Edward, NY November 28, 1879

FENTON Lansen age 87y in Ft. Ann, NY November 26, 1879

FOAMES Hattie C. age 3m 11d dau of James and Mary in Battenville, NY November 29, 1879

WELLS David age 71y in Cambridge, NY December 7, 1879

HOPKINS Eleanor age 60y widow of Thomas in Argyle, NY December 6, 1879

TANZY Julia M. age 32y wife of M. at Fathers G. H. **STEWART** in Ft. Ann, NY December 5, 1879

MORRISON William age 75y in N. Granville, NY (newspaper date December 18, 1879)

COMISKEY Charles age 8y son of James and Anna in Greenwich, NY December 21, 1879

BLANCHARD Victor age 18m son of James in E. Greenwich, NY December 10, 1879

DIXON Mrs. Robert age 22y in Argyle, NY December 16, 1879

LOW John age 60y in Buskirks Bridge, NY December 13, 1879

BYRNE Margaret age 40y in Cambridge, NY December 10, 1879

HYDE Arunda age 48y 10m in Hoosick, NY December 7, 1879

MOSIER Mrs. Charlotte D. age 55y in Eagle Bridge, NY December 17, 1879

GIDDINGS Julia age 62y in Sandy Hill, NY December 16, 1879

GREEN Mrs. Adeline ae 42y in Ft. Ann, NY December 19, 1879

STEWART Maria L. age 71y wife of S. N. in Greenwich, NY December 11, 1879

DILL John age 66y in Hoosick, NY December 11, 1879

SHILL Darius J. age 34y in Greenwich, NY December 27, 1879

DUERS infant dau of M. A. in Sandy Hill, NY December 18, 1879

WROATH Oscar age 30y in Schuylerville, NY December 19, 1879

BEAN Emma age 18y in Schuylerville, NY December 23, 1879

DONNELLY Willie age 5y son of John in Northumberland, NY December 22, 1879 and Ella age 8y died December 13, 1879

KINGSLEY Mrs. Minerva age 86y in Ft. Miller, NY December 20, 1879

WOLL Mrs. ____ age 36y in Ft. Edward, NY December 23, 1879

SMITH Justin A. age 61y in Whitehall, NY December 30, 1879

BEVERIDGE Archie A. age 15y in Greenwich, NY December 31, 1879

POLLOCK William age 77y in N. Argyle, NY December 26, 1879

ROGERS Mrs. Cornelius age 48y in White Creek, NY December 22, 1879

TIERNEY Miss Mary in Argyle, NY December 30, 1879

WELLING Richard P. age 82y in Valley Falls, NY December 25, 1879

VANDENBURGH ____ age 12d son of Edward and Lizzie M. in Cambridge, NY December 25, 1879

MC CLELLAN Mrs. Sally age 77y in Cambridge, NY December 31, 1879

WASHINGTON COUNTY POST
May 17, 1837 - December 26, 1879

WHEELER W. H. in his 12th yr in Salem, NY May 12, 1837

MARSHALL Charles age 78y in Easton, NY May 10, 1837

HOY Agnes age 92y widow of James in Jackson, NY May 14, 1837

CLEVELAND Daniel R. age 56y formerly of Salem, NY in Macon, Ga. May 1, 1837

GRIFFIN Emma age 47y wife of Howard in Union Village, NY May 22, 1837

HIGGINS John age 21y in Hebron, NY May 21, 1837

DENNIS Mrs. ____ widow of George abt 90y in Argyle, NY May 20, 1837

BROWN George Mairs'in his 21st yr in Argyle, NY June 6, 1837

MARVIN Nancy age 23y dau of George **FORBES** of Ft. Ann, NY in York, Mi. May 14, 1837

HOWE Jesse in Albany, NY June 16, 1837

RICE Catherine age 67y widow of Col. Clark Rice in Whitehall, NY June 10, 1837

GOUGH Mrs. Mary Ann age 19y dau of Col. Curtis **COLE** of Galesville, NY in Albion, NY June 1, 1837

BELL Esther age 55y wife of Ebenezer in Union Village, NY June 7, 1837

BENNETT Betsey age 22y wife of Phineas in Galesville, NY June 8, 1837

LANNING Abraham C. age 59y 10m 4d in Lansingburgh, NY June 18, 1837

COGSWELL Capt. John age 78y Revolutionary Soldier in Whitehall, NY June 18, 1837

IRVING Robert in his 65th yr in Salem, NY June 28, 1837

WHELDON Peter in his 69th yr in Cambridge, NY July 5, 1837

SMITH Capt. Gordon age 38y in Granville, NY July 1, 1837

OLDS Liberty in his 39th yr in Jackson, NY July 9, 1837

HUGHES Phinehas in his 19th yr in Easton, NY September 11, 1837

BARNUM Capt. Horace L. formerly of Cambridge, NY in Cincinnati, Ohio August 20, 1837

LEE Cornelius Wendell youngest son of Martin in Granville, NY September 26, 1837

WHEADON Samuel H. in Salem, NY September 22, 1837

SAFFORD Margaret age 37y wife of William C. in Salem, NY September 26, 1837

ELDRIDGE William C. age 74y formerly of Salem in Penfield, NY August 29, 1837

PARKER James Henry age 1y son of Col. Joseph in Rupert, Vt. October 1, 1837

BURDETT Martin Van Buren age 1y 8m son of Samuel drowned at Whitehall, NY September 13, 1837

MARTIN Lock abt 50y in Salem, NY October 19,1837

HOPKINS Polly age 34 dau of Joel in Hebron, NY October 8, 1837

SMITH Caleb in Hebron, NY November 12, 1837

BREWSTER Sally abt 40y suicide in Hebron, NY November 4, 1837

GRAY Margaret age 51y wife of Dr. Henry in White Creek, NY November 22, 1837

BENJAMIN David age 20y in Whitehall, NY December 15, 1837

HASTINGS Mrs. L. wife of Major Hastings in Dresden, NY December 11, 1837

BROWN William G. age 20m son of William in Dresden, NY December 11, 1837

CLEVELAND Mrs. Harriet in her 36th yr in Sandgate, Vt. December 2, 1837

CROWL Frances Maria age 2y 4m 25d dau of Lyman and Maria in Albany, NY December 11, 1837

SAFFORD Cynthia age 52y wife of Gideon Jr. in Argyle, NY December 19, 1837

ATWOOD John Francis age 3y 3m son of Abiathar and Margaretta M. in Troy, NY January 12, 1838

HAMILTON George Lansing infant son of James and Elizabeth in Salem, NY January 27, 1838

CULVER Nathan in his 34th yr in Jackson, NY January 31, 1838

STOCKWELL Ann Elizabeth age 2y 2m 22d dau of F. in Whitehall, NY February 12, 1838

CUNNINGHAM John in Watertown, NY February 3, 1838

MC MORRIS John in Salem, NY February 25, 1838

STEEL Eleanor in her 75th yr consort of John in Salem, NY March 1, 1838. Native of Scotland, came to Salem in 1772

SAFFORD Gideon age 83y in Salem, NY March 7, 1838. Born Preston, Conn. 12 children all living, 91 grandchildren, 66 great grandchildren, 17 great-great grandchildren

BARNARD Sarah infant dau of William S. in Salem, NY March 15, 1838

SMITH Samuel age 57y in Whitehall, NY April 16, 1838

BLANCHARD Elizabeth M. wife of Anthony in Albany, NY April 13, 1838

ALLEN Edward age 6m son of Cornelius in Salem, NY May 7, 1838

BLOSSOM Elizabeth age 63y wife of John in Salem, NY May 15, 1838

LAKIN Martha age 5y dau of Lemuel in Salem, NY May 14, 1838

JOHNSON Mary Ann age 11y 11m dau of Jedediah and Elizabeth in Whitehall, NY May 2, 1838

DUNHAM Moses in his 15th yr son of Abram in White Creek, NY May 14, 1838

PORTER Huldah S. age 44y dau of Col. **MARTINDALE** of Dorset, Vt. in Hebron, NY April 23, 1838

AMES Charles F. in Salem, NY May 5, 1838

MC NISH Alexander Jr. in his 16th yr in Salem, NY June 2, 1838

BASSETT Mary age 20y wife of Thomas in Salem NY May 6, 1838

STEEL Capt. John in his 80th yr a Revolutionary Soldier in Salem, NY May 25, 1838. Born June 9, 1753 in Ireland. Settled in Salem 1772

STEBBINS E. Eliza age 27y wife of Calvin in Union Village, NY June 9, 1838

BASSETT George age 1y son of Alexander in Union Village, NY June 11, 1838

REAB Maj. George age 84y a Revolutionary Soldier in Salem, NY June 20, 1838

BINNINGER Harriet age 3y 11m died June 17, 1838 and Caroline W. age 1y 9m died June 22, 1838 children of Isaac and Glory Ann in Salem NY

CROWL Miss Janet in her 27th yr in Salem, NY July 22, 1838

MC CRACKEN Daniel abt 64y formerly of Salem, NY in Murray, NY July 14, 1838

MC FARLAND John M. age 3y 5m son of John in Salem NY August 19, 1838

STEEL Joshua Jr. age 3y 3m son of Joshua August 28, 1838

PARKER Joseph S. age 4y son of Joseph in Rupert, Vt. August 30, 1838

GRAVES Sophronia M. age 48y wife of Rufus in Granville, NY August 23, 1838

ROOT Cyrus in Hebron, NY September 9, 1838

RUSSELL David age 1y 17d son of William A. and Clarissa in Greenwich, NY August 12, 1838

HEWLET Daniel a Revolutionary Soldier formerly of Conn. died August 27, 1838 in Pawlet, Vt. Wife Abigail age 83y died July 12, 1838. Married 63 yrs, 3 sons and 8 daughters

WILLIAMS Elizabeth wife of Roderick in Battenville, NY September 17, 1838

BUNNELL Rev. Seth age 26 in Glenville, NY September 1, 1838

CONKEY Silas A. formerly of Salem, NY in New Berlin, NY September 11, 1838

NICHOLS Horace age 34y formerly of Sandgate, Vt. in Stafford, NY August 10, 1838. Bro Henry of Salem NY

MARTIN Abigail age 18y grand dau of Asa **FITCH** in Salem, NY October 2, 1838

DOUGERY James in his 53rd yr in Lansingburgh, NY October 10, 1838

THURSTON Martha Cornelia age 2y 3m dau of Daniel and Mary Ann in Granville, NY October 4, 1838

STILES Harriet age 19y dau of Beriah and Esther in Mendon, NY October 2, 1838

STEVENSON Dr. Robert M. in his 37th yr in Salem, NY October 18, 1838

CLEVELAND Frederick age 51y formerly of Salem, NY in Calhoun Co. Mi. September 15, 1838

RICE Daniel in his 61st yr in Salem, NY October 13, 1838

POTTER Levi drowned in Lake Champlain October 15, 1838

MC ALLISTER Mary age 44y formerly of Salem in Albany, NY October 8, 1838

SPRAGUE Sarah in his 15th yr in Union Village, NY December 1, 1838

BACHOP Alexander abt 60y in Argyle, NY (newspaper date December 13, 1838)

LOOMIS Jeduthan in her 61st yr in Cambridge, NY November 22, 1838

BROWN William age 35y in Whitehall, NY December 12, 1838

PENNELL Robert in Whitehall, NY December 11, 1838

QUILLOS Phillip fell from wagon in Whitehall, NY December 2, 1838

PROUDFIT Mary Elizabeth age 2y 6m died December 14, 1838 and Emily age 11m died December 21, 1838 children of James formerly of Salem in White Pigeon, Mi.

STEVENS Susan age 38y wife of Samuel in Albany, NY January 7, 1839

LAKE Sarah in her 77th yr widow of James in Salem, NY January 4, 1839

CRANE Hector H. age 44y in Albany, NY November 27, 1838

THOMPSON William age 69y in Salem, NY January 23, 1839

SKINNER Clarissa in her 45th yr wife of Reuben in Granville, NY January 15, 1839

PULLMAN Lucy age 64y wife of Jonathan in Union Village, NY February 1, 1839

MOREHOUSE Stillman age 1y son of Ansel in Hebron, NY February 12, 1839

STEVENSON Andrew age 38y in Salem, NY February 28, 1838

NICHOLS Malcolm age 15m son of James B. and Mary in White Creek, NY February 7, 1839

TAYLOR Diantha G. age 27y wife of Seth R. formerly of Salem, NY in Guilford, Ohio January 22, 1839, son Alexander H. age 18m died February 20, 1839

STEWART Calvin M. formerly of Sandy Hill, NY in Buffalo, NY March 1, 1839

JOSLIN Ruth in her 39th yr wife of George W. in Hebron, NY March 23, 1839

WHIPPLE John F. age 73y in Union Village, NY March 19, 1839

SEARLE Mrs. Abigail age 88y in Salem, NY April 20, 1839

LANSING John H. youngest child of W. Lansing in Greenwich, NY May 8, 1839

SHEPPARD Marciline age 2y dau of Samuel in Galesville, NY May 6, 1839

EDWARDS Rachel age 28y wife of Daniel in Galesville, NY May 8, 1839

TRIPP Mrs. Mary age 23y in Greenwich, NY May 11, 1839

BEATY Hannah (**DEWEY**) wife of Samuel 2nd died May 14, 1839, son Josiah Rising age 4y died May 12, 1839, dau Sarah Maria age 7m died May 16, 1839 in Salem, NY

CROSBY Ellen D. in her 41st yr wife of A. Crosby in Cambridge, NY May 22, 1839

WALLER Anna age 49y wife of Elisha in Union Village, NY May 14, 1839

DAY Eunice age 75y consort of Capt. Solomon Day in Sandy Hill, NY May 28, 1839

ALMY Obadiah in Glens Falls, NY May 31, 1839

PIERCE William Julius in his 8th yr son of Julius in Whitehall, NY June 10, 1839

MC NISH James in his 44th yr in Salem, NY July 5, 1839

DOBBIN Charity age 23y wife of David formerly of Jackson, NY in Rennelsburg, Ohio June 14, 1839

COLE Roxanna age 73y wife of David and dau of late Daniel BARBER in Kingsbury, NY June 20, 1839

LAW Mary abt 73y widow of Thomas in Salem, NY July 11, 1839

GREEN Mrs. Parmelia age 67y in Troy, NY July 30, 1839

PRINDLE Griffin age 16y son of Lazarus G. drowned in Argyle, NY August 9, 1839

REYNOLDS George age 53y in Moreau, NY August 11, 1839

MARTIN Henry age 18m son of Lansing in Salem, NY August 24, 1839

STOCKWELL Frederick in his 25th yr in Whitehall, NY August 28, 1839

PARMELEE Ira age 68y in N. White Creek, NY August 19, 1839

CARTER John abt 18y in Jackson, NY September 1, 1839

MC NAUGHTON Isaac age 33y formerly of Washington Co. in Cincinnati, Ohio September 1, 1839

GILLETTE Susan in her 4th yr dau of Rev. A. D. Gillett formerly of Jackson, NY in Philadelphia, Pa. September 2, 1839

SKIDMORE Caroline age 29y in Salem, NY September 18, 1839

LAW Joseph age 29y attny in New York at bro in Tarrytown, NY September 19, 1839. Buried Washington Co.

LEWIS Jane wife of Joshua S. and dau of James ROGERS of Greenwich, NY in Petersburgh, NY September 12, 1839

WARNER Dr. John age 66y formerly of Sandgate, Vt. in Starkey, NY September 4, 1839

LAWRENCE Lewis Henry in his 24th yr son of Lewis of Stillwater, NY in Mechanicsville, NY September 15, 1839

MOORE John Jr. age 23y of Salem, NY in Schuylerville, NY September 25, 1839

WITHERELL Rev. George age 55y formerly of Hartford, NY in Spring, Pa. August 19, 1839

MYERS Mary in her 29th yr wife of Michael J. and dau of Peter J. H. Myers in Whitehall, NY October 7, 1839

WILLIAMS William age 67y formerly of Salam, NY in Hadley, Ill. September 26, 1839, grandson John Moore age 3y son of John C. died August 28, 1839, dau Sarah Smith age 8m died September 10, 1839 and son George Ashley age 8y died September 13, 1839

BURR George age 33y November 6, 1839

GRAY David D. in his 67th yr in Salem, NY November 18, 1839

GOODRICH William Jr. abt 38y in Jackson, NY November 12, 1839

ATWOOD Samuel H. of Troy, NY son of Zacheus at bro Anson Atwoods November 12, 1839

DODDS James age 24y in Salem, NY November 22, 1839

ALLEN Cornelius Lansing infant son of C. L. Allen in Salem, NY November 4, 1839

CLEVELAND Martha widow of Parmer November 13, 1839

CHAMBERLAIN Elizabeth age 59y wife of Andrew in Salem, NY November 13, 1839

CRANDALL Sarah in her 75th yr wife of Joseph in Easton, NY November 16, 1839

CLARK Aurinda age 52y consort of Dr. Russell in Sandy Hill, NY December 6, 1839

BROWN Slade D. in his 46th yr in Hartford, NY December 15, 1839

SAWYER Prudence age 82y in Salem, NY December 15, 1839. Native of Andover, Mass. dau of Daniel **ABBOTT**, married age 21y moved to Amherst, NH later Salem

CLEVELAND Levi age 20y (son of Martha who died 5 wks ago) December 17, 1839

FAIRLEY William age 29y in Salem, NY December 26, 1839

DAWSON Mrs. Elizabeth age 74y in Cambridge, NY December 29, 1839

COWAN Mrs. Polly in her 74th yr in Jackson, NY December 21, 1839

SAVAGE Edward age 26y Prof. of Union College in Quincey, Fl. January 4, 1840

LIDDLE Thomas in his 54th yr in Salem NY January 29, 1840

BOIES Albert R. in his 27th yr in Whitehall, NY January 6, 1840

MILLER Mrs. Amanda age 42y in Union Village, NY January 27, 1840

COREY David in Battenville, NY February 5, 1840

BRADLEY Roswell age 23y in Sandy Hill, NY January 28, 1840

BLANCHARD Mary Elizabeth age 16y dau of Anthony in Albany, NY February 8, 1840

ROSS Elizabeth age 37y wife of Samuel in Argyle, NY February 9, 1840

CURTIS David in his 40th yr in E. Rupert, Vt. December 25, 1839

GIBSON John C. age 52y formerly of Salem, NY in Chicago, Ill. January 27, 1840

ALLEN Sarah H. infant dau of Cornelius in Salem, NY February 15, 1840

BURROUGHS Steven in Three Rivers, Ontario, Canada January 23, 1840

GRIFFITH Maria B. age 26y consort of Samuel in Sandy Hill, NY February 20, 1840

HENRY Simeon formerly of Sandy Hill, NY in Niles, Mi. January 27, 1840

COLLINS Sarah age 66y wife of Nathan in Jackson, NY February 28, 1840

GOODRICH Richard in his 33rd yr in Jackson, NY February 29, 1840

BRISTOL Mary Ann age 19y dau of Alvah and Emily in Dorset, Vt. January 16, 1840

DYER Amherst in his 81st yr a Revolutionary Soldier in White Creek, NY March 3, 1840. Native of RI, lived here 50 yrs.

PARMELEE Elias in his 66th yr in Lansingburgh, NY March 16, 1840

QUA William H. age 66y in Hebron, NY March 30, 1840

KIMBERLY Abel B. in his 72nd yr in Sandgate, Vt. March 30, 1840

WOODWORTH Cornelia age 16y dau of Ira in Salem, NY April 7, 1840

SCOTT Margaret in her 74th yr wife of Benjamin in Jackson, NY April 10, 1840

PRATT Levi in his 80th yr a Revolutionary Soldier in Dresden, NY February 26,

1840. Native of Bridgewater, Mass.

CHAMBERLAIN Andrew in his 64th yr in Salem, NY March 26, 1840

HAMMOND James in his 37th yr in Union Village, NY April 22, 1840

WILLIAMS Israel in his 56th yr formerly of Washington Co. in Albany, NY April 26, 1840

WALDO E. in W. Granville, NY April 16, 1840

TOMB Mehetable age 71y widow of Rev. Samuel at son-in-laws Rev. **SEARLE** in Coxsackie, NY April 22, 1840. Native of Rowley, Mass. Husband died Salem, NY March 28, 1832

WELLS Capt. Daniel age 86y a Revolutionary Soldier in Cambridge, NY May 6, 1840. Native of Hebron, Conn. Married March 1776 Hannah **LOTHROP** dau of Rev. Elijah Lothrop. Came first to Cambridge, NY in 1775. 16 children

BROWN Dr. Seth in his 69th yr in Salem, NY May 26, 1840

BELL Ebenezer age 65y in Union Village, NY June 6, 1840

GARDINER Sarah age 43y wife of John in Whitehall, NY May 23, 1840

COON Mary Elizabeth age 1y 25d dau of William and Rebecca in Salem, NY July 6, 1840

CROSBY Julia E. 2nd age 16y dau of A. in Cambridge, NY June 17, 1840

LEE Cornelia W. age 24y dau of Martin in Granville, NY July 18, 1840

DUTTON Ephram age 86y a Revolutionary Soldier in Ludlow, Vt. July 18, 1840

ALLEN Newell age 27y son of Dr. Abram Allen in Salem, NY August 15, 1840

BASSETT Miss Eliza in her 26th yr in Salem, NY August 16, 1840

OSBORN Deborah in her 26th yr wife of Cornelius formerly of Union Village, NY in Marshall, Mi. March 4, 1840

WRIGHT Jane E. age 26y wife of Sidney in Granville, NY August 24, 1840

GRAY Louisa age 1y 22d dau of William H. and Louisa in Lansingburgh, NY August 25, 1840

WOODWORTH Lot in his 75th yr in White Creek, NY August 20, 1840

BASSETT Joel in his 58th yr in Salem, NY September 5, 1840

COOPER Sophia age 15y dau of David of Salem in Troy, NY September 7, 1840

MC DONALD Margaret age 68y wife of Daniel in Hebron, NY September 10, 1840

WELLS Lemuel age 69y in Whitehall, NY August 30, 1840

REYNOLDS Jonathan age 100y a Revolutionary Soldier in Whitehall, NY September 16, 1840. Native of Dutchess Co. Oldest man ever in Whitehall except Joseph **FRANCISCO** who lived to be 136 yrs old.

NASH Sarah M. wife of Hollis in Union Village, NY September 7, 1840

WELLS Edward age 16m son of Edward in Whitehall, NY September 23, 1840

MC NISH Jane age 42y in Salem, NY October 6, 1840

PHILLIPS Eunice age 71y consort of Burdin in Kingsbury, NY October 1, 1840

SAUNDERS Jane in her 30th yr wife of Philander in Whitehall, NY October 24, 1840

COLLINS Archibald in his 25th yr in Whitehall, NY October 29, 1840

VIELE Stephen L. age 57y in Ft. Miller, NY October 26, 1840

BARTHOLOMEW William age 65y in Whitehall, NY November 16, 1840

FRANK John age 72y in Granville, NY March 24, 1841

ALLEN Miriam in her 72nd yr wife of Dr. Ephraim Allen in Salem, NY April 16, 1841. Last of the family of Gen. Timothy **NEWELL** of Sturbridge, Mass.

MURDOCK Russell B. age 17y 7m in Salem, NY April 16, 1841

LYTLE Samuel B. age 55y in Salem, NY April 22, 1841

REED Silas age 61y formerly of Fulton Co. NY in Red Creek, NY April 5, 1841

FITCH Elizabeth dau of Rev. Eli T. and Abby M. **MACK** in Granville, NY April 24, 1841

BLAIR Charlotte dau of Lewis and Catherine Ann (**AUSTIN**) in Salem, NY April 17, 1841

WOODWORTH Susan age 71y in Salem, NY May 9, 1841. Native of Franklin, Conn. Husband Ezra died 5 yrs ago in Ludlow, Vt.

DAY Ellen Augusta age 11m dau of Hiram and Matilda in Cambridge, NY May 4, 1841

ELDRICH infant son of Ahira and Polly age 5m of White Creek, NY April 21, 1841

TUTTLE David in his 72nd yr in Lansingburgh, NY May 17, 1841

JONES Elizabeth D. S. age 26y wife of Rev. Zebulon Jones of Peterboro, NH and dau of Seeley **SHERMAN** of Salem, NY in Salem, NY July 31, 1841

BAKER Ebenezer age 80y in W. Granville, NY August 23, 1841

WRIGHT Rebecca in her 70th yr widow of Alexander in Salem, NY August 21, 1841

CHAMBERLAIN James H. age 29y 10m in Salem, NY August 25, 1841

MC NISH Andrew in his 78th yr in Salem, NY October 8, 1841

COLLINS John abt 42y in Jackson, NY October 7, 1841

BARBER Elizabeth K. age 55y wife of Thomas in Marshall, Mi. September 18, 1841, Had 14 children, 13 living

WHITE James fell from apple tree in Salem, NY October 12, 1841

FULLER Maria age 5y in Salem, NY October 23, 1841

MAIRS Rev. George Sr. in his 31st yr in Argyle, NY October 11, 1841

CRAWFORD Margaret in her 29th yr dau of Mathew in Salem, NY October 10, 1841

TAYLOR Sarah Maria age 13m in Salem, NY October 21, 1841

DWYER John in his 8th yr son of James and Jane in Salem, NY January 9, 1842

SAFFORD Aden age 65y in Salem, NY January 14, 1842

ROBERTSON Susan age 44 wife of David died January 14, 1842, oldest son Robert age 18y died January 13, 1842 and Isabel age 4y youngest child died January 15, 1842 in Argyle, NY

TUTTLE Mrs. Nancy age 57y late of Lansingburgh, NY in Cuyahoga Falls, Ohio (newspaper date January 19, 1842)

WALKINSHAW Alsander age 29y in Salem, NY January 21, 1842

HAYES Margaret age 9y died February 3, 1842, Catherine age 6y died February 3, 1842, John age 7m died February 5, 1842 children of Owen and Mary in Salem, NY

MARTIN Aaron age 74y in Salem, NY February 8, 1842

BOARDMAN Lewis infant son of Rev. A. B. in Salem, NY February 14, 1842

CORBETT Melinda age 46y wife of Elijah in Jackson, NY February 10, 1842

SKINNER Mrs. Joseph February 19, 1842. Leaves 5 small children

MC CLELLAN infant son of Chester and Christianna age 4m February 24, 1842

SAFFORD Benjamin in his 60th yr February 26, 1842

SMART Miss Sarah age 32y in Salem, NY February 28, 1842

BROWN Simeon Earl age 2y 6m son of Benjamin R. and Deidamia (newspaper date March 9, 1842)

SHELDON Martha Ann age 4y 8m 17d dau of Ira F. and Rosina in Rupert, Vt. March 6, 1842

MC FARLAND Mitchell abt 40y in Salem, NY March 4, 1842

WILSON Catherine Maria age 33y 2m 28d wife of William in W. Troy, NY March 13, 1842

MURDOCK Samuel age 64y 9m in Salem, NY March 25, 1842

CRARY Catherine age 7y 3m 20d dau of John C. and Sarah in Salem, NY March 26, 1842

MC LEAN Almeda age 23y wife of Thomas in Jackson, NY March 25, 1842

SHELDON Harriet Smith age 4y 5m 16d only child of David S. and Mary L. in Rupert, Vt. February 12, 1842

STILLMAN Elizabeth abt 52y in Jackson, NY April 4, 1842

ELDRIDGE Mrs. Sarah in her 69th yr in Cambridge, NY April 5, 1842

MC MORRIS Ephraim in Salem, NY February 10, 1842

MC MORRIS Isabella in her 73rd yr in Salem, NY March 22, 1842

GRAY Andrew age 25y in Lansingburgh, NY May 21, 1842

LAW Annis Potter age 5m 21d dau of Daniel in Jackson, NY May 5, 1842

BEATY Elizabeth Matilda age 9m 10d dau of J. H. and Nancy M. in Salem, NY May 17, 1842

WESTON Lewis age 1y 10m son of Charles and Delane May 24, 1842

METCALF Edward age 16y in Salem, NY June 6, 1842

THOMPSON Alexander age 3y 3m 9d son of David B. and Jane in Salem, NY June 2, 1842

CLARK Caroline in her 11th yr dau of Loraness in Sandy Hill, NY May 26, 1842

SHERMAN Capt. Isaac age 72y in Sandgate, Vt. June 26, 1842

DARROW Stephen age 53y in Hebron, NY June 18, 1842

MC GEE Oliver Austin age 1y 9m son of Calvin and Susannah in Salem, NY June 2, 1842

WARNER Freelove Maria age 7m dau of Jonathan and Maria in Jackson, NY June 13, 1842

WESTON Lydia age 60y wife of Ephraim in Salem, NY June 29, 1842

VAN CURLER Aaron age 99y 6m 14d formerly of Salem, NY in Manchester, Vt. June 26, 1842

SHERMAN Lemuel age 84y in Cambridge, NY July 10, 1842

HARKNESS Sarah age 1y 7m 5d dau of William B. and Caroline in Salem, NY July 21, 1842

MC INTYRE George Earl age 2y 8m son of Gideon and Minerva in Salem, NY July 21, 1842

MERRILL George age 9y son of Oliver in Salem, NY August 2, 1842

NICHOLS Charles age 67y formerly of Sandgate, Vt. in Mina, NY July 27, 1842. Leaves son Henry of Salem, NY

HARDER Peter age 90y 4m 18d in Argyle, NY August 14, 1842

WOODS Judge David abt 65y formerly of Cambridge, NY in Cambria, NY September 15, 1842

MC CLAUGHRY Thomas age 63y in Salem, NY September 19, 1842

STEVENSON Joseph age 35y in Salem, NY September 15, 1842

HALLEY Ebenezer Erskine age 21m son of Rev. E. in Salem, NY September 9, 1842

ABBOTT Charles Sanders age 5m son of William S. and Charlotte S. of New York in Salem, NY September 7, 1842

REED Kitchell age 88y in Greece, NY September 14, 1842

ADAMS Elizabeth R. age 21y 3m dau of William K. formerly of Salem, NY in Marshall, Mi. September 20, 1842

MC CRACKEN Caroline age 18y dau of James C. in Arlington, Vt. July 29, 1842

RICE Col. Clark abt 50y October 20, 1842

THOMPSON Andrew in his 76th yr October 24, 1842

STEELE Alexander age 53y formerly of Salem, NY in Lewis, NY October 26, 1842

WATSON Lydia age 37y wife of James in Greenwich, NY October 25, 1842

SAFFORD Lucy Maria age 3m 28d dau of Gideon F. and Sarah in Salem, NY November 14, 1842

BASSETT Mary Ann formerly of Salem, NY in Schenectady, NY November 12, 1842

DILLINGHAM Lucy Jane age 3y dau of William and S. C. in Granville, NY November 20, 1842

BARNES Jared age 85y in Arlington, Vt. November 12, 1842

ALLEN Rev. Edward D. son of Mrs. Hester Allen of Lansingburgh, NY in Albany, NY December 20, 1842

BRAYMER Anna S. age 28y wife of Frederick and dau of Roswell **FLOWERS** of Rupert, Vt. in Hebron, NY December 30, 1842

MC DONALD Donald age 14y son of John and Margaret in Salem, NY January 13, 1843

MOORE Margaret age 23y dau of widow Moore of Salem, NY January 13, 1843

CRAMER Charles age 55y in Granville, NY February 5, 1843

FRASER Elam age 54y in Hartford, NY February 12, 1843. Born Salem, NY

WENDELL Rebecca in her 70th yr wife of Gerritt of Cambridge, NY at son-in-laws John A. **RICE** in Adrian, Mi. January 29, 1843

JOHNSON Thias age 60y in Jackson, NY March 6, 1843

COOK Edward age 68y in Cambridge, NY March 9, 1843

SHAW Alexander in his 79th yr in Greenwich, NY March 23, 1843. Native of Scotland, emigrated in 1789. Wife died February 1842

REAB Abigail age 70y widow of George in Salem, NY March 16, 1843

STILES Esther would be 47 in 3 days wife of Beriah formerly of Cambridge, NY in Mendon, NY April 2, 1843

HUGGINS Caroline age 19y dau of William R. and Mary K. late of Granville, NY in Bethany Center, NY March 8, 1843

CRATTY John age 29y in Salem, NY April 18, 1843

DUNCAN Robert age 31y in Salem, NY April 28, 1843

WHITESIDE Edward abt 35y in Salem, NY April 25, 1843

BOIES Ashley age 34y in Jackson, NY April 23, 1843

HITCHCOCK Warren F. abt 55y in Whitehall, NY May 5, 1843

YOUNGLOVE Lewis age 50y in Union Village, NY May 6, 1843

RATHBUN Elizabeth in her 30th yr wife of Benjamin in Whitehall, NY May 10, 1843

STEELE Joshua age 77y in Salem, NY May 17, 1843

PHILLIPS Squire M. age 26y in Salem, NY May 23, 1843

MARTIN Artemus abt 70y in Jackson, NY June 9, 1843

COON Maria age 19y in Salem, NY June 9, 1843

ADAMS John Henry age 6y son of John in Salem, NY June 12, 1843

SHERMAN Fortunatus in his 45th yr in Cambridge, NY June 22, 1843

GOURLAY Thomas age 79y in W. Hebron, NY June 24, 1843, came from Scotland abt 50 yrs ago

DRESSER Mary Jane age 14m dau of Joel and Belinda in Granville, NY July 15, 1843

BUTTON Gideon in his 78th yr in Hebron, NY June __, 1843

PRESTON Mary in her 81st yr in White Creek, Ny August 5, 1843

DAY Dan H. in his 22nd yr in Lansingburgh, NY August 22, 1843

DAY ____ age 1y child of William in Granville, NY August 18, 1843

ROSE Joseph in his 69th yr in N. White Creek, NY August 25, 1843

BOWEN Abner C. age 1y 6m 6d son of David and Jane S. in Salem, NY September 15, 1843

GREEN William C. in his 23rd yr in Cambridge, NY September 19, 1843

WELLS Lucy in her 51st yr wife of Joseph formerly of Salem, NY in Constantine, Mi. September 15, 1843

WILLETT Samuel age 93y a Revolutionary Soldier in Cambridge, NY August 30, 1843. Native of NJ

MARTIN John R. age 32y formerly of Salem, NY in Albany, NY September 25, 1843

BRISTOL Peter in his 79th yr in Salem, NY September 14, 1843

BISHOP Arch age 2y son of Arch and Ann in Granville, NY September 26, 1843

HARVEY James age 79y in Salem, NY October 4, 1843

COVILLE Gen. William age 60y in S. Hartford, NY September 24, 1843

ARCHIBALD Alexander age 6y son of David in Salem, NY October 16, 1843

WHEELER Solomon King age 31y 6m formerly of Salem, NY in Peoria, Ill. September 30, 1843

THURSTON Samuel age 78y in M. Granville, NY October 19, 1843

ADAMS Melinda age 42y in Union Village, NY October 13, 1843

WING Almira age 15y dau of D. W. Wing in Ft. Edward, NY October 5, 1843

JACKSON Stephen age 71y of Ridgeway, NY, formerly of Easton, NY at bro James Jackson in Salina, NY September 24, 1843

STEVENSON James in his 82nd yr formerly of Washington Co. at son-in-laws Ward **CHILDS** in Strykersville, NY October 9, 1843

MC NEIL Margaret Ann in her 20th yr died September 20, 1843 and Catherine Eleanor age 13y died October 8, 1843 children of Daniel and Ann in Argyle, NY

WALKER Ann age 14y dau of Daniel and Jane in Argyle, NY October 24, 1843

DOBBIN William 2nd formerly of Jackson, NY in Columbus, Ohio October 10, 1843

MORSE Samuel age 26y accidental discharge of gun in Whitehall, NY November 3, 1843

HASCALL Minerva S. age 26y wife of John H. and dau of late Robert W. **OLIPHANT** of N. Granville, NY in Baltimore, Md. October 11, 1843

FISH Harriet E. in her 18th yr in M. Granville, NY October 24, 1843

STEVENSON Dan age 3y son of William Jr. in Cambridge, NY November 1, 1843

ROUSE Amy Ann in her 23rd yr consort of George of Northumberland, NY and dau of Jesse **MOTT** Jr. of Greenwich, NY At Fathers October 28, 1843

ROGERS Harriet E. age 26y dau of Samuel in Greenwich, NY October 24, 1843

PRIEST Rhoda age 52y wife of John in Salem, NY November 5, 1843

BREWER Simon age 45y in Easton, NY November 15, 1843

SHEARER Lewis age 72y in Union Village, NY November 8, 1843

CARLISLE James in his 75th yr in Hartford, NY October 7, 1843

HENRY Mary S. in her 24th yr wife of William and dau of Archibald **ROBERTSON** of Argyle, NY in Greenwich, NY December 2, 1843

HALLEY Eliza age 4y dau of Rev. E. Halley in Salem, NY December 13, 1843

WHIPPLE Martin age 34y in Easton, NY December 27, 1843

VAUGHN Mrs. Harriet W. age 37y in Whitehall, NY December 23, 1843

BOWE Amos age 75y in Wells, Vt. December 1, 1843

WOODWORTH Dolly age 34y 4d wife of C. V. K. Woodworth in N. White Creek, NY December 31, 1843

BARBER Martha dau of John in White Creek, NY December 24, 1843

MANNERY George abt 40y in Salem, NY January 4, 1844

ANDREWS Denison in his 74th yr in Mechanicsville, NY January 16, 1844

NELSON Mrs. Mary age 77y in Sandgate, Vt. January 13, 1844

BEATTIE Robert B. in his 27th yr son of Mrs. Elizabeth Beattie of Salem, NY in Prairie Du Chen, Wis. December 16, 1843. Born Salem, NY

STEELE Jane age 32y wife of Joshua and dau of John **MC MURRAY** in Salem, NY February 15, 1844

BLIVEN Rebecca age 69y in N. Hebron, NY February 15, 1844

ANDERSON Mary Elizabeth age 4y 8m dau of William and Margaret February 25, 1844

MC LEAN James in his 78th yr in Jackson, NY March 8, 1844

DORR Margaret age 73y relict of Jonathan in N. White Creek, NY March 11, 1844

FERGUSON John age 16y son of Duncan in Jackson NY March 9, 1844

SMITH Mrs. Anna in her 75th yr in Sandgate, Vt. February 24, 1844

SIMPSON Laura age 55y wife of Robert and dau of Ebenezer **BILLINGS** in Jackson, NY April 10, 1844

GRANDY Mrs. Hannah age 93y in Easton, NY April 6, 1844

WRIGHT Margaret in her 54th yr wife of Alvin and dau of late William **MC CLEARY** of Rupert, Vt. in Colebrook, Conn. March 29, 1844

THURSTON Elisha P. age 2y son of Daniel and Mary Ann in M. Granville, NY March 7, 1844

COOK John age 20y son of Isaiah in Granville, NY March 20, 1844

WHYTE Ellen M. age 23y dau of Rev. James Whyte of Salem, NY in Inverness, Scot. March 4, 1844

CARTER Mary G. age 32y wife of Dr. Carter and dau of Henry **GRAY** of White Creek, NY in Weston, Vt. May 9, 1844

HEUSTIS Catherine in her 73rd yr widow of Jacob and dau of late Archibald **CAMPBELL** of Cambridge, NY in Chesterfield, NY May 9, 1844

LAW Robert R. abt 66y in Jackson, NY April 29, 1844

OVIATT Isaac abt 73y May 11, 1844

LYTLE Maj. Andrew in his 69th yr in Hebron, NY May 21, 1844

COOK Caroline in her 29th yr wife of Isaac in Chicago, Ill. April 21, 1844

SHILAND John abt 76y of Cambridge, NY at son-in-laws Daniel **MC FARLAND** May 25, 1844

ATWOOD Sarah Ann age 8y 28d dau of Anson and Mary in Troy, NY June 9, 1844

FAIRLEY Catherine abt 52y wife of Hugh in Salem, NY June 15, 1844

SMITH John Nelson age 15y son of John L. drowned in Whitehall, NY June 8, 1844

CLOUGH Ithamer in his 93rd yr in Hartford, NY May 18, 1844

MC DOUGAL Mary age 39y consort of Nathaniel in Greenwich, NY July 3, 1844

WILSON Caroline abt 20y consort of David of Whitehall, NY in Sandy Hill, NY July 9, 1844

STEVENSON William age 73y in Cambridge, NY July 9, 1844. Native of Scotland

LAW Margaret Ann age 32y wife of David and dau of Gilbert **ROBERTSON** of Argyle, NY in Salem, NY July 20, 1844

WELLS Henry Clay age 14m son of Leonard and Eliza A. in Cambridge, NY July 25, 1844

DURELL Nicolas in her 68th yr of Bradford, NH at sons Samuel Durell in N. White Creek, NY July 20, 1844

MAIRS Julia in her 18th yr dau of Rev. George Mairs in Argyle, NY July 29, 1844

PALMER Henry Clay age 6m 16d son of John and Margaret B. in N. White Creek, NY August 12, 1844

BEAMAN Betsey age 51y wife of Luke in Fairhaven, Vt. August 17, 1844

CHURCH Diademe in her 90th yr relict of Bethuel in Shushan, NY August 15, 1844. 9 children, 4 living

RICE Phebe in her 69th yr wife of Roswell in White Creek, NY August 28, 1844

BARNARD Abner S. age 14m 22d son of Abner C. and Lucy J. in E. Greenwich, NY September 8, 1844

GRAY Margaret age 79y widow of John in Salem, NY September 16, 1844

HALL Thomas age 87y in Salem, NY September 14, 1844

LYTLE William B. age 28y in Salem, NY October 3, 1844

FITCH William in his 73rd yr in Salem, NY October 7, 1844

SNYDER George age 4y 6m 9d son of George W. and Elizabeth September 23, 1844

DECKER Jacob age 66y in Cambridge, NY (newspaper date October 9, 1844)

BEATY Lamira S. wife of Samuel 2nd and dau of Perez **HARWOOD** of Bennington, Vt. in Rupert, Vt. October 14, 1844

BILLINGS Adelia age 4y 5m dau of Derick and Ann in Argyle, NY October 16, 1844

RHODES Mindwell age 49y wife of Nathan in N. Granville, NY October 24, 1844

SLADE Catherine in her 24th yr wife of Barton and dau of Gerritt **QUACKENBUSH** of Salem, NY in Sempronius, NY October 27, 1844

SHERMAN Abby E. wife of Enoch S. and dau of William **HASELTINE** of Pembroke, NH in W. Rupert, Vt. November 11, 1844 and dau Abby H. age 9w died December 27, 1844

WING Mariette in her 31st yr wife of Lorenzo B. in Salem, NY October 27, 1844

HUGHES Rubic age 43y wife of Maj. John Hughes formerly of Cambridge, NY in

Cleveland, Ind. November 15, 1844

STOWELL Asa age 84y a Revolutionary Soldier from Wilmington, Conn. at Crown Point, NY December 8, 1844

GILSON Peter in 82nd yr a Revolutionary Soldier, native of Craton, Mass. in Cambridge, NY (newspaper date January 1, 1845)

AUSTIN Ann Elizabeth age 4m dau of Abner Jr. and Ann in Salem, NY December 24, 1844

HOPKINS Joel abt 70y in Hebron, NY December 27, 1844

FENTON Harriet Maria age 3y dau of Buel and Nancy in Cambridge, NY January 11, 1845

WARNER Sarah relict of Kirkland Warner in Jackson, NY January 15, 1845

MC ALLISTER Jerusha abt 59y wife of Charles formerly of Salem, NY in White Pigeon, Mi. January 10, 1845

WINCHESTER Esther Mary in her 22nd yr in Lansingburgh, NY February 2, 1845

GILLETTE Daniel H. age 32y son of Dr. F. B. Gillette of Cambridge, NY in City of Mobile February 9, 1845

GORDON David formerly of Salem, NY in Trinidad, W. Indies December 30, 1844

NICHOLS Abigail P. in her 17th yr dau of Marshall formerly of Sandgate, Vt. in Hannibal, NY February 7, 1845

CHURCH Clarissa age 49y wife of Leonard formerly of Brattleboro, Vt. in Salem, NY March 10, 1844

CLARK Mary age 2m 15d dau of James and Ruth in Salem, NY February 27, 1845

BISHOP Huldah in her 28th yr in Lansingburgh, NY March 7, 1845

MC CLELLAN Lydia age 63y wife of Jonathan in Jackson, NY March 14, 1845

GIBSON Cornelia in her 3rd yr dau of James in Salem, NY March 26, 1845

WRIGHT Martin Lee age 8m son of William in White Creek, NY March 27, 1845

GILLETTE Philander G. in his 53rd yr son of late Dr. F. B. Gillette of Cambridge, NY in Fairport, Chemung Co. NY March 29, 1845

BASSETT Elizabeth age 64y widow of Joel in Salem, NY April 7, 1845

TAYLOR Ednah in her 25th yr in Argyle, NY April 1, 1845

STOVER Martin age 87y in Pittstown, NY April 14, 1845. 9 children 8 living, 76 grandchildren 53 living, 52 great grandchildren 41 living

LAKE Cetesa age 52y 6d wife of Salmon and dau of Rev. Obed **WARREN** of Salem, NY in Pomfret, NY April 11, 1845. Mother was sister of Rev. C. **BLOOD**, pioneers in Baptist Church

SHIPLEY Sarah Mary age 1y 3m dau of Simeon and Jane in Salem, NY May 16, 1845

HURD Laura age 23y relict of Charles in Rupert, Vt. last week (newspaper date May 21, 1845)

HOPKINS Ebenezer age 7m son of George and Eliza J. in Salem, NY May 15, 1845

WHELDON Mary Ann age 3m dau of Darius and Abigal in Easton, NY May 5, 1845

DARROW Betsey in her 30th yr wife of Jedediah in Salem, NY May 13, 1845

MEEKER Margaret in her 34th yr wife of Lifelet and sister of Mrs. Betsey **DARROW** in Sandgate, Vt. May 25, 1845

MOORE Robert age 38y native of Ireland drowned Sprakers Basin, NY June 16, 1845

DUNHAM Anna in her 20th yr dau of late Nahum in Jackson, NY July 30, 1845

BRISTON Mrs. Jemima age 35y in Camden, NY June 26, 1845

NILES Maria N. age 37y wife of David and dau of Paul **CORNELL** in White Creek, NY July 30, 1845

RUGGLES Charles age 22y at Fathers in Jackson, Mi. (newspaper date August 13, 1845)

CLARK Ines age 2y 5m 23d dau of Thomas and Margaret in Kingston, NY August 15, 1845

MC DOUAL Alexander in his 81st yr in Cambridge, NY August 12, 1845

FERGUSON Mary Elizabeth age 2y 7m 9d dau of George and Margaret in Jackson, NY August 20, 1845

POTTER Almira M. age 8y 7m dau of Ephram in Granville, NY September 3, 1845

CLEVELAND Dorotha age 28y in Salem, NY September 25, 1845

MC WHORTER Mary wife of George formerly of Salem, NY in New Berlin, Wis. October 8, 1845 and dau Sarah died August 15, 1845

BAXTER Moses age 95y a Revolutionary Soldier in Ft. Ann, NY October 26, 1845.

Came from Mass. 7 children, abt 50 grand children one is Albert L. **BAKER** of Salem, NY

WATKINS Terza in her 62nd yr wife of John in Jackson, NY November 5, 1845

WHEELER Grace age 24y wife of Aaron and dau of John **THOMPSON** of Salem, NY in Alton, Ill. October 31, 1845

FORD Abraham of Hoosick Falls, NY in W. Troy, NY March 3, 1849

NORTON Austin age 22y in White Creek, NY March 7, 1849

KERR Margaret in her 49th yr wife of Andrew and sister of George **ROBERTSON** of Salem, NY in Schenectady, NY March 6, 1849

WARNER Elizabeth in her 80th yr widow of Sylvester in Jackson, NY May 6, 1849

CARSWELL Nathaniel age 71y formerly of Salem in Racine, Wis. April 13, 1849

KING Mary Jane in her 26th yr wife of Alexander in White Creek, NY May 10, 1849

WILLIAMS Frances age 65y wife of John of Salem in Albany, NY May 11, 1849

FISHER Esther Ann abt 16y in White Creek, NY May 16, 1849

ASHTON James in his 63rd yr in Argyle, NY May 30, 1849

STEVENS Charles Knox age 13y 11m 8d son of John and Jane in White Creek, NY July 8, 1849

LOOMIS Mary Ann in her 30th yr in White Creek, NY July 13, 1849

BINNINGER Elizabeth age 82y widow of Isaac in Camden Valley, NY July 13, 1849

DUNHAM Russell N. in his 26th yr in Jackson, NY July 29, 1849

GOODFELLOW Harriet in her 31st yr wife of Thadeus and dau of Erastus **BEEBE** of Jackson, NY in Sandy Hill, NY July 27, 1849

STONE Nancy wife of Reuben in Jackson, NY July 8, 1849

MC CLELLAN Adelaide age 21y dau of Charles and Sally in White Creek, NY July 31, 1849

MOORE Harriet age 20y 2m wife of John in Jackson, NY August 25, 1849

GRAHAM John age 39y formerly of Salem in Reynoldsburg, Ohio August 19, 1849

DOBBIN John 2nd abt 45y in Jackson, NY August 29, 1849

ATWOOD Mrs. Abiathar age 46y of Troy, NY in Salem, NY August 24, 1849

GRAY Edward Beebe age 19y son of Harry in Arlington, Vt. August 25, 1849

ARNOLD Burr K. abt 3y son of Henry and Margaret in Arlington, Vt. September 13, 1849

JOHNSON Ellen Jane age 2y 7m 1d dau of John and Lydia in White Creek, NY September 21, 1849

MC CLELLAN Reuben in his 89th yr in Oberlin, Ohio June 19, 1849

HASLEM Joseph age 53y in Jackson, NY October 10, 1849

LIVINGSTON William age 62y of Jackson, NY in Salem, NY October 5, 1849

SAFFORD Mrs. Mary age 65y in E. Greenwich, NY October 6, 1849

ATWOOD Zacheus in his 74th yr in Salem, NY November 11, 1849

BOWEN Patty in her 66th yr wife of Eddy in Shushan, NY October 15, 1849

DUNHAM Anna age 64y widow of Nahum in Jackson, NY November 14, 1849

WELLS Austin a Revolutionary Soldier in White Creek, NY December 8, 1849. Born February 14, 1759 in Hebron, Conn. Came to Cambridge in 1773

GETTY Capt. John abt 58y in Hebron, NY December 12, 1849

DUNHAM Samuel D. abt 40y in Jackson, NY December 5, 1849

HILL David S. age 25y in Salem, NY December 19, 1849

MC KIE Elizabeth age 84y widow of James in White Creek, NY December 27, 1849

MARTIN Clark V. B. in his 30th yr at Glens Falls, NY December 21, 1849

CHASE Humphrey abt 35y in White Creek, NY December 28, 1849

GORDON Phillip in his 67th yr in White Creek, NY January 5, 1850

JOHNSON Albinus age 50y formerly of Cambridge in New York January 8, 1850

CROCKER Kate Elizbeth age 4m 1d dau of R. E. and Sarah J. in White Creek, NY January 11, 1850

CROCKER Rev. A. B. in his 37th yr in White Creek, NY January 10, 1850

HOWE Charles Albert age 1y 7m son of C. M. in White Creek, NY January 18, 1850

IRELAND Sarah Ann in her 34th yr wife of Lorenzo D. and dau of Solomon **WRIGHT** of Salem, NY in Lyons, NY December 23, 1849

HEATH Amarilla in her 72rd yr wife of Arden formerly of Jackson, NY in Northeast, Pa. January 29, 1850

BILLINGS George in his 27th yr in Jackson, NY February 20, 1850

PIERSON Sam son of Job of Troy, NY in San Francisco, Cal. January 27, 1850

CROSS Lucinda wife of David and dau of Elijah **SLOCUM** of White Creek, NY in Shaftsbury, Vt. February 27, 1850

LAKIN Robert age 88y in Salem, NY March 13, 1850

TICE Mrs. Ann age 92y 5m 19d in White Creek, NY April 18, 1850. Born Middletown, NJ

ACKLEY Mrs. Mary in her 85th yr in White Creek, NY April 17, 1850

SOUTHWELL Julia A. age 23y formerly of White Creek, NY in Moriah, NY April 17, 1850

ORCUTT Lydia age 26y wife of William in Jackson, NY April 23, 1850

ROBERTSON Nancy age 60y wife of James in Greenwich, NY April 15, 1850

TAYLOR Samuel age 87y a Revolutionary Soldier in Hartford, NY May 5, 1850. Native of Concord, Mass.

NELSON Earl S. age 4m son of Wesley and Mary P. in Hebron, NY May 8, 1850

KENYON Mumford abt 30y formerly of Cambridge, NY in San Francisco, Cal. March 1, 1850

MONTGOMERY John abt 25y in Jackson, NY May 24, 1850

LARKIN Henry M. in his 19th yr in N. Hoosick, NY May 23, 1850

LARMON Eleanor age 19y in Cambridge, NY May 31, 1850

PRATT Rufus in his 75th yr in Cambridge, NY June 3, 1850

HODGES Abel in his 93rd yr in Salem, NY June 2, 1850

HUTCHINGS Bulkeley age 83y a Revolutionary Soldier in Pawlet, Vt. May 16, 1850

HAWES George P. age 45y formerly of Cambridge in Lockport, NY May 23, 1850

MOORE Sarah age 12y dau of Paschal D. and Maria in Jackson, NY June 15, 1850

GILCHRIST Archibald in his 76th yr in N. Argyle, NY June 12, 1850

DAVIS Eugene age 5y son of Peter from a fire in Jackson, NY June 18, 1850

ELDRICH Bethiah in her 90th yr widow of Zoeth and Mother of Ahira of White Creek, NY in Willington, Conn. June 24, 1850

LONG Harriet M. age 32y wife of Rev. Walter R. formerly of Cambridge, NY in Meridan, Conn. July 2, 1850

COON Solomon advanced age in White Creek, NY July 31, 1850

MILLIMAN Esther age 55y wife of Thomas in Salem, NY July 26, 1850

CLOUGH Phebe in her 69th yr widow of Elijah in Hebron, NY July 20, 1850

CALL Content abt 60y wife of John in Cambridge, NY July 20, 1850

BARBER Charles in his 24th yr in Greenwich, NY (newspaper date August 15, 1850)

STEVENSON James M. in his 43rd yr in Cambridge, NY August 22, 1850

DIBBLE Betsey age 19y dau of Solomon and Mary in Granville, NY August 27, 1850

CROSBY Aaron age 64y formerly of White Creek, NY in Springfield, Ill. August 24, 1850

LAMBERT Boardman A. age 10m 16d son of Dr. T. S. in Salem, NY September 8, 1850

OUDEKIRK Clark age 22y of Shushan, NY in Troy, NY August 31, 1850

CHURCH Ada Rowena age 1y 10m dau of Leonard and Ann in Shushan, NY September 5, 1850

MALBLE Harvey age 40y in E. Arlington, Vt. September 6, 1850

COOK Ann Maria age 30y wife of Dr. John T. Cook and dau of Samuel **GILMORE** of Cambridge, NY in Jewett City, Conn. September 15, 1850

MOODY Leroy Chase age 14m son of Simeon and Mary in Cambridge, NY September 22, 1850

HURD Amy D. in her 16th yr dau of Isaac in Spring, Pa. September 22, 1850

DOBBIN Jane in her 30th yr dau of John in Jackson, NY September 24, 1850

MC LEAN Lewis in his 47th yr in Jackson, NY October 9, 1850

LARKIN John E. in his 45th yr at Galway, NY October 6, 1850

WELLS Hannah A. in her 31st yr adopted dau of George and Susan **RUSSELL** of E. Salem, NY in Troy, NY October 23, 1850

LEIGH Jesse S. age 65 in Argyle, NY November 6, 1850

TAYLOR Mrs. ____ drowned in Union Village, NY December 1, 1850

HILL Charles age 2y son of Peter and Clarissa in Jackson, NY November 30, 1850

DOXY Mrs. Mary age 73y in Whitehall, NY November 27, 1850

RICHARDSON James in his 85th yr in White Creek, NY December 13, 1850

ROBERTS Col. John son of Thomas in Argyle, NY November 5, 1850

LEE Marshall age 2y 8m 7d son of Elisha and Esther in White Creek, NY (newspaper date January 9, 1851)

LAUDERMAN Edward formerly of Cambridge, NY in Livingston Co. NY (newspaper date January 16, 1851)

CHAPMAN Ebenezer age 87y Revolutionary Soldier in Hebron, NY December 9, 1850

TERRY Mrs. Sarah J. age 23y at Ft. Edward, NY January 6, 1851

GRAHAM Susan age 6y 3m dau of F. B. in Schuylerville, NY January 21, 1851

DYER Cynthia in her 88th yr widow of Amherst a Revolutionary Soldier in White Creek, NY January 4, 1851. Born Swansey, RI, moved to Shaftsbury, Vt. age 9, lived White Creek 62 yrs

PARKER Charlotte dau of Mathew **CORNELL** in Greenwich, NY January 8, 1851. Born 1813 in Schaghticoke, NY

AUSTIN Marinus F. in his 6th yr son of Lewis and Catherine in Salem, NY January 31, 1851

YOUNG Foster in his 76th yr in Buffalo, NY January 8, 1851

ROBERTSON James P. age 4y 6m son of Peter V. K. and Jane C. A. in White Creek, NY February 24, 1851

TIMMERMAN Jane E. age 42y consort of John formerly of Argyle, NY in Waterford, NY February 8, 1851

HANNA Robert abt 80y in Salem, NY February 15, 1851

MC FARLAND Mary Elizabeth age 7m 8d dau of James A. and Elizabeth in Salem, NY February 16, 1851

ROBERTSON George W. age 61y in Cambridge, NY March 3, 1851. Born Redpath, Scotland, came to US age 4y

NORTON Tolley age 58y wife of William in Union Village, NY March 1, 1851

WHITE Moses H. age 63y in Union Village, NY March 2, 1851

ADAMS John abt 65y formerly of Salem, NY in Troy, NY March 7, 1851

WALKER Mrs. ____ abt 80y in Salem, NY March 7, 1851

HALL Martha abt 45y in Cambridge, NY March 15, 1851

BURROUGHS Daniel abt 45y in Troy, NY March 15, 1851

MC NISH Sarah age 96y widow of Alexander in Salem, NY March 23, 1851

ROGERS John L. age 10m son of Elizabeth in Salem, NY March 26, 1851

SHIELDS Mary in her 87th yr widow of James formerly of Salem, NY in Guilford, Ohio December 13, 1850

MC CLELLAN John abt 93y in Jackson, NY March 21, 1851

CORNELL Edwin age 1y 5m son of Zina and Mary in Cambridge, NY March 21, 1851

CORNELL Walter M. age 3m 8d son of Thomas and Patience M. in Cambridge, NY March 20, 1851

COLEGROVE Joshua age 6y son of Asa and Charlotte in Cambridge, NY March 31, 1851

PERRY Henry in his 23rd yr son of Elihu in White Creek, NY April 9, 1851

MC KIE Henry W. in his 22nd yr son of George in Cambridge, NY April 21, 1851

BEATTIE Alexander abt 38y in Cambridge, NY April 9, 1851

STEVENS Henry abt 26y in Shushan, NY April 22, 1851

MC MANN Eliza age 24y wife of Michael in Salem, NY April 19, 1851

STARKS Julia abt 21y in Granville, NY April 14, 1851

SWEET Benjamin G. abt 21y in Hoosick, NY April 24, 1851

BARTON Hiram A. age 19y son of Hiram of Shaftsbury, Vt. in Cambridge, NY April 24, 1851

RANDALL Lucy age 72y of Rutland, Vt. at sons Josiah in Swansey, NH April 16, 1851

SAFFORD Harriet age 11y dau of John and Deborah in Union Village, NY April 28, 1851

CROCKER Eleazor in his 69th yr formerly of White Creek, NY at bro Deacon B. Crocker in Niles, Mi. April 1, 1851

RICHARDSON Manassah age 49y in Whitehall, NY May 8, 1851

ROWAN John age 18y son of Archibald M. and Mary in Argyle, NY May 11, 1851

SAFFORD Frances M. age 4y 4m 2d dau of Chester and Malinda in Troy, NY May 5, 1851

CLARK Hannah age 21y dau of Charles in Jackson, NY May 28/June 4, 1851

MALADY Mary age 36y wife of James in Jackson, NY May 20, 1851

SANDERS Mary wife of A. C. and dau of late Daniel **WELLS** of Cambridge, NY in Salem, NY June 3, 1851

BULLIONS William in his 26th yr son of Rev. Alexander Bullions at brother-in-law's Dr. William O. **NELSON** in Cambridge, NY June 19, 1851

BOYD Mary in her 27th yr wife of James and dau of David D. **GRAY** in Salem, NY June 7, 1851

PARKER Miss Mary A. age 20y in Pattens Mills, NY June 8, 1851

DEMING Martin age 62y in Arlington, Vt. June 21, 1851

JONES Jacob in his 81st yr in Coila, NY July 7, 1851

BINES Robert M. of New Orleans, La. at res. of Isaac W. **BISHOP** in Granville, NY June 25, 1851

BANCROFT George P. abt 40y at Ft. Edward, NY July 13, 1851

MC INTOSH Isabella in her 4th yr dau of Hiram and Helen of Princeton, NY in Jackson, NY July 17, 1851 while visiting grandfather Robert **KERR**

SMITH William E. age 16m son of Charles E. and Hellen B. in White Creek, NY July 18, 1851

SMART Anna Maria in her 42nd yr wife o Rev. John G. formerly of Baltimore, Md. dau of late William **STEVENSON** in Cambridge, NY July 20, 1851

WOOD John age 33y in White Creek, NY July 23, 1851

WOLCOTT William age 85y at sons Dr. W. G. in Whitehall, NY July 13, 1851

COOK Chester in his 74th yr in Kingsbury, NY July 25, 1851

NEWTON Emeline age 28y wife of John H. in Kingsbury, NY July 27, 1851

GRAVES Rufus age 59y in Granville, NY August 1, 1851

BREESE William age 41y in Salem, NY August 6, 1851

GRAHAM William Gillette age 10y son of William and Eunise in Jackson, NY August 13, 1851

(issues missing until January 5, 1854)

WRIGHT Lauchlin at son-in-laws Lemuel **SHERMAN** in Cambridge, NY January 9, 1854

MC MORRIS Mary in her 20th yr dau of Thomas in Jackson, NY January 22, 1854

CORNELL Mathew in his 67th yr in White Creek, NY January 30, 1854

MC MILLAN Henry Clay in his 6th yr in Argyle, NY February 4, 1854

SAYLES Fannie A. age 6m dau of Dr. Sayles in White Creek, NY February 28, 1854

CALHOUN Mary Jane in her 15th yr in Greenwich, NY February 15, 1854

VOLENTINE Thomas age 30y in Jackson, NY January 30, 1854 and Leonard in his 48th yr died February 4, 1854, their Father Daniel age 76y died March 11, 1854

FOWLER Martha Ann age 24y wife of James P. in Cambridge, NY March 11, 1854

BOSS Joseph in his 43rd yr in White Creek, NY February 28, 1854

LYMAN Arthur Duane age 5m 11d son of Elbridge and Elvira in Shushan, NY March 2, 1854

CROSBY Lucy in her 85th yr at sons S. W. in White Creek, NY April 5, 1854

ELDRICH Francis W. in his 22nd yr in Cambridge, NY March 27, 1854

HASKELL Fanny in her 29th yr wife of Judson in Whitehall, NY April 4, 1854

INGRAHAM Almira L. in her 36th yr wife of H. April 4, 1854

BROCKWAY Edward Augustus in his 13th yr in White Creek, NY April 10, 1854

COOK Benajah age 67y in White Creek, NY May 16, 1854

DOVER George abt 72y May 31, 1854, buried in Cambridge, NY

MC CLELLAN Eliza age 45y in Pittsfield, Ohio June 3, 1854

PECK Baldwin age 41y in Sandgate, Vt. June 15, 1854

MARSH Catherine in her 65th yr at son-in-laws Benjamin J. **LOOMIS** in White Creek, NY June 18, 1854

MC DOUGAL Mrs. Sarah age 86y in Schuylerville, NY June 28, 1854

SHARP Mary age 66y in White Creek, NY July 20, 1854

BARBER Julia Ann age 61y wife of John in N. White Creek, NY July 17, 1854

WHYTE Robert A. in his 27th yr July 4, 1854

RUSSELL Henry age 72y in White Creek, NY August 1, 1854

MERRITT Benjamin age 77y formerly of White Creek, NY in Cleveland, Ohio July 4, 1854

NUTTING Sarah E. age 4y dau of Byron and Sarah J. in Cambridge, NY August 16, 1854

HUNTINGTON Elias in Shaftsbury, Vt. September 9, 1854

JACKSON James age 51y in White Creek, NY September 27, 1854

MAYNARD Burroughs age 61y in Hartford, NY September 26, 1854

MAXWELL John age 14y son of William in Reynoldsburg, Ohio September 24, 1854 and father William abt 50y died September 25, 1854

MC FARLAND Robert age 25y son of Daniel in Jackson, NY September 27, 1854

HORTON Nancy B. age 54y wife of Dennis in Oberlin, Ohio (newspaper date October 13, 1854)

GRAHAM Betsey age 47y wife of Benjamin in Bennington, Vt. September 24, 1854

DEAN Joel age 80y in Cambridge, NY October 11, 1854

ALLEN Mary age 31y wife of Quincey in White Creek, NY September 17, 1854

CONNEL Elenor in her 65th yr wife of James formerly of Hebron, NY in Reynoldsburg, Ohio October 17, 1854

WOODS William in his 40th yr of Cambridge, NY in Earslville, Ill. (newspaper date December 1, 1854)

PRATT Lydia E. age 27y wife of Alanson in New York November 24, 1854

JOSLIN William age 68y in Cambridge, NY December 16, 1854

CROCKER Ellen Frances in her 5th yr dau of Lott W. and Ellen H. in Albany, NY January 6, 1855

DEWEY Jesse in his 72nd yr in White Creek, NY January 5, 1855

CRANDALL Dr. abt 60y in Union Village, NY January 30, 1855

WING George age 55y in Easton, NY January 13, 1855

GARDNER Ella age 2m 5d dau of Edward and Miriam in Orange, NJ January 28, 1855

ALLEN John age 81y in White Creek, NY February 3, 1855 and dau Eleanor abt 28y

MINER B. F. age 21y in E. Salem, NY February 18, 1855

THOMPSON Andrew age 3y 10m son of David and Cornelia in E. Salem, NY March 4, 1855

CENTER Sullivan age 46y in White Creek, NY March 23, 1855

HAMLIN Sophia in her 25th yr wife of Rev. James Hamlin and dau of Rev. Joseph **PARRY** of Ft. Edward, NY in Mattetuck, NY April 2, 1855

BULLIONS Mary wife of Rev. Alexander Bullions in Coila, NY April 30, 1855

RANDALL Mary Elizabeth age 11m 22d dau of Daniel and Jane in White Creek, NY April 20, 1855

CORBETT Eney age 35y wife of Simeon in White Creek, NY May 16, 1855

TRUMBULL Horace age 81y in Rupert, Vt. May 14, 1855, dau Mrs. David **FISHER**

FISHER Delight in her 85th yr May 13, 1855. Leaves son David Fisher

SMALL Phebe **(THOMAS)** in her 71st yr in Cambridge, NY June 8, 1855

MC MILLAN James age 66y from Branch Co. Wis. in Jackson, NY June 8, 1855

WRIGHT Roxana in her 83rd yr widow of Laughlin at sons in Scriba, NY July 14, 1855, buried White Creek, NY

VOLENTINE Mary E. age 13y dau of Joel and Lydia in Shushan, NY July 15, 1855

WILLIAMS Nehemiah age 56y in White Creek, NY July 22, 1855

MOORE Virginia age 1y 2m 5d dau of Ira H. and Ruth Ann in Williamsburgh July 23, 1855

PERRY Miss Cornelia age 44y in White Creek, NY August 13, 1855

FOSTER Agnes M. wife of John and dau of William **LYMAN** in Schenectady, NY August 16, 1855

FOWLER Dewitt C. age 27y in White Creek, NY September 6, 1855

VAN VECHTEN Dr. Isaac abt 62y in Cambridge, NY September 1, 1855

PATCHIN Sarah Maria age 7y 10d dau of Henry and Margaret **(ARNOLD)** in White Creek, NY August 29, 1855

DORR James D. age 47y formerly of White Creek, NY in Bath, NY (newspaper date September 14, 1855)

ROBERTSON Mrs. Elizabeth in Jackson, NY September 18, 1855

WALSH Charles age 21y son of David in Battenville, NY September 22, 1855

SMALL Edward in his 78th yr in Coila, NY October 28, 1855

GRAHAM Sarah age 75y formerly of White Creek, NY in Mc Grawville, NY October 13, 1855

WATERS Ann wife of late W. W. and dau of late Jonathan **DORR** Sr. October 23, 1855

STEVENSON William age 17y son of William in Coila, NY October 31, 1855

TEFFT James C. (missionary) age 39y formerly of White Creek, NY in Kaw Mendi, W. Africa October 16, 1855 and son James Benton Tefft died September 16, 1855

HARRINGTON Freelove in her 43rd yr wife of John in White Creek, NY November 15, 1855

SMITH John C. formerly of White Creek, NY in Shaftsbury, Vt. December 16, 1855

MC FARLAND Electa M. in her 20th yr wife of William of Jackson, NY at Fathers J. **BENNETT** in Manchester, Vt. December 28, 1855

WARNER John age 6m 3d son of Abner K. in Jackson, NY January 13, 1856

BROWN John age 73y in Jackson, NY January 11, 1856

MC KIE Peter age 48y in Jackson, NY January 11, 1856

WELLS Amelia P. age 32y in White Creek, NY January 24, 1856

LOVELAND Margaret age 34y in White Creek, NY February 6, 1856. Husband died in Cal. a few months ago.

DUNLAP A. W. age 45y in Arlington, Vt. March 5, 1856

PORTER Ralph in his 65th yr in White Creek, NY March 10, 1856

WHITNEY Chauncey age 78y in White Creek, NY March 4, 1856

HAXTUN Mary Frances age 6y dau of James D. in Cambridge, NY March 29, 1856

BARKER Jane C. age 30y wife of George in White Creek, NY April 2, 1856

FOWLER Isaac age 101y in White Creek, NY April 16, 1856

RICHARDSON Aurelia age 87y widow of James in White Creek, NY April 20, 1856

SLOCUM Mandana age 23y in Cambridge, NY March 27, 1856

ELDRIDGE Dorris age 53y in Cambridge, NY April 30, 1856

WILSON Ward Jr. age 58y in White Creek, NY May 4, 1856

SANDERSON Mary E. age 29y 6m wife of E. I. late of San Francisco, Cal. at parents in Union Village, NY May 8, 1856

BALLOU Mrs. Sarah in her 61st yr in N. White Creek, NY May 19, 1856

BEVERIDGE Andrew age 25y in Greenwich, NY May 20, 1856

GRAY Norman of Troy, NY in White Creek, NY June 26, 1856

DAY Mrs. Eliphalet formerly of Cambridge, NY in Spencers Basin, NY June 18, 1856

FENTON Erastus age 85y in Cambridge, NY July 11, 1856

COOK Dr. John T. age 38y in White Creek, NY July 25, 1856

FENTON Edward T. in his 19th yr son of A. H. formerly of Shushan, NY in Aurora, NY July 16, 1856

PHELPS Adah age 50y wife of Julius in Cambridge, NY July 26, 1856

MC CREARY Maria age 17y in Cambridge, NY July 29, 1856

MOSHER Jerome D. in his 59th yr at Buskirks Bridge, NY July 13, 1856

VAN VECHTEN Walter age 53y in White Creek, NY July 26, 1856

LAKIN Nellie age 9y dau of William H. and Jane in White Creek, NY August 5,

1856

GAYLORD Henry in his 68th yr of Whitehall, NY at son-in-laws J. C. **HOUSE** in Waterford, NY July 17, 1856

HOZELL Helen Elizabeth age 4y dau of Myron and Catherine in Ft. Edward, NY August 2, 1856

WEBB Phebe abt 50y wife of Abell in Cambridge, NY September 17, 1856

HOAG Rhoda B. wife of Abram formerly of White Creek, NY in Otsego, Mi. September 11, 1856

TILTON Levi M. age 34y in White Creek, NY October 3, 1856

WELLS Ann Eliza (**JOHNSON**) age 36y wife of Joseph in Easton, NY November 9, 1856

DENNIS Elizabeth in her 63rd yr wife of Charles in Battenville, NY January 2, 1857

DONELSON Jennette abt 25y wife of James in Salem, NY February 11, 1857

MOORE Jane age 11m dau of John D. and Agnes in Shushan, NY February 12, 1857

FOWLER Philena M. age 64y wife of Jonathan in White Creek, NY February 16, 1857

MC LEAN Francis age 63y at bro Thomas in Reynoldsburg, Ohio February 4, 1857

ROBERTSON Eliza M. age 38y in Ashtabula, Ohio February 17, 1857

ALLEN Hannah age 71y in Cambridge, NY February 28, 1857

MC SHELLIE Marta V. K. age 6y 6m 22d dau of Thomas and Jane in Cambridge, NY March 5, 1857

FURLONG Rev. Jonathan abt 60y in White Creek, NY March 5, 1857

MC NAUGHTON Duncan J. formerly of Cambridge, NY son of late James in Philadelphia, Pa. March 6, 1857

CORNELL Abigail age 76y relict of Paul in Cambridge, NY March 19, 1857

ROSE Aura age 32y wife of John in Grenby Center, NY March 28, 1857 and John abt 50y formerly of White Creek, NY died April 8, 1857

MANLY Minerva M. in her 26th yr wife of William R. and dau of Gen. Orville **CLARK** in Sandy Hill, NY March 29, 1857

MILLIMAN Joseph Edward age 7y son of Ira in White Creek, NY April 4, 1857

ARCHER Joseph I. age 57y in Cambridge, NY April 10, 1857

VAN VECHTEN James T. age 22y 21d son of Walter and Emily in White Creek, NY March 28, 1857

MATOON Isabella wife of William in Springfield, Mass. March 28, 1857

WAIT Hon. S. in Kingsbury, NY April 20, 1857

WOODARD Eli age 18y son of Daniel and Anna in Hebron, NY April 13, 1857

WOODARD Nancy age 50y wife of Lyman in Battenville, NY April 14, 1857

SHERMAN Miss C. M. formerly of Cambridge in Washington, Io. March 29, 1857

RUSSELL William in his 90th yr in Cambridge, NY March 29, 1857

CROCKER Esther age 30y wife of William C. in Newtonville, NY March 28, 1857

CURTIS Simmons age 80y 5m in Warrensburgh, NY April 17, 1857

DILLON Thomas age 63y in E. Salem, NY May 2, 1857

CENTER Sheldon age 76y in White Creek, NY May 11, 1857

MUNROE Miriam age 79y in Shaftsbury, Vt. May 9, 1857

COOK Martin E. age 22y formerly of White Creek in Sonoma, Cal. April 16, 1857

GORDON Mary (**HAY**) age 78y widow of James of New York in Andes, NY April 30, 1857. Leaves son Rev. Peter Gordon of Cambridge, NY

ROBERTSON Christy Ann age 42y in E. Greenwich, NY May 17, 1857

DAY Horace B. age 20y son of Hiram in Albany, NY May 17, 1857

COMSTOCK Sarah age 17y in White Creek, NY May 30, 1857

PRENTISS Sarah E. in her 15th yr dau of Mason in White Creek, NY June 7, 1857

LAW George age 13m 11d son of Robert and Jennett in Putnam, NY May 26, 1857

BEACH Minerva O. age 25y dau of John in Sandy Hill, NY May 20, 1857

PATTISON Emma E. age 27y dau of John in Ft. Miller, NY May 24, 1857

STEWART Jennette Ann age 27y dau of William and Sarah in Jackson, NY May 29, 1857

HOAG Mary M. age 26y wife of Jonathan E. in Easton, NY May 30, 1857

CRANDALL Polly age 60y wife of Alexander in Easton, NY June 6, 1857

FENTON Martha age 38y wife of A. H. of Aurora, Ill. in Cambridge, NY June 23, 1857

HAWLEY Lemuel age 57y in W. Arlington, Vt. June 25, 1857

BULLIONS Rev. Alexander age 78y in Coila, NY June 26, 1857. Born Scotland

WILBUR Tryphena in her 63rd yr widow of George of White Creek, NY in Momence, Ill. June 9, 1857

AUSTIN Maria in her 50th yr wife of Henry and dau of late Solomon WARNER of Jackson, NY in Mexico, NY June 13, 1857

AUSTIN Sophia in her 52nd yr wife of Daniel in Mexico, NY July 7, 1857

LEE Julia Augusta age 1y 6m dau of Hiram and Jane July 22, 1857

MAY Harriet N. age 39y wife of Dr. John May in Pittstown, NY August 19, 1857

BREWER Johny age 2y 1m 10d son Hiram J. and Mary A. in Oneonta, NY August 28, 1857

WELLS Daniel L. age 79y son of late Daniel of Cambridge, NY in Hoosick, NY September 11, 1857

MC AULEY Martha age 68y of Williamstown, NY at bro E. MC LEAN in Cambridge, NY September 22, 1857

FOWLER Thomas age 74y in White Creek, NY September 28, 1857

RICHEY Agnes (ROBERTSON) age 48y 8m 7d wife of Judge R. W. and dau of Samuel and Jennett GREEN of Washington Co. in Oquawka October 19, 1857

NOBLE Charles age 17y 9m son of A. S. in Coila, NY October 26, 1857

BREWER Sidney age 18y in Union Village, NY October 19, 1857

QUA Mrs. Martha age 72 of Hebron, NY in White Creek, NY October 10, 1857

BRIGGS Sylvia C. in her 49th yr wife of Christopher in Ft. Covington, NY October 14, 1857

ROBERTSON William in his 74th yr in Coila, NY November 1, 1857

NICHOLS Mary H. age 66y wife of James B. in White Creek, NY November 6, 1857

WOODS Andrew age 37y in Cambridge, NY November 8, 1857

MARTIN Andrew age 77y in Salem, NY November 9, 1857

PARISH Hiram age 58y in Jackson, NY November 9, 1857

COMSTOCK Ward age 17y son of Thomas in White Creek, NY November 15, 1857

FISHER Mrs. Rebecca age 70y formerly of White Creek, NY in Onondaga Hill, NY November 11, 1857

MARSH Abigail age 82y in E. Salem, NY November 15, 1857

CROSBY Mrs. S. W. age 39y in White Creek, NY December 1, 1857

BARNETT George age 57y 2m in Putnam, NY December 10, 1857

MAXWELL Jane Louisa age 6m dau of Robert and Elizabeth in Putnam, NY December 13, 1857

BLOUNT Oscar F. formerly of Whitehall, NY in Milwaukee, Wis. January 6, 1858

WILSON Hannah in her 73rd yr wife of Robert in Salem, NY January 21, 1858

SAYRE Charles age 74y in Sandgate, Vt. January 14, 1858

PRINDLE Elizabeth in her 59th yr wife of L. G. in Argyle, NY January 14, 1858

SIMPSON Susannah age 72y wife of Anderson in Jackson, NY February 7, 1858. Born September 11, 1786 in White Creek, NY dau of Benjamin and Margaret **SCOTT**. Married April 14, 1812

DOIG Mrs. Catherina age 43y in Cambridge, NY February 17, 1858

BURT Angeline age 46y wife of T. R. in Shushan, NY February 16, 1858

STEVENSON Fannie age 1y 9m dau of H. K. and M. C. (**LUSK**) in Manchester, Vt. February 16, 1858

HILL Sarah in her 93rd yr widow of Thomas at son-in-laws N. A. **SISSON** in White Creek, NY February 28, 1858

LEE Jane abt 35y wife of Hiram W. in White Creek, NY March 18, 1858

NILES Mary Ann abt 35y wife of Nathaniel M. in White Creek, NY March 12, 1858

WELLS Hannah Miriam age 67y wife of Sidney in Cambridge, NY April 2, 1858

AUSTIN Margaret Hannah age 6m dau of David L. and Emily W. in Jackson, NY March 7, 1858

ARCHER Esther abt 70y widow of Joseph in Jackson, Ny April 2, 1858

WALKER Mary Jane in her 21st yr wife of T. H. and dau of B. F. MC NITT in White Creek, NY April 12, 1858

HILL Alexander age 52y son of Col. Whiteside in Cambridge, NY April 13/18, 1858

BARTON Helen M. age 24y wife of Henry O. in White Creek, NY April 21, 1858

BARTON Nettie W. wife of M. P. Barton 2nd in White Creek, NY May 3, 1858

HUNT James age 73y 3m in White Creek, NY May 4, 1858

SAYLES Anna R. wife of Dr. C. formerly of White Creek, NY in Delevan, Wis. May 8, 1858

SLAFTER Sylvanius in Lewisville, Va. May 5, 1858

MC DONALD Daniel in his 90th yr in Salem, NY May 23, 1858

COON Margaret in her 25th yr wife of Russell B. in Salem, NY June 10, 1858

CRAIG Joseph in his 88th yr in Hebron, NY June 10, 1858

HUNT Annie age 63y widow of Hugh at son-in-laws D. N. BROWNELL June 11, 1858

WOODARD Elizabeth age 36y wife of James in Jackson, NY June 13, 1858

RIDER Elizabeth in her 55th yr wife of Zerah in White Creek, NY July 6, 1858

MC LEAN Henry R. abt 56y in Battenville, NY July 5, 1858

ANTHONY Martha in her 88th yr widow of Richard July 2, 1858

DOIG Robert age 22y son of John in Salem, NY July 4, 1858

GOODELL Tirsa age 73y in Hartford, NY June 24, 1858

COULTON George R. age 46y in Hartford, NY June 27, 1858

TAYLOR Nathan W. in Hartford, NY June 28, 1858

SAVAGE Jane in her 70th yr wife of Thomas in Argyle, NY July 9, 1858

MC CARTY Daniel age 1y son of Dennis and Hannah in Salem, NY July 30, 1858

OATMAN Daniel age 78y in N. Hartford, NY July 26, 1858

GETTY Jane age 77y widow of Isaac in Salem, NY July 27, 1858

PARRY Araminta C. wife of Joseph Jr. formerly of Washington Co. and dau of V.

S. BECKER of Easton, NY in Davenport, Iowa July 27, 1858

DOIG Mrs. abt 80y widow of Thomas at sons David in Cambridge, NY (newspaper date August 20, 1858

BARTON child of Henry of White Creek, NY in Schuylerville, NY August 15, 1858

ELLIS Mary in her 71st yr in White Creek, NY August 17, 1858

BLANCHARD Hamilton in his 25th yr son of Anthony in Salem, NY August 28, 1858

MENTON Sarah E. age 40y wife of Michael and dau of John S. **NORTHUP** of N. Hartford, NY in Kingsbury, NY July 30, 1858

CRANDALL Hannah age 70y in Easton, NY August 23, 1858

COVEY Aaron age 50y 1m 4d in Sandgate, Vt. August 18, 1858

HOYT David abt 6y son of E. Hoyt in Sandgate, Vt. August 18, 1858

SMITH Maria age 54y wife of Platt formerly of White Creek, NY and dau of Gerritt **WENDELL** in Adrian, Mi. August 17, 1858

JOHNSON Jane M. age 6y dau of W. W. and Anna in White Creek, NY September 2, 1858

MURDOCK Chester S. age 29y son of Peter and Jane of Argyle, NY in Salem, NY August 18, 1858

FOWLER Artie age 1y 4m son of Horace and Adelia in Salem, NY August 16, 1858

RIPLEY James C. age 42y son of Allen in N. Granville, NY September 5, 1858

BEDOE Salem abt 100y former slave in White Creek, NY September 13, 1858

FOWLER Cornelia M. in her 5th yr dau of late Dewitt C. and Henrietta E. in White Creek, NY September 12, 1858

HARRINGTON Henry W. in his 51st yr in Arlington, Vt. October 4, 1858

WILCOX Robert abt 80y in White Creek, NY October 9, 1858

WHITE Mary G. in her 2nd yr dau of Charles A. and Joanna N. in Albany, NY October 25, 1858. Another child age 4y died a few days earlier

SMITH Calvin age 76y formerly of Jackson, NY in Ogden, NY October 14, 1858

BROWN Philenda age 88y formerly of Jackson, NY in Ogden, NY October 22, 1858

MOREY William T. age 37y in Sandwich, Ill. July 13, 1858

LEE Charles Henry in his 16th yr son of Elisha and Esther in N. White Creek, NY November 23, 1858

LOOMIS Ezekiel age 45y formerly of White Creek, NY in Granby, NY November 18, 1858

AUSTIN Lewis W. age 37y in White Creek, NY November 19, 1858

STEWART John K. age 26y 1m in N. Argyle, NY October 29, 1858

MC LEAN John age 65y in Salem, NY December 5, 1858

SLOCUM Jonathan age 83y in White Creek, NY December 2, 1858

CLEVELAND D. D. age 37y formerly of Jackson in Troy, NY December 1, 1858

HURD Julia C. age 26y dau of Merritt in White Creek, NY December 10, 1858

FAIRLEY Miss Jane in her 57th yr in Salem, NY December 7, 1858

TWISS Mrs. Russell abt 30y in Cambridge, NY December 24, 1858

SPRAGUE John in his 65th yr in Salem, NY December 21, 1858

AUSTIN Job age 75y in Camden, NY December 23, 1858

FORT Nathaniel age 19y son of Gerritt in Cambridge, NY December 24, 1858

PLAISTED Edwin G. age 28y in White Creek, NY January 6, 1859

RATHBONE ____ age 2y son of Stephen in Easton, NY January 13, 1859

LEGRYS Louisa age 31 wife of Thomas in White Creek, NY January 11, 1859

WARNER Dr. Kirtland T. age 54y in Jackson, NY December 16, 1858

ROBERTSON Marriam age 14y dau of Charles in White Creek, NY January 26, 1859

MORRISON Sarah Ann in her 34th yr wife of Robert late of Jackson, NY in Florence, Lambton Co. Canada W. January 16, 1859 and William Morrison in his 70th yr same place January 25, 1859

SKELLIE Emily in her 49th yr in Cambridge, NY February 3, 1859

OVIATT Esther in her 43rd yr in Shushan, NY January 23, 1859

RICE Thomas in his 64th yr in N. White Creek, NY February 8, 1859

MC CREARY James abt 30y in Cambridge, NY February 10, 1859

DOBBIN Sarah Jane age 38y widow of John in White Creek, NY February 16, 1859

LAMBERT David G. abt 42y in White Creek, NY February 16, 1859

RALSTON Lottie (**TAYLOR**) age 22y wife of V. F. of Quincey, Ill. at parents in N. White Creek, NY February 21, 1859

MONEYPENNY John in New York City February 14, 1859

CHURCH Bethewel age 74y formerly of Shushan in Tallmadge, Mi. January 10, 1859

CUMMINGS William in his 67th yr at Putnam, NY February 13, 1859

EASTON Jennett age 38y 10m wife of David in Putnam, NY February 28, 1859 and son John Dayton Easton age 2y 3m died February 13, 1859

GUNN Dud age 80y formerly of White Creek at Ft. Covington, NY March 2, 1859

ALLEN George age 15y son of Samuel and Esther in Granville, NY March 14/19, 1859

MATTISON Mrs. Jonathan abt 60y drowned at White Creek, NY March 23, 1859

WOOD Elizabeth Louisa age 18y dau of Daniel in Cambridge, NY April 4, 1859

BROWN Phebe R. age 70y widow of John in Jackson, NY April 16, 1859

NELSON John age 53y in Salem, NY May 3, 1859

ARNOTT George in his 84th yr in Jackson, NY April 23, 1859

KING Miriam Annette age 3y 7m 22d dau of Daniel and Caroline in Battenville, NY May 22, 1859

PARRY John in his 37th yr in Ft. Edward, NY May 13, 1859

BEEBE Roderick in his 82nd yr in Salem, NY May 18, 1859

STROW Mrs. Abigail age 63y in Hartford, NY May 13, 1859

SELLECK Ann age 87y sis of Timothy **STOUGHTON** in Ft. Edward, NY (newspaper date May 27, 1859)

EDMONSON Catherine Ann age 43y wife of John G. in Easton, NY May 14, 1859

AGAN B. F. in his 45th yr in Granville, NY May 23, 1859

CLEVELAND Miriam in her 48th yr wife of Levi H. in Salem, NY May 30, 1859

TAYLOR Lydia in her 55th yr dau of Simeon in Union Village, NY May 30, 1859

PARISH John age 39y in Jackson, NY June 27, 1859

PECKHAM Jesse W. age 48y yr formerly of White Creek, NY in Clyde, NY June 22, 1859

DAY Eliphalet age 70y formerly of White Creek, NY in Ogden, NY June 28, 1859

LOWE William R. age 35y in Ft. Edward, NY July 28, 1859

ROBERTSON Margaret age 72y wife of John formerly of Battenville, NY in Ashtabula, Ohio July __, 1859

JUDSON Joshua age 77y late of Arlington, Vt. in Cambridge, NY September 27, 1859

PRATT Eli age 35y in Cambridge, NY August 4, 1859

WARREN Sylvia wife of William in White Creek, NY August 17, 1859

MC LEAN William C. age 91y in Jackson, NY August 16, 1859

HOES R. F. in his 29th yr in Manitowne, Wis. July 30, 1859

IRVINE Mary W. widow of Rev. James formerly of Hebron, NY in New York July 26, 1859

OLIN Gideon C. in his 56th yr in White Creek, NY August 25, 1859

LIVINGSTON Mrs. Anna age 49y in Cambridge, NY August 13, 1859

MILLER Mary Jane age 22y dau of late James and present Mrs. Ellen **ROBERTSON** in Cambridge, NY September 14, 1859

ROBERTSON Moses K. age 17y son of Peter V. K. September 15, 1859

MILLER William John age 12y 4m 29d son of John W. and Margaret F. in Ft. Edward, NY September 6, 1859

LAMPSON Mrs. Hannah in Granville, NY September 22, 1859

NEWCOMB Mary age 19y dau of S. Newcomb and Eliza L. **GRAVES** in Granville, NY October 24, 1859

MC ARTHUR Thomas in his 43rd yr in Jackson, NY October 11, 1859

BROWNELL Nathan age 69y in Cambridge, NY December 4, 1859

PRUYN Henry N. age 76y in Cambridge, NY December 7, 1859

WEBSTER George age 32y son of Simeon D. of Hebron, NY in Australia September 2, 1859

MC GOWAN Clarance D. age 1m son of Micas and Mary A. in Shushan, NY December 29, 1859

NELSON Eliza Mary in her 45th yr widow of Dr. William G. and dau of late Dr. Alexander **BULLIONS** in Cambridge, NY January 15, 1860

BASSETT Sarah E. age 53y wife of Pardon in Union Village, NY January 22, 1860

ALLEN William C. age 35y 10m in Union Village, NY January 25, 1860

AUSTIN Abner in his 78th yr in Salem NY January 31, 1860

GETTY Jane age 2y 8m dau of John H. and Jane G. in Salem, NY February 2, 1860

YOULEN Rachael in her 66th yr wife of Benjamin in Salem, NY February 5, 1860

MC ARTHUR Robert age 44y 2m in Putnam, NY February 9, 1860

MC COY Helen dau of William T. and Margaret in Argyle, NY January 30, 1860

MC EACHRON David age 63y in Ft. Edward, NY February 2, 1860

WHITESIDE Miss Ann age 69y in W. Cambridge, NY February 27, 1860

BARTLETT Leroy E. age 7y 7m son of Emrie and Cornelia in White Creek, NY February 11, 1860

DEWEY Mrs. Aletha age 49y in White Creek, NY February 21, 1860

GALUSHA Electra age 50 clothes caught fire at County Home February 20, 1860

SMITH Lucy age 64y of White Creek, NY at the County Home February 20, 1860

GRAHAM Ann Elizabeth age 5y 10m died March 11, 1860, Mary Jane age 2y died March 12, 1860, Robert Denslo age 7y 8m died March 14, 1860 and James Russell age 5m died March 15, 1860, children of Isaac and Charlotte of Putnam, NY

HIGGINS Jane age 92y 1m 5d widow of Cornelius at son-in-laws Joel **RICH** in White Creek, NY March 20, 1860

HAYS Elizabeth age 75y in Delaware Co. NY February 17, 1860

CLAPP Stephen in his 74th yr in Salem, NY March 19, 1860

ROCHESTER James B. age 49y brother-in-law of Mrs. H. B. **WILLIAMS** of Salem, NY in Auburn, NY March 22, 1860

DAWLEY Charles Herbert age 1y 2m son of Morgan and Ellen in Union Village, NY March 9, 1860

MURDOCK Russell age 14y son of Samuel in Salem, NY March 16, 1860

MC LEAN John C. age 60y in Battenville, NY March 25, 1860

SHARPE Jane age 87y wife of H. K. and dau of Andrew MARTIN of Salem, NY in Cambridge, NY April 5, 1860

SHIPLEY George S. age 1y 11m 16d son of Simeon and Jane in Cambridge, NY April 5, 1860

SKELLIE Hannah age 30y dau of John and Sabra in Jackson, NY March 13, 1860

BASSETT Anna age 75y widow of Russell at son-in-laws William COON in Salem, NY April 5, 1860

FAIRLEY Maggie F. age 2y 9m dau of William D. and Kate E. in Salem, NY April 3, 1860

MYERS Willis son of William and Mary Jane in Schaghticoke, NY April 11, 1860

SMART Mary Frances in her 13th yr dau of Hugh and Frances in Salem, NY April 11, 1860

SAFFORD Thomas infant son of Joseph and Ellen in Salem, NY April 7, 1860

CROWL Lyman formerly of Salem, NY in Forest, Mi. March 19, 1860

CROWL Alice A. age 6y 6m 13d twin dau of Alvin and Mary A. in Salem, NY April 14, 1860

CRONIN William T. age 1y 2m son of Timothy and Helen M. in Salem, NY April 14, 1860

SHAW Lucy J. age 7m 11d dau of Cornelius and Helen in Salem, NY April 15, 1860

WALKLEY Sarah E. Wife of W. in White Creek, NY April 25, 1860

FOWLER Abram V. T. in his 42nd yr in Aurora, Ill. April 19, 1860

PORTER Susie M. age 2y dau of Charles and Phebe A. in N. White Creek, NY May 6, 1860

ROBERSON Ann Eliza age 50y relict of Charles in White Creek, NY May 6, 1860

WEBSTER Simeon D. age 65y of Hebron, NY at son-in-laws William J. BOCKES in White Creek, NY May 13, 1860

LARMAN Miss Freelove age 30y in Cambridge, NY May 14, 1860

GUNN Annie age 80y of White Creek, NY at dau Mrs. D. M. QUA in Ft. Covington,

NY May 12, 1860

WARNER Martha age 41y wife of Abner in Jackson, NY May 21, 1860

RUSSELL Laurens age 80y widow of Thomas in White Creek, NY May 28, 1860

AUSTIN Emily W. age 30y 9m 17d widow of David L. in White Creek, NY June 3, 1860

STACKHOUSE Mary Jane age 20y in White Creek, NY May 11, 1860

CENTER Miss Marion age 42y in White Creek, NY June 15, 1860

BROWNELL Miss Minerva age 35y at bro Smith H. in Shushan, NY June 18, 1860

SHARPE Peter in his 78th yr at Buskirks Bridge, NY June 4, 1860

ALEXANDER Jennette age 21y dau of John in Greenwich, NY June 15, 1860

MORGAN George age 18y son of Carlos in Glens Falls, NY June 11, 1860

SHILAND Amelia Campbell age 9y 9m dau of Thomas in Cambridge, NY July 17, 1860

HAWLEY James age 9y son of Rev. B. Hawley in White Creek, NY July 22, 1860

SAFFORD Lucy age 13y died June 22, 1860, William J. age 11y died July 10, 1860 and Nathaniel C. age 9y 6m died July 16, 1860, children of Gideon F. and Sarah of Salem, NY

STOVER Henrietta age 10y dau of George in Greenwich, NY July 18, 1860

BARKER Albert P. age 1y 3m 26d son of Phineas and Amelia E. in Salem, NY July 9, 1860

POOR M. age 80y wife of W. C. of Albany in White Creek, NY August 7, 1860

GILLIS James W. in his 11th yr son of Archibald in Salem, NY August 4, 1860

STEELE Daniel age 50y in Salem NY August 6, 1860

MC LAUGHRY Martha age 2y 7m dau of James and Margaret J. in Salem, NY June 28, 1860

LONG Edward in Cambridge, NY August 10, 1860, born November 19, 1787 in Salem, NY

HOUGHTON Mary age 4m dau of E. S. and Julia in White Creek, NY August 13, 1860

RUSSELL Paul age 32y in White Creek, NY September 2, 1860

NICHOLS James B. in his 71st yr in White Creek, NY September 13, 1860

REID Mrs. Sarah age 74y of Argyle, NY in Coila, NY August 30, 1860

PALMER Nelson and Neland twin sons of J. Hill and Martha E. in Jackson, NY September 19, 1860

HAWLEY Louisa Maria wife of David of New York and dau of James WHITESIDE of Cambridge, NY at Mothers September 18, 1860

SOPER John L. age 61y in Dorset, Vt. September 15, 1860

ARNOLD Henry M. age 50y in White Creek, NY October 1, 1860

VOLENTINE Harvey age 57y in Jackson, NY October 1, 1860

FITCH Cynthia age 27y wife of Charles L. of White Creek, NY in Arlington, Vt. October 13, 1860

ROUSE Joseph age 80y in Argyle, NY October 12, 1860

ADAMS Thurdon F. age 27y son of Robert B. and Lydia in E. Salem, NY November 7, 1860

HODGE Eugene B. age 27y in White Creek, NY November 13, 1860

COOK James R. age 35y in White Creek, NY December 13, 1860

BEADLE Daniel in his 38th yr in Waterloo, NY November 23, 1860

HOUSE Haines B. in his 38th yr son of John of White Creek, NY in Dresden, Tenn. December 1, 1860

SISSON John age 76y in White Creek, NY December 22, 1860

RANSOM Elizabeth dau of Francis and Ann CROCKER formerly of White Creek, NY in Louisville, Va. December 21, 1860

VAN VECHTEN Dow age 17y 10m 4d son of Cornelius and Caroline in White Creek, NY November 24, 1860 and dau Julia age 16y 7m 13d died December 24, 1860

LAKE James age 70y in White Creek, NY January 3, 1861

ROBERTSON Frankie son of John and Minerva in Cambridge, NY January 8, 1861

CHAPPELL Alansing B. in his 47th yr in Cambridge, NY January 10, 1861

STEVENS Mary Ann dau of John WILSON in Salem, NY January 1, 1861

CROCKER Laura M. age 16y 9m 4d dau of James M. and Mary A. in Charlton, NY January 23, 1861

LAWTON Cynthia age 13y in White Creek, NY January 20, 1861

MILLIMAN Throop in his 11th yr son of N. B. in Ft. Edward, NY January 13, 1861

GAVETTE John abt 90y in Greenwich, NY January 19, 1861

BUGBEE Adelia A. in her 42nd yr wife of A. and dau of Eleazor **CROCKER** formerly of White Creek, NY in S. Bend, Ind. January 26, 1861

BILLINGS C. son of Walter formerly of Greenwich, NY in Clarenceville, Canada December 13, 1860

DUEL Isaac abt 70y in Cambridge, NY February 14. 1861

VOLENTINE Clark abt 35y in Shushan, NY February 12, 1861

TUTTLE Joseph age 87y in Sandgate, Vt. February 15, 1861

BISHOP Isaac W. age 57y in Granville, NY February 24, 1861

HOWE Mary L. age 3y 4m dau of Henry and Helen M. in White Creek, NY March 17, 1861

DOBBIN John in Jackson, NY March 22, 1861

BAKER Charlotte age 13y dau of Reuben and Laura in Salem, NY March 22, 1861

SHERMAN Job in his 87th yr in Cambridge, NY April 8, 1861

MC CLAREN Malcolm age 21y son of Rev. D. C. of Geneva, NY in Redwing, Minn. April 5, 1861

ASHTON John age 61y formerly of White Creek, NY in Groton, NY April 10, 1861

STAPLES Elery age 77y of Danby, Vt. at son-in-laws Abram **ELDRIDGE** Jr. April 13, 1861

DAVIS Maria A. (**SIMPSON**) age 30y wife of Harvey formerly of White Creek, NY in Springfield, Mi. April 19, 1861

KINNEY Eunice T. age 72y wife of Silas and sis of Rev. E. H. **NEWTON** in Newfane, Vt. March 31, 1861

WHITCOMB Betsey age 67y wife of J. Whitcomb in White Creek, NY May 11, 1861

NORTON William age 76y in Union Village, NY May 10, 1861

SMALL Thomas Edward age 8y 9m son of James in Cambridge, NY May 18, 1861

CAMERON Willie age 3y 1m son of Duncan in Jackson, NY May 21, 1861 and father Duncan age 53y died June 4, 1861 in Coila, NY

SMART Francis Wardell age 11y son of Rev. J. G. in Coila, NY May 27, 1861

RICHARDSON James age 67y in Poultney, Vt. May 26, 1861

ALEXANDER Robert age 53y in Jackson, NY May 24, 1861

STRONG Isabel age 56y sister of George **ROBERTSON** of White Creek, NY in Reynoldsburg, Ohio (newspaper date June 7, 1861)

HARPER Ann Isabella age 4y 5m dau of James in Coila, NY June 4, 1861

MC ARTHUR Mary age 86y widow of John at sons Robert in Jackson, NY June 6, 1861

MC CLAREN James Stevenson age 19y son of Rev. D. C. in Geneva, NY June 17, 1861

CRUIKSHANK Maggie A. age 1y 2m 12d died May 31, 1861 and John R. age 2y 8m 6d died June 12, 1861 children of James A. and Sarah R. in Salem, NY

MERRILL Mary E. age 25y in White Creek, NY June 24, 1861

STARR Mary Jane age 20y dau of S. P. and M. A. in Cambridge, NY June 27, 1861

CARPENTER Mary age 20y dau of Sullivan at Buskirks Bridge, NY July 8, 1861

BAIN Anna M. in her 30th yr (no date) W. J. Bain in his 16th yr died July 14, 1861, children of John B. in S. Argyle, NY

HARRINGTON Jesse age 8y son of Widow H. H. in Arlington, Vt. June 24, 1861

HAWLEY William Chauncey age 22y son of Ransom and Margaret July 18, 1861

VAN TUYL Jane age 68y wife of Abraham August 16, 1861. Born Cambridge, NY

WATKINS Mr. ____ age 82y in White Creek, NY August 10, 1861

BROWNELL J. G. in Appleton, Wis. July 24, 1861

MC FADDEN Alexander age 44y in Argyle, NY August 2, 1861

THOMPSON Julia Jennett age 3y dau of James in White Creek, NY August 10, 1861

NEWMAN R. B. age 47y formerly of Easton, NY in New York August 24, 1861

MUNROE David age 89y September 15, 1861

QUA Susie Bell age 10m dau of John C. in White Creek, NY September 25, 1861

WRIGHT Mary **(FISHER)** age 31y wife of William in Cambridge, NY November 19, 1861

NILES Richard O. age 2y 3w son of Stephen and Sophia L. in Shaftsbury, Vt. November 7, 1861

CROSBY Maria F. age 39y dau of late Aaron of Springfield, Ohio in Chillecoth, Ohio September 15, 1861. Born Cambridge, NY

NELSON William Henry age 17y 9m son of late Dr. William G. Nelson in Va. a mem. of 3rd Vt. Reg. (newspaper date November 29, 1861)

WILSON N. Albert mem. of Ellsworth's Reg. at Washington DC November 22, 1861. Buried Salem, NY

HATCH Mary age 57y in Jackson, NY December 12, 1861

FISHER John age 67 in White Creek, NY December 12, 1861

BURTON Simon age 61y in Easton, NY December 6, 1861

WHELDON William P. age 2y 11m 24d died December 1, 1861 and Harriet age 6y 7m died December 5, 1861, children of Francis J. and Mary in Easton, NY

BUCKLEY D. Mosely abt 35y in White Creek, NY January 1, 1862

SLOAN Margaret C. wife of Rev. J. R. W. and dau of Rev. D. C. **MC CLAREN** in Geneva, NY December 21, 1861

KETCHUM Willie L. age 7y 1m 9d son of Peter and Julia in Cambridge, NY December 25, 1861

RALSTON Josie W. age 5y grand dau of William **TAYLOR** in N. White Creek, NY December 28, 1861

FENWICK Miss Margaret age 48y in White Creek, NY January 27, 1862

HEDGES Ida age 11y in White Creek, NY February 1, 1862

TRULL Mrs. Catherine age 57y of Syracuse, NY at brother-in-laws W. **MC ALLISTER** in Salem, NY January 27, 1862. Native of Jackson, NY

WILSON Emma A. age 13y 9m 1d dau of James Mc C. and Catherine in W. Hebron, NY February 3, 1862

SMITH Mrs. Hannah in her 97th yr in Hebron, NY February 1, 1862

MONEYPENNY Mary Ann in her 57th yr relict of John January 24, 1862

ROBERTSON Miss Ellen age 75y in Cambridge, NY February 9, 1862

TEFFT George E. age 13y son of Samuel and Emeline **(COTTRELL)** in White Creek, NY February 16, 1862

GREEN Mrs. R. formerly of White Creek, NY in De Kalb Co. Ill. February 12, 1862

LARMON Alexander age 2y 9m son of John and Frances in White Creek, NY March 13, 1862

BAKER Miss Cornelia age 42y dau of Col. J. in White Creek, NY March 5, 1862

CLARK Orville age 61y of Sandy Hill, NY in Des Moines, Iowa March 19, 1862

KEHOE Mary Genevieve age 2m 25d dau of Lawrence and Sarah E. in New York March 28, 1862

HOUSE John age 80y in White Creek, NY April 11, 1862

STEWART James Mitchell age 30y son of William H. in Salem, NY April 4, 1862

JOHNSON Sarah in her 72nd yr widow of Thias at sons Rev. William M. Johnson in Stillwater, NY April 15, 1862

MC KIE Neil W. age 48y in Cambridge, NY April 27, 1862

WOODWORTH Lott age 76y in White Creek, NY April 30, 1862

AKIN Rhoena age 65y wife of Eliakim in White Creek, NY May 15, 1862

TRULL Miss Sally age 75y in White Creek, NY March 31, 1862

MC CLAREN Findlay age 31y of Milwaukee, Wis. son of Rev. D. C. Mc Claren in Geneva, NY May 16, 1862

ROBERTSON Jennette P. age 26y in Coila, NY May 26, 1862

SKELLIE Andrew in his 55th yr in Cambridge, NY May 2, 1862

COOK Dr. Oliver age 49y in White Creek, NY June 2, 1862

THURBER Hannah age 74y a widow in White Creek, NY June 5, 1862

TABER Henry abt 65y in Easton, NY June 24, 1862

SANFORD Mrs. Clarissa age 86y in White Creek, NY June 21, 1862

COLE Robey age 71y sister of Curtis Cole in Jackson, NY June 28, 1862

LAKE Augustus H. age 4y 10m son of Thomas and Lydia in White Creek, NY June 26, 1862

CROSBY E. G. age 68y formerly of White Creek in Hartford, Conn. July 1, 1862

BINNINGER John in his 63rd yr son of Isaac the Revolutionary Soldier in Bellville, Can. June 16, 1862. Born Salem, NY, removed to Canada in 1817

ALLEN Sarah H. in her 57th yr dau of David **RUSSELL** in Salem, NY July 12, 1862

WEBSTER Orrin H. age 62y in Hampton, NY July 10, 1862

HALL William R. age 15y son of Joseph in Cambridge, NY August 7, 1862

PATTERSON Jane abt 55y wife of Samuel in Eaglevile, NY August 6, 1862

PIERCE William H. age 22y 28d Corp. in Co. G. 93rd Reg. NY Vol. at Fortress Monroe July 10, 1862

DWINNELL William in his 77th yr in White Creek, NY July 9, 1862

BRISTOL Jane R. age 53y wife of L. in White Creek, NY August 20, 1862

WILLARD Sally age 57y wife of Levi in White Creek, NY August 27, 1862

WOODWORTH Miss Maria B. age 29y dau of C. V. K. Woodworth of Cohocton, NY at sis Mrs. L. **CROUCH** in White Creek, NY August 17, 1862

SHERWOOD infant child of Dr. Sherwood in White Creek, NY August 22, 1862

MC FARLAND William in his 73rd yr in Salem, NY August 30, 1862

CARSWELL Marthy Elizabeth in her 10th yr dau of James H. and Isabel in Salem, NY August 26, 1862

THOMPSON Jane in her 59th yr wife of David B. in Salem, NY August 31, 1862

RICH Ebenezer age 8y son of Allen and Margaret in Salem, NY September 1, 1862

COLE Curtis in his 79th yr in Jackson, NY August 26, 1862

PRATT George Smith age 2y son of Edward and Delia in White Creek, NY September 1, 1862

GORRIE Mrs. Mary age 52y in Coila, NY September 20, 1862

DUNHAM Abraham age 77y in Jackson, NY September 18, 1862

FULLER Linus William age 6y 6m died September 30, 1862 and Wilhelmina age 3y 6m died October 9, 1862 children of Linus and grandchildren of Rev. Peter **GORDON**

of Cambridge, NY

SIMPSON Anderson in his 75th yr in Jackson, NY October 14, 1862

WOOD Mercy E. age 10y died October 24, 1862 and Elizabeth L. age 3y died October 26, 1862, children of H. K. and Emily C. in White Creek, NY

MC AULEY Lucy wife of William formerly of Arlington, Vt. in N. Adams, Mass. October 28, 1862

SKELLIE William abt 24y of Cambridge, NY in 123rd Reg. NY Vol. at Harpers Ferry November 3, 1862

TRIPP Frederick Eugene age 8y 26d son of Stephen and Amelia in Cambridge, NY November 3, 1862

GILBERT Charles abt 50y in White Creek, NY November 13, 1862

WOOD Mary E. age 1y 5m dau of George B. and Delia E. in Cambridge, NY November 13, 1862

PORTER Phebe Ann age 39y wife of Charles in White Creek, NY November 15, 1862

QUA Howard Nixon age 5y 10m 15d son of John C. and Jane in White Creek, NY November 19, 1862

WALSH Bell dau of Peter in Cambridge, NY December 1, 1862

MORRISON Mrs. R. W. dau of Peter **WALSH** in Tamarack, Ill. November 19, 1862

GIFFORD Louise Antoinette age 5y 2m 2d dau of Jeremiah and Lydia in Cambridge, NY November 28, 1862

HURLEY John Jr. age 3y 7m 12d in E. Salem, NY December 17, 1862

WHITESIDE William W. in his 73rd yr in Cambridge, NY December 20, 1862

WRIGHT Ebenezer age 54y in Cambridge, NY January 8, 1863

STACKHOUSE William abt 27y in Cambridge, NY January 5, 1863

WYATT William Henry age 20y 10m 4d son of Elijah and Candace W. in Battenville, NY January 10, 1863

EAGER Eugene M. age 5y son of Abraham and Mary in Galesville, Ill. November 9, 1862

BILLINGS Moses age 28y in Nashua, Iowa December 6, 1862

MILLER Peter age 34y in Camp Union Mills, Va. January 10, 1863

MC ARTHUR Robert in his 63rd yr in Jackson, NY February 11, 1863

PORTEOUS Alexander age 47y at residence of Solomon Culver February 8, 1863. Born Dumfrieshire, Scotland

BENNETT Mrs. Elizabeth age 67y formerly of White Creek, NY in New Haven, NY February 3, 1863

STARBUCK James age 94y in Cambridge, NY February 14, 1863

EDGERTON _____ age 4y dau of E. S. in White Creek, NY March 2, 1863

SPENCER Charlie age 2y 9m 23d son of D. Carlton in White Creek, NY March 23, 1863

HARVEY Clarissa D. age 61y wife of Francis in Albany, NY March 30, 1863

NOBLE Charles Holmes age 2y 8m 24d son of Henry and Sarah M. in White Creek, NY April 28, 1863

KIMBERLY Mrs. Currance in her 90th yr formerly of Sandgate, Vt. in Salem, NY May 4, 1863

WHITE John Franklin age 10w son of N. I. and Sarah J. in Salem, NY May 1, 1863

MURDOCK Samuel age 58y in Salem, NY May 3, 1863

MC FARLAND Daniel A. age 67y in Salem, NY April 23, 1863

RUGGLES Miss Ann age 83y in White Creek, NY May 18, 1863

LONG Charity widow of Edward of Cambridge, NY at son-in-laws James **HALL** in Argyle, NY June 2, 1863

NOBLE Ransom age 86y in Essex, NY June 6, 1863

CARPENTER Ephraim age 83y in Strafford, Vt. June 11, 1863

ARNOLD John W. age 20y of Co. D. 22nd Reg. in White Creek, NY June 21, 1863

ROBERTSON James F. age 80y in White Creek, NY July 8, 1863

QUA Ida age 2y dau of D. V. T. and M. A. in Shushan, NY on birthday July 12, 1863

ANDREWS Mary E. in her 32nd yr wife of J. M. and dau of Samuel **RUSTE** formerly of White Creek, NY in Aurora, Ill. July 5, 1863

NICHOLSON Lewis age 61y in White Creek, NY July 10, 1863

SHEDD Alanson abt 50y in White Creek, NY July 14, 1863

BAKER Nancy age 70y at sons Fletcher in White Creek, NY July 29, 1863

HANKINS Mrs. ____ age 54y in Jackson, NY July 31, 1863

MONROE Darius abt 40y in White Creek, NY August 3, 1863

LOVEJOY ____ age 7m child of H. in White Creek, NY August 4, 1863

COWAN David S. age 21y formerly of White Creek, NY in Lafayette, Ind. August 1, 1863

ARCHER George J. age 9m 7d son of James H. and Julia A. in Cambridge, NY July 23, 1863

BRISTOL William R. age 17y son of Levi in White Creek, NY August 17, 1863

NORTON Miss Charlotte abt 40y in E. Salem, NY August 18, 1863

GOW Nathan C. age 4y 9m son of John and Martha in Coila, NY August 25, 1863

GILMORE Samuel age 72y 3m 20d in Cambridge, NY August 31, 1863

SMITH Harriet J. age 32y 7m 12d wife of Ebenezer in White Creek, NY September 26, 1863

RUSTE Harriet J. age 66y wife of Samuel in Aurora, Ill. October 2, 1863

COULTER Clarence L. age 20y 3m in Co. G. 123rd Reg. in Alexandria, Va. October 26, 1863

MC NAUGHTON Nellie age 9m 17d dau of John C. and Annie C. in Salem, NY October 3, 1863

NORTHUP John E. in his 71st yr in Hartford, NY September 17, 1863

BEATTIE Sarah age 73y widow of David in Salem, NY September 30, 1863

SPRAGUE Joseph in his 46th yr in Salem, NY October 6, 1863

STEELE James age 69y in Salem, NY October 15, 1863

LOOMIS Jeduthan abt 50y formerly of White Creek in Galway, NY October 9, 1863

OLIN Ephraim age 47y in White Creek, NY November 3, 1863

SHEPHERD Sarah (MC AULEY) age 70y in Ft. Miller, NY October 31, 1863

ALLEN Harvey W. age 9m son of Squire W. and Abbie in New York November 11, 1863

ASHTON David Henry age 10y 17d son of David G. and Harriet in White Creek, NY November 17, 1863

SKELLIE J. L. age 24y of Co. D. 123rd Reg. in Cambridge, NY October 21, 1863

GOODMAN T. Irving age 10y son of H. N. and Eliza in Syracuse, NY November 21, 1863

PINNEY Walter A. age 11m 28d son of Alden and Lizzie formerly of Salem, NY in Rutland Vt. October 29, 1863

BECKER David abt 40y in Borodino, NY November 19, 1863

PALMER Henry in his 74th yr in Clifton Park, NY December 9, 1863

CROCKER Lizzie Mari age 5m dau of R. K. and S. J. in White Creek, NY December 19, 1863

BLAKELEY Margaret age 85y relict of Jonathan in Greenwich, NY December 22, 1863. Son Billings

WILCOX Calista age 48y wife of Oliver in Greenwich, NY December 18, 1863

PINNEY Lizzie in her 24th yr wife of Alden and dau of Lysander and Hannah R. **WHEELOCK** in Eagle Bridge, NY December 18, 1863

DAY Caroline M. in her 22nd yr dau of Hiram in Cambridge, NY December 28, 1863

GURNETT Anna B. age 23y dau of Zerah **RIDER** in White Creek, NY January 5, 1864

OVIATT Francis W. age 39y in White Creek, NY December 31, 1863

FOSTER John in his 72nd yr in White Creek, NY December 24, 1863

CENTER Obadiah in his 75th yr in Cambridge, NY December 17, 1863

WILDER Dr. A. H. in Newark, NJ December 2, 1863

HARRIS Eveline M. age 34y wife of James E. in Hartford, NY December 2, 1863

FRATO Joseph age 26y in White Creek, NY Janury 8, 1864

BENWAY David age 88y in Buskirks Bridge, NY January 9, 1864

SELLECK Adeline M. age 38y wife of Perry M. in Greenwich, NY January 10, 1864

MOSHER David age 51y in White Creek, NY January 13, 1864

HUGHES John age 63y in Euclid, Ohio November 3, 1863

WOOD Daniel age 73y in Cambridge, NY January 18, 1864

WAIT Zera age 55y in White Creek, NY January 18, 1864

DECKER Henry age 16y son of Jacob in White Creek, NY January 19, 1864

DOBBIN Nealie age 1y dau of John W. and Anise in E.Greenwich, NY January 10, 1864

NILES Charles age 76y in White Creek, NY January 28, 1864

BARTON Hiland age 28y son of Eli of White Creek, NY in Hoosick Falls, NY February 5, 1864

BAKER Col. J. in his 74th yr February 3, 1864

RICHARDS Mrs. Sarah abt 77y in White Creek, NY February 10, 1864

KEECH Rev. Israel in his 67th yr in Grooms Corners, NY February 8, 1864

BROWN Alice M. age 19y dau of William and T. C. of Salem, NY February 5, 1864

COLLINS Anna age 58y wife of Julius in Jackson, NY February 5, 1864

HUTCHINS Lydia C. age 14y dau of John S. and Lydia C. in White Creek, NY February 17, 1864

BARTON Currance age 69 wife of Mial in White Creek, NY February 24, 1864

ELDRIDGE Rhoda J. age 38y wife of Ahira Jr. in White Creek, NY March 7, 1864

VANDENBURGH Jacob abt 74y in White Creek, NY March 11, 1864

FISHER Emily C. formerly of White Creek, NY March 3, 1864

WILCOX Rachel in her 82nd yr at sons G. W. in White Creek, NY March 10, 1864

SWEET Walter C. age 3y son of Hyde and Martha A. in White Creek, NY March 1, 1864

WRIGHT Delia Addie age 3y dau of William W. in Cambridge, NY March 31, 1864

JOHNSON Ella age 11y dau of John in White Creek, NY March 30, 1864

NEWTON Isaac in his 73rd yr in Newfane, Vt. March 24, 1864

LAW Elizabeth widow of John March 20, 1864. Born June 1773 in Co. Downs Ireland, came to Salem, NY 1789. Married 1798, husband died June 16, 1835

HUBBARD Mrs. Margaret in her 79th yr in Sandgate, Vt. April 9, 1864

HUBBARD Alice age 78y wife of Jonathan in White Creek, NY April 15, 1864

LEWIS Esther Ann age 27y 4m 5d dau of James R. and Sarah **COMSTOCK** formerly of Washington Co. in Naticoke, NY (newspaper date April 29, 1864)

LANSING Ella age 15y 3m 20d dau of Jacob C. and Louisa Ann in Brighton, NY April 26. 1864

RALSTON Capt. V. Y. son of Dr. J. N. of Quincey, Ill. and son-in-law of William **TAYLOR** of White Creek, NY in St. Louis, Mo. April 19, 1864

MERRYMAN Lottie age 1y 7m 15d died April 21, 1864 and Lizzie age 3y 8m died May 3, 1864 children of William and Rebecca A. in Jackson, NY

OLIN ____ age 8m 6d son of William and Elizabeth S. in White Creek, NY May 13, 1864

BAKER Robert age 77y in White Creek, NY May 18, 1864

THIGUE Charles age 17m died May 24, 1864 and William Henry age 5y died May 29, 1864 sons of Leonard and Margaret C. in Jackson, NY

NOBLE Harmon age 58y in Essex, NY May 24, 1864

LEE Anna age 71y in Granville, NY May 15, 1864. Born July 10, 1793 dau of Garrett **WENDELL**. Married November 7, 1811 Martin Lee

TINKHAM Casindra age 78y 7m 14d wife of Rev. Daniel in White Creek, NY June 15, 1864. Born Shaftsbury, Vt.

WARNER William S. age 59y in White Creek, NY June 22, 1864

CAMPBELL Elizabeth P. age 43y in Putney, Vt. June 23, 1864, son Arthur age 6y died June 24, 1864

CORNELL William age 66y in Jackson, NY July 16, 1864

LAMBERT Sarah B. in her 54th yr wife of Rev. A. B. and dau of Rev. Dr. **GUNN** of New York July 31, 1864

MC NEIL Miss Jane age 70y in Argyle, NY September 4, 1864

BISHOP Bertie age 2y 9m son of Merritt and Annie in White Creek, NY September 8, 1864

KING Mary age 68y wife of John in White Creek, NY September 5, 1864

CHASE Aaron in his 67th yr formerly of Cambridge, NY in Bloomington, Ind. August 29, 1864. Born Alsted, NH

MC KIE John age 75y in White Creek, NY September 10, 1864

DOWNER Sally age 68y wife of Silas in Arlington, Vt. September 30, 1864

BULLIONS Rev. David G. in W. Milton, NY September 29, 1864, buried nr White Creek, NY

SLOCUM George abt 21y in White Creek, NY October 6, 1864

COOK Henry R. age 25y of Battery K. 16th NY Heavy Artillery in battle before Richmond October 7, 1864

TRULL John age 71y Veteran of War of 1812 in Cohoes, NY October 21, 1864

HOLLIS Alfred Henry age 6y 9m son of Harvey and Maria L. in White Creek, NY November 5, 1864

STEVENS Hannah age 73y wife of John and dau of Paul CORNELL in White Creek, NY October 24, 1864

MORRIS Phillip V. N. abt 70y in Cambridge, NY November 13, 1864

DYER Fordyce A. age 24y Lieut. in Mass. Heavy Artillery formerly of Cambridge, NY in Newburne, NC October 26, 1864

ROBERTSON George Edward age 4y son of George and Susan J. in Cambridge, NY November 16, 1864

DARBY Julia age 36y wife of A. L. formerly of Pittsfield, Mass. in White Creek, NY December 5, 1864

HILLMAN Charles H. age 6y son of James H. and Lydia in Salem, NY December 10, 1864

HOWE William P. age 30y in White Creek, NY December 21, 1864

RICE Miss Sarah Jane age 30y dau of Harvey in Jackson, NY December 19, 1864

SAVAGE Rev. John A. son of Abram of Salem, NY and bro of Dr. James Savage of Argyle, NY in Waukesha, Wis. December 14, 1864

TAYLOR John Barbour age 25y 6m January 4, 1865

CHAPMAN Hepzibah age 61y widow of John W. and Dau of James GIBBONS of Albany, NY January 8, 1865. 2 sons James G. and William of Syracuse, NY

FASSETT B. F. age 65y in N. Bennington, Vt. January 10, 1865

CRANDALL James W. age 38y formerly of Greenwich, NY in Quaker Springs, NY February 7, 1865

FENTON Zina in her 78th yr wife of Amariah in Jackson, NY February 12, 1865. Born December 24, 1787 in Wellington, Conn. Married (1) 1803 Daniel **RICE** who died 1838. Married (2) 1848

SKINNER Alice (**ARMSTRONG**) age 39y 3m wife of William in Argyle, NY January 23, 1865

FULLER William G. age 53y in White Creek, NY February 20, 1865

KELLOGG Laura in her 75th yr wife of O. in White Creek, NY February 23, 1865. Born May 1790 dau of Jacob **BACON** of Williamstown, Mass.

BLAIR Hannah abt 82y in White Creek, NY March 1, 1865

SHILAND Miss Ann in her 46th yr in Cambridge, NY February 26, 1865

WEIR Almina wife of William in Jackson, NY February 21, 1865

MARSHALL Louisa age 11m 16d dau of David and Lydia in White Creek, NY March 9, 1865

FITCH William age 17y son of S. S. in White Creek, NY March 27, 1865

ACKLEY Lot age 57y formerly of White Creek, NY in Troy, NY March 30, 1865

MILLER Miss Mary R. age 35y in Salem, NY March 30, 1865

MAYNARD Jennie (**BROMLEY**) age 29y wife of X. J. in N. White Creek, NY April 10, 1865

ARNOLD John in his 91st yr at sons Jesse in White Creek, NY April 11, 1865

MC ARTHUR Mary age 54y 6d wife of Rev. Samuel and dau of late Edward **SMALL** of Cambridge, NY in Birmingham, Iowa November 23, 1864

MASON William abt 36y from fall at Academy 3 yrs ago in White Creek, NY April 17, 1865

BATES Louisa N. in her 62nd yr widow of Rev. Chandler Bates and sis of late Rev. E. H. **NEWTON** in Parma, NY April 17, 1865

TILFORD David S. age 27y son of widow Mary in Jackson, NY April 25, 1865

SIMPSON Nelson R. in White Creek, NY May 10, 1865

NOBLE Adonijah S. age 57y 2m 19d in Cambridge, NY June 8, 1865

MAXWELL Sarah wife of James and dau of James **GREEN** of Cambridge, NY in Jackson, NY May 12, 1865

MUZZY William L. age 26y in Coila, NY June 15, 1865

WARNER Capt. Garrett W. in his 53rd yr in Vasalia, Cal. June 1, 1865. Born Cambridge, NY. Went to California in 1853

MAXWELL James age 2y 6m son of James in Jackson, NY July 7, 1865

FISHER Flora L. age 16m dau of Stephen R. And Frances in White Creek, NY July 12, 1865

HOUSE Mary relict of John of White Creek, NY in Troy, NY July 24, 1865. Born October 31, 1785 in Marlboro, Vt.

AUSTIN Elijah age 40y in Salem, NY August 7, 1865 and Maria age 16d dau of Elijah and Esther Jane August 8, 1865

HYDE Mary in her 78th yr wife of Iram in Jackson, NY August 3, 1865

FISHER Willie J. age 1y 4m 13d son of Rev. J. and Laura E. in Newark, NJ July 27, 1865

COOK Mrs. Lucy C. age 76y in White Creek, NY August 13, 1865

LIVINGSTON Mrs. Elizabeth age 67y of Cambridge, NY in Manchester, NH August 24, 1865

MILLER Sarah E. age 17y dau of Lewis P. and Larinda of Cambridge, NY in Ballston, NY August 29, 1865

HART Joel age 48y in White Creek, NY August 29, 1865

GORDON Peter abt 63y in S. Easton, NY September 6, 1865

ROBERTSON Mrs. George in her 48th yr dau of late James **WOODS** of Cambridge, NY in White Creek, NY September 2, 1865

COOK Florence age 8y in White Creek, NY September 5, 1865

ROBERTSON Jesse abt 80y in Cambridge, NY September 26, 1865

BISHOP Sarah age 84y in Easton, NY September 7, 1865

KING Anna age 51y 10m wife of John in Coila, NY September 22, 1865

HIGGINS Martha Ann age 38y wife of Mason A. of White Creek, NY and dau of

Simeon **REED** of Putney, Vt. October 1, 1865

SKELLIE Henry age 30y in Cambridge, NY October 18, 1865

WOODWORTH Frances H. age 18y in White Creek, NY October 22, 1865

VAN VECHTEN Caroline age 59y wife of Cornelius in White Creek, NY October 29, 1865

AKIN Judith Sophia age 30y in White Creek, NY October 16, 1865

WELLS Leonard age 64y son of Daniel of Cambridge, NY October 30, 1865

CROSBY Flavel age 61y formerly of White Creek, NY in Palatine, Ill. October 24, 1865

SHILAND James age 64y in Jackson, NY November 27, 1865. Born Cambridge, NY

GUTHRIE George Jr. age 30y in Hebron, NY December 9, 1865

CHAPPELL George T. age 21y in Castleton, Vt. December 14, 1865

ARMITAGE Margaret age 77y in Coila, NY December 16, 1865

ARCHER Johny age 18m son of J. W. in Cambridge, NY December 15, 1865

MOORE Maria Prime **(PRATT)** age 36y wife of E. R. in Portsmouth, Ohio December 10, 1865

COMSTOCK Esther age 87y at sons Thomas in White Creek, NY January 9, 1866

MAYNARD John T. in his 21st yr in W. Junius, NY January 8, 1866

SIMPSON Hettie age 51y wife of Anderson in Jackson, NY January 11, 1866

REA Mrs. John M. abt 40y in W. Hebron, NY January 7, 1866

QUA Emily age 48y wife of Abner in White Creek, NY January 20, 1866

BLANCHARD Catherine age 18y in White Creek, NY January 18, 1866

BENTLEY Alvin J. age 12y in White Creek, NY January 18, 1866

THOMPSON Thomas age 65y in Jackson, NY January 30, 1866

WELLS Samuel age 84y in Cambridge, NY January 29, 1866

HAWKINS Mattie C. age 20y wife of Warren E. and dau of Abner **QUA** in Cambridge, NY January 31, 1866

MC COY Emily (ALLEN) age 26y 5m in Sunderland, Vt. January 25, 1866

HURD Laura M. age 5y dau of Herman and Florence in Johnsonville, NY January 30, 1866 and Florence age 26y 9m dau of Daniel HILT died February 4, 1866

KING Sarah M. wife of Col. Edward A. and dau of James MC NAUGHTON formerly of Cambridge, NY in Dayton, Ohio February 7, 1866

FENTON Amariah formerly of White Creek, NY in Erie, Pa. February 9, 1866

FLEMING John age 48y in Salem, NY March 12, 1866

FAIRLEY Wallace age 1y 3m 4d son of W. D. and K. M. in Salem, NY March 7, 1866

BURBY Francis age 2y 4m son of Thomas and Margaret in Sandy Hill, NY March 19, 1866

WOODARD Russell age 55y in Hebron, NY March 15, 1866

MC COLLOUGH ___ age 3m son of Michael and Mary in Hebron, NY March 14, 1866

GROVE Eliza A. age 64y in Hoosick, NY March 16, 1866

HOWD Addie J. dau of Sidney W. WRIGHT late of Granville, NY in New York April 23, 1866

KEEFE Susie age 25y wife of Daniel in Sandy Hill, NY May 8, 1866

BRUCE Mrs. Sarah age 78y in Salem, NY May 8, 1866

SKINNER Nancy age 77y widow of Reuben in M. Granville, NY May 18, 1866

WORTH Edward age 64y formerly of Easton in St. Croix Falls, Wis. April 26, 1866

COX Esther age 67y in Cambridge, NY June 24, 1866

QUA Anna age 24y wife of William C. in Cambridge, NY July 1, 1866

CLARK Lucy age 44y wife of Andrew in Poultney, Vy. July 9, 1866

GLENHOLMES William James age 5y son of Francis and Eliza in Hebron, NY July 5, 1866

WALSH Theresa age 18m dau of Michael in Cambridge, NY July 23, 1866

KEHOE Sarah Elizabeth (ORCUTT) age 30y wife of Lawrence native of White Creek, NY in New York July 18, 1866

RICH Nial in his 77th yr formerly of White Creek, NY in Hoosick Falls, NY August 7, 1866

RYAN Thomas age 1y 3m son of John in Cambridge, NY August 1, 1866

WALLACE Margaretta Ross age 18y 8m 17d in Lansingburgh, NY July 28, 1866

NORCROSS Walter age 6m son of Phillip in E. Greenwich, NY August 15, 1866

PARISH Learned age 74y in Hebron, NY August 25, 1866 and wife Jane age 72y died August 19, 1866

WRIGHT Mercy age 74y wife of Robert in Cambridge, NY September 2, 1866

BILLINGS William age 62y in E. Arlington, Vt. September 4, 1866

ASHTON Margaret age 67y in Salem, NY September 5, 1866

MC GEOCH Mary Agnes age 17y dau of George in Jackson, NY September 6, 1866

BARNETT Benajah age 5y 8m 28d dau of Darius and Sarah J. **(STANLEY)** in Shushan, NY September 8, 1866

COTTRELL Evie age 4y died September 17, 1866 and Clarence nr 9y died September 20, 1866 children of Charles C. and Eunice

PERRY Elihu age 70y in White Creek, NY September 18, 1866

ROBINSON Ira age 87y in Cambridge, NY September 22, 1866

SWEET J. B. Ryan age 29y in Hoosick, NY September 23, 1866

KENNEDY Robert age 56y in Stillwater, NY September 25, 1866

SMITH Miss Nancy age 42y in White Creek, NY September 27, 1866

MAHAFFY Samuel in his 75th yr in Salem, NY October 3, 1866

TIERNEY James age 8y 2m 14d son of Michael and Bridget in Salem, NY October 11, 1866

ADAMS William age 35y in White Creek, NY October 8, 1866 and son Willie age 21m died September 29, 1866

EDGERTON ____ wife of E. S. formerly of Cambridge, NY in St. Joseph, Mo. October 13, 1866 and son Ralph age 6y died October 14, 1866

CHURCH Leonard a Revolutionary Soldier in Shushan, NY October 22, 1866, born October 13, 1771 in Salem, NY, 2 sons Bethuel Jr. and Leonard in Civil War

COLLIER Harriet age 68y widow of J. E. in Sandy Hill, NY October 24, 1866

ORR Louise age 2y 11m dau of David and Lovica in Salem, NY October 28, 1866

CROCKER Helen J. age 43y wife of N. S. P. formerly of Cambridge, NY in Spencerport, NY (newspaper date November 2, 1866)

MC CLELLAN John age 1y 8m son of Henry B. and Mary in Cambridge, NY October 20, 1866

WATERS Mary age 75y in Jackson, NY October 27, 1866

RICE Anna M. age 22y wife of Clark and dau of George **ROBERTSON** in Cambridge, NY November 2, 1866

DURFEE Mrs. Sophia age 59y in Cambridge, NY October 29, 1866

OVIATT Samuel age 60y in Jackson, NY November 7, 1866

CONNORS Daniel age 45y in Cambridge, NY November 10, 1866

MICKLEJOHN Elizabeth E. age 26y 4m wife of A. and dau of James **LEDGERWOOD** in Putnam, NY October 31, 1866

AMIDON Betsey age 77y in Granville, NY November 5, 1866

CHERRY Luenda age 19y dau of James and H. A. in E. Greenwich, NY October 20, 1866

HARVEY Jane age 73y in Jackson, NY November 18, 1866

PARKE Mrs. Hannah in her 78th yr in Whitehall, NY November 12, 1866

LAW Andrew in Whitehall, NY November 14, 1866

BAKER Alfred E. age 26y son of Silas and Amanda in Ft. Ann, NY November 1, 1866

PRIEST Mary Ann age 45y wife of Henry in Cambridge, NY November 21, 1866

GUNN Loomis W. age 48y in Cambridge, NY November 22, 1866

GREEN Jane age 89y in Cambridge, NY December 3, 1866

ARNOTT Joseph age 5y son of Samuel M. and Jennett A. in Jackson, NY December 6, 1866

HOWE Lydia age 62y wife of Horace in Cambridge, NY December 8, 1866

RICE James age 78y formerly of Cambridge in Lansingburgh, NY December 9, 1866

POWELL Garrett age 32y in Hebron, NY December 28, 1866

JOHNSON Miss Elizabeth age 45y in Cambridge, NY December 20, 1866

MATHEWSON Hettie age 8y 2m dau of D. and L. E. in Sandy Hill, NY December 18, 1866

PERRY William H. age 32y in White Creek, NY December 25, 1866

CHASE Isabell age 53y wife of Christopher in N. Hoosick, NY December 29, 1866

GRAY Levi in his 70th yr in Camden Valley, NY December 29, 1866

HENRY Mary E. age 24y wife of William E. in Granville, NY December 21, 1866

WEAVER Jacob age 82y in the County Home December 29, 1866

MURPHY Maria age 34y in Easton, NY December 28, 1866

LAW Margaret abt 39y wife of George in Jackson, NY December 30, 1866

BAKER Ellen age 39y wife of Fletcher in Cambridge, NY December 31, 1866

SHELDON Dewitt C. son of late Gen. Thomas Sheldon of Westfield, Mass in Salem, NY December 31, 1866

LONG Margaret E. age 48y wife of Col. Barry in Cambridge, NY January 4, 1867

PENDLETON Charles age 78y in Cambridge, NY January 9, 1867

MURPHY Elizabeth age 74y in Sandy Hill, NY January 1, 1867

RUSSELL Perris age 73y wife of John in Anaquasicoke, NY January 10, 1867

MATTISON Jonathan age 73y in White Creek, NY January 15, 1867

TINKHAM Daniel in his 84th yr in White Creek, NY January 13, 1867

LAW Ann Eliza age 8y 8m dau of George in Jackson, NY January 17, 1867

CHALMERS Peter in his 91st yr in Whitehall, NY January 11, 1867

NORCROSS Clara age 21y dau of Phillip and Miranda in E. Greenwich, NY January 11, 1867

SMITH John age 46y in Whitehall, NY January 17, 1867

WAIT William age 59y in Whitehall, NY January 19, 1867

SULLIVAN Daniel Jr. age 20y 11d in Whitehall, NY January 24, 1867

EATON Edwin John age 6m 22d son of Alvin R. and Kate in Whitehall, NY January 22, 1867

WALDO Mrs. Huldah age 86y in Argyle, NY January 8, 1867

RANSOM Nelson in E. Poultney, Vt. January 28, 1867

AYLSWORTH Sarah V. (MARTIN) age 52y wife of E. M. in E. Arlington, Vt. January 29, 1867

WOODWORTH Betsey age 65y wife of Daniel P. formerly of White Creek, NY in Scriba, NY January 12, 1867

BLISDELL John age 87y in Kingsbury, NY January 30, 1867

MC KNIGHT Mrs. Catherine in her 72nd yr Mother of John M. REA in Hebron, NY February 8, 1867

PATTERSON Nancy age 76y wife of Hugh in Hebron, NY February 10, 1867

MC KIE Maria age 36y 11m 11d wife of E. J. in Cambridge, NY Febuary 8, 1867

CORNELL G. L. age 36y in Granville, NY February 19, 1867

WRIGHT Isaiah age 25y in Granville, NY February 16, 1867

NORTON Mrs. William S. age 63y in Ft. Edward, NY February 27, 1867

GALUSHA Dan R. age 6y son of Russell and Eliza M. in Ft. Miller, NY February 12, 1867

MC OMBER James age 65y in White Creek, NY March 4, 1867

MORSE Horace M. abt 26y in S. Granville, NY March 6, 1867

MC KERNON John age 66y in Cambridge, NY March 4, 1867

NILES Maria age 3m 21d dau of W. C. and Josephine in White Creek, NY March 6, 1867

PLUNKETT Mary age 6m dau of Michael in Cambridge, NY March 6, 1867

LEE John age 85y in Cambridge, NY March 9, 1867

BARKER Sarah age 76y widow of Benjamin in Granville, NY March 1, 1867

BURDETT Aaron E. abt 30y in Whitehall, NY March 10, 1867

CLARENDON George age 39y in Whitehall, NY March 10, 1867

TILFORD Mrs. Elizabeth age 70y in Ft. Edward, NY March 6, 1867

GRAVES Azel age 81y in Salem, NY March 11, 1867

MC MAHON Lizzie age 13y dau of Ann in Salem, NY March 11, 1867

MOORE Elizabeth age 60y in Salem, NY March 10, 1867

WOODWORTH William age 62y formerly of Cambridge, NY Westfield, Ind. March 11, 1867

MC COTTER Julia B. in her 59th yr in Whitehall, NY March 16, 1867

CORNING Ella age 13y dau of James and Mary in Ft. Ann, NY March 13, 1867

CLEMENTS Susan wife of Augustus M. and dau of Col. William Clements of Sandy Hill, NY In Ft. Edward, NY March 16, 1867

SHERMAN Abram age 62y in Ft. Ann, NY March 16, 1867

TEFFT Chloe age 85y wife of Joseph in Kingsbury, NY March 3, 1867

GRIFFIN Freddie G. age 1y 8m son of E. J. in Cambridge, NY March 25, 1867

ADAMS Albert D. age 9m son of James in White Creek, NY March 22, 1867

FERGUSON George age 56y in Jackson, NY March 22, 1867

ARCHER Nancy age 70y in Cambridge, NY April 2, 1867

MONROE Isaac T. in his 21st yr in S. Granville, NY March 24, 1867

SMALL Elizabeth age 52y widow of Alexander in Jackson, NY April 3, 1867

COULTER James H. age 14m son of John and Nancy in Jackson, NY April 1, 1867

MC FARLAND Sarah L. age 60y wife of William in Jackson, NY April 5, 1867

HEDGES George age 48y in Jackson, NY April 5, 1867

DOIG Bertie age 6m 6d son of William J. and Mary in Jackson, NY April 6, 1867

SULLIVAN John age 30y in Cambridge, NY April 8, 1867

COULTER Caroline age 55y wife of Robert in Cambridge, NY April 7, 1867

RANSOM Rev. W. H. age 54y in E. Dorset, Vt. March 24, 1867

CROFF Maj. George E. age 29y in Danby, Vt. March 21, 1867

DERBY Lizette age 30y widow of Benjamin in Poultney, Vt. March 29, 1867

POOR infant son of Rev. W. H. and Louisa R. in Poultney, Vt. March 29, 1867

MOORE Sarah in her 83rd yr widow of John in Salem, NY March 20, 1867

CLEVELAND Joel in his 61st yr in Salem, NY April 3, 1867

HATCH Horatio in his 74th yr formerly of Washington Co. in Logan, Ohio January 24, 1867

BOWKER Mrs. Mary age 83y in Granville, NY April 9, 1867

MILLER Augustus age 59y in Sandy Hill, NY April 9, 1867

BATES Jesse age 28y in N. Bennington, NY Arpil 12, 1867

TILFORD Robert age 64y in Jackson, NY April 13, 1867

MC INERNEY Patrick age 29y in Cambridge, NY April 17, 1867

MORRISON Margaret age 51y wife of John in Salem, NY April 21, 1867

YULE George in his 84th yr in Whitehall, NY April 12, 1867

SHAW Isabella C. age 27y wife of Rufus R. in Greenwich, NY April 10, 1867

FARRAN Loraine O. age 45y in Rupert, Vt. April 23, 1867

HUGHES Esther, Mother of Charles in Kingsbury, NY April 15, 1867

NORTHUP Maryette wife of John H. in Sandy Hill, NY April 21, 1867

HOUSE Sarah age 50y dau of late John of Cambridge in Troy, NY April 27, 1867

KENYON Anna Maria age 24y wife of P. M. and dau of F. P. **STARR** in Urbana, NY April 22, 1867

DA LEE Mehitable (**DEMING**) age 67y wife of John formerly of White Creek, NY in Harvard, Ill. April 25, 1867

HAY James age 64y formerly of Cambridge, NY in Sonora, Cal. (newspaper date May 10, 1867)

PIERSON Lettie J. age 15y dau of E. in W. Arlington, Vt. April 30, 1867

MAHAR Johanna age 26y wife of Thomas in Easton, NY May 4, 1867

MINTON Henry J. age 22y in Sandy Hill, NY May 1, 1867

MILLIMAN Jennie age 18y dau of Joseph in Cambridge, NY May 14, 1867

BILLETT Adelia age 11y dau of S. A. in Whitehall, NY May 4, 1867

GRIFFIN Harvey in his 35th yr in Ft. Ann, NY May 3, 1867

FOSTER James M. Md. age 62y in Hebron, NY May 3, 1867

PRINDLE Betsey Ann in her 72nd yr in Salem, NY May 14, 1867

CONWAY John age 15d son of Michael and Sarah in Cambridge, NY May 15, 1867

GREEN ____ age 2m 3d dau of William in Shushan, NY May 13, 1867

MALONEY Bridget age 5m dau of Michael and Bridget in Shaftsbury, Vt. May 15, 1867

GIFFORD Ira age 79y in Schaghticoke, NY May 12, 1867

SHERMAN Sarah D. age 68y in Cambridge, NY May 17, 1867

GEARY Daniel age 58y in Jackson, NY May 21, 1867

PIERCE William age 82y in W. Sandgate, Vt. May 26, 1867

FERRIS Charles age 7y 2m son of Walter and Eliza in Sandy Hill, NY May 14, 1867

SCRANTON Howard age 4m son of William and Mary in Jackson, NY May 21, 1867

BUCK Jane E. age 45y wife of David in White Creek, NY (newspaper date May 31, 1867)

CLARENDON Emma F. age 28y wife of Charles in Whitehall, NY May 19, 1867

FAULKENBURY Mathew age 80y in Whitehall, NY May 24, 1867

MATHEWS Col. David age 82y in Sandy Hill, NY May 28, 1867

HODGEMAN Jemima age 38y in Ft. Edward, NY May 23, 1867

ROBERTSON Mary L. age 51y wife of Thomas in Lakeville, NY May 25, 1867

MECHIM John age 17y in Jackson, NY June 2, 1867

DODDS Alice age 5y 10m dau of Walter in Buskirks Bridge, NY June 12, 1867

WARREN Barton age 76y of Hartford, NY in Lynnville, Ill. June 3, 1867

MC CLEARY Alexander age 75y in Jackson, NY June 13, 1867

BUCK Ella Mary age 7y 6m 4d dau of James P. and Eliza in Kingsbury, NY June 7, 1867

MOORE Sarah O. **(DUNHAM)** in her 50th yr wife of William A. formerly of Jackson, NY in Alexandria, Va. June 15, 1867

BROUGHTON Experience age 83y in Jackson, NY June 28, 1867

ROBERTSON Margaret M. C. age 57y in E. Greenwich, NY June 30, 1867

WALDO John C. age 54y in Ft. Ann, NY June 27, 1867

MC AULEY William age 56y in Arlington, Vt. July 3, 1867

GREEN Capt. James age 70y in Cambridge, NY July 3, 1867

SMITH Maria age 55y wife of James Y. in Coila, NY July 10, 1867

SAVAGE William age 61y in M. Granville, NY July 3, 1867

CENTER Ellen age 38y wife of Edward and son Willie age 4m in Ft. Edward, NY June 24, 1867

COULTER Peter age 61y in Arlington, Vt. July 13, 1867

MOORE Elizabeth **(GRAHAM)** age 56y wife of James in Troy, NY July 11, 1867

WILSON Christopher age 75y in N. Argyle, NY July 9, 1867

TULL Mrs. Mary age 66y in Greenwich, NY July 20, 1867

BUEL Josie age 1y 11m 5d dau of Rev. Clarence and Laura E. **(DAVIS)** in Cambridge, NY July 22, 1867

GILLETTE Adelbert G. age 18y in Whitehall, NY July 24, 1867

VANDENBURGH Mrs. Solon age 44y in Whitehall, NY July 23, 1867

WRIGHT Elizabeth age 13y dau of Benjamin and Ann in Whitehall, NY July 28, 1867

ASHTON Benjamin age 68y in White Creek, NY July 29, 1867

LINEHAN Mary age 14y in Cambridge, NY July 28, 1867

DIBBLE Laura Louise age 19y 6m 11d dau of Horace and Louise in Kingsbury, NY July 21, 1867

FOSTER Maggie age 17y dau of Robert in Salem, NY August 6, 1867

BROWNELL Elijah suicide in Easton, NY August 2, 1867, an elderly man

RIDER Zerah abt 70y in Cambridge, NY August 3, 1867

FREEMAN Ira Jr. age 2y 6m 1d in Sandy Hill, NY July 19, 1867

MATTISON Smith age 76y in W. Exeter, NY July 26, 1867

COMSTOCK Adah age 7m 2d in Cambridge, NY August 10, 1867

WARNER Sylvester K. age 19y 5m 16d son of Mary A. in Brooklyn, NY August 8, 1867, buried in Woodlands cem. Cambridge, NY

COWAN Mary J. abt 31y in Cambridge, NY August 13, 1867

LINSENBARTH Lilly age 6y in Salem, NY August 6, 1867

ROGERS Solomon age 91y 14d in Whitehall, NY August 13, 1867

BROWN Theda age 7m 21d dau of Hiram in Cambridge, NY August 17, 1867

DUNHAM Mrs. Mary H. in her 57th yr in Jackson, NY August 15, 1867

DURFEE Pardon age 58y in Cambridge, NY August 15, 1867

YOUNG Malinda age 64y wife of Custis in W. Arlington, Vt. August 17, 1867

BROWNELL Henry W. age 2m son of Gideon and Laura in White Creek, NY August 20, 1867

SHERMAN Polly D. age 54y wife of Joseph in S. Granville, NY August 19, 1867

STARR Anna Mary age 8y 4m 6d grand daughter of S. P. in Cambridge, NY August 26, 1867

BLANCHFIELD Mary age 4y in Cambridge, NY August 24, 1867

VANDENBURGH Sarah age 75y in White Creek, NY August 30, 1867

KING Henrietta age 7w dau of W. F. in Cambridge, NY August 29, 1867 and Pheba A. age 37y wife of W. F. died September 3, 1867

KING Mary Florence age 5m 13d dau of A. B. and E. C. in Sandy Hill, NY September 3, 1867

MC GRATH Edward abt 30y in White Creek, NY September 8, 1867

BENWAY Catherine age 90y in Cambridge, NY September 11, 1867

MILAN Michael age 55y in Whitehall, NY September 6, 1867

BRUSH Mrs. Joanna age 62/82y in Sandgate, Vt. September 14, 1867

WHITLOCK Nancy age 62y wife of William in W. Hebron, NY September 16, 1867

STIDFOLE Mary J. age 30y wife of Alfred H. in Whitehall, NY September 24, 1867

HOPKINS Aaron age 75y in Salem, NY September 8, 1867

PUTNAM John P. age 81y in Cambridge, NY October 10, 1867 last surviving descendant of Gen. Israel Putnam of Revolutionary fame

FLETCHER Robert M. in his 20th yr son of Rev. J. of White Creek, NY in the 17th Reg. US Infantry in Hempstead, Tx. September 22, 1867

BOWKER George age 16y son of Henry and Clarissa in Granville, NY October 5, 1867

CRAVER Sally age 74y wife of Stephen Sr. in Whitehall, NY September 23, 1867

PARKE John age 30y in Whitehall, NY September 20, 1867

SHERMAN James age 29y of Whitehall, NY drowned in Montreal October 2, 1867

NEVILLE John H. in his 26th yr in Granville, NY October 4, 1867

PATTERSON Maria age 49y widow of William in Whitehall, NY October 7, 1867

STIDFOLE Frankie age 22d in Whitehall, NY October 6, 1867

LANGWORTHY Mrs. Serina age 64y dau of late Dr. S. **DEAN** of Cambridge, NY in Greenwich, NY October 15, 1867

BANE John age 28y in Cambridge, NY October 13, 1867

ASHTON Elizabeth age 77y wife of Thomas in Argyle, NY October 9, 1867

PRATT Mary L. age 39y wife of Orson S. in Cambridge, NY October 14, 1867

MC DONALD Charles in his 33rd yr in Ft. Edward, NY October 12, 1867

KELLEY Jane (**CUNNINGHAM**) age 27y wife of John in Sandy Hill, NY October 14, 1867

GRANT Wallace age 2y son of Charles H. in N. Granville, NY October 11, 1867

HARRIGAN Michael age 40y in Whitehall, NY October 11, 1867

JILLSON Ann age 81y wife of Joseph in Whitehall, NY October 11, 1867

RHODES Nathan age 79y in N. Granville, NY October 12, 1867

LAKE Sarah age 17y niece of Robert **MC DOWELL** in W. Hebron, NY October 17,

1867

BROWNELL Simeon age 25y formerly of Rennsalaer Co. nephew of Isaac Brownell of White Creek, NY in Galveston, Tx. (newspaper date November 8, 1867)

RANDALL Henry age 19y son of Daniel in Hoosick, NY November 2, 1867

ROBERTSON Archibald age 23y late of 93rd Reg. in Lake, NY November 7, 1867

GILBERT Jordan age 8m 17d son of Judson and Helen A. J. W. in Harlem, NY November 4, 1867

STEVENSON Maggie age 18y dau of Dr. John in N. Argyle, NY November 17, 1867

BEATTIE Alexander H. age 21y son of John H. and Nancy in Salem, NY November 28, 1867

CORNELL Lydia F. age 79y relict of Mathew formerly of Cambridge, NY in Genesee Co. NY November 28, 1867

VAUGHN Curnell age 28y in Salem, NY December 4, 1867

SCHERMERHORN Bartholomew age 78y in Buskirks Bridge, NY December 1, 1867

CANFIELD Lamina age 60y wife of Harmon in Arlington, Vt. December 1, 1867

BARNUM Margaret age 68y wife of Harman in Cambridge, NY December 11, 1867

THOMAS Lucas age 76y in Salem, NY December 8, 1867, served War of 1812

NORTHUP Martha J. age 40y wife of James in Hartford, NY November 30, 1867

SMITH Ezra age 84y in Cambridge, NY December 17, 1867

PITNEY Aramantha C. age 24y wife of E. B. in Cambridge, NY December 20, 1867

CORSE Mrs. Susanna age 55y in Shushan, NY December 21, 1867

SAFFORD Thomas in his 73rd yr in Salem, NY December 24, 1867

MC FARLAND Col. John in his 75th yr in Jackson, NY December 27, 1867

GRISWOLD Sarah abt 55y wife of A. H. in Whitehall, NY December 25, 1867

BLACK Samuel in his 89th yr in Whitehall, NY December 21, 1867

WHEELER James age 82y in Whitehall, NY December 25, 1867

BROWN Eliza age 19y dau of John and Ellen in Salem, NY January 1, 1868

POTTER Anna age 28y wife of Lewis in Easton, NY December 31, 1867

LOOMIS Mrs. Abigail age 66y in Cambridge, NY January 14, 1868

GIBBONS Aaron age 45y in White Creek, NY January 8, 1868

WEST Mrs. Polly age 82y in Jackson, NY January 6, 1868

BARNETT John age 83y in Hoosick, NY January 20, 1868

WALKER John age 96y in Cambridge, NY January 20, 1868

BUCKLEY Mary Frances age 9y in Easton, NY January 14, 1868

REDFIELD Frank A. age 33y 10m in Arlington, Vt. January 27, 1868

PERCY Sarah age 77y in Hoosick, NY January 25, 1868

COULTER James age 30y in Arlington, Vt. February 3, 1868

KIELEY Edward age 22y in Jackson, NY February 7, 1868

MC FARLAND Colin age 89y in Salem, NY February 6, 1868

FONDA William Henry age 41y in Salem, NY February 5, 1868

DOUGLAS Evander M. age 31y in Whitehall, NY February 6, 1868

CONANT Belle abe 26y wife of C. B. in Ft. Edward, NY February 5, 1868

BENSON Caroline abt 40y wife of Hiram in Pittstown, NY February 11, 1868

MONTGOMERY John W. in his 85th yr in Salem, NY February 15, 1868

MC NISH Jane in her 48th yr widow of Ephraim in Salem, NY February 9, 1868

MYERS Nelson age 13y son of William in Schaghticoke, NY February 16, 1868

HOWARD Emma abt 18y dau of Lyman in Jackson, NY February 19, 1868

AUSTIN Daniel in his 68th yr formerly of Washington Co. in Mexico, NY February 12, 1868

BLIVEN Polly age 71y in Kingsbury, NY February 18, 1868

CLARK Mary Edith age 5y dau of Guy W. and Deborah in Sandy Hill, NY February 15, 1868

FISK Thomas B. age 45y in Shushan, NY February 20, 1868

MOORE Hattie G. age 19y dau of John in Jackson, NY February 23, 1868

ROBERTSON Mrs. Jane abt 56y in Jackson, NY February 27, 1868

BILLINGS Abbie age 54y in Arlington, Vt. February 27, 1868

LANGWORTHY Robert age 68y in Greenwich, NY March 4, 1868

HARRELL Sarah Emily age 32y wife of S. L. formerly of White Creek, NY in Syracuse, NY February 16, 1868

JOHNSON Erastus age 27y in White Creek, NY March 7, 1868

O'LEARY Abigail age 39y wife of James in Eagle Bridge, NY March 8, 1868

PARMELEE Sarah age 81y at son-in-laws Rev. **FLETCHER** in Cambridge, NY March 15, 1868

WARNER Maggie W. age 1y 6m dau of Charles D. and Anna in Cambridge, NY March 18, 1868

LYONS Bridget age 28y wife of Patrick in Cambridge, NY March 14, 1868

BARNETT Nathaniel age 76y in Cambridge, NY March 16, 1868

MC MURRAY Mary in her 60th yr wife of Ebenezer in Salem, NY March 15, 1868

WALDS James age 70y in W. Hebron, NY March 17, 1868

MACUMBER Dorcus abt 70y in Cambridge, NY March 23, 1868

MC GILL Sarah age 61y in Hebron, NY March 21, 1868

CRAIG Betsey age 73y in Hebron, NY March 22, 1868

STEVENS _____ age 13m son of Martin in Shushan, NY April 1, 1868

SLOCUM Mrs. Perry abt 80y in Jackson, NY April 1, 1868

MILLIMAN Isaac G. abt 65y in White Creek, NY (newspaper date April 3, 1868)

FOSTER Catherine age 39y wife of William P. in Camden, NY March 31, 1868

SMITH Ella age 16y in Shaftsbury, Vt. April 2, 1868

PARISH John in his 71st yr in Jackson, NY March 21, 1868

MURRELL Hiram abt 86y in Ft. Ann, NY March 19, 1868

MILLER Miss Zeporah age 82y in Cambridge, NY April 5, 1868

WARD John age 5y son of John and Mary in Eagle Bridge, NY April 4, 1868

COLBY Charles Lafayette age 5m 6d son of Abner and Sarah M. in Jackson, NY April 4, 1868

GOULD Abram age 79y in Shushan, NY April 9, 1868

WALLACE Joseph age 68y in White Creek, NY April 7, 1868

ORCUTT Caleb in his 87th yr in Jackson, NY April 10, 1868

FLACK Martha (**FOSTER**) age 38y wife of George in White Creek, NY April 14, 1868

BROWN William age 58y in Cambridge, NY April 11, 1868

PATTERSON Louise age 42y wife of J. C. in Cambridge, NY April 16, 1868

ARNOLD William Henry age 38y in Cambridge, NY April 24, 1868

HALL Henry Merchant age 32/82y (illegible) son of J. Dorr of White Creek, NY in Greenwich, NY April 20, 1868

GRAHAM Thomas formerly of 123rd Reg. in Hebron, NY April 13, 1868

TRIPP Willie age 18m son of Lewis in Cambridge, NY April 20, 1868

BILLINGS Libbie age 4y 1m dau of Henry and Maggie in Jackson, NY April 26, 1868

MC KNIGHT Miss Libbie age 30y in Hebron, NY April 22, 1868

STEVENSON Libbie age 9m dau of William in Cambridge, NY May 12, 1868

MAXWELL Walter J. abt 60y in Jackson, NY May 13, 1868

MC NITT Mary abt 52y wife of B. F. in Cambridge, NY May 14, 1868

CURTIS Samuel in his 60th yr in Greenwich, NY May 1, 1868

BOWER Phebe age 69y 11m wife of Nehemiah in Jackson, NY May 18, 1868

HERMAN Sarah age 31y dau of Merritt **GIFFORD** in Easton, NY May 19, 1868

BROWN Solomon age 65y in Salem, NY May 22, 1868

BARNES Willie L. age 8m son of Horace H. in Salem, NY May 23, 1868

KNAPP Harriet age 24y wife of Merritt in Shushan, NY May 22, 1868

O'BRIEN Mrs. Elizabeth age 70y in Johnsonville, NY May 24, 1868

FOSTER Agnes L. age 22y in Shushan, NY May 27, 1868

ALLEN John age 82y in Cambridge, NY June 2, 1868

IRVIN Mrs. D. J. abt 38y in Hebron, NY June 8, 1868

WHITTAKER Michael age 68y in Cambridge, NY June 21, 1868

RICE Harvey age 66y in Jackson, NY June 21, 1868

MC KIE Almy age 66y in Cambridge, NY June 24, 1868

HILLS Moses age 60y in Hartford, NY June 20, 1868

GARRETT Mrs. Betsey age 92y in Hartford, NY June 20, 1868

SMITH U. Platt age 66y formerly of White Creek in Wyandotte, Mi. June 10, 1868

DUNLOP Sarah Maria age 17y in Sandgate, Vt. June 21, 1868

MILLIMAN Joseph E. in his 33rd yr in Cambridge, NY July 9, 1868

WARNER Solomon W. age 51y in Cambridge, NY July 6, 1868

ROBINSON Charles age 53y in Cambridge, NY July 6, 1868

MILLER Mattie age 97y in N. Greenwich, NY July 12, 1868

MURPHY Ann age 53y wife of Timothy in Salem, NY July 14, 1868

GAINER James abt 36y in Salem, NY July 15, 1868

BOCKES William J. age 52y in Cambridge, NY July 26, 1868

PRATT Ivy J. age 29y wife of William J. in White Creek, NY July 30, 1868

RANSOM Stephen formerly of Washington Co. in Cleveland, Ohio July 28, 1868. Born April 22, 1777 in Watertown, Conn.

HOWE Norman H. age 10m 3d son of Lucien in Cambridge, NY July 29, 1868

RANSOM Eva M. age 3m dau of Edwin in White Creek, NY August 1, 1868

LYNCH Andrew P. age 23y in Cambridge, NY August 11, 1868

PERCY John age 75y in Hoosick, NY August 10, 1868

KITT William age 23y in Hoosick, NY August 7, 1868

HUTCHINS Tyler age 67y in Jackson, NY August 9, 1868

HAYES Bridget age 18y in Buskirks Bridge, NY August 10, 1868

DORR Valentine age 41y in Salem, NY August 14, 1868

BURKE Thomas age 4m son of Daniel and Julia in White Creek, NY August 18, 1868

DYER Miss Ann age 83y at bro John K. in White Creek, NY August 14, 1868

BOWE Maria age 16y in Shushan, NY August 16, 1868

PERCY Jane Maria age 1y 5m 17d dau of Alanson and Amelia A. in Cambridge, NY August 5, 1868

ROBERTSON James S. age 37y in Cambridge, NY August 19,1868

WYATT Alanson age 9m 1d son of A. P. and Adelia E. in Cambridge, NY August 24, 1868

ROWAN Mrs. Susan age 72y in Cambridge, NY August 22, 1868

STEVENS Maria A. age 41y wife of Milton in Shushan, NY September 1, 1868

COULTER Jennett age 30y wife of Alexander in Jackson, NY August 30, 1868 and dau Jennie age 3y died August 11, 1867

PERKINS Joseph age 70y in Salem, NY September 7, 1868

BASCOM Edward S. age 70y in Whitehall, NY September 8, 1868

SWEET Miss Josephine in her 24th yr in Hebron, NY September 3, 1868

BROWNELL Rebecca age 85y in White Creek, NY September 25, 1868

FISK Hannah M. age 31y wife of Peran in Shushan, NY September 21, 1868

WYATT David age 87y in Cambridge, NY September 19, 1868

WHITE Willard W. age 66y in Greenwich, NY September 12, 1868

NORTON Leroy age 47y in Greenwich, NY September 14, 1868

FLOWERS Dewitt age 21y in Salem, NY September 26, 1868

JACKSON Willie E. age 4m 8d son of Edward and Maria S. in Cambridge, NY October 5, 1868

SISSON Burton age 22y in White Creek, NY September 26, 1868

DUEL Stephen age 53y in Buskirks Bridge, NY October 11, 1868

NEWMAN Katie J. **(CONKEY)** age 19y 3m wife of Joel L. in Cambridge, NY October 2, 1868

HUGGINS Mary in Argyle, NY October 7, 1868

ENGLISH Frances A. age 22y 14d dau of Abram J. and Cornelia M. in Cambridge, NY October 21, 1868

BILLINGS Maggie wife of Henry and dau of late Col. John **MC FARLAND** in Jackson, NY November 4, 1868

CLEVELAND Martha age 64y in Salem, NY November 2, 1868

DONAHUE Patrick abt 30y in Salem, NY November 9, 1868

RELIHAN Dennis age 78y in Eagle Bridge, NY November 1, 1868

AGAN Bridget age 70y wife of James in Cambridge, NY November 9, 1868

RICE Hiram A. age 82y in Cambridge, NY November 11, 1868

CORNELL Mary T. in her 68th yr widow of William late of Jackson, NY in Timber Ridge, Vt. October 18, 1868

SHALER May E. age 22y wife of Andrew and dau of Jeremiah **HAXTON** in Cambridge, NY November 23, 1868

BROWN Anna age 44y wife of Daniel in Buskirks Bridge, NY November 21, 1868

PROVAN Keziah age 83y in Sandgate, Vt. November 5, 1868

COLEMAN Nelson M. age 21y in Sandy Hill, NY November 24, 1868

EGERY Miss Jennette age 56y in Poultney, Vt. November 9, 1868

TAFT Henry age 22y of Whitehall, NY in Euclid, Ohio? November 10, 1868

MILLER Mary Ann age 48y wife of William in Cambridge, NY November 28, 1868

SCUDDER Betsey age 55y wife of Benjamin and sis of Mrs. E. B. **HOYT** of Cambridge, NY in Hobart, NY November 26, 1868

MATTISON Reuben age 64y in Shaftsbury, Vt. December 5, 1868

GILLIGAN Katie A. age 22y wife of Ambrose in Whitehall, NY December 11, 1868

JONES Edward age 4y son of Edward S. and Julia A. **(HOUGHTON)** in Cambridge, NY December 17, 1868

HOLCOMB Olive age 19y in Dresden, NY December 12, 1868

MANVILLE Bennett age 63y in Whitehall, NY December 14, 1868

WRIGHT Minnie age 12y in N. Easton, NY December 20, 1868

LIDDLE James I. age 52y of Salem, NY in Utica Asylum December 11, 1868

KING Hugh abt 40y in Argyle, NY December 20, 1868

KINNEY Julia age 45y in Argyle, NY December 21, 1868

SHEPHERD Jennie E. age 30y wife of Julian in Greenwich, NY December 21, 1868

OVIATT George Lamb age 8y 3m 22d son of Amanda F. and late Clark in Shushan, NY December 22, 1868

MC DONALD Patrick age 38y in Salem, NY January 1, 1869

TISDALE Susan age 21y dau of H. G. in Whitehall, NY December 29, 1868

RATHBUN Mariette age 21y wife of William in Whitehall, NY December 20, 1868

HOVER A. D. abt 21y in Cambridge, NY January 4, 1869

HULST Jemima age 60y 6m in Easton, NY (newspaper date January 15, 1869)

STONE Col. Charles in her 83rd yr in Sandy Hill, NY December 31, 1869

CULVER Isaac W. in his 80th yr in Jackson, NY January 8, 1869

HYDE Frances Elizabeth age 30y wife of James T. and dau of C. L. ALLEN in Salem, NY January 17, 1869

BENTLEY Hiram age 22y in Cambridge, NY January 14, 1869

ENSIGN Stephen age 50y in Easton, NY January 16, 1869

BENNETT Benjamin age 56y in White Creek, NY January 16, 1869

STEWART Sarah F. in her 73rd yr widow of David in Salem, NY January 23, 1869

BROUGHTON Ira age 76y of Salem, NY in Hampton, NY January 19, 1869

CORNELL Augustus age 21y in Easton, NY January 23, 1869

CULVER James S. age 36y formerly of Greenwich, NY in Iowa City, Iowa January 25, 1869

SANFORD Cora age 36y wife of Milo in Whitehall, NY January 28, 1869

WILSON Mattie age 10m 13d dau of Oliver and Christy A. in Salem, NY February 1, 1869

SWEET Louisa age 28y wife of Loren in White Creek, NY February 5, 1869

TUCKER Dennis age 41y in Sandgate, Vt. February 8, 1869

WICKERSON Joseph age 77y in Sandgate, Vt. January 22, 1869

SHERMAN Theresa L. age 21y dau of Henry O. and Hulda in Greenwich, NY February 28, 1869

JOHNSON Mary age 85y in White Creek, NY February 14, 1869

MC NAMARA Kieran age 60y in Jackson, NY February 15, 1869

WHITNEY Erastus age 78y 7m in Center Falls, NY February 15, 1869

FAXON Millie M. age 16y in Greenwich, NY February 14, 1869

TILTON William age 77y in Buskirks Bridge, NY February 14, 1869

MC CLELLAN James R. age 36y in Jackson, NY February 18, 1869

HOOSE Sarah E. age 24y in Jackson, NY February 20, 1869

LOURIE Mary H. wife of James L. in Greenwich, NY February 21, 1869

GRAHAM Adeline (**BILLINGS**) wife of Rev. E. in Canada (newspaper date February 26, 1869)

COTTRELL Delia age 38y wife of Charles H. in Greenwich, NY March 2, 1869

DOBBIN Maria age 59y wife of John in Greenwich, NY March 2, 1869

CURTIS Lydia Ann age 65y wife of John B. February 27, 1869

BARTON Richard age 69y in Cambridge, NY February 28, 1869

MERRILL Henry C. age 34y of Cambridge, NY in New York February 27, 1869

MC FARLAND John age 74y in Greenwich, NY March 1, 1869

ROBERTSON Sarah Ann age 42y wife of James in Cambridge, NY March 9, 1869

MC FARLAND Daniel age 76y in Jackson, NY March 9, 1869

WILMARTH Josephine age 24y wife of George in Greenwich, NY March 12, 1869

ROBERTSON William in his 31st yr in Salem, NY March 15, 1869

PORTER Aurelia age 74y in Cambridge, NY March 13, 1869, sons Charles and Addison

CHUBB Mrs. Betsey age 78y in Greenwich, NY March 3, 1869

MASTERS Blanche age 2y dau of N. M. M. in Greenwich, NY March 10, 1869

ASHTON Thomas age 75y in N. Argyle, NY March 22, 1869

CRUIKSHANK Bertha age 6m dau of James A. and Sarah E. in Salem, NY March 12, 1869

WORKS Alida I. wife of Prof. Adam Works in Ft. Edward, NY March 12, 1869

FOWLER Reynolds age 57y in Eagle Bridge, NY May 12, 1869

MUNSON William age 76y in Hebron, NY March 26, 1869

BRADFORD Alonzo abt 36y in Belcher, NY March 30, 1869

MC GEOCH Mary Eliza in her 21st yr in Hebron, NY March 25, 1869

CONNELLY Margaret abt 21y in W. Hebron, NY March 24, 1869

RICHARDS Andrew age 5y died March 27, 1869 and Hattie age 3y children of A. D. and Mary E. in Greenwich, NY

MC DOUGAL Alex E. abt 66y in Argyle, NY March 29, 1869

BARBER Jane age 33y wife of Capt. Erastus in Greenwich, NY March 17, 1869

ROBERTSON Fred A. age 5y son of Alfred and Mabel in Greenwich, NY March 27, 1869

MC CLELLAN Johnie E. age 4m son of John and Emeline in Jackson, NY March 16, 1869

MC CLELLAN Emma E. age 4y dau of William and Charlotte in Jackson, NY April 5, 1869

SMITH George age 60y formerly of Jackson, NY in N. Adams, NY April 3, 1869

ROBERTSON Martha age 17y dau of William and Agnes in Jackson, NY April 5, 1869

WITHERELL Alanson age 64y in Eagle Bridge, NY April 2, 1869

BROWNELL Otis D. age 24y in Easton, NY March 24, 1869

HAWLEY Ransom age 71y in Cambridge, NY April 11, 1869

POOR Julia age 58y wife of David and Mother of Clark in Saratoga Springs, NY April 12, 1869

TEFFT Asael age 43y in Galesville, NY April 7, 1869

OSGOOD Maria in her 53rd yr wife of Rev. David in Argyle, NY March 30, 1869

JENNENS William Henry age 6y son of B. W. in Greenwich, NY April 11, 1869

KING Fenner E. age 43y formerly of Cambridge in Corydon, Io. March 30, 1869

CAREY Catherine widow of John of Belcher, NY in Troy, NY April 18, 1869

WEIR Edwin age 43 in Cambridge, NY April 9, 1869

GILLIS Lucy F. in her 77th yr in Salem, NY February 18, 1869

DAVIS Jonathan in his 85th yr in N. Granville, NY April 19, 1869

ADAMS Roxanna age 69y in Greenwich, NY April 18, 1869

TEFFT Harriet wife of John H. in Easton, NY April 27, 1869

BUCK Eliza age 51y wife of James P. in Kingsbury, NY April 14, 1869

MATTOCK Anna (**JONES**) age 53y in Sandy Hill, NY April 18, 1869

HOLBROOK Fremont age 9y son of Amariah in Sandy Hill, NY April 8, 1869

WHITE Charles J. Md. age 65y in Hebron, NY April 25, 1869

HAYWARD Layman age 80y in Whitehall, NY April 21, 1869

TANNER Sarah age 67y wife of Joshua in Cambridge, NY April 26, 1869

MAXWELL Margaret age 78y wife of George in Jackson, NY May 2, 1869

HUNT Emily abt 21y wife of Lewis in Buskirks Bridge, NY May 4, 1869

MOORE Francis F. age 27y in Whitehall, NY April 30, 1869

JAMES Henry G. age 29m son of Rev. D. T. in Whitehall, NY April 26, 1869

BOSWORTH Eunicy age 24y wife of Harvey M. in Center Falls, NY April 30, 1869

BROOKS Matilda age 48y in Easton, NY April 30, 1869

MC MILLAN John age 48y in Argyle, NY April 30, 1869

MC KIE James age 64y in White Creek, NY May 5, 1869

STACKHOUSE Jerusha age 53y wife of Joseph in Cambridge, NY May 6, 1869

DURFEE Martha C. age 42y wife of Mathew in Cambridge, NY May 8, 1869

JONES John age 56y in White Creek, NY May 9, 1869

MARCH Lorenzo D. abt 54y in Hoosick, NY May 13, 1869

SPENCER Amy age 6m 6d died April 18, 1869 and Claudia age 2y 11m died May 9, 1869 children of Almon and Caroline in Cambridge, NY

BARNHART Joseph age 79y in Eagle Bridge, NY May 13, 1869

BROWN Jenet age 94y in Hartford, NY May 13, 1869

BOISE Mrs. ____ age 80y relict of Joseph in Greenwich, NY May 16, 1869

REMINGTON Ethan age 2y son of Luke and Margaret in Easton, NY May 12, 1869

FLOOD James age 18y in Salem, NY May 17, 1869

NILES Elizabeth age 23y 10m 27d wife of Henry G. in White Creek, NY May 19, 1869

MC MILLAN George age 73y in Argyle, NY May 15, 1869

GAY Amanda T. age 71y wife of Joel in White Creek, NY May 22, 1869

ARMSTRONG Elizabeth age 63y wife of George in Jackson, NY May 22, 1869

OSTRANDER Richard age 77y in Hoosick, NY May 12, 1869

MC GOWAN Michael age 30y in Easton, NY May 14, 1869

PRUYN William N. age 52y 13d in White Creek, NY May 23, 1869

SHERMAN Isaac in his 72nd yr in Salem, NY April 17, 1869

NORTON Ann Maria age 2m dau of William S. and Katie in Salem, NY May 19, 1869

COLLINS Mrs. ____ age 33y widow of John formerly of Granville, NY in Troy, NY May 21, 1869

BALCH John H. age 45y in Cambridge, NY May 30, 1869

DAILEY Mary C. age 27y 4m 15d wife of C. A. in Ft. Miller, NY May 12, 1869

ROBERSON Alfred age 42y in Greenwich, NY May 29, 1869

SHIELDS William H. in his 51st yr in Salem, NY May 25, 1869

CLARK Maggie J. age 1y 9m dau of John M. and Mary in Salem, NY May 22, 1869

MONTGOMERY Betsey E. age 73y widow of Hugh in Hebron, NY May 25, 1869

MILLER Agnes age 27y in Greenwich, NY May 31, 1869

DUNSON Miss Martha J. in her 21st yr in Whitehall, NY June 1, 1869

SHELDON Nancy E. age 20y dau of William in Rupert, Vt. June 7, 1869

CORNELL Jane in her 83rd yr in Argyle, NY June 5, 1869

LEARD John age 26y in Hampton, NY June 2, 1869

JONES Thomas age 23y in White Creek, NY June 9, 1869

HERRINGTON Mrs. Bentley age 42y in Greenwich, NY June 7, 1869

BROWNELL Emily age 5y in Cambridge, NY June 10, 1869

CLEVELAND Fannie age 24y wife of Henry and dau of C. **ADAMS** in Shushan, NY June 12, 1869

WEBSTER Nancy age 71y in Cambridge, NY June 12, 1869

PIERCE Hosea A. age 25y in White Creek, NY June 12, 1869

HOY James age 77y of Hobert, NY formerly of Cambridge, NY at brother-in-laws James **ROBERTSON** in Cambridge, NY (newspaper date June 18, 1869)

LEACH Gertrude age 10m dau od Charles B. in Argyle, NY June 14, 1869

SMITH Frederick age 7y 6m son of Russell and Louvina in Salem, NY June 13, 1869

FREEMAN Marvin age 68y in Salem, NY June 13, 1869

FORD Mrs. Jane age 81y in Whitehall, NY June 9, 1869

MC COY Charles A. age 4m 1d son of Charles and Margaret in Salem, NY June 21, 1869

PRUYN Franklin age 77y in Buskirks Bridge, NY June 19, 1869

LANE Clark D. age 55y in Shaftsbury, Vt. June 21, 1869

REID Alexander age 80y in Argyle, NY June 23, 1869

LANE Mrs. Amy E. age 29y in Shaftsbury, Vt. June 24, 1869

MC NAUGHTON Gen. John in his 80th yr in Salem, NY June 27, 1869

WATT Mrs. Jane age 45y in Shushan, NY June 26, 1869

PATTISON Samuel in his 58th yr in E. Salem, NY June 27, 1869

KENYON Mrs. Joseph age 26y in Greenwich, NY June 28, 1869

SPENCER Frances age 30y wife of David in Cambridge, NY June 23, 1869

CLARK Daniel in his 80th yr in Hebron, NY June 28, 1869

MC NISH Frances Maria wife of Thomas of Cambridge, NY at bro A. M. BINNINGER in New York July 4, 1869

WRIGHT Nelson age 24y 1m 13d in Putnam, NY July 14, 1869

PURCELL Michael age 23y in Hebron, NY July 17, 1869

MC DOUGAL Jane age 59y widow of John in Argyle, NY July 29, 1869

SHANNON Robert abt 55y in Argyle, NY August 4, 1869

ANDERSON Amanda P. in his 17th yr in Putnam, NY August 2, 1869

LAMB Mary Lucy age 9m dau of Leroy and Sarah M. in Ft. Ann, NY July 29, 1869

WILSON Mrs. ____ age 90y Mother of George in Hebron, NY July 27, 1869

WEIR Emeline in her 58th yr wife of Justin in Greenwich, NY July 29, 1869

WOODARD Xenothon age 62y in Greenwich, NY August 3, 1869

KERSLAKE Robert Arthur age 3m son of Thomas and Jane in Salem, NY August 9, 1869

SAFFORD Leroy Adelbert age 16y son of J. B. in Greenwich, NY August 4, 1869

RUSSELL George H. age 24y 6m in White Creek, NY June 7, 1869

LAMB George E. age 5y 2m in Ft. Edward, NY August 13, 1869

HARRIS Eva age 10y in Ft. Edward, NY August 12, 1869

CHASE Elizabeth age 34y wife of Julius and infant son in Ft. Ann, NY August 18, 1869

MC MAHON Ann S. widow in her 47th yr in Salem, NY August 19, 1869

CARTER Stevie age 2y son of Henry and Jennie in Whitehall, NY August 20, 1869

O'DONNELL James age 46y in Jackson, NY August 26, 1869

GORDON Maria abt 58y in Pittstown, NY September 7, 1869

JONES Daniel age 20y in Shaftsbury, Vt. September 4, 1869

DECKER Abram age 45y in Cambridge, NY September 8, 1869

DUNHAM Abigail age 79y in Jackson, NY September 9, 1869

COOK C. C. age 59y in Greenwich, NY September 4, 1869

BURDICK Daniel age 24y son of David in Easton, NY September 1, 1869

ROBEDEAU Nellie age 22y 7m 10d wife of C. T. and dau of J. **WINN** of Ft. Edward, NY in Salem, NY September 9, 1869

ALLEN Mrs. Margaret age 67y formerly of Cambridge, NY in Lawrence, Ks. August 26, 1869

BIGELOW Anson in his 75th yr of White Creek, NY at son-in-laws George M. **GRIFFIN** in Albany, NY September 15, 1869

GIFFORD Benjamin abt 45y in Cambridge, NY September 14, 1869

MURPHY Jerry abt 60y in Arlington, Vt. September 13, 1869

AMOS William age 22y (colored) in Argyle, NY September 14, 1869

CORBETT Mary E. in her 20th yr wife of Albert and dau of Simeon F. **FOSTER** in Shushan, NY September 17, 1869

WALKER Willie C. age 14d son of William and Mary H. in E. Greenwich, NY September 1, 1869

WELLING Margaret age 60y wife of R. P. in Cambridge, NY September 18, 1869

DUNLOP James age 18y son of William in Sandgate, Vt. September 22, 1869

GREEN Edward age 2y son of Alex and Sophia in Coila, NY September 23, 1869

BOWKER James Henry age 15y son of Almon and Sarah Jane in Jackson, NY September 24, 1869

SAFFORD Elizabeth age 67y wife of Thomas in Salem, NY September 30, 1869

ROSS Sarah M. age 30y wife of William in Salem, NY October 2, 1869

GOODRICH Nancy age 59y widow of Alvin in Salem, NY September 28, 1869

HOYT Franklin J. age 47y in Lansingburgh, NY September 28, 1869

BENNETT Martha age 1y 2w dau of Thomas in Cambridge, NY October 9, 1869

EDIE William J. age 26y son of William in E. Salem, NY October 11, 1869

ANDREWS Miss Mary age 20y in Shaftsbury, Vt. October 12, 1869

PEASE Mrs. Sybil abt 70y in Arlington, Vt. October 1, 1869

CLEMENTS Mrs. Daniel age 59y in W. Hebron, NY October 4, 1869

BOSWORTH Eveline age 38y wife of Henry in Pittstown, NY October 14, 1869

LYTLE Rev. David age 43y in Rock City Falls, NY October 13, 1869

SMITH Pauline Y. age 27y dau of James in Coila, NY October 17, 1869

DECKER Emily age 37y wife of Charles in Easton, NY October 17, 1869

ARMITAGE Dell age 14y dau of James and Eliza in Hoosick, NY October 20, 1869

RUSSELL Francis age 48y in Belcher, NY October 20, 1869

PRATT Lennie age 1y 7m son of Henry L. and Katie in Smiths Basin, NY October 13, 1869

GROAT Allen age 54y in Arlington, Vt. October 23, 1869

COWAN Tracy age 46y of Whitehall, NY in Shushan, NY October 25, 1869

DIMMICK Emma age 15y dau of William in Cambridge, NY October 24, 1869

HYLAND Nicolas D. age 38y in Sandy Hill, NY October 23, 1869

CASEY James age 32y in M. Granville, NY October 19, 1869

CONKEY Matilda age 28y wife of William in Arlington, Vt. October 29, 1869

MATHERS Mary P. age 31y 15d wife of Alfred S. and dau of Artemus **PRATT** of Clarendon, Vt. in Rutland, Vt. October 28, 1869

ADAMS Charles E. age 20y son of George in Whitehall, NY October 26, 1869

BIRGE Thadeus age 85y formerly of Whitehall, NY Father of Mrs. Walter J. **DONNELLY** of Northampton, Mass. October 27, 1869

ARMITAGE Margaret age 76y in Cambridge, NY November 5, 1869

WEIR George H. age 31y in Cambridge, NY November 6, 1869

ROSS William age 30y in Salem, NY November 5, 1869 and Fannie age 2y 9m 10d dau of William and Sarah M. died November 19, 1869

CLARK Mrs. Addie S. age 27y in Salem, NY November 14, 1869

HALL Jane wife of David in Sandy Hill, NY November 13, 1869

SMITH Maria dau of widow Smith in Sandy Hill, NY November 13, 1869

THOMPSON Dr. Cephas in his 80th yr in S. Granville, NY November 20, 1869

ALBRO Charlie age 4y son of Charles in Ft. Edward, NY November 23, 1869

CARLETON Orville N. age 48y in Kingsbury, NY November 20, 1869

VAN RENSSELAER Jane age 72y 10m wife of Henry P. and dau of Gen. J. A. **FORT** in Clarack, NY November 25, 1869

SOVERN Sarah E. age 27y wife of William in Cambridge, NY November 26, 1869

WOOD Squire M. age 19y in White Creek, NY November 28, 1869

ROBERTSON Alexander L. son of Mary and late William of Cambridge, NY in Hempstead, Tx. November 25, 1869

SEARLE Frank age 28y in Easton, NY December 9, 1869

PLACE Miss Phoebe age 78y in Greenwich, NY November 24, 1869

MALADY Patrick age 45y in Cambridge, NY December 12, 1869

TINKHAM Anson abt 3y son of Daniel and Huldy in Bennington, Vt. November 30, 1869

RUSSELL Laura in her 25th yr wife of Henry and dau of Orrin **HOWARD** in Ft. Ann, NY December 15, 1869

HUDSON Charles Edward age 11w son of James and Hannah in White Creek, NY December 22, 1869

SULLIVAN Margaret age 45y wife of Patrick in Cambridge, NY December 20, 1869

CLARK Eliza R. age 28y wife of Myron in Shaftsbury, Vt. December 26, 1869

KINNERSON Mrs. Nathan abt 60y in Easton, NY December 25, 1869

BLANCHARD Miss Guly age 45y in Greenwich, NY December 26, 1869

PERRY Alexander age 24y 5m in S. Easton, NY January 2, 1870

TAYLOR John T. age 76y in Ft. Edward, NY December 24, 1869

BRADLEY Jeremiah age 36y in Ft. Edward, NY December 21, 1869

CARROLL Owen age 68y in Sandy Hill, NY December 23, 1869

WELLS Mrs. Elizabeth age 77y in Cambridge, NY January 4, 1870

LOCKROW William A. age 58y in Cambridge, NY January 9, 1870

BUTTON Margaret age 51y wife of C. N. in Cambridge, NY January 10, 1870

KIERNAN George N. age 21y in Whitehall, NY January 4, 1870

GIBBS Arthur G. age 1y 6m son of Dr. L. in Ft. Ann, NY January 2, 1870

BRIGGS George age 6y son of D. O. in Ft. Ann, NY January 3, 1870

MAXWELL Alexander B. age 24y son of Alexander of Jackson, NY in Kenosha, Wis. December 29, 1869

LATIMER Joseph age 31y formerly of Cambridge in New York January 13, 1870

COLEMAN Lettie S. (THOMAS) age 26y wife of Warren D. in Sandy Hill, NY January 8, 1870

WAIT Martha and Mary age 7w twin dau of L. R. in Ft. Ann, NY January 4, 1870

BREWER Charley abt 7y son of Leroy and Manima in Greenwich, NY January 16, 1870

RUSSELL Jane age 50y 10m 9d in White Creek, NY January 17, 1870

WOODCOCK Lucinda age 69y Mother of Israel in Dresden, NY January 5, 1870

DENNIS George age 57y in Whitehall, NY January 17, 1870

CARPENTER Hannah age 28y wife of David in Greenwich, NY January 7, 1870

SPENCER Harry age 2y 10m son of William and Emma in Greenwich, NY January 10, 1870

MOORE Eli age 86y 7m 28d in Queensbury, NY January 16, 1870

LESLIE Libbie A. age 13y dau of George and Catherine in Argyle, NY December 20, 1869

HATCH Solomon age 74y in Jackson, NY January 22, 1870

AYLSWORTH Edward M. age 54y 11m 4d in Arlington, Vt. January 21, 1870

MC LEAN Alexander age 77y bro of Ebenezer formerly of Cambridge, NY in Manchester, Vt. January 29, 1870

ODBERT Mrs. Rose Ann age 69y in Salem, NY February 6, 1870

MOFFIT Polly age 78y widow in Hebron, NY January 25, 1870

HORTON Hiram age 72y in Jackson, NY February 9, 1870

WILSON James in E. Hebron, NY February 14, 1870

MC INTYRE Mrs. John in W. Hebron, NY February 17, 1870

MILLER Adeline age 54y wife of Nicolas in Battenville, NY February 14, 1870

SHALEY Willie age 2m son of William G. and Seraph in Jackson, NY February 11, 1870

LYONS George R. age 29y 7m in Easton, NY January 15, 1870

LINDSAY Jane abt 2y dau of Peter and Ann in Cambridge, NY February 20, 1870

KELLEY William abt 6y son of William and Bridget in Cambridge, NY February 21, 1870

GLASCOW Phoebe Ann age 41y dau of John **ROBERTSON** of Coila, NY in Washington, Iowa February 11, 1870

SMITH Julia M. age 28y wife of Charles A. and dau of Galvin **FENTON** in Greenwich, NY February 15, 1870

WAIT A. D. Jr. age 7y 11m in Ft. Edward, NY February 25, 1870

WILSON Lemuel in his 74th yr at son-in-laws J. F. **CLARK** in Whitehall, NY February 24, 1870

WAIT Job age 30y formerly of Cambridge, NY in Muncie, Ind. February 28, 1870

MAYNARD X. J. age 37y in Cambridge, NY March 5, 1870

SKINNER William M. age 32y son of F. B. in Houston, Tx. March 1, 1870

WALDO Mrs. Jane age 62y in Hebron, NY February 13, 1870

LAW Narcissa A. age 22y dau of Rev. James and A. B. formerly of Cambridge, NY in Philadelphia, Pa. March 14, 1870

SKINNER Elizabeth in her 79th yr in Argyle, NY March 11, 1870

EDIE Anna Mary age 19y dau of Robinson in Cambridge, NY March 14, 1870

FOSTER Charles H. in his 24th yr in Greenwich, NY March 15, 1870

FORSYTHE Hattie age 2y 6m dau of J. C. and P. M. in Salem, NY March 21, 1870

WRIGHT David P. age 76y formerly of White Creek in Scriba, NY March 17, 1870

FORT E. age 6w son of Elmer and Maggie E. **VANDENBURGH** in White Creek, NY March 20, 1870

BROWN Rufus in his 67th yr in Sandy Hill, NY March 12, 1870

LANGWORTHY Seth in his 58th yr in Greenwich, NY March 19, 1870

RICE Dr. P. Hilton age 53y son of late Clark in Liberty, Miss. March 1, 1870

DAWLEY Addie age 28y wife of George P. in Greenwich, NY March 23, 1870

ROWLAND Ruth age 68y wife of Jeardus in White Creek, NY (newspaper date April 1, 1870)

AUSTIN Thomas age 75y in Cambridge, NY March 30, 1870

SELLECK Aaron age 72y in Greenwich, NY April 4, 1870

ELDRIDGE Job age 77y in Easton, NY April 5, 1870

KERKIN Maggie age 21y dau of Thomas and Mary in Jackson, NY April 1, 1870

DEXTER Elijah abt 78y in Cambridge, NY April 2, 1870

WRIGHT Mrs. La Vendee age 75y in Ft. Edward, NY April 13, 1870

LAW Agnes E. age 31y wife of William in Shushan, NY April 19, 1870

MC INTYRE Mary age 3y 9m dau of Freeman and Sarah M. in W. Hebron, NY April 18, 1870

LAW Johnie Potter age 11d son of William in Shushan, NY April 23, 1870

CANFIELD Anson M. age 26y in Arlington, Vt. April 25, 1870

BREWER Parmelia age 65y relict of Peter in Shushan, NY April 25, 1870

HICKS Joseph in M. Granville, NY April 24, 1870

DWELLE Elizabeth M. age 38y dau of Alphonso in Greenwich, NY April 29, 1870

BURCH Henry age 92y in Easton, NY April 28, 1870

DAY William age 77y in Greenwich, NY May 1, 1870

ENGLISH Barnabus age 63y in Cambridge, NY April 30, 1870

FOWLER William J. age 13y 8m son of James P. in Cambridge, NY April 30, 1870

WEIR William W. age 24y in Salem, NY May 1, 1870

AKIN Amanda age 69y in Cambridge, NY May 9, 1870

MC LEAN Elizabeth in her 43rd yr dau of T. K. in Greenwich, NY May 13, 1870

WEEKS James Edward age 14y son of Charles in Greenwich, NY May 13, 1870

JOSLIN Maria (**WAIT**) age 62y in Hoosick, NY May 12, 1870

ARNOTT Prudence in her 50th yr in Coila, NY March 7, 1870

ARNOTT Mary Ann in her 63rd yr in Coila, NY March 28, 1870

ROBERTSON Harriet age 54y wife of Barber in Greenwich, NY May 23, 1870

STEVENSON Jane Florence age 6m 2d dau of John A. and Elizabeth in Coila, NY May 23, 1870

HUTTON Alexander age 35y in Greenwich, NY May 25, 1870

ROBERTSON Isabel age 85y wife of James in Borodino, NY May 18, 1870

SAFFORD Sarah age 53y wife of Gideon in Salem, NY May 31, 1870

JOHNSON Edward age 72y in Ft. Ann, NY June 5, 1870

ACKLEY Rhoby age 63y in Cambridge, NY June 7, 1870

HERRINGTON Esther age 44y wife of John in Cambridge, NY May 29, 1870

MEADER Lydia J. in her 24th yr in Greenwich, NY June 11, 1870

NOBLE Hiram K. age 69y in Troy, NY June 19, 1870

CROCKER Anna age 31y wife of William C. in Washington, DC June 17, 1870

SPENCER Oscar age 40y in Greenwich, NY June 18, 1870

DONAHUE David age 46y in Greenwich, NY June 19, 1870

TRIPP Lucy abt 65y in Argyle, NY June 12, 1870

BRIENAN Mary age 30y in Argyle, NY June 19, 1870

MC GEOCH William age 31y in Jackson, NY June 20, 1870

WRIGHT Robert age 78y in Cambridge, NY June 26, 1870

DELANEY Katie age 22y wife of John in Cambridge, NY June 20, 1870

STEELE William J. age 56y 10m in Shushan, NY July 1, 1870

BURNHAM Anna Maria age 69y relict of William E. in Greenwich, NY July 5, 1870

TINGUE George in his 33rd yr son of Charles of Cambridge, NY in Greenwich, NY July 3, 1870

POTTER James age 71y in W. Ft. Ann, NY June 24, 1870

WEST John abt 3y son of Morris and Kate in E. Salem, NY July 9, 1870

HUBBARD Jonathan age 81y in Cambridge, NY July 9, 1870

THORNTON Thomas age 57y in Cambridge, NY July 11, 1870

SHERMAN Betsey age 87y widow of Seeley in Salem, NY June 29, 1870

SMITH Parmelia age 68y widow of Edward in Sandgate, Vt. (newspaper date July 15, 1870)

SHEELIEU Bartholomew age 3y 8m son of Edward and Mary in Cambridge, NY July 13, 1870

HALL Susan age 41y wife of J. Dorr in Cambridge, NY July 12, 1870

MOWRY Charles T. in Greenwich, NY July 11, 1870

KETCHUM Peter age 66y in Cambridge, NY July 20, 1870

HAGGERTY Thomas age 23y in Cambridge, NY July 14, 1870

FISHER Kate age 6m dau of Wesley and Eliza in Cambridge, NY July 18, 1870

HAMLIN John in his 84th yr in Camden, NY June 24, 1870

SAVAGE Mrs. Susan age 62y in Granville, NY July 5, 1870

LARMAN Harry R. inf. son of John and Frances in Eagle Bridge, NY July 9, 1870

HARVEY Julia B. age 57y wife of George in Saratoga, NY July 19, 1870

HUNT John P. in Cambridge, NY July 18, 1870

BURDICK Winter in Easton, NY July 13, 1870

MC MORRIS Anna M. age 28y dau of William and Anna Eliza of Salem, NY in

Jerseyville, Ill. July 19, 1870

CLEVELAND John W. in his 74th yr formerly of Salem, NY in Wethersfield, NY (newspaper date July 29, 1870)

BULLIONS Lewis H. age 24y in Racine, Wis. (newspaper date July 29, 1870)

HAYWOOD Charles age 40y in Hoosick, NY July 24, 1870

HUNT Mrs. Nancy abt 73y in W. Easton, NY July 24, 1870

COYNE Margaret A. age 4m dau of Patrick and Bridget in Cambridge, NY July 24, 1870

FERGUSON Sarah age 25y dau of William in Hebron, NY July 28, 1870

MAYNARD Elisha abt 65y in Hebron, NY July 26, 1870

WHITTAKER Eliza wife of Benjamin C. in Jackson, NY July 26, 1870

HERRINGTON Sarah Ann wife of Job in Cambridge, NY July 30, 1870

HAWKINS William H. age 26y in Argyle, NY August 6, 1870

ROBINSON Charles age 36y in Shushan, NY August 17, 1870

JOY Frankie B. age 6y son of Benjamin and Helen M. in Hoosick NY August 8, 1870

ELDRIDGE Polly in her 72nd yr wife of Ahira August 23, 1870

CHASE Ida A. age 4y dau of John B. and Ann H. August 19, 1870

ALLEN Fannie W. age 5m 20d dau of James H. and Maria formerly of Salem, NY in Emporia, Ks. August 16, 1870

GETTY Miss Jane W. age 79y 7m in Salem, NY August 22, 1870

INGALLS Loretta age 15y dau of James and Susan in Belcher, NY August 21, 1870

CRARY Nellie age 7m dau of John S. in Salem, NY August 22, 1870

NILES ____ age 2m son of L. in White Creek, NY August 25, 1870

FORT Garrett age 75y in Cambridge, NY August 17, 1870

CLARK John B. age 75y in Lake, NY August 20, 1870

GILCHRIST Alexander age 71y in Cambridge, NY August 27, 1870

GILCHRIST Lena age 11w dau of Archibald and Mary in White Creek, NY August

30, 1870

CRAMER Peter in his 83rd yr in Ft. Ann, NY August 31, 1870

HALL Ira in his 74th yr in Ft. Ann, NY August 18, 1870

BAIN David abt 60y in Argyle, NY August 9, 1870

RUSSELL Kate May age 15m dau of William A. and Mattie in Salem, NY August 29, 1870

ROACH John age 3y son of Thomas and Margaret in Eagle Bridge, NY September 1, 1870

COFFIN Lizzie May age 2m 17d dau of Robert A. and Minnie M. in Cambridge, NY August 20, 1870

FOLEY Thomas in his 74th yr in Cambridge, NY September 6, 1870

TEFFT Margaret age 48y wife of Lewis in Galesville, NY August 27, 1870

ROCK George W. age 6y in Eagle Bridge, NY September 3, 1870

MARSHALL Agnes abt 3y died September 2, 1870 and Rose Emma age 1y 8m 16d died September 17, 1870 children of Richard and Ann in Eagle Bridge, NY

YOULEN Lucy age 86y widow of Jeremiah in W. Rupert, Vt. September 6, 1870

GILES B. F. in Pawlet, Vt. September 6, 1870

SAFFORD Mrs. Nathan age 87y in Argyle, NY September 9, 1870

HERMAN Eva age 6m dau of Charles and Lydia in Schuylerville, NY September 11, 1870

HOVER Charles age 6y son of Henry and Anna Maria in White Creek, NY September 14, 1870

MC FARLAND Will age 21y son of Samuel in Jackson, NY September 14, 1870

BATES Eliza A. age 67y widow of Merritt in Traverse City, Mi. August 27, 1870

KEITH Lyman B. age 66y formerly of Jackson, NY in Otsego, Iowa August 2, 1870

WOODWORTH Jennett age 54y wife of C. V. K. in N. Smithfield, Pa. (newspaper date September 22, 1870)

RICE Henry age 79y in White Creek, NY September 17, 1870

ARMITAGE Freddie age 2y 6m son of James in Hoosick, NY September 18, 1870

CRANDALL John age 31y in White Creek, NY September 19, 1870

RUSSELL Mrs. Dolly age 76y in White Creek, NY September 19, 1870

DOIG Paul in his 70th yr in Jackson, NY September 6, 1870

DENNIS James abt 80y in Argyle, NY September 19, 1870

YOULEN John P. age 60y in W. Rupert, Vt. September 19, 1870

JOHNSTON Jane age 46y wife of David in Salem, NY September 17, 1870

LINCOLN John age 87y in Hebron, NY September 20, 1870

SCOTT Eddy age 16m son of Abner Q. and Sarah in Argyle, NY September 14, 1870

NORTON Abigail age 70y wife of Warren E. in Salem, NY September 21, 1870

BURKE Annie Louisa age 10y dau of S. M. in Greenwich, NY September 23, 1870

WILLIAMSON Jane age 33y wife of James in Argyle, NY September 22, 1870

THOMPSON Jane M. age 47y widow of Isaac in Jackson, NY September 28, 1870

WILLIAMS Nathan in his 40th yr in Salem, NY (newspaper date October 7, 1870)

GILLIS Miss Eliza M. age 30y in Argyle, NY September 27, 1870

RELIHAN Maggie age 3y 3m dau of Cornelius in White Creek, NY October 10, 1870

SWEET Minerva age 24y wife of John in Hoosick, NY October 11, 1870

SALISBURY John age 57y in Jackson, NY October 11, 1870

BINNINGER Abram Merritt age 69y in New York October 17, 1870

WHITE Willie age 3y 8m son of Charles and Sarah E. in Argyle, NY (newspaper date October 21, 1870)

WEED Charles A. age 61y in Jackson, NY October 20, 1870

MC AFEE William age 62y in Jackson, NY October 22, 1870

AUSTIN Lewis in his 60th yr in Salem, NY October 24, 1870

WHITLOCK William T. age 3y 5m 6d son of Arthur in Salem, NY October 30, 1870

MC DERMONT Thomas age 67y in Salem, NY October 30, 1870

BROWNELL Albert C. age 26y formerly of White Creek, NY in Peoria, Ill. October

23, 1870

MC ARTHUR John P. abt 45y in Jackson, NY November 4, 1870

BLAIR Robert age 4y 10m son of John and Frances **LARMAN** October 13, 1870

BROWN Betsey age 56y wife of Thomas formerly of Hebron, NY and dau of late Isaac **CLARK** in Pewankee, Wis. October 23, 1870

HIGGINS Bridget age 16y in Cambridge, NY November 11, 1870

BARNARD Marion L. dau of late John in Greenwich, NY November 15, 1870

BROWN Laura H. S. widow of Slade D. of Hartford, NY and dau of Daniel C. **SANDERS** of Meadfield, Mass. in Meadifled October 23, 1870

ELDRIDGE James M. age 24y formerly of Cambridge, NY in Washington DC November 16, 1870

HILL Mary D. C. age 30y 3m 5d wife of Judge Edwin Hill formerly of Argyle, NY in Vicksburg, Miss. November 15, 1870

JOHNSON Clarissa age 48y wife of C. P. in Ft. Edward, NY November 24, 1870

COTTRELL Edward G. age 37y formerly of Argyle, NY in Monmouth, Or. October 24, 1870

SMITH Hannah age 18y in Hoosick Falls, NY November 23, 1870

COMSTOCK Mrs. Hannah in her 92nd yr in Cambridge, NY November 28, 1870

ACKLEY Adelaide age 26y wife of David W. in Salem, NY November 26, 1870

O'NEIL Mrs. Johannah in her 75th yr in Salem, NY December 6, 1870

GORDON David age 83y in N. Easton, NY December 3, 1870

REYNOLDS Porter age 66y in Galesville, NY December 1, 1870

STREETER Sarah A. age 33y wife of Dr. M. H. in Granville, NY December 2, 1870

MC KERROW Martha J. age 46y wife of Robert in Argyle, NY November 30, 1870

LUNDY infant child of John M. in N. Argyle, NY December 1, 1870

LIDDLE John abt 63y in N. Argyle, NY November 17, 1870

SKELLIE Jennette age 41y wife of Andrew in Jackson, NY December 11, 1870

BRODIE John age 34y in Reeds Corners, NY December 9, 1870

STEVENSON James age 73y in Coila, NY December 16, 1870

COAN Ellen age 53y in Hoosick, NY December 15, 1870

WALKER Susan age 72y in Salem, NY December 11, 1870

BARKLEY Charles age 24y in Argyle, NY December 26, 1870

LITTLE Mrs. Phebe age 91y in Sandy HIll, NY December 23, 1870

LINCOLN George W. age 42y in Sandy Hill, NY December 18, 1870

BANCROFT Jonathan Barber age 79y in Granville, Mass. December 28, 1870

ELDRIDGE Dewitt Filmore age 26y son of A. G. formerly of Cambridge, NY in Washington DC January 5, 1871

COX Mary Jane age 21y in Hebron, NY January 4, 1871

MC DOUGAL James age 59y in Argyle, NY January 7, 1871

GRAVES Mary Louise age 33y wife of George E. in Rutland, Vt. January 4, 1871, grand daughter of Hezekiah **NILES** formerly of Washington Co.

WATERS Smith abt 70y formerly of White Creek, NY in Cruso, NY January 2, 1871

HOVER Ann Marie age 38y wife of Henry formerly of White Creek, NY in Hoosick, NY Janaury 10, 1871

MC FARLAND Alexander age 27y in Cambridge, NY January 10, 1871

KELLOGG Isabella age 36y wife of O. T. in Cambridge, NY January 12, 1871

BUCKLEY John M. abt 25y in Cambridge, NY January 12, 1871

THOMPSON Emma (**GIFFORD**) wife of Simon in Cambridge, NY January 9, 1871

ABEL ____ age 2d dau of Lester A. in Cambridge, NY January 14, 1871

SHANAHAN Joseph age 11y son of Gregory in Cambridge, NY January 17, 1871

RIDER Benjamin W. age 28y in Jacksonville, Fl. January 11, 1871

SHEARMAN Nettie age 21y 4m dau of Robert formerly of White Creek, NY in Greene, NY January 11, 1871

CHURCH Mary E. age 26y wife of William in Salem, NY January 14, 1871

CLOSSON Mary Ann age 26y 10m wife of Robert E. in Cambridge, NY January 16, 1871

DORR Hettie G. widow of Dr. Jonathan of Lansingburgh, NY at son-in-laws Charles A. **WHITE** in Albany, NY January 11, 1871

HANKS Uriah age 81y formerly of White Creek, NY in Hunter, NY January 13, 1871

MC COY Eleanor age 86y in Argyle, NY January 21, 1871

DANFORTH Henry age 55y in E. Salem, NY January 23, 1871

GOODSPEED Merritt age 31y in Pawlet, Vt. January 26, 1871

WEIR Hattie wife of John F. in Angelica, NY January 8, 1871

SHEEHEY John abt 27y in Cambridge, NY January 27, 1871

BONAS William age 44y in Jackson, NY January 29, 1871

TEFFT David L. in his 27th yr in Whitehall, NY January 22, 1871

POTTER Amanda age 36y wife of Shedd in White Creek, NY February 2, 1871

ASHTON Isaac age 74y in White Creek, NY February 3, 1871

HILLMAN Susie age 3y 8m dau of Daniel and Louisa formerly of Cambridge, NY in Oakland, Mi. February 7, 1871

BEATTIE David age 51y in Salem, NY February 10, 1871

COULTER James W. age 64y 5m 14d formerly of Cambridge, NY in Clinton, Mass. February 14, 1871

RISING Sarah C. age 37y wife of Jacob L. formerly of Buskirks Bridge, NY in Rutland, Mi. (newspaper date February 24, 1871)

SHILAND Freddie age 7m 4d son of Albert and Mary formerly of White Creek, NY in Iowa February 15, 1871

HOWLET Miss Sarah age 60y in W. Rupert, Vt. February 15, 1871

PARKER Mary J. age 21y wife of Henry in Cambridge, NY February 17, 1871

RANNEY Ann (**CURTIS**) age 46y wife of E. W. in New York February 23, 1871

HAMMOND Emeline age 32y wife of George F. in Pawlet, Vt. February 23, 1871

GRANT Howard son of Francis S. and Margaret in Whitehall, NY February 21, 1871

MC LEAN Elizabeth age 42y wife of Henry in Hoosick Falls, NY February 26, 1871

LOTRIDGE Ann age 27y wife of John in Hoosick, NY February 26, 1871

ROBINSON Alice C. age 5y dau of Charles and Hannah in Arlington, Vt. February 27, 1871

STEVENSON Jane in her 63rd yr widow of William in Coila, NY March 2, 1871

WOOD Deborah E. age 78y at sons H. W. in Brooklyn, NY January 2, 1871

CHASE Alphonso age 49y in Eagle Bridge, NY March 6, 1871

BAUMES A. age 63y in Galesville, NY March 6, 1871

BREWER Amos age 26y in Greenwich, NY February 24, 1871

REID Arthur age 64y in S. Argyle, NY March 5, 1871

BRIGHAM M. E. age 36y wife of J. M. in Whitehall, NY March 1, 1871

CUNNINGHAM Robert age 86y in Oquawka, Ill. January 20, 1871

COWAN S. H. age 78y in Shushan, NY March 10, 1871

SIMPSON George F. age 47y in Ft. Edward, NY March 9, 1871

TUTTLE R. G. age 32y in Arlington, Vt. March 16, 1871

SKELLIE Sabra in her 49th yr in Jackson, NY March 16, 1871

ALLEN Martha C. age 4y dau of Peter and Rosilla in Jackson, NY March 15, 1871

MC LEAN Sarah age 2y 4m dau of James and Sarah in White Creek, NY March 20, 1871

BARBER Mary Lois age 4y 7m 20d dau of Benjamin and Lois in Eagle Bridge, NY March 20, 1871

COBB Catherine W. wife of M. L. in Sing Sing, NY March 25, 1871

THOMAS Henrietta age 39y wife of William in White Creek, NY March 24, 1871

SLOCUM Alexander age 52y in Easton, NY March 26, 1871

BAILEY Jennie age 49y in Greenwich, NY April 1, 1871

ELLIS Elizabeth age 22y wife of William in Argyle, NY April 1, 1871

BROWNELL Charity M. age 22y 5m dau of Mack in Cambridge, NY April 3, 1871

GOOD Lydia abt 6y dau of Alson and Hannah in White Creek, NY April 5, 1871

WILDER Nancy age 66y 6m 6d widow of Merrick in Ft. Edward, NY April 2, 1871

BAKER Phillip age 77y in Valley Falls, NY April 6, 1871

WELCH Mary age 8y dau of James and Katie in Cambridge, NY April 3, 1871

VANDENBURGH Adelbert age 1m son of Edwin and M. Libbie in White Creek, NY April 10, 1871

BRODIE James age 4m son of Martin and Bridget in White Creek, NY April 9, 1871

CONANT John age 78y in White Creek, NY April 17, 1871

GRAY Margaret Ann age 59y wife of David and sis of J. C. BEATTIE formerly of Salem, NY in Onarga, Ill. April 6, 1871

LEONARD Charles E. formerly of Greenwich, NY in Grinnell, Iowa March 28, 1871

STAPLES infant son of John in M. Granville, NY April 15, 1871

GRIFFIN Mrs. Shemuel age 60y in Kingsbury, NY April 13, 1871

SMITH Henry P. age 41y in Greenwich, NY April 20, 1871

HILL Thomas age 38y in Greenwich, NY April 21, 1871

BAKER Mrs. _____ abt 80y in Pittstown, NY April 27, 1871

HICKOK Frank age 46y 7m in N. Greenwich, NY April 27, 1871

ROWAN Mary Jane age 3y 6m in Easton, NY May 5, 1871

CHIPMAN Isaac age 86y in Crown Point, NY May 10, 1871

SCHERMERHORN Harvey age 20y 6m in Salem, NY May 14, 1871

BIGBY George age 3y 4m son of John E. and Mary REXSTRAW in Argyle, NY May 17, 1871

PRATT Mrs. Sarah age 74y relict of Walter S. in White Creek, NY May 5, 1871

CUNNINGHAM Elizabeth age 5y dau of Thomas in Cambridge, NY May 16, 1871

WELCH John age 17y son of Michael formerly of White Creek, NY in Pownal, Vt. May 17, 1871

DOYLE Wallie age 8y in Salem, NY May 17, 1871

CRARY Esther age 30y formerly of Salem, NY in Troy, NY May 18, 1871

GAGE Mary Ann in her 26th yr in Greenwich, NY May 13, 1871

WILLIAMS ____ eldest child of Ellis in M. Granville, NY May 19, 1871

GREEN Mrs. ____ age 74y at sons Charles in Argyle, NY (newspaper date May 26, 1871)

HALL John age 51y in Argyle, NY May 21, 1871

ENSIGN Margaret age 39y wife of Fred in M. Granville, NY May 26, 1871

HILL Mary E. age 21y 5m dau of John and Mary in Greenwich, NY May 22, 1871

DONALDSON Joseph age 33y in Argyle, NY June 4, 1871

WETHERBEE Isaac age 89y in Ft. Ann, NY May 30, 1871

DEMOTT Elizabeth age 28y 11m in Hoosick Falls, NY May 31, 1871

PARKER William Henry age 4m in Cambridge, NY June 1, 1871

ROBERTSON Agnes age 49y wife of W. E. in Jackson, NY June 2, 1871

SKIFF James M. age 73y in Easton, NY June 8, 1871. Son Samuel

MC ALLISTER William abt 80y in Salem, NY June 9, 1871

HILLMAN Delina age 71y widow of Mathew in Jackson, NY May 29, 1871

NEEDHAM Mrs. Sally age 61y in Ft. Ann, NY June 11, 1871

MONAHAN Nellie age 15y in Ft. Ann, NY June 14, 1871

BEEBE George N. age 9y 20d son of George and Marie in Salem, NY June 18, 1871

GOODHUE Julius D. age 35y in Anaquasicoke, NY June 19, 1871

HILLMAN Hiram M. age 42y in Cambridge, NY May 23, 1871

ABEL Jennie Elizabeth age 5y 1m dau of Lester A. and Josephine in Cambridge, NY June 26, 1871

MEADER Frankie L. son of Lyman and Elizabeth in Greenwich, NY June 26, 1871

LOY Mrs. Barney in Argyle, NY June 21, 1871

EDWARDS Charles age 26y at Bald Mountain, NY July 2, 1871

CLOSSON Mrs. Mary at Bald Mountain, NY July 2, 1871

HILL John in Greenwich, NY July 3, 1871

BROWN Polly age 82y in Castleton, Vt. June 26, 1871, Mother-in-law of Andrew **CLARKE** and grandmother of Mrs. I. V. **BAKER** Jr.

WELCH Margaret age 45y in Salem, NY July 4, 1871

BARNHAM Gertie age 2y dau of M. J. and Sarah A. in Ft. Edward, NY July 4, 1871 and dau Blanche age 6y died July 14, 1871

HOLMES Catherine age 12y in Ft. Edward, NY July 6, 1871

KINNEY Mattie May dau of James G. and May in Ft. Edward, NY July 5, 1871

ANDREWS George age 2y son of Taylor in Ft. Edward, NY July 5, 1871

HUNT Jennie age 10m dau of John and Nancy in Eagle Bridge, NY July 13, 1871

SMITH Ida age 10y 7m dau of Ebenezer and Harriet J. in Albany, NY July 10, 1871

LIDDLE Lottie (**FREEMAN**) age 36y wife of Leonard M. in Salem, NY July 17, 1871

SHERMAN Caleb age 76y in Cambridge, NY July 20, 1871

FULLER Eliza A. wife of Sidney formerly of Greenwich, NY in Oshtema, Mi. July 20, 1871

BENNETT Eddie son of James and Sarah in Greenwich, NY July 20, 1871

MARTIN Frankie age 3m son of Harvey and Mary in Cambridge, NY July 28, 1871

BALDWIN David abt 55y in W. Hoosick, NY August 4, 1871

PRATT Ida age 2m dau of Amasa and Mary in Cambridge, NY August 5, 1871

PARIS Thomas N. age 62y in Galesville, NY August 6, 1871

STEVENS Winifred dau of Edwin R. and Ruth S. in Greenwich, NY August 7, 1871

MC MILLAN Frankie in Argyle, NY August 5, 1871

SNOW Henry age 72y in Ft. Ann, NY August 5, 1871

BROUGHTON Orville age 2y son of Lyman and Maria in Ft. Ann, NY August 12, 1871

HARWOOD Mary J. age 21y dau of W. P. in Cambridge, NY August 13, 1871

AKIN Charles H. age 23y formerly of White Creek in Beria, Ohio August 12, 1871

CONKEY Abigail age 82y in Eagle Bridge, NY August 17, 1871

THOMPSON George age 4m 17d son of John and Marion in Putnam, NY August 17, 1871

QUACKENBUSH Miss Sophia age 71y 6m in Salem, NY August 18, 1871

SCOTT Mrs. Heman age 82y in White Creek, NY August 19, 1871

ANDREWS Mrs. Laura in her 89th yr in Greenwich, NY August 21, 1871

BOSWORTH Eddie age 12y son of George in Greenwich, NY August 20, 1871

BARBER Lyman age 43y in Easton, NY August 21, 1871

WILLIAMS John formerly of Argyle, NY in Ft. Miller, NY August 12, 1871

WAIT Ann Eliza age 45y wife of Anson in White Creek, NY August 24, 1871

GOODING _____ age 6m son of Hiram and Charlotte in Buskirks Bridge, NY August 25, 1871

LYONS Annie age 1y 8m 3d dau of Charles and Susan A. in Shushan, NY August 26, 1871

MC GUIRE William age 5m 15d son of Patrick and Hannah in Jackson, NY August 28, 1871

VOLENTINE Elizabeth age 1y dau of Dwight and Catherine in Jackson, NY August 29, 1871

ROBINSON Charles H. age 2y 1m 6d son of W. L. and Sarah E. in Cambridge, NY August 29, 1871

MILLETT James age 11m son of John and Bridget in Jackson, NY August 31, 1871

ARNOLD Margaret F. in her 61st yr in Cambridge, NY August 31, 1871

MC KINNEY Florence age 25y wife of James in Cambridge, NY September 2, 1871

HASTINGS Sarah Ann age 47y 3m wife of Lewis M. in Troy, NY September 6, 1871

BAKER Catherine M. age 81y in Cambridge, NY September 7, 1871

ALLEN John age 75y in Cambridge, NY September 8, 1871

FERGUSON Violetta age 14y dau of James and Mary in Johnsonville, NY September 14, 1871

KENNERSON Nathan age 75y in W. Cambridge, NY September 14, 1871

HEATH Sarah S. age 53y wife of Morgan in Greenwich, NY September 6, 1871

BLAWIS Martha H. age 50y wife of Erastus in Jackson, NY September 2, 1871

RAY Samuel age 25y in Argyle, NY September 10, 1871

MC INTYRE Anna died September 6, 1871 and Alice died September 17, 1871 twin daus of Robert and Cynthia C. in Argyle, NY age 5m

SHILAND Jane age 64y widow of James in Coila, NY September 14, 1871

AUSTIN Mrs. Susan age 81y in Salem, NY September 17, 1871

HEGEMAN Louisa age 58y in Easton, NY September 13, 1871

COULTER Florence age 2y 10m dau of Henry and Phebe P. in White Creek, NY September 14, 1871

HAYS Mary age 28y in Buskirks Bridge, NY September 16, 1871

CAMPBELL Charlotte A. age 51y wife of George in Jackson, NY September 17, 1871

WRIGHT Anna age 1y 10m dau of Benjamin D. and Margaret G. in Cambridge, NY September 18, 1871

KING John age 83y in Buskirks Bridge, NY September 19, 1871

SIDILEAU Miss Agnes age 20y in S. Granville, NY September 17, 1871

OVERACKER Margaret E. age 6m dau of George and Nettie in Cambridge, NY September 22, 1871

ACKERMAN Charles of Ft. Miller, NY in Argyle, NY September 20, 1871

HILL Miss Mary age 30y in Salem, NY September 22, 1871

WATERS Mrs. Lucy age 81y in Jackson, NY September 20, 1871

SHEEHAN Edward age 2y 9m son of Edward and Mary in Buskirks Bridge, NY September 24, 1871

EDIE Margaret age 91y in Cambridge, NY September 27, 1871

POLLOCK William formerly of Salem, NY in Grand Mound, Io. September 11, 1871

FERGUSON Edna age 7w dau of R. E. and Addie in Greenwich, NY September 22, 1871

BURDETT Mrs. ____ age 74y in W. Ft. Ann, NY September 29, 1871

STRANG Moses abt 70y formerly of White Creek, NY in Reynoldsburg, Ohio October

8, 1871

SAVAGE John R. age 45y in Salem, NY October 8, 1871

MANCHESTER Iram age 76y 4m in W. Hoosick, NY October 14, 1871

BARRY Mrs. A. age 84y in Sandy Hill, NY October 17, 1871

ROBERTSON Gilbert age 21y son of W. D. in S. Argyle, NY October 22, 1871

WILCOX Charles age 6y 7m son of George in Eagle Bridge, NY October 22, 1871

BULDRICK Alexine age 6m son of Joseph Cambridge, NY October 22, 1871

ROBERTSON George A. age 21y in Argyle, NY October 22, 1871

STEELE Thomas B. in his 26th yr son of Joseph of Salem, NY in Blairstown, Iowa October 26, 1871

MAHAR Alice age 60y wife of Michael in Jackson, NY October 28, 1871

VAN VECHTEN Rebecca age 76y widow of Isaac in Buskirks Bridge, NY October 27, 1871

MALADY Catherine age 23y 8m in Bennington, Vt. November 1, 1871

PLANT Erastus in his 16th yr in Greenwich, NY October 23, 1871

HILL James age 63y in Argyle, NY November 5, 1871

VALENTINE Warren E. in his 30th yr son of Joseph in Roseville, Ind. (newspaper date November 10, 1871)

GEER Emma Lucy age 3y 5m 21d dau of Augustus and Lucy in Cambridge, NY November 21, 1871

MC GUIRE Sarah age 63y wife of Joseph in Rochester, NY November 13, 1871

THOMAS Mrs. David age 48y formerly of White Creek, NY in Elmira, NY November 22, 1871

FAIRLEY William D. age 41y 8m in Salem, NY November 20, 1871

HOLMES Mrs. Nancy M. in her 74th yr in Greenwich, NY November 29, 1871

WATERS Joseph age 54y in Jackson, NY November 24, 1871

WRIGHT John age 67y in Greenwich, NY November 24, 1871

KENYON Alonzo abt 38y formerly of Jackson, NY in Schaghticoke, NY November

28, 1871

GOODING Abt 45y in White Creek, NY November 28, 1871

BAKER Josiah age 2y 9m died November 18, 1871 and Henrietta age 13y 6m 18d died October 18, 1871 children of Benjamin and Eunice in Eagle Bridge, NY

DEUEL Abigail age 80y in Buskirks Bridge, NY November 28, 1871

ROBERTSON Mrs. Sarah abt 82y in Cambridge, NY November 29, 1871

RICH Joel age 85y in Cambridge, NY December 2, 1871

COVEY John B. age 57y in Sandgate, Vt. December 4, 1871

HOWARD Mrs. Jane A. age 56y wife of Orrin in Ft. Ann, NY November 27, 1871

ARCHIBALD Anna age 23y wife of David in Cambridge, NY December 14, 1871

BAKER Helen E. age 17y dau of Fisher and Elizabeth in Pittstown, NY December 14, 1871

BURGESS John age 9y 6m son of John and Helen in White Creek, NY December 13, 1871

WETSELL Daniel F. abt 54y formerly of Ft. Ann, NY in Glens Falls, NY December 14, 1871

PARISH Mrs. ____ age 85y widow of William of Ft. Ann, NY in Dresden, NY December 14, 1871

DAWLEY Eliza age 36y wife of William in Greenwich, NY December 20, 1871

ENGLISH Sally age 29y wife of Stephen in Easton, NY December 19, 1871

CAMERON David age 63y in Putnam, NY December 22, 1871

MURPHY James age 2y son of John and Catherine in Cambridge, NY December 21, 1871

WARNER Asaph E. in his 65th yr in Jackson, NY December 24, 1871

PRATT David age 78y in Cambridge, NY December 24, 1871

MAHAN Catherine age 5y 5m dau of Patrick and Bridget in White Creek, NY December 25, 1871

CARNES Diana abt 90y in Jackson, NY December 25, 1871

BATES James T. age 86y in W. Rupert, Vt. December 28, 1872

MC CONLEE John age 37y in Argyle, NY December 17, 1872

SMALLEY John age 63y formerly of Salem, NY in Green Isle (newspaper date January 3, 1873)

KERR Robert age 85y in Jackson, NY December 27, 1872

WING Sarah Isabella age 20y dau of Osborn and Abigail L. formerly of Shushan, NY in Aurora, Ill. December 25, 1872

CRONKHITE Eliza age 26y wife of Harrison in Hoosick, NY December 30, 1872

SWEET Emery T. age 30y in Walloomsac, NY December 30, 1872

GRAY Mrs. Allanta age 63y in Shushan, NY January 2, 1873

SARGENT Helen age 28y in Pawlet, Vt. December 24, 1872

SKELLIE John age 76y in Jackson, NY December 19, 1872

CLEVELAND Fannie age 77y in Jackson, NY December 31, 1872

LARKIN Harmon H. formerly of Salem NY in Dorset, Vt. December 27, 1872

RICHMOND Paris age 69y in Galesville, NY December 29, 1872

BLAKE Mrs. ____ age 75y in E. Greenwich, NY December 30, 1872

WILSON William age 17y son of Andrew in Greenwich, NY December 28, 1872

GREEN Caleb abt 70y in E. Greenwich, NY December 30, 1872

SMITH Jason age 80y in Granville, NY December 26, 1872

HAWLEY Adda wife of Dr. H. T. formerly of White Creek, NY and sis of Mrs. E. B. **HOYT** in Tittalewassee, Mi. January 3, 1873

PERCY Minerva A. age 1y 3m 8d dau of Lansing and Amelia in Cambridge, NY January 8, 1873

BATTY Stephen age 76y in Easton, NY January 4, 1873

CRANDALL David age 62y in Easton, NY January 9, 1873

ACKLEY Charles A. age 39y in Cambridge, NY January 14, 1873

NORTON Warren age 83y in Cambridge, NY January 15, 1873

SPRAGUE Rev. D. G. age 76y in Salem, NY January 11, 1873

BEEBE Oliver C. age 46y formerly of Salem, NY in Cal. January __, 1873

MC GILL Mrs. Catherine age 93y in Cambridge, NY January 22, 1873

BACON Kittie A. age 26y 6m in Whitehall, NY January 21, 1873

WEST Mary abt 61y wife of Samuel in Northumberland, NY January 14, 1873

DENSLOW John age 35y in Whitehall, NY January 23, 1873

MC INERNEY Bridget age 62y in Cambridge, NY January 24, 1873

TURNER C. G. age 72y in Arlington, Vt. January 24, 1873

MOSS Henry Erwin age 1y son of Erwin and Jennie in Ft. Edward, NY January 27, 1873

HUTCHINS Mrs. Waty age 70y in E. Salem, NY February 3, 1873

HALL William age 78y in E. Greenwich, NY February 2, 1873

SAFFORD Esther age 28y dau of Gideon F. in Salem, NY February 3, 1873

WILSON Gillis age 19y in Argyle, NY February 6, 1873

MC ALLISTER Jesse age 2y 5m son of Oliver and Christianna **WILSON** formerly of Coila, NY in Wolcott, Ind. February 3, 1873

DRISCOLL Johanna age 30y wife of John in White Creek, NY February 19, 1873

BRAYTON infant child of Marcus and Susan in White Creek, NY February 13, 1873

BENNETT Georgey age 5d son of George and Harriet in Shaftsbury, Vt. February 9, 1873

GILCHRIST Maggie age 40y of Argyle, NY in S. Adams, NY February 3, 1873

PHILLIPS James Hawley age 7m 22d son of Dr. W. S. in Arlington, Vt. February 22, 1873

TEFFT Stephen A. age 83y in Buskirks Bridge, NY February 25, 1873

BROCKWAY Dr. Josephus age 78y in Cambridge, NY February 26, 1873

WATKINS Mary J. age 42y wife of John and dau of Buel **FENTON** of White Creek, NY in Granville, NY February 27, 1873

DOWLING John age 31y in Salem, NY March 2, 1873

ARNOTT infant child of Samuel W. and Jennie in Jackson, NY March 4, 1873

HODGE Herbert E. age 19y son of Jerome in Cambridge, NY March 1, 1873

CARTER Alexander age 75y in Benson, Vt. February 13, 1873

CROCKER Platt S. age 55y formerly of Cambridge, NY in Arlington, Va. February 26, 1873

FOWLER Gardner age 68y in Glens Falls, NY February 7, 1873

SMITH Mrs. Elizabeth in S. Bay, NY (newspaper date March 7,1873)

BLANCHARD Mrs. Betsey age 30y in S. Bay, NY February 10, 1873

ADAMS Gussie age 2y only child of Martin M. and Christina, J. in Welch Hollow, NY January 28, 1873

NILES Susan age 84y Mother of N. E. in White Creek, NY February 14, 1873

HASTINGS Loren age 84y in Shushan, NY March 7, 1873

MOSELEY Pardon in his 73rd yr in Hoosick, NY March 9, 1873

FOSTER Boardman age 4m son of Joshua and Mary E. in Salem, NY March 8, 1873

NOYES William age 82y in Greenwich, NY February 28, 1873

WOODWORTH Mary age 37y 10m wife of George in Greenwich, NY February 2, 1873

HORTON Joel in his 85th yr in Jackson, NY March 4, 1873

KING Sarah T. age 8y 5m 5d dau of George and Theresa in Pittstown, NY March 17, 1873

NOONAN Patrick age 26y in Salem, NY March 3, 1873

HILL Abner age 68y in Salem, NY March 10, 1873

ARMITAGE William J. in his 58th yr in Rochester, NY March 8, 1873

HOLLEY Jefferson age 56y in Cambridge, NY March 24, 1873

CONGDON Albert abt 25y in Hebron, NY March 22, 1873

HALL Mrs. William in E. Greenwich, NY March 20, 1873

HALL Marion E. age 4m dau of William and Mary in Jackson, NY March 24, 1873

HITCHCOCK Ida in her 7th yr dau of John R. in Cambridge, NY April 3, 1873

BROTT Frankey age 11y son of Daniel and Charlotte in Mechanicsville, NY March 27, 1873

TEFFT Delia dau of William and Maria in Mechanicsville, NY March 28, 1873

DONSLEY Eliza Jane age 19y wife of Daniel in Mechanicsville, NY April 2, 1873

WRIGHT Mary Cornelia age 4y dau of John and Melissa in Salem, NY April 2, 1873

RISING Clarence age 4y 10m adopted son of John E. **HITCHCOCK** in Cambridge, NY April 5, 1873

RICHARDS Lemuel J. age 1y 6m son of Alber W. and Annie E. in Argyle, NY April 9, 1873

ANDREWS George C. age 36y in Arlington, Vt. March 30, 1873

HUBBARD Lyman age 79y in Jackson, NY April 5, 1873

LANE Martin S. age 60y in Shaftsbury, Vt. April 5, 1873

MILLER William age 41y in Jackson, NY April 12, 1873

FREEMAN Harvey in his 44th yr in Salem, NY April 12, 1873

SKINNER Freddie S. age 8m 1d son of Charles in Welch Hollow, NY April 18, 1873

SHELDON Franklin W. age 11y son of Walter and Lucinda in White Creek, NY April 23, 1873

VOLENTINE Fannie E. age 19y 2m dau of Daniel and Sarah J. in Aurora, Ill. (newspaper date April 25, 1873)

JERMAIN Catherine in her 51st yr wife of James B. and dau of late Clark **RICE** of Cambridge, NY in Albany, NY April 21, 1873

JUDSON Mabel Graham age 13m dau of J. R. and Virginia in E. Arlington, Vt. April 23, 1873

NOBLE Sarah Irene age 31y 8m 23d wife of Henry and dau of late Richard **BARTON** in Cambridge, NY April 25, 1873

DAVIS Benjamin age 86y in W. Arlington, Vt. April 23, 1873

HARRISON Martha age 26y wife of William Henry formerly of Washington Co. in Boston, Mass. April 17, 1873

PORTER William D. age 39y in Salem, NY April 19, 1873

CROSIER Joseph age 63y in Hebron, NY April 29, 1873

LA BARRON Amelia age 22y wife of John in Jackson, NY May 3, 1873

LUDDY David abt 3y son of William and Mary in Sandgate, Vt. May 8, 1873

REID Margaret age 89y in Argyle, NY May 8, 1873

DOUGLAS Wilbur F. age 78y in Whitehall, NY May 6, 1873

BADGLEY Henry age 42y in Stillwater, NY May 16, 1873

BENTLEY Reuben age 17y in White Creek, NY May 16, 1873

FITCH Harriet A. age 52y wife of Samuel in Barkers Grove, NY May 17, 1873

WELLS Henry Morgan age 69y in Shushan, NY May 18, 1873

KENNEDY Dr. L. W. age 40y in Cambridge, NY May 18, 1873

SQUARES Hattie age 28y in White Creek, NY May 19, 1873

WILLIAMS Barber age 89y in Easton, NY May 2, 1873

CARPENTER Timothy age 32y in Dinning Corners, NY May 23, 1873

BECKER Martha age 21y wife of James in Easton, NY May 9, 1873

ALEXANDER Jennie age 26y wife of William in Lake, NY May 19, 1873

NELSON Mrs. Mary age 79y in Rupert, Vt. May 25, 1873

MARSH Daniel H. age 21y in W. Arlington, Vt. May 20, 1873

PARISH James M. in his 36th yr in Spring Valley, NY May 3, 1873

RUSSELL Clara E. wife of Cornelius L. in Santa Barbara, Cal. June 3, 1873

RUSSELL Susan abt 76y wife of George of White Creek, NY in Rochester, NY June 18, 1873

SALTER William Holmes age 16y in Easton, NY June 21, 1873

BELDEN Fred S. age 30y in Granville, NY June 11, 1873

CULVER Mrs. Amy age 84y in Cambridge, NY June 13, 1873

STROW John W. age 37y formerly of Granville, NY in Delevan, Wis. May 30, 1873

BROWN Dentia A. age 36y wife of S. S. and dau of W. Z. **WAIT** formerly of Hebron, NY in Pawlet, Vt. June 11, 1873

GARDNER Mrs. Mattie age 36y wife of Rufus in Sandy Hill, NY June 13, 1873

KING Olive age 1y 4m 7d dau of Benjamin and Mary A. in Sandy Hill, NY June 16, 1873

SMALLEY George F. age 29y in Shushan, NY June 28, 1873

WATERS Mrs. ____ age 56y in E. Salem, NY July 7, 1873

TREMBLEY Mitchell age 82y in Sandy Hill, NY July 18, 1873

WEST Charles age 21y son of Edward in E. Salem, NY July 15, 1873

COLBY Margaret age 30y wife of Abner in Shushan, NY July 16, 1873

BULLIONS Annie age 5y 3m dau of Rev. J. and Mary Gray Anderson and grand daughter of D. H. C. **GRAY** of White Creek, NY in Martin, Mi. July 15, 1873

BRADSHAW Walter E. age 6w 2d son of Frederick and Emily in Whitehall, NY July 20, 1873

REID Mrs. Mary in Argyle, NY (newspaper date August 1, 1873)

PRATT Jennie L. age 23y wife of Amasa and dau of Orrin **SHERMAN** of Pittstown, NY in Canterbury, Del. July 24, 1873

JOSLIN Susie E. age 5y dau of Thomas C. in Hoosick Falls, NY July 28, 1873

REA Belle age 30y dau of John in Salem, NY July 28, 1873

FENTON Mary Nancy age 1y 3m dau of George J. and Cornelia B. in Cambridge, NY August 3, 1873

YOUNG Mrs. Lovina in Ft. Ann, NY July 29, 1873

GRAVES Lucy age 39y wife of Lyman and dau of late William **MC AULEY** in Arlington, Vt. August 6, 1873

LUNDY Mrs. John age 35y in Argyle, NY August 7, 1873

BATCHELDER Estella May age 7m 5d dau of Orestus and Hattie A. in Ft. Ann, NY August 18, 1873

BAKER Mary age 1y 15d dau of William in Salem, NY August 14, 1873

MALTHANER John age 13m son of Phillip in Salem, NY August 21, 1873

HEDGES ____ age 6w child of Samuel in Cambridge, NY August 21, 1873

BARTLETT Lyman age 74y in Shushan, NY August 25, 1873

FLOWERS Willie age 22y in Salem, NY August 23, 1873

JOHNSTON ____ age 7m son of David and Kate in Salem, NY August 22, 1873

HALL Bertha age 7m dau of J. F. and Miranda in Cambridge, NY September 3, 1873

DUEL Alida J. age 42y wife of Morgan in Cambridge, NY September 2, 1873

KINCAID Herbert B. age 6m son of W. H. in Argyle, NY August 28, 1873

HAGGERTY infant son of James in Cambridge, NY August 25, 1873

KINCAID Alexander age 74y in Hoosick Falls, NY August 21, 1873

GRAY infant child of Henry in S. Cambridge, NY September 1, 1873

ROBERTSON John age 87y 4m in Coila, NY September 2, 1873

OTIS Marcia dau of Sardis in Granville, NY September 1, 1873

WHYTE Col. William H. age 77y in Argyle, NY September 4, 1873

HYDE Iram age 75y formerly of Jackson, NY in Wolcott, Ind. September 3, 1873

BARRY infant dau of John in Whitehall, NY September 5, 1873

WRIGHT James H. age 75y formerly of White Creek, NY in Saugatuck, Mi. September 12, 1873

PLUTE Mary age 2y dau of John in Whitehall, NY September 5, 1873

HOPE Willie infant son of Joseph in Whitehall, NY September 10, 1873

MOORE Mrs. Morgan S. age 63y in Napoleon, Mi. September 12, 1873

MERRILL J. H. age 6m in Stillwater, NY September 16, 1873

MILLER Margaret M. age 21y dau of William in Cambridge, NY September 19, 1873

FENTON ____ age 10m son of George in Shushan, NY September 16, 1873

BOYLE Willie age 3m son of James in Whitehall, NY September 20, 1873

ROCK ____ age 3w son of Charles in Whitehall, NY September 20, 1873

MARTIN Harris age 65y in Easton, NY September 20, 1873

MC GOWAN Hattie J. age 5m 23d in N. Argyle, NY October 4, 1873

SARGENT Minerva age 70y in Bristol, Pa. September 28, 1873

SMITH Margaret age 64y widow of Alexander in Argyle, NY September 26, 1873

COTTRELL Nathan age 80y in Hoosick, NY October 7, 1873

WELLER Sally at Beadle Hill, NY October 14, 1873

BARRY Edward age 15y in Sandy Hill, NY October 4, 1873

WATSON John age 73y in Greenwich, NY October 5, 1873

KIMBALL Charlie son of H. W. in Greenwich, NY October 4, 1873

PRESTER Emily age 52y in Argyle, NY October 11, 1873

ALLARD Elizabeth age 72y at son-in-laws William **LIVINGSTON** in Cambridge, NY (newspaper date October 24, 1873)

HANNA H. Amanda in her 56th yr wife of Robert and dau of Samuel **RUSTE** formerly of Cambridge, NY in Aurora, Ill. October 14, 1873

MC LEAN Mary L. age 19y dau of Ebenezer in Jackson, NY October 22, 1873

HATCH Jennie age 7m 22d dau of John in Jackson, NY October 29, 1873

MOORE Percy age 11m son of George S. in Whitehall, NY October 18, 1873

SIMPSON Ebenezer age 72y formerly of Shushan, NY in Allegeny, Mi. rec. (newspaper date October 31, 1873)

GORDON S. C. age 73y widow of Rev. P. formerly of Cambridge, NY in Kent, Conn. October 30, 1873

LAWRENCE Anna V. S. age 38y wife of Jacob formerly of Cambridge, NY in Amsterdam, NY October 31, 1873

HALL Mrs. John age 76y in Argyle, NY October 31, 1873

SMITH Donald in his 20th yr in Argyle, NY November 4, 1873

BALDWIN Cornelia age 19y dau of John in Buskirks Bridge, NY October 23, 1873

BROWN Milo F. age 54y in Whitehall, NY October 25, 1873

RICH Mrs. Caroline age 53y in Whitehall, NY October 26, 1873

WEST S. M. age 66y in Arlington, Vt. November 12, 1873

SCOTT Donald age 20y in Argyle, NY November 4, 1873

KENYON Alvah age 67y in Ft. Ann, NY November 17, 1873

DERBY Paul age 20y in Whitehall, NY November 12, 1873

MC ARTHUR Ellen S. age 22y wife of Thomas S. in Putnam, NY November 9, 1873

COON Stillman G. age 30y formerly of Cambridge, NY in Juvenile Asylum in New York November 13, 1873

WHITMAN George B. age 49y in Arlington, Vt. November 21, 1873

DOUGLAS Elmer age 11y 11m 5d son of Morgan and Mary J. (Mother dec.) formerly of Cambridge, NY in Breckenridge, Mo. August 2, 1873

SPENCER Carrie May age 8y 1m 9d dau of Dr. D. C. and Levina in Augusta, Wis. November 28, 1873

KENYON Martha M. age 75y 2m 19d wife of Joseph C. formerly of Granville, NY in Elgin, Ill. died on husbands 81st birthday November 2, 1873

LUSK Mrs. Betsy age 86y in Whitehall, NY December 1, 1873

CULVER Eliza M. age 50y widow of O. F. in Tuxpan, Mexico November 13, 1873

CALLERY John age 24y in N. Hoosick, NY December 6, 1873

WING Lillian M. age 10 in N. Hoosick, NY December 11, 1873

SANDERSON Mrs. B. H. age 51y in Cambridge, NY December 7, 1873

TOWNSEND Louisa age 9y dau of Edward in Hartford, NY November 2, 1873

BALDWIN James age 24y in Camden, NY December 2, 1873

MATTISON Lena age 6m dau of Job and Ada in Arlington, Vt. December 21, 1873

FOWLER Polly age 74y wife of Noah in Mendota, Ill. December 18, 1873

LYONS John abt 30y in Whitehall, NY December 19, 1873

OLIVER Anna May age 6w dau of Joseph and Abbie T. in Salem, NY December 18, 1873

STEWART Eunice age 54y wife of Walter G. in Lakeville, NY December 18, 1873

CAREY Matilda age 84y in White Creek, NY November 24, 1873

FISHER William age 72y formerly of White Creek, NY in Belvidere, Ill. December 25, 1873

MAHAN Mary age 17y in Eagle Bridge, NY December 30, 1873

MC CLELLAN Mrs. Joanna age 27y formerly of White Creek, NY in Ogden, Ill. (newspaper date January 2, 1874)

CROSS Helen Estella age 13y dau of Samuel and Clarissa in Sandy Hill, NY December 23, 1873

FIFIELD Hannah L. age 25y wife of Frank N. in Salem, NY December 16, 1873

MC MURRAY Mary Grace age 53y wife of Ebenezer of Salem, NY in New York December 27, 1873

FISH Imogene E. age 24y in Eagle Bridge, NY January 1, 1874

CULVER Nathan age 74y in Coila, NY January 7, 1874

CULVER Capt. J. W. age 31y 9m 20d of the 123rd Reg. NY Vol. formerly of Washington Co. in Iowa City, Iowa January 5, 1874

GREEN James age 28y formerly of Cambridge, NY in Vassar, Mi. December 7, 1873

ALLEN Miss Helen formerly of Greenwich, NY in Troy, NY December 27, 1873

O'HERRON Ann age 47y in Battenville, NY January 9, 1874

DARROW Eddie age 17m son of Nelson in Cambridge, NY January 12, 1874

HOLLEY L. J. age 19y dau of late Jefferson in Cambridge, NY January 13, 1874

HITCHCOCK Mary F. age 16y dau of W. E. in Cambridge, NY January 13, 1874

MC CLELLAN William A. age 3y son of William in Jackson, NY January 19, 1874

MC CLELLAN George age 16y son of John in Jackson, NY January 20, 1874

BURCH infant son of Russell in Johnsonville, NY January 20, 1874

MC MORRIS Elizabeth age 64y wife of Thomas in Jackson, NY January 11, 1874

WILSON Edgar age 3y son of John and Fannie in Easton, NY January 14, 1874

WRIGHT Catherine age 63y 2m 12d wife of J. G. in Cambridge, NY January 19, 1874

MARTIN Miriam age 63y dau of late Artemus in Jackson, NY January 21, 1874

EDIE Lillie J. age 8y dau of Henry in Jackson, NY January 22, 1874

BAKER Edgar age 26y formerly of Cambridge in N. Adams, Mass. January 17, 1874

WOOD Samuel age 77y in Granville, NY December 31, 1873

FLYNN Thomas age 62y in Cambridge, NY January 23, 1874

WAIT George age 29y in Shushan, NY January 28, 1874

JONES Adelbert W. son of Adelbert G. and Julia (**WATSON**) in Greenwich, NY January 18, 1874

MC NEIL Alexander age 78y in Argyle, NY January 20, 1874

MALTHANER Maria E. age 3m 4d in Salem, NY January 19, 1874

MATHEWS Edward C. age 3m 9d son of Horace P. and Ellen in Salem, NY January 19, 1874

TALMADGE Celia age 15y in Ft. Ann, NY January 26, 1874

GILLESPIE Thomas age 74y in Shushan, NY February 3, 1874

SWEET John T. age 23y in Hoosick, NY February 4, 1874

MONROE William age 76y in Pawlet, Vt. January 30, 1874

CULVER Betsey age 56y wife of Samuel in N. Pawlet, Vt. January 30, 1874

LAMB Olive age 83y widow of George in S. Granville, NY February 3, 1874

CLARK Bathsheba age 78y wife of Charles formerly of Jackson, NY in Northeast, Pa. January 28, 1874

VANCE George A. age 23y in Battenville, NY February 1, 1874

COLTON George age 23y in Salem, NY February 3, 1874

KENT Margaret age 72y in Cambridge, NY February 9, 1874

CROSS Sally abt 80y of Ft. Ann, NY in the County Home (newspaper date February 20, 1874)

HOUGHTON George M. age 33y 5m 3d son of Andrew and B. in Buskirks Bridge, NY February 12, 1874

WHITCOMB Joel in his 88th yr in Ft. Miller, NY February 13, 1874

HALL Mary E. age 27y wife of William A. and dau of James B. **WEIR** in Jackson, NY February 11, 1874

WILLIAMS Coomer M. age 59y in Sandy Hill, NY February 9, 1874

LESTER David age 90y in N. Argyle, NY February 8, 1874

MC MILLAN Lucy age 84y in Shushan, NY February 12, 1874

SHEDD Mercy (FOWLER) age 88y widow of Jared formerly of White Creek, NY in N. Hoosick, NY February 13, 1874

BURGESS Mrs. Ruth age 67y in Hoosick, NY February 18, 1874

PRUE ____ age 6m son of Horace and Eliza in S. Bay, NY February 16, 1874

TURNER Carrie age 9y dau of W. J. and M. E. in W. Sandgate, Vt. February 22, 1874

KING Susie age 5y 11m dau of John and Elizabeth in Salem, NY February 16, 1874

WEEKS Katie age 7y dau of H. C. and Lucy in Salem, NY February 17, 1874

YOUNG Cora M. age 3y 8m dau of Zadoc and Electa in Greenwich, NY February 16, 1874

MC LEAN Mary J. age 25y wife of Francis in Washington DC February 19, 1874

VAN VRANKEN Charles age 20y in Salem, NY February 21, 1874

HUBBARD infant child of A. P. in Shushan, NY March 2, 1874

STATIA Martha age 21y wife of Henry in Ft. Ann, NY February 24, 1874

SKELLIE Hugh age 78y in Cambridge, NY February 28, 1874

GREEN Mrs. Esther age 34y in Easton, NY March 7, 1874

SMITH Mrs. Catherine age 77y in Easton, NY December 23, 1873

FENTON Parnell E. age 73y 24d wife of Simon in Cambridge, NY March 8, 1874

CROCKER Benjamin age 85y in Cambridge, NY March 10, 1874

MARTIN Margaret age 55y wife of William in White Creek, NY March 7, 1874

MC AULIFFE Ellen age 1y died March 10, 1874 and John Jr. age 2y died March 16, 1874 children of John of Cambridge, NY

GREEN Emily P. age 15y dau of S. W. in Eagle Bridge, NY March 14, 1874

MATTISON Lydia age 77y in White Creek, NY March 14, 1874

LEE Winnie age 1y 2m dau of Mrs. Juliette and grand daughter of James HAY 2nd in Greenwich, NY March 8, 1874

MAGEE Fannie age 21m dau of Austin and Mary J. in Salem, NY March 4, 1874

BUTTON Allie D. age 13y dau of William and Almira in Salem, NY March 10, 1874

STEWART Hannah B. in her 44th yr in Salem, NY March 7, 1874

LEE Josephus age 17y 11m in Salem, NY February 18, 1874

MAGEE George V. age 29y in Salem, NY March 13, 1874

BAUMES Sarah E. age 19y 6m 20d dau of Hiram and Sarah C. formerly of White Creek, NY in Schenectady, NY March 27, 1874

BOWEN Julia age 74y wife of Sylvester in Buskirks Bridge, NY March 5, 1874

MC CLELLAN J. Lourie age 3y 6m died March 26, 1874 and George E. age 5y 4m died March 27, 1874 children of Chester L. and Mary E. in Cambridge, NY

ASHTON Joseph age 7y son of Michael and Jennette in Salem, NY March 22, 1874

BUTTON Charles N. age 61y in Cambridge, NY April 8, 1874

HORTON William age 57y in White Creek, NY April 6, 1874

LE GRYS Herbert J. age 2w 4d son of Thomas in White Creek, NY April 7, 1874

LONG Elizabeth age 54y 11m wife of Rev. W. R. in Buffalo, NY March 31, 1874, buried in Cambridge, NY

HUTCHINSON Samuel T. age 53y in Moreau, NY March 18, 1874

ROBINSON Emeline age 36y wife of John A. in Belcher, NY March 26, 1874

BENTLEY Caleb age 57y in White Creek, NY April 13, 1874

PALMER Charlotte age 93y in Cambridge, NY April 13, 1874

MC CLELLAN Joanna dau of George R. and Joanna in Ogden, Ill. April 9, 1874

RANDALL R. M. son of Charles and Martha in Sandgate, Vt. April 17, 1874

BANE Mrs. Elizabeth in her 86th yr in Greenwich, NY April 11, 1874

QUACKENBUSH Mrs. Mary age 92y in Greenwich, NY April 22, 1874

HARRIS Marvin C. age 62y in Kingsbury, NY April 28, 1874

NEDDO Mrs. J. age 89y in Whitehall, NY April 26, 1874

KETCHUM Mrs. ____ age 28y in Jackson, NY April 27, 1874

ELLSWORTH Sarah age 47y in Kingsbury, NY April 10/19, 1874

GIFFORD Abram age 54y formerly of Cambridge in Atkinson, Ill. April 30, 1874

WAIT William abt 68y formerly of White Creek in Wheatland, Wis. April 30, 1874

BOWEN John age 66y in Mission, Ill. April 28, 1874, buried White Creek, NY

GAVETTE Mrs. Asahel age 61y formerly Mrs. David FISHER in Greenwich, NY May 3, 1874

JACKSON Freddie age 11m 10d in Sandy Hill, NY April 27, 1874

VANDENBURGH Carrie age 8y dau of George and Cornelia in Sandy Hill, NY May 3, 1874

GREEN Mrs. Zina in her 26th yr in Greenwich, NY May 5, 1874

WOOD Mattie E. age 43y dau of late Samuel in Greenwich, NY May 8, 1874

FREEMAN Fannie A. in her 15th yr dau of late Harvey in Salem, NY May 6, 1874

BEATTIE Mary A. age 36y 10m 11d wife of James M. and dau of Joshua STEELE in Salem, NY May 6, 1874

BARTHOLOMEW Sarah in her 16th yr dau of Alvah in Whitehall, NY May 15, 1874

WILLIAMS Adelaide age 4y 8m dau of John S. and Rebecca in Salem, NY May 18, 1874

KELSEY Don in his 27th yr in Whitehall, NY May 23, 1874

MILLER Jesse A. infant son of A. H. in Greenwich, NY May 30, 1874

MC LEAN William Francis age 4m son of Francis and Mary J. in Washington DC June 11, 1874

RUSSELL Catherine age 85y in Pittstown, NY June 11, 1874

SCOTT Mrs. Margaret A. age 50y in Argyle, NY June 23, 1874

WILSEY John age 76y in Whitehall, NY June 22, 1874

PEARL Polly age 88y widow of Elijah C. in Amsterdam, NY June 25, 1874

CANFIELD Almira in her 88th yr relict of N. S. in Arlington, Vt. June 30, 1874

KING Calvin W. age 78y formerly of Cambridge, NY in Alden, NY June 17, 1874

KEITH Amasa abt 60y in Saratoga Springs, NY June 30, 1874

RILEY Jane Ann age 41y dau of Peter WALSH in Cambridge, NY June 30, 1874

HAXTON King A. age 76y in Cambridge, NY June 27, 1874

BRAY _____ age 7m dau of A. in Oak Hill, NY June 27, 1874

HENRY Harry A. age 7m son of George and Lucy in Granville, NY June 30, 1874

HAY Mrs. Lois age 44y wife of James in Greenwich, NY June 29, 1874

MACE Sady age 8y in Putnam, NY June 27, 1874

PARTRIDGE Adriel age 84y in Shushan, NY June 27, 1874

HURD Bryant age 64y in Sandgate, Vt. July 2, 1874

LAMBERT Ida May age 10m 8d dau of Horace and Phebe A. in Cambridge, NY June 23, 1874

BENNETT Robert N. age 21y son of John and Serena in White Creek, NY June 21, 1874

EDWARDS Margaret age 30y wife of Hugh in Granville, NY July 9, 1874

GERO Minnie age 15m dau of Thomas and Margaret in Granville, NY July 8, 1874

CASE Sylvia age 68y wife of David in W. Hoosick, NY July 4, 1874

GLIDDEN George age 74y in Arlington, Vt. July 1, 1874

DWINNELL Mary E. age 11y in White Creek, NY July 17, 1874

SKINNER Calvin age 76y formerly of Cambridge, NY in Herndon, Va. July 11, 1874

BAIN Phillip J. age 61y in S. Argyle, NY July 16, 1874

BRAYMAN Seth age 73y in Argyle, NY July 19, 1874

POOR Nellie age 9y dau of W. C. in White Creek, NY July 16, 1874

FERGUSON Francis age 70y of Whitehall, NY in the County Home July 15, 1874

THOMPSON Mary age 13y dau of Oscar and Mary in Granville, NY July 21, 1874

ROGERS Clarissa A. age 77y wife of Zebulon in Whitehall, NY July 14, 1874

BARKER Mrs. O. M. in her 72nd yr in Adamsville, NY July 17, 1874

GILMAN Miss Alvira A. age 32y in Salem, NY July 16, 1874

MC FARLAND Alice V. in her 15th yr in E. Greenwich, NY July 19, 1874

ARCHER Thomas abt 56y of Jackson, NY in the County Home August 5, 1874

GREGORY Joey age 9m 18d son of Thomas C. and Abby A. in Salem, NY August 6, 1874

COMSTOCK Peter age 80y native of Ft. Ann, NY in Port Kent, NY August 5, 1874

GREEN Patrick age 6y son of Patrick and Julia in Whitehall, NY August 12, 1874

GREEN Warren age 6m son of A. H. and Lenora in Granville, NY August 16, 1874

SHEAHAN ____ age 2y 6m dau of John in Whitehall, NY August 17, 1874

WOODARD Irene age 10m 25d dau of T. S. and Fanny H. **KETCHUM** and grand daughter of Rev. B. **HAWLEY** in Glens Falls, NY August 12, 1874

WEIR Robert I. age 26y formerly of Cambridge in Mayville, NY August 17, 1874

GRAVES Edmond age 48y in Camden Valley, NY August 11, 1874

RUSSELL Prince age 87y in Pittstown, NY August 4, 1874

BUTLER James age 35y of Ft. Edward, NY in the County Home August 20, 1874

FULLER George age 16y in Shaftsbury, Vt. August 21, 1874

PARKER Jerusha age 58y in Shushan, NY August 22, 1874

JACKSON Edward age 55y of Ft. Edward, NY in the County Home August 27, 1874

HARWOOD Miss Julia age 23y in Rupert, Vt. August 20, 1874

KEDARE John age 67y in Ft. Ann, NY August 19, 1874

WILCOX William age 2d son of Henry and Mary in Hoosick Falls, NY August 30, 1874

HERRINGTON Nancy age 33y in White Creek, NY August 31, 1874

MC MURRAY Mrs. H. A. age 58y in Whitehall, NY September 2, 1874

LA BERNE John age 80y in Argyle, NY September 2, 1874

LOWELL Caroline age 73y wife of James if N. Granville, NY August 31, 1874

WHITLOCK Martha M. age 31y wife of William in Salem, NY September 10, 1874

GRADY John age 58y in Whitehall, NY September 2, 1874

O'SHAUNESSEY __ age 10w child of Malachi in Cambridge, NY September 8, 1874

POWERS ____ age 2m child of Thomas in Hoosick Falls, NY September 11, 1874

COULTER Earland D. age 4m son of George in Jackson, NY September 17, 1874

HARVEY Mrs. David age 62y in Sandy Hill, NY September 13, 1874

MILLIMAN Gray M. age 3m 11d dau of Henry in Hoosick Falls, NY September 23, 1874

VINCENT Walter age 8y in Cambridge, NY September 26, 1874

BELL Mary age 9y dau of Edward in Ft. Ann, NY September 22, 1874

BARTLETT Julia D. age 16y in Cambridge, NY September 26, 1874

PERRY Josephine age 52y in Whitehall, NY September 25, 1874

GIBBS Arabella age 40y wife of A. D. in Whitehall, NY (newspaper date October 2, 1874)

KINNEY Harvey M. age 86y in Whitehall, NY September 26, 1874

DIMES Mary age 47y wife of William in Whitehall, NY September 24, 1874

ALLEN Sarah E. age 4m 21d dau of C. L. Jr. and Ada in Salem, NY September 18, 1874

SPRAGUE Edward Deering age 9w son of Edward F. and Sarah D. in Salem, NY September 25, 1874

GREEN Thomas J. age 8m son of Alexander in Coila, NY October 4, 1874

PETTIT Maggie age 34y dau of Horace **WEIR** in Cambridge, NY October 7, 1874

GREGORY Frankie age 4y 6m in Whitehall, NY October 2, 1874

CARRINGTON infant son of Luke H. in Whitehall, NY October 3, 1874

WILLIAMS Mrs. Hannah M. age 71y in Ft. Miller, NY October 3, 1874

HILL John age 48y in Salem, NY October 3, 1874

MOORE Perley age 4y son of Martin H. and Delia M. **DEMING** in Arlington, Vt. October 8, 1874

CALLIGAN Mary age 20y in Ft. Edward, NY (newspaper date October 16, 1874)

QUILLION Michael age 54y in Eagle Bridge, NY October 11, 1874

GRACE Hannah age 32y in Buskirks Bridge, NY October 12, 1874

LYONS ____ age 3m child of C. in Shushan, NY October 9, 1874

AIKEN Katie age 21y wife of William in Whitehall, NY October 9, 1874

FISHER Mrs. Frank age 33y in Whitehall, NY October 10, 1874

WEIR David abt 65y in Jackson, NY October 11, 1874

FAIRLEY Charlie age 2m son of James M. and Jane in Salem, NY October 11, 1874

HARVEY Adelia age 26y wife of Joel in Ft. Ann, NY October 15, 1874

KEECH Mrs. Lucinda age 74y in Kanes Falls, NY October 16, 1874

EATON Charlie age 9y son of Levi in Ft. Ann, NY October 16, 1874

BLAKELEY Hattie in Pawlet, Vt. October 4, 1874

FOSTER Henry C. age 10y in N. Hoosick, NY October 15, 1874

CHRISTOPHER Mary age 75y in Murray Hollow, NY October 19, 1874

WILLIAMS Desire age 85y in Argyle, NY October 14, 1874

LATTIMORE ____ age 3y son of Peter in Whitehall, NY October 18, 1874

VAYETTE ____ age 2y 9m dau of Isaac in Whitehall, NY October 16, 1874

DEMAR Charles age 6y died October 15, 1874, James age 2y died October 10, 1874 children of Charles and Elizabeth in Whitehall, NY

POTTER Mrs. Hiram H. in her 52nd yr formerly of Cambridge, NY in Aurora, Ill. October 24, 1874

DOIG Rhoda B. (CULVER) in her 58th yr wife of David formerly of Cambridge, NY in Washington, Iowa October 20, 1874

WEIR Elisha age 56y in Cambridge, NY October 26, 1874

MATTISON Ellen age 24y in White Creek, NY October 24, 1874

RAY Mrs. Samuel age 87y formerly of Argyle, NY in Saratoga, NY October 22, 1874

CAPERS Levi age 44y in Granville, NY November 2, 1874

BARTLETT Martha age 20y in Cambridge, NY November 5, 1874

SWEET Mrs. Ruby age 35y in N. Hoosick, NY November 3, 1874

RYAN Willie in his 5th yr in Whitehall, NY October 31, 1874

THOMPSON John age 72y in Salem, NY November 1, 1874

HANNA Sarah age 78y in White Creek, NY November 6, 1874

FACTO Emma P. age 7y in Whitehall, NY November 14, 1874

PAPENIEU ____ dau of Frank in Whitehall, NY November 14, 1874

BAKER Alexander age 20y in Pittstown, NY November 16, 1874

BROWN Rumsey D. age 52y 7m in Whitehall, NY November 14, 1874

BROUGHTON Miss Sylvia age 40y dau of Amos in Ft. Ann, NY November 11, 1874

ESTABROOK John age 4y son of E. R. in Hoosick Falls, NY November 14, 1874

LAW Miss Lina age 72y in Granville, NY November 12, 1874

FOSTER Julius age 2y 8m in Whitehall, NY November 24, 1874

HERRINGTON Mrs. Huldah age 76y in Pittstown, NY November 13, 1874

BOWEN Eddie age 87y in Cambridge, NY November 20, 1874

THOMPSON Louise age 52y wife of James in Cambridge, NY November 25/26, 1874

NELSON Wesley age 27y in Hebron, NY November 17, 1874

DOUGLAS Mary age 73y wife of Erastus in Whitehall, NY November 20, 1874

MOSES Dr. Salomon age 82y in Hoosick Falls, NY November 25, 1874

COTTRELL Mrs. Nathan in her 76th yr formerly of Schaghticoke, NY in Victor, Iowa (newspaper date December 4, 1874)

ROBINSON infant son of Orville C. in Argyle, NY November 30, 1874

HUBBARD Mary C. age 47y in Shushan, NY December 1, 1874

FORTIN ____ age 2y dau of George in Whitehall, NY December 4, 1874

MABBITT Willie T. age 5y son of T. G. in Whitehall, NY December 5, 1874

STOCKWELL Fred abt 4y in the County Home December 5, 1874

HAWLEY John age 17y in Greenwich, NY December 17, 1874

SMITH Amanda age 28y wife of Walter and dau of late Ebenezer **SIMPSON** of Shushan, NY in Allegany Mi. December 1, 1874

MARTIN Mary E. age 17y in Cambridge, NY December 17, 1874

REAP William P. age 16y in Jackson, NY December 23, 1874

ARNOTT George E. in his 30th yr in Salem, NY December 23, 1874

SALISBURY Mary abt 60y formerly of Cambridge, NY in Hinsburgh, NY December 6, 1874

LARMON William age 90y in Cambridge, NY December 30, 1874

MAHAR Mary age 40y 3m wife of Thomas in Cambridge, NY January 4, 1875

MOORE ____ age 5m dau of Benjamin in Whitehall, NY January 2, 1875

PARRY ____ age 4y dau of J. in Whitehall, NY January 2, 1875

PETTIBONE Marietta age 67y in Whitehall, NY January 4, 1875

PARKER Gracie age 2y dau of Franklin and Anna in S. Granville, NY December 28, 1874

KISSEL Mary age 4m dau of William and Mary F. in Ft. Edward, NY December 29, 1874

HOAG Andrew age 20y son of George in Hoosick, NY January 3, 1875

TODD Gracie age 18m dau of Edward and Clemmie in Saratoga, NY January 9, 1875

LACKEY Mary age 12y dau of William in Argyle, NY January 11, 1875

MORAN John age 52y in Cambridge, NY January 13, 1875

SHERMAN Etta M. age 23y in Buskirks Bridge, NY January 7, 1875

LACKEY Miss Peggy age 70y in Hartford, NY January 4, 1875

TODD Louise (CORLISS) age 33y wife of A. S. formerly of Washington Co. NY in Sterling, Ill. December 18, 1874

WRIGHT Walter age 78y 6m formerly of Cambridge in Adrian, Mi. January 30, 1875

DOWNS A. F. age 51y in Sandy Hill, Ny January 22, 1875

PATTERSON Kittie age 3y dau of E. J. in Hoosick Falls, NY January 25, 1875

SMITH Mrs. Jane age 57y in Kingsbury, NY January 28, 1875

PARK Mrs. Almena age 82y in Jackson, NY February 6, 1875

GOODALE Mrs. M. age 88y in Whitehall, NY February 5, 1875

PLUDE _____ age 2y son of Anthony in Whitehall, NY February 7, 1875

BAIN Harry age 18y son of William in Argyle, NY February 4, 1875

HERRINGTON Lucina age 12y in W. Hoosick, NY February 3, 1875

SIMPSON Robert age 91y in Anaquasicoke, NY February 13, 1875

HALL W. S. age 52y in Cambridge, NY February 16, 1875

COREY Mrs. Joseph abt 30y in Hoosick, NY February 4, 1875

MAXWELL Annie in her 36th yr wife of Walter in Kenosha, Wis. (newspaper date February 19, 1875)

BENEDICT Abel age 84y in W. Arlington, Vt. February 11, 1875

SHIPLEY William age 15y in Cambridge, NY February 13, 1875

HERRINGTON Philo age 71y in Cobbtown, NY February 17, 1875

MC COY Hannah age 16y in Argyle, NY February 24, 1875

OATMAN Aurilla age 75y in Pumpkin Hook, NY March 5, 1875

DOYLE Phil abt 50y in Hoosick Falls, NY March 7, 1875

JOSLIN Jessie E. age 4y 9m dau of Henry P. and Emma in Hoosick Falls, NY March 24, 1875

MANCHESTER Elizabeth A. age 63y wife of E. in Hoosick Falls, NY March 24, 1875

MITCHELL Robert age 18y in Hoosick Falls, NY March 29, 1875

HASTINGS John abt 50y in Anaquasicoke, NY April 7, 1875

THOMAS Everett age 17y in Middle Falls, NY April 7. 1875

PAOZA Mrs. Rhoda age 84y at Moss St. April 3, 1875

HEDGES Donald in his 21st yr son of George in Shushan, NY April 8, 1875

VAN WAGER Mrs. Annie E. age 28y in Cambridge, NY April 10, 1875

AUSTIN Orland age 21y in Cambridge, NY April 12, 1875

LARMON Nancy dau of late Alexander of Cambridge, NY in Mansville, NY April

3, 1875

WARNER Charlie age 12y in Greenwich, NY April 15, 1875

MILLER Freddie B. age 2y son of Robert and Ann in Cambridge, NY April 24, 1875

BALL Mrs. L. Chandler age 60y in Hoosick Falls, NY April 21, 1875

MORROW Lizzie age 2y 25d dau of William and Lottie in Lake, NY April 5, 1875

TEFFT Barton age 79y in Buskirks Bridge, NY April 9, 1875

BLAIR Mrs. Catherine age 83y in Cambridge, NY April 24, 1875

MC CLELLAN John B. age 43y in Jackson, NY April 27, 1875

BENNETT Alice A. age 21y in Greenwich, NY April 21, 1875

TANNER William S. age 73y formerly of Greenwich, NY in N. Andover, Mass. April 25, 1875

GEARY Annie Jane age 3y in Sandgate, Vt. April 20, 1875

SHERMAN Nancy age 30y in Eagle Bridge, NY April 30, 1875

WELCH infant child of Mike in Whitehall, NY May 11, 1875

BALCOM Johny in his 7th yr son of E. S. in Ft. Edward, NY April 24, 1875

WHEELER Olive age 91y in S. Shaftsbury, Vt. May 6, 1875

MC EACHRON Lettie age 78y widow of John (died 3 yrs ago) in Annsville, NY May 5, 1875

MILLS Sarah F. age 61y wife of Thomas in Cambridge, NY May 6, 1875

FERGUSON John age 69y in Salem, NY May 6, 1875

TOWNE Archelaus age 93y Father of E. of Cambridge in Langden, NH May 5, 1875

KILBURN Georgie age 10m son of Harvey and Mary in Welch Hollow, NY May 13, 1875

EDIE Matilda age 71y relict of David W. in Grattan, Mi. May 23, 1875

SNOW Ann B. age 68y relict of Henry of Ft. Ann, NY in Hoosick Falls, NY May 18, 1875

BENNETT J. L. age 75y in Cambridge, NY May 22, 1875

SCOTT Mary Lillian age 16y 10m 8d dau of Olin and Celeste E. in Bennington, Vt. May 27, 1875

WHITNEY Anna M. age 34y wife of Leroy in Sandy Hill, NY May 26, 1875

ALLEN Almy age 79y in Buskirks Bridge, NY May 20, 1875

QUINN John I. age 18m 10d son of Michael and Hannah in Hoosick Falls, NY June 5, 1875

FITZGERALD Timothy age 32y in Hoosick Falls, NY June 9, 1875

STEWART Carrie abt 24y dau of Solomon in Hoosick Falls, NY June 8, 1875

LUCEY Mrs. Daniel age 34y widow in Hoosick Falls, NY June 7, 1875

CONNORS Katie age 4y 3m dau of John in Hoosick Falls, NY June 4, 1875

GAMBLE Willie A. age 4m son of Abraham in Cambridge, NY June 10, 1875

EARL Mrs. Phebe age 70y in Buskirks Bridge, NY June 14, 1875

FOSS I. H. age 68y in Sandgate, Vt. June 20, 1875

RYAN Mrs. Bridget age 74y in Eagle Bridge, NY June 24, 1875

WELCH Michael age 8y son of John and Catherine in White Creek, NY June 14, 1875

PITNEY Mary age 62y wife of Bingham of Eagle Bridge, NY in Onieda, NY (newspaper date July 16, 1875)

WILSON Josiah age 11y 1m son of Charles and Ellen A. **(GRAHAM)** in Cambridge, NY July 13, 1875

DOUGHERTY John age 16y in Hoosick Falls, NY July 11, 1875

BRODIE John age 6y son of Patrick and Mary in Troy, NY July 20, 1875

MEADER Eliza age 65y wife of Robert in Easton, NY July 11, 1875

CARPENTER Phillip Naher infant son of James H. and Anna J. of Troy, NY July 19, 1875

LAMBERT Charles W. age 6w in Jackson, NY July 7, 1875

JOSLIN Daniel age 74y in W. Hoosick, NY July 17, 1875

JACKSON Mary age 6w in Oak Hill, NY July 20, 1875

EYCLESHYMER Nicolas age 87y in Buskirks Bridge, NY July 27, 1875

CONWAY Bridget age 70y wife of Michael in Buskirks Bridge, NY July 20, 1875

BRIGGS Freddie age 1y 6m son of Charles and Elizabeth in White Creek, NY July/August 8, 1875

PROSPER infant son of A. in Whitehall, NY August 27, 1875

O'BRIEN Katie age 13y of Troy, NY in Oak Hill, NY Agust 21, 1875

MC ARTHUR Ida age 19y dau of Elsie and late W. in Putnam, NY August 23, 1875

GORDON James age 2m 11d son of James J. and Anna A. (BENNETT) in Ft. Edward, NY Spetember 1, 1875

FOWLER David age 63y in White Creek, NY September 6, 1875

MILLER Harry age 1y 4m son of George in Cambridge, NY September 5, 1875

MOORE Hattie age 8m dau of Benjamin in Hoosick, NY September 7, 1875

HURLEY Lucy age 67y in E. Salem, NY September 4, 1875

FOWLER infant child of David D. and Hannah A. in Argyle, NY September 7, 1875

BUTTERFIELD Lorana Lawton age 66y 2m 11d in Ash Grove, NY September 10, 1875

HAY Frank age 1y 5m son of C. W. and E. D. in Granville, NY September 2, 1875

HARSHA Charles G. age 54y in Cambridge, NY September 19, 1875

WILLIAMS Harrison abt 55y of Argyle, NY in the County Home September 19, 1875

GIFFORD Lydia abt 19y of Ft. Edward, NY in the County Home September 20, 1875

HACKETT Anna Mary age 15y 7m dau of John and Catherine in Bennington, Vt. September 15, 1875

WILLIAMS Eddie age 25d in the County Home September 23, 1875

SPAFFORD Ellen abt 52y of Cambridge, NY in the County Home September 24, 1875

HIGGINS Hanora age 22y in Cambridge, NY September 23, 1875

LYONS John age 5y son of Edward in Whitehall, NY September 28, 1875

NORTON James M. age 60y in Hartford, NY September 28, 1875

MILLER Mrs. David age 45y in Ft. Edward, NY October 6, 1875

FORREST Bertha L. age 14m 25d dau of Darwin and Maria in Salem, NY September 31?, 1875

HAMMOND George age 3m son of J. H. and M. S. **(DERBY)** in Sandy Hill, NY October 18, 1875

SOLES Guy D. age 11y son of Ira in Whitehall, NY November 7, 1875

CULVER James age 58y in W. Hoosick, NY November 11, 1875

BLANCHARD ____ age 17y son of J. in Whitehall, NY November 17, 1875

HALL Jane age 35y wife of William D. in Argyle, NY November 12, 1875

HILL Jane age 42y in Cambridge, NY November 26, 1875

PITTINGER Lillian age 3y 2m dau of Edward in Whitehall, NY November 29, 1875

WAIT Jennie age 16m dau of H. R. in Whitehall, NY November 27, 1875

GEORGE John Henry age 7y 5m son of Washington in Whitehall, NY December 1, 1875

NILES Nathaniel M. age 68y in Shaftsbury, Vt. December 11, 1875

MYERS Addie B. age 9y dau of David and Hattie in Harts Falls, NY December 13, 1875

HILLIBERT Mrs. Eliza age 77y in Ft. Ann, NY December 22, 1875

BUCKLEY Edna A. age 24y in Greenwich, NY December 23, 1875

CONE Zena King age 59y bro of A. B. of Cambridge, NY in Winhall, Vt. December 24, 1875

SMITH Thomas age 72y in White Creek, NY December 22, 1875

HERRINGTON ____ age 2m child of Martin and Gertrude in Jackson, NY December 25, 1875

BROWN Emily **(VOLENTINE)** age 41y wife of William Q. formerly of Jackson, NY in Irvington, NY January 1, 1876

SIMPSON Mrs. W. D. age 33y in Ft. Edward, NY January 1, 1876 and son George W. age 7m died November 6, 1875

SWEET Lewis age 2y 3m son of Freeman and Emma in White Creek, NY January 3, 1876

PENFIELD Sarah A. age 61y 1m in Whitehall, NY December 31, 1875

SANFORD ____ age 2y son of Milo in Whitehall, NY January 1, 1876

PENDERGRASS James age 77y in Argyle, NY December 20, 1875

BATEMAN Abigail age 84y in Granville, NY December 22, 1875

WATKINS Cornelia B. age 32y wife of John in Granville, NY January 17, 1876

WELLS Julian age 5y 3m 20d son of Henry and Annie in Whitehall, NY January 17, 1876

GREEN Ruth age 72y in Cambridge, NY January 21, 1876

HAYNES John C. age 94y in Hoosick, NY January 22, 1876

HAMILTON Ann age 44y in Easton, NY January 13, 1876

PARKER Mrs. Sarah in Middle Falls, NY January 14, 1876

THOMPSON David B. in his 75th yr in Salem, NY January 16, 1876

BABCOCK Marvin Md. age 31y in Middle Falls, NY January 13, 1876

MYNDERSE Nancy age 86y in Easton, NY (newspaper date January 28, 1876)

RICE Mrs. John age 62y in S. Argyle, NY January 21, 1876

JEMERY Luella Belle age 3m 21d dau of Joseph and Louise in Whitehall, NY January 27, 1876

DILL Theodora M. age 3m 6d dau of Hannah and late Theodore in Whitehall, NY January 28, 1876

WHEELER Mrs. ____ agt 70y in S. Argyle, NY January 28, 1876

DYER Frank age 43y in Greenwich, NY January 31, 1876

DONALDSON John B. age 68y in N. Greenwich, NY January 30, 1876

MC COLLUM Thomas age 74y at res of Zina **TUCKER** in Ft. Miller, NY (newspaper date February 18, 1876)

LIVINGSTON Stella M. age 2w dau of Fred B. and Stella in Burlington, Vt. February 16, 1876

HAYNER Charles age 31y in Whitehall, NY February 15, 1876

STARKS Mrs. Catherine age 75y in Arlington, Vt. February 24, 1876

SPENCER ____ age 1y child of Almon in Easton, NY February 25, 1876

BENNETT John J. age 3y 7m son of James in Battenville, NY February 29, 1876

HENRY Alexander in his 67th yr formerly of Washington Co. NY in Freeland, Ill. February 23, 1876

MC DOUAL Elsie age 89y in Jackson, NY March 4, 1876

DERBY Anna age 95y widow of Abner in Rupert, Vt. March 2, 1876

LEWIS infant dau of William and Mary in Rupert, Vt. March 2, 1876

SAFFORD John L. age 57y in Ft. Miller, NY March 7, 1876

COWAN Kezia age 63y wife of Thomas M. formerly of Cambridge, NY in Courtland, Mi. (newspaper date March 17, 1876)

SWEET Benjamin G. age 80y in Hoosick, NY March 18, 1876

BLOSSOM Fidelia age 58y in W. Pawlet, Vt. March 19, 1876

HARRINGTON ____ age 4y son of Richard in Easton, NY March 8, 1876

CORBETT James J. age 2y 10m son of L. in Whitehall, NY March 12, 1876

MC LAUGHLIN Isaac age 28y in Putnam, NY March 7, 1876

BAILEY Mrs. Franklin age 43y in Ft. Ann, NY March 11, 1876

RICE James R. age 44y 10m 12d son of Dr. James in Ft. Ann, NY March 13, 1876

HENRY Maria age 53y 8m wife of Walter in Buskirks Bridge, NY March 19, 1876

MORRISON Mary Ann abt 22y of Salem, NY in the County Home March 17, 1876

WRIGHT Maria age 60y wife of Sidney in Cambridge, NY March 29, 1876

MC COLT ____ age 6w dau of Oscar and Helen in Salem, NY March 29, 1876

PRINDLE Edwin age 56y formerly of Argyle in Saratoga Springs, NY April 1, 1876

COBB Hannah age 85y sis of Leonard **WELLS** of Cambridge, NY in Cleveland, Ohio March 30, 1876

ROBINSON Fannie age 9m dau of John and Adelaide in White Creek, NY March 31, 1876

HENRY Stephen age 1y 6m in Arlington, Vt. April 5, 1876

WARNER William H. age 25y in Cambridge, NY March 25, 1876

PARK Jane abt 70y wife of John Jr. formerly of Hartford, NY in W. Liberty, Iowa March 9, 1876

KEALEY Barron age 74y in Hoosick, NY April 2, 1876

BRIMMER Daniel in his 90th yr in Hoosick, NY April 2, 1876

FAULKENBURY Lafayette age 51y in Whitehall, NY April 5, 1876

DORR Franklin age 72y in Waymart, Pa. April 7, 1876

ALMY Prudence age 76y in Buskirks Bridge, NY April 7, 1876

WILLIAMSON Mary A. age 39y in N. Argyle, NY April 17, 1876

DAVIDSON Sarah Ann age 20y in Dunhams Basin, NY April 7, 1876

PEARSONS Helen in Ft. Edward, NY April 8, 1876

JENKINS Mrs. Joanna in Center Falls, NY April 2, 1876

BOLAN James age 46y in N. Greenwich, NY March 31, 1876

WILEY Mary Ann age 18y in Battenville, NY April 3, 1876

WARNER William age 72y in Northeast, Pa. April 3, 1876

ROBERTSON Jeremiah age 70y in Greenwich, NY April 15, 1876

DOBBIN Samuel age 86y in Greenwich, NY April 18, 1876

VALENTINE Mrs. Margaret A. age 67y in Ft. Edward, NY April 22, 1876

RICE Hercules age 71y formerly of White Creek, NY in Otsego, Mi. (newspaper date May 5, 1876)

HUNT Margaret age 2y 6m dau of William and Hannah in Indian Lake, NY April 27, 1876

BLANCHARD Frank age 2y son of Edward in Indian Lake, NY April 16, 1876

STEWART Joseph age 30y in Eagle Bridge, NY May 1, 1876

BURDETT Israel in his 85th yr in Whitehall, NY May 4, 1876

SULLIVAN John age 7y in Murray Hollow, NY May 3, 1876

GILL Mary B. age 37y of New York in Greenwich, NY May 14, 1876

SPRAGUE Susan age 77y relict of John in Salem, NY May 6, 1876

BRIGGS Mrs. David age 88y in Ft. Ann, NY May 18, 1876

MC INTOSH Mrs. S. age 64y in Camden, NY May 23, 1876

ALMY Willie age 14m son of Frederick and Margaret (**BLANCHARD**) in Easton, NY May 25, 1876

PARISH Daniel age 71y 11m 12d in Salem, NY June 9, 1876

MC MILLAN Ebenezer age 47y in Salem, NY June 12, 1876

RUSSELL Abijah age 76y of Hartford, NY in the County Home June 4, 1876

FOWLER Henry age 2y son of David D. in Argyle, NY (newspaper date June 16, 1876)

WELLS Delia A. age 1y dau of E. S. and E. in Sandy Hill, NY June 2, 1876

SCHERMERHORN Roscoe C. age 8y son of Dr. B. and Anna of Buskirks Bridge, NY run over by horses in Esperance, NY June 8, 1876

MC NEIL William age 68y formerly of Argyle, NY in Hayesville, Ohio June 7, 1876

HUNTINGTON Deborah D. wife of William D. and dau of Otis **DILLINGHAM** of Granville, NY in E. Randolph, NY June 6, 1876

TIERNEY ____ age 15m son of Phillip in N. Argyle, NY June 17, 1876

BRIMMER Vashti age 23y in Eagle Bridge, NY June 15, 1876

HAYNES John age 70y in Athens, NY June 23, 1876

GROESBECK Nicolas age 77y in S. Cambridge, NY June 28, 1876

COULTER Susie May age 2y 9d dau of W. G. and Angeline in E. Arlington, Vt. June 29, 1876

VANCE Eliza age 54y wife of William in Battenville, NY July 7, 1876

CADY Almira M. age 67y Mother of Mrs. O. L. **WHITCOMB** of Argyle, NY in Wethersfield, Vt. June 20, 1876

BARTHOLOMEW Mrs. Florence age 64y in Whitehall, NY July 9, 1876

COOKE J. R. age 8m 5d son of R. C. in Whitehall, NY July 30, 1876

NOLT Sarah age 22y wife of Barney in W. Hoosick, NY August 6, 1876

CONWAY Anna age 15d dau of Peter and Bridget in Oak Hill, NY August 8, 1876

BURTON Richard age 9m in Whitehall, NY August 11, 1876

SHARROCK William age 39y at Fathers in Mechanicsville, NY August 16, 1876

BARNES Harry age 1y 4m son of Walter and Alice in Hoosick Falls, NY August 22, 1876

MILLER Aaron age 66y of Easton, NY in the County Home August 21, 1876

SHANKS Ethel Harriet age 5m dau of Robert and Sophia in Greenwich, NY August 25, 1876

MARTIN Sidney age 4y son of Martin and Esther (**ROBERSON**) in Sandgate, Vt. (newspaper date September 1, 1876)

CHALMERS Mrs. Margaret age 89y in Mooers, NY August 22, 1876

GLEASON Mary age 54y wife of Michael in Ft. Edward, NY August 22, 1876

HARCOURT Willie age 13m son of Robert and Mary J. in Middle Falls, NY September 1, 1876

RUSSELL W. A. in his 64th yr in Salem, NY September 1, 1876

FOWLER William age 76y in White Creek, NY September 6, 1876

SHERMAN George W. age 18m in Eagle Bridge, NY August 24, 1876

GRAVES Nathan age 87y 10m in W. Rupert, Vt. (newspaper date September 8, 1876)

WILSON infant son of James in Whitehall, NY September 2, 1876

MILLER Myron abt 50y in Comstocks, NY September 2, 1876

MOFFATT Oscar age 4m son of Philander and Alice in Rupert, Vt. September 7, 1876

PETTEYS Charlie age 11y 9m son of Horace and Phebe in Jackson, NY September 9, 1876

WHITESIDE Maria Jeanette age 27y dau of W. P. and Maria J. in Maysville, NY September 1, 1876

GILMORE Jemima age 66y wife of John in Chili, NY September 19, 1876

GILCHRIST William L. in his 64th yr in Hebron, NY September 16, 1876

WALLER Mrs. Lydia age 82y in S. Hartford, NY September 25, 1876

BIXBY Rev. John age 60y in Cambridge, NY September 27, 1876

NOXON James P. age 77y in White Creek, NY September 28, 1876

BARTON Eunice age 76y in Cambridge, NY September 26, 1876

WING D. Smith age 65y formerly of Sandy Hill, NY in Saratoga Springs, NY September 23, 1876

DOBBIN Anna **(WELLS)** age 36y wife of John W. in Salem, NY September 22, 1876

MANNING William H. age 33y in N. Argyle, NY October 4, 1876

HARRINGTON Freelove age 78y in Argyle, NY October 4, 1876

SINSENBARTH Emma J. age 2y 7m dau of Frederick and Louisa in Salem, NY October 11, 1876

SINNOT Ella **(WELCH)** age 27y wife of William in Whitehall, NY October 11, 1876

DUNTON Phebe age 62y in Cambridge, NY October 15, 1876

MILLER Anna age 76y wife of Moses W. in Jackson, NY October 3, 1876

EYCLESHYMER Herbert A. age 26y in Eagle Bridge, NY September 27, 1876

MC GEOCH Mrs. Phebe age 73y in Coila, NY October 3, 1876

PLATT Carrie E. age 10y dau of Andrew K. and Hannah I. in Buskirks Bridge, NY October 4, 1876

MC CLELLAN Henry age 72y in Brighton, Ohio September 15, 1876

WHITE Hannah age 79y in N. Hebron, NY October 18, 1876

SMITH Jeremiah abt 65y in N. Hebron, NY October 18, 1876

CONGDON Duncan age 37y in Shushan, NY October 20, 1876

HORTON Lucien M. age 43y in Cambridge, NY October 19, 1876

MC FARLAND Mrs. Daniel in her 84th yr in Hebron, NY October 18, 1876

ROWE Mary age 78y in N. Granville, NY October 21, 1876

NORTHUP ____ age 17y dau of John in Granville, NY October 22, 1876

REYNOLDS ____ age 6y child of Thomas in Granville, NY October 22, 1876

BOWEN Sylvester age 80y in Cambridge, NY October 28, 1876

WANDELL Betsey abt 65y in Argyle, NY October 27, 1876

HANNAN Elizabeth age 68y in Arlington, Vt. October 30, 1876

LAW Catherine age 82y in W. Salem, NY October 27, 1876

EDDY Ann age 67y wife of J. W. in Cambridge, NY November 1, 1876

SKELLIE Elizabeth age 72y wife of William formerly of Cambridge, NY in Syracuse, NY November 5, 1876

WRIGHT Clarissa in her 73rd yr in White Creek, NY November 6, 1876

JOHNSON Miss Annie age 17y 3m in Durkeetown, NY November 11, 1876

BOCKES James A. age 69y 8m 1d in W. Hebron, NY November 8, 1876

MARTIN Lydia (CLARK) age 84y 2m 19d widow of Mason in Hartford, NY November 7, 1876

MONROE Joseph age 101y 1m in Whitehall, NY November 7, 1876

WATERS infant son of Merritt in Whitehall, NY November 8, 1876

BUSTARD ____ age 15m son of William in Whitehall, NY November 9, 1876

EYCLESHYMER Mrs. Herbert abt 28y in Eagle Bridge, NY November 4, 1876

HANNON William age 4y 5m son of Michael in Cambridge, NY November 6, 1876

HOGABOOM Louisa age 13y dau of Almira in Cambridge, NY November 14, 1876

GREEN Charles B. age 17y in Argyle, NY November 9, 1876

HAVILAND Charles abt 60 formerly of Easton in Saratoga, NY October 27, 1876

BAKER Patience age 74y wife of Simeon in Easton, NY November 5, 1876

BAKER Moses age 75y in Easton, NY November 7, 1876

DAY Mary Ann age 60y wife of Oel in Cambridge, NY November 20, 1876

BURROUGHS H. abt 55y in Cambridge, NY November 20, 1876

MOULTON Nancy age 40y wife of C. F. and dau of Orlando HORTON of Cambridge, NY in Yonkers, NY November 22, 1876

JOHNSON James age 19y 6m son of James and Bridget in Durkeetown, NY November 17, 1876

ROGERS Louisa age 47y wife of James M. in Hebron, NY November 26, 1876

MC FERRON Mrs. Aseneth age 74y in Whitehall, NY November 23, 1876

LYONS Theodore age 69y in Whitehall, NY November 20, 1876

MC EACHRON Margaret Y. age 71y wife of Henry in E. Greenwich, NY November 25, 1876

SMITH Daniel age 78y in Post Corners, NY December 5, 1876

KING James age 88y in Argyle, NY November 30, 1876

SHELDON James age 85y in Rupert, Vt. November 27, 1876

GARDEPHE Maggie age 45y 6m 22d wife of Modesta in Glens Falls, NY November 26, 1876

MC NITT Cassandra **(COOKE)** age 45y wife of B. F. in Cambridge, NY November 27, 1876

PRATT Lydia age 81y in White Creek, NY November 29, 1876

GORDON Dr. A. B. in Ft. Edward, NY December 2, 1876

WINSHIP Mrs. Mary age 30y in W. Pawlet, Vt. December 2, 1876, son age 2y died last week

BULL Gifford age 63y in Ft. Ann, NY December 9, 1876

WHITE Harriet **(FENTON)** age 49y wife of John in Cambridge, NY December 16, 1876

MC CLELLAN Mrs. Christian F. age 71y in Shushan, NY December 20, 1876

COPELAND Libbie **(BROWN)** age 35y in N. Argyle, NY December 17, 1876

CRAWFORD James H. age 41y in Hebron, NY January 3, 1877

TILFORD Charlie Rowan age 13y 6m son of Rev. J. H. and grand son of A. M. **ROWAN** in Tipton, Ind. December 28, 1876

KILMER Mrs. George age 62y in Argyle, NY January 5, 1877

PRATT Eva F. age 2y 11m dau of Andrew K. and Hannah J. in Cambridge, NY January 3, 1877

MC MURRAY Mrs. Anna age 57y in Brattleboro, Vt. January 6, 1877

RICE James formerly of Cambridge, NY in Granby Ctr. NY December 23, 1876

BUCK Mina age 89y in Arlington, Vt. January 5, 1877

TOWNSEND Joel B. age 73y 10m in Whitehall, NY January 11, 1877

MC INTYRE Peter age 78y in Ft. Edward, NY January 5, 1877

SWEET Aruna H. age 77y in Hoosick, NY January 13, 1877

WELCOME _____ age 5m child of Peter in Cambridge, NY January 19, 1877

BRAYTON Harriet E. **(DEWEY)** age 41y wife of Eli Jr. in Troy, NY January 19, 1877

GIFFORD Jane M. age 51y wife of Col. H. formerly of Easton, NY in Richland, Mi. January 15, 1877

HOLBROOK Amariah age 60y formerly of Sandy Hill, NY in Golden, Col. January 22, 1877

NEWTON Asahel age 75y in Hartford, NY January 20, 1877

TUCKER Mercy age 91y in N. Greenwich, NY January 18, 1877

RIVETT Joseph age 68y in Whitehall, NY January 22, 1877

WAIT Walter W. age 10m son of A. D. and Celina in Ft. Edward, NY February 5, 1877

LAMBERT John in Greenwich, NY February 6, 1877

VAUGHN W. Scott age 28y in Ft. Ann, NY February 2, 1877

LEE Howard abt 32y in Eagle Bridge, NY February 14, 1877

LIVINGSTON Frank age 19y son of George Jr. and Anna and grand son of Duncan of Cambridge, NY in New York February 13, 1877

MUNSON James E. age 54y in N. Argyle, NY February 19, 1877

DURKEE Frankie W. age 3y 10m son of John R. and Eliza in Durkeetown, NY February 24, 1877

HUGGINS Mary M. age 54y in N. Argyle, NY February 21, 1877

TERRY Reconcile age 73y nr Ft. Miller, NY (newspaper date March 2, 1877)

DARBY Leonard age 90y 6m in Hoosick Falls, NY February 23, 1877

INGALLS Mrs. Barbara age 65y in W. Hebron, NY February 2, 1877

MC INTYRE Miss Mary age 16y 8m in W. Hebron, NY February 22, 1877

DENNIS Lonnie son of S. H. in Greenwich, NY February 19, 1877

ROBERTSON Ellen I. age 64y formerly of Washington DC in Cambridge, NY March 8, 1877

CULVER George R. age 21d son of Ensign and Kate in Juneau, Wis. March 2, 1877

ROSS Susannah (**BLANCHARD**) age 73y widow of Henry P. in Essex, NY February 26, 1877

POWELL Mrs. Phoebe age 77y in Granville, NY February 24, 1877

HICKS Mrs. Jerusha age 83y in Granville, NY February 24, 1877

WEBSTER George former Pastor Baptist Church in Sandy Hill, NY in New York February 23, 1877

DUNHAM Samuel age 83y in Dunhams Basin, NY February 28, 1877

LYMAN Mrs. Betsey age 67y in Anaquasicoke, NY March 1, 1877

MILLETT John age 3m son of John and Bridget in Oak Hill, NY March 7, 1877

MC LEAN Miss Mary K. age 68y in Jackson, NY March 4, 1877

COOK Clarence age 8m son of Palmer in Whitehall, NY February 28, 1877

ST CLAIR Lucy age 42y in Whitehall, NY March 3, 1877

SMITH Hannah S. age 86y in Whitehall, NY March 5, 1877

MC CLELLAN Mrs. Margaret age 64y formerly of Salem, NY in Yorktown, Ill. February 22, 1877

HARRIS Emery D. in his 39th yr in Ft. Edward, NY March 7, 1877

CRANDALL Mary E. age 56y wife of Gideon in Durkeetown, NY March 1, 1877

CAVANAUGH Mary age 58y widow in Sandy Hill, NY March 6, 1877

WHITNEY Chauncey age 61y of White Creek, NY in County Home March 2, 1877

MC KEAN Catherine age 85y in White Creek, NY March 4, 1877

HOAG Robert age 81y of Easton, NY in Cambridge, NY March 10, 1877

LASHWOOD Matilda in her 49th yr wife of Levi formerly of Granville, NY and dau of Thomas and Chloe J. **WAIT** in Berlin, Mi. (newspaper date March 16, 1877)

CADY Sarah E. abt 30y wife of James and dau of S. W. **WRIGHT** of Cambridge, NY in St. Louis, Mo. March 9, 1877

TYRELL Richard age 65y of Whitehall, NY in the County Home March 15, 1877

MAXWELL Daniel age 85y in Argyle, NY March 17, 1877

MORRIS Mrs. Surette E. age 36y in Hebron, NY March 16, 1877

SULLIVAN ____ age 18m son of John in Whitehall, NY March 17, 1877

FORT Eunicy age 68y in Easton, NY March 9, 1877

EYCLESHYMER Peter in Easton, NY March 9, 1877

CARSWELL Mrs. Alexander age 73y in Ft. Miller, NY February 24, 1877

MILLER Sidney B. age 69y in Dunhams Basin, NY March 14, 1877

STICKNEY William in his 71st yr in Kingsbury, Ny March 11, 1877

DARDIS Mrs. Christopher abt 50y widow in Sandy Hill, NY March 13, 1877

CRAWFORD Hannah M. age 35y in Greenwich, NY March 9, 1877

WASHBURN Thomas age 53y in Hartford, NY March 13, 1877

PILLING Louis age 7m son of Charles and Carrie in Salem, NY March 13, 1877

GALVIN Mrs. John age 45y in Easton, NY March 19, 1877

LYLE Mary age 64y in W. Hebron, NY March 18, 1877

KILBURN Nellie Viola age 24y 17d wife of E. Jerome in Brandon, Vt. March 20, 1877

BASS Mrs. Sally age 83y in Post Corners, NY March 23, 1877

HAGGERTY Michael age 75y in Buskirks Bridge, NY March 26, 1877

BOURNE Orson age 43y in Sandy Hill, NY March 23, 1877

BROWN Charles H. abt 28y formerly of Cambridge in Burlington, Vt. April 2, 1877

HALL Julia B. age 19y in Cambridge, NY April 2, 1877

DANFORTH Lydia M. age 48y wife of Isaac in N. Hoosick, NY April 4, 1877

SANDERS Catherine age 34y of Ft. Miller, NY in the County Home March 28, 1877

HUGHES Frank age 6y of Whitehall, NY in the County Home March 29, 1877

WHEELER E. M. age 88y of Argyle, NY in the County Home March 27, 1877

MONROE Asa age 79y of Dresden, NY in the County Home March 31, 1877

TINKEY Stephen age 79y in Argyle, NY April 1, 1877

COPELAND ____ age 15m dau of W. J. in N. Argyle, NY March 27, 1877

CALDWELL Wallace E. age 58y formerly of Whitehall, NY in New York March 22, 1877

JILLSON Mrs. Harriet age 62y in W. Hebron, NY April 8, 1877

BRYAN Michael age 3m of Granville, NY in the County Home April 9, 1877

RODD David abt 35y in Menominee, Mi. April 5, 1877

BARKLEY Henry in his 81st yr in Salem, NY April 11, 1877

STOTT James A. age 22y in Argyle, NY April 10, 1877

KING Delevan G. age 82y in Buskirks Bridge, NY April 11, 1877

BENNETT Mary age 60y widow of Benjamin in Kankekee, Ill. April 11, 1877

CAVANAUGH Daniel age 77y in Cambridge, NY April 16, 1877

SHERMAN Elizbeth M. age 77y wife of Zina in Cambridge, NY April 19, 1877

WILLIAMS infant dau of Alfred and Julia in Durkeetown, NY April 12, 1877

SKINNER Mary E. age 61y widow of Calvin formerly of Cambridge, NY in Herndon Va. April 4, 1877

GIFFORD Jeremiah age 61y in Cambridge, NY April 23, 1877

PALMER John age 56y of Salem, NY in the County Home April 21, 1877

MATHEWS Sidney age 89y in S. Argyle, NY April 18, 1877

HAWES Walter E. bro of Maria of Cambridge in S. Boston, Mass. April 24, 1877

MATTISON Zina H. age 67y in Sandy Hill, NY April 15, 1877

WILLIAMS Mary age 86y wife of Eli S. in Salem, NY April 14, 1877

STOVER George age 66y in Cambridge, NY April 20, 1877

DONNELLY John age 81y 10m in Hartford, NY April 23, 1877

MC INTYRE Miss Polly in W. Hebron, NY April 28, 1877

CUMMINGS Edward abt 40y in Salem, NY April 23, 1877

WHEADON Mrs. abt 80y widow of David in W. Pawlet, Vt. April 25, 1877

GALLOWAY Sally age 4y of Buskirks Bridge in the County Home April 25, 1877

MC MURRAY Robert James age 29y in Argyle, NY April 26, 1877

HAYS Edward age 19y in Putnam, NY May 5, 1877

HARRINGTON Arnold age 77y in White Creek, NY May 7, 1877

DEACON William age 72y in Hebron, NY May 10, 1877

KINNE Grant in his 13th yr son of Asa and Maryette in Rupert, Vt. May 6, 1877

WALSH Almira age 74y 2m 21d wife of Peter in Cambridge, NY May 15, 1877

LEWIS Amasa age 63y of Wells Vt. in Eagle Bridge, NY May 7, 1877

NELSON Mrs. age 79y formerly of N. Adams Mass.in N. Argyle, NY May 19, 1877

JACOBS Jennie age 84y of Kingsbury, NY in the County Home May 20, 1877

BELL Mary age 14y dau of Sidney in Ft. Edward, NY May 8, 1877

DEACON Martha age 75y relict of William in Hebron, NY May 19, 1877

GRIFFIN John age 29y in Hartford, NY May 8, 1877

MC GOWAN Mrs. Catherine age 76y in Argyle, NY May 15, 1877

LA ROSE Joseph age 49y in Whitehall, NY May 16, 1877

LAWRENCE Alpheus L. in his 68th yr in Albany, NY May 27, 1877

BROWN William age 58y in Hartford, NY May 24, 1877

FERGUSON Mary age 82y of Salem, NY in the County Home May 26, 1877

WEIR William abt 55y of Jackson, NY in the County Home May 20, 1877

GODOU Francis age 73y in Whitehall, NY May 25, 1877

LIDDLE Margaret age 72y in N. Argyle, NY June 9, 1877

GRAHAM William I. in his 79th yr native of Washington Co. in Reynoldsburg, Ohio June 3, 1877

WELCH Alvira age 62y wife of Abel S. at Fitchs Point, NY June 8, 1877

MC NAUGHTON Capt. John D. age 34y 3m 22d of the 188th Reg. NY Vol. son of D. R. of Mumford, NY in Washington DC May 9, 1877, buried Caledonia, NY

LEWIS Willie age 10y son of E. P. and Mary A. in Jackson, NY June 20, 1877

CORNELL George T. son of F. B. in Cambridge, NY June 14, 1877

THOMPSON Margaret age 71y in Anaquasicoke, NY June 10, 1877

MC NEIL John R. age 69y in Argyle, NY June 14, 1877

MURRAY Margaret abt 65y in N. Argyle, NY June 15, 1877

WALSH Ada F. age 23y in N. Argyle, NY June 18, 1877

RIGGS Ebenezer age 74y of Argyle, NY in the County Home June 16, 1877

BARRYDON Mary age 27y of Granville, NY in the County Home June 13, 1877

MELLOR Elizabeth widow of Thomas in Ft. Edward, NY June 13, 1877

EDWARDS Eunice in her 70th yr widow of Job in Martinsville, Ill. June 13, 1877

TIERNEY Margaret age 45y wife of Patrick in White Creek, NY June 25, 1877

OVIATT Lydia age 26y in Cambridge, NY June 29, 1877

CHASE Mrs. Nancy age 68y in Cambridge, NY July 4, 1877

WALKER Sayles age 20y in Cambridge, NY July 4, 1877

BARBER David age 81y in Cambridge, NY June 22, 1877

O'REILLY Miss Emma age 21y at sis Mrs. **WARNER** in Whitehall, NY July 2, 1877

LELAND L. B. age 55y in Whitehall, NY June 30, 1877

CRANDALL Warren age 63y in Easton, NY July 3, 1877

MURDOCK Catherine in her 57th yr wife of Stephen formerly of Salem, NY in Detroit, Mi. July 3, 1877

LEE Norman age 66y in M. Granville, NY June 30, 1877

NEWMAN Mary A. age 26y dau of John H. and Sylvia A. formerly of Cambridge,

NY in Sing Sing, NY June 17, 1877

DUNCAN Patience (**CARTER**) in her 74th yr wife of David in Salem, NY July 6, 1877

GUY Timothy age 88y formerly of Kingsbury, NY in Benton, Mi. June 30, 1877

DRECE Byron age 5y of Easton, NY in the County Home July 12, 1877

GREEN Anna M. age 10m dau of Ambrose in Cambridge, NY July 18, 1877

FOSTER Mrs. Mary E. age 61y in Whitehall, NY July 11, 1877

GAY Charles N. age 18y 6m son of J. W. and Anna in White Creek, NY July 14, 1877

QUA Mrs. Sarah E. age 76y in Belcher, NY July 20, 1877

HARPER Miss Elizabeth age 62y in S. Argyle, NY July 21, 1877

BURLINGTON George age 35y in Cambridge, NY July 27, 1877

LAMPRA Catherine age 25y in Whitehall, NY July 23, 1877

CHATFIELD Jessie age 4y 9m dau of H. S. and S. M. in Hoosick Falls, NY July 26, 1877

BURDICK Jennie age 37y in Eagle Bridge, NY July 27, 1877

MOSELEY Charlotte A. age 68y in Eagle Bridge, NY July 30, 1877

PADDEN John age 45y in E. Greenwich, NY July 30, 1877

WRIGHT Mary E. abt 73y wife of Walter formerly of Whitehall, NY in Tabor, Iowa July 25, 1877

MC NEIL Dale C. age 1y 24d son of Dr. J. S. and Josephine in Argyle, NY August 7, 1877

NICHOLSON Mary E. age 23y wife of L. E. in Cambridge, NY August 2, 1877

THOMPSON Squire in his 79th yr in N. Granville, NY August 6, 1877

GILCHRIST James H. age 72y in Ft. Edward, NY August 1, 1877

BECKETT Michael age 87y in Whitehall, NY August 6, 1877

CULL Mrs. Mary E. age 36y in Whitehall, NY August 11, 1877

HURD Frankie A. age 15m dau of D. D. and M. F. in Buskirks Bridge, NY August

14, 1877

HUTCHINS Benjamin age 86y brother-in-law- of R. S. **FISH** of Cambridge, NY in Mechanicsville, NY August 21, 1877

ROACH William age 28y in S. Glens Falls, NY August 15, 1877

HEWITT Nannie age 3y 11m dau of S. M. and Mary in White Creek, NY August 18, 1877

WARD William Mathias age 2y 10m son of William and Sarah D. in Ft. Ann, NY August 24, 1877

STYLES _____ age 2y dau of Samuel in Easton, NY August 17, 1877

HOADLEY Marion B. age 9m dau of George A. and Ida M. in Argyle, NY August 27, 1877

SKELLIE Jennie wife of Edward formerly of Cambridge, NY in Mina, NY August 16, 1877

HAYES Margaret age 76y in Murray Hollow, NY August 29, 1877

BLAIR Maggie age 2y dau of James and Agnes in Putnam, NY September 6, 1877

IRVIN Susan wife of Alexander Proudfit Irvin and dau of Robert L. **TAYLOR** in New York September 9, 1877

HAMMOND Edson formerly of Ft. Edward, NY in St Louis, Mo. September 2, 1877

HALL Edwin age 75y 8m in Auburn, NY September 8, 1877

QUA Mrs. J. A. age 70y formerly of Washington Co. in Ft. Covington, NY (newspaper date September 28, 1877)

TIERNEY Hugh age 84y in N. Argyle, NY September 22, 1877

HURD Merritt C. age 16y son of Chauncey formerly of Cambridge, NY in Sandgate, Vt. September 5, 1877

ALLEN Laura **(RICE)** widow of F. S. in Monmouth, Ill. August 28, 1877

REID James E. age 63y formerly of Argyle, NY in Racine, Wis. September 9, 1877

HARSHA Henry M. age 60y in Ft. Edward, NY September 25, 1877

RICKERT James age 70y in Putnam, NY September 30, 1877

MAXWELL Mrs. William age 66y in W. Hebron, NY September 25, 1877

WILLIS Lucinda age 84y wife of Antipas in Granville, NY October 13, 1877

BURDOU Antoine age 48y in Whitehall, NY October 11, 1877

TANNER Joshua age 83y in Cambridge, NY October 5, 1877

MC GILL Elizabeth wife of W. A. in Hebron, NY October 17, 1877

DUGAN James Augustine age 2y 6m son of Henry in Cambridge, NY September 29, 1877

DUGAN Ellen age 67y wife of Hugh in Cambridge, NY October 13, 1877

SPRAGUE Sara age 16m dau of Joseph in Arlington, Vt. October 19, 1877

MANGARVIN Julia age 19y in White Creek, NY October 17, 1877

DE LURY Mrs. Alice age 70y in Salem, NY October 21, 1877

KETCHUM Austin age 6y 7m son of William and Eunice in Cambridge, NY October 29, 1877

MONCRIEF Mrs. Hepsibah P. age 87y in Shushan, NY October 31, 1877

COPELAND Josie F. age 26y dau of John and P. S. in Glens Falls, NY October 27, 1877

MC CLELLAN John age 5y 5m in Cambridge, NY October 31, 1877

ANDERSON William Sr. age 94y in Putnam, NY October 25, 1877

WRIGHT Mrs. Amanda age 65y in Ticonderoga, NY November 5, 1877

TOBEY Francis M. age 82y in Easton, NY November 8, 1877

GRIFFIN Thomas age 77y in Adamsville, NY October 27, 1877

DOBBIN Mrs. Joseph age 72y in Lakeville, NY November 8, 1877

FISH Mary L. age 28y wife of Marcus in Eagle Bridge, NY November 9, 1877

ALLEN Mrs. Martin age 51y in Ft. Edward, NY October 7, 1877

BURBANK John S. age 72y in N. Granville, NY September 29, 1877

WHITCOMB Elliot Fairbanks abt 70y brother-in-law of A. B. **CONE** of Cambridge, NY in Munson, Mass. November 7, 1877

KERR Elizabeth age 93y 5d in Jackson, NY December 5, 1877

WEEKS Richard age 77y in Pawlet, Vt. December 3, 1877

BUCK Franklin age 71y in Cambridge, NY December 8, 1877

BUCK Charles age 73y in Arlington, Vt. December 6, 1877

ASHTON William abt 76y formerly of Cambridge, NY in Tanganoxie, Ks. December 9, 1877

HUNT Cora E. age 4y 11m 15d dau of Darius and Jane in Schaghticoke, NY December 29, 1877

SANFORD Milo age 58y in Whitehall, NY January 20, 1878

BRADLEY Ephraim L. abt 60y in Easton, NY January 21, 1878

INGALLS Mrs. Myron abt 40y in Benson, Vt. January 24, 1878

ROSS Oliver age 77y formerly of Greenwich, NY in Normal, Ill. January 14, 1878

HODGE Jerome M. age 38y in Cambridge, NY February 2, 1878

GREGORY Julia age 21y formerly of Ft. Edward in Buffalo, NY January 25, 1878

MOSHER Sophia H. in Ovid, NY February 21, 1878

HATCH Catherine M. age 49y in Greenwich, NY March 1, 1878

GILBERT C. age 21y in Ft. Edward, NY March 12, 1878

CARR Sarah age 2y in Kanes Falls, NY March 13, 1878

CARR William age 34y in Kanes Falls, NY March 15, 1878

HILL William M. abt 40y in S. Granville, NY March 20, 1878

BARTLETT Prudence age 83y in Sandgate, Vt. March 15, 1878. Son Danforth

PRATT Mrs. Mary L. in Alabama, NY April 17, 1878

PAYTON Mrs. Mary age 81y in Whitehall, NY April 25, 1878

HOLLISTER Miss Jane age 66y in N. Pawlet, Vt. May 7, 1878

MC EVOY Marcella ae 26y wife of Patrick in Cambridge, NY May 7, 1878

WHITCOMB Rhoda C. age 70y widow of E. F. and sis of A. B. **CONE** in Munson, Mass. May 5, 1878

SLOAN Jane P. age 78y in S. Bay, NY May 17, 1878

NORTON Eleanah M. (**WHEELOCK**) age 40y 11m wife of Albert C. in Greenwich, NY May 31, 1878

HOYT Frederick D. in his 72nd yr in W. Arlington, Vt. July 17, 1878

DINGS George age 12y son of Casper and Jane in Lake, NY July 31, 1878

SALTER Mrs. John in Barkers Grove, NY August 6, 1878

MASON William L. age 50y in Ft. Ann, NY August 6, 1878

NORTON Mary age 92y widow of Russell formerly of Cambridge, NY in New Haven, NY July 29, 1878

COMSTOCK James abt 75y in Center Village, NY August 19, 1878, bro of late Thomas of Cambridge, NY

MC CLELLAN George B. in Jamestown, NY July 17, 1878

MC KEAN Catherine (**BEDELL**) abt 80y in Ft. Edward, NY August 22, 1878

COLLINS Mrs. Zilpha age 87y in Whitehall, NY September 9, 1878

COMBS Mrs. E. M. age 41y in Whitehall, NY September 10, 1878

BENSON Mrs. Lydia in her 84th yr in White Creek, NY September 8, 1878

HASTINGS Charles age 72y in Ft. Ann, NY September 17, 1878

GREEN Mrs. Betsey age 79y in Greenwich, NY September 19, 1878

MOORE Orra H. age 72y 9m 12d wife of Rev. W. W. September 25, 1878

SNELL Patience age 68y 8m 18d in Cambridge, NY September 12, 1878

HARLOW George C. age 74y in Whitehall, NY September 25, 1878

WALLACE Robert age 2w son of Rev. Oliver A and Helen J. **BROWN** in Gloversville, NY October 13, 1878

HAWES L. A. abt 41y in Poultney, Vt. October 2, 1878

MC CONLEE Neil age 67y in Argyle, NY October 2, 1878

AGAN Bennie F. age 31y 4m 23d in Cambridge, NY October 10, 1878

MOSHER Mary D. age 23y wife of Fred D. of Eagle Bridge, NY and dau of late Dr. J. D. **STEWART** in Boston, Mass. October 16, 1878

CHASE Marvin in Ft. Ann, NY October 27, 1878

KENNEDY Michael age 20y in W. Granville, NY October 27, 1878

HELP Jesse age 61y of Cambridge, NY in the County Home November 10, 1878

CADARR Mrs. John age 87y in Ft. Ann, NY November 6, 1878

PARKS George age 36y in Sandy Hill, NY November 14, 1878

WING Emma B. age 81y widow of Nelson H. in Greenwich, NY November 30, 1878

BROWN Miss Polly in N. Argyle, NY December 8, 1878

FENTON E. P. age 63y formerly of Cambridge in Syracuse, NY November 20, 1878

HOLLISTER Freddie E. age 12y 7m son of Fred M. in Troy, NY December 7, 1878

GILES Braman F. age 21y in N. Pawlet, Vt. (newspaper date December 13, 1878)

BARNES Mrs. Maria age 72y in Greenwich, NY December 8, 1878

LA HUE Philista age 65y wife of John in W. Granville, NY December 14, 1878

WRIGHT Jane A. age 65y widow of Dr. Albert Wright of Brooklyn, NY in Cambridge, NY December 21, 1878

BARRELL Washington age 77y in S. Hartford, NY December 18, 1878

PRUYN John age 86y in Buskirks Bridge, NY December 27, 1878

HAMILTON Susie dau of Frank in W. Cambridge, NY January 6, 1879

AKIN Mary Elizabeth age 61y in Cambridge, NY January 7, 1879

SHANAHAN Michael age 17y in Greenwich, NY February 5, 1879

WELLING Frank age 5y son of Edgar M. in Easton, NY February 10, 1879

DEWEY Moses abt 55y in Argyle, NY February 13, 1879

WILBUR Elijah age 4y son of Stephen in Easton, NY February 17, 1879

DURFEE Lura V. age 2m 15d dau of Merritt and Vandilla in Easton, NY March 1, 1879

MOSHER Parmelia age 82y in Eagle Bridge, NY March 1, 1879

KASSON Mrs. Mary age 47y in Greenwich, NY March 8, 1879

CRAVEN Mrs. Emily Huntington 'at the cure' Castle, NY February 25, 1879

THORNE Mrs. Eunice at Griswold Mills, NY March 15, 1879

POTTER Lucinda in her 80th yr formerly of Greenwich, NY at son-in-laws Thomas B. **WHYTE** in Troy, NY March 30, 1879

WRIGHT Eva age 1y 3m 7d dau of H. A. and D. C. in Hartford, NY April 2, 1879

PEETS Leslie F. age 8y son of James and Ruth in S. Granvile, NY March 20, 1879

HODGE Susan C. age 43y in Anaquasicoke, NY March 28, 1879

BARRETT Elijah abt 68y in Pawlet, Vt. April 13, 1878

ADAMS Ezekiel abt 70y in Shushan, NY May 1, 1879

BELGARD Lewis age 45y in Whitehall, NY May 1, 1879

SWIFT Nathan age 69y in N. Pawlet, Vt. April 24, 1879

LANSING Jacob C. age 55y in Cambridge, NY April 24, 1879

GRIFFIN Amanda (**BRAYTON**) age 46y in Sandy Hill, NY May 7, 1879

LEIGH Victor son of Darwin in Putnam, NY May 5, 1879

LOCKROW Mary A. age 71y in Cambridge, NY May 3, 1879

RUSSELL Jane age 32y 4m wife of Christopher in White Creek, NY April 19, 1879

WARNER Betsey age 75y Mother of H. H. of Greenwich, NY in Leicester, NY April 22, 1879

DOUGLAS Mary E. age 9y in Whitehall, NY June 2, 1879

DOUGLAS Joseph age 30y in Whitehall, NY June 2, 1879

CRAFTS Elizabeth J. age 75y in Whitehall, NY May 28, 1879

GRISWOLD Isaac Chester age 69y 15d in Whitehall, NY June 8, 1879

STOTT Hedelia age 8y dau of George of Ticonderoga, NY drowned in Whitehall, NY June 8, 1879

SMITH John age 35y in Sandy Hill, NY June 15, 1879

KEECH Mrs. Elizabeth age 78y in Sandy Hill, NY June 18, 1879

CROWL Samuel H. in his 66th yr in Cincinnati, Ohio June 27, 1879

HOWLAND Mrs. Susan M. age 90y in Sandy Hill, NY July 7, 1879

SEELEY Mrs. David in Pattens Mills July 2, 1879

WOODWARD Mrs. Anderson age 69y in Pawlet, Vt. June 29, 1879. Dau Mrs. MC ANDRUS of Cambridge, NY

SMITH Capt. Seth age 93y in Sandy Hill, NY July 16, 1879

BAILEY Mrs. S. G. in Granville, NY July 11, 1879

INGALLS Mrs. John abt 60y in Granville, NY July 13, 1879

DAWSON Mary age 19y dau of George in M. Granville, NY July 6, 1879

SMITH Lucy age 23y wife of C. O. in Granvile, NY July 14, 1879

MATHEWS Esther age 87y widow of Abraham in Argyle, NY July 16, 1879

BROKES Welcome age 9m son of William and Mary J. in Buskirks Bridge, NY July 24, 1879

GILLIGAN Mary Frances age 6y 3m 10d dau of Ambrose in Whitehall, NY July 21, 1879

GATES Harvey age 82y in Hartford, NY July 16, 1879

SMITH Cornelius V. age 80y in White Creek, NY July 19, 1879

LAWRENCE William formerly of Shushan, NY in Aurora, Ill. July 26, 1879

THOMPSON Pierre Burden age 4y son of George S. in N. Hoosick, NY (newspaper date August 1, 1879)

RISING Dora Age 14y dau of William in Hoosick Falls, NY (newspaper date August 1, 1879)

BLACK Mrs. Mary age 90y in Whitehall, NY July 31, 1879

TERRY Mary Elizabeth age 1y 1m 6d dau of Isaac in Whitehall, NY July 25, 1879

MULLIGAN Mary age 62y in Whitehall, NY July 26, 1879

HILL Mrs. William age 64y in N. Argyle, NY July 26, 1879

WILSON Henry W. age 70y in Sandy Hill, NY July 30, 1879

DOTY Walter age 65y in Ft. Edward, NY July 28, 1879

BURNS James age 27y in Whitehall, NY July 23, 1879

WINEGAR Russell age 87y of Ft. Ann, NY in Whitehall, NY August 2, 1879

KENYON Mrs. Otis in N. Greenwich, NY August 6, 1879 and dau age 6y died August 1, 1879

CARROLL Frankie age 2y 10m dau of Frank and Maggie in N. Granville, NY August 2, 1879

JOHNSON Orville age 65y in Ft. Ann, NY August 7, 1879

RICHARDSON Charles age 21y in N. Granville, NY August 10, 1879

BRIGGS Cornelius age 68y in Saratoga Springs, NY August 17, 1879

CASE Jonathan age 79y in Hoosick, NY August 26, 1879

LUCCA Horace W. age 40y in Milwaukee, Wis. August 24, 1879

RANDALL Sarah A. abt 60y wife of R. R. in Sandgate, Vt. August 20, 1879

WHEELER Betsey age 87y in Whitehall, NY August 30, 1879

FITCH Chester age 73y in Hartford, NY September 5, 1879

MC CARTY George age 19y of Hartford, NY in Battenville, NY September 5, 1879

BECKER Clarence age 5y son of Nathaniel and Phelena in N. Cambridge, NY August 21, 1879 and Johnie B. age 10y died September 10, 1879

EDIE David R. age 16y in N. Cambridge, NY September 4, 1879

PHELPS Laura R. age 59y wife of Julius formerly of Cambridge, NY in Newark, NY August 23, 1879

HILL Alexander age 76y in N. Cambridge, NY August 26, 1879

RICHARDS Orson age 68y of Sandy Hill, NY at Shroon Lake September 4, 1879

MC CLANTY George age 20y in Greenwich, NY September 5, 1879

FELCH Chester age 73y in Hartford, NY September 5, 1879

ANDRUS Margaret abt 32y wife of Cleve in Danby, Vt. September 18, 1879

MERRICK _____ age 7m dau of Delmar in Pawlet, Vt. September 28, 1879

LACKEY _____ age 2y 4m son of Alexander and Helen in Ft. Edward, NY September 23, 1879

COOK Charles J. age 31y in Hoosick Falls, NY (newspaper date October 10, 1879)

COX Robert age 70y in Glens Falls, NY October 2, 1879

HAMMOND Rhoda age 91y late of Ballston, NY in Argyle, NY October 25, 1879

KILMER Hannah abt 20y in Kirwin, Ks. September 5, 1879

BRANNAN James age 38y in Sandy Hill, NY October 25, 1879

BOLAND Minnie age 9y 4m in Cambridge, NY (newspaper date November 7, 1879)

HOLLIS Carrie age 2y dau of Henry and Maria in Eagle Bridge, NY November 3, 1879

MC CLELLAN Fannie Kate age 6y 9m 18d dau of Chester L. and Mary E. in Beatrice, Neb. November 18, 1879

SWEET Aruna **(HYDE)** age 48y 10m 19d in Hoosick NY December 7, 1879

WHITEHALL CHRONICLE
September 1851 - February 10, 1877
scattered issues

FAULKENBURY Ezra age 60y in Whitehall, NY October 16, 1853

ROOT Roxeynthia in her 67th yr wife of John in Ft. Ann, NY October 9, 1853

MIDDLETON Mrs. Robert age 63y in N. Granville, NY February 5, 1856

SIMONS Ebenezer age 97y 10m 8d in Whitehall, NY February 19, 1856

FAULKENBURY Miss Cynthia in her 39th yr in Whitehall, NY March 12, 1856

CHAPIN Joseph William age 1y 8m 13d son of Charles and Lovisa H. in Whitehall, NY March 12, 1856

TAFT William in his 27th yr in Whitehall, NY March 12, 1856

WILLIE Hannah Jane age 22y 9m dau of Col. A. and Margaret in Putnam, NY March 9, 1856

WRIGHT Hannah in her 52nd yr wife of Dr. Ira in Whitehall, NY March 26, 1856

HAYNES Martha Jane age 4y 3m dau of Dr. S. and Isabel in Putnam, NY March 14, 1856

MICKLEJOHN William F. age 1y 3m 7d son of George and Hannah Jane in Putnam, NY March 21, 1856

BELL John Quincey Adams age 1y 9m 8d son of Joseph and Eliza in New York March 21, 1856

MC NAIR Mrs. Elizabeth in her 34th yr in Decatur, Wis. March 27, 1856

CULL Phebe age 60y relict of John formerly of Whitehall, NY in Decatur, Wis. March 19, 1856

DOE Mary age 68y widow of Walter in Saratoga Springs, NY (newspaper date June 6, 1856)

JAMES David age 21y accident at powder works in Hampton, NY May 30, 1856

RICHARDS son of Capt. Frank Richards age 6y drowned in canal July 15, 1856

KINNEY Abba M. age 3y 12d in Whitehall, NY July 21, 1856

HARPER Lillis wife of Reuben in Munson, Ohio June 13, 1856. Born December 12, 1793 in Ft. Ann, NY. After marriage, moved to Galen, NY and to Ohio in 1843.

HOPKINS Mary W. wife of Henry J. C. formerly of Granville, NY in Madison, Wis. July 29, 1856

LEE Stephen age 84y in Sandy Hill, NY August 23, 1856

CULL Jennette age 35y wife of John in Whitehall, NY September 5, 1856

SULLIVAN Mary Ann age 20y dau of John in Whitehall, NY September 10, 1856

ABELL S. P. in his 58th yr in Westhaven, Vt. September 17, 1856

THOMAS Nancy R. age 25y wife of William H. in Ft. Ann, NY December 12, 1856

DOUGLAS George age 84y in Whitehall, NY April 12, 1857

PATTON Mary Jane age 17y in Whitehall, NY April 10, 1857

CHAMBERS Lucy A. age 22y 19d wife of Thomas and dau of James **ADAMS** of Westhaven Vt. in Elmira, NY April 8, 1857

MORRELL Stephen age 66y in S. Hartford, NY May 19, 1857

FRANK Elizur W. in his 50th yr in Omer, Wis. May 21, 1857. Born Granville, NY

O'RILEY _____ dau of John and Betsey in Whitehall, NY July 16, 1857

SMITH Permela in her 74th yr in Whitehall, NY August 28, 1859

DOREN John age 2y 3m 15d son of James and Arabella in Whitehall, NY June 11, 1860

HILLETT Freddie age 24d son of James F. in Whitehall, NY June 24, 1860

DUNSON Carrie age 1y 8m dau of George and Phebe in Whitehall, NY July 30, 1860

LUTHER Allen age 30y in Whitehall, NY July 31, 1860

FAULKENBURY Jemima age 63y widow of Ezra in Whitehall, NY December 26, 1860

KENNEDY Andrew age 48y in Whitehall, NY June 17, 1861

WILSON _____ age 11y dau of James and Sarah in Whitehall, NY August 9, 1862

HIGLY Eunice wife of C. D. in Hartford, NY August 23, 1862

BARNEY George age 74y of Hatch Hill in Whitehall, NY January 15, 1863

AVERY Lucy P. age 10y 7m 27d died January 7, 1863 and Charles H. age 5y 11m 27d died January 14, 1863, children of Hiram and Lucy in Hartford, NY

RICE Edward M. in his 22nd yr of Ft. Ann, NY in Washington DC Hospital. Member of Co. D. 137th Reg. NY Vol. Buried Ft. Ann, NY December 25, 1862

BASCOM Josiah age 77y in Whitehall, NY January 24, 1863

TAYLOR George P. age 26y formerly of Vt. son of Rev. Chauncey Taylor at Central City, Col. Terr. February 5, 1863

BROWN L. M. D. at Arlington Heights Hospital December 16, 1862. Buried Boardman's burying ground in Whitehall, NY

HERRING Samuel age 20y adopted son of Seth **MC FARREN** in Whitehall, NY January 9, 1864

SHERMAN Mary age 106y in Cambridge, NY January 9, 1864

JUCKET Michael age 92y in Ft. Ann, NY January 9, 1864

ADAMS Henry C. age 3y 13d died January 3, 1864 and "Tutie" age 5y 1m 13d died January 6, 1864, Children of Henry and Marcia in Westhaven, Vt.

LACCA Ira Jr. funeral held Whitehall, NY January 24, 1864

ROBINSON Alexander in his 87th yr at Ft. Miller, NY January 29, 1864. Born Scotland, married age 26

HEMINWAY Asa in his 74th yr in N. Granville, NY February 16, 1864

JONES Salina in her 65th yr widow of Walter in Whitehall, NY March 10, 1864

(issues missing from 1864 - 1874)

MC LAUGHLIN Salina age 22m dau of Patrick in St. Hartford, NY January 17, 1874

COON John in his 83rd yr of Salem, NY at son-in-laws George **RUDES** in Starkey, NY January 19, 1874. Buried Salem, NY

MARTIN Mariane age 63y in Jackson, NY January 21, 1874

BARTHOLOMEW Amanda age 25y wife of Lewis R. formerly of Comstocks Landing, NY and dau of Samuel **KINGSLEY** in Andover, Ohio (newspaper date January 31, 1874)

MARNES Miss A. age 29y in Whitehall, NY January 24, 1874

JEMERY Bertha Mabel age 6w dau of Joseph in Whitehall, NY January 28, 1874

FOLLETT Randall age 53y in Jersey City, NJ February 16, 1874

SMITH Charity age 76/79y in Whitehall, NY February 14, 1874

FACTO Mrs. Jane age 27y in Jersey City, NJ February 21, 1874, buried Whitehall

MURRELL Mrs. Jane widow of Stephen in Hartford, NY February 18, 1874

WRIGHT Warren E. of Aurora, Ill. in RR accident at Madison, Wis. (newspaper date February 28, 1874). Born Granville, NY, married 8 yrs, moved to Aurora 7 yrs ago.

HOLCOMB Alice abt 30y wife of James in Whitehall, NY March 2, 1874

DAVIDSON Frankie in his 17th yr dau of William in S. Hartford, NY March 2, 1874

ALLEN John K. in Granville, NY March 7, 1874. Buried Saratoga Springs, NY

ELWOOD Mrs. Ellen age 93y in Ft. Edward, NY last week (newspaper date March 21, 1874)

KEITH Mr. ____ buried March 15, 1874 in Hampton, NY

SMITH Eli in his 70th yr in Hebron, NY March 13, 1874

MARTLING James age 80y at sons Joseph G. in Whitehall, NY March 17, 1874

ADAMS Frank age 19y of Detroit, Mi. in Whitehall, NY March 16, 1874

O'REILLY Betsey age 54y wife of John in W. Huron, Vt. March 16, 1874

KELLY Henry abt 50y in Westhaven, Vt. March 15, 1874

DRISTOL Mrs. ____ age 74y in Whitehall, NY March 14, 1874

KELLOGG Myers age 30y of Whitehall, NY in Bloomington, Ind. March 11, 1874

COLLINS John of Hampton, NY March 14, 1874

WILLIAMSON Mary in her 64th yr wife of Daniel in Putnam, NY March 22, 1874

DILL Martha Austin age 7w dau of E. M. in Whitehall, NY March 24, 1874

RICH Charles age 64y in Whitehall, NY March 30, 1874. Lived Whitehall 53 yrs.

NORTHUP George Sr. age 94y 6m at sons George Jr. in N. Granville, NY Marvh 30, 1874

DOUGLAS George H. age 10m son of Charles in Whitehall, NY March 27, 1874

SPAULDING Henry G. in his 55th yr in N. Granville, NY March 29, 1874

UNDERHILL Minerva in her 58th yr wife of Samuel and dau of Harden **BAILEY** (newspaper date April 4, 1874)

HATHAWAY Benjamin in his 80th yr in Hartford, NY March 9, 1874

NOBLE Mrs. Calista age 57y of Washington Co. at nephews John **SATTERFIELD** in Aurora, Ill. March 28, 1874

FENTON Clark age 70y in Welch Hollow, NY April 9. 1874

SHINE Peter in his 71st yr in S. Hartford, NY April 17, 1874

TOBIN Lavinia age 54y wife of B. C. in Whitehall, NY April 21, 1874

RAYDER Nellie C. age 10y dau of C. P. in Pattens Mills, NY April 10/15, 1874

GILCHRIST Elmiraett in her 64th yr in Ft. Edward, NY April 13, 1874

LUTHER Nathan in his 64th yr in Moreau, NY April 13, 1874 and wife Delinda in her 31st yr died April 17. 1874

WEBSTER Capt. Phineas suicide at Roundout April 23, 1874, buried Whitehall, NY

JACKWAY Thomas age 82y in Westhaven, Vt. April 25, 1874

NEDDO Mrs. J. age 39y in Whitehall, NY April 25, 1874

BARTHOLOMEW Sarah J. age 15y dau of Alvah in Whitehall, NY May 15, 1874

SELDEN Alonzo age 79y in Whitehall, NY May 15/16, 1874

TAYLOR Ida age 18y in Whitehall, NY May 15/16, 1874

LOING Jane P. age 16y dau of Uzziel in N. Hebron, NY funeral May 10, 1874

WILSEY John age 76y in Whitehall, NY June 22, 1874

COOK Mrs. W. W. in Whitehall, NY June 30, 1874. Born September 1805 in Middletown, Vt. Father was bro of Gen. Jonas **CLARK** and Mother was sister of Rev. Dr. **CULVER**

ABELL Ella age 28y dau of Olif and Carrie in Wolcott, Vt. June 29, 1874

MACE Adie age 7y in Putnam, NY June 26, 1874

BARKER Mrs. O. M. age 71y wife of Rev. J. R. in Hartford, NY July 17, 1874

DOTA Edward age 96y in Whitehall, NY July 19, 1874

MC GOWAN Roseta age 31y in Whitehall, NY July 19, 1874

BUCKLE Miss Eva age 18y overdose of morphine in Dresden, NY July 27, 1874

SILL Dr. Richard in his 85th yr in S. Hartford, NY July 23, 1874

STONE Lewis age 5y in Whitehall, NY August 3, 1874

CAMELL ____ age 11y son of S. in Whitehall, NY August 20, 1874

BRIDGE Lizzie Dory age 4y dau of Ellen in Whitehall, NY August 20, 1874

RAYMOND Aurelia age 6y dau of E. Raymond in Whitehall, NY August 17, 1874

LEPORD infant son of Theodore in Whitehall, NY August 15, 1874

ASHLEY infant son of C. in Whitehall, NY August 16, 1874

CAMPBELL infant son of Samuel in Whitehall, NY August 18, 1874

ADAMS Hiram F. age 9m 9d son of Robert and Fanny in Whitehall, NY August 16, 1874

PHOENIX Emma age 6y dau of Saul and Katherine in Whitehall, NY August 31, 1874

GRADY John age 58y in Whitehall, NY September 2, 1874

PERKINS ____ age 6y dau of H. Perkins in Whitehall, NY September 7, 1874

MEERS Mary age 8y in Whitehall, NY September 8, 1874

PRATT Frank age 5w son of Charles in Whitehall, NY September 4, 1874

MONARQUE Willie died September 10, 1874, Nathan R. age 2y 6m died September 11, 1874 and Mary F. age 7y 3m died September 15, 1874, children of Frank in

Whitehall, NY

MC FARREN Ida age 13y 5m in Whitehall, NY September 10, 1874

LAMB Lydia Jane age 21y wife of Joseph in Whitehall, NY September 14, 1874

REED ____ son of John in Whitehall, NY September 18, 1874

TEFFT Simeon age 86y grandson of Nathan who was born March 14, 1717 in N. Kingston, RI and died April 3, 1789. Wife Isabel was born August 13, 1716 and died 1787. Their children were Stanton born July 9, 1744 and died 1811, Isabel born March 14, 1746, Nancy born December 14, 1749. Nathan 2nd (father of Simeon) was born August 2, 1752 and died September 18, 1828, John born March 13, 1756, Mary born May 2, 1758, Sarah born August 14, 1762. Nathan 2nd suceeded his father on the farm. His wife Dorcas was born December 12, 1753. Their children were Benjamin born October 16, 1773 and died May 2, 1847, Nathan 3rd born March 10, 1776 and died January 24, 1848, Isabel was born November 27, 1778 and died March 16, 1857, Gardner was born August 13, 1780 and died November 8, 1803, Sarah was born January 23, 1783 and died October 6, 1863, Dorcas was born June 1, 1786 and died April 2, 1865, Simeon (subject of this obit) was born August 20, 1788 and died August 30, 1874, Mary was born January 28, 1791 and died October 28, 1816, Phebe was born November 2, 1796 and is only survivor. Simeon was married over 60y, his wife surviving and had 8 children, 7 living

BARRETT Hattie age 6m dau of Cornelius and Ida in Whitehall, NY September 20/29, 1874

LAKE ____ age 18m child of George in Whitehall, NY September 21, 1874

MONARQUE J. B. age 3y died September 25, 1874 and Mary J. age 3y 4m died September 28, 1874 in Whitehall, NY

MC GUE Glosten age 5y dau of Frank (newspaper date October 3, 1874)

BROOKS Mrs. ____ age 22y in Whitehall, NY September 28, 1874

JILLSON Samuel T. age 82y 4m 26d formerly of Whitehall, NY in Lima Centre, Mi. August 29, 1874

BARBER ____ age 6/8y dau of Ralph in Whitehall, NY October 10, 1874

BOCK Peter age 4y in Whitehall, NY October 12, 1874

BECKWITH Ira S. age 51y in Orwell, Vt. October 15, 1874

RODD Mrs. R. L. age 34y in Whitehall, NY October 16, 1874

MC CABE Alonzo age 24y in Ft. Ann, NY October 14, 1874

SMITH Wheaton funeral at N. Hebron, NY October 20, 1874

ADAMS Katie C. age 17y dau of J. P. Adams in Whitehall, NY October 24, 1874

HALL P. P. age 15y in Whitehall, NY October 23, 1874

WATERS Mrs. William age 30y in Whitehall, NY October 23, 1874

ROBATOR ____ age 4y dau of P. Robator in Whitehall, NY October 26, 1874

GARDNER Eli H. age 45y drowned in canal at Ft. Ann, NY October 31, 1874

HORTON Moses age 60y in Westhaven, Vt. October 29, 1874

SKEELS infant son of H. B. Skeels in Whitehall, NY October 27, 1874

LUSHER Miss Rasmond in Whitehall, NY November 4, 1874

ADAMS Christia A. wife of Martin B. in Ft. Ann, NY November 9, 1874

CROWLEY John age 5y in Whitehall, NY November 10, 1874

PERO infant son of Joseph in Whitehall, NY November 8, 1874

BAILEY Carrie E. age 15y in Whitehall, NY November 15, 1874

FLAGLER Thomas age 15y son of Jonas in S. Hartford, NY November 15, 1874

WAIT Jennie BOYD age 27 at Auburn, NY July 31, 1876

WAIT Horace L. age 10m son of A. D. in Ft. Edward, NY February 5, 1877

BAKER Robert D. age 38y formerly of Granville, NY in Milwaukee, Wis. January 30, 1877

MC GOWAN Michael age 79y in Whitehall, NY February 2, 1877

WHITEHALL DEMOCRAT
January 6, 1847 - February 20, 1847

WRIGHT Eleanor age 85y widow of Silas in Weybridge, Vt. December 20, 1846. Husband died May 1843 age 84y, married 61 yrs

HOLLISTER Happylona age 46y wife of Dwight in Whitehall, NY December 31, 1846

STARR Weltha Ann in her 63rd yr wife of J. J. in Burlington, Vt. January 6, 1847

DENNISON Lorane Eliza age 20y dau of Stephen H. and Maria in Castleton, Vt. January 9, 1847

SNODY Elizabeth M. age 29y wife of Daniel in Whitehall, NY January 11, 1847

TORREY Lydia age 83y in Benson, Vt. January 12, 1847

GRISWOLD Frederick age 6m son of George S. in Whitehall, NY February 14, 1847

WHITEHALL TIMES
January 25, 1864 -December 27, 1882
scattered issues

HERRINGTON Ophelia age 15y 5m dau of David in Easton, NY February 5, 1864

AUSTIN William Thomas age 5m son of John in White Creek, NY February 5, 1869

CARPENTER Cora Augusta age 6m dau of Newton in Greenwich, NY February 5, 1869

ASHLEY Nancy age 79y formerly of Troy, NY in Cambridge, NY February 9, 1869

CRAMER Mrs. Noble age 36y in Benson, Vt. February 13, 1869

RICE Miss Sarah M. age 27y in Ft. Ann, NY August 5, 1871

DAHN George age 61y in Whitehall, NY August 29, 1871

HENNESSY George T. age 4m 17d son of John and Marion in Putnam, NY August 17, 1871

BUNCE Joseph A. age 36y formerly of Whitehall, NY in Chicago August 21, 1871

HJORTSBERG J. age 24y in Whitehall, NY February 11, 1877

BUNCE Joseph age 76y in Whitehall, NY February 9, 1877

FILE 226
FILLMORE 150, 276
FINCH 47, 55, 67, 74, 116, 203, 206
FINN 55
FINNIGAN 255
FISH 75, 77, 96, 159, 231, 311, 413, 444, 445
FISHER 20, 29, 78, 109, 113, 168, 170, 181, 184, 203, 231, 270, 290, 317, 326, 332, 344, 351, 355, 389, 412, 417, 421
FISK 67, 73, 77, 191, 200, 369, 373
FITCH 13, 35, 139, 154, 187, 197, 285, 299, 305, 314, 341, 354, 408, 451
FITTS 143
FITZGERALD 108, 126, 129, 264, 426
FLACK 23, 111, 112, 123, 284, 371
FLAGLER 107, 157, 254, 459
FLAHERTY 149, 230
FLANDREAU 90, 115
FLANNERY 284
FLATTEY 235
FLEMING 51, 79, 357
FLETCHER 50, 90, 187, 191, 195, 263, 367, 370
FLOOD 24, 274, 379
FLOWERS 50, 309, 373, 410
FLOYD 104
FLYNN 36, 240, 285, 414
FOAMES 294
FOILS 67
FOLEY 391
FOLGER 133
FOLLETT 225, 455
FONDA 122, 138, 160, 185, 369
FOOT 11, 34, 145
FORBES 56, 59, 63, 296
FORBUSH 19, 184
FORD 151, 292, 317, 380
FORGEY 22
FORREST 244, 428
FORSYTHE 198, 387
FORT 6, 44, 105, 251, 280, 335, 384, 387, 390, 439
FORTIN 128, 422
FOSS 21, 426
FOSTER 16, 19, 23, 33, 47, 51, 62, 72, 80, 109, 144, 224, 229, 240, 254, 283, 284, 327, 350, 364, 365, 370-372, 382, 387, 406, 421, 422, 443
FOURNEY 284
FOWLER 26, 33, 51, 54, 85, 161, 242, 259, 324, 327-329, 331, 334, 339, 377, 388, 406, 412, 415, 427, 432, 433
FOX 250, 278
FRANCISCO 305
FRANK 305, 453
FRANKLIN 199
FRASER 78, 111, 309
FRATO 350
FRAZER 13
FREEBORN 146
FREEMAN 26, 49, 57, 183, 203, 205, 217, 263, 279, 366, 380, 399, 407, 417

FREIDENBURGH 277
FRENCH 37, 133, 136, 139, 157, 191, 286, 292
FRISBIE 96
FROST 66, 173, 184, 185, 214
FULLER 15, 52, 96, 102, 113, 145, 167, 177, 180, 185, 205, 223, 253, 257, 275, 306, 346, 354, 399, 419
FULLERTON 156
FURLONG 329
FURSMAN 241
GAGE 397
GAILBRAITH 42, 261
GAINE 7
GAINER 372
GALE 52, 168, 181, 211, 217
GALLIGAN 89
GALLOT 121
GALLOWAY 77, 441
GALLUP 291
GALUSHA 94, 338, 361
GALVIN 439
GAMBLE 139, 426
GANDEL 17, 58
GANNON 158, 281
GANSEVORT 9
GANTZ 25, 238
GARDEPHE 184, 192, 436
GARDINER 304
GARDNER 13, 64, 105, 135, 326, 409, 459
GARDON 143
GARRETT 101, 372
GARRITY 123
GARVEY 53
GARVIN 173
GASTON 107
GATES 65, 149, 153, 244, 278, 283, 293, 450
GAUVREN 257
GAVETTE 205, 342, 417
GAVIN 129
GAY 253, 379, 443
GAYLORD 329
GEARY 364, 425
GEER 59, 69, 176, 402
GEOLIN 276
GEORGE 93, 103, 428
GERART 62
GERMAIN 52
GERO 418
GETTY 1, 18, 28, 34, 45, 115, 185, 270, 278, 318, 333, 338, 390
GIBBONS 353, 369
GIBBS 29, 94, 145, 214, 385, 420
GIBSON 12, 27, 28, 63, 73, 89, 137, 159, 269, 303, 315
GIDDINGS 204, 295
GIDLEY 168
GIFFORD 41, 43, 195, 230, 276, 281, 347, 364, 371, 382, 394, 417, 427, 437, 440
GILBERT 8, 99, 118, 135, 178, 193, 240, 253, 269, 279, 282, 347, 368, 446
GILCHRIST 14, 40, 83, 85, 124, 142, 162, 164, 177, 234, 241, 269, 320, 390, 405, 433, 443, 456

GILES 215, 391, 448
GILL 130, 132, 155, 431
GILLESPIE 414
GILLETTE 57, 301, 315, 365
GILLIGAN 374, 450
GILLIS 110, 197, 340, 378, 392
GILMAN 28, 91, 95, 197, 237, 280, 418
GILMORE 15, 36, 286, 320, 349, 433
GILSON 78, 168, 182, 315
GLADSTONE 254
GLASBY 155
GLASCOW 386
GLEASON 6, 137, 160, 231, 254, 282, 433
GLENHOLMES 277, 357
GLIDDEN 418
GLINN 276
GLOVER 196
GODOU 441
GOKEY 142
GOLDEN 259
GOOD 396
GOODALE 13, 88, 132, 424
GOODELL 82, 288, 333
GOODFELLOW 317
GOODHUE 398
GOODICH 128
GOODIN 45
GOODING 400, 403
GOODMAN 254, 350
GOODRICH 4, 24, 50, 56, 105, 302, 303, 382
GOODSPEED 4, 5, 395
GOODWIN 80
GORDON 123, 154, 315, 318, 330, 346, 355, 382, 393, 411, 427, 436
GORHAM 148
GORRIE 346
GOSS 97
GOUGH 296
GOULD 3, 41, 162, 371
GOURLAY 1, 135, 310
GOURLEY 27, 140, 292
GOURLIE 84
GOW 78, 349
GOWAN 268
GOWRAN 123
GRACE 58, 285, 420
GRADY 419, 457
GRAHAM 5, 11, 12, 14, 21, 24, 30, 31, 36, 48, 85, 86, 104, 116, 131, 134, 152, 179, 193, 257, 284, 290, 317, 321, 324, 325, 327, 338, 365, 371, 376, 426, 442
GRANDY 188, 313
GRANGER 168, 207, 241, 274, 275
GRANT 86, 161, 225, 249, 274, 284, 367, 395
GRAULICH 288
GRAVES 2, 62, 107, 199, 209, 299, 324, 337, 362, 394, 409, 419, 433
GRAY 1, 8, 12, 16, 18, 20, 23, 24, 26, 27, 49, 50, 52, 62, 109, 116, 121, 157, 158, 166, 167, 186, 189, 193, 202, 213, 254,

139, 163, 164, 187, 263,
284, 439

WATERS 54, 72, 90, 107, 113, 144,
145, 180, 182, 198, 205, 244,
246, 251, 267, 270, 277, 327,
359, 394, 401, 402, 409, 435,
459

WATKINS 2, 23, 29, 31, 100, 317,
343, 405, 429

WATSON 6, 16, 24, 33, 34, 71,
162, 173, 231, 279, 309, 411,
414

WATT 381

WEATHERHEAD 152

WEAVER 122, 360

WEBB 161, 259, 329

WEBSTER 7, 49, 223, 337, 339,
346, 380, 438, 456

WEED 114, 231, 392

WEEKS 41, 58, 73, 190, 226, 388,
415, 446

WEIR 37, 88, 169, 220, 225, 230,
236, 354, 378, 381, 383, 388,
395, 414, 419-421, 441

WELCH 46, 78, 88, 100, 133, 150,
185, 224, 244, 252, 397, 399,
425, 426, 434, 442

WELCOME 437

WELLER 80, 411

WELLING 42, 155, 253, 280, 295,
382, 448

WELLS 13, 19, 20, 53, 57, 62, 73,
98, 105, 119, 143, 146, 156,
173, 209, 215, 234, 258, 268,
293, 294, 304, 305, 310, 314,
318, 321, 323, 327, 329, 331,
332, 356, 385, 408, 429, 430,
432, 434

WENDELL 11, 199, 309, 334, 352

WENTWORTH 163

WEST 96, 150, 205, 369, 389, 405,
409, 411

WESTCOTT 75, 108, 135, 161, 282

WESTFALL 290

WESTINGHOUSE 260

WESTON 24, 30, 73, 179, 207, 217,
307, 308

WETHERBEE 152, 398

WETSELL 403

WHALEN 40

WHALEY 196, 235

WHEADON 40, 202, 297, 441

WHEATON 5

WHEELER 3, 53, 146, 148, 247,
252, 260, 281, 296, 311, 317,
368, 425, 429, 440, 451

WHEELOCK 48, 194, 261, 350, 447

WHELDON 166, 170, 175, 185,
187, 219, 296, 316, 344

WHIPPLE 14, 18, 50, 169, 181,
183, 184, 192, 194, 198, 200,
210, 213, 215, 217, 230, 235,
300, 312

WHITBECK 159

WHITCOMB 3, 4, 20, 22, 23, 121,
125, 154, 167, 243, 342, 414,
432, 445, 446

WHITE 2, 12, 17, 33, 63, 74, 75,
93-95, 105, 119, 131, 140, 169,
177, 192, 198, 209, 211, 212,

214, 219, 221, 234, 237,
251, 288, 306, 322, 334,
348, 373, 378, 392, 395,
434, 436

WHITESIDE 15, 36, 72, 176, 245,
263, 271, 310, 338, 341, 347,
433

WHITLOCK 126, 136, 367, 392,
419

WHITMAN 85, 412

WHITNEY 54, 64, 99, 110, 126,
138, 193, 267, 328, 376, 426,
438

WHITTAKER 207, 259, 372, 390

WHYTE 136, 175, 179, 263, 313,
325, 410, 449

WICKERSON 376

WICKS 69, 239

WIGGINS 148, 160

WILBUR 23, 71, 76, 108, 198, 240,
262, 278, 285, 331, 448

WILCOX 28, 127, 131, 140, 180,
188, 190, 195, 207, 209, 212,
221, 224, 225, 233, 235, 248,
255, 261, 263, 281, 334, 350,
351, 402, 419

WILDER 107, 201, 219, 288, 350,
396

WILEY 256, 431

WILKIE 70

WILKINSON 52

WILKISON 23

WILLARD 26, 29, 67, 126, 199,
271, 346

WILLETT 21, 98, 163, 311

WILLIAMS 1, 4, 6, 28, 35, 36, 45,
79, 82, 108, 112, 115, 119, 124,
130, 154, 168, 173, 182, 188,
195, 200, 202, 226, 238, 239,
246, 249, 252, 279, 299, 302,
304, 317, 326, 338, 392, 398,
400, 408, 414, 417, 420, 421,
427, 440

WILLIAMSON 5, 29, 44, 64, 109,
122, 147, 237, 266, 392, 431,
456

WILLIE 452

WILLIS 93, 115, 132, 156, 197, 445

WILMARTH 174, 175, 181, 185,
376

WILSEY 417, 457

WILSON 26, 27, 38, 46, 48, 56, 62,
65, 85, 112, 121, 126, 129, 133,
141, 152, 163, 175, 176, 188,
208, 221, 222, 224, 228, 232,
242, 243, 251, 258, 277, 281,
286, 288, 290, 307, 313, 328,
332, 341, 344, 365, 376, 381,
386, 404, 405, 413, 426, 433,
450, 454

WILTSIE 70, 81, 84, 90, 126

WINAN 7

WINCHESTER 2, 315

WINEGAR 86, 115, 450

WING 40, 62, 66, 94, 162, 165, 228,
259, 270, 311, 314, 326, 404,
412, 434, 448

WINN 254, 277, 382

WINNEY 169

WINSHIP 436

WITHERELL 302, 377

WOLCOTT 14, 135, 324

WOLF 215, 217, 219

WOLL 295

WOOD 18, 36, 38, 76, 92, 110,
113, 130, 132, 136, 151, 162,
163, 210, 235, 252, 268, 283,
288, 323, 336, 347, 351, 384,
396, 413, 417

WOODARD 5, 40, 110, 141, 169,
182, 190, 226, 267, 330, 333,
357, 381, 419

WOODCOCK 105, 385

WOODRUFF 87, 174, 284

WOODS 182, 192, 308, 325, 331,
355

WOODWARD 11, 19, 64, 450

WOODWORTH 16, 22, 32, 56,
60-62, 75, 117, 139, 162, 169,
196, 237, 264, 265, 303-305,
312, 345, 346, 356, 361, 362,
391, 406

WORKS 377

WORTH 71, 357

WRAY 6, 78, 165

WRIGHT 2, 9, 21, 32, 34, 44, 47,
71, 72, 93, 94, 106, 111, 144,
150, 152, 153, 155, 166, 172,
177, 179, 185, 206, 207, 209,
210, 216, 219, 220, 222, 224,
227, 228, 230, 255-258, 273,
285, 288, 290, 304, 306, 313,
315, 319, 324, 326, 344, 347,
351, 357, 358, 361, 365, 375,
381, 387, 389, 401, 402, 407,
410, 413, 423, 430, 435, 439,
443, 445, 448, 449, 452, 455,
459

WROATH 212, 281, 295

WROTH 83, 119

WYATT 178, 257, 347, 373

WYLIE 196

WYMAN 104, 114

YARMER 86

YARTER 142, 246

YATES 294

YOLT 150

YOULEN 189, 222, 338, 391, 392

YOUNG 15, 20, 28, 32, 97, 137,
165, 174, 180, 183, 192,
214, 216, 222, 245, 259, 321,
366, 409, 415

YOUNGLOVE 8, 175, 310

YULE 162, 258, 363